DATE DUE

DEC 0 7 2000	
DEC 1 6 2003	

BRODART, CO.   Cat. No. 23-221-003

AMERICAN MINORITY PEOPLES

HARPER'S SOCIAL SCIENCE SERIES

F. STUART CHAPIN, EDITOR

AMERICAN MINORITY PEOPLES

A STUDY IN
RACIAL AND CULTURAL CONFLICTS
IN THE UNITED STATES

BY

DONALD YOUNG

Assistant Professor of Sociology
University of Pennsylvania

HARPER & BROTHERS PUBLISHERS
NEW YORK AND LONDON

DEDICATED TO
THE AUTHOR'S FRIENDS OF MINORITY STATUS
IN THE HOPE THAT THEY WILL REMAIN
HIS FRIENDS

CONTENTS

EDITOR'S INTRODUCTION

PROBLEMS of economic reconstruction have grown so insistent of late that our attention has wandered from other important subjects. Not the least of these are the problems of race relations. Irrespective of the economic fortunes of particular periods of history, race and culture remain. Fortunately a considerable amount of careful study dealing with social attitudes and cultural change has been carried on since the close of the World War. Race relations have become susceptible to impartial scientific analysis as systems of attitudes and conflicts of culture traits and in the process of acculturation. Professor Young has assembled the facts and principles of these researches, but more than this he has given the whole problem new interest and reorientation by virtue of his emphasis on the minority peoples of America.

F. STUART CHAPIN

FOREWORD

Both pride and lack of confidence in blood and nationality make the study of the alien peoples and colored races in the United States a thankless task. Such minorities are sensitive, and observations which do not reflect credit on their rôle in this country are likely to be condemned as evidence of race prejudice. The old American majority in turn tends to resent not only the slightest praise, but even academic tolerance of the peoples whom they have contemptuously, yet partly in fear, classified as lesser breeds. Still, even thankless tasks must be undertaken, and the one here essayed is no more hopeless than others which have been profitably attacked.

The Southerner's claim of complete understanding of the Negro has come under the fire of the Negro's counter-claim that no white man knows the Negro, but that Negroes know the white man. There is enough of a mixture of truth and falsity in both of these defensive assertions of superior knowledge to permit the layman to accept that side of the argument toward which he may be already inclined. The fallacy in both arguments is that Southerners, Negroes and white men are not homogeneous groups of individuals as similar as peas in a pod. Being born and reared a white man in the South does not automatically qualify a person as an expert on all things relating to the darker peoples of the world, nor does it bar one from ever appreciating or making an unprejudiced study of the qualities of our colored population. On the other hand, being born and reared a Negro neither qualifies nor disqualifies one as an authority on all things relating to Negroes. Neither the white man nor the Negro can avoid being prejudiced by the circumstances of birth and rearing; all of us are members of some racial group with which we must identify ourselves and be identified by others.

Skin color and other inborn racial characteristics, however, are not the only bases on which mankind has divided itself into conflicting groups. Wealth, education, pride of family, nationality, language, religion, beliefs and customs in general, are some of the more common rocks on which the split may be made. Out of these have grown social classes and castes with conflicting interests and objectives, so that even the people of the United States with their traditional lip service to the doctrines of democracy and equality are divided and subdivided without end into a complicated pattern of interest groups. Of these, we have here selected those based on the differentiating features of race and alien cultures for study, with the full realization that they are but a part of the picture of class and caste conflict in the United States, a part which has many essential similarities with the rest of the whole.

It is unfortunate that the author is perforce a member of one of the groups under discussion. As such, he will be told repeatedly that which he already knows—that he can never really understand the feelings, emotions, beliefs, problems, and behavior of the groups to which he does not belong. Of course it is impossible for a white man of old American stock to put himself in the place of a Negro, an Oriental, an Indian, a Latin American or south European immigrant. Of course he must interpret the life of American minority peoples without having participated fully in it and in the light of his own cultural heritage. A colored sociologist who read most of the following chapters in manuscript remarked that they were in many respects naïve in that they seemed to have been written by one who was unfamiliar with the personal squabbles, jealousies, and conflicting interests involved in some of the situations discussed. The interpretation, he continued in what seemed to be a vein of mixed approval and regret, might be described as that of an academician who was either unaware of or indifferent to personalities and all else save pertinent sociological facts and principles. There is much truth in his remarks, for the author could not avoid the naïveté of an outsider, nor did he believe it necessary for his purpose to do so.

The purpose of this book is to give new perspective to academic discussions of American race relations as well as to summarize and interpret the outstanding facts in the history and present condition of our minority peoples. It is written primarily for the use of the native white majority. There have been any number of books written on the Negro, the various immigrant groups, and the Indian, and their status as minorities in this country. A few have discussed more than one minority. The impression conveyed, however, has been in the main that Negro-white relations are one thing, while Jewish-Gentile, Oriental-white, and other race relations are vastly different from each other, even to the extent of kind rather than degree. The view here presented is that the problems and principles of race relations are remarkably similar, regardless of what groups are involved; and that only by an integrated study of all minority peoples in the United States can a real understanding and sociological analysis of the involved social phenomena be achieved.

Race, in the strict meaning of the term, is not the subject of this study. We are primarily concerned with social behavior; and the people whose behavior is under consideration neither know nor care whether the Jew, the Italian, the Scandinavian, the American Negro, the Mexican, or even the "American," is a representative of a particular race in the strict biological sense. With superb disdain for the findings of the scientists, popular belief lumps biological, language, cultural, political, and other groups under the one heading of "race," and behaves accordingly. Our use of the term race, then, must conform to that of the ordinary citizen, for it is his behavior, not that of the scientists, that we are studying.

There is, unfortunately, no word in the English language which can with philological propriety be applied to all these groups, that is, which includes groups which are distinguished by biological features, alien national cultural traits, or a combination of both. For this reason, the phrases, "minorities of racial or national origin," "American minorities," or "minority peoples" are here used as synonyms for the popular usage of the word race. To most of us the word "minority" has political connotations in that it calls to mind a political party which is not in power. Since it is never used with that meaning in this book, no confusion should result from its present special application.

Several friends who read the manuscript called attention to the fact that many of the statistics cited were gathered more than a decade ago. To some extent this is cause for regret, especially where due to the unavailability of 1930 census data at the time of writing. Nevertheless, since this volume is designed as an interpretation rather than as an encyclopedia of American race relations, the statistics included are intended to be illustrative of social processes and not proof of present status. Their date is never their most important attribute.

Acknowledgment must be made to at least a few of those who contributed to this work through inspiration, advice, and tedious reading of manuscript. The greatest debt is to Dr. Carl Kelsey, who not only read the manuscript while it was still in a formative, almost illegible state, but also gave the author his first instruction in the subject of race relations, yet never in thirteen years of close acquaintance as teacher and friend consciously exercised the slightest intellectual domination.

Dr. Thorsten Sellin, who would have been a co-author except for the unavoidable pressure of other work, aided materially in the planning of the volume, and contributed particularly to the discussions of leisure-time activities, education, mental capacity, and art. Dr. Sellin, Dr. W. W. Weaver, and Mr. D. K. Bruner made many valuable suggestions while they were colleagues of the author in the teaching of Sociology 3B, American Race Relations, at the University of Pennsylvania. Dr. Ray Abrams also read the entire manuscript and offered helpful criticisms. Dr. Stuart Rice was most helpful in his comments on the nature and measurement of social attitudes and on methodology. Mr. Phelps Soule, of the University of Pennsylvania Press, not only made literally hundreds of technical corrections in the manuscript, but also gave the full benefit of his years of experience as a publisher in his criticisms of the entire project. The permission of numerous authors and publishers to quote from their works deserves appreciation. The anonymous contributions of innumerable friends of minority status must receive acknowledgment above all else.

Lest some blame be attached to these friends for their kindnesses, it should be emphatically stated that none of them agreed with all of the interpretations here presented.

DONALD YOUNG

Philadelphia
January, 1932

AMERICAN MINORITY PEOPLES

CHAPTER I

RACIAL PREJUDICES

The historical origin of race prejudice is unknown. Some students of humanity assume that mankind is endowed by nature with a powerful drive to hate, despise and fear strangers of alien ancestry; others look to the social environment and tradition for an understanding of group antagonisms. Whatever their origin, every American community has its mythical beliefs and discriminating attitudes which act as social barriers and establish the social status of racial minorities.

WHAT WE BELIEVE

Few native-born white Americans accept any Negro as a social equal. Even the illiterate Florida cracker knows that "niggers are niggers," and he would rather be his poverty-stricken self than a Dumas. "Orientals would drive the white man out of the Pacific coast states if they got a chance." "American labor must be protected from destructive competition by European immigrants." "North Europeans have more brains and greater emotional stability than any other people in the world." "The torch of civilization will be carried furthest if intrusted to the care of old American stock free from dilution by the admixture of colored or recent immigrant strains." The man who does not subscribe to such beliefs as these is not a representative citizen of the United States, even though all his ancestors came to this continent on the *Mayflower*.

Racial theories and antagonisms, however, are not confined to representative Americans. Negroes have as many and as bitter prejudices about white folk as white folk have about them. They agree that the heathen Chinee is peculiar, that Jews are unscrupulous, and that recent immigrants are

1

"trash." Jews, in turn, come to this country with some unflattering beliefs concerning Gentiles, and rapidly acquire the racial prejudices prevalent in their land of adoption, including a species of anti-Semitism. There is not a minority in the United States of whatever racial or national origin which has not brought with it or acquired group antagonisms and prejudices concerning the capacities and characteristics of other minorities and of the majority of old American stock. Not a single individual in the United States is permitted by his own beliefs and by the controlling attitudes of his group to regard his fellows as individuals rather than as members of some class or caste based on racial or national ancestry, and characterized thereby.[1]

Using race in its popular but unscientific meaning to include political, cultural, and biological human groupings, we are constantly faced with the necessity for governing our conduct in accordance with ready-made race attitudes. These attitudes affect beliefs in inborn qualities, limit employment, fix the place of residence, influence forms of recreation, and go so far as to prescribe permissible varieties of social relationships. They vary from group to group, are never identical in all parts of the country, and are altered radically in the passage of time. Although rigidity is not a characteristic of American group distinctions, their observance is required of all who fear the penalties of social disapproval.

Attempts to measure racial attitudes, to determine definitely their nature and extent, have thus far yielded doubtful results.[2] The very definition of an "attitude" is still a matter

[1] The development of the concept of social attitudes, including racial attitudes, owes much to the pioneer work of William I. Thomas. Special reference may be made to his major publication, in joint authorship with Florian Znaniecki, *The Polish Peasant in Europe and America*, Alfred A. Knopf, New York, 2nd edition, 1927, vol. i, pp. xv + 1116; vol. ii, pp. vi + 1117-2250.

For a well rounded discussion of social attitudes in symposium form, see Kimball Young, editor, *Social Attitudes*, Henry Holt & Company, Inc., New York, 1931, pp. xii + 382. Chapter XII, "Attitudes and the Mexican Immigrant," by Emory S. Bogardus, and Chapter XIII, "The Negro and the Immigrant," by Herbert A. Miller, are of particular importance to the student of racial attitudes. Well selected bibliographies are included.

[2] For bibliographies of reports on racial attitudes and their measurement, see Kimball Young, "The Field of Social Psychology," *Psychological Bulletin*,

of dispute among the experts, the social psychologists. To cut the Gordian knot with one stroke, an attitude may be here defined as a tendency to respond to a social or physical stimulus in some particular manner because of either biological inheritance or cultural conditioning, or both. Thus the Southerner who walks out of a northern restaurant because a Negro is being served is giving expression to a racial attitude, while the white patrons who remain may be free from this particular tendency. More likely, they possess other attitudes influencing them to continue their meal which are stronger than their distaste for dining in the same room with a colored person. The employer who refuses to hire Negroes, Jews, Orientals, Mexicans, or aliens also demonstrates the possession of racial attitudes, as does the Negro who refuses to work for a Jew, the Oriental who will not accept employment from a Negro or Mexican, or the Irishman who would rather go hungry than obey the orders of a French-Canadian foreman. Whether such attitudes are the product of nature or nurture is a moot point. Their existence is undisputed.

In a recent study of the willingness of students at Syracuse University to admit individuals of certain races and nationalities to intimate personal relationships, the most antagonistic attitudes were found to be against Negroes, Orientals, Hindus, and Turks, the last three of which were rated about as acceptable as Bolshevists, anarchists, loafers, and people of unconventional morals. A bit up the scale came the Greeks, Armenians, Poles, and other Slavic peoples, about on a par with agnostics. Slightly greater toleration was shown for American Indians, Italians, Jews, reactionaries, socialists, students whose families had a jail record, and queer-looking or personally unattractive individuals. Nordics, of course, were the most acceptable stock.[3]

Willingness to admit individuals of minority racial and

vol. xxiv, No. 12, December, 1927, pp. 661-691; Kimball Young, *Source Book for Social Psychology*, Alfred A. Knopf, New York, 1927, chaps. xviii and xix, Gardner Murphy and Lois B. Murphy. *Experimental Social Psychology*, Harper & Brothers, New York, 1931.

[3] Daniel Katz and Floyd Allport, *Students' Attitudes*, The Craftsman Press, Inc., Syracuse, 1931, pp. 145ff.

nationality status to intimate personal relationships is apparently rationalized in terms of innate ability and other group qualities, both desirable and undesirable. A few years ago, the the present writer obtained the judgments of 450 students in his courses on race relations concerning their beliefs as to the *inborn capacities* of twenty-four American minority peoples. This investigation was confined strictly to the question of the potential ability of these peoples to achieve or adopt successfully a complex civilization similar to that existing in the United States, and no reference whatever was made to the willingness of the students to associate with them in any way. The ranking of minorities obtained in this study is approximately the same as numerous rankings secured by other investigators who attempted to measure only "social distance" between racial and national groups, and disregarded entirely the question of popular beliefs concerning racial differences in innate mentality. The following descending rank order is typical of practically all such studies:[4]

1. White	13. Norwegian
2. American	14. Italian
3. German	15. Spanish
4. Nordic	16. Japanese
5. Scandinavian	17. Greek
6. English	18. Yellow
7. Jewish	19. Russian
8. Scotch	20. Chinese
9. French	21. American Indian
10. Dane	22. Turk
11. Swede	23. Mexican
12. Irish	24. Negro

The group names in this study, distinctly "unscientific" in some instances, were purposely selected so as to be those which were in familiar use among the students and so as to overlap for purposes of checking. It may be noticed that the Nordic

[4] Donald Young, "Some Effects of a Course in American Race Relations on the Race Prejudices of 450 Undergraduates at the University of Pennsylvania," *Journal of Abnormal and Social Psychology*, October-December, 1927, vol. xxii, pp. 235-242.

received a high rating, but that Danes, Swedes and Norwegians, actual immigrant nationalities in comparison with the abstract Nordic, received a relatively low rating. Similarly, the yellow peoples as a whole, an abstraction, were rated higher than their two major components, the Chinese and Japanese. The table is full of illogical comparisons, and reflects not scientifically established racial facts but popular attitudes, rationalized in terms of group capacities.[5]

The attitudes of racial and national minorities in the United States are strikingly similar to those of the native white majority. Professor Bogardus has demonstrated this in his study of the reactions of 202 native American Negroes to seventeen "races" and of 178 native-born Jews to eighteen "races." Negroes, of course, expressed the greatest willingness to marry Negroes, and Jews to marry Jews, preferably German Jews. The rankings for these two native-born minorities, arranged in descending order of favorable reactions to close kinship by marriage with members of the other "races," were as follows:[6]

Negroes	*Jews*
1. Negroes	1. Jews, German
2. Mulattoes	2. Jews, Russian
3. French	3. English
4. Spaniards	4. French
5. English	5. Germans
6. Canadians	6. Irish

[5] An analysis, by E. S. Bogardus, of the racial attitudes of 1725 native-born Americans of many different stocks, but mostly northern European, obtained results similar to those of Katz and Allport and of the present writer. Professor Bogardus secured verbal reactions of his subjects to several different forms of intergroup relations ranging in intimacy from intermarriage to mere presence in the United States. The ranking of forty different "races," arranged in a descending order of favorable reactions to the idea of close kinship by marriage with members of the groups listed, was as follows: English, American (native-white), Canadians, Scotch, Scotch Irish, Irish, French, Welsh, Germans, French Canadians, Swedes, Dutch, Norwegians, Danes, Spaniards, Finns, Russians, Italians, Portuguese, Poles, Hungarians, Roumanians, Armenians, Czecho-Slovaks, Indians, German Jews, Bulgarians, Russian Jews, Greeks, Syrians, Serbo-Croatians, Mexicans, Japanese, Filipinos, Negroes, Turks, Chinese, Mulattoes, Koreans, Hindus. Emory S. Bogardus, *Immigration and Race Attitudes*, D. C. Heath & Company, New York, 1928, p. 25.

[6] *Ibid.*, pp. 27-28.

7. Mexicans

8. Americans (native white)

9. Hindus

10. Japanese

11. Germans

12. Italians

13. Chinese

14. Jews, Russian

15. Greeks

16. Russians

17. Turks

7. Scotch

8. Spaniards

9. Armenians

10. Italians

11. Mexicans

12. Japanese

13. Turks

14. Greeks

15. Chinese

16. Hindus

17. Filipinos

18. Negroes

While the rankings quoted are far from identical, they do show the existence of prejudices which are somewhat similar to those of the entire population, prejudices whose major differences are obviously not the result of inherent antagonisms but rather an expression of cultural backgrounds.[7] There have been numerous similar studies of racial antipathies, studies of college students and of the less favored classes, of rural

[7] Goodwin B. Watson, in a study of American attitudes toward oriental peoples and questions, found that the section of the United States in which his subjects resided was of trifling importance in comparison with their occupations, information concerning the Orient, general education, magazine reading, and religion. College students of the East, South, Middle West and the Pacific states showed differences in attitudes which were "almost negligible." California business men were "not clearly different from those of the East." "California labor is more like Ohio labor than it is like the business men of California."

In spite of the fact that this study was somewhat hurried, was entirely restricted to the questionnaire method (3,000 questionnaires were returned out of 9,000 sent out, with some evidences of poor sampling in the returns), and that one of the specific purposes of the enterprise hinged on the belief that "individuals who tried to express opinions upon the questions would be stimulated to a keener interest in the problems of the Far East and in the part which the United States should play in their solution" (p. 2), the final report deserves careful consideration both as to content and as to method. The stereotyped occidental attitudes toward oriental peoples and problems disclosed by this study throw much light on our policies in regard to oriental immigration and international relations.

See Goodwin B. Watson, *Orient and Occident,* a private report issued by the American Group of the Institute of Pacific Relations for the use of the members of the 1927 Conference of the Institute in Honolulu. For a partial digest of this report, see Goodwin B. Watson, "Orient and Occident," *Religious Education,* 1929, vol. xxiv, pp. 322-328.

and urban samplings, of Easterners, Westerners, Northerners and Southerners, and all agree that native Americans, regardless of color, national origin, and social status, prefer the north European, the south European, the Indian, the Asiatic, and the African in a descending order as listed.

Few investigators claim that they have been able accurately to measure the racial attitudes of their subjects. Since an attitude is a tendency to act, either antagonistically or favorably, in response to a stimulus—a way of being "set" for or against something—one may not be sure that a verbal expression of an attitude in answer to a hypothetical question corresponds to the subject's actual behavior in life situations. Such situations, unfortunately, are difficult to observe under experimental conditions, with the consequence that investigators have relied on opinions which may be rationalizations, unconsciously misleading, or deliberate falsehoods. It is, nevertheless, likely, in view of the pronounced similarity of the results of all investigators of racial attitudes, and of the correspondence of these results with observable phenomena in everyday life, that approximately correct indices of reaction tendencies have been achieved.

If, however, absolute accuracy of measurement is the goal in studies of racial attitudes, it must be admitted that no valid methodology has as yet been developed. Attitudes can hardly be reduced to such definite units as inches or quarts. In fact, there is some question whether the unfavorable attitude of an individual toward, say, Negroes, may properly be considered as no more than a variation in degree from an unfavorable attitude toward, say, Germans. There may be a difference in kind involved. If, however, it is merely a difference in degree, shall the variations be measured in terms of deviation from scientific fact or by a unit arbitrarily determined by the opinions of individuals willing to express their ideas of the favorability or antagonism of a given type of action or belief? The latter is the common practice. Professor L. L. Thurstone is the most prominent exponent of the quantitative expression of attitudes, but even his technique has yet to receive unqualified acceptance by sociologists, social psychologists, or statisticians.[8]

MAY WE BELIEVE OTHERWISE?

Crude as they are, existing studies of racial attitudes confirm the prevailing belief of cultural anthropologists and others who emphasize environment rather than heredity, that race prejudice as evidenced by tendencies to antagonistic reactions is the result of a process of socialization rather than an inborn abhorrence. It is well known that Europeans of the same stock as white Southerners in this country are possessed of different group antipathies and are relatively free from prejudice against peoples with whom they have had little contact, such as the Negro. "In many ways, the most satisfactory study of interracial attitudes yet published is that of

[8] See L. L. Thurstone and E. J. Chave, *The Measurement of Attitude,* University of Chicago Press, Chicago, 1929, pp. xii + 96; L. L. Thurstone, "An Experimental Study of Nationality Preferences," *Journal of General Psychology,* 1928, vol. i, pp. 405-425, and "Attitudes Can Be Measured," *American Journal of Sociology,* No. 4, January, 1928, vol. xxxiii, pp. 529-554; Stuart A. Rice, *Statistics in Social Studies,* University of Pennsylvania Press, Philadelphia, 1930, chap. xi; Gardner Murphy and Lois B. Murphy, *op. cit.,* chap. xi.

Professor Thurstone's complicated technique for the measurement of social attitudes, borrowed from the methodology of psychophysics, involves the creation of scales ranging from the greatest to the least degree of favorability and divided into approximately equal intervals. The degree of favorability is determined by the opinions of several hundred representative individuals, chosen almost at random, who sort the proposed questionnaire statements not in regard to their truth, but on the basis of their friendliness or antagonism to the subject of investigation. When the opinions of the sorters concerning a particular statement are too widely dispersed, or when the statement is apparently irrelevant, that is, does not reflect an attitude, the statement is discarded. The scale is then constructed on the basis of the remaining statements so that belief or disbelief in any one of them may be plotted in accordance with its degree of favorability thus established. The results of Professor Thurstone's method in studies of racial attitudes do not differ much from those of studies with less involved techniques.

Nevertheless, it seems that the methods of psychophysics promise the best results in the study of race attitudes. For purposes of comparison, it is suggested that Professor Fernberger's studies of weight discrimination be examined. See S. W. Fernberger, "The Effect of the Attitude of the Subject upon the Measure of Sensitivity," *American Journal of Psychology,* October, 1914, vol. xxv, pp. 538-543, his "Instructions and the Psychophysical Limen," *American Journal of Psychology,* July, 1931, vol. xliii, pp. 361-376, and "Die Ungewissheitsurteile in der Psychophysik," *Archiv für die gesamte Psychologie,* Band 80, Heft. ¾, 1931.

Lapiere.[9] Relying upon interview rather than printed questionnaire, and concealing the purpose of his inquiry, he gathered data from hundreds of persons in France and England as to their attitudes toward colored people. In France he took occasion wherever he happened to be on his travels to put to 428 people some form of the question, 'Would you let a good Negro live at your home?' . . . For reasons which he does not fully explain, he found it necessary to alter the form of his question [in England], so that the resulting data must not be regarded as in all points comparable. In various parts of England he asked people of various social classes some form of the question 'Would you let children, your own, or of your class associate with those of good colored people?' "[10] In France, there was much more prejudice against Negroes in the cities than in the rural districts. The French lower and middle classes evidenced anti-Negro feeling only rarely, while in the upper class it predominated. Of the thirty-one hotel proprietors interviewed in France, twenty-four expressed their willingness to accept colored guests, and most of the others were apparently influenced in their policy by tourist patronage, especially that of American tourists. Sixteen out of twenty hotel managers interviewed in England were unwilling to accept Negro guests. This country was also distinguished by a more even distribution of anti-Negro feeling throughout all social classes, although the lower class was more prejudiced than the upper. The specific expressions of such varied attitudes must be the product of cultural conditioning.

It is still logically possible, however, that a general predisposition toward racial antipathies, particularly strong against peoples who vary greatly in outward characteristics from the prejudiced individual, may be the inherited biological foundation on which superstructures of conditioned responses are built. It is even possible that within a given race there may be individuals with a much greater or a much weaker inherent receptivity to racial prejudices. An analogy

[9] R. T. Lapiere, "Race Prejudice: France and England," *Social Forces,* September, 1928, vol. vii, No. 1, pp. 102-111.
[10] Gardner Murphy and Lois B. Murphy, *op. cit.,* pp. 632ff.

from our knowledge of sex is timely, for in spite of the startling differences in the sex practices of races, nations, and
even of individuals within a given group, it is conceded that
there is an underlying biological sex impulse which may find
expression in diverse ways.

Even the additional argument against the possibility that
if there were some inherent tendency favoring, perhaps demanding, the development of racial animosities, it would find
expression in children at an earlier age than is generally the
case, is not conclusive. Bruno Lasker makes much of the fact
that young children of all races are apparently free from feelings of disgust, hatred or even mild dislike for persons of another race until they have learned the lesson of prejudice
from their elders.[11] It is possible, if unlikely, that racial attitudes, like the sexual attitudes of maturity, may normally
be delayed in their development.

The belief in an inherent predisposition favoring the development of racial prejudices, more common among laymen
than among social psychologists and sociologists, rests almost entirely on the reasoning that a social phenomenon of
such wide distribution must have an inbred foundation. No
doubt it has, in the same sense that every human action has
a biological basis. It is only when the attempt is made to cor-
relate race prejudice with a specific inbred tendency that the
argument falls from lack of support.

Race prejudice may be compared with such personality
traits as radicalism and conservatism, emotional excitability
and stability, receptivity and resistance to suggestion, careful thinking and jumping to conclusions, or high and low general intelligence. Thus far, however, investigators have been
unable to show that there is any necessary correlation between either the acceptance of or freedom from antagonistic
racial attitudes and a single one of these traits. Furthermore,
these traits themselves have not yet been adequately analyzed
with regard to the relative importance of nature and nurture
in their development. It is usually thought that the American

[11] Bruno Lasker, *Race Attitudes in Children*, Henry Holt & Company, Inc.,
New York, 1929, pp. xvi + 394.

free from antagonistic racial attitudes is likely to be something of a general radical, emotionally unstable, quick in
judgment, able and anxious to think for himself, and a bit
better than average in ability, if perhaps a trifle unbalanced.
Actually, he may be the exact opposite in any or all of these
characteristics. The verdict must be the Scottish one of "not
proven." Whatever may in the future be found to be the biological basis of unfavorable racial attitudes, it is so varied
in its manifestations today, and has been so varied during
all that period of human history of which we have records,
that it may undoubtedly be sublimated or even entirely suppressed with no danger to the individual's personality.[12]

Racial attitudes, friendly or antagonistic, may be the product of objective and accurate observations, but they are more
likely to be based on limited and faulty knowledge, distorted
by the minds through which they have been relayed, and by
the subjective interpretations of their possessor. Human experience is limited, but personal opinions may be posited on
limited and false information. Even a stupid person who
has never studied chemistry will hesitate to hazard a guess
as to the product of a mixture of sulphuric acid and zinc, but
such diffidence is rare when it comes to the expression of an
opinion concerning the outcome of social processes. What
American has not spoken his mind on sovietism, on the qualifications of dozens of persons for the presidency, on prohibition, on imperialism, and on inherent racial characteristics,
from information so limited and uncertain that its counterpart in chemistry, physics, or biology would be good reason
for flunking a high-school student? What Walter Lippmann
has so aptly called "the pictures in our heads" make it possible for us to be dogmatic about social questions with which
we are as unfamiliar as we are with the possibilities of life
on Mars.

These "pictures in our heads" may be definite mental images

---

[12] The best discussion of the innate factors in the formation of attitudes,
together with critical summaries of the investigations of G. W. Allport, E.
D. Starbuck, I. Husband, H. T. Moore, M. F. Washburn, G. B. Vetter and
others who have made contributions to this field of knowledge, is to be found
in Gardner Murphy and Lois B. Murphy, op. cit., pp. 655ff.

or verbal characterizations. They are shortcuts to conclusions on everything under the sun. They are commonly so uniform throughout all kinds of population groupings that Lippmann's term "stereotypes" may be applied with propriety. "When we use the word 'Mexico' what picture does it evoke in a resident of New York? Likely as not, it is some composite of sand, cactus, oil wells, greasers, rum-drinking Indians, testy old cavaliers flourishing whiskers and sovereignty, or, perhaps an idyllic peasantry à la Jean Jacques, assailed by the prospect of smoky industrialism, and fighting for the Rights of Man. What does the word 'Japan' evoke? Is it a vague horde of slant-eyed yellow men, surrounded by Yellow Perils, picture brides, fans, Samurai, banzais, art and cherry blossoms? Or the word 'alien'? According to a group of New England college students, writing in the year 1920, an alien was the following:

'A person hostile to this country.'
'A person against the government.'
'A person who is on the opposite side.'
'A native of an unfriendly country.'
'A foreigner at war.'
'A foreigner who tries to do harm to the country he is in.'
'An enemy from a foreign land.'
'A person against a country,' etc. . . .

"Yet the word alien is an unusually exact legal term, far more exact than words like sovereignty, independence, national honor, rights, defense, aggression, imperialism, capitalism, socialism, about which we readily take sides 'for' or 'against.' "[13] The significance of stereotyped "pictures in our heads" in race relations will be evident if the reader will pause a moment to visualize and verbally characterize his concepts of the typical Negro, Oriental, Italian, Swede, German, Jew, Englishman, Canadian, Mexican, and other American minorities of racial and national origin.

[13] Walter Lippmann, *Public Opinion*, The Macmillan Company, New York, 1927, pp. 68-69. Mr. Lippmann's quotation is from *The New Republic*, December 29, 1920, p. 142. Reprinted with the permission of the publishers.

Popular notions of group traits, physical or social, are never accurate either in detail or in broad outline. There are more points of similarity between the most widely differing races of mankind than there are dissimilarities, yet stereotypes invariably emphasize the variant characteristics. Individuals within any racial or nationality group in the United States differ far more in inborn characteristics and cultural attainments than the "typical" or "average" members of any two such groups differ from each other. There is, of course, always more than one stereotype applied to American minorities. Thus we have stereotypes of the German, English, or Portuguese Jew at odds with that of the Russian "kike," mental pictures of fat, beer-drinking Germans and of arrogant Prussians, of Russian Bolshevists, and of Russian aristocrats, of "darkeys" and "bad niggers," of "greasers" and of Latin Americans. These sub-stereotypes, however, cannot be sufficiently multiplied to take account of all significant variations within a minority, nor are they necessarily any more accurate because of their limited application. Inadequate, faulty observations and misinterpretations are not automatically corrected by such pseudo-refinement.[14] Racial stereotypes are necessarily false because they, like Procrustes, mutilate the individual to fit a preconceived notion of what a person should be like. Because Negroes have been stereotyped as "primitive," "animal-like," "unmoral," and "emotionally unstable," the individual Negro is popularly assumed to be oversexed, thieving, care-free, and irresponsible. Because the Jew is visualized as obsessed by the desire for wealth, individual Jews must be unscrupulous, shrewd, and money-mad. Peculiarly enough, where a member of one racial group becomes intimately acquainted with some member of another race, the individual is admitted to be an exception to the accepted stereotype of his group; but, no matter how many such exceptions are dis-

[14] For an analysis of the rôle of stereotypes in politics which demonstrates their inherent inaccuracies as well as their importance in social relations, see Stuart A. Rice, *Quantitative Methods in Politics,* Alfred A. Knopf, New York, 1928, pp. xxii + 331, and "Stereotypes: A Source of Error in Judging Human Character," *Journal of Personal Research,* November, 1926, vol. v, No. 7.

covered, the stereotype is still retained for the rest. This is
the explanation of the common observation that while the
South hates Negroes in general, it loves and protects the individual Negro. Jews have a saying that every Gentile has his
pet Jew, which, being interpreted, means that even anti-
Semites make exceptions to their general prejudices when
they happen to become really acquainted with a member of
the hated minority. Cultural barriers, however, so restrict
the number of such intergroup contacts that stereotypes, fat-
tened by ignorance, are not destroyed thereby.

Yet racial attitudes and stereotypes do change. They
change, however, not because of exceptional intimate and
understanding friendships between individuals of antagonistic groups, but when the basic conditions which have produced
group hatreds are removed. Science has taught us that there
must be causes for every effect, and that only by eliminating
causes may their consequences be prevented. It seems, however, that we in the United States are unwilling or unable
to apply this principle in the social world as we do in the
material. If a polluted stream is spreading disease we promptly
seek the source of pollution to destroy it. If soil is infertile
it is analyzed to determine whether potash, nitrates, or phos-
phates should be added to improve the yield. Forgetting
this rule, when social ills stir us into action, the cause is then
assumed to lie in human perversity or ignorance of proper
standards, and we apply the ineffective remedies of moral
exhortation and instruction, neglectful of factors which are
beyond the influence of sermons and academic lectures.

In the author's previously mentioned attempt to measure
the beliefs of his students concerning the inborn capacities of
twenty-four races, nationalities and culture groups, he also
tried to discover changes in student attitudes produced by
his course in American race relations. Identical questionnaires
were submitted to the students during the first and last fifteen minutes of a thirty-hour course which included lectures,
assignments, and class discussions of the concept of race,
the cultural backgrounds of American minorities, their present status, and a constant emphasis on the importance of the

physical and social environment in cultural achievement. Among the points persistently stressed was the author's belief that although there may well be inherent differences in potential ability between races, their extent and nature have not yet been scientifically established, that the overlapping between races is known to be far more important than the divergencies, and that such closely related peoples as the English, French, German, Scandinavian, and white American, primarily political and cultural groupings, may not be contrasted in regard to native intelligence on the basis of our present meager knowledge of race psychology. The results of this experiment showed remarkably few changes in student attitudes.

There were thirty-one students who said they thought that all races were about equal in native ability in the questionnaires returned before the course began. This number was increased to forty-eight by a semester's instruction. There is, however, reason to doubt the sincerity of some of these expressions of disbelief in any relationship between race and civilization, for some students were unquestionably inspired in their liberality by a desire to please their teacher. The majority, nevertheless, were frank enough to register the same opinions concerning the relative inherent abilities of racial, national, and cultural groupings after taking the course as before, as is evidenced by the following coefficients of correlation:

Ranking by first-term group before course to ranking
    by same group after course.................... .98
Ranking by second-term group before course to ranking by same group after course............... .96
Ranking by first-term group before course to ranking
    by second-term group before course........... .92
Ranking by first-term group after course to ranking
    by second-term group after course............ .95

All of these figures are so near +1 that the variations become insignificant. Apparently the fifteen weeks of logic, facts and figures in thirty classroom hours of a semester course is not an adequate counterirritant to fifteen years or more of attitude building in life situations.

It should not be implied that there were no worth-while changes in the racial attitudes of these students. If nothing more was accomplished than the development of a willingness to argue, to realize that there is more than one side to racial problems, the course in race relations may be considered to have been relatively successful. There is, furthermore, the question of whether or not it is the function of a college course in this subject to influence student attitudes. Perhaps nothing more should be attempted than a presentation of facts. If so, the students investigated in this study obtained all the profit that may have been properly expected, for their formal examinations showed an adequate knowledge of the subject. Knowledge and attitudes, it seems, may actually contradict each other, for students who made term grades of 85 per cent and over, indicative of the accretion, if not of the assimilation, of racial facts, retained prejudiced stereotyped racial attitudes with no apparent mental conflict.

The results of this investigation suggested that racial attitudes, the highly emotionalized products of years of exposure to life situations, might better be changed by an emotionalized teaching method involving actual life situations, than by logical, formalized pedagogy, perhaps more adapted to the teaching of mathematics and chemistry than to instruction in social science. To test this suggestion, a group of sixteen graduate students were in the following year given a factual background in American race relations during the first semester and then put through a term's work consisting largely of unusual contacts with Negroes who were in startling contrast with popular racial stereotypes.

These graduate students visited a Negro hospital and watched a skillful colored surgeon perform a delicate major operation, listened to colored doctors explain the recent rapid advances in the medical arts made by their people, and seemed impressed by what they saw and heard. They were entertained at a tea in the home of a wealthy and cultured Negro couple. They met a charming colored girl who was an excellent pianist and heard her play difficult classical compositions on a Steinway in a home which they might all have been proud to own. Week after week they found their stereotyped attitudes toward the Negro in conflict with new experiences. It should be emphasized that when this project was suggested to them —they were given an absolutely free choice between a formal lecture and discussion course and the experimental one which they unanimously selected—they were eager to cooperate and discover what might happen to their racial attitudes. At the end of the academic year an involved questionnaire which they had filled out in the early fall was again submitted to them and the results "before and after taking" were compared. They had also been given a psychological examination by Dr. Samuel W. Fernberger, of the University of Pennsylvania Department of Psychology, in the hope that some correlation might be discovered between attitude flexibility and individual psychological qualities.

The results were characterized by a lack of uniformity. Some students showed less prejudiced attitudes after the course than before. However, the student who was least antagonistic to the Negro before the course apparently acquired a nice set of violent prejudices as the result of his exposure to contacts with exceptional Negroes. Most of the variations were slight, although the increase in prejudice was smaller in proportion than the increase in tolerance. No correlation could be made between the results of Dr. Fernberger's tests and the changes in attitudes. The number of students examined was, of course, too small to justify statistical treatment, but the absence of any pronounced trend in the resulting changes in racial attitudes, either in the nature of the changes or in their extent, supports a skeptical view of the influence of even emotionalized classroom treatment of racial attitudes.

Not all investigators of changes in student attitudes have reported negative results.[15] Indeed, a majority of such studies

[15] For more optimistic statements of belief in the possibility of fundamental changes in racial attitudes due to classroom instruction, see Rachel Davis Du Bois, "Building Tolerant Attitudes in High-School Students," *The Crisis*, October, 1931, pp. 334-336; Katherine Gardner, "Changing Racial Attitudes,"

report increases in tolerance, liberalism and radicalism following in the wake—somewhat far behind, it must be admitted—of higher education. Such correlations, however, must be heavily discounted to allow for the difference between verbalized opinions and actual attitudes, for the confusion in comparisons of results caused by increased information and better interpretation of questions which produce a semblance of changes in attitudes, and for general defects in measurement techniques. For example, before taking a course in race relations a student may check as true the statement that "Negroes are all right as long as they stay in their place," and then at the end of a semester's study of American racial minorities mark the same statement as false. Does this necessarily indicate a change in his attitude toward the Negro? It may, but it is more likely to mean that he wants to prove to his teacher that he was a worthy student, that the meaning of the statement has been changed for him, that he is trying to be intellectually honest in spite of a continuing prejudice against Negroes, or that he has come to recognize ethical implications in the statement to which he is unwilling to subscribe—implications which have not altered his traditional mode of behavior when faced with the necessity for action instead of merely registering an opinion. If we know so little about changes in attitudes produced by college courses, it may be assumed that confidence in the socializing power of scattered lectures, sermons, articles, and books is only an evidence of wishful thinking.

Before we may talk of increasing interracial understanding and cooperation, of destroying racial prejudices, of giving reality to the doctrine of the brotherhood of man, should we not first take thought of the reasons for group animosities? Why do French-Canadian, Irish, German, and Polish Catholics need to worship in separate buildings? If the brotherhood of man means anything, how can the fact that every racial and nationality group in the United States supports its own

The Crisis, October, 1931, pp. 336-337; Ruth Wanger, *High School Study of the Negro,* The Friends Committee on Race Relations, 20 South 12th Street, Philadelphia, 1931, p. 4.

monotheistic sects be explained? One might imagine that monotheistic religions would be the leading forces drawing mankind together into harmonious natural communities, yet it seems that racial prejudices are stronger than religious beliefs, for they are a major cause of differentiation in worship.[16] Further, if education is a cure for racial prejudices, how explain the fact that they are found among scholars as well as among the illiterate, and that they are more widespread and powerful in the civilized world of today, a world which makes a fetish of its democracy in education, than they were before the spread of the public-school system? The answer is that we preach and teach, accept and follow, current beliefs and not millennial ideals. Social leaders and reformers who are out of step with their times obtain few converts. There must be something in our times which breeds group antagonisms. If so, not until we know its nature may a program for a change in racial attitudes be initiated with any hope of success.

Our task, then, is one of understanding the causes of racial friction. This requires a knowledge of the manifold activities of American minorities of racial and national origin—how they earn their living, their relations with the government, their family life, their physical and mental qualities, and even the ways they spend their leisure time. Some apparently minor personality trait may make an individual unpopular and an outcast; some equally minor group characteristic may lead to social segregation, economic discrimination, and political exclusion. Every contact between races and culture groups of foreign extraction must be scrutinized. A large order, it may be said; but if the emphasis is on interpretation rather than on minute details, a survey within the scope of a single volume may be profitable if not all inclusive. Forgetting our stereotyped racial attitudes whenever possible, realizing their mythi-

---

[16] See Clifford Kirkpatrick, *Religion in Human Affairs*, John Wiley & Sons, Inc., New York, 1929, chap. x; H. Richard Niebuhr, *The Social Sources of Denominationalism*, Henry Holt & Company, Inc., New York, 1929, pp. viii + 304.

cal origins when they will not be put out of mind, we may proceed in our undertaking by examining the characteristic activities of American minorities and their impacts on the happiness and welfare of the majority, the native-born, white descendants of old American stock.

CHAPTER II

RESTLESS PEOPLES

WITHOUT migration there would be no problems of conflict between the established population and minorities of racial and national origin. By migration is meant any population movement except those of a temporary nature by individuals who never become affiliated with the communities which they visit, such as tourists or envoys who may be residents in but not members of an alien neighborhood. It might be proper to include even these as migrants, but their motives and affiliations are so distinct that doing so would serve no useful purpose in migration analysis. Human migrations involving more than a superficial relationship to the new home and its existing population are the subject of our study.

It is possible to differentiate between a number of types of such human migrations. Whole tribes or communities may change their residence, or the unit of migration may be the individual or the family. The movement may be from a well populated region of complex culture to one less well developed, or the reverse. Sheer weight of numbers may enable a simple folk to overwhelm a more advanced people. Armed forces and a few camp followers have often been the entering wedge for civilian migrants who came later. The migrants may become subject to the authority of the political powers existing in their new home, or they may extend the boundaries of their own nation. The old allegiance may be retained, or it may be lost through some form of naturalization.[1] These are some of the variations between forms of migration, but the main form which we shall need to keep separate in our thoughts is that in which the individual or the family is the migrating

---

[1] For a concise classification of the forms of migration, together with a discussion of their social effects, see H. P. Fairchild, *Immigration*, The Macmillan Company, New York, 1928, chap. i.

21

unit and in which the political authority of the land to which the migrant moves is recognized, either with or without a change in citizenship status.

THE POPULATION OF THE EARTH

For the sake of perspective, let us preface our discussion of migration to and within the United States by a brief statement concerning the distribution and growth of the world population. The best and most recent summary of the known facts on this subject is to be found in *International Migrations*, Volume II, edited by Walter F. Willcox. Chapter I, from which the table and chart below have been taken, was prepared by Dr. Willcox himself.

For graphic presentation of the essential data in Table I, the accompanying chart, also by Dr. Willcox, is reproduced. It shows in vivid form the terrific increase in the population of the world during the last two hundred and eighty years, only a brief part of the hundreds of thousands of years man has been on earth. The inclusion in this chart of the dots and solid line to represent contemporary estimates of world population is valuable if only because the wide variations between these estimates indicate the danger of error in such guesses. Dr. Willcox would be the last to claim infallibility for his figures, for he has said that, "The figures [in the chapter from which the table and chart have been taken] may be left with the comment of an eighteenth-century predecessor upon his own results. 'They are not to be viewed with much confidence but they are a first step towards the truth. The proper way to criticize them is to displace them by more accurate figures. They are more like old maps of unexplored parts of the world, useful or even necessary until rectified by new discoveries.' "[2] Perhaps we may be allowed to think of Dr. Willcox's estimates as new maps of partially explored territory, useful guides to students of migration, because in spite of probable errors in detail, existing fragmentary data were suffi-

[2] Walter Willcox, *International Migrations*, National Bureau of Economic Research, Inc., New York, 1931, p. 82. His quotation is from Moheau, *Recherches et considérations sur la population de la France* (1778), p. 62.

TABLE I

ESTIMATED POPULATION OF THE EARTH AND THE CONTINENTS, 1650—1929[3]

(In Millions)

Continent	Year						Area[a] in Million Square Miles
	1650	1750	1800	1850	1900	1929	
Asia	250	406	522	671	859	954	16.7
Europe	100	140	187	266	401	478	3.8
North America	7	6.3	15.4	39	106	162	9.4
Africa	100	100	100	100	141	140	10.8
South America	6	6.1	9.2	20	38	77	7.3
Australasia and Polynesia	2	2	2	2	6	9	3.3
Total	465	660.4	836.6	1098	1551	1820	51.3
Annual increase per 100,000	....	351	474	549	693	553	.....

Per Cent Distribution							
Asia	53.8	61.5	62.5	61.1	55.4	52.4	32.6
Europe	21.5	21.2	22.4	24.2	25.9	26.3	7.4
North America	1.5	1.0	1.8	3.6	6.8	8.9	18.4
Africa	21.5	15.1	12.0	9.1	9.1	7.7	21.0
South America	1.3	0.9	1.1	1.8	2.4	4.2	14.2
Australasia and Polynesia	0.4	0.3	0.2	0.2	0.4	0.5	6.4
Total	100.0	100.0	100.0	100.0	100.0	100.0	100.0

[a] Excluding the uninhabited Polar lands; based on International Statistical Institute *Aperçu de la démographie . . . du monde, 1929*, pp. iv, 25–40.

cient to enable some checking which, together with shrewd estimating based on years of experience, has furnished us with a diagram accurate in broad outline, at least.

Two observations may be made with assurance in their accuracy: first, that the population of the earth has long been distributed over its surface most unevenly, even making due allowance for arability, and, second, that the rapid increase of world population has not been the result of population increase in all continents with anything like approximate equality.

[3] *Ibid.,* vol. ii, p. 78.

Asia has had a bit more than half of the world population since 1650 at least, with but 32.6 per cent of the world's area. Europe, with 7.4 per cent of the area, has maintained about a quarter of the earth's people for not less than three centuries. Africa, with 21.0 per cent of the land area, has had her proportion of the world population drop from 21.5 per

FIGURE 1[4]
CONTEMPORARY ESTIMATES (DOTS AND SOLID LINE) AND PRESENT ESTIMATES
(DASH LINE) OF THE POPULATION OF THE EARTH AT VARIOUS DATES
BETWEEN 1650 AND 1929

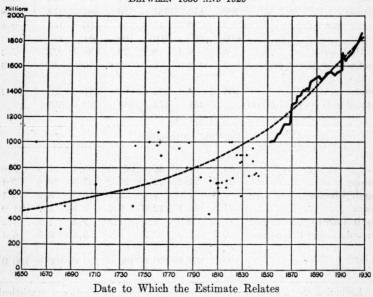

Date to Which the Estimate Relates

cent to 7.7 per cent. The largest proportionate gain has gone to North and South America, particularly to the United States. These shifts in population have not been the simple result of the balance of births and deaths, but, especially in the case of the Americas, have been complicated by migrations of all varieties.

MIGRATION TO THE UNITED STATES

Except the American Indians, of whom there are perhaps some 50,000,000, the rest of the people of the Americas,

[4] *Ibid.,* p. 79.

amounting to about a quarter of a billion, are all migrants or the descendants of migrants who came to these continents since the days of Columbus. Considering the United States alone, only a handful of the aboriginal inhabitants have survived, and only a few thousand of these, mostly in the southwest, are living anywhere near their pre-Columbian homes. In other words, practically every person in the United States belongs to a migrant group which has moved to its present home within the last three centuries. Further confusion results from the fact that these wanderings, both within the country and from beyond its borders, have been taking place continuously since the days of the first European settlers.

TABLE II

POPULATION OF THE UNITED STATES FOR 1930 BY RACE AND NATIVITY

Race or Nativity	Number	Per Cent
Total population	122,775,046	100
White	108,864,207	88.7
Native	95,497,800	
Native parentage	70,136,614	
Foreign parentage	16,999,221	
Mixed parentage	8,361,965	
Foreign-born	13,366,407	
Negro	11,891,143	9.7
Mexican	1,422,533	1.2
Indian	332,397	0.3
Chinese	74,954	0.1
Japanese	138,834	0.1
Filipino	45,208	.....
Hindu	3,130	.....
Korean	1,860	.....
All other	780	.....

European migrants who came to the United States before 1820, when our immigration records begin, together with their children may be considered the original, almost the colonial, white population of the United States. Since that time the total reported immigration has been 37,672,012, mostly Europeans. If this may be considered as a single population movement, it is the greatest migration known in the history of the world. Distributed by decades, the detailed figures are as follows:

TABLE III

IMMIGRATION TO THE UNITED STATES, 1820–1930[5]

Years	Number
1820	8,385
1821–30	143,439
1831–40	599,125
1841–50	1,713,251
1851–60	2,598,214
1861–70	2,314,824
1871–80	2,812,191
1881–90	5,246,613
1891–1900	3,687,564
1901–10	8,795,386
1911–20	5,735,811
1921–30	4,107,209
Total	37,762,012

These statistics of immigration take no account of aliens

[5] *Annual Report of the Commissioner General of Immigration for 1930,* p. 198. To this total should perhaps be added the 250,000 aliens estimated by the Commissioner to have arrived between the close of the Revolutionary War and 1820.

The value of these figures for purposes of comparison from year to year is impaired by statistical defects in their collection. According to the Commissioner, *loc. cit.,* "For 1820 to 1867 the figures are for alien passengers arriving; for 1868 to 1903, for immigrants arriving; for 1904 to 1906, for aliens admitted; and for 1907 to 1930, for immigrant aliens admitted. The years from 1820 to 1831 and 1844 to 1849, inclusive, are those ending September 30; from 1833 to 1843 and 1851 to 1867 those ending December 31; and beginning with 1869 and thereafter those ending June 30. The other periods cover 15 months ending December 31, 1832; 9 months ending December 31, 1843; 15 months ending December 31, 1850; and 6 months ending June 30, 1868."

who entered the United States surreptitiously, probably a considerable number, but impossible to estimate. They also take no account of those who left the country after being legally admitted, and hence they must not be interpreted as the actual increase to our population through immigration. Dr. Willcox estimates that out of the gross immigration of 37,762,012 individuals, only 26,180,000 may be said to be a net increase to our population.[6]

Until the year 1921, when the first quantitatively restrictive legislation applying to European immigrants was enacted, variations in the volume of admissions from year to year were reflections of increased or diminished desire on the part of aliens to enter our country. Oriental exclusion went into effect before the number of arrivals from the East was large enough to disturb the general contour of the waves of immigration as shown on the accompanying chart. Since up to 1921 aliens who could pass the negative requirements for admission were admitted freely, it is permissible to examine fluctuations in the volume of immigration in the hope that some light will thereby be thrown on the causes of immigration.

For example, it will be noticed that the periods of the Civil War, the Spanish American War and the World War, are periods of low ebb in immigration, obviously a relationship of cause and effect. The sharp declines in immigration after 1921 and after 1924, however, bear no relation to the causes of immigration, since the numerical restrictions of the quota acts passed in these years are sufficient to account for the declines.

Beginning in the second decade of the nineteenth century, there is a gradual increase in the volume of immigration, speeding up in the 'forties and 'fifties, reaching a peak in 1854, and then declining sharply, cut almost in half in one year, to the low point of the Civil War. The succeeding wave of immigration reached its crest in 1873, with a trough following rapidly so that the bottom was reached by 1877. Then follow peaks in 1882, 1892, 1907 and 1914, with corresponding low points in 1886, 1897, 1909 and 1918. Panics or recessions occurred in the United States in 1854, 1873, 1883, 1893, 1907

[6] Walter Willcox, *op. cit.*, p. 89.

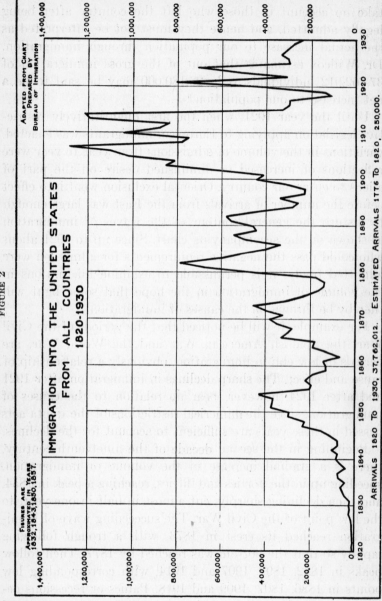

FIGURE 2

IMMIGRATION INTO THE UNITED STATES FROM ALL COUNTRIES 1820-1930

ADAPTED FROM CHART PREPARED BY BUREAU OF IMMIGRATION.

FIGURES ARE APPROXIMATED IN YEARS 1832, 1843, 1850, 1857.

ARRIVALS 1820 TO 1930, 37,762,012.   ESTIMATED ARRIVALS 1776 TO 1820, 250,000.

and 1913, dates which are nearly the same as those for immigration crests.[7]

The interpretation of this correlation is that economic conditions in the United States are the most important immediate cause of gross immigration. Economic upsets are preceded by boom times, with a pyramiding of credit, production and corresponding opportunities for labor. The fact that immigration on several occasions, notably 1873 and 1907, reached the crest of the wave in the panic years themselves—an unfortunate situation since it meant the addition of hundreds of thousands of laborers to an already overstocked labor market—may be explained by the time it takes for news of panics to reach Europe, for immigrants already on the way to arrive or change their plans, and by the fact that fiscal years do not correspond to calendar years. Thus the fiscal year 1907 included six months of 1906, a year of prosperity, and had adjustments been made for this fact in the chart the volume credited to 1907 would be much lower, in spite of the fact that momentum acquired in the prosperous preceding years carried thousands of immigrants into the midst of American hard times.

Hard times have been blamed on everything conceivable, even on spots in the sun, and the immigrant has not been exempt. The correlation between the volume of immigration and economic conditions in the United States has been seized upon as proof that the immigrant has been a cause of financial depressions. Certainly he has made hard times harder by his presence, especially in the panics of the two decades before the World War. He has also aided the overexpansion of agriculture and industry by furnishing a ready-made labor supply,

[7] A careful analysis of the correlation between the volume of immigration and economic conditions both in the United States and in the countries of emigration is to be found in Harry Jerome, *Migration and Business Cycles*, National Bureau of Economic Research, Inc., New York, 1926, p. 256. A conclusion of this study is that "In brief, whatever may be the basic causes of migration, there is a close relation between the cyclical oscillations of employment and those of immigration and emigration, and a moderately close resemblance in the respective seasonal fluctuation, with considerable reason to believe that this similarity, particularly in the cyclical oscillations, is due to a sensitiveness of migration to employment conditions" (p. 243).

always at hand during the past century when overconfidence encouraged overexpansion and hastened economic collapse. Excepting these two factors, to say that immigration causes depressions is to put the cart before the horse, for the conditions which lead up to depressions are responsible for drawing the immigrant to the United States in greatest numbers, so that he becomes one of the victims even as he aggravates our own suffering.[8]

There is a popular impression in the United States that, while the recent immigrant has come to the United States for economic betterment, the older stocks came more for political and religious freedom. Some appearance of truth is given this belief by the fact that religious and political oppression in Europe was more common a generation or two ago under governments less representative than the more responsible ones of today. The importance of these forms of oppression has been overestimated, perhaps because most of us have ourselves had migrant ancestors, and it is more flattering to claim that they migrated because they would not knuckle down to tyranny than because of economic failure in the old country.

Of course conditions in Europe, including oppression of all types, have always been a factor in emigration. People rarely sever all home ties and move to a strange land if they are well off where they were born. There must be a "push" to give

[8] According to Jerome, "As to cyclical fluctuations in unemployment, it would appear that, directly at least, migration is probably not a primary cause of such variations in unemployment; and that in some instances it is an ameliorative influence, in that in limited portions of depression periods it is withdrawing more workers than it is contributing. More frequently, however, it is a contributory factor to the evils of unemployment. This conclusion is based in part upon the fact that the timing of migration changes to cyclical changes in employment is imperfect; and secondly, upon the fact that the peaks and troughs of industrial activity frequently coincide in the countries of immigration and of emigration, in which case migration cannot be well adjusted to conditions in both countries. Also, although a decline in employment is usually followed by a decline in immigration, the incoming stream does not dry up entirely, and in those portions of depression periods in which there is a net immigration—a not uncommon phenomenon—migration is feeding into industry more men than it is taking out. Lastly, the very fact of a known source of additional labor available through immigration in boom periods probably has lessened the pressure for regularization of industry" (*ibid.*, p. 243f.).

incentive to leave one place, and a "pull" of opportunity to help in the choice of a new home. Both the incentive to leave the homeland and the attraction of some other locality may and frequently do include the desire for greater personal liberty. The evidence from the financial status of arriving immigrants, who are without financial resources almost to a man, from the fluctuations in immigration from year to year in correspondence to American economic conditions, and from the economic conditions of the countries of emigration, conclusively establishes the hope for greater economic opportunity as the basic motive in migration. This is so obvious in the case of primitive folk wanderings that it is now taken for granted; immigration is not such a different form of migration that it need be made an exception to the general rule that the search for food is the prime motive in migration.

The Puritans, the Quakers, the Huguenots, the Mennonites, and the Jews are often cited as evidence against this conclusion. The same is true of the German revolutionists of 'forty-eight, the impoverished Irish, especially those who came during the periods when England's hand was heaviest, the racial minorities in Austria-Hungary before the World War, the Armenians, and other refugees. A better perspective is obtained if we recall that in all these cases more of these same oppressed peoples remained at home than emigrated to the United States. Undoubtedly persecution by the church, the state and by dominating majorities was a factor which helped drive out these emigrants, but a greater number of their brothers in oppression stayed at home and fought it out to a successful conclusion. Those who emigrated were not the most successful at home, although it must be assumed that their economic failures were to an unknown extent the result of persecution.

Among the causes of immigration are customarily included the advertising and agents of steamship and other transportation companies, of the American state and federal governments, of land companies, and of industrialists in need of labor. Letters of immigrants to friends in the home country and returned immigrants, with their accounts of success in their adventures, encourage others to emigrate. Such things as these, however, are only secondary causes of immigration, in that they merely spread or exaggerate information of attractive opportunities and help make up the minds of potential immigrants already dissatisfied with their condition.

TABLE IV

EUROPEAN IMMIGRATION, 1820–1930[9]

Years	Northern and Western[a]	Southern and Eastern[b]
1820–30	103,119	3,389
1831–40	489,739	5,949
1841–50	1,592,062	5,439
1851–60	2,431,336	21,324
1861–70	2,031,642	33,628
1871–80	2,070,373	201,889
1881–90	3,778,633	958,413
1891–1900	1,643,492	1,915,486
1901–10	1,910,035	6,225,981
1911–20	997,438	3,379,126
1921–30	1,284,023	1,193,830
Total	18,331,892	13,944,454

[a] Comprising Belgium, Denmark, France, Germany, Luxemburg (1925–1930), Netherlands, Norway, Sweden, Switzerland, and England, Ireland, Scotland, Wales, and United Kingdom not specified.
[b] Southern and eastern Europe comprises all countries on that continent not listed above.

If the chart of the annual volume of immigration were broken up into a dozen or more charts of the year-by-year influx of aliens from the main emigrant countries, the European causes of dissatisfaction would be more evident. This, however, would require more detailed analysis than seems necessary, and it will be sufficient to serve our purposes if it is pointed out that until some time after the Civil War the new immigrant, predominantly from southeastern Europe, was numerically unimportant, and that the volume of immigration from this source did not exceed the immigration from

[9] *Annual Report of the Commissioner General of Immigration for 1930,* p. 200.

northwestern Europe until the decade 1891-1900. There has been, of course, immigration from all sections of Europe throughout our history, but we are interested here only in significant variations in source. The quota acts artificially regulated the sources of immigration so that we are compelled to leave the relative proportions of old and new immigrants since 1921 out of consideration in our discussion of causes.

It has been argued that during the first period of immigration the attraction for immigrants was free or cheap land, and that this drew English, German, Scandinavian and other desirable north European immigrants to the United States. As a corollary to this belief, it has been stated that with the exhaustion of the public domain and the shift to industry as the major opportunity for aliens, the northwestern Europeans lost interest, and the allegedly less desirable new immigrants began swarming to our shores, lured by work which the natives and the better class of immigrant would not accept. This interpretation is inaccurate.[10]

Considering the state of economic development, Europe may be said to have been overpopulated during the first half of the nineteenth century. This was especially true of the British Isles and Germany. In Ireland, for example, some eight million people were supported at a squalid level of existence in this period, and with the subsequent failure of the potato crop and abuses of the landlord system, surplus millions were forced to migrate for economic reasons which were, as previously explained, rationalized into religious and political excuses. Similar conditions, though perhaps not so sharply defined, existed throughout other parts of Europe with similar results up to the time when industrial development gave employment to added millions who could not have existed in an agricultural society.

Historically the appropriation of public land, the earliest incentive to immigration, may be divided into two periods:

[10] The author is indebted to *The Annals* of the American Academy of Political and Social Science and to Dr. W. Wallace Weaver for permission to adapt and reprint in this chapter sections of an article prepared jointly by himself and Dr. Weaver on "The Public Lands and Immigration" which originally appeared in *The Annals*, Publication No. 2234, March, 1929.

(1) that prior to 1862, during which the public lands were regarded as a source of revenue, and (2) that since 1862, during which the object of the government has been to secure the development of the lands as rapidly as possible. The year 1862 does not mark a sharp transition from a policy of sales to one of free land, for sales continued on a considerable scale until quite recently, but after that year any person desiring a farm could secure it free of charge by fulfilling the requirements of the Homestead Act.

Under the land acts prior to 1862, land was sold in tracts as small as forty acres and as large as a half million acres. The price ranged from one to two dollars per acre, though the bulk was sold at a dollar and a quarter per acre. The peak of sales was reached in 1836, when over 20,000,000 acres were sold for approximately $25,000,000. Few other years approached this in volume of sales, but between 1796 and 1862 about 157,000,000 were disposed of at a sum exceeding $186,-000,000. In addition to this, some 68,000,000 acres allowed as bounties to soldiers were disposed of under acts passed prior to 1862. Much of the land alienated during this period found its way into the possession of immigrants, especially in the Northwest Territory.

The years following 1862 are marked by an extravagant disbursement of lands, not only through free homesteads, but also through grants to railroads, education, Indians, forest reserves, parks, and special grants. By 1890 the best of the public agricultural lands were exhausted, and settlers began to turn to semi-arid, cut-over, and swamp land. Sales of Indian lands, reclamation projects, and liberal grazing grants have continued to offer inducement to immigrants, but the opportunities witnessed during the years between 1862 and 1890 can never be duplicated. Since the beginning of federal control a total of 1,397,000,000 acres has been distributed.[11]

After the free lands were used up, the immigrant neither supplied food for the non-agricultural worker nor speeded the exploitation of rural areas. Instead, he became a severe com-

[11] B. H. Hibbard, *A History of the Public Land Policies,* The Macmillan Company, New York, 1924, p. 570.

petitor of the masses and as such was voted into minor importance by restrictive immigration legislation. His usefulness gone, he was deserted even by his brother immigrants.

The explanation that the recent immigrant does not go to the farm because there is no farm land within reach of an immigrant's purse, now that the public domain has been depleted, apparently has not occurred to many who shudder at the rapid rise of the city. At a time when farms are being abandoned as unprofitable by native American owners who have slaved to make a living on them, but have been driven to salvage what they could before hiring out in the mills, the immigrant would have to be an alchemist if, without capital or credit, he could make agriculture his major occupation.

It is alleged that he is now of a racial type which does not take to rural life, in spite of the fact that in Europe farming was his main occupation. It is said that he wishes to have the fellowship and aid of his own kind by living in communities where his own language and customs prevail, although it is well known that the German and the Swede had no difficulty in finding such communities in Wisconsin and Minnesota. The claim is made that he is only a temporary immigrant, intending to return to his native land as soon as a little money has been laid by, regardless of the common knowledge that he shows a relatively slight tendency to do so. The sixth revision (1926) of that standard text on *The Immigration Problem* by Jenks and Lauck, in two sections entitled "Why the Immigrant Does Not Go to the Land," and "Getting the Immigrant on the Land," does not even mention the scarcity and high cost of land today as a factor. Changes which are considered undesirable must apparently be blamed on the immigrant and not on ourselves. Yet the fact is almost self-evident that the new immigrant from southern and eastern Europe stays in the industrial areas as much as he does and engages in industry or commerce largely because there is nothing else for him to do.

The claim, then, that the exhaustion of public lands has resulted in a shift in the race and nationality of our immigrants from the land-loving northern and western European to the wage-working southern and eastern European peasant, is patently in error. Since almost all immigrants migrate primarily for economic reasons, and those who have come to the United States are no exception to the general rule, it is to be expected that they will settle where the returns are the greatest. It so happens that the economic discontent which drove the English, Scandinavians and Germans to our country occurred early when free land was still available, while the Italians, Greeks, Slavs, and other new immigrants did not have sufficient incentive and knowledge to migrate to America until industry offered the prime opportunity for economic improvement. It should be remembered that the Italian who migrates to Brazil is easily persuaded to become a rural dweller, and that even in the United States, as will be explained later, hundreds of thousands of new immigrants earn their living by agricultural pursuits, the number being about in proportion to the opportunities available.

Had the European incentives to emigration been reversed in time, it would have been the southeastern European who settled out west on the farms and the northwestern European who manned our factories and mills as unskilled labor. This does not mean that there are not some small groups who prefer the cities in any case. The majority, however, go where the opportunities are greatest.

Only the causes of European immigration have thus far received specific attention, although only 85.4 per cent, or 32,276,346, of the total of 37,762,012 immigrants who came to the United States between 1820 and 1930 were from Europe. What of the others? Did they, too, come for land and wages? The common assumption is that they did. We white people are ever more ready to ascribe materialistic motives to red, yellow, and brown immigrants with whom we claim no kinship, than to the white, our ancestors, who simply must have been idealistic in their motives for migration!

Table V contains the decennial immigration totals for non-European admissions. The totals in this table are subject to the same statistical criticisms as have been previously mentioned in our criticism of immigration statistics in general.

TABLE V

IMMIGRATION TO THE UNITED STATES, 1820–1930, FROM NON-EUROPEAN SOURCES [12]

Source	Years											Total 111 Years 1820–1930
	1820–30	1831–40	1841–50	1851–60	1861–70	1871–80	1881–90	1891–1900	1901–10	1911–20	1921–30	
Canada and Newfoundland	2,486	13,624	41,723	59,309	153,878	383,640	393,304	3,311	179,226	742,185	924,515	2,897,201
Mexico	4,818	6,599	3,271	3,078	2,191	5,162	1,913	971	49,642	219,004	459,287	755,936
West Indies	3,998	12,301	13,528	10,660	9,046	13,957	29,042	33,066	107,548	123,424	74,899	431,469
South America	542	856	3,579	1,224	1,397	1,128	2,304	1,075	17,280	41,899	42,215	113,499
Other America	107	44	368	449	95	157	404	549	8,192	17,159	15,800	43,324
Total America	11,951	33,424	62,469	74,720	166,607	404,044	426,967	38,972	361,888	1,143,671	1,516,716	4,241,429
China	3	8	35	41,397	64,301	123,201	61,711	14,799	20,605	21,278	29,907	377,245
Japan	0	0	0	0	186	149	2,270	25,942	129,797	83,837	33,462	275,643
Other Asia	12	40	47	58	143	473	4,399	30,495	93,165	87,444	34,031	250,307
Total Asia	15	48	82	41,455	64,630	123,823	68,380	71,236	243,567	192,559	97,400	903,195
Total, other sources	33,350	69,965	53,199	29,379	18,317	12,062	14,220	18,378	53,915	23,017	15,240	341,042

Excluding Europe, America and Asia, as specified; including Africa, Australia, New Zealand, and appertaining islands, other Pacific Islands, and countries not specified.

[12] From Annual Report of the Commissioner General of Immigration for 1930, p. 202.

In addition, there has probably been more smuggling of aliens in some of these non-European groups than in the case of Europeans. Paul S. Taylor, for example, believes the number of Mexican laborers who have surreptitiously crossed our borders to be dangerously large.[13] The illegal entry of Orientals has long been a sore subject in the west and in Congress. There is no way accurately to check illegal entries, for even a comparison of those aliens known to have been properly admitted with the number found in the United States at a given time is dangerous evidence, since it must be corrected against the number of births, deaths and emigrants. However, it may be assumed that the number of legal admissions of aliens of any nationality is roughly proportionate in fluctuations to the pressure against our borders at other than officially designated ports of entry, allowing for the varying accessibility of different nationalities to our territory. Restrictive legislation destroys this relationship.

Mexican immigrants have been peasants, mostly of mixed Indian and white blood, with a slight, unnoticeable Negro infusion, and a goodly proportion of pure Indians and a few whites. This is in accordance with the racial origins of the total Mexican population of about 14,250,000 persons, of whom 9.8 per cent are white, 59.3 per cent Mestizo, 20.2 per cent Indian, with only 1.7 per cent Oriental, Negro, foreign-born or unknown.[14] There has been religious conflict in Mexico. Political disturbances and oppression of the inferior classes from whom immigrants are drawn have been present with varying intensity since before Mexican immigration to the United States became heavy. Study of Mexican immigration to the United States shows that its volume depends more on labor opportunities in this country than on persecution of a religious or political nature. Opportunities in construction work, in the agricultural development of California and the South-

[13] See Paul S. Taylor, *Mexican Labor in the United States: Migration Statistics*, University of California Press, Berkeley, 1929.

[14] *Ibid.*, p. 239. Taylor believes the proportion of white people is overestimated by the Mexican census, and quotes Ernest Gruening, *Mexico and Its Heritage*, The Century Company, New York, 1928, p. 70, who estimates that the number cannot be over 500,000 (p. 238).

west, the need for labor created in Texas by the northward migration of Negroes, these are the sort of immediate causes which may most easily be related to Mexican immigration. Dissatisfactions with home conditions must be supplemented by definite economic opportunities in another region before they become effective as causes of migration.

Chinese immigration was non-existent until the decade 1851-1860, when 41,397 arrived in response to the need for labor in California. After the discovery of gold and the resulting influx of adventurous white men from other parts of the United States, there was work to be done which was despised by white men who preferred more lucrative occupations than washing clothes, cooking, trucking, road building, and the like. Until the completion of the first transcontinental railroad in the late 'sixties it was a long, hard, and frequently expensive journey from the east to California, whether one went across the plains or took a water route. Cheap Chinese labor was the only abundant labor supply in sight, and the oriental stream, once started by all kinds of inducements, swelled to fair size until it was checked by the exclusion act of 1882. Conditions in China had little to do with its actual volume.

Japanese immigration had but a brief unrestricted span. Until 1868 Japanese were forbidden by their own government to go abroad, and even the first mitigation in this year of their own "seclusion law" of 1638 applied only to the higher classes and not to workers who might wish to migrate, for free emigration was not legalized for all Japanese subjects until 1885.[15] Opportunities for improvement in the United States, especially in the agricultural regions of the Pacific coast, soon became known to them, and within a decade were taken advantage of by thousands. Many of these belonged to the despised Eta caste, which, although abolished by law in Japan, was still a serious handicap. Overpopulation, however, rather than class oppression, furnished the main stimulus for emigration. It may nevertheless be said that persecution was

[15] Yamato Ichihashi, *International Migration of the Japanese,* in Walter Willcox, *op. cit.,* p. 618.

a more important factor in Japanese emigration than in Chinese, if only because of the indirect evidence that the Japanese left their home with the intention of establishing permanent residence in the United States to a far greater extent than did the Chinese, whose common intention of returning to the Orient after a temporary residence here indicates the relative absence of a persecution motive in their migration.

This latter type of indirect evidence of motives for immigration can be applied to all immigrants. In the years from 1908 to 1930, inclusive, 4,015,381 aliens (not including naturalized immigrants) departed from the United States after officially expressing their intention of taking permanent residence in another country. Of this number, 3,238,230, mostly of European origin, gave their intended future residence as a European country. China was given as the intended permanent residence of 74,645, and Japan of 48,786. The rest were destined for the other countries of the western hemisphere, and a few to others not here mentioned. Only an economic motive, gratified or finally abandoned, can account for most of these departures. These aliens were returning to all nations from which other aliens were emigrating to the United States. Home conditions had in but few instances altered perceptibly during their absence, in regard to group persecutions other than economic. Few had been so successful in this country as to elevate their status much beyond that of their original inferior social class. The major changes which permitted their return, however, were in the departing aliens themselves. They were older. Their days of greatest effort to achieve a competence were past. They had had their fling in the promised land of golden opportunity.

MIGRATION WITHIN THE UNITED STATES AND ITS POSSESSIONS

So far we have spoken only of aliens who have migrated from one sovereign country to our own. The basic economic motive in migration becomes more evident when we consider trends in group migration within the United States itself. We are to a surprising degree a migrant nation, in the sense that our people have not taken root in the soil and become fixed in one locality from generation to generation or even for the duration of a single generation. A new nation, tens of thousands of square miles still unsettled within the past century, and with the frontier spirit not yet quenched, must perhaps be so, even without the disturbance of industrial adjustment.

The migrations of the old stock do not seriously concern us, except as their movement from the country to the city has brought intolerant provincials into contact with minorities whom they cannot understand. There has been, however, sufficient internal migration by colored minorities to serve as the basis for the present discussion.

The colored inhabitants of our insular possessions will serve as one example. The most recent addition to our territory, the Virgin Islands, has sent us a few thousands of her small population who became discouraged with the meager resources of their insular home. President Hoover has gratuitously referred to these small islands as a "poorhouse," and while his remark may have been in bad taste after a welcomed visit to them and in view of our military reasons for their purchase from Denmark, the description was so accurate that it stung the natives, 90 per cent Negro, who felt their poverty no fault of their own. The first American civil governor, Dr. Paul Pearson, has announced a well-planned agricultural and industrial program for economic rehabilitation which in itself is proof of the motive which has led many, too discouraged to carry on the struggle at home, to leave for the mainland. Similar but less pronounced poverty of local economic resources had led many Porto Ricans to migrate to continental United States. The Porto Ricans are accepted as Latin Americans (to be distinguished from Mexicans) and the Virgin Islanders disappear among the native Negroes, so that neither creates any special issue of race relations.

Although most people in the United States would fail to recognize a Filipino if they saw one, the migrants from the Philippines do not lose their group identity on the mainland. Concentrating on the west coast in the wake of the other Orientals now excluded, their small total of less than 50,000 in the entire country, mostly laborers (79.4 per cent of their immigration has been between the age of 16 and 30, while 93 per cent has been of males), has remained a focus of public attention easily watched because it is the only brown-skinned group in the district.[16] The Filipino rejects and is rejected by other Orientals and by Negroes, so that he is forced to draw companionship from his own group, or, particularly if he wants feminine company, to make the acquaintance or win the friendship of non-Filipino individuals who are likely to be ostracized by their own group, be it white, yellow or Negro, if they accept his advances.[17]

The table of contents of Bruno Lasker's *Filipino Immigration* lists the following as causes of their emigration: Artificial Stimuli, Labor and Traffic Recruiting; Influences of Americanization, the School System, and the Press and Moving Picture; Predisposing Economic Factors, Backward Economic Development, Asiatic Immigration, Lack of Homestead Facilities, Special and Seasonal Causes of Poverty; Economic Pull, Reports of Opportunity and Demonstration of Opportunity. On page 234 he quotes from a mimeographed report of the Philippine Islands Bureau of Labor, issued in December, 1929, what it considers the important causes of emigration. These are:

"1. The unevenness of the distribution of population.

2. The unemployment in large urban centers, such as Manila and other large cities.

3. Due to lack of opportunities, farm laborers can only eke out a hand-to-mouth existence.

4. The waste of man-power due to forced idleness during off-season.

5. The small farmers and tenants barely able to earn

[16] E. S. Bogardus, *Anti-Filipino Race Riots, a Report Made to the Ingram Institute of Social Science, of San Diego,* May 15, 1930, p. 24. The percentages quoted by Dr. Bogardus are from W. J. French, *Facts About Filipino Immigration into California,* Department of Industrial Relations, San Francisco, 1930, p. 12.

[17] Filipinos have mixed in the Islands with Chinese immigrants, so that there is a considerable infusion of Chinese blood in our immigrants from this possession. Differences in cultural and economic status on the Pacific coast hold these two minorities well apart on the mainland.

      enough to support and maintain their families from
their share of their products.

6. The lack of incentives for agricultural workers in the
Philippine Islands.

7. Letters to relatives at home relating the labor conditions in Hawaii, such as high wages, good working
conditions, abundance of work, and the thousands
of *pesos* in money orders exchanged in the post of-
fices of the Ilocos provinces serve as potent pro-
moters of the present exodus."

Filipino migration to Hawaii has been directly proportionate
to the labor needs of the sugar plantations. The presence of
a large proportion of other Orientals in Hawaii is also explained in terms of the need for a ready labor supply to meet
the requirements of rapid agricultural exploitation. There
is possibly some significance in the fact that Filipinos began
coming to the mainland shortly after the World War and immigration restriction prevented the importation of European
labor as well as of alien Orientals.

With minor modifications, Bruno Lasker's table of causes
of Filipino migration and that of the Philippine Islands Bureau of Labor could be made to serve as a basis for the discussion of the causes of European immigration. The strength of
the economic motive becomes more apparent with the recognition of two additional facts, first, that the Filipinos are
under the same political sovereignty both before and after
migrating, and enjoy citizenship privileges in the Islands but
are mere residents without the privileges of political participation on the mainland, and, second, that they are more the
objects of personal persecution in their new residence than
in the old. The desire for personal freedom and political participation is thus minimized as a cause of their migration.
A similar observation may be made in regard to Chinese and
Japanese immigrants who have also been denied American
citizenship, been segregated economically and socially, and
been religiously oppressed if they attempted to follow their
alien forms of worship openly. For people such as these the

United States may be an economic "haven of refuge," but it is hardly a "land of liberty."

The greatest internal migration of any minority in the United States has been that of the Negro, a migration which has continued since he first landed on this continent. How many were actually imported to the territory which is now the United States is unknown. There are numerous documents as to the nature of the trade and the details of individual enterprises, but accurate total statistics can hardly be derived from them. "As early as 1734 one of the captains engaged in it [the slave trade] estimated that a maximum of seventy thousand slaves a year had already been attained. For the next half century and more each passing year probably saw between fifty and a hundred thousand shipped. The total transportation from first to last may well have numbered more than five million souls. Prior to the nineteenth century far more Negro than white colonists crossed the seas, though less than one-tenth of all the blacks brought to the western world appear to have been landed on the North American continent. Indeed, a statistician has reckoned, though not convincingly, that in the whole period before 1810 these did not exceed 385,000."[18]

It is useless to attempt to determine from what parts of Africa and from what tribes these slaves were brought. The shipping center, of course, was on the west coast, and many slaves were native to that region, but slave coffles were marched a thousand miles or more on occasion from all sections of the continent. Since tribal lines have been destroyed by intermixture, the matter of tribal origin is now of academic interest only. This is hardly to be regretted except sentimentally, for variations in inherent tribal abilities have not been demonstrated. It may be added that what tribal selection chanced to occur in the trading with Latin America, as separated from the region north of Mexico, was so random and slight as to justify the conclusion that distinctions need not

[18] U. B. Phillips, *American Negro Slavery*, D. Appleton & Company, New York, 1918, p. 39. The captain referred to is Snelgrave, in *Guinea and the Slave Trade*. The statistician is H. C. Carey, *The Slave Trade, Domestic and Foreign*, Philadelphia, 1853, chap. iii.

be made between the Negroes in Brazil, Venezuela, Haiti, Santo Domingo, Cuba, other tropical American regions and the United States. Furthermore, there was an early interchange of Negroes between the United States and the West Indies.

The cause of this involuntary migration from Africa was entirely economic. After landing in the colonies of North America or, later, in the United States, involuntary migration of Negroes continued as slave owners shifted them about, supplemented by the voluntary changes of residence of free Negroes both before and after the Civil War. The movement of free Negroes, although not always entirely voluntary in that they were frequently compelled to leave the place of their emancipation during slave days, was naturally influenced by motives other than opportunity for self-support.

Although Negroes were originally introduced into all colonies—northern Yankees were prominent in the trade—their extensive use was soon restricted to southern areas. At the time of the first census, the center of Negro population was found to be in Virginia. From then it moved south and west during each succeeding decade, until it reached northeastern Alabama in 1910. Within the ten years from 1910 to 1920 it shifted back nine and one-half miles east and nineteen and one-half miles north of the 1910 location.[19] This northeastward movement continued on an extensive scale well into the decade from 1920 to 1930.

There are several misconceptions current concerning this last major change in the geographical distribution of the American Negro. It has been described as though it were the first and only northward drift, as though it were essentially an escape from the south to the north and as though its primary causes were the prejudices of the south and a belief in the north as a "promised land." All three of these descriptions are sufficiently inaccurate to be branded as false.

Throughout the period from 1790 to 1910 characterized by

[19] For statistics of the distribution and movements of Negro population, see E. B. Reuter, *The American Race Problem*, Thomas Y. Crowell Company, New York, 1927, chap. iii; Charles S. Johnson, *The Negro in American Civilization*, Henry Holt & Company, Inc., New York, 1930, chap. ii.

the predominant southwestward drift of the colored population of the United States, there was a lesser but significant
stream of Negroes finding its way into the northeastern and
middle-western states of the northern tier. This stream was
fed, however, not so much by the Negro population of the
lower south as by that of the upper states of southern tradition. Virginia, Maryland, Delaware and Kentucky have long
been sending a small but steady supply of Negroes into New
Jersey, Pennsylvania, New York, Ohio, Indiana and Illinois.
A scattering of colored migrants came from farther south, and
some were diffused more widely. There has been, however, a
definite, if weak, current moving in this direction since before
the Civil War. It is traceable in the ancestry of the older, more
aristocratic colored families in Philadelphia, New York, Boston, and Chicago, and even in the border cities, such as Washington and Baltimore. Recent migrants tend to be looked
down upon and held at arm's length by members of their own
race who preceded them by a generation or more, although
other factors than precedence are involved in this class distinction.

What has happened has been that the bulk of Negro migrants have been pulled southwestward by agriculture, which
was early restricted by land abuses in the south Atlantic states,
and drawn away by cheap acreage suited to the growth of
long staple cotton which required a warmer climate than was
offered by Virginia and adjacent territory. Planters, their
younger sons, the landless in general, saw opportunity to
prosper in the sparsely populated, virgin soil of areas to the
southwest, capable of being cultivated in ways they understood. Industrial and urban development, as in the Birmingham region, played its part in later times, but farming was
the basic attraction which drew the migrants, white and black
alike.

Meanwhile, there were always Negroes who heard of and
believed in opportunities in other parts of the country. The
greatest number of these were naturally in those states closest
to the north, and the opportunities they heard of were in the

cities with which communication was most easily established. This accounts for the original Negro northward migration.

It is perhaps misleading to describe any migration of Negroes as "northward." The point of the compass toward which they have moved has been incidental. The Atlantic Ocean kept them from going east, and there was little chance to earn a living in the west or northwest by the time they were able to go there. The description "northward" blinds us to the larger aspects of Negro migration during the past fifteen or twenty years, for there were hundreds of thousands of Negroes who participated in the same population movement without ever leaving the southern states. What has happened has been in answer to the call of industrialism, a call which has drawn both Negroes and whites into all cities needing labor for manufacture and commerce.

It so happens that most industry is carried on in the north, but if, by some trick of fate, the south were the manufacturing and commercial center of the nation, few Negroes would have left it in spite of its traditional prejudice and discrimination against them. The best evidence of this is that prosperous southern urban centers have drawn their proportionate share of colored workers from the farm no less easily than have the northern. This population movement should be referred to as the industrialization or urbanization of the Negro, or as his cityward migration, if a proper perspective is to be maintained.

When the urban drift of Negroes was observed in 1915 and for some time thereafter, academic explanations of the migration dressed it in the garb of another flight from Egypt to the Land of Canaan. Southern segregation, lynching, disfranchisement and oppression were vividly described as making the life of the Negro unbearable. So, without any Moses to lead them, Negroes undertook the journey to the northern land of milk and honey where life and property were secure, citizenship conferred civil rights, prejudice was a minimum and segregation nonexistent!

Such a sentimental explanation had enough basis in fact to make it plausible, both to Northerners who admired themselves in the humanitarian rôle, and to Southerners who had guilty consciences. The observation that if there had been any change at all in the southern attitude toward Negroes it was in the direction leading to the improvement of race relations, while the north showed signs of increasing prejudice which made it difficult to account for the sudden migration in terms of search for freedom, was met by the retort that jobs had to be available and that an awakening to opportunity was needed before the march to social liberty could begin. Such a retort twists the facts so as to make the tail wag the dog.

There was no change in racial attitudes coincident with the migration which could account for it. Lynching in the south was on the decrease. Further, the movement of Negro population cannot be correlated with lynching, for counties which have permitted atrocious lynchings have been known to have increases in colored population soon thereafter. The fact that districts which lost Negro population as a rule also lost white population should have been enough to show that discrimination against the Negro played but a minor, predisposing rôle in the redistribution of the colored population. Thus it is misleading to say, "The southern agricultural Negro did not migrate, any more than other peoples have migrated, motivated primarily by the hope of obtaining a better paying job or a more comfortable house or any of the other animal needs, but rather was his migration a quest for happiness—'to have a better time'—'to get more enjoyment out of life'—as many of them have expressed it. . . . The better paying job, for instance, was only a means to this end."[20] The job is always a means to an end, and the end is always happiness. The Negro searching for work followed agriculture into

[20] Forrester B. Washington, "Recreational Facilities for the Negro" in Donald Young, editor, "The American Negro," *The Annals* of the American Academy of Political and Social Science, November, 1928, vol. cxxxx, p. 272.

The most recent reliable investigation of Negro mobility concludes that "the intensity of the demand for industrial labor was so great in the years from 1919 to 1924 as to make it the predominant factor in the movement of the Negro." By way of prophecy this same investigation has led to the conclusion that "Fortunately or otherwise, the industrialization of the colored man seems destined to go on." Edward E. Lewis, *The Mobility of the Negro*, Columbia University Press, New York, 1931, pp. 130, 132.

the deeper south during the days of its prosperity as readily as he followed industry into the north.

Another exaggerated factor was the "liberating influence" of the World War on the rural Negro. It was pointed out that thousands of drafted colored men left the small radius of their home community for the first time when they were sent to army training camps, where a new glimpse of the world was given them. Those who reached France saw still more of the world, a part where race prejudice was less evident. Thus a broader horizon, restlessness, and a hitherto unknown self-confidence bred of military travel was assigned a prominent place in explanations of Negro migration. If this was so important, why did the migration begin in 1915, some time before the United States even entered the war? *C'est la guerre* is a phrase used to cloak ignorance.

The World War was of the greatest importance in the migration, but in a different way. It checked the flow of unskilled immigrant labor at a time when old industries were expanding and war industries created demands for workers which could not be met by local supplies. There was but one place to turn to fill the partial labor vacuum so created, and that was to the farm. American Negroes happened to include hundreds of thousands of farmers and farm laborers who could be easily attracted, for southern agriculture even in the boom wartimes had several years of failure, and the Negro's high visibility, coupled with traditional attitudes, created the impression that his migration was different from that of white farmers who left their plows in response to the same economic opportunity. Actually, it was unique only in that racial attitudes added a confusing stimulus to migration, one which was nevertheless impotent by itself.

Charles Johnson has called attention to this fact by a comparison of Jewish and Negro migrations. "There is a natural parallel in Negro migrations with the immigration of Jews from Russia. Prior to 1880, immigration from Russia was negligible. There were prosperous conditions in the United States and persecution in Russia. But although persecution continued, this migration slumped after 1882, and continued low for several years, then with the return of prosperity in the United States rose to 81,511 in 1892. Despite the fact that the Jews were expelled in 1891 from Great Russia by Imperial Edict, in 1893 the numbers arriving in the United States began to decline, due to depression in this country. With the later industrial development occurring along with depression and pogroms in Russia this immigration began to take on vast proportions and in 1906 there were 263,000 arrivals."[21] Any other immigrant might as well have been selected, for, as we have been endeavoring to show, the parallel is almost universal in migrations.[22]

An apparent exception to this rule is found in the post-Columbian migrations of American Indian tribes. Where the Indian originally came from we do not know. He has been "explained" as a remnant of the ten lost tribes of Israel, on the untenable evidence of a so-called Jewish cast of countenance and in answer to an understandable desire to solve a historical mystery. Some have spoken of the Indians as descendants of a single or multiple migration by way of an almost complete land bridge from the Orient. Others think in terms of venturesome sailors from Asia, Australia, Polynesia, Easter Island and even from across the Atlantic.[23] We may be sure, however, that racially and culturally the Indian is related to the Oriental. An acceptable, simple theory of origin has not yet been advanced, and probably never will be, for there are such great differences in physical type and appearance of different tribes, the popular stereotype to the contrary notwithstanding, that a simple origin may be accepted only if we have faith in a much longer residence on this continent permitting more extensive natural selection and differentiation than seems probable.

[21] Charles Johnson, *op. cit.*, p. 19.

[22] For a careful analysis of the recent Negro migration, see Louise Venable Kennedy, *The Negro Peasant Turns Cityward*, Columbia University Press, New York, 1930. The bibliography at the end of this volume deserves special mention.

[23] W. Christie MacLeod, *The American Indian Frontier*, Alfred A. Knopf, New York, 1928, chap. i. In addition to a short discussion of some of the theories of the origin of the American Indian, this chapter in its footnotes also suggests bibliographical sources on the question.

Estimates as to the total number of Indians living in the fifteenth century are unreliable. So far as the United States is concerned, they range from the now discredited statement that there are about as many Indians in this country today as there were when the first settlers arrived—that is, somewhat less than half a million—up into the millions. MacLeod has set his estimate at three million, with an additional twelve million for the rest of the Americas.[24] Willcox, after a survey of the available evidence, too meager for certainty, believes that the United States supported about a million Indians before the whites arrived.[25] We need not further complicate the question by hazarding a guess of our own, for it is sufficient for us to know that the number was radically reduced by the white man's policies in the West Indies, where the Indian has been exterminated, and in the United States, where only a handful of pure bloods remain. With the exception of Argentina, Brazil, and the West Indies, the Indian has not only survived but has also increased in number in Latin America.

The Latin conquerors and settlers were able to live in the same territory with the natives, while the English drove them out. The French, for example, felt no need to exterminate the Indians in their settlements. The Spaniards, with a different policy, completely subjugated the native tribes, were brutally ruthless in their conquests, enslaved the natives who survived, but did not as a rule murder them for the purpose of extermination. The conquests of Mexico and Peru are notorious for their cruelty, but Indians still form the largest element in the population of these countries. The Puritans were remembered for their piety, but Indians are now a curiosity in the regions which they Christianized. To the non-Latin pioneers Indian warfare was a killing expedition on which an area was "mopped up" as clean as possible of stragglers who survived pitched battle, with age and sex a matter of slight concern. Perhaps the fact that the Spaniards depended more largely on the natives for labor and support than did the peaceful north Europeans, who were more willing to work

[24] *Ibid.*, p. 16.
[25] Walter Willcox, *op. cit.*, p. 55.

with their own hands, is an explanation of their different policies in terms of selfish motives. Regardless of motives, the Indian fared better as a race under the brutal Latins than under the pious Protestants.

Unfortunately for the Indian race, the Latins were unable to retain the footholds they originally obtained in the territory which is now the United States. It was the north European who killed off or drove out the Indians from southeastern United States after it was lost to the Spaniards. The Louisiana Purchase which meant the elimination of the French from this continent lead to more Indian deaths. When California was added to the Union there were far more Indians living there peacefully than survived the murders by miners and landgrabbers who flooded the territory from the east. What land the north European acquired he wanted for his sole possession. To this the Indian was an obstacle which had to be removed.

He was removed not only by warfare and murder, but also by being driven to vacant territory in out-of-the-way places not yet needed by the white man. Away from the coast, out of the fertile valleys, into the swamps and hill country ranging from the Everglades to the hills of New England, the Indian retreated. He crossed the Alleghenies, the Ohio and the Mississippi. A few remnants of tribes held on in the east well into the first third of the nineteenth century. By 1840 the only Indians left in the east were either scattered individuals or such insignificant bands as the Senecas of New York—they were fortunate to locate in the eastern state which has best treated its Indians; the Seminoles of Florida; the Abnaki of Maine—most of these had gone to French Canada; or the Cherokees of North Carolina—mountain refugees from the westward migration of their brothers under military escort.

When the eastern lands were cleared of their Indian encumbrances and filled with undisputed white successors, there was soon need for more land farther and farther to the west. In less than a century after President Monroe, in 1825, suggested the forced migration of the eastern Indians to an area which is now included in Oklahoma and Arkansas, not only was his program accomplished, but the western Indians were also dispossessed of their lands by removal to Indian Territory, restricted to reservations a fractional size of their original holdings and not always in the same locality, or, as in California, just dispossessed and told to go anywhere so long as they stayed out of the white man's way. Here, then, we have an illustration of a racial minority migrating from desirable to undesirable regions, the reverse of the migrations previously mentioned.

It was the reverse because it was always involuntary. It was the kind of migration which can occur only when the impelling force is a migration of a more powerful people driving all before it. The basic motive of economic advancement was in the minds of white men, not of the Indians, who had no choice in the matter. So the Negro drove the poor whites to the barren hills of West Virginia, Kentucky and Tennessee and other harsh environments under the competition of slavery. While the immigrant has displaced as well as replaced his predecessors, it is only to a limited extent, since he has been less powerful than his competitors. Forced migrations in the United States seem to be a thing of the past. Without slavery, bloodshed would be involved, and that is too costly a method of obtaining economic advantage in densely populated industrial areas. It is one reason why modern warfare is unprofitable, for there are insufficient thinly peopled habitable regions to be captured as a place for the migration of surplus population.

One more question remains. To what extent, if at all, have migrations to and within the United States been biologically selective? Did the colonists possess some inherent superior quality which gave them the power and incentive to endure hardships as migratory pioneers? Have immigrants been superior or inferior stock, or have they been random biological samples of their people? Are the Negroes who have come north endowed with qualities of the better sort? The question implies the possibility of a biological cause in migration heretofore omitted from our discussion.

The evidence in support of such a theory boils down to the

fact that migrants in general have been more successful in acquiring worldly goods than their fellows who were content to remain at home. The United States has enjoyed a rapid prosperity greater, in a material sense at least, than that of the countries from which her people came. The same may be said of Australia, Canada, South Africa and New Zealand. A widely used text in business geography holds that New Zealand, for example, is prosperous, has a low death rate, and is well governed at least partly because, being so far from the home country of its inhabitants, only the better stock with ability, health and inherent initiative have been willing or able to make the journey in the hope of improving their lot.[26] It is perhaps unfair to single out this one illustration when the viewpoint is so common, but one example must suffice. Like all other possible illustrations, this statement rests not on evidence from the biological sciences but on the interpretation of cultural phenomena in biological terms.

This is always dangerous. It is so much more direct and simple to explain the prosperity of such countries, that is, those populated by recent migrants, in terms of available resources and freedom from hampering tradition. The so-called inherent pioneer spirit thus becomes freedom from the re-

[26] "New Zealand as an Example of Natural Selection.—The same process of natural selection which has helped to make the Chinese of northern Manchuria so active and competent has probably been a factor in making New Zealand one of the most prosperous and progressive of countries. When migration to a new country takes place, there is a strong tendency for those who are physically weak and of a timid temperament to stay at home. On the other hand, among those who migrate, the ones who go farthest are likely to be those with sturdy bodies, strong wills, and a spirit of adventure and initiative. They are also likely to have at least enough money to pay their fare and still have something left to start with in their new homes. In general, this means people who are thrifty and industrious. New Zealand is the most remote of the places to which European colonists have gone in the last century. Apparently that fact has helped to give New Zealand an unusually fine type of colonist. That is one reason why New Zealand stands at the very top of productivity, and is renowned for its progressive social legislation and its general prosperity and comfort." Ellsworth Huntington and Frank E. Williams, *Business Geography*, John Wiley & Sons, Inc., New York, 1926, p. 84.

For further details of Professor Huntington's theory of the relationship between migrations and natural selection, see his *The Character of Races*, Charles Scribner's Sons, New York, 1924, pp. xvi, 393. The "List of References" in this volume furnishes an adequate bibliography of the subject.

straint of custom in a country where custom has not had time
to solidify. Unexploited forests, mines and virgin soil yield
high returns for little effort. Furthermore, since it is the unsuccessful who migrate, not those who are able to win out
at home against severe competition, considerable rationalizing
is necessary to show that their original lack of success was in
spite of superior inherent qualities. To say that there is an
"indefinable something," a kind of "indomitable spirit," which
impels some individuals to endure the hardships of migration
rather than accept the alleged easy escape of bowing to the
will of fate, is sheer speculative nonsense.

The Puritans, Quakers, Huguenots, German revolutionists,
Irish rebels and Jewish outcasts who fought their battles in
Europe showed not a bit less courage, initiative or ability
than those who ran away from the fight by coming to America. The Negroes who left the south for northern industry
required no great intelligence to see their opportunity, nor
bravery and spirit to undertake the journey. If we may believe contemporary accounts, the pioneers who crossed the
Alleghenies, the Plains, and the Rockies were no great loss
to their home communities, and only a few of them achieved
contemporary respect and approbation. Who stays at home
and who strikes out to an unknown land seems to be less a
matter of stock than of knowledge of opportunity, freedom to
accept, and chance personal inclination.

On the other hand, there is equally slight justification for
assuming that migrating stock is likely to be inferior just because it is composed mainly of economic failures. Failure may
be due to many causes unrelated to ability, especially in well
established communities with class and caste distinctions
firmly fixed in the social order. Ease of migration is also supposed to be correlated with the quality of the migrants, so that
as difficulties of transportation and perils in the country of
destination diminish, so too the caliber of the migrants is
alleged to diminish. The fact that this would mean that the
colonists were biologically superior to immigrants, and that
the old immigrants were superior to the new, makes one
suspicious that the passage of time has added glory to past

generations while the faults of recent arrivals have not been obscured by aging.

Since we are all the descendants of migrants, it is only natural that we should tend to invest our ancestors with in-bred superior qualities which would automatically be passed along to ourselves. Those of us untainted by the blood of recent immigrants would also tend to restrict such superiority to the older migrants. Wishful as well as careless thinking must bear the blame for attributing to biology the effects of social accidents.

So keen an observer of race relations and of conditions in the United States as Viscount Bryce held the belief that the problems growing out of friction between Negroes and white people in this country would be increasingly geographically restricted if not eliminated by a pronounced degree of auto-matic segregation of our colored population in the more trop-ical states of the south. "As the races of northern Europe have been hitherto unable to maintain themselves in the torrid zone, so the African race, being of tropical origin, dwindles away wherever it has to encounter cold winters. . . . It is in the lower regions that lie near the Gulf Stream and the Gulf of Mexico, and especially in the sea islands of South Carolina and on the banks of the lower Mississippi that he [the Negro] finds the conditions which are at once most fav-ourable to his development and most unfavourable to that of the whites. . . . It is thus clear that the Negro center of popu-lation is more and more shifting southward, and that the Afri-can is leaving the colder, higher, and drier lands for regions more resembling his ancient seats in the Old World."[27] Bryce's objective evidence for this conclusion was the steady south-ward drift of the center of Negro population as measured by the census returns from 1790 to 1910. His interpretation of this movement in terms of the Negro's adaptation to a tropi-cal environment rests on no more secure facts than these. As water finds its level if unimpeded, so the Negro was supposed to be finding the American environment for which tropical

<hr />

[27] James Bryce, *The American Commonwealth*, The Macmillan Company, New York, new edition, 1923, pp. 512-513.

natural selection had fitted him during his thousands of years of residence in Africa. The northeastward shift in the center of Negro population in the decade between 1910 and 1920 made clear to later observers the economic determinant in his migrations and utterly destroyed Bryce's theory—a pity, since its truth could have assured us of an unplanned but certain solution of the "Negro problem" through segregation. It is also a pity that the theory of selective migration cannot be substantiated, for it would explain our past prosperity, condemn unnecessary new immigration, and assure the future eminence of the United States!

CHAPTER III

MINORITY FARMERS

FARMERS have only one characteristic in common: they are employed in growing and disposing of crops or livestock. Their work may involve intensive hand culture of barren soil, or it may utilize the power of animals and tractors on lands capable of repaying such capital investments. A money crop of cotton, tobacco, wheat, hogs, cattle, or other salable commodity may be the main dependence of a farmer who purchases most of the necessities of life, or sufficient diversification may be practiced so as to make a few acres supply nearly all of the wants of the occupants. High-grade morons have been known to acquire the reputation of successful farmers, and well-trained agriculturists have been bankrupted through no fault of their own. The words "agriculture" and "agriculturist" are no more definite in their meaning than the word "sick," for they convey a minimum of description unless supplemented by specific details.

THE CALL OF THE LAND

The agricultural training of American minorities of racial and national origin is a matter of temporary and slight importance in so far as the determination of their occupation in the United States is concerned. They may be converted into profitable farm laborers overnight, even if lacking in intelligence, provided inertia or some attraction holds them on the land for a season. Given a little more time, they may learn to operate farms for themselves as tenants or owners. The farm hand need be no more than semi-skilled, to use an industrial term, and the independent farmer may prosper if he is a skilled worker in the sense that he knows how to apply the rules of thumb.

Consequently the foreign occupation of our immigrants is

not the basic determinant in their choice of occupation in the United States; it is rather a question of personal inclination and opportunity in this country. Thus in the past immigrants and colonists who were traders, domestic servants, artisans and wage workers in Europe have turned to farming after their arrival if they thought it the most profitable occupation. On the other hand, farmers have turned into industrial workers with equal facility. Further, the differences in technique between the intensive peasant farming of Europe and the extensive methods adapted to a new country where land is abundant and cheap seriously reduce the advantage of a European farm background through the necessity for learning new agricultural methods. The English colonist faced different problems in freshly cleared lands along the Atlantic coast of the New World than he did abroad. Southern planters did not ask whether newly imported Negro slaves were acquainted with the culture of tobacco, indigo, hemp, rice, sugar or cotton. Mexicans, Filipinos and Japanese working in the California fruit orchards and truck farms today came to them with no previous experience in these types of agriculture. Bohemians and Italians are succeeding in the United States as farmers working with crops, climate, soil and marketing conditions which bear slight resemblance to those with which they may have been familiar in Czecho-Slovakia and Italy. If farmers and farm laborers are needed, an adequate supply may quickly be trained from any race or nationality.

Certain races and nationalities, however, have acquired a reputation as either agriculturists or industrialists, supposedly limited by inherent nature to one or the other types of occupation. North Europeans are believed capable in any form of economic endeavor. South Europeans are reputed to lend themselves better to wage work in factory and mill. Mexicans, Japanese and Filipinos have the reputation of being well fitted for farm labor. Chinese immigrants are thought of as urban dwellers. Negroes are said to belong on the farm, in the kitchen, or, as unskilled labor only, in some industries. Jews, of course, seem to be born traders and are alleged to have no capacity for agriculture. The "capacity" of these minorities for success in industry and the professions is not easy to ascertain, but their agricultural abilities may be examined in the light of American experience. It is pertinent to remark that industry is a recent development in the history of man, that commerce has never furnished a major occupation for the people of any minority but is a development of the more complex cultures, while every minority has had a long acquaintance with agriculture.

The accompanying tables are sufficient proof that American minorities do not go to the farm or stay on the farm in proportions equal to those of the native white stock:

TABLE I

FARMERS IN THE UNITED STATES, 1920[1]

All farmers....................	6,448,343
Total white farmers[a]...........	5,498,454
Native white.................	4,917,386
Foreign-born white..........	581,068
Total colored farmers..........	949,889
Negro.......................	925,708
Indians.....................	16,680
Chinese....................	609
Japanese...................	6,892

[a] 12,142 Mexican farmers were included in the number of white farmers.

In this table the "farm population," counted for the first time in the census of 1920, includes both farm operators and farm laborers, and may be said to be a reasonably accurate classification.

The fact that more than half of the Indians were found to be farm residents is not surprising, for it not only is in keeping with their tradition but is also a necessary consequence of their enforced migration to Indian Territory and their segregation on reservations in rural regions. Had the eastern Indians not been moved out of the white man's way it is probable that

[1] From the *Fourteenth Census of the United States*, 1920, vol. vi, part i, p. 20. Attention is called to the fact that this table includes only the heads of families actually operating farms, and bears no definite relationship to the total farm population or the number of farm owners.

TABLE II

FARM, VILLAGE, AND URBAN POPULATION OF THE UNITED STATES, BY RACE,
NATIVITY AND PARENTAGE: 1920[2]

Race, Nativity and Parentage	Total Population	Farm Population	Village Population	Urban Population (excluding urban-farm)
Total..............	105,710,620	31,614,269	20,047,377	54,048,974
White..............	94,820,915	26,313,654	18,128,031	50,379,230
Negro..............	10,463,131	5,112,253	1,803,695	3,547,183
Indian..............	244,437	142,714	86,593	15,130
Chinese............	61,639	4,287	7,518	49,834
Japanese............	111,010	39,504	19,881	51,625
Other races[a].........	9,488	1,857	1,659	5,972
Native white........	81,108,161	24,842,614	16,205,684	40,059,863
Native parentage....	58,421,957	21,045,836	12,958,707	24,417,414
Foreign "	15,694,539	2,326,166	2,107,206	11,261,167
Mixed "	6,991,765	1,470,612	1,139,771	4,381,382
Foreign-born white....	13,712,754	1,471,040	1,922,347	10,319,367

[a] Filipinos, Hindus, Koreans, Hawaiians, Malays, Siamese, Samoans, and Maoris.

the proportion of those urbanized would be much larger than it is. There is also the fact to be considered that an unknown but significant number of people with sufficient Indian blood to be classified as Indians if living in Indian country, have passed into the white or Negro groups among which they live in our cities.

The small proportion of Chinese included in the farm population is accounted for in terms of occupational choice rather than lack of agricultural capacity. They were originally brought to the United States as wage workers, and a majority were probably wage workers in Canton and south China before they left. Their opportunities in stores, importing houses, restaurants, laundries and domestic service have been plentiful, and have well repaid their efforts. Further, farming is for them an occupation which implies permanent residence in

[2] Leon E. Truesdell, *Farm Population of the United States*, Bureau of the Census, Department of Commerce, Washington, D. C., 1926, p. 96.

the United States rather than a brief working period for the purpose of earning enough money to provide for a return to the home country, in spite of the fact that in the 1870's some 70 per cent of all California farm laborers were Chinese. Farm laborers, of course, may be temporary immigrants, as in the case of many Mexicans, but farm wages are not so lucrative as urban occupations and, other things being equal, aliens who have not given up the idea of a return to the land of birth—some Italians might be included with the Chinese in this classification—prefer the better paid occupations.

The fifty-eight and a half million native white people of native parentage in the United States in 1920 were 55.3 per cent of our total population. They furnished 66.6 per cent of the farm population and 45.2 per cent of the urban population. The thirteen and three-quarters million foreign-born white people, 13 per cent of the total population, showed a different tendency, for they contributed only 4.7 per cent of the total farm population and 19.1 per cent of the urban. Those born of foreign or mixed parentage, about twenty-two and a half million in number, were 21.4 per cent of the total population and contributed 12.1 per cent of the farm and 28.9 per cent of the urban population.[3]

In spite of the fact that the foreign-born whites were the smallest farm group in the United States as a whole or taken by major geographical sections, there was nevertheless an appreciable number of foreign-born farmers, 1,471,040, of whom 581,068 were farm operators. These were found somewhat concentrated in three groups of states, one along the north Atlantic coast, comprising Massachusetts, Rhode Island, Connecticut and New Jersey (percentage of foreign-born in farm population in these states varying from 13.5 to 20.8). Another was in the middle west and included Michigan, Wisconsin, Minnesota, North Dakota, South Dakota and Montana (percentage of foreign-born in farm population from 13.2 to 21). The third was in the far west, and included California, Washington, Nevada and Arizona (percentage of foreign-born in farm population from 15.1 to 18.4). The foreign-

<hr />

[3] Leon E. Truesdell, *loc. cit.*

born farmers in the north Atlantic states included a high proportion of recent arrivals from south Europe who engaged in intensive cultivation, such as truck farming for the metropolitan markets of New York and Philadelphia.[4] Those in the middle-western group of states were mostly older immigrants from north Europe, and were engaged in extensive farming. In the far west, Mexican farm laborers were important in raising the percentage of foreign-born farmers, with Italians, Danes, Portuguese and Japanese representative of the farm operators. No important immigrant district was located in the south.

The groups of foreign origin which have the greatest proportion of their numbers in agriculture include the Norwegians (35.9%), Danes (34.2%), Dutch (30.0%), Swiss (27.8%), Finns (25.3%), Swedes (24.5%) and Germans (21.1%). The immigrants who have shown the least interest in farming include the Greeks (1.2%), Roumanians (1.7%), Italians (2.9%), Poles (3.9%), Irish (4.0%), Hungarians (4.5%), and Russians (5.9%). The Scots (7.6%), Welsh (9.3%), English (8.3%), Canadians (11.0%) and French (10.1%) can be compared with the Austrians (13.3%) and the Portuguese (16.0%).[5] The proportion of farm population among Mexican and Filipino immigrants is not given, for at the time of this census (1920) their number was so much smaller than it has been in later years that the figures gathered at that time are no longer representative of their distribution. We do know, however, that they have been more largely attracted to the United States by agricultural wages and labor conditions than have European immigrants, and that they will desert the fields for the city, and *vice versa*, as opportunity and higher wages offer.

Paul S. Taylor has made excellent sample studies of the Mexican as an agricultural laborer in the three widely sepa-

[4] A rough sketch of the agricultural life of immigrants who went to the land during the first two decades of the present century, including a description of their lands and activities, their difficulties in acquiring the holding farms, and a proposal of the land policy, can be found in the first part of Peter A. Speek, *A Stake in the Land*, Harper & Brothers, New York, 1921. Part Two deals with the education of these immigrants and their children.

[5] Leon E. Truesdell, *op. cit.*, p. 105.

rated centers of Mexican immigration of the Imperial Valley, California, the valley of the South Platte, Colorado, and Dimmit County, Texas. In his own words, "Not only do environments and American populations vary, but the Mexican populations of each area are fed largely by streams from different sources of emigration in Mexico; they are parts of different flows of seasonal migrations within the United States, and they comprise varying proportions of the resident populations of each area, ranging from about 6 per cent in northeastern Colorado to over 35 per cent in Imperial Valley, California, and over 70 per cent in Dimmit County, Texas.

"Imperial Valley, California, leads the United States in production of cantaloupes, and has extensive acreages of lettuce and cotton. A large part of its Mexican population leaves home in the spring and early summer, moving from the border northward by train, stage, or automobile across the Tehachapi ridge, to harvest the deciduous fruits, grapes, and cotton of the Valley of California. In the fall the Mexicans return southward for the winter lettuce harvest in Imperial Valley.

"The leading sugar beet growing area in the United States is the Valley of the South Platte River in northeastern Colorado. To this region, as to others in the Middle West from Montana to Michigan, Mexican families are transported each spring at the time for thinning sugar beet plants; in the fall at the conclusion of the harvest they return to the places whence they came, go to northern cities, or remain in the towns and on the farms of the valley. Many of the laborers come originally from Mexico by way of Texas: many others, largely Spanish Americans, come from southern Colorado and New Mexico.

"Dimmit County, lying in the Winter Garden district of South Texas, leads the United States in production of Bermuda onions, and raises large acreages of spinach. The Mexicans, both native and foreign-born, transplant and harvest the onion crop by hand between November and May; during the remaining months of the year a large proportion of them join the migration of cotton-pickers who assemble near Corpus Christi on the Gulf of Mexico, and follow the opening cotton

northward to Fort Worth and westward across the plains of
West Texas. In November and December they return to their
homes in the Winter Garden."[6]

This does not mean that Mexican laborers are confined to
the southwest, for there are Mexican industrial laborers scattered throughout the middle west and the east in groups ranging in size up to several thousands of individuals. Chicago,
for example, has quite a Mexican center, and few northern
cities are without a Mexican colony. They have also been engaged in railroad and other construction work of a temporary
nature. The deeper they penetrate into the United States the
less likely they are to take their families with them, with a resulting disturbance of their sex ratio and age distribution, a
socially undesirable condition.

The Filipinos have not yet distributed themselves widely
in industry, but have remained on the west coast in agricultural labor and in a limited number of other occupations, as
in domestic and personal service, fish canneries, saw mills,
box plants, marine service and some public employments,
such as in navy and post office work. Their major occupation,
however, is in the field working for wages, as in the extensive
truck farms and orchards of California. There have been sufficient instances of wage cutting to arouse the antagonism of
white competitors for their work and to inspire anti-Filipino
agitation among laboring groups not yet in serious competition with them. For the most part, however, they are engaged
in occupations which would otherwise be filled by Mexican,
Negro or immigrant labor, for the older American stock has
shown no inclination to supply the market for "stoop labor"
in agriculture and for the poorer paid, harder work in canneries, saw mills and other industries where the Filipino has
penetrated.[7] Even the Chinese and Japanese have been leaving such undesirable work when circumstances have made it
possible for them to do so.

The Negro farmer has been restricted to the south, where he

[6] Paul S. Taylor, *Mexican Labor in the United States: Bethlehem, Pennsylvania,* University of California Press, Berkeley, 1931, pp. 1-2.

[7] For details of Filipino occupations, see Bruno Lasker, *Filipino Immigration,* University of Chicago Press, Chicago, 1931, pp. xxii + 445.

furnishes a large proportion of the agricultural population except in West Virginia, Oklahoma, and Kentucky, states which are not truly southern although usually so listed. He was first brought to this continent as an agricultural worker on rice, indigo, sugar, hemp, and tobacco plantations—cotton needed his labor only after the introduction of long-staple, semi-tropical varieties and the use of machinery in its ginning and manufacture into cloth—during a period when there was too much cheap and free land available to expect migrants to do farm labor for hire except under the duress of slavery.

While slavery taught the Negro habits and methods of work quite different from, and from an American point of view much better than, those to which he was accustomed in Africa, neither slavery nor the farm tenancy and limited ownership which followed emancipation equipped him for independent, profitable agriculture. Incentive to thrift and hard work has been slight under both slavery and the post-Civil War southern caste system. The extensive use of money crops, especially cotton and tobacco, limited agricultural instruction to an easily supervised, routine procedure, and required little development of intelligent planning. Not all Negroes either during or after slavery were farmers or farm hands, for many were domestics and skilled artisans, more so in *ante bellum* days than later. The bulk of our colored population has been from the beginning and still is agricultural, fortified with a minimum of training and incentive for efficient work.

The common error should not be committed of assuming that the South is a uniform agricultural region with a Negro farm population suffering from the same ills or enjoying identical blessings in all districts, for regional variations are even greater than those already mentioned in regard to the Mexicans of California, Colorado and Texas. Climate, soil, crops, race attitudes, finances, land ownership and agricultural methods are so different in the region around Durham, North Carolina, from those in the alluvial lands of Mississippi—to select just one comparison from the multitude possible—that a capable Negro farmer from one region would be at a loss in the other. Without attempting to make a regional survey of the agricultural South, we may quote Dr. Carl Kelsey to show the necessity for exercising extreme caution in generalizing about the southern Negro farmer. Dr. Kelsey's geographical divisions are significant in that they call attention to territorial differences which are well known but frequently overlooked.

"City conditions are more or less uniform in all sections of the south. The geographical location of the farmer, however, is a matter of considerable importance not only as determining in large measure the crop he [the Negro] must raise, but as limiting the advance he may be able to make under given conditions. . . . For convenience we may divide the territory into five districts: (1) Virginia and Kentucky, above the limit of profitable cotton culture. (2) The Atlantic Sea Coast. (3) The Central belt running from Virginia to Central Mississippi. This includes several different soils, but general conditions are fairly uniform. (4) The Alluvial Lands, which may be subdivided into the cotton and the cane districts. (5) Texas."[8] Texas is not included in his study of *The Negro Farmer,* which nevertheless remains the best analysis of the subject today. A new comprehensive survey is demanded by the changes which have come about since the World War. Dr. Kelsey found even his own classification inadequate, for he was compelled to subdivide these districts and to qualify his cautious generalizations about them so that the problem is seen to be one of limited localities rather than one of large areas, with only a few threads of prejudice, of varying strength, insecurely tying the whole together.

The extent and broad geographical distribution of American farmers belonging to racial and nationality minorities has been indicated. Instead of making the rounds of the Italians of New Jersey, New York, and California, the Germans of Wisconsin, the Swedes of Minnesota, the Russians of North Dakota, the Mexicans of Texas, the Canadians of Michigan, the Orientals of the Pacific coast, and the Negroes of a dozen southern districts—an impossible task—it seems wiser to focus attention on the two aspects of agriculture which are basic,

[8] Carl Kelsey, *The Negro Farmer,* Jennings and Pye, Chicago, 1903, p. 21.

namely, the agricultural products raised, and the underlying financial structure, including wages, land tenure, and credit.

In a given agricultural area farming tends to be either extensive or intensive, diversified or more or less restricted to a money crop. If land is cheap and of good quality the temptation is to cultivate a large area with a minimum of effort per acre, and trust to the bounties of nature to bring forth a generous crop. Barring drought and other catastrophes, disappointment under such conditions is rare and prosperity is as certain as it can be on this earth. On the other hand, areas which are well populated and have long been cultivated require more labor and capital, and smaller farms are the rule except where large holdings can be cultivated by machinery or by hired hands. So far as crops are concerned, there is a temptation to specialize in cotton, tobacco, melons, celery, fruit, wheat, etc., where soil and climate are favorable and a market seems probable at planting time. Modern transportation, with its conveniences of warehouses and elevators, express speeds, canning factories, stockyards, refrigeration, and produce markets, all designed to bring the farmers' crops to an increasing number of non-agricultural consumers in all parts of the country and abroad, has encouraged the farmer to depend less on his own acreage for consumption goods and more on purchases from middlemen. Minorities have chosen from these alternatives in accordance with the opportunities offered them.

Good farms readily available in the public domain encouraged the immigrant up to the last decade of the nineteenth century to be a farm operator and owner rather than a laborer. The isolation of the farms added to the area under cultivation before the days of railroad development and automobiles forced diversified agriculture, even where the immigrants specialized in corn or wheat for the market. Cattle raising, hardly a form of agriculture in its romantic western period, was a one-crop system which was too expensive and speculative to survive in competition with immigrant homesteaders who needed no financing but planned from the first to produce sufficient consumption goods to pull them through lean years.

Plenty of homesteaders failed miserably, but many more would have had to give up their claims had they depended on money to buy any considerable portion of their necessities. This statement applies not only to homesteaders, but also to the other migrants to our farms from Europe until the present century.

The need for working capital and credit followed the exhaustion of the free lands, and this fact almost by itself checked the operation of farms by immigrants as either owners or tenants and increased crop specialization, particularly on the accessible, fertile lands. Apple orchards of the backyard variety lost their importance. Grapevines on the smokehouse, peach, plum and cherry trees along the fences, no longer were a main source of supply for urban or even village consumers. Farmers began buying potatoes and canned vegetables at the store. Hog killing, with its techniques of ham curing, sausage making, and other forms of food preserving, is almost a lost art in the farm home, and few of the younger generation would know what to do with a side of beef if it were presented to them already dressed. It may be that the immediate cost of such products raised and prepared by specialists and marketed in the modern manner is less to rural and city resident alike than if each ten-acre lot were more nearly a self-sufficient economic unit. The quality of everything bought at the grocery store, from apples to cottage cheese, may be superior to the home product, and undoubtedly it is more uniform and sanitary. Most of all, the farmer's only chance for real prosperity today lies in intensive dairying, raising poultry or live stock, fruit, cereal, truck or the raw materials of industry. The old-fashioned farmer may be able to eke out a living, but he cannot get rich. The advantages of cash-crop farming, however, have their parasitic penalties in a general lack of the security characteristic of the old-style rural life, a risk gladly accepted by most, who are eager and able to compete for material rewards equal to those of industry and commerce.

Thus in the north and west we no longer think so much in terms of farm communities, but rather in terms of potato, corn, wheat, fruit, dairy and other "belts." There has been an increase in production per farmer, largely due to increasing use of machinery. Farms are growing in acreage by consolidation. Estimated farm mortgages have increased from $3,320,000,000 in 1910 to $7,858,000,000 in 1920.[9] This indicates that the farmer has learned lessons in specialization and finance from industry, and is no longer content to make his acres yield a living but no cash. Not only has he less control over the conditions favorable to production than has the industrialist, but his market also is likely to be poorest in those years when crops are good and his competitors flood it with surplus products. Without capital resources—and few farmers have been able to build a cash reserve—the chances of flat failure or miserable survival are extraordinary.

This has meant an increasing flow of farmers and farmers' sons to the city for wages. It is surprising that a million and a half immigrants, including 581,000 farm operators, had gone to or had stayed on the land in 1920. Their success has in no small measure been the result of crop specialization and hard work, although many of these, particularly the old immigrants in the middle west, are still profiting from the advantages of arrival during the days before the public domain was thoroughly exploited. The more recently arrived farming immigrants to the Atlantic coast and the far west have had to break into agriculture under the handicaps of specialization, costly land and a money farm economy.

"Most of these later immigrants went first to the cities and worked and saved until they had accumulated enough to purchase land. Thus, in one Wisconsin community studied, there were Polish families from New York, Pittsburgh, Chicago, Milwaukee, and one of the southern cities. In a number of other centres the farmers had come from the coal mines of the central competitive field. In one area visited, two-thirds of the operators had reached their farms only after an industrial experience. The flow of foreign-born into the cut-over lands of northern Wisconsin and Michigan has been inversely proportional to the prosperity of the coal industry in

* Leon E. Truesdell, *op. cit.*, p. 6.

the central middle west, according to the testimony of agricultural leaders in these states. Other southern Europeans have made their first contact with the soil they now till through their experiences as migrant workers either on railroads or highways, or as laborers at harvest time. So, too, the influx of southern Europeans and Slavs to the farms of Connecticut and Massachusetts has largely come from the cities."[10]

Once on the land, the recent immigrant farmer has been forced into the intensive cultivation of specialized crops. The cheap, abandoned, neglected and unreclaimed cut-over acreage which forms the bulk of his recently acquired holdings can be made to compete with industry as a source of livelihood only if the whole family bends itself for long hours in the painstaking labor of raising foods for the produce markets. Raising food for home consumption is a necessary but incidental means of economy which permits saving to pay off the mortgage, to buy machinery, to build up the soil, and makes the ultimate reward of agriculture adequate and attractive.

Where immigrant farmers have been reported as using agricultural methods and planting crops different from those of neighboring native white farmers, it has commonly been observed that by so doing they were securing better results than those to which the community was accustomed. Usually these differences have been in a disproportionate use of hand labor during the first years of operation, but tractors, trucks and other machines have lightened the human load as soon as savings warranted the expense of their purchase. Further, as newcomers, they have not been bound by local traditions, nor, as migrants, has their early training in European methods been applicable to American farming except in a general way, so that they have been more free to respond to new demands for farm products not traditionally supplied by the regions in which they have settled.

There is a difference between the new immigrant's specialization in fruit and vegetables in response to the food de-

[10] Edmund de S. Brunner, *Immigrant Farmers and Their Children*, Doubleday, Doran & Company, Inc., Garden City, N. Y., 1929, pp. 31-32.

mands of growing urban communities, and the habitual planting of time-honored money crops by older immigrants, native
whites and Negroes in the corn and hog, cattle, wheat, tobacco
and cotton belts. This is similar to the difference between the
progressive farmer who devotes his land to dairying or poultry in answer to the effective demand of city populations
within profitable shipping distance, and the rule-of-thumb,
unintelligent planting of cash crops to which the soil is
adapted and the community accustomed without regard for
probable overproduction and devastating crop failures, just
because prices have been high and killings have been made
in the past. Of course trucking, dairying and poultry raising
may also be overdone, with disastrous results to the enter-
prising farmer if not to the purchaser who benefits by an oversupply of farm products; but both demand and price tend to
be steadier and adjustments to market conditions can be
made more easily than in the forms of specialization usually
spoken of as the "one-crop system."

The Negro has been the particular minority sufferer from
the one-crop system, to use the term in its popular meaning.
Most Negroes are still farmers, and they farm in regions where
tradition demands that everything be risked on the chance
of a bountiful yield and a high price for a staple crop, conditions which rarely go together in modern industrial society,
where rapid communication and transportation permit the
farmers of the whole world to be competitors with each other.
To use cotton culture as the outstanding illustration, the region which leans too heavily on this crop is always in an insecure economic position. Drought, frost or the boll weevil
may lay waste plantation after plantation, and what little is
salvaged may go on the market when bumper crops in the
rest of the country or in some other part of the globe have
driven prices to a low level. If the perils of nature are avoided,
there is still the problem of sale in a market over which the
planter has no control. Yet the lesson, not so much of diversification as of intelligent specialization with a view to crop
possibilities and to the market, is not easy to teach to those

who recall that the past prosperity of the South was founded on traditional cash crops and who are unfamiliar with the safer farm methods. Every cotton and tobacco planter of the South knows the dangers of carrying all the eggs in one basket just as well as do the specialists in wheat and corn, and perhaps better than those who supply the produce markets. Land and climate may, however, be unsuitable for safer crops, markets may be too far distant, money for a change may not be available, and, after all, there is always the chance that the next year will be the year to wipe out the failures of the past.

Individuals have grown wealthy under the one-crop system, and some are still able to make more than a bare living out of it. Whole regions have rolled in the wealth produced by plunging everything on some one cash crop. The South in its heyday has shown that it can be done. Since then, however, new fields capable of producing any crop have been brought into world competition, new competitive products have been put on the market, and the old careless, wasteful farm methods no longer bring undeserved prosperity because of a practical monopoly of supply.

To continue with our illustration, in the days before the Civil War one of the most prosperous agricultural regions in the world was to be found in the sea islands off the coast of South Carolina and Georgia, islands especially suited for the raising of the superior sea-island cotton, a cotton then of unrivaled quality. Its yield was heavy, slave labor was reasonably cheap, a market at a high price was certain. The climate has not changed, nor has the soil been so exhausted that it could not be reclaimed. Wages on these islands are low, and labor is available. The quality of sea-island cotton, however, can be matched by the product of many other regions. Silk is cheap, and artificial silk is cheaper, and both are more attractive to the modern consumer. The boll weevil has entered the islands. Some cotton is still raised, but other crops are being planted for low returns in fields which once were capable of paying for themselves in a year or two of cotton. These crops include corn, to which greater acreage was given than to cotton even before 1920, sweet and Irish potatoes, sugar cane, peanuts and rice.[11]

The white owners of the sea islands were driven out during the early years of the Civil War, and their land was sold to former slaves after federal confiscation on the excuse of non-payment of taxes. Negroes still own most of the land—few white people live on the islands today—but efforts to bring back any semblance of the old prosperity have failed. Agricultural education by the Penn School, an excellent institution established by northern white philanthropy, has undoubtedly improved the lot of the islanders, but they are still living in what to a New York State farmer would be abject poverty, although conditions in other parts of the rural south are far worse. The case is cited here to show how the one-crop system has failed in spite of good soil well adapted to high-grade cotton—the boll weevil appeared there first in 1920—and that, so far as the Negro is concerned, his chances of agricultural progress have been slight, and not necessarily from lack of land ownership, for here for seventy years he has owned and cultivated his land continuously with a minimum of white domination.

The evils of the one-crop system as developed in the south have by no means lain solely in the financial risks involved. It has been unhappy in other respects as well. It has meant, for example, local stagnation, in that change and adaptation to new ideas, inventions and modern economic processes were discouraged. Cotton culture was reduced to a routine, and this routine included not only the purely agricultural aspects such as planting, cultivating and harvesting, but also the necessary non-agricultural accompaniments of financing, marketing, education, diet, legislation, and family and community life in general. A social stratification originating under slavery tended to persist beyond its original usefulness, handicapping poor whites and Negroes alike in their endeavors to rise, and holding impoverished "quality folks" in a rut which led nowhere. This is not intended to be an interpretation of southern

---

[11] For a readable survey of one of the sea islands, see T. J. Woofter, Jr., *Black Yeomanry*, Henry Holt & Company, Inc., New York, 1930, pp. x + 291.

life entirely in terms of the one-crop system, for it is not likely that the development of the South would have paralleled that of the North, the West, or any other section of the United States had the plantation production of money crops never existed. There is no question, however, but that the economic and social growth of the South could have been greater had it been possible to destroy the agricultural reliance of large regions on cotton, rice, corn or tobacco soon after the early monopolistic advantage of the South vanished.

There is no geographical reason why any important part of the South should be doomed to follow ancestral agricultural methods. A warm climate forbids some crops, such as wheat, but these limitations are balanced by the possibilities of cane, semi-tropical fruits, and other warmth-loving, frost-abhorring plants. Transportation is also a problem, but if cheese and butter can be shipped with profit to the east from Wisconsin, vegetables and fruits from the Pacific coast or from states bordering on the Gulf of Mexico, and from foreign countries, the restrictions of southern agriculture must be primarily those of the economic and social order.

It may be admitted that the sandy soil, such as that of the sea islands, and the lands worn out by the excessive drains of successive tobacco crops need scientific farming if they are to be used to the greatest advantage. Coastal marsh and swamp land, and the hill country of the interior, both offer obstacles of isolation and a natural poverty which at best permits them to be marginal lands. The soils along the Atlantic are "largely from crystalline rocks and . . . are reputed less fertile than the gulf soils. The alluvial lands of the Mississippi and other rivers are beyond question the richest of all. . . . Next to these probably stand the black prairies. In all states there is more or less alluvial land along the streams, and this soil is always the best. It is the first land brought into cultivation when the country is settled, and remains most constantly in use. Each district has its own advantages and its own difficulties. In the metamorphic regions, the trouble comes in the attempt to keep the soil on the hills, while in the flat lands the problem is to get proper drainage."[12] In every state in the Union there are whole counties of land which may at best be described as marginal, although some southern states perhaps have more than their due; but this is no barrier to the intensive cultivation of the remainder of better quality, provided not too much marginal land is kept under cultivation.

Possibly the best evidence of what can be done is what has been done. Florida has switched thousands of acres to fruit and truck, many of them only recently reclaimed from worthless swamp. Texas shipments of similar products to markets all over the north have brought solvency to individuals and communities once thought beyond financial salvation. There is not a southern state in which similar agricultural adjustments have not been made since the World War, and with the advantages which they hold in the way of low wages, cheap land and early harvests, they may be made not only to compete with but also to supplement the products of other farm regions. Other areas, unfortunately for the South, have obtained a control of the important markets which is hard to break in times like these when there seem to be too many farmers in the world. In the long run, selling advantages are not fixed by nature but are rather the results of man's strategy, and cannot be maintained in the face of intelligent, determined attack.

Intelligent attack implies an adaptability to market demands and an economy in production which is characteristic of few rural communities, especially if a natural isolation prevails. Adaptability, however, is a matter of attitude and education, both of which are already responding to the onslaughts of modern communication. Attitudes and education favoring adaptive change, however, cannot perform miracles of adjustment until they are materialized. This materialization must show itself in the adoption of modernized economic materials and methods before a revival of prosperity can be expected by either black or white farmers in any part of the country. Economic interdependence, a characteristic of the social organization of the United States, requires that all units in the produc-

[12] Carl Kelsey, *op. cit.*, pp. 9-10.

tive and distributive machine be geared to each other. Scored parts, broken cogs and outmoded mechanisms must be replaced in agriculture as well as in industry, only the need is not so evident, since the farmer may survive under inefficiency where the industrialist would starve. In the south it is an outworn, broken-down financial structure more than a lack of strategic location, racial prejudice and other narrow-mindedness, which is lowering the efficiency of the entire rural population.

WAGES, LAND TENURE AND CREDIT

The Negro farmer may be owner, tenant, or wage worker. His wages may be supplementary to other sources of support, or they may be his main reliance. Tenancy may be on the basis of any one of a number of common forms of crop sharing, or it may involve a fixed rental independent of productivity. Even ownership has its variations between the farmer free from debt and the one laboring under a mortgage or other obligation.

Complete, year-round dependence on wages by colored agricultural laborers is found best exemplified in the sugar-cane district of Louisiana. Cane apparently does not lend itself to the small-farm system or to any of the types of tenancy so common in other parts of the South. The concentration of selling and manufacture is in the control of a limited number of corporations which must meet the competition not only of cane products from other countries, such as Cuba, but also of sugar beets which can be raised in more temperate climates. The fresh-cut cane must be taken to costly mills where the first steps of manufacturing are completed, after which the crude products are refined and offered for sale in a world market. There is an essential difference between this process and that by which corn, wheat, cotton or tobacco are offered for sale. The cereals may be stored or sold immediately after harvest without further expense except transportation. Tobacco can be prepared for sale by the farmer himself in an inexpensive barn. Cotton can be baled in a local mill at little cost. Cane, however, cannot be stored, but must be started on its manufacturing process without delay, and it must be handled on a large-scale production plan. This comes near to being industrialized agriculture.

Wages on the cane plantations are not high, and the labor is arduous, so that there has been difficulty in keeping the workers from migrating to other occupations. Italian laborers have been tried as substitutes for the Negroes, but with little success. Homes, furnished by the owners, usually include a vegetable patch, and are perhaps a trifle better than those available to Negroes on the ordinary plantation. Corporation policy regarding Negroes is less influenced by local white prejudices, if only because dividends automatically become the major interest of absentee stockholders and even direct owners of the large investments required. It seems that the greatest handicap of Negro wage workers in the cane region is that, owing to the necessity for large-scale production, there is practically no opportunity for rising from the wage class to that of small-farm ownership except by migration.

While the cane fields furnish opportunity for wage labor throughout the year, other agricultural wage employment is seasonal. The cultivation of rice, for example, furnishes employment for only about six months in the year, and the income so obtained must be supplemented by some other occupation. Usually, however, wages earned by Negroes in farming supply the supplementary income, while most of their time is devoted to some other occupation such as personal service, odd jobs and small farms of their own operating. Strawberries, peaches and other fruits, as well as cotton, cereals and vegetables, require seasonal labor if cultivated on anything except a small scale, so that there is no part of the South where there is not some opportunity to earn a little money seasonally without going into the lumber camps, coal and phosphate mines, fishing, domestic service, odd jobs or industry in nearby centers. With an abundance of cheap labor, white and black, wages and conditions of labor have remained at an unhealthy, starvation level which permits no great improvement in social welfare. Savings have been practically out of the question, and the absence of training in thrift is supplemented by a lack of incentive when there is so little to save. Migrations to the city, however, have been the most powerful force in driving wages upward and in the introduction of improved working and living conditions, for a scarcity of workers in any locality adds bargaining power to those available.

Immigrant wage workers have been more fortunately situated. With few exceptions they have stayed out of the South, some south European governments having gone so far as to warn their emigrants not to go to such states as Louisiana and Mississippi both because of prejudice in these states against south Europeans and because of intolerable working conditions. When immigrants have gone to the farm as hired hands they have selected the regions where there was sufficient need for them to make it worth their while both in wages and in opportunity for advancement. Negroes, on the other hand, were settled in farm regions in the days of involuntary servitude when they had no choice in the matter and before the post-Civil War slump in southern agriculture. The only effective demand for their labor on farms has been from the deeper South and a few border states, where even a slight differential was able to attract them from worn-out and more backward regions. The farms of the North and West found immigrants more desirable and sufficiently abundant during the days of need.

In the north the farm has had to compete directly with industry for hands, and in the west homesteads and cheap land have been plentiful until so recently that non-operating labor has been difficult to hold, and only the most inefficient workers could be attracted by low wages. Casual labor from the cities in the east and of migrant workers in the west has been depended on for the larger seasonal demands, while the small farmer has relied on the cooperation of his neighbors. The immigrant, further, has been trained in thrift and instilled with the idea of ownership, so that he has eagerly seized free lands where available and purchased cheap lands with hoarded wages in well populated districts. The immigrant farm hand has consistently had before him the objective of farm ownership, and wages have been but a means to an end, one much more readily achieved in northern and western regions than in the southern states.

Thus the farm immigrants of the Pacific coast, with the exception of the Mexicans and the Filipinos, who have included many intending to stay in the United States only temporarily, have accepted work in the orchards and on the truck and other farms, shifting constantly with the demand and with wages, to the end that they might lease and own agricultural lands for themselves. In this the Japanese have been successful, increasing their holdings, at least through 1920, in spite of the alien land law of 1913 which was designed to drive them out or keep them as hired hands. This process of transition from farm employee to farm owner has been more common among immigrants from Europe and Asia than among Negroes, wherever the immigrant has gone to the land. It is interesting to observe that while the people of the United States are generally more in favor of immigrants who become farmers than of those who become industrial workers, federal and state laws have restricted their right to the ownership of agricultural lands in all sections of the country.

Since there is a parallel between the attitude expressed in these land-ownership laws and that of many Southerners toward the acquisition of farms by Negroes, brief consideration of them may be given at this point.

The best-known example of alien land laws is that found in California, directly inspired by the success of Japanese farm laborers, well liked and gladly hired by agricultural employers as wage hands, in changing their status to farm operators. Acting under an amendment of 1894 to the state constitution, the California legislature enacted its first alien land law in 1913, later to be strengthened in 1921 and 1923. The effect of these enactments is to prevent aliens ineligible to citizenship from the ownership of or the holding of any interest in agricultural lands. Consequently, Orientals, if of foreign birth, may not acquire title to farms either directly or through some subterfuge such as incorporation, nor may they operate farms as tenants, croppers or in the disguise of "employees" with wage and bonus agreements. Essentially similar laws directed against Orientals are in effect in Oregon, Washington, Arizona, Idaho and Montana.[13]

Such laws, if not contrary to existing treaties, have been repeatedly held constitutional, and there is ample precedent for them. While California was the first state to use the qualifying clause "ineligible to citizenship," a classification of aliens held to be reasonable by the United States Supreme Court, the common law has long recognized a distinction between the rights of citizens and aliens in property ownership. This applies, however, to real and not to personal property, which has generally been permitted alien ownership under both common and statute law. An alien who has not formally declared his intention of becoming an American citizen is not permitted to take title to public lands under the Federal Homestead Act. A federal act of 1887 restricted the right of aliens to land ownership in federal territory. In addition to the states already mentioned, Eliot Mears cites Pennsylvania, Missouri, Delaware, Illinois, Kansas, Kentucky, Minnesota, Nebraska and Texas as states limiting the ownership of real property by aliens. Treaties, since they are on a parity with acts of Congress, must be respected by such state legislation, and in no case has the ownership of all kinds of real property under all circumstances been forbidden to aliens.

To quote the summary of Charles Maxson, "At common law, says Wise, an alien 'may take real estate by act of the parties or by deed or grant, or devise, or by other act of purchase, but cannot hold it except upon such terms as may be described by the state.' Though he may take by will, he may not take by descent, and he cannot transmit his land by descent but it vests immediately in the state. In theory, at least, our states began with this system, and some few states still hold to it, but 'Massachusetts, Ohio, and Wisconsin are three states which have removed the disabilities of aliens with respect to the possession, enjoyment, or descent of property.' Between these extremes a great variety of law may be

---

[13] For an excellent concise statement concerning alien land laws in the United States, see Eliot Grinnell Mears, *Resident Orientals on the American Pacific Coast*, University of Chicago Press, Chicago, 1928, chap. vii.

found. . . . . All these discriminations against aliens would appear to be in violation of the equal protection clause of the Fourteenth Amendment, but that amendment, interpreted in the light of history of the times, was not intended to invalidate the land laws of the majority of the states and of the United States."[14] It is understood, of course, that citizenship, either by naturalization or by birth in the United States, prevents such legislative restrictions. If this were not the case, it is certain that the force of existing land laws would, in the Pacific states at least, be extended to the descendants of aliens ineligible to citizenship, perhaps even to the children of some Europeans, especially in the states which polled strong nativist votes in the 'thirties, 'fifties, 'nineties and post-World War anti-foreign agitation.

At first thought it may seem that Indians and Negroes have escaped this type of discrimination. Confusion is caused by the fact that these minorities were so differently situated from the oriental and European immigrants that it was possible to accomplish the fundamental purpose of restricting agricultural competition by them through even more stringent legal measures. Legalized appropriation of Indian farm lands, frequently but not always disguised as treaty and purchase, with accompanying compulsory migration, generally achieved the white man's purpose. In California, without the ratification of any treaty or the semblance of purchase, the native Indians were completely dispossessed in so far as the white man wished during the first half century of United States possession. Thousands of Indians unwillingly sold their land in eastern states in the first third of the nineteenth century when they were moved west by the federal government. Except in two or three areas of concentration, Indian farmers today are unimportant agricultural competitors, as they have been since the latter part of the past century. The federal government, however, still finds it necessary to hold title to the lands of many Indians

[14] Charles H. Maxson, *Citizenship*, Oxford University Press, New York, 1930, pp. 221-222. Dr. Maxson's first quotation is from J. S. Wise, *American Citizenship*, p. 270; his second, from F. A. Cleveland, *American Citizenship*, p. 139.

lest the several states and private individuals be too careless in their regard for Indian property.

Negro farm laborers before the Civil War, with the exception of freedmen amounting to something less than eleven per cent, many of whom were not farmers, were under the restraints of slavery, and consequently could not legally own property of any kind. "In civil transactions slaves had no standing as persons in court except for the one purpose of making claim for freedom; and even this must usually be done through some friendly citizen as a self-appointed guardian bringing suit for trespass in the nature of ravishment of ward. . . . It may fairly be said that these laws for the securing of slave property and the police of the colored population were as thorough and stringent as their framers could make them, and that they left an almost irreducible minimum of rights and privileges to those whose function and place were declared to be service and subordination."[15] Even free Negroes had their rights restricted by law and practice during the slave period, although they were usually neither sufficiently numerous nor prosperous to constitute a threat to the agricultural prosperity of the white people in a community. Further, they could be compelled to leave a community if they became obnoxious, or even through no fault of their own. Why, under these conditions, need there have been any further legal restraints to reduce their competition? Now, of course, they, like the Indians, are citizens, and efforts to keep them out of the land-owning class must be extra-legal. There is evidence in the not uncommon attitude of Southerners, who do not look with favor on the too prosperous Negro farmer and sometimes go so far as to refuse to sell their land to colored people, that there would be Negro land laws if it were not obvious that they would be unconstitutional.

Legislation, however, cannot prevent land ownership by individuals of any minority in the United States. Just as native white people in the city will sell their residences to a person of any color or creed if the price is right, almost regardless of

[15] U. B. Phillips, *op. cit.*, pp. 500-501.

what they and their neighbors might prefer, so farm owners will generally sell if it seems advantageous to do so.

TABLE III

FARMERS IN THE SOUTH, BY COLOR AND TENURE, 1925[16]

Tenure

Total	White	2,299,963
	Colored	831,455
Full owners	White	1,173,778
	Colored	159,651
Part owners	White	150,875
	Colored	34,889
Managers	White	10,259
	Colored	667
Tenants	White	965,051
	Colored	636,248
Cash tenants	White	103,854
	Colored	78,760
Croppers[a]	White	278,736
	Colored	344,322
Other tenants	White	582,461
	Colored	213,166

[a] The croppers here listed operated 22,985,660 acres in 1925.

In 1925, according to the census of agriculture, there were almost 200,000 Negro farm owners in the south, although about 35,000 of these did not own all the land they cultivated, many of this latter number holding title to only small patches of ground. This is a slight decrease from the number reported owning farms in 1910, perhaps accounted for largely by the recent migration to the city. The number of southern Negro farm owners in 1925 should be contrasted with the number of tenants, not quite 640,000, and with less than a thousand managers, as well as with a total of over 2,250,000 white farm operators in the same area, of whom about 1,325,000 were full or part owners.[17] It can be seen from this comparison that the

[16] United States Census of Agriculture, 1925, Government Printing Office, Washington, D. C., part i, p. 14.

[17] An excellent running account of Negro farm laborers and operators can be found in Carter G. Woodson, The Rural Negro, The Association for the Study of Negro Life and History, Washington, D. C., 1930, chaps. ii, iii and iv.

Negro does not achieve ownership so readily as the white man in the south. "The size of the farms of colored farmers in the south compared with that of the white throws further light on the question. The farms of the white owners in the south averaged 149.7 acres in size in 1920, with 59.7 acres improved, as compared with an average size of 64.7 acres and 33.3 acres improved for colored owners. The farms of the white tenants averaged 90.4 acres in size, with 49.2 acres improved, as compared with 38.2 and 28.9 acres respectively for the total and improved acreage operated by colored tenants.

"The value of the land thus operated, too, will further illuminate the situation. Reporting on the total value of farm property such as land, buildings, implements, machinery, and live stock on farms operated by whites in 1920, 69.5 per cent was returned for farms operated by owners, 33.4 per cent for farms operated by tenants, and 4.1 per cent for farms operated by hired managers. In the case of the colored farmers the corresponding figures were 27 per cent for the owners, 71.6 per cent for tenants, and 1.4 per cent for managers."[18]

Whether the responsibility for these discrepancies between the success of the colored and white farmers of the south lies in race prejudice, the one-crop system and ignorance of improved farm methods, tenancy and peonage, poor soil, credit and finance, low wages, the Negro as a race, or in some combination of these and other factors, is a disputed point. All except the argument of race must be considered interlocking, contributory causes.

According to the agricultural census of 1920, the immigrant farmer is highly successful if farm ownership is any test. "The proportion of farm owners among immigrants exceeds the proportion of native-born white farm owner-operators in the total native-born groups in every one of the nine census divisions, except New England, where the difference is less than one-tenth of 1 per cent. Of the 4,760,406 native-born white owners and tenants, 66.4 per cent own the land they cultivate. Of the 573,880 foreign-born white farmers, other than operating managers, 90.8 per cent have achieved ownership. The

[18] *Ibid.,* pp. 30-31.

holdings of this group constitute 83.5 per cent of the total land operated by foreign-born farmers of the owner and tenant groups."[19]

The average size of the farms operated and owned by native-born white people in 1920 was 165 acres, valued at $10,019.00; the foreign-born owner and operator cultivated an average farm of 184 acres, valued at $13,484.00. Native-born tenants operated farms of an average size of 132 acres, valued at $11,996.00, while the foreign-born tenant operated one averaging 191 acres, valued at $21,706.00. The variations in average size and value of the farms operated by owners or tenants of the different European nationalities is without great significance in the determination of their relative success as farmers, for much depends on the time of arrival, whether their farms were bought or taken under the Homestead Act, whether they lie in densely or sparsely populated regions, and on the crops raised on them. Indeed, this also holds true in comparisons of the value and size of farms operated by Negroes, by native-born white people, and by immigrants, so that at best we have in such facts only a rough measure of success of minority and majority farmers. They do, however, show the trend in regard to the rôle played by the various minorities in our agricultural life, and are sufficient proof that all may be relied upon, should an unlikely shortage of farm labor and operators become imminent.

Farm tenancy, especially the forms prevalent among the colored minorities, has been criticized as a major factor in agricultural retardation. While under most circumstances it appears to be advantageous for the operator to have a permanent interest in the soil he cultivates, the practice of farm leasing need not inevitably lead to disaster for either landlord or tenant.

The tenant's payment for the use of farm land may be a

[19] Edmund de S. Brunner, *op. cit.*, p. 41. This study of the foreign-born farmers and their children has culled the important facts from the recent census publications on white minorities of European, Mexican and Canadian national origin, has made them available in readable form, and has given them keen interpretation in the light of special field work and research more penetrating than that possible in general census procedure.

sum of money agreed to in the lease, a definite proportion of the crops, or a fixed amount of produce not varying with the yield. The landlord's obligations may be limited to the furnishing of the land to be cultivated, or they may be extended to include farm implements, livestock, seed, fertilizer, or even advances for the living expenses of the tenant and his family. It is obvious that payment will vary with the extent of the landlord's obligations, and that any number of types of leases is possible.[20] We may, however, center our attention on four most important types, namely, cash tenants, whose payments are independent of the yield and who receive nothing from the landlord except the land and perhaps buildings; standing renters, who pay a stated amount of farm produce and frequently receive practically everything needed by a farmer during the period before harvest; croppers, who give a high proportion of the produce to the landlord since they furnish little except their labor; and ordinary share tenants, who pay a share of the crops lower than that paid by the croppers, since they furnish not only labor but also the farm machinery, livestock, fertilizer, etc., required on the farm. Tenants who have an insufficient reserve to meet living expenses generally receive credit from the landlord, the storekeeper or the bank; in those forms of tenancy where the landlord does not furnish the necessary farm equipment as a part of the contract, similar sources of credit for this purpose are usually available.

Since cash tenants and ordinary share tenants receive the least from the landlord, that is, usually nothing more than the land and empty buildings—and not always buildings—

[20] "A step below the Negro cash tenants came the largest group of Negro farm operators—the share tenants. There are varying degrees of share tenancy, but the most common procedure was to rent the Negro forty or fifty acres of land, the landlord taking a part of the crop as rent. The share of the crop taken depended upon what the laborer furnished. If the tenant gave nothing but his labor, the landlord received two-thirds of the crop; if he fed himself, the landlord received one-half of it; if the laborer also furnished implements and work animals, the landlord received from one-third to one-fourth. Of course, the fertility of the soil, the locality, and the character of the contracting parties all influenced such details." Lorenzo J. Greene and Carter G. Woodson, *The Negro Wage Earner*, The Association for the Study of Negro Life and History, Inc., Washington, D. C., 1930. Chapters IV and XI deal with the Negro in agriculture both before and after the World War. An extensive bibliography is included.

the landlord has risked less on their ability and industry and therefore interferes the least with their freedom to live and farm as they please. The poorer the land and the market, the more likely these systems are to be used, for where the soil is infertile and when agricultural prices are low there is slight incentive to throw good money into the cultivation of a farm. Absentee landlords who are unable to keep an eye on their tenants, or who do not find it practicable to employ someone else to do so for them, also tend to adopt the systems which require the least effort and expenditure on the part of the owner. It is notorious that such farm tenants, with no stake in the land but a high investment in labor and capital, are likely to be "miners" rather than farmers, that is, to take everything possible out of the soil and put nothing back by the way of crop rotation, fertilizer, weed control and repairs. The longer the lease, of course, the greater the tenant's interest in the quality of his leasehold, so that this danger may be offset by renting for a considerable period of time.[21]

When, on the other hand, the owner has expectations of good returns from his land, he is more inclined to give it his personal attention and to invest his own or borrowed capital in it. Thus, the better the land the more nearly the tenant comes to resembling a wage worker through leases which require of him little more than the labor of himself and his family. Under the cropping system and the standing rental system, both generally providing for a greater return per acre to the owner than cash rental or ordinary share tenancy, there is a tendency for the landlord to attempt to protect his investment by methods which approximate and not infrequently actually constitute peonage.

In the south, where farm tenancy is most common, all of

---

[21] J. A. Dickey and E. C. Branson, in a survey of two townships in Chatham County, North Carolina, the results of which were published in a pamphlet, *How Farm Tenants Live*, by the University of North Carolina Press in 1922, found the following daily cash incomes for farmers: 135 white owners, 34 cents; 41 black owners, 32 cents; 38 white renters, 14 cents; 13 white croppers, 8 cents; 66 black renters, 16 cents, and 36 black croppers, 10 cents (p. 15). The living conditions of both white and colored tenants and owners can be inferred from these incomes which, although based on data gathered in one locality, are not exceptional.

these systems with a multitude of variations may be found in the same locality. Cash rental and cropping leases may be found on adjoining farms, although one form or the other usually prevails, so that no absolute generalization concerning the conditions determining their use will be accurate. Cropping, however, is by far the most common type of tenancy in the south as a whole. In 1925 it was between four and five times as common among Negro tenants as cash rental, and the almost 350,000 colored croppers exceeded by about one-third of that number the total of all other types of tenantry combined except cash rental. In round numbers, there were 80,000 cash tenants, 350,000 croppers and 215,000 other types of tenants among southern Negroes according to the agricultural census of that year. Perhaps a lack of confidence in ill-trained, penniless farmers, both white and black, predisposes the southern owner to the use of a lease system which requires a dangerous outlay of funds but permits, by common practice if not by law, supervision and restraint beyond that allowed an industrial employer over his labor. A paternalistic tradition, of course, favors the practice.

It is so easy for a crop to be lost by improper cultivation and neglect that owners with a share in the yield have forced intolerable leases as well as excessive physical supervision on their tenants in their efforts at self-protection. A portion of a sample lease will suffice for illustration:

"Said tenant further agrees that if he violates the contract, or neglects, or abandons or fails (or in the owner's judgment violates this contract or fails) to properly work or cultivate the land early or at proper times, or in case he should become physically or legally incapacitated from working said lands or should die during the term of his lease, or fails to gather or save the crops when made, or fails to pay the rents or advances made by the owner, when due, then in case of full possession of said premises, crops and improvements, in which event this contract may become void and cancelled at the owner's option, and all indebtedness by the tenant for advances or rent shall at once become due and payable to the owner who may treat them as due and payable without further notice to the tenant; and the tenant hereby agrees to surrender the quiet and peaceable possession of said premises to the owner at said time, in which event the owner is hereby authorized to transfer, sell or dispose of all property thereon the tenant has any interest in, and in order to entitle the owner to do so, it shall not be necessary to give any notice on any failure or violation of this contract by the tenant, the execution of this lease being sufficient notice of defalcation on the part of the tenant, and shall be so construed between the parties hereto, any law, usage or custom to the contrary notwithstanding."[22]

In fairness it must be said that there are thousands of plantation owners who either demand no such lease or who would consider it unworthy of a gentleman to take advantage of its provisions except in a case of the most outrageous violation of contract by a worthless tenant. Yet other thousands of owners compel the acceptance of such terms by white and colored tenants, and enforce the provisions when whim or possible advantage favors such a course of conduct.

Peonage, or involuntary labor other than as a penalty for crime, has been a failure when attempted by law but has had some success when enforced by the common consent of the ruling classes in the south. The vagrancy laws by which southern states immediately after the Civil War attempted to compel Negroes to work where and when the white people wanted them to work, and without gain, were promptly nullified. Although modeled after laws found in northern states, they were abused in interpretation and enforcement to secure the involuntary labor of freedmen on the pretext that vagrancy, broadly defined in law and practice, justified wholesale round-ups of Negroes who were subsequently given into the custody of white men who needed their labor. Later attempts, persisting into the twentieth century, to make debts the basis of involuntary servitude also failed. This method of attack was invariably found unconstitutional when tested in the Supreme Court of the United States, although some of the lower

---

[22] Quoted by Carter G. Woodson, op. cit., p. 49, from the American Statistical Association, Quarterly Publication, vol. xiii, pp. 82-83.

courts originally supported it. Between the Civil and the World Wars, however, the Negro farm laborer or tenant who fell into debt found it difficult to leave the service of the employer or landlord to whom he was indebted in such states as Alabama, Florida, Mississippi, Georgia, North Carolina, and South Carolina.

Debts in the process of being worked out on the farm not infrequently became larger instead of smaller during months and years of labor. Crop and market failures, improvidence and, on occasion, unscrupulous practices connived to keep workers tied to the land. The fact that it was to the interest of the landowner to keep satisfactory hands and tenants on his place tempted him to advance money too freely for luxuries, to falsify accounts and gouge wherever possible; and no doubt those who succumbed to temptation comforted themselves by the rationalization that it was all for the good of the Negro, who was thus kept under their paternalistic guidance. In case of dispute concerning the amount of debt, the Negro's word was practically worthless. Planters who refused to stoop to such practices were not strong enough to check the trickery and thieving of the others, so that the luckless individual who was caught in the system had little opportunity to escape until his creditor willed it. If he decamped surreptitiously, there was the problem of where to go. By what might ironically be called a "gentlemen's agreement" it was customary in many districts for one planter to refuse to employ an applicant or lease to him until he was assured that previous obligations, however unjust, had been met. Bankruptcy offered no way out. There is reason to believe that even this thieves' code of honor was violated readily enough when a planter needed labor badly, but such violations furnished inadequate relief for only a few peons.

In recent years several factors have tended to disrupt the peonage system. A shortage of labor resulting from migration has made some planters less particular about the previous obligations of their tenants. A number of public scandals involving brutality along with peonage have created open public sentiment against it even in the South itself. Most of all, the opening of industry to unskilled colored labor has given a refuge to debtors, for it would be a rare factory management which would attempt to inquire into the previous financial record of its employees or do without valuable laborers because a gentlemen's code bound them to some landowner. Corporations have been said to be soulless, and in this respect their alleged defect is a source of freedom to colored serfs.

It has been said with much justice that the basic defect of the southern agricultural system under which Negroes and whites suffer has been neither tenancy nor peonage, but the credit system which has dominated owner, tenant, and wage worker together. Southern money crops have demanded financing, and it has been the exceptional owner or tenant who could long survive without an extension of credit from some source or other. The landowner, if not already heavily mortgaged, as has too often been the case, has been able to depend on the local banks. Reputable planters, of course, could obtain personal loans in addition to mortgage money, and it has been the rule that they have financed their operations by borrowing money at interest in spite of the certainty that they would be pressed for payment regardless of crop failures. Interest rates in the south have been notoriously high and burdensome. The money so obtained has been reloaned to tenants for the purchase of everything from seed, mules, fertilizer, and bacon to calico, tobacco, candy, and automobiles. The risk of crop failure because of a caprice of nature or the laziness, ignorance and dishonesty of tenants has been covered by both open and disguised exorbitant interest charges. Thus an unsound banking relationship has been established between landlord and tenant, with ill feeling resulting from high charges, from pressure for payment in hard times as well as in good, and from the mere fact of a debtor-creditor connection.

In those cases where the storekeeper has extended credit in order to get business, the situation has been no better, and has probably been worse. The landlord at least had an in-

terest in his tenants growing out of a desire that his share
of the crops should be as large as possible, with the incidental
result that the tenants' share was also increased by any
supervision and guidance given. The storekeeper, however,
made his sole profit out of purchases across his counter,
and cared little about their nature so long as he was reasonably certain that the sale of crops would cover indebtedness
to himself. Purchases could be limited by his estimates of
seasonal advantages and disadvantages and by his judgment
of the individual patron. The only advice his interests dictated was in the direction of encouraging large purchases of
goods in which there was the greatest profit. Some bad debts,
of course, were unavoidable, but these were usually more
than covered by the mark-up on all prices. If an occasional
storekeeper weighed his thumb with the bacon, added his
columns generously, or delivered less than the accounts
showed, who could challenge him in a community where
Negroes were illiterate and few professed to believe them
against any white man's claim? One dishonest storekeeper
in a county was more than ample to convince most Negroes
that they were being cheated by all. The legend of the storekeeper who charged a Negro patron the price of the three bales
of cotton which his shrewd customer said was his entire
crop, and then found an error in his addition exactly equal
to the price of a fourth bale which he discovered had been
concealed, may be a fiction, but its currency is evidence of
the colored attitude in such matters. Granting that most storekeepers are as honest as they can be, there is still the fact
that they, like the landlord, are indulging in banking, while
their primary interests in selling conflict with sound principles of money lending. Even the fertilizer companies, which
have been forced into extending credit unwisely, are compelled to charge too much for the service, and are tempted to
sell more fertilizer than is needed in order to swell profits
for the company and commissions to the agents. Neither race
prejudice nor thievery is the basic flaw in this form of credit
extension; it is the temptation to, and the practical necessity

for, the use of unsound banking methods by individuals who are not and cannot be good bankers.[23]

It may be claimed that the landlord and the seller of commodities who profit by their dealings with Negroes are the only practical sources of Negro farm credit. Their interests compel them to make advances of money or goods in order that they may reap a profit on the use or sale of the money or goods. The hope of ultimate gain, however, exerts a pressure to make advances to all tenants and to all customers, and at the same time to guard against loss by unreasonable or dishonest charges. The trouble has been that southern banking has been inadequate and reactionary, so that no other means for handling the situation have been in sight. The answer lies in the observation that lending is the function of banks and bankers, and that if they find it unprofitable to lend to Negro tenants no one else can make a profit out of the practice except by unethical or crooked means. Unreliable Negroes should no more be given credit than unreliable white men, nor should poor farmers be given financial advantages denied poor business men. If tenants were compelled to go directly to the banks for all appreciable loans and be scrutinized just as any other applicant is scrutinized, the undesirable tenants would be

[23] Roland B. Eutsler, in an article in *Social Forces*, vol. viii, nos. 3 and 4, March and June, 1930, entitled "Agricultural Credit and the Negro Farmer," reports his findings as to the use and cost of credit as summarized in the following table:

PROPORTION OF FARMERS USING CREDIT AND COST OF CREDIT

Type of Credit	Percentage Using Credit	Cost of Credit
Mortgages	51.0	6.0
Short-time Cash	43.0	16.8
Fertilizer	65.5	37.2
Merchant	52.4	26.0

Personal interviews with 588 Negro farmers, 313 of whom were farm owners, living in twelve counties in the eastern and central section of North Carolina, supplied the data on which this table is based. One hundred and twenty of the farm owners rented additional land. The counties included cotton-tobacco-peanut, cotton-tobacco, and cotton belts, with truck represented in two counties. While no sectional study of agricultural credit would be strictly typical of the entire South, a sufficient variety of crops, tenant systems and sources of credit is found in these twelve counties to indicate the general defects of the southern agricultural organization.

forced into the wage class, and southern agriculture would be better off without them.

The argument that no bank would lend money to a Negro is not only based on false assumptions but is also contrary to southern experience. There are banks throughout the south which have found Negro borrowers profitable. Many tenants have property other than real estate which can be mortgaged. While both are used, banks seem to prefer endorsed notes to crop liens. Money may also be lent on no other security than the character of the borrower, and every southern community has Negroes who would justify the confidence of the local banker. The drifters and the improvident may deserve sympathy, and landed proprietors may think they need their labor, but the policy of financing them has been ruinous to whole communities in the south. It would not be tolerated in the north. Those who may brand this argument as "theoretical" and "impractical"—damning epithets in America—will be confounded if they but examine the experience of progressive southern banks, increasingly common since the World War.

Tenancy and farm credit have presented no problems of similar magnitude to the other minorities of racial and national origin in the United States. Mexicans and Filipinos are primarily wage workers on the farm. The Orientals of alien birth are slowly being driven off the farms in the states where they have settled, now that they are no longer content with being hired hands as they were during the first years after their arrival. All immigrants, from Europe, from the Orient and from other countries in the western hemisphere alike, have seen fit to become tenants or to strive for farm ownership only when they were convinced that the odds against their success were not overwhelming, as is witnessed by their avoidance of the south. Any attempt to force them to accept impossible leases and exorbitant credit charges would have been the signal during later years for a turn to industry even greater than it was; during the free-land period such an attempt would have been unthinkable. They were migrants coming to the United States in search of promised opportunity for advancement, and the fact that they were migrants gave them freedom to pick and choose which the Negro will not experience for years to come.

Minorities need not be encouraged to go or to stay on the farm. To the extent that they are mobile they will rush to grasp opportunities for self-advancement without urging. Those who are not yet mobile, and this refers chiefly to the Negroes, may be helped but not freed from poverty by reputed panaceas such as scientific farming education (as at Hampton and Tuskegee and their swarm of imitators), and federal farm credit, which cannot reach the Negro through administrators and agents who are not permitted by tradition to have confidence in him or understanding of his needs. Farm programs designed for minorities all have their weakness in that by their very limitation to a fraction of the population they are restricted to dealing with symptoms and not with basic causes of farm distress, which is a community or national problem and not one of racial or national origin.

CHAPTER IV

INDUSTRY, THE PROFESSIONS, AND TRADE

IT IS a part of the American credo that all immigrants who came to the United States before 1890 had their ambitions fired by the call of fertile soil awaiting the plow of the pioneer. Even that involuntary migrant, the Negro, has been invested with the qualities of a born agriculturist who only recently has had the effrontery to invade industry. Like most popular beliefs, this one too is false, except as it reflects a trend evidenced by the majority of early migrants. Division of labor as between agricultural and other workers existed in Europe before Columbus, and was brought to this continent by the first settlers. The proportions of the population distributed in the specialized, non-agricultural occupations, however, were decidedly smaller than they are today, so that with the passage of years our attention has focused on the more prominent agricultural features of bygone days and manners. Thus there is today not a single comprehensive study of the *ante bellum* village and city Negro, and only a few brief or superficial papers or chapters in larger works, while the plantation Negro has dwarfed his urban brother almost to the point of invisibility in scientific literature and fiction alike. So, too, the early European migrant has come to be stereotyped as a farmer, to the neglect of the less numerous, but significant, non-agricultural element. Now, of course, we are reversing the process, and forgetting the minority farmer who has been relegated to the background by the greater prominence of the migrants to our cities. The non-agricultural gainful occupations of minorities include today, and always have included—although to a lesser degree formerly than now—mining, industry, transportation, personal service, business, law, medicine, teaching and the other professions.

THE CALL OF INDUSTRIALISM

Charles Wesley, in summarizing the relation between slavery and industrialism, has shown that "Upon the plantation, in skilled and unskilled labor, Negro workers were found. In various parts of the south they were used with measures of success in such manufacturing plants as the economic development of the south permitted. A talented number emerged from the larger group, demonstrated the possession of the special skill which the town and the plantation demanded and made themselves a necessity to a class of individuals who knew neither the value nor the process of labor."[1] Of the free Negro, he has said: "Individual free Negroes, as the urban tabulations reveal, were filling during slavery important places in the mechanical occupations, even in the midst of unfavorable circumstances, but also in the field of achievements, in the inventions, in the professions, in business organization, and in the accumulation of wealth."[2] In the north, where Negro population fell from 3.4 per cent in 1790 to 1.7 per cent in 1860, the colored worker was restricted by the very smallness of his numbers to agriculture and domestic service until well after the Civil War, although there were an appreciable number of individuals in business, the professions and the skilled trades.[3] It was in the south, where the agricultural system and slavery had concentrated wealth in the hands of a small proportion of the white people and had impoverished the others who could not compete with slave labor even in the skilled trades, that the Negro first achieved outstanding success in non-agricultural pursuits. In fact, before the Civil War, free and slave labor practically monopolized southern occupations of the artisan and other classes requiring apprenticeship, except in those regions where the poor whites fled for refuge from the devastating competi-

[1] Charles H. Wesley, *Negro Labor in the United States,* Vanguard Press, Inc., New York, 1927, p. 24. This volume contains an extensive bibliography.
[2] *Ibid.,* p. 65.
[3] For details of Negro occupations from colonial times up to the present, see Lorenzo J. Greene and Carter G. Woodson, *op. cit.* A bibliography is included.

tion of Negroes brought to the United States originally for unskilled agricultural labor.

There was a fierce resentment against the Negro and against slavery on the part of the millions of poor whites in the south who were not ignorant of the cause of their poverty. "Southern society at the outbreak of the Civil War was made up not of two classes, white masters and Negro slaves, but of four classes. These were: first, the slave-holding families, about 350,000 in number, representing about 1,750,000 individuals; second, the Negro slaves, nearly 4,000,000 in number; third, the free Negroes who numbered about 500,000 throughout the whole country and about 260,000 in the south; fourth, the 'poor white' small farmers, artisans, laborers, and tradesmen, who numbered more than 5,250,000."[4] So long as legalized slavery kept the political and social control of the south in the hands of the slave owners, the Negro was secure in his occupations against any onslaughts by "white trash." Emancipation, however, led to political and economic reorganization which gave control to the long-suffering but hitherto ineffective masses who at last achieved power through sheer force of numbers. This accomplished, there began a steady drive to take over more and more of the traditional "nigger jobs," such as bricklaying, barbering, shoe shining, carpentry, masonry, and even the better agricultural opportunities, until today there is no type of work in which the Negro is as secure from white competition as he was before emancipation. Thus, excepting a limited amount of agricultural progress, the Negro is economically worse off in the south now than he was before a flood of white workers, released by the abolition of slavery, descended upon him and denied him the opportunity of using the skills required under slavery.

The colonists and later immigrants had no such leashed labor reserve impatiently and resentfully waiting to come down from the hills and out of the barren lands to demand occupations in which to establish itself. The early European migrants

---

[4] Sterling D. Spero and Abram L. Harris, *The Black Worker*, Columbia University Press, New York, 1931, p. 3.

were always at liberty to turn to the soil for relief if a preferred urban occupation was found to be crowded, and the native-born competitors who felt themselves crowded by alien workers had and frequently accepted the same opportunity for escape. Periods of unemployment, of course, recurred at intervals, but they tended automatically to check further immigration from abroad even before the exhaustion of the free lands of the west. Had the native white population in immigrant districts been as economically unfortunate as the great majority of southern white people, the immigrant would not have dared to come to the United States, just as he did not dare to go to the South.[5] It may be observed, further, that the European immigrant, having no permanent stigmas of minority status, could not long be held in an inferior caste, but passed as a member of the native majority as soon as language, dress and manner were adapted to American custom, as did the Irish, Germans and Scandinavians, while the south Europeans are rapidly accomplishing the same end. Even the oriental and Mexican immigrants, who do have permanent stigmas of their origin, have been able to avoid withering competition by refusing to migrate to regions where an abundance of labor could already be found. The Negro, however, being a slave, could not refuse to be an involuntary migrant to districts where his labor was wanted because its cost was little more than subsistence on a bare existence basis. even if it meant entering unwilling competition with free white workers.

At the present time, however, no minority people in the United States is occupationally distributed in proportions

[5] It has been claimed that the immigrant has stayed out of the South because he could not or did not wish to compete with the Negro. This claim is usually based on the statistical evidence that there has been a negative correlation between the proportion of Negroes and immigrants in the population of any given locality. The fact of this negative correlation is indisputable, but its interpretation does not seem so simple. It may well be that the immigrant was not so much deterred by fear of competition with the Negro as he was by the lack of economic opportunity in the south and by the impossibility of competing with other white people in the south, the poor whites, who constituted an available labor reserve and wage threat which could not be overcome, as could perhaps the Negro, by a new arrival's claim for work based on white superiority.

similar to those of the native-born white population of native parentage. Agricultural disproportions, high for some minorities and low for others, have already been discussed. Disproportions in the non-farming pursuits are no less startling.

"In the present [economic] structure the native whites still lead in the advanced occupations, which include architects, chemists, civil engineers, dentists, electrical engineers, lawyers and judges, physicians, teachers, manufacturing officials, bankers, brokers, etc. The mixed-parentage group leads in the number of manufacturers, builders and contractors, foremen, city and county officials and inspectors, mail carriers, detectives, policemen, electricians, stationary engineers, jewelers, mechanics, millwrights, varnishers, paperhangers, structural ironworkers, tinsmiths, toolmakers, switchmen, semi-skilled workers in glass, iron, furniture, lumber, metal (other than iron and steel), rubber, clerks and collectors. These, it will be noted, are the highest-paid skilled and petty official positions.

"The foreign-born lead in number of blacksmiths, brickmasons, cabinetmakers, carpenters, metal grinders, iron molders, plumbers, tailors, shoemakers, semi-skilled workers in house building, slaughter houses, railroad shops, beverage industries, automobile factories, textile industries, and laborers in practically all lines providing unskilled work.

"The Negro workers show a fluctuating importance among the industries, coming with greatest numbers into places most difficult to fill. Their largest proportion is in blast furnaces and rolling mills, where they constitute 19.7 per cent of all the workers. The next highest proportion, 8.01 per cent, is in the semi-skilled positions in steam-rolling mills; the next, 5.2 per cent, is in the slaughtering and packing houses; and the next, 4.6 per cent, in brass mills. As crane-men and derrick-men they provide 4.5 per cent of all the workers. This latter is a skilled process. The largest proportions among all the occupations are in personal and domestic service, where they contribute 29.6 per cent of all the porters (not in stores).

13.5 per cent of all the servants, 20.8 per cent of all the waiters, and 9.05 per cent of the janitors.

"If they do not count seriously in numbers as compared with the groups of larger total population in the city, they are significantly massed in certain lines, thus rendering their comparatively small numbers important. They exceed their proportion in the population in more than forty fairly important occupations. For example, the Negro proportion of stationary firemen, furnace-men and chauffeurs is over twice as large as their population proportion; the proportion of crane-men, four times as large; semi-skilled workers in rolling mills, and janitors, eight times as large; domestic servants and rolling-mill laborers, more than twenty times as large as their population proportion."[6]

The chart facing this page, based not on total population but on the number of individuals ten years of age and over who were gainfully employed in 1920, is designed to represent graphically the degree of dependence of the United States on minority workers of all kinds except those receiving no direct pecuniary reward. Native white people of native parentage furnish 55.3 per cent of the total population but, as shown on the chart, only 49.3 per cent of the gainfully employed. Individuals of foreign or mixed parentage supply 21.4 per cent of the total population, and 20.1 per cent of the gainfully employed. The Negro, on the other hand, furnished 9.9 per cent of the total population, and 11.6 per cent of the gainfully employed, although in this instance the percentages are so small as to be without significance.

The foreign-born, especially the unnaturalized, have been openly discriminated against in government service, while the Negro has been unofficially limited in his employment by the federal, state and municipal governments. Even a naturalized alien may not become President of the United States, and nativism has been so successful as to restrict the employment of non-citizens as public school teachers, elective and appointive officials and ditch diggers on public works. The

---

[6] Charles S. Johnson, op. cit., pp. 35-36. The occupational figures on which this quotation is based are for 1920.

FIGURE 3

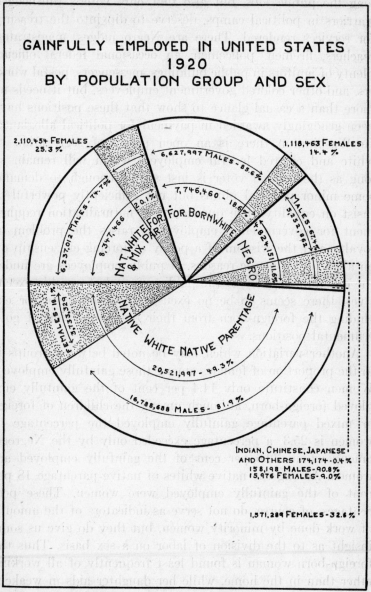

GAINFULLY EMPLOYED IN UNITED STATES
1920
BY POPULATION GROUP AND SEX

2,110,454 FEMALES
25.3 %

1,118,463 FEMALES
14.4 %

6,627,997 MALES - 85.6%

7,746,460 - 18.6%

MALES - 67.7%
5,252,983

8,347,466 - 20.1%

6,237,012 MALES-74.7%

NAT. WHITE
& MIX. PAR.

FOR. BORN WHITE PAR.

824,151-11.6%

NEGRO

FEMALES 18.1%
5,733,329

NATIVE WHITE NATIVE PARENTAGE

20,521,997 - 49.3%

16,788,688 MALES - 81.9%

INDIAN, CHINESE, JAPANESE
AND OTHERS 174,174-0.4%
158,198 MALES-90.8%
15,976 FEMALES-9.0%

1,371,289 FEMALES-32.6%

Based on Niles Carpenter, *Immigrants and Their Children*, Census Monograph VII, Government Printing Office, Washington, D. C., 1927, pp. 272-73

spoils system means not only that to the political victor belong the public jobs, but also that only voters, full-fledged
warriors in political camps, deserve to dip into the treasury
for services rendered. There are Negro judges, magistrates,
teachers, firemen, policemen, an occasional federal official,
plenty of janitors in public buildings, messengers, postal workers, and other colored government employees, but it needs no
more than a casual glance to show that these positions have
been grudgingly awarded in payment for political allegiance.
In Washington there is an open policy of segregation of
white and colored federal employees which will remain so
long as the colored voter is just strong enough to demand
some minor political plums but not sufficiently powerful to
insist on equality. The question of a naturalization requirement for governmental employment raises the problem of
loyalty and the wisdom of a policy of forcing citizenship on
an alien for economic reasons. If public employees are under
the constant scrutiny of the public eye and of capable executives, there seems to be no excuse except nativism for excluding the foreign-born from their due proportion of governmental positions.

Another variation which may be noted between groups is
in the proportion of females among those gainfully employed.
Women constitute only 14.4 per cent of the gainfully employed foreign-born, although among the children of foreign
or mixed parentage gainfully employed the percentage of
women is 25.3, a percentage exceeded only by the Negroes,
among whom 32.6 per cent of the gainfully employed are
women. Among the native whites of native parentage 18 per
cent of the gainfully employed were women. These percentages, of course, do not serve as indicators of the amount
of work done by minority women, but they do give us some
insight as to the division of labor on a sex basis. Thus the
foreign-born woman is found least frequently of all working
other than in the home, while her daughter aids in weakening the family as an economic unit by working for hire more
than do the women of any other white population group. The
individualistic, poverty-stricken Negro woman, of course,

spends more of her time outside of the family circle working for pay than do the women of any other racial or nativity element in the population of the United States. One should be cautious in generalizing concerning these percentages, for no statistical corrections have been made for varying sex ratios, age distribution, place of residence, and other differential factors.

Just as Americans like to think of themselves as a people who do not permit their women-folk to be overworked at home or employed outside of it, so they express horror at the thought of child labor. Perhaps home drudgery for wife and daughter is decreasing, and perhaps the work feminine members of American families are finding in mill, store and office is lighter, more pleasant, than women's chores of the past generation. No doubt even the child labor of today would on the whole seem like recreation to the over-burdened children of the poorer classes, say, in England two centuries ago. By no such rationalizations, however, should we be allowed to justify the working conditions under which we permit over eight and one-half million women of all racial and national origins to be gainfully employed as we did in 1920, nor, when we realize that there are over a million children between the ages of 10 and 15 years gainfully employed, should our consciences be appeased by the thought that the number decreased almost a million from 1910 to 1920 and that the lot of the remaining million is not so bad in comparison with what it might have been a century ago.

Since Negroes live mostly in the south where agriculture predominates and child labor legislation is apparently thought to be an unwarranted interference with the divine rights of parents, it would be expected that their proportion of children gainfully employed between the ages of 10 and 15 years would be the highest of any population group—as it is—with a percentage of 21.9 of all such children in 1920. The corresponding percentage for foreign-born children is 9.4; for native-born children of foreign or mixed parentage, 5.8; for Indians, Chinese, Japanese and other small colored groups, 6.6; and for native white children of native parentage, 7.0.

The percentage for the last-named group is of course raised by the fact that many of them live in the south, while the foreign-born rate is reduced by the fact that they have concentrated in the east and west where compulsory education and child labor legislation reduce parental exploitation of children.[7] One thing is certain from even a casual survey of child labor statistics over a period of years, and that is that the rates for all racial and nationality minorities show a rapid tendency to approximate that of the majority in the community where they live in so far as a caste or class system will permit.

In respect to type of non-agricultural occupation, division of labor on a sex basis, and child labor, it is thus evident that minorities show significant variations from the characteristic rates for the gainfully employed native white people of native parentage. While we may not claim that the majority rates are the most desirable, it is permissible to assume that they come closest to the prevailing national ideal of economic stratification and organization. Under a democratic-capitalistic system such as we have, it is reasonable to suppose that a normal occupational distribution of workers could be diagrammed as a pyramid, with the unskilled laborers as the base, supporting a smaller block of semi-skilled workers, with the skilled, the "white-collar," and the professional blocks piled on top in decreasing numbers in the order named. Without any attempt to represent actual proportions, this could be diagrammed as in the chart facing this page.

Whether this is an ideal scheme or not—and many economic radicals might well dispute the point—it is an approximation of actual conditions in so far as the native white people of native parentage are concerned. Negroes, however, as may be seen by the accompanying tables of occupational distribution, do not even approximate such a regular pyramid, nor do the other colored peoples, while the new immigrants, the old immigrants, and the native-born children of foreign or mixed parentage, approach, in the order named, the oc-

[7] All statistics of the employment of women and children in 1920 quoted in this section are taken from Niles Carpenter, *Immigrants and Their Children*, Census Monographs, No. VII, Government Printing Office, Washington, D. C., 1927.

FIGURE 4

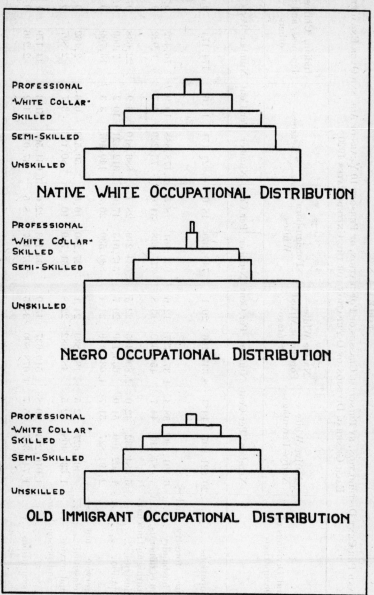

PROFESSIONAL
"WHITE COLLAR"
SKILLED
SEMI-SKILLED
UNSKILLED

NATIVE WHITE OCCUPATIONAL DISTRIBUTION

PROFESSIONAL
"WHITE COLLAR"
SKILLED
SEMI-SKILLED
UNSKILLED

NEGRO OCCUPATIONAL DISTRIBUTION

PROFESSIONAL
"WHITE COLLAR"
SKILLED
SEMI-SKILLED
UNSKILLED

OLD IMMIGRANT OCCUPATIONAL DISTRIBUTION

PROBABLE RELATIVE OCCUPATIONAL DISTRIBUTION OF SELECTED
POPULATION GROUPS

TABLE I

NUMBER AND PER CENT DISTRIBUTION, BY PRINCIPAL CLASSES OF POPULATION, OF PERSONS 10 YEARS OF AGE AND OVER ENGAGED IN EACH GENERAL DIVISION OF OCCUPATION FOR THE UNITED STATES 1920 [8]

General Divisions of Occupations	Native White—Native Parentage		Native White—Foreign or Mixed Parentage		Foreign-born Whites		Negroes		Indian, Chinese, Japanese, and all others	
	Number	Per Cent	Number	Per Cent	Number	Per Cent	Number	Per Cent	Number	Per Cent
All occupations	20,521,997	49.3	8,347,466	20.1	7,746,460	18.6	4,824,151	11.6	174,174	0.4
Agriculture, forestry and animal husbandry	6,391,480	58.4	1,374,777	12.6	931,561	8.5	2,178,888	19.9	76,452	0.7
Extraction of minerals	487,314	44.7	150,620	13.8	377,138	34.6	73,229	6.7	1,922	0.2
Manufacturing and mechanical industries	5,384,332	42.0	2,890,495	22.5	3,634,249	28.4	886,810	6.9	22,638	0.2
Transportation	1,562,409	51.0	633,170	20.7	547,613	17.9	312,421	10.2	7,969	0.3
Trade	2,194,827	51.7	1,033,446	24.4	860,530	20.3	140,467	3.3	13,709	0.3
Public service (not elsewhere classified)	404,627	52.5	185,839	24.1	127,280	16.5	50,552	6.6	2,162	0.3
Professional service	1,339,408	62.5	489,682	22.8	231,719	10.8	80,183	3.7	2,897	0.1
Domestic and personal service	1,016,293	29.8	510,637	15.0	769,193	22.6	1,064,590	31.3	44,179	1.3
Clerical occupations	1,741,307	55.7	1,078,800	34.5	267,177	8.5	37,011	1.2	2,246	0.1

[8] Niles Carpenter, op. cit., p. 273.

cupational distribution of the old American stock. Roughly, the diagrams of Negro and old immigrant occupational distribution would be as indicated in the accompanying chart.

The economic problem of minorities in its simplest form thus becomes one of determining the reasons for the irregularities in their pyramids of occupational distribution. These pyramids, it should be borne in mind, are not intended to include agricultural workers, although it is not likely that their relative form would vary much if they were included. Logically, the explanation of the differences in proportion between minority and majority workers in the various types of non-agricultural occupations must lie in the minorities themselves, in the demands of their majority employers and patrons, in their fellow workers of other stocks, or in some combination of all three. The physical environment, of course, may also be a factor, but in view of the fact that all minorities in the United States engaged in non-agricultural pursuits, with but few exceptions and these mostly among the Negroes, have fairly recently and voluntarily migrated to their present locality and are still free to migrate to some other physical environment, this factor will receive no consideration here.

BARRIERS TO LABOR

Minority Traits.—Limited economic opportunities for minorities are most commonly explained in terms of minority characteristics, both inherent and acquired. Innate mentality, for example, has been said to furnish the basic reason for the lack of Negro and alien success in the more desirable occupations. The argument here has been that instead of having a normal curve of distribution of intelligence as is supposed to be the case with the old white American stock, Negroes, Orientals, south Europeans, French Canadians and Mexicans are alleged to have their curve skewed toward the lower levels as indicated in Figure 5.

If this diagram represented the known facts it would be a comforting justification for educational, political, economic, and other forms of group discrimination, for obviously society should not waste its time and money attempting to give equal

intellectual, political, and occupational opportunities to
minorities who have fewer individuals in the upper intelligence
levels than has the majority. As a theory it has something
of the appearance of a modern scientific substitute for the
older theory of the inherent or divine right of the upper classes
to enjoy the fruits of the lower, who were supposed to be
what they were because nature or a supreme being so ordered

FIGURE 5

ALLEGED DISTRIBUTION OF MENTAL ABILITY OF POPULATION GROUPS OF RACIAL AND NATIONAL ORIGIN

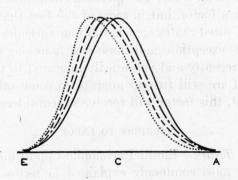

E   C   A

—— OLD WHITE AMERICAN STOCK A · GREATEST INNATE MENTAL ABILITY
—·— NEW IMMIGRANT   C · MEDIAN INNATE MENTAL ABILITY
—— ORIENTAL IMMIGRANT   E · LOWEST INNATE MENTAL ABILITY
····· NEGRO

the universe. Since the inherent educational capacity of
minorities is discussed elsewhere it seems inappropriate to do
more here than cite the major conclusion of a later chapter,
which is that while differences in capacity may exist between
the races of mankind, they have not yet been established, nor,
on the basis of known evidence, is it probable that any which
may be discovered in the future will be of such a nature as to
brand any one people as so decidedly inferior to another as
this theory implies to be the case.

To put this defense of the existing order, as developed by credulous or hopeful research mechanics familiar with the tools of science but incautious in their use, into its more popular form, most minority peoples are not only supposed to be without the "brains" to participate fully in the civilization of the more advanced nations, but they are also alleged to be the possessors of specific traits and characteristics which deny them certain occupations and fit them for others, usually the least desirable of all.

Negroes are glibly described as lazy, impulsive, childlike, lacking in "moral sense," imaginative, without initiative, in need of constant supervision, good farm laborers but not operators, fitted for the "hot jobs" in industry, fitted for the wet tropics but not for the temperate zone, and without the capacity for foresight required of all who are to do well in modern civilization. If these were characteristics of the Negro race—and the list is far from complete—it is obvious that colored people should be discouraged from attempting to improve their lot. Such a policy is given definite expression, for example, by the Ku Klux Klan which claims publicly, and undoubtedly has many members who sincerely believe, that true friends of the Negro will keep him from reaching for the moon, the false lure to advancement which must always remain beyond his grasp. As the child is unhappy and a failure when given the duties and responsibilities of an adult, so, says the Klan, would the Negro fare if his radical leaders and their misguided Yankee sympathizers had their way. Few Negroes seem in any immediate danger of having their lives ruined by opening to them opportunities for advancement, and those few seem willing to take a chance. For the present, the rest are either out of work—this is written during the worst unemployment period in the history of the United States—or are being saved from themselves by an economic caste system which restricts their employment to tasks which match their alleged characteristics.

Now there is no doubt that the American Negro includes in his numbers many, almost certainly an overwhelming majority, who may with propriety be described by one or more of the undesirable traits just mentioned. But are they race traits? Are Negroes restricted to the inferior tasks because of their racial limitations, or have they been temporarily conquered and beaten into inefficient economic cogs by the poverty of the tasks assigned them? Laziness may be due to anything from the hook worm to lack of training and incentive under a system which denies workers the fruits of labor, but a race of lazy humans would be an oddity requiring a less specious explanation than the *a priori* argument that life in the tropics has made them so. A world-famous geographer who ought to know better has cited the example of certain tropical peoples who are so lazy that they work fewer days if their pay is a dollar a day than if it were fifty cents, on the theory that there is a fixed income needed to live and the sooner it is acquired, the more days there will be left for loafing. The implication was that this was a tropical racial trait. It has the earmarks of the American story of the Negro—Indian, Mexican, South American, etc., in other versions—who when asked whether he wanted to earn a quarter declined the suggestion with the remark that he had a quarter. No doubt such incredible attitudes as the one evidenced by this answer are common among minority peoples, but their explanation is social, not biological, and is essentially the same as that of the millionaire who retires because he has all that he wants under the existing order, and further increments to his fortune would involve greater sacrifices than returns. So the Negro who "has a quarter" has reached the point of diminishing returns in the social position in which he finds himself and from which he knows he cannot escape.

So the other Negro traits which are offered as the basis of his inferior economic station may also be explained. Why speak of a "childlike" or "infantile" race when what we mean by maturity is actually no more than a store of knowledge and the development of judgment through both formal and informal educational processes denied the Negro? Why invent a "moral sense," an absolute fiction, to explain by its absence the petty thievery of cooks, maids, and housemen whose immediate forbears were legally denied the rights of property and who themselves suffer only light penalties for their peculations in a society which dismisses such trifling dishonesty with a warning and a shrug? Need we account for the concentration of Negroes in the hard, dirty, hot, wet, backbreaking, soul-killing jobs except as a matter of opportunity? To say that races bred in the shade of the date palm and the banana tree cannot produce such men as Daniel Boone and the early pioneers or their descendants, who have beaten their plough-shares and rifles into typewriters and adding machines, as a psychologist of international reputation has said within the past decade, is an extension of the theory of natural selection which no reputable biologist could support. One is reminded of the report on the Negro's adaptability to various types of work which claimed that he could not profitably be employed near water except under closest supervision because of his *penchant* for going fishing.

With minor variations to meet local conditions, the general charges of industrial aptitude, or lack of it, are monotonously the same, regardless of the racial origin of the minority involved. The argument that some peoples are "born agriculturists" has been considered in a previous chapter. Now that the farmer has become a ridiculed "hick" and only "gentlemen farmers" or "scientific farmers" are conceded intelligence and granted enviable social status, any outcast is admitted to have the capacity for agriculture of a sort, except the Jew, who has been turned into a "born trader," but one without ethics, by the good old stand-by, natural selection. The fight is now for industrial, commercial and professional supremacy, so that minorities are at present attacked as unfit for any but the poorest paid, least desirable tasks in urban rather than in rural occupations. A selected few of the popular defenses of occupational discrimination against minorities, be they migrants from Europe, Asia, Africa, or Latin America, may be cited. All of them will be found to be cultural in nature, and none will be without some foundation in fact.

"Minorities constitute a threat to our standard of living." This is perhaps the most common charge of all. It is based on the twin observations that migrants come from lands with low standards of living and that they bring these standards with them and are consequently willing to work for wages which the native American considers so poor as to permit little more than bare subsistence. It is probably safe to say that no recent migrant group gets the same pay that native white labor would get for the same job. It is also true that most minorities of racial and national origin can maintain themselves on starvation wages with less discomfort than could persons who had become so accustomed to plenty that former luxuries were turned into necessities. It is another matter, however, to say that minorities refuse to accept higher standards, that their competition forces down the income of the majority, and that there is anything more than a cultural foundation for such phenomena.

A low standard of living and economic inadequacy cannot be measured by the proportion of inmates in institutions for paupers. A much quoted study of the alien, which incidentally includes the Negro, as an institutional ward for reasons of dependency, mental defect, crime and disease, is the report by Dr. Harry H. Laughlin of the Carnegie Institution's Eugenics Record Office to the Congressional Committee on Immigration and Naturalization, published in 1923. Restricting his study to state and federal institutions, Dr. Laughlin found that inmates because of dependency included about one-third more foreign-born white paupers than would be expected if they furnished the same proportion of total dependents that they furnished of the total population of the United States. The children of mixed and foreign parentage furnished about the same proportion of dependent inmates in relation to their total number as did the native white people of native parentage in proportion to their total number in the country. The various nationalities, however, supplied both surprisingly high and surprisingly low proportions of pauper inmates in proportion to their numbers. The Irish headed the list with six times the proportion to be normally expected, followed by the British with about two and one-fifth times the normal expectation. At the bottom were the immigrants from Austria-Hungary, with one-quarter; from Italy, with two-fifths, and the Negroes, with one-quarter of their normal expectation of inmates. It is common knowledge that Negroes are the most poverty-stricken minority in the United States, yet they made a showing as good as any, and far better than most. This fact alone established the statistical inadequacy of Dr. Laughlin's measure of dependency, and of other minority defects as well.[9]

Since Dr. Laughlin's data were so vigorously used to justify our present policy of discrimination against the recent immigrant, it is desirable to point out the major defects of his method for determining the quality of immigration. He restricted his study to federal and state institutions, and did not obtain reports from all of these, many failing to reply to his questionnaire and others failing to furnish data on the birthplace of all of their inmates. City and county institutions, as well as private institutions, were omitted, a fact which loads the study against the foreign-born. The low returns for Negro dependents suggests the fact that minorities are not admitted freely to all custodial institutions with the exception of the prisons, where it has been suspected their welcome has been too warm. The need of institutional care for dependency also depends on age grouping, sex, the possession of interested relatives and friends, the amount of outdoor relief available, and occupation. What Dr. Laughlin actually measured was nothing more than the proportion of foreign-born and Negroes in state and federal custodial institutions, a valuable bit of information to have at one's disposal, but by no means an index of minority poverty or pauperism. The only excuse for citing this study here is the national prominence

[9] For Dr. Laughlin's original data, see *Analysis of America's Modern Melting Pot,* United States, House of Representatives, 67:3, Hearings before the Committee on Immigration and Naturalization. Serial 7C. Government Printing Office, Washington, D. C., November 21, 1922, pp. ii + 725-831; *Europe as an Emigrant-Exporting Continent and the United States as an Immigrant-Receiving Nation,* United States, House of Representatives, 68:1, Hearings before the Committee on Immigration and Naturalization. Serial 5-A. Government Printing Office, Washington, D. C., March 8, 1924, pp. v + 1,231-1,437.

which it has achieved and, perhaps, its value as a warning how not to analyze minority economic failures.[10]

We have been too prone to attribute the high standard of living current in the United States to the superior quality of our older white stock. The plain truth is that we have been fortunate in having a favorable ratio of population to available resources. If a fixed amount of wealth is available to a small number of individuals, it is obvious that they may and will, since human wants have the capacity for expansion beyond known limits, consume more goods per capita than if their number were doubled or tripled, assuming that the point of diminishing returns has been reached. Childhood training or individual idiosyncrasy may, of course, keep persons down to living on a crust in a hovel, but such cases are exceptional among all people, once the opportunity for increased consumption is offered them. Orientals and the peoples of the crowded regions of Europe depend more on plant foods and deny themselves meat more than we do in this country, not because of choice, but because of necessity, since it takes several times as much land to produce the animal food equivalent of cereals and potatoes. Migration itself is evidence of the desire for a higher standard of living.

No one knows what the present American standard of living would be if the last twenty million immigrants had been refused admission. Perhaps the native population would have increased more rapidly without the threat of their competition. On the other hand, perhaps agricultural and industrial expansion would have been retarded to such an extent that the per capita yield would have been smaller than it has been. One thing is certain, and that is that all migrants have raised their standards as soon as possible along with the rest of us, and while there may have been some displacements of native white workers, the general tendency has apparently been to push the older labor up into better positions as the new took their place on the bottom rung of the economic ladder.

The really important question concerns the danger of over-

---

[10] For a detailed criticism of Dr. Laughlin's study see H. S. Jennings, "Undesirable Aliens," *The Survey*, December 15, 1923.

population. While the United States can support hundreds of millions of additional people at the present stage of the industrial and agricultural arts, in spite of recurrent periods of unemployment, there must be a point somewhere, barring revolutionary economic discoveries, at which the standard of living must begin declining solely because of the inadequacy of available resources. Defining the optimum population as that number of individuals of ordinary capacity which will produce the greatest per capita yield in a given area, what is the optimum population for the United States or for the thousands of natural economic areas within the country each of which has its separate optimum? Granting that it takes about two and a half acres of land under cultivation per person to support a people at a reasonable standard of living, such as that of Germany before the World War, it might be concluded that the population of the United States could increase for several generations at the present rate without necessitating a restriction in individual consumption. This would absolve the immigrant from any blame of causing overpopulation of the United States as a whole, but there are so many assumptions in such simple estimates that they had better be used only in clarifying the problem, and not as solutions to it.

"Immigrants and Negroes weaken the bargaining power of labor" is a second charge. All of our present restrictive immigration legislation, whether it be against the Oriental or the European, has been enacted because of the power of the labor vote. Capitalists notoriously have been anxious to secure labor reserves of migrants so that they could dictate terms of employment to an autocratic degree impossible where a shortage gives strength to labor's demands. Any mobile labor supply which is willing to be rushed from place to place constitutes a threat to the economic security of all labor which does not depend on some special skill or quality to maintain its position. The lower the standard of living of a minority, the more easily it can be thrown into the conflict between capital and labor as the last crushing argument that those who don't like their jobs as they are may give way to a new supply.

Fresh, tractable workers could formerly be imported from Europe or the Orient without limit, now can be brought in from Latin America, and will always be available within the country itself so long as caste restrictions keep the Negro from a community interest with white labor.

Immigrant labor would be less of a threat to native workers were the system by which employment is obtained improved. Thus far it has been too much a matter of chance and capitalistic eagerness to have a bountiful labor supply secured in the easiest manner to permit an equitable distribution of foreign labor to the points where it would disturb wages and working conditions the least. Employers' recruiting agents, private labor agencies and "padrones," together with haphazard inquiries by the aliens themselves, have been the almost exclusive means for connecting the immigrant with the job. Employers' labor agents have had but one interest at heart, the desire to secure cheap labor and plenty of it. Labor agencies look only to private profit, and require close governmental supervision to prevent exploitation of the immigrant. The "padrones," foreign-born men who earn their living by supplying groups of workers of their own nationality for commissions and for "concessions" such as the exclusive right to operate commissaries, also care nothing for the welfare of either immigrant or native workers. Hiring and firing, wage scales and conditions of labor involve the antagonistic interests of the employer, the employed and the unemployed, and the middleman, and it seems that only an impartial arbiter, such as the state or federal government, can be expected to balance the three. This explains the increasing agitation for state and federal employment services, for which the only substitute is detailed regulation and control of private agencies.

Among the conditions not previously mentioned which make it possible for minorities to be used as a coercive tool in the hands of employers are their lack of education and their unfamiliarity with the industries in which they suddenly find themselves; their abject poverty, for if they were not without resources they would not submit to such exploitation; their "tractability," for the impoverished stranger may readily be

bent to the will of the master; and the fact that they are not
attached to any particular occupation or locality but drift toward opportunity for even temporary advantage. There is not,
and never has been, a minority of racial or national origin
in the United States to which these characterizations could
not at some time have been applied, and they have usually
been applicable just so long as and no longer than their
minority status remained evident. Today they have the appearance of being special attributes of the recent immigrant,
of the Negro, rather than of the old immigrant or even of
the Orientals other than the Filipino, but this is an illusion
resulting from the advanced stage of assimilation of the
earlier arrivals from Europe and the Orient. One gains the
impression from such works as that of Jenks and Lauck, *The
Immigration Problem,* and from the report of the Congressional commission established in 1907 on which their book
is based, that "illiteracy and inability to speak English,"
"necessitous condition," "low standards of living," "lack of
permanent interest," and "tractability" are peculiarities of
recent immigrants; but they have been equally true of the
Germans, the Scandinavians, the Irish, the English, and the
colored peoples, except for the fact that north European
schools have been generally superior to those of south Europe,
and that some of them have been familiar with the English
language, both exceptions being of temporary importance in
view of the nature of the positions available and of the ease
with which even subnormal people learn a new language if
necessary. The recent industrialization of tens of thousands of
Pennsylvania Germans affords a parallel to the transforma-
tion of European immigrants seemingly ill adapted to a machine civilization. Another parallel is to be found in the recent
utilization of southern "hill billies" and "poor whites" who,
except for the lack of language handicap, suffered from all the
disabilities of the recent immigrant in the way of poverty,
tractability, low standards of living, etc., and were even advertised in the trade journals by local chambers of commerce
as constituting an ideal, easily handled, low-wage labor supply capable of being exploited (although that was not the

word used) if textile and other industries would only move to the reviving South.

"The very nature of American economic organization has had to be altered because of the industrial inefficiency of the immigrant," say other critics, and no doubt the entrance of the Negro into industry will later lead to a similar charge against him. What is meant is that the apprentice system has disappeared, skilled artisans have been replaced by machines, foremen and other petty supervisors have been multiplied to direct unskilled labor, and that, generally speaking, American workers are now mere tools of the machine instead of masters of their tools. How much more true this is today than it was a century or more ago the author does not know. Some skeptics consider it little more than a clever remark with enough truth behind it to make it sound convincing. Certainly in the sense that the old skilled worker who could carry a process through from beginning to end has disappeared from some trades and is rare in others, the point may be conceded, although its social significance is another matter.

Machinery and the accompanying division of labor have indeed done away with the man who could make a pair of shoes from start to finish, who could construct a house from masonry to shingles, who could build a wagon from iron tires to tailboard. No longer does flax raised on the farm become homespun linen without leaving the hands of a single family. It now takes less than two weeks to train a productive coal miner to tend a machine which cuts free from the vein more fuel in a day than a number of Welsh miners, imported because of their skill resulting from years of apprentice labor, could prepare for hoisting to the surface in the same time. Bottles are blown by machine, iron is forged by machine, stone is carved by machine, type is set by machine, but what have minorities to do with this? Did unskilled minorities call the machines into existence, or did the machines give them the opportunity to become productive in manufacturing and commerce without a long and costly period of apprenticeship? No doubt the fact that the only supply of labor available for industrial expansion was without training in the techniques thereof gave stimulus to the invention of robots, but it must also be conceded that minorities would have stayed where they were had not the machine given them the opportunity for immediate high wages. Machines without labor are even more useless than labor without machines. If either is to be given priority as a cause, it must be the advance in technical knowledge of the processes of large-scale production and the development of mechanical power.

Out of this industrial trend have grown a multitude of better-paid jobs, a hierarchy of foremen, superintendents, executives and administrators. Unskilled operators of expensive machinery, semi-skilled and skilled workers who are limited to some tiny process in a long chain which leads to the ultimate product, need supervision to dovetail their efforts with those of thousands of other workers, to supply their tools and raw materials, to tell them what to make, to see that they do not waste time and materials, and to market the finished product. The old-style craftsman who owned his tools, bought his raw materials, made what he thought proper, and sold it to the consumer, has gone, not because the immigrant drove him out of business, but because he could not compete with the efficiency of increasing specialization. His going made possible higher incomes for the hundreds of thousands of workers who were pushed up to positions of responsibility in the system, and led to a wider distribution of wealth. It is no more reasonable to blame minorities for the evils of this automatic system of production which puts men into monotonous jobs with little opportunity for creative self-expression than it is to give them credit for affording individuals the opportunity of rising in the economic scale in such numbers and to such heights as were undreamed of by our great-grandfathers.

"It would be better if all this had been accomplished by native-born labor of old white stock," is the next complaint when it is shown that minorities have been the tool of an economic expansion which became inevitable when man discovered the possibilities of power and large-scale production. In so far as this contemplates a selfish policy of restricting the advantages of material progress to the people of white complexions who happened to have ancestors who fled to the American continent from failure abroad several generations ago, a logical defense of the statement is impossible, and sentiment based on petty provincialism must be used to support it. What difference does it make except to sentimentalists whether one's fellow worker or competitor comes from north or south Europe, from Asia or Latin America, so long as the optimum population has not been reached and both cooperation and competition can be regulated as we, the majority, demand? Culture conflict, which we have done little to reduce, has been the largest fly in the ointment, but even that one is quickly removed by the inevitable process of assimilation which has tended to mold all residents of the United States to the prevailing pattern of their community.

There is, of course, a cost to the country which may be expressed in both social and economic terms, in adjusting minority cultures to the American. Neglect of effective conscious effort to accomplish the required adjustments is responsible for a considerable portion of the penalty we have paid and are still paying for permitting minority cultures to persist as disrupting influences in the midst of our economic development. If there is any blame to be fixed, it falls not on the immigrant, who, except for the small percentage of intended temporary residence, generally wishes to become acculturated and identified with the natives, but on ourselves, on those of us who have been indifferent to the inadequacies of minorities except as they have annoyed us. Fixing blame, however, does not remove the penalty, so that in this respect at least the charge must stand that minorities have disturbed the even tenor of our growth. There has been the cost of reeducating adults to American industrial needs, the cost of imposing our standards of industrial and business conduct, the cost of accidents and inefficiency, the cost of grudging cooperation and sabotage because of misunderstanding, all of which would have been less had we depended on labor more amenable to our desires and needs because of native birth.

The claim that the United States suffers economically on

account of the large amounts of money sent to immigrants' relatives and friends abroad, or taken back home by those who have made their stake and wish to spend their declining years in the land of their birth, is based on false premises. It is true that hundreds of thousands of immigrants have gone home to live on resources acquired here, and that millions have forwarded part of their earnings to dependents in foreign lands. What of it?

The wages an immigrant receives are only a fraction of the value of the goods he produces by his labor. Some of these wages he must spend to house, clothe, and feed himself, be he ever so miserly. What he sends or takes abroad can thus represent only a small fraction of the values he has created. Even so, it may be replied, it would be better for the rest of us if even that small fraction were to remain in this country. This argument is also without weight, for what he sends or takes abroad is not capital goods, tons of steel, barrels of pork, cases of shirts, but credit. What actually happens is that a piece of paper is purchased in this country which is later bought by a third party and used to extinguish a foreign obligation to someone in this country. Neither goods nor gold need cross the border in the immediate transaction by the returned immigrant. There is sufficient foreign trade with all emigrant nations to absorb these credit transactions, and with the billions of dollars owed the United States today such transactions might actually be called helpful to our economic condition in that they would help make it possible for Europe to meet her obligations to us if only they were large enough really to matter. Compared with our total international transactions they are insignificant, and do not even compare with the American credit used abroad by tourists. If such trifles are to be mentioned, we may as well include the fact that there is an economic saving by the United States because the immigrant's unproductive years of childhood and old age are spent abroad.

Enough has been said to convict minorities of the possession of group traits or characteristics of such a nature as to limit their occupational distribution, but all of the group stigmas have been cultural in origin, and therefore capable of elimination. At the risk of anticipating some of the conclusions developed in our section on the educational capacity of races, a few sentences may be culled from the summary of T. R. Garth's study of race psychology. "The real problem of race psychology is to determine whether there are mental differences belonging to one of the so-called races as distinguished from another. . . . It may be stated as a fact that races do not differ in sensory traits either qualitatively or quantitatively. . . . Practically all races of men have been studied with some kind of psychological test. . . . As for racial differences in intelligence, quantitative results certainly indicate group differences in the findings, but these are open to the criticism that the factor of nurture has not been equalized between the two races compared with as much success as would seem fair to both races. . . . While the measures of intelligence indicate great differences between races, it must be remembered that even these measures must be taken with this fact in view, i.e., that I.Q.'s have been changed with euthenical procedures. . . . Only when so-called inferior races have been favored with such euthenic treatment could the measures be taken as final. . . . In regard to the esthetics of different races it is held that regardless of the crudity of primitive art or the virtuosity of cultured peoples there is but one esthetic impulse. . . . Though much has been said popularly about personality due to race, the studies so far made do not justify the belief that it exists. . . . The study of community of ideas of races reveals no differences in the association process of the races so far tested where the environmental factor has been controlled. . . . The conclusion then which must be drawn in the light of such scientific investigations as have been made is that there are no sure evidences of real racial differences in mental traits. While heredity operates according to laws, qualitatively considered, mental traits are distributed among all races, for all possess these human traits."[11] Where a compendium of all the scientific data on

[11] Thomas R. Garth, *Race Psychology*, McGraw-Hill Book Company, New York, 1931, pp. 207ff. An apology is perhaps due the reader for stringing to-

race psychology such as that of Professor Garth leads to such
negative conclusions, it would be foolhardy to attribute group
industrial specialization or limitations to hereditary factors,
especially when the traditional and environmental influences
are so plain, as are also the errors of popular misconceptions
with which economic differentiation is so glibly explained.

Antagonisms of Employers and Patrons.—Not all the cultural reasons for minority economic differentiation lie in the
minorities themselves. Beliefs and attitudes on the part of
employers and patrons must also be considered. Ask the educated Negro why the large department stores refuse to employ
Negroes behind their counters, and he will be certain that it
is partly because the executives doubt the capacity of Negroes
as salespeople, are afraid of labor trouble with their white employees, and do not wish to offend customers who may have
an aversion to dealing with a colored person. The attitude of
white workers toward Negro competition deserves consideration in a section by itself, but the opinions of employers and
customers, both of lesser importance in the total situation, may
now be briefly analyzed.

As a starting point, it may be stated that employers as a
class will hire anyone whose labor they believe will result in
the greatest profit for the firm. No doubt individuals can be
found who will consciously sacrifice profit to race prejudice,
but they are rare and, as a rule, will not long survive in the
fierce competition of the modern system where even a slight
advantage means the difference between success and failure.
If Negro, Indian, Chinese, Japanese, Italian, Swedish, or
French Canadian labor of the proper quality is available at a
price more profitable than that of native white labor of old
American stock, one may be sure that it will not go begging.

Illustrations are plentiful, but perhaps the best ones can be
drawn from the experiences of Negroes, for if prejudice against
them can be subjected to the desire for profit, no other minority will fare worse. So long as an immigrant labor supply was

gether this series of quotations without including the qualifying and connecting sentences, but it is believed that no false impressions will be created by
doing so in this particular instance.

available at low wages, northern employers denied the capacity of Negroes for even the unskilled work in industry. When this supply of cheap workers was cut off by the World War, the railroads, the automobile factories, the steel mills, the clothing industries, all the great employers of immigrant labor promptly forgot the old disqualifications of the colored race and literally begged them to accept work for which they were previously believed incompetent. Where white skilled labor was available—and few Negroes who migrated cityward could call themselves industrially skilled—they were of course given the preference, but there are numerous examples of skilled as well as semi-skilled occupations which were first opened to Negroes at this time. The common practice was naturally for white workers to move up a step or two to the better jobs, while the Negro, as the most recent entry into industry, started at the bottom. There was not a single industry, however, in which some shortage of labor did not develop in the semi-skilled ranks in one locality or another and in which a few Negroes did not soon find themselves. In fact, the Negro has been found to be a superior employee in comparison with the immigrant on unskilled and semi-skilled work, and he acquires industrial skills as rapidly as any alien. This is to be expected if we consider his familiarity with our language and with the American point of view, although his greater efficiency against that of the foreigner has surprised many an employer. The clothing industry used quite a number of Negro men and women to replace foreigners, the automobile industry did not keep all its colored employees at crude labor, and the packing companies found that Negroes could do any work previously performed by immigrants. It was so much simpler, however, to move white labor up from the ranks that Negro opportunities for advancement were comparatively few. There was also a common practice of carrying Negroes on the payroll as unskilled labor even when they were employed at labor which would have been called skilled if the workers' skins had been white, so that the actual number of skilled Negro employees tended to be underestimated, and with considerable saving in wages to the employers who so indulged their prejudices at a profit. However few skilled Negro employees there may have been during and immediately after the World War, there were enough to show what attitude the employers would take in case of necessity.

Even where Negro labor is cheaper than white labor of equal or perhaps lesser quality, it has been and still is a common practice to employ the white. This does not destroy our basic statement that profit, not race, will ultimately determine employment, for in such instances it can usually be shown either that the employer feared labor trouble, or that there was a threatened loss of sales. The manager of a leading Philadelphia hotel recently discharged his colored elevator girls and replaced them with white operators at higher wages, even though he considered the colored girls more efficient. He claims he found it necessary to do so because a few of his patrons complained that they did not wish to ride in stuffy elevators with colored help, and in a business so crowded with competitors the loss of even a few patrons spells failure. School boards in the north commonly assert that the major reason they employ no colored school teachers for white pupils, no matter how well qualified, is because the children's parents would protest. The management of one of the largest and best department stores in the east has been reported as saying that colored clerks would be employed if it were not that customers would be lost, and the report is supported by the fact that this particular store is noted for its liberal policy toward Negroes, going so far as to show no discrimination against them in its restaurant. There are cases in which such fear has been proved to be a ghost which did not materialize when the experiment was tried, but these are probably exceptional, and for some time to come we may expect Negro employees to be kept in the inferior positions or in those which require no contact with customers.

It is this fear, real or fictitious, which keeps many firms from employing Negroes of a quality higher than that of present white employees, as in the case of the hotel elevator operators just mentioned, even where they may be obtained at lower wages. One Chicago merchandising house, however, has taken advantage of the situation by employing colored girls in its wrapping and shipping department, and has profited because it could obtain workers who had at least some high school education but were forced into a routine, dead-end job because all other doors were closed. The white people who previously had done this work were of the poorer sort, for those with real capacity and training either refused such employment or soon left it for opportunities not open to Negroes. A similar condition prevails in the teaching profession in large northern cities such as Philadelphia, where the number of positions available to Negroes is so much smaller than the supply of teachers that those who do find work are likely to be superior in ability and training. Still another example may be found in domestic service, one of the few places where work is open to Negro women. Having no other outlet, they include the higher types of individuals, willing to be servants, while white women of equal capacity would scorn to be cooks or maids. This condition offers profitable opportunities for employers who need workers not in contact with customers and are so organized that trouble with white labor can be avoided, to secure excellent labor at low cost.

Customers' objections to being served by Negroes may be explained largely in terms of status. Employers, with the employer-employee status firmly fixed, are little bothered by any threat to their personal prestige. The customers of a hotel, a restaurant, a store, an automobile agency, however, include many who are not confident of their own position in the social order, who are themselves employees, often in capacities similar to those of the employees who serve them. Where the status of the white patron is assured in his own mind, only slight objection to being served by a colored person is found. Thus the southern white man has not objected to being shaved by a Negro, but the Northerner, who is not sure of the rules governing Negro-white relationships, generally fights shy of colored barber shops. In regard to this point, it is worth observing that the replacement of colored by white barbers in the south has been at the instance of the white barbers, not of the white patrons of secure status. In restaurants, too, those

which serve the highest type of white patron find the least
objection to colored waiters. The catering establishment which
serves the most socially elect clientele in Philadelphia is entirely owned and staffed by Negroes. To those who look on
the cook, the clerk, the waiter, the barber, the carpenter, the
bricklayer, the mechanic, and similar employees, as of a status
which in no way competes with their own, or who fear no
danger of lessening their own status through contact of a
purely business nature with colored people in such positions,
there is nothing unseemly in the employment of Negroes in
these capacities. The majority of people, of course, feel that
the Negro must be kept in his place, and the further down
the place of the white man may be, the further down is his
concept of the Negro's proper place.

Another factor which influences the white man's concept of
proper employment for Negroes is tradition. There are in the
south what have been called "nigger jobs," and even in the
north there are certain occupations—those of cooks, waiters,
janitors, etc.—which may be held by Negroes without exciting
comment. It is a mistake, however, to assume that "nigger
jobs" are fixed either as between one locality and another or
from time to time. Barbering has been colored work in the
south but not in the north. However, whenever white people
have found employment difficult or have seen an opportunity
for profit in an occupation traditionally Negro in character,
they have hesitated only briefly in taking over "nigger jobs."
One of the Negro's loudest complaints is that while he is told
to stay in his place and not try to enter white men's occupations, the white men are showing no compunctions in taking
his away from him, so that he is left with a smaller and smaller
field of possible employment. This has worked particular hardship on the Negro in the south, where today there is not a
single occupation reserved for him, as was the case in various
communities before the World War. There are, of course, no
exclusively "nigger jobs" in the north either, so that in times
of unemployment the Negro is the first fired, to hold employment open to white workers, and, when unemployment is re-
lieved, he knows he will be the last hired. Regardless of how

the Negro hates occupational segregation, if it actually existed he would at least have the comfort and security of knowing that he could not be driven out of a few of the less desirable occupations.

What has been said about employers' and customers' attitudes toward Negro workers could also be said in principle about the attitudes of both groups toward other minorities. With the employers it is essentially a question of profits, and with the patrons it is largely a matter of status. Californians have consistently hired Orientals when they thought they could get good service at low wages without offending purchasers of their products, the danger of labor troubles, of course, always being taken into account. The fishing industry from Alaska to San Diego has employed Chinese, Japanese and Filipinos. The farmers have given plenty of work to these three groups of Orientals and to the Mexicans.

Orientals and Mexicans, like the Negroes, have had to be kept as much from contact with customers as possible, but so have recent immigrants under the handicap of the prejudices attendant upon minority status. No ordinary university or college employs Jews as freely for faculty members as it does Gentiles. An outstanding exception to this rule is a university whose students go there more from necessity than choice, and realize they will gain less social status than if they went to Yale, Harvard, or Princeton. There are any number of corporations which will not knowingly employ Jews, and others which will use them only on inside or special work. Armenians, Italians, Greeks, Bohemians, and Portuguese are disqualified today by customers' whims, regardless of ability, and they are only experiencing discriminations which were suffered by the Germans, the Irish, and the Scandinavians in former times. If the utmost sales and profits are to be made, customers must not be offended by being asked to deal with employees of inferior minority status, for there are many customers of inferior or insecure status themselves who dare not run the risk of contact, even in a business way, with "untouchables."

A revealing exception to this generalization about customers is in the case of establishments operated by minorities for the sale of some commodity which is peculiarly characteristic of their race or nationality. Any white man or woman feels perfectly free to enter a store in Chinatown for the purchase of lichee nuts, coolie coats, or other curiosities. Here they may patronize the Oriental who serves them, and their feeling of superiority is fed by the contact. So the tourist buys trinkets from the wayside Indian from Niagara Falls to the pueblos. Oriental, Italian, and Russian restaurants afford diners a similar feeling of exaltation. Negro cabarets and shows produce the same assurance of superiority. This is the peculiar delight of slumming, and by its obvious appeal through the enhancement of the status of the patronizing customer partially explains the nature of the objection to exactly similar transactions with minority individuals who have attempted to remove their badge of inferiority by being employed at other than their proper stereotyped occupations.

As in the case of the Negro, the stereotyped occupations of immigrant races and nationalities are far from fixed, although the tendency is for the immigrant to drift to a higher level, deserting voluntarily some one type of work in a given locality when a later and socially inferior migrant takes his place as he moves up to a better job. The Negro, however, has had his traditional occupations taken against his protest by a socially superior class. Today there is a concentration of Italians, Poles and Slovaks in coal mining, where there were formerly Welsh and Irish. These groups also furnish a large proportion of laborers in blast furnaces and on steam railroads, having replaced such widely different predecessors as the Irish and the Chinese, and they are in turn being replaced by later migrants. The Irish today furnish over 10 per cent of the alien foremen and overseers in manufacturing, in spite of the fact that they were originally preponderantly unskilled workers at the very bottom of the immigrant economic ladder. The evidence is clear that both employers and customers respond quickly to changes in minority status forced on the country, usually by economic necessity.

The Attitude of Labor.—Since minority economic characteristics and majority attitudes of the employer and cus-

tomer classes may be shown to be variables capable of trans-
formation almost overnight, the persistence of occupational
discrimination against minorities which, except in times of
economic emergency, usually lasts as long as minorities retain
their social visibility, requires a more extended explanation.
This may perhaps be found in the attitude of the majority
working classes who would be subjected to increased minority
competition were racial and nationality economic barriers removed. Native white ditch-diggers, doctors, carpenters and
clerks face a real threat to their economic security if all minorities are admitted freely to competition for their jobs. The
person who is economically secure as a rule cares little about
the color or nationality of individuals who also achieve material success, although he may borrow prejudiced attitudes
which originated among the classes who have reason to fear
minority competition. Were it not for the masses of native
white workers who consciously or otherwise dread the added
competition of European, Asiatic, and Mexican immigrants
and of migratory Negroes in the north and of all Negroes in
the south, it is unquestionable that there would be far less
occupational discrimination in the United States against these
peoples than now exists. It is always to the economic advantage of a group of workers to keep their number as small
as possible; and if racial and nationality barriers can be utilized to bar millions of potential Negro competitors and tens of
millions of potential alien competitors, every resource, including group hatreds and physical violence, may be expected to
be brought into play to accomplish the purpose.

The most definite evidence in support of this position can be
found in the attitudes of the labor unions. As the members
of continental guilds of earlier times limited the number of
their competitors by apprenticeship requirements, so modern
labor unions tend to control their membership, and thereby
their competitors, by every practical device. Since most labor
today is of such a simple nature that only a brief apprenticeship is required to obtain the necessary skill involved, almost
any occupation could be flooded with newcomers if artificial
restraints were not available. If all Negroes, for example, can

be barred from a union, almost 10 per cent of the potential competitors already in the United States can at one stroke be eliminated from the picture. This has been a common device whereby white men have held on to their jobs and kept up wages, although it must not be assumed that even a majority of union members supporting such a policy have been conscious of this purpose, for race prejudice with its roots in competition existed before the unions and obscures the basic reasons for Negro exclusion from all except the most clear-sighted.

"The official American labor movement consists of associations of boilermakers and bricklayers, plumbers and carpenters, machinists and railway switchmen, bookbinders and stationary engineers, each interested in its own particular job, jealously guarding its jurisdiction against all encroachments, and highly suspicious of every brother organization whose field approaches its own. The craft is a sort of exclusive club consisting of those who now belong. The smaller it is kept the higher will be the value of the craftsman's service. It is therefore made as difficult as possible for new members to join If whole classes, such as Negroes, can be automatically excluded, the problem of keeping the membership down is made that much easier. The organizations may carry the slogan of unity on their banners, but the ideals of labor solidarity and the brotherhood of all industrial workers have little practical bearing on their conduct. All that they want are signed agreements with employers. Collective negotiation upon a business basis is the ideal which really moves their lives. The American Federation of Labor is an agency set up to keep craft separatism from defeating its own ends. Its purpose is to settle disputes among the unions, to handle matters of common concern, particularly where legislation is needed, and to care in some manner for the organization of those workers who might, if not brought into the system in some way, ignore its claims and threaten its continuation. The American Federation of Labor is after all a creature of the trade unions. While it must have some measure of authority over them in order to fulfill its purpose, it can hardly, in view of its nature, rise to higher levels than its dominating elements—the craft internationals.

"Although the Negro is but one of the victims of American craft unionism, he is a victim upon whom the burden falls with special weight, for his peculiar situation in American society makes it particularly difficult for him to cross craft barriers. To the white trade unionist the Negro is not merely an outsider trying to get into the union, but a social and racial inferior trying to force the white man to associate with him as an equal. And the Negro knows that the white worker wants to keep him out of the union not merely as a potential competitor but as a member of a race which must not be permitted to rise to the white man's level. For three hundred years the Negro has been kept in a position of social and economic inferiority, and white organized labor, dominated by the hierarchy of the skilled crafts, has no desire to see him emerge from that condition."[12]

The union ideal of labor solidarity, regardless of race and creed, has been in conflict with the motivation of economic security, which is the real reason why workers pay dues and obey union orders. Idealism usually suffers when it opposes material advantage. There are, however, some occupations where it is to the advantage of union members to admit Negroes. Generally speaking, Negroes have obtained union recognition only where they were a greater threat to the organization members from without than from within the ranks. The result is that about 10 per cent of the white workers in non-agricultural occupations are unionized and only about 2 per cent of the Negroes similarly engaged enjoy the advantages of labor organization.

Race prejudice and the forces of competition for work have produced a wide variety of types of Negro union membership. Some Negroes belong to separate unions affiliated with the American Federation of Labor but with no white members.

[12] Sterling D. Spero and Abram L. Harris, *op. cit.*, pp. 461-462.

For further discussion of the Negro and unionism, see also Charles H. Wesley, *op. cit.*; Ira De A. Reid, *Negro Membership in American Labor Unions*, The National Urban League, New York, 1930; Lorenzo J. Greene and Carter G. Woodson, *op. cit.*

The Pullman porters have such a union, but with only a small proportion of the total number of porters belonging; and even though this type of work is restricted to Negroes it was not until 1929 that it was recognized by the Federation, no doubt because added colored representation was not desired in its councils. Negro freight handlers also have a small separate organization affiliated with the Federation, and there are a number of local colored unions scattered throughout the country, but of no particular importance, which have been granted special permission by the Federation to organize. Skilled workers are almost entirely excluded from union membership by ritual, constitution or by distortion of organization rules which on their face show no racial discrimination. Such unions include the Railway Carmen, Boilermakers, Dining Car Conductors, Sleeping Car Conductors, Railway Conductors, Machinists, Engineers, Firemen, Switchmen, Telegraphers, Train Dispatchers, Trainmen, Yardmasters, Railroad Workers, Wire Weavers, Clerks, Freight Handlers, Express and Station Employees, Masters, Mates and Pilots, the Railway Mail Association, the Neptune Association, the Electrical Workers, the Sheet Metal Workers, the Plasterers, and the Plumbers and Steam Fitters.

The less skilled a trade is, the more chance the Negro has of union organization. Longshoremen, of whom about 30 per cent are Negroes, included the first colored workers effectively organized, and they are today admitted in both separate and mixed locals. Hod Carriers and Building Laborers also admit Negroes. Hotel and Restaurant Employees, Journeymen Barbers, Laundry Workers, Tobacco Workers, United Textile Workers, Cooks and Waiters have permitted Negroes to join their organizations, but only in separate unions. The Musicians, representing a skilled occupation, also admit Negroes to separate unions, and this exception to the general practice of refusal to organize skilled Negroes is perhaps explained by the fact that the manner of employment of musicians is such that the Negro can more easily be used in competition with white musicians than is the case in most skilled trades.

"Other unions, like the Carpenters and Joiners, the Painters, and Bricklayers admit Negroes but do not solicit their membership. The only exception to this has been in the South, where the Negro could seriously handicap the white artisans by underworking them. . . . In the South, the Negroes have unions of their own; in the North they are usually taken, when permitted to affiliate, into mixed unions."[13]

Where a union represents an industry rather than a craft, the Negro has the best opportunity for inclusion in the organization. This does not mean that industrial unions will always admit Negroes on a parity with white workers, for, as Spero and Harris point out, "the Railway Carmen, an American Federation of Labor union, and the American Federation of Railroad workers, an independent union, do not. . . . A union having jurisdiction over a whole industry would imperil its own existence by neglecting any large section of workers in that industry."[14] Even though there is discrimination against the Negro varying with local conditions in such unions as the United Mine Workers, the International Ladies' Garment Workers, the Amalgamated Clothing Workers and the Industrial Workers of the World, they have shown a greater willingness to admit Negroes to their benefits than have the more specialized crafts unions. There has been a tendency for these unions to be more radical in their economic outlook, which, together with an alien membership proportionately greater than that of crafts unions, such as, for example, the Big Four of the railroads, has reduced the force of traditional prejudice against the Negroes.[15] It is not without significance that the now defunct Knights of Labor, a radical organization in its time with a special appeal to the unskilled worker, sought Negro members and gave them their first real contacts with the labor movement.

[13] Lorenzo J. Greene and Carter G. Woodson, *op. cit.*, p. 349. Lists of unions cited in this section without specific reference have also been taken from this volume, pp. 347ff.

[14] Sterling D. Spero and Abram L. Harris, *op. cit.*, pp. 325-326.

[15] Accurate statistical data concerning union membership in the United States are practically unavailable, especially in regard to race and nationality. Color and country of birth are frequently not recorded for membership records because of indifference to such facts which do not directly enhance the unions' power, and quite commonly the omission is for the purpose of concealing discrimination contrary to announced principles and official policy.

While the Negro is held by both workers and employers to be incapable of effective union organization, the recent immigrant is charged not only with being a threat to the solidarity of American labor through his ignorance of and indifference to collective bargaining, but also with being a fomenter of union agitation. The facts are that he, like the Negro, has been used to break strikes, has been barred or unwelcome in some unions, has been given free access to others and has been the controlling factor in the organization and operation of still others. There have even been separate locals of some unions specially created for Italians, Poles, Lithuanians, and others in order to facilitate the organization of these minorities with a minimum of prejudiced conflict. Discrimination against aliens, as in the case of the Negro, has been by ritual, constitution, and by unofficial barriers. Since unionism has been strongest in the industrial centers where the recent immigrant has concentrated, it is natural that he has turned to it for protection and has been admitted more readily than the Negro, who has moved to mill and factory only recently and is still a lesser factor in labor conditions than is the alien. The Negro has needed the union less than the immigrant, and the union has been less in danger from unorganized Negroes than from similar immigrants. Neither group has been familiar with American union practices before its entry into industry. Neither group is either "racially unfitted" for unionization or particularly difficult to organize if the majority wish it and the benefits are made evident.

When union troubles with minorities are brought to the attention of the organized workers, their first reaction is that "hunkies," "dagos," "wops," "niggers" and such are inferior breeds who have not the finer human trait of sacrifice and co-operation for the sake of the common good. This is the easy way in which the untrained, prejudiced mind explains group differences today. Experience has shown, however, that any group of American workers can be thoroughly organized to meet an emergency if minority traits are not disregarded.

South European immigrants were brought into the ranks of the United Mine Workers of America after it was generally conceded that they could not be organized. In the anthracite fields, for example, the prejudices of the natives and the older immigrants had first to be placated, and then organizers were carefully selected from among the ranks of the new immigrants themselves, and local unions of Italian, Slav, or other origin were formed. Except where minority workers are but a few scattered among those of native white stock, it is apparently safer to provide separate locals for the more sharply delineated minorities. This seems only reasonable, since cooperative bargaining for wages and conditions of labor requires a united front which is not easily obtained in a local including Germans, Irish, native Americans, Italians, Slavs, French Canadians, Portuguese, or any two or three of these. Relatively unmixed locals, however, may readily cooperate in their bargaining with other locals of any race or nationality through representatives and a central organization, so that the effectiveness of a union is increased rather than weakened by a policy which would be resented by Negroes, and is sometimes resented by aliens as well, as undemocratic segregation. No doubt prejudice is a factor in the need for the organization of such "segregated" locals for aliens as well as for Negroes, but racial antagonisms are definite facts which labor must take into account in its strategy; and even if it were entirely eliminated, there would still be the certainty of disruptive cultural conflict if free admission of minorities were the universal practice except where they were an unimportant element which could be disregarded in the formation and execution of policies. Once minority assimilation has gone so far as to produce common attitudes toward wages, hours of labor, working conditions, standards of living, and the like, separate organizations will tend to automatic disappearance, as in the case of the natives, the Irish, and the Germans today. It will be many years, however, before cultural differences will have so far disappeared that all minorities, particularly the south European and the colored, will be able whole-heartedly to identify themselves with labor.

The history of the clothing workers illustrates this point. When the Jews felt that they were not being treated fairly by the United Garment Workers—and there is no question but that racial prejudice and cultural conflict were rife in the organization—they split off from the main body in 1914, were followed by the Poles and Italians, and formed the Amalgamated Clothing Workers of America. This new union since then has had to exercise extreme caution in dealing with its Jewish, Polish, Lithuanian and Negro membership, but has so far succeeded in holding widely differing minorities together by giving all of them adequate representation in its councils, even going so far as to publish papers in seven different languages for the benefit of its members. The International Ladies' Garment Workers has also been able to hold various nationalities and, more recently, numerous Negroes in its membership effectively. The United Garment Workers, a Federation union, has remained conservative and nativistic, so that it has no colored membership and apparently wishes none. The Amalgamated Textile Workers, competing with the United Textile Workers, was organized by immigrants with radical tendencies when they found themselves the subject of discrimination—even the conservative immigrants were not wanted by the United Textile Workers—and has had considerable success from New England to Pennsylvania and New Jersey. The I.W.W. has generally attempted to organize immigrant outcasts from the more conservative unions, as it has also tried to do with the Negroes, but with little success, and its strength today among any group is negligible. Much of the minor success which it has sporadically enjoyed could have been avoided had the conservative unions recognized the peculiar needs of minorities who they refused to believe could be organized.

Immigrant workers in the packing industries and in iron and steel were also neglected. In these industries, as in most, the skilled workers organized first, and since the skilled workers were natives, Irish, Germans, English and other older immigrants, the new immigrants and their later successors, the Negroes, found their opportunities in rough labor unprotected and indifferently regarded by the unions already in the field. This attitude of superior indifference was changed somewhat in all industries when it was discovered that unskilled labor could move up to the skilled ranks in times of strikes, many of which were broken by this process.[16]

Strangely enough, it has been through the use of recent immigrants and Negroes as strikebreakers that they have gained a knowledge of union principles and been given an incentive and opportunity for organization. Immigrants were an important factor in such strikes as that in the bituminous mines in 1897, in anthracite in 1900 and 1902, in the packing industry in Chicago in 1904, in the Homestead strike of 1892, the Pittsburgh steel strike of 1919, the Lowell textile strike of 1903, the Lawrence textile strike of 1918, the cloak-makers' strike of 1910, and countless others.[17]

The Negro did not achieve his prominence in industrial labor disturbances outside of the southern coal mines of Alabama and West Virginia and the steel mills of Alabama and Maryland, and in a few other states of lesser importance in these industries, until the World War. While he has always been a factor in labor disputes in the south, only a few minor importations of colored workers to northern industries were effected prior to 1914, for until then European immigrants were readily available to employers in most emergencies. In those instances where immigrant strikebreakers could not be effectively used prior to 1914, it seemed equally unwise to attempt the use of unskilled Negroes. For accuracy's sake it should be mentioned that practically every large industry in the north made some temporary use of the Negro in times of labor disputes between the Civil and the World Wars, but the total labor situation was little affected by him in comparison with the influence of the immigrant. Since the World War, however, no northern strike involving unskilled and semi-skilled labor has been fought to its conclusion free from the participation of the Negro as a real or potential strikebreaker unless, as in

[16] For excellent brief accounts of the rôle of the recent immigrant in the unionization of the workers in the mines, the packing houses, the iron and steel industries, the textile mills and in the clothing industry, see William M. Leiserson, *Adjusting Immigrant and Industry*, Harper & Brothers, New York, 1924, chaps. ix-xii.

[17] *Ibid.*, pp. 185ff.

the case of the anthracite mines of Pennsylvania, an adequate white labor reserve was already at hand to meet the needs of the operators.

Immigrants and Negroes have little reason to trust the unions which, taken by and large, have done their best to keep them from the better jobs and to relegate them to such crude labor as they themselves did not want or could not supply. This is not only an organized labor attitude, but also the common attitude of native white workers. In fact, even minority workers of one variety have openly shown their antagonism to workers of some other race or nationality. Both immigrants and Negroes have been built into labor reserves, eking out an existence from the crumbs of employment while held in waiting for labor disturbances which would give them their opportunity, an opportunity which too frequently lasted only as long as the strike. The few outstanding exceptions where minority strikebreakers were retained on their jobs after the settlement were not sufficient to decrease distrust of employers as well as of majority workers. Further, most minorities have migrated from districts where the functions of the union and of the strike were unknown, for practically all of the Negroes and most of the immigrants who have served as strikebreakers came to industry from the farm. The immigrant learned rapidly, and so lost his industrial tractability, for he had a background favorable to class cooperation and group solidarity. The Negro, however, learned the rudiments of western civilization as a slave, was trained as an individualist, and thought in terms of a personal employer to whom personal loyalty was but natural. Only when, but just as soon as, a consciousness of community of interests with other workers has been instilled, and the knowledge of discrimination by both employers and competing laborers, together with the fear of unemployment and low wages because of minority status, are all removed from the minds of immigrant and colored workers will they cease to be a threat to organized labor.

While our discussion of workers' attitudes toward the employment of minorities in the effort to determine the explanation for their unequal occupational distribution has been confined to that of labor organizations, it is not difficult to see that union attitudes are identical with those of non-union workers, except that the latter are less definitely expressed. The non-union workers of the South have feared and hated the Negro ever since he drove them out of the rich plantation districts to the harsh environments where slave labor was unprofitable. West Virginia, Arkansas, Kentucky, and Tennessee hill farmers, with comparatively few Negroes in their communities, have not forgotten that their ancestors would have remained in the more fertile alluvial lands had not Negroes unwittingly deprived them of the opportunity to earn a decent living there. It is still the poor folks of the South whose denunciation and hatred of the black man is most open and bitter and least tempered by sympathy and understanding. In the southwest and on up into the State of Washington it is the poor white farmer and laborer who participates in riots against the Mexican and the Oriental. In El Paso, a southern city, the Mexican bears the brunt of racial prejudice since there he, and not the Negro, is the native white man's real competitor for work. In the clothing trades it is the Russian Jew, and, to a lesser extent, the Italian and the Pole, who are the objects of the native workers' animosity. It is also the Jew, who has made the greatest success in manufacturing and trade, who is today the most hated immigrant minority, for he is the competitor so far as the commercial native working classes are concerned. Where direct competition enters, there group antagonism reaches its height. The inference is undeniable that it is not the minorities themselves and their characteristics, not the employers of labor or their customers, but those whose livelihood is threatened who furnish the real explanation of minority occupational discrimination.

It will be noticed that the Indian has been left entirely out of this discussion of occupational distribution. This is because he is so unimportant a factor in the industrial life of the nation that he is free to work wherever he wishes provided he is capable of doing so. "Data supplied by 16,534 pupils in Indian schools regarding the employment of their fathers showed that 10,011 of them are engaged in agriculture as 'farmers' or 'ranchers.' The next largest group was laborers, 856, followed by carpenters, 151, railroad employees, 142, and lumbermen, 138, with the rest scattered among some eighty-six distinctive occupations."[18] This distribution may be taken as roughly typical, so far as Indians who have not been completely assimilated are concerned, and shows why the occupations of Indians are of only sentimental interest to white workers and capitalists alike, except for a few localities where there is a concentration of aboriginal population. The Indian has found industrialization distasteful because of tradition, and inconvenient because of rural habitat. If, however, we were to consider the white worker's and employer's attitude toward non-agricultural Indians in the early settlements when the ratio between white and red population was nearer 1:1 than it is now, a quite different attitude would be found, one which classed Indians as tricky, thieving, lazy, unreliable, profitable workers only under the closest supervision and, in short, not even always on a par with Negro workers. It was not an accident that Hampton Institute was built to educate both Indians and Negroes to work with the hands.[19]

THE PROFESSIONS AND BUSINESS

We have now to consider the economic activities of minorities in the professions and in business. The Mexican and the Filipino immigrants have not had time to achieve any prominence in these occupations. All other alien groups and their children have made such notable contributions in law, medicine, education, the ministry, manufacturing, and trade, that few question the fact that their numbers include sufficient individuals with such capacities as to compare favorably with the old native white stock. The Negro, however, has produced few outstanding commercial and industrial leaders, and his contributions to the professional world are of importance in spite of their poverty only because of their service to the col-

---

[18] Lewis Merriam, *The Problem of Indian Administration,* Johns Hopkins Press, Baltimore, 1928, p. 387.

[19] For details of Indian occupations, see G. E. E. Lindquist, *The Red Man in the United States,* Doubleday, Doran & Company, Inc., New York, 1923, p. 461; Lewis Merriam, *op. cit.,* especially chap. x.

ored race, otherwise given only grudging attention by white preachers, doctors, lawyers, and teachers. It is even more difficult to find outstanding professional and business men among the American Indians than among the American Negroes, although the red man is popularly conceded to be mentally superior to the black. This last fact alone should make one suspicious that in these superior occupations, as in the wage classes, differential occupation is more a matter of culture than of biology.

Two colored groups, the Chinese and Japanese, like the Latin Americans, have escaped the worst effects of racial antagonisms by sending their advanced students to universities in regions removed from the centers of prejudice against them. As is explained later in our discussion of professional education for minorities, the white people of the United States have come to think of Orientals and Latin Americans as divided into two classes, the despised working class, and the respected wealthy and professional class. The former class was a threat to the native white population of the communities to which it migrated, while the latter was well received, in spite of racial identity, because it came into contact only with the more secure white classes who had no fear of its puny competition and could not appreciate the feelings of the working people. Most of the superior Orientals and Latin Americans who intended to remain permanently in the United States confined their business and professional relations to their own people or were engaged in some special occupation which was conceded to be their field, such as importing from the country of their origin. Others came to this country only for an education and were recognized as visitors. Their lot was easy compared with that of the Negro having similar ambitions.

Negroes have been regarded as just Negroes, whether they were rich or poor, educated or illiterate, doctors or cooks. The professional unions, if we may call them such, have limited their admission no less than the trade unions. The American Medical Association, for example, has been powerless to give recognition to Negro doctors when the local units have denied them admission, as has been the common practice in the south. While the national body does not support racial discrimination in principle, it has permitted its local units to act as they pleased in the matter. It is unquestionably true that the average Negro doctor does not measure up to the average white doctor, but it is also true that thousands of Negro doctors have been barred from membership in professional associations for no other reason than color. The response has been the formation of the National Medical Association, a separate union for colored doctors. Discrimination against Negroes by the American Bar Association has called into being the colored National Bar Association. Preachers in the south, and sometimes in the north, are also organized in separate associations on a color basis. Frequently this is carried so far as to necessitate separate Negro denominations. White teachers have also found it difficult to work with their colored fellows, and segregation in educational associations is only a reflection of the almost universal policy of not permitting Negroes to teach white students. The most socially select profession of all, that of officering the military and naval forces of the United States, may be considered closed to Negroes, since the attitude of the white officers and of West Point and Annapolis has created an intolerable situation for colored aspirants to commissions. The engineering and architectural professions, overcrowded with qualified white workers, offer few opportunities for Negroes.[20]

[20] "The slowness of the increase in the number of Negro physicians and lawyers when compared with the number of Negro preachers and teachers is indicated by the fact that in 1890 the United States census reported 12,159 preachers, 15,008 teachers, 431 lawyers and 909 physicians and surgeons. . . .

"In 1920 the census reported 950 Negro lawyers; 3,495 physicians and surgeons; 19,571 preachers and 35,563 teachers. . . .

"Under freedom there was a rapid development in professions other than the ministry, teaching, law and medicine. The more notable of the increases in these other professions from 1890 to 1920 were: actors, from 180 to 1,973; artists and teachers of art, from 150 to 259; dentists, from 120 to 1,109; musicians and teachers of music, from 1,881 to 5,902; photographers, from 190 to 608; religious, charity and welfare workers, from 0 to 1, 231; trained nurses, from 0 to 3,341." Monroe N. Work, "The Negro in Business and the Professions," in Donald Young, editor, "The American Negro," *The Annals* of the American Academy of Political and Social Science, November, 1928, vol. cxxxx, p. 139.

On the same page of this reference is found the number of white and colored people for each white and colored member of the leading professional classes.

Members of white minorities, however, may succeed in any of the professions, with only the Jew encountering any real opposition. Strangely enough, even the Jew may minimize the prejudice against his origin by making a success of the medical, literary or teaching professions, although not so easily in the legal. This is recognized by Jewish parents and children, and, together with a traditional respect for education, helps to explain the high proportion of this minority who enter these fields.[21]

Industry and trade have made countless wealthy men of European immigrants. It is only natural that of the millions of immigrants who have started as day laborers, clerks and peddlers, a reasonable proportion would achieve success as measured by income. In an acquisitive society where the goal is to buy for little and sell for more, one pays slight attention to the national origin of those with whom business relations are maintained. Handicaps of prejudice have stood in the way of all European minorities, but they have been overcome with sufficient frequency to justify a belief in American economic democracy.

The Negro, however, has found it otherwise. Negro banking has remained insignificant during a period when immigrants have become financial leaders of their communities and of the entire nation. The few Negro insurance companies combined do less business than one white company does with Negroes alone. Negro stores are of the neighborhood corner variety, and poor ones at that. There are a few Negro contractors, a scattering of manufacturers, some caterers, and little more. The Negro has been a farmer under pauperizing conditions, and farmers do not make business successes as a rule unless they migrate to business centers. Furthermore, when the Negro did migrate to business centers he found all his needs

---

The number of persons per each minister in 1920 were: white, 983, colored, 543; per each teacher, white, 145, colored, 291; per each physician, white, 748, colored, 2,993; per each nurse, white, 725, colored, 3,131; per each dentist, white, 1,924, colored, 9,434; per each lawyer, white, 870, colored, 11,013; per each minister, white, 874, colored, 534.

[21] Interesting illustrations and interpretations of the status of Jews of the business and professional classes may be found in Bruno Lasker, editor, *Jewish Experiences in America,* The Inquiry, New York, 1930, pp. xiv + 309.

served by existing commercial institutions, and, since he was given no opportunity to learn business methods through employment in responsible positions by banks, stores, factories, and mills, and has thus been left without training as well as without capital, it is understandable that his measure of industrial and commercial success has been limited.[22] Real estate has been as easy a source of Negro wealth as any, as might be expected from the fact that the Negro has in all cities been a transitional tenant, occupying blocks in the path of business expansion after it lost its residential desirability but before it reached its greatest value for business purposes. In the few instances where he was able to acquire title to such land, and hold it, he was sure to profit. No specialized training is required for the acquisition of wealth in this way, and racial antagonism can hardly interfere. In fact, racial prejudice may be an advantage, for it encourages white people to sell their property below its real value when Negroes encroach upon it, so that the colored purchaser may drive a better bargain after an entry has been gained in a residential section. The fact that the Negro has made most of his fortunes in land, the type of business where race prejudice imposes the least handicaps, characterizes Negro business in its entirety. There is truth to the remark that the Negro started with nothing and still has it.

A solution to the lack of opportunity for professional and business development of Negroes which finds favor among many colored people and is just about taken for granted by white people is that the Negro should be encouraged to build up a colored clientele for his own services and products. This amounts to a suggestion that a dual economic structure be erected with a division based on color alone. In support of it may be cited the fact that Negro doctors, lawyers, preachers, teachers, tradesmen, bankers, and other successful leaders

[22] "The chief problems of Negro business of every sort are efficient management and sufficient capital, including credit in its various forms to successfully carry on the enterprises. The average Negro business man, unlike the average white business man, until recently had no special opportunity to obtain business training. The first Negro bank was established by a preacher. The largest of the life insurance companies was established by a barber." Monroe N. Work, op. cit., p. 144

have thus far, with few exceptions, founded their achievements on colored patronage. The Madam Walker Manufacturing Company, which brought its founder over a million dollars before she died in 1919, is an illustration of this type of business which was forced to be so because its products were beautifying preparations made especially to meet Negroes' needs. There are other Negro enterprises which must depend on colored patronage because of their nature, such as hotels, restaurants and southern amusement parks, but these are in the minority, and by far the greater portion of Negro businesses today could just as well serve white and colored together, from an economic point of view, if they were sufficiently attractive and well operated, which they are not. The fact that they are limited to the patronage of a poverty-stricken minority is but another reason for their underdevelopment. Colored people, being poor, must watch their pennies, and the economic motive is as strong in them as in anyone else, so that they have shown a distinct tendency to buy where they get the most for their money, and are shrewd enough to know that the white stores can generally give them better service than the colored. Why should they buy Negro newspapers when the others are as cheap, and far better? Why should they patronize colored theaters, grocery, drygoods, furniture and other stores when the white are available and less expensive? The prejudices of white owners and clerks, doctors and dentists, may drive them to patronize colored enterprises, but race consciousness will not. They are individualists, they are jealous of their successful fellow Negroes, and, above all, their dollar must go far.

Further, if Negro race consciousness could in some manner be developed so that the Negro would do his best to patronize only fellow Negroes, the white men would be the first to protest against the loss of trade. The most prejudiced white man is willing enough to take the Negro's money if he can do so without losing caste, and there seems to be little difficulty in accomplishing this purpose. The white man needs Negroes to work for him. He needs the patronage of Negro consumers. Our economic organization is so constructed that every resident in the country is in a measure dependent for his living on members of every minority of whatever racial and national origin, as well as of the native white majority. Harlem has been touted as an example of what may be done to secure independent economic organization for the Negro, but even there the far greater share of Negro wages goes to pay white men for consumption goods. The land itself in Harlem is mostly owned by white landlords. Every city in the United States with an appreciable colored population can furnish a few examples of Negroes who have secured a competence by supplying the needs of other Negroes, but these are comparatively rare exceptions, and must remain so, if for no other reason than that the white man will insist on it. A program of economic segregation is the least possible of all segregation policies.

That such a program is not the road to minority economic progress is indicated by the fact that the business leaders of no alien group have followed it. Where there is a distinctly personal service involved, as in the relation between doctor and patient, preacher and communicant, teacher and pupil, lawyer and client, we may expect a considerable degree of economic segregation. For such personal services the north European, the Italian, the Jew, the Oriental, and the Negro show a pronounced tendency to patronize members of their own minority, but only so long as their culture remains distinct. When the element of personal relationship is diminished —and in nearly all forms of trade it is at a minimum—group consciousness gives way to competitive bargaining.

Children of minorities against whom occupational discrimination is maintained for more than a generation face an insoluble problem if they are truly ambitious to be more than wage workers or lesser business and professional people serving only their own minority. We may illustrate the economic choices which lie before them by reference to the occupational opportunities open to American-born children of Orientals.

The child born in the United States of Chinese parentage, for example, may choose between three roads, all of which are strewn with well-nigh insuperable obstacles. He may remain in this country and accept the lot assigned him by the white majority. This means that he must force himself to be content with the lot of a servant, cook, waiter, laborer, farmer or laundryman. This is the easiest road of the three, for it involves only the passive acceptance of inferior status. If, however, he cannot resign himself to such a subordinate rôle, he may still elect to remain in the United States but decide to strive for professional or financial leadership. If he does, he knows that he must depend on the patronage of Orientals or on that which white people will give to Orientals only if they are engaged in some stereotyped occupation, such as operating a Chinese restaurant, a store selling Chinese goods, an importing house, or perhaps a farm. Since there are less than a quarter of a million Orientals in the country, it is understood that their patronage is limited, and there are also limits to the number of Chinese enterprises which the white population will support. Furthermore, it is galling to be restricted to selling chop suey and curios with the knowledge that that is all one is deemed fit to do in life. The third road is usually described by thoughtless Americans as "going back to China," when only a moment's consideration will remind one that he has never been there. Still, it may be argued, he has the advantage of acquaintance with American civilization, and should therefore succeed more readily in competition with natives of the country of his ancestors who have only an oriental education. This is a false assumption, for his American birth and training would be a handicap in China, where his race would call forth the expectation that he should fit into oriental civilization in spite of his occidental rearing. Social and economic non-conformities which would be excused in a white man living in China—being white he could hardly be expected to know any better!—would lead to his ostracism, for his Chinese ancestry destroys the excuse of ignorance but not the ignorance itself. This road turns out to be the most difficult of the three.[23]

[23] This illustration of the "three roads" is adapted from Kazuo Kawai, "Three Roads, None Easy," *The Survey Graphic*, May, 1926, vol. lvi, No. 3, pp. 164-166.

The American-born child of Japanese parentage has the same three roads before him. So, for that matter, does the American-born child of Jewish or Negro parentage, with the difference in the last two cases that there are a greater number of Jews and Negroes in the United States to furnish patronage for a fellow minority member and that, in the case of the Jew, there is greater opportunity for professional and commercial success dependent on majority patronage permitted by the lesser prejudice against a white minority. In any event, the road of "going back" to Jewish centers in Europe or to Negro Africa is closed to American Jews and Negroes, who would be strangers in a strange land if they did so, worse off among their non-migrating cousins than if they were no kin at all. Thus while the rapidly assimilable minorities must put up with occupational discrimination only temporarily, the more fixed minorities, once tainted by American manners, customs, and ideals, must choose between an uphill struggle in which they never quite achieve equality with their majority competitors, and a resigned acceptance of inferior economic status. To offer them the opportunity of "going back where they came from" is but an empty gesture. If they accepted such an alternative to American prejudice they would still be an inferior minority, outcasts in the lands of their fathers.

CHAPTER V

PEACE THROUGH SEGREGATION

STRANGE races and nationals make no trouble if they are kept out of the way of our own people. This statement, so obviously true in theory yet so disappointingly false when tried as a complete practical program, is perhaps the most widely accepted plan for the solution of the problems of minority-majority relationships, not only in the United States but also throughout the world. It is so simple. Dogs cannot fight if they are not allowed in the same yard. So, the theory in the United States has run, let us restrict European immigration, especially that from south Europe, bar Asiatics, put Indians on reservations and keep Negroes "Jim Crowed." In other words, segregation is to be accomplished by keeping out alien minorities, and by the use of a caste system and deportation for those who are already in our midst. No, dogs cannot fight if they are fenced apart. State and federal governments have been building and tearing down and again building all conceivable varieties of fences between clashing human groups since before the Revolutionary War. With what success?

THE RESTRICTION OF EUROPEAN IMMIGRATION

The Declaration of Independence complains that the King of Great Britain "has endeavored to prevent the population of these States; for that purpose obstructing the laws for the naturalization of foreigners; refusing to pass others to encourage their migration hither, and raising the conditions of new appropriations of lands." From this it would seem that the colonists favored relatively free migration and feared no trouble from the admission of minorities. In the light of their earlier history, however, this is an unlikely interpretation. Not a single colony has a record free from all immigration restriction. Pennsylvania, one of the most liberal toward new-comers, required that settlers should be Christians, tried to keep out felons, and for a brief period also taxed foreigners and Irish servants. Roman Catholics were generally unwanted, and even Maryland, something of a Catholic refuge, legislated against members of that Church. Quakers were banned as undesirable colonists in Virginia and in the New Haven Colony, and were unpopular with other colonists even in Pennsylvania, where they were at least legally welcome. Germans were looked upon quite commonly as the south European is today regarded, that is, of some economic worth but with socially undesirable characteristics probably outweighing their positive contributions. There was a confusion of opinions from New England to Georgia as to who was to be admitted and who was to be barred. There was no confusion, however, as to the means to be taken to save any particular colony from minorities, religious, national, or racial. Restrictive immigration legislation, brutally honest with the self-confidence of intolerance born of an unquestioned certainty of righteousness, left no doubt in the minds of minorities that they were not wanted.[1]

Banishment, the ancestor of modern deportation, was a vigorous process. Jesuits who returned to Massachusetts Colony after having once been driven out might be executed, although the law charitably allowed those who were shipwrecked time to leave. There was no polite, delicate restraint in explaining why groups were not wanted, as there is in our modern laws, but then those were rough days when tolerance and doubt had not softened the hand of punishment. Nor were international relations as complicated as they are now. Above all, colonial laws were in the hands of relatively homogeneous lawmakers, with less of the modern conflict of group interests and traditions.

Let it not be thought, however, that, because conflict of religions was the most common basis for exclusion, it was the only one or that it was so very different from our modern

[1] For a brief summary of colonial restrictions on immigration, see the *Annual Report of the Commissioner General of Immigration for 1930*, pp. 2ff.

excuses. Convicts were excluded by at least one colony, Maryland. Nationalities other than those of the mother country were frequently subject to discrimination. Religion itself was in those days more of a measure of other qualities, so that when the Catholics or the Quakers were excluded, it was also a culturally undesirable group, possibly of undesirable stock, from whom the colony was being saved.[2]

The need for strong and willing hands, no matter to what variety of minority body they were attached, was constantly at war with the controlling majority's efforts to insure continued homogeneity and to prevent group disintegration. After the severance of political ties with England, the thirteen original states and their later-born sister states of the West yielded to the demands of the vacant lands for settlers, and in the hope of immediate, unfailing prosperity gave up attempts at selective immigration and welcomed all who were willing to come. For a century following the War of Independence the dangers of minorities were forgotten except by an ineffectual few in the scramble for people—any people—who would develop the vast available acreage of untilled soil.

There were, of course, periods in our history when waves of anti-alien sentiment, always rippling over the country, reached their crest, but even then it was not powerful enough to secure restrictive immigration legislation. The organization of the Native American Party in 1835 marks the crest of one such wave, although it accomplished nothing in its attempts to save the United States from aliens. The later adoption of a goodly proportion of its members and principles by the Whigs was equally ineffective in this respect.

"In 1850 was organized in New York the Supreme Order of the Star Spangled Banner, also known as the Sons of the Sires of '76. This organization came to be known as the Know-Nothing Order. It was an oath-bound secret fraternity composed of a national council, with state and local councils. Members were admitted only after a searching examination and an elaborate ritual. A candidate had to be descended from

---

[2] The facts of colonial policies toward minorities just cited, but not their interpretations, have been taken from *ibid.*, pp. 1-4

at least two generations of American ancestors. Neither he nor his wife nor any of his ancestors for two generations could have been members of the Roman Catholic Church. The candidate had to be vouched for by a select committee of the council. Obviously there could be no trace of salt-water in a Know-Nothing lodge. When a member was asked about the order, he invariably replied 'I don't know' or 'I know nothing.' From this it came that members were dubbed 'Know-Nothings,' although they called themselves members of the Native American party. . . .

"In the beginning of its meteoric career the principles of the Know-Nothing party were secret, but before long they became public property. It advocated the repeal of all naturalization laws, none but native Americans for office, a pure American common-school system, war to the hilt on Romanism, opposition to the formation of military companies composed of foreigners, hostility to all papal influences, more stringent and effective immigration laws, the sending back of all foreign paupers on our shores, and, summing everything up, 'our country, our whole country, and nothing but our country.' "[3]

In spite of the success of this group in the election of numerous candidates to public office, much of which was really a protest against the two major political parties rather than an acceptance of Know-Nothing principles, its existence was of short duration and its imprint on immigration legislation invisible.

The two organized successors to this party, the American Protective Association of the last decades of the nineteenth century and the modern Ku Klux Klan following the World War, created the illusion of effectiveness in immigration legislation largely because they came into existence after the tide of public opinion had begun to turn against free immigration. Their programs were essentially the same in spirit, if not identical in specific proposals, in so far as alien minorities were concerned. There is no reason to believe, however, that our

[3] George M. Stephenson, *A History of American Immigration*, Ginn & Co., Boston, 1926, pp. 112-113.

immigration legislation today would be in any way different from what it is, had neither of these organizations ever existed.

Once the public domain was fairly well exhausted, and in spite of the need for crude labor in the rapidly expanding industries in the latter part of the nineteenth and the beginning of the twentieth centuries, which drew millions of Europeans into the United States before they could be checked, public sentiment against the unrestricted admission of aliens automatically increased in volume until it culminated in the immigration legislation of 1924. From the 1880's to the present, more and stricter immigration laws have been enacted, each major law more restrictive than its predecessor.

In the early years of the United States, as today, there were always some states which suffered more than others from the undesirable effects of immigration. Massachusetts and New York, for example, with adequate populations of their own acquired early, were troubled because they contained the two most important harbors through which immigrants arrived—Boston and New York City. The almshouses, hospitals, jails, and charities were forced to care for many aliens who fell by the wayside in their march to the west. The extent of this burden has been exaggerated, and these eastern states also actually profited from their gateway position and from those aliens of good quality who remained in them, but so long as they believed they were getting a bad bargain they could be expected to protest.

One form of protest was state immigration legislation. Head taxes on immigrants, barriers against convicts and other types of aliens who seemed obviously unfit to support themselves were enacted. The State of California passed numerous anti-Chinese laws. The various forms of self-protection, however mistaken the propagandist bases may have been, were not as a rule unreasonable, and many are now represented in our federal laws. The United States Supreme Court, however, held in 1849 and again in 1875 that such legislation was beyond the power of the several states, and even went to the unusual length of suggesting federal remedies for an increasingly intolerable burden on the states.

Congress, under the spell of the expansion movement, took its time in passing even the simplest qualitative restrictions, apparently indifferent or in fear of the restrictive influence on the immigrant streams which any discouraging laws might have. Federal legislation until the last quarter of the nineteenth century definitely encouraged immigration. Lands were made available to immigrants, who were told by government propagandist literature of the golden opportunities awaiting them in the United States. "The very title of an act passed by Congress on July 4, 1864, *i.e.,* 'An Act to *Encourage* Immigration,' while not truly descriptive of its purposes, was nevertheless of this deep rooted sentiment [supporting an open-door policy.]"[4] This bill was repealed in 1868, for shortly after the end of the Civil War the anti-alien feeling took root and grew to real importance in our legislative councils.

Although 1875 is perhaps the year which should be cited as that in which the federal government first barred any special classes of immigrants—for it was in this year that involuntary Asiatic immigration and the importation of women for immoral purposes was forbidden—it was not until 1882 that any worth-while relief was given. In this year Congress recognized the necessity for protective measures by enacting restrictive legislation copied almost verbatim from state regulations which had been declared unconstitutional. A head tax of fifty cents was levied on aliens entering the United States by water. Among other things, but most important of all, "The act [of 1882] excluded idiots, lunatics, persons likely to become public charges, and convicts, excepting those convicted of political offenses."[5] Leaving the colored aliens out of consideration for the time being, since this year Congress has extended this list of socially undesirables in a number of acts, the most important of which were passed in 1907 and 1917, so that the following classes are now included in the barred group:

---

[4] *Annual Report of the Commissioner General of Immigration for 1930,* p. 5.

[5] *Ibid.,* p. 5.

Persons who suffer from loathsome or dangerous contagious diseases, including tuberculosis, ringworm, trachoma, syphilis, gonorrhea, and leprosy.

Persons who are mentally defective. This includes people who suffer or have suffered from insanity, the feeble-minded of various types, and the epileptic.

Persons who are deemed morally undesirable. This includes those who have been convicted of or who have admitted committing a serious crime, paupers, inebriates, prostitutes, and polygamists.

Persons who hold certain radical political views. This includes anarchists, people who believe in the overthrow of government by violence, and members of organizations opposed to organized government.[6]

In addition to this somewhat miscellaneous, catch-all list, apparently the result of years of sporadic effort by our legislators to think of all the types of persons for whom there was an emotional distaste on the part of their constituents, there were a number of bases for exclusion written into the law which deserve special mention because of the social philosophy underlying them and because their consequences are in dispute. While one may regret the unscientific, scatter-shot manner in which the above-listed hodge-podge of "undesirables" was made a part of the law of the land in a half-century of effort (1875-1917), and while some of the tests for admission were palpably ridiculous, if only from an enforcement point of view, some, such as those relative to physical and mental health, are at least minimum requirements, and the rest, if they do no great good, also do no great harm. We shall later return to a discussion of these miscellaneous traits,

[6] For a more detailed but simple statement of the reasons for barring aliens as immigrants, see Marian Schibsby, *Handbook for Immigrants to the United States,* Foreign Language Information Service, 222 Fourth Ave., New York, 1927. See also Jeremiah W. Jenks and W. Jett Lauck, *The Immigration Problem,* Funk & Wagnalls Company, New York, 6th edition, 1926, Appendices A and B. These appendices contain copies of the important immigration laws. Not all restrictive or regulatory immigration is included, for there are today fifty-eight acts or parts of acts in force, exclusive of Chinese immigration legislation, according to the statement of the Commissioner General of Immigration in his 1930 report.

but first a description of the outstanding immigration law is required.

The immigration law of 1864, previously mentioned, provided, among other features encouraging to immigration, for a legalized system of contract labor. Immigrants had been, of course, arriving under contract to work since the time of the colonial indentured servants or redemptioners, and they continued to arrive after this law was repealed. The law is here referred to in order to emphasize a governmental attitude toward contract labor quite different from that which first obtained legal expression in the toothless law of 1885, strengthened by supplementary legislation in 1887, which forbade the entrance of immigrants under contract to work. The law of 1864 naturally was one designed to be of value to the employer rather than to the laboring man; but since the latter part of the nineteenth century the laboring people have had their own way with immigration legislation, so that there is no further danger that capitalists will bring in strikebreakers and intimidating labor reserves under contract by the boatload, as was done while it was still legal in enough cases to constitute a definite threat to the workingman's bargaining power in wage disputes.

Although we must be careful not to picture capitalists as eager vultures, ever poised ready to beat down wage scales with the aid of such devices, some did use such tactics and others have shown themselves ready and willing to use them again if permitted, so that justification for this law exists. In its present form, however, it is hard to defend.

Immigrants under agreement to work at definite jobs in the United States cannot be legally admitted. The minor exceptions to this rule do not appreciably soften its effect. Artists, ministers, professors, nurses, actors, and domestic servants are exempt from this law. It is also possible to bring in a workingman skilled in some occupation not yet developed in this country, provided no similarly skilled workman can be found available in the United States. This requires the unwinding of much red tape and is not often done. The purpose of the law, of course, is to prevent the competition or the threat of competition of cheap foreign labor with our own, a socially expedient purpose.

It can, however, be carried to extremes. When Mike, a fine young Greek boy, upon arrival frankly tells the immigration inspector that he is going to work in a fruit store managed by his brother in Detroit, he is sent back home as a contract laborer. But when Tony, perhaps a worthless vagrant from Naples, tells the inspector that he has no prospect of work, that he does not know where he is going, and, in short, that he is without plans of any kind, he is promptly admitted so far as this law is concerned. This seems unfair, and unwise from the standpoint of the social welfare of the United States itself. In theory, it is so; in practice, it is not so bad. The immigrant by this time knows enough, if he is given rudimentary advice by friends, to deny any knowledge of a job when asked, and thus gets into the country quite easily. On the other hand, if any employer were to attempt to bring in a sufficient number of contract laborers to constitute a wage threat, there would be little likelihood that his plot could escape detection. Thus the main purpose of the law is accomplished, and without much hardship on the desirable immigrant with a job who does not mind a bit of evasion. The law could, of course, be rewritten to avoid this feature, but the labor leaders look on it as something of a sacred cow, not to be touched for fear of profanation. Ninety-three contract laborers were caught trying to enter the United States during the fiscal year 1930, and only four of these at seaports. Possibly if college professors, artists, actors, and ministers were politically more powerful, they too could be protected from alien competition.

The Immigration Act of 1917, in addition to a long list of undesirable types of aliens previously mentioned and a provision excluding all oriental immigrants except Japanese, included a literacy test which provided that, with certain exceptions based on youth or old age, religious persecution, and the presence of certain relatives willing to give support in the United States, ability to read and understand what is read in a language to be selected by the immigrant is necessary for admission.

It would seem at first glance that a literacy test of such a character—and the tests as given are very simple—could hardly be criticized; so the fact that Presidents Cleveland, Taft, and Wilson vetoed literacy test bills (the one now in force being passed over President Wilson's second veto) requires explanation.

The test as now provided for by law and as enforced is no test of mental ability. Any person who is able to pass the direct mental examination has the ability to learn to read the small vocabulary of everyday words required. Since English is not required, it cannot be said that this requirement is primarily designed to aid the immigrant in his new home, although the ability to read any language is actually of some aid. It does not even favor those with "a desire and sufficient initiative to get an education," as has been claimed; to do that it would have to be much more difficult. These are the usual arguments in its favor. The argument which secured its passage was quite different.

In actuality, it was a subterfuge, as admitted by some of its supporters, designed to restrict the new immigration from southeastern Europe. The hope was that since the public educational systems of the old immigrant countries were better established than those of the new, a nationally selective immigration would be achieved, if only slightly, without the necessity for open discrimination. This hope was not realized. Since more recent quota legislation has openly accomplished this end in a way that no literacy test can ever do, there is no valid excuse for the continuance of the literacy test in its present form except to fool constituents into the belief that it is a Congressional bulwark against inferior immigrants, which it is not. It should consequently either be repealed or made into a real educational test.

Until 1921 there was no numerical restriction on immigration, except in the case of those oriental countries from which no immigration at all was permitted. In this year the first quota act was passed, introducing a new and popular method of numerical restriction, followed by the act of 1924, which included a temporary quota based on the place of birth of our foreign-born population as determined by the census of 1890, and a permanent one based on the national origins of our total white population in 1920.

The Quota Act of 1921 provided that the number of immigrants of any nationality to be admitted in a given year should be limited to 3 per cent of the number of people who had been born in that country but were living in the United States in 1910. This act was rushed through Congress as a temporary stop-gap to check the rapid increase in immigration after the World War. When the number of immigrants again started to increase, after a severe decline as the law first went into effect, the act of 1924 replaced it.

This act provided that until July 1, 1927, the number of immigrants of any nationality to be admitted in a given year should be 2 per cent of the number of people who had been born in that country but were living in the United States in 1890. Census figures were of course used as the base. However, this same act provided that "The annual quota of any nationality for the fiscal year beginning July 1, 1927, and for each fiscal year thereafter, shall be a number which bears the same ratio to 150,000 as the number of inhabitants in continental United States in 1920 having that national origin . . . bears to the number of inhabitants in continental United States in 1920, but the minimum quota of any nationality shall be 100."

Later sections of the law provided that the colored population, not of European origin, was to be excluded from this computation, and that the determination of national origins should be through rates of population increase, statistics of immigration and emigration, and other reliable data, and not by an attempt to trace back the ancestry of particular individuals. Owing to delays in agreement upon quotas and political maneuvering, this national origin provision did not go into effect until July 1, 1929.

Quota limitations could not, of course, be applied to everyone, and generous exceptions have been made. Without going

into technical details, immigrants from Canada, Newfound-
land, and the independent countries of the western hemisphere
have been exempted from quota restrictions, although they
must comply with the other immigration requirements. Government officials, their families and official staffs, aliens traveling for business or pleasure or in continuous transit through
the United States, students, certain relatives of American
citizens, and others who may logically be put in special classifications have not been assigned to quotas. Since we are not
considering the technical administration of the laws, we may
leave these exceptions out of our discussion except as they
may tend to weaken the original legislative purpose.

Essentially, the quota has had two purposes. It has served
as a check on the total number of immigrants admitted, and
it has been used to favor immigrants of some nationalities as
against some others. The effectiveness and desirability of quota
legislation, then, should be judged by the way it has kept
the United States from unwanted numbers of immigrants and
from immigrants of unwanted nationalities, and by the scientific justification for the Congressional objectives which they
attempt to achieve. Knowing that Congress has long desired
to limit the new immigration and favor the old, a tabulation
of the three quotas provided in the laws of 1921 and of 1924
should make obvious their relative effectiveness in accomplishing this purpose and this is given on page 164.

This table is adapted from the *Annual Reports* of the Commissioner General of Immigration to the Secretary of Labor
for 1924 and 1930. Some quota countries are omitted because
of their lack of significance for our purposes. The quotas in
the first column are based on the 1910 foreign-born population
of the United States; in the second, on the 1890 foreign-born
population; in the third, on the national origins provision.
A critical analysis of the quota system, with a viewpoint differing from ours, may be found in Roy L. Garis, *Immigration
Restriction*.

The first quota law, it can readily be seen, was primarily
an attempt to reduce the numbers of immigrants, while at the

TABLE I

QUOTA COUNTRIES	ACTUAL QUOTAS IN FISCAL YEARS		
	1922	1925	1930
Albania........................	288	100	100
Austria........................	7,451	785	1,413
Belgium........................	1,563	512	1,304
Bulgaria........................	302	100	100
Czechoslovakia.................	14,282	3,073	2,874
Danzig, Free City of............	301	228	100
Denmark.......................	5,694	2,789	1,181
Finland........................	3,921	471	569
France.........................	5,729	3,954	3,086
Germany.......................	68,059	51,227	25,957
Great Britain and Ireland.......	77,342		
Great Britain and Northern Ireland		34,007	65,721
Greece........................	3,294	100	307
Hungary.......................	5,638	473	869
Irish Free State................		28,567	17,853
Italy........................	42,057	3,845	5,802
Latvia.........................		142	236
Lithuania......................		344	386
Netherlands....................	3,607	1,648	3,153
Norway........................	12,202	6,453	2,377
Poland........................	25,827	5,982	6,524
Portugal.......................	2,520	503	440
Roumania......................	7,419	603	295
Russia........................	34,284	2,248	2,784
Spain.........................	912	131	252
Sweden........................	20,042	9,561	3,314
Switzerland....................	3,752	2,081	1,707
Turkey........................	656	100	226
Yugoslavia....................	6,426	671	845

same time distributing them among all European nations in
rough proportion to the number arriving within the last generation. The shift from 3 to 2 per cent and from the census
of 1910 to that of 1890 in the temporary quota provisions of
the act of 1924 was an attempt not only to reduce the amount
of immigration, but also to favor the old immigrant stock still

more. There were several surprises, however, when the quotas on the national origins basis were finally announced, for certain north European countries whose immigrants were considered most desirable had their allotments seriously curtailed, to the advantage of England in particular. Germany, for example, dropped from 51,000 to 25,000, Norway from 6,000 to 2,000, Sweden from 9,000 to 3,000, while Italy, Austria, Belgium, Yugoslavia and several others gained, although not tremendously, much to the surprise of those who were confident that before the influx of the new immigrant toward the end of the nineteenth century this country had been almost exclusively "Nordic."

There is undoubted justification for limiting the number of immigrants who may be admitted to the United States, but, as will be suggested later, it might be well to make that limit flexible instead of a flat figure based on population percentages or at an arbitrary figure like 150,000. There is also some justification for awarding larger quotas to countries whose cultures more nearly approximate our own than others. To some extent both the 1890 census base and the national origins provision serve this purpose. It is, for example, easier for us to "digest" socially immigrants from England and Germany than those from south European nations, and the quotas in the last two columns of the table are somewhat in accord with this fact.

We have now rapidly surveyed the outstanding laws by which the United States restricts European immigration, and thereby demonstrates its acceptance of the theory that the easiest way to prevent conflict with minorities is by keeping them from contact with her citizens. There are, of course, other motives involved in this legislation, such as the prevention of overpopulation, unemployment, disease, radicalism, and so on, but these objectives might all be attempted through other programs of a quite different nature. The essence of our immigration policy during and since the last quarter of the nineteenth century has been segregation. How well this policy has been achieved can be discovered only through an analysis of the laws themselves and of their enforcement.

IMMIGRATION LAW ENFORCEMENT

Efficient enforcement of the present immigration laws of the United States is impossible. This is true in spite of the fact that public opinion is convinced of the need for rigid immigration restriction and deportation legislation. Ordinarily it is an easy matter to secure a reasonably strict enforcement of legislation which is so fully in accord with popular sentiment as our immigration laws seem to be. Where dissenting voices are so loud and so frequent as they are in opposition to the Volstead Act, common disregard for the law is to be expected. The immigrant problem, however, appears to be different, in that the law is popularly approved yet not enforced.[7]

This non-enforcement is in large measure due to exceptional circumstances found in the United States rather than to neglect or inefficiency on the part of the Immigration Service. While it is not within our province to comment on such a technical question as the efficiency of the personnel of this service, it seems proper to say that the immigration officials have done their work remarkably well when their financial, geographical, legal, and other handicaps are considered. These handicaps will become apparent as our discussion proceeds.

The most obvious problems of enforcement of any set of immigration laws in the United States should be mentioned, but require no discussion. They include the following:

(1) The thousands of miles of United States boundaries, varying in character from swamp seacoast to arid desert wastes.

(2) The opportunities for the maintenance of a high standard of living in the United States, which naturally attracts multitudes from foreign congested areas.

(3) The millions of aliens already in the United States, who by their presence make it difficult to apprehend the illegal foreign resident.

---

[7] The following discussion of the effectiveness of immigration legislation is reprinted, with adaptations, by permission of the publishers, from the author's article on "Immigration Law Enforcement," *The Scientific Monthly*, May, 1927, vol. xxiv, pp. 439-447.

(4) The immense areas of our cities and country districts which afford security to hunted aliens.

(5) The necessity for the United States to do the pioneer work in the field of immigration legislation. No other country has had our problems, although many of the newer lands, such as Australia, Brazil, Canada, and South Africa, are beginning to meet them on a smaller scale. They have the advantage, however, of being able to look to our experiments for advice, and have apparently done so.

Such handicaps as these are no one's fault, and cannot be avoided. An examination of the legislation itself, previously sketched in brief outline, may show defects or omissions in some measure avoidable. We shall begin our examination by an analysis of the admissibility requirements established by Congress for prospective immigrants.

Certain prospective immigrants are considered undesirable because of (a) race or nationality, (b) individual defects of mind or body, (c) personal ideals and conduct, or (d) unfavorable economic or social conditions in the United States. Resident aliens may also be deported for reasons of the first three types mentioned, but not for the fourth. It may be that a share of the enforcement difficulties encountered by our immigration officials lies in the nature of the undesirability tests legally provided.

From the most ancient recorded times it has been the accepted practice to judge the merits of an individual by the color of his skin, the shape of his nose, the clothes he wears or even the language he speaks. Foreign characteristics, cultural or biological, apparently significant or obviously unimportant, have been sufficient to classify a man as necessarily inferior. "Barbarian" and "Gentile" were rarely intended as terms of praise. This state of mind is as common today as ever. Certainly our immigration legislation evidences its wide acceptance by the "barred zone" exclusion of Orientals in 1917, the "aliens ineligible to citizenship" provision of 1924, and the veiled discrimination of the quota bases of the same act, favoring aliens of the "old stock."

This attitude of racial discrimination was one of the first

important causes of modern immigration law violations, and it is becoming increasingly important as our national pride develops and is written into our alien legislation. Beginning with our timid Chinese exclusion act of 1882, growing more bold with its continuation during the next quarter century and with the extension of the principle of racial exclusion in the Gentleman's Agreement in 1907, the "barred zone" provision of 1917, and in the quota acts of 1921 and 1924, we now say quite frankly that we do not want any oriental immigrants and only a few of the "new" immigrant stock. We have with growing assurance asserted a belief in our own superiority. As each additional "race" has been put on the undesired list, thousands of its members have attempted to smuggle themselves across our borders, and with no little success.

Part of the difficulty here lies in the inability of the "inferior" excluded and restricted peoples to appreciate our point of view. Why should Italians be restricted while Mexicans are allowed in, almost without limit? Why should the Slav, with his centuries of glorious history, be less desired than the Irish? Why should Negroes from tropical America and from Africa, Filipinos and Porto Ricans be given a chance to gain admittance, but not Chinese, Japanese, and other Orientals, even though they be well educated and financially secure? As a result of such discriminations as these, the so-called "inferior races" feel no compunction about entering our country illegally, for they are sure that our law is founded upon an error, and while its violation may be a crime, as it legally is, it is to them no moral wrong. So long as they have an incentive to leave their native lands for ours, they will continue to run our borders. No adequate way has been devised to stop them, although millions of dollars have been spent in the attempt.

This is not to be misunderstood as an argument that all races and nationalities should be admitted in equal numbers or proportions. There may be biological reasons for their exclusion, but none have been scientifically established, in spite of the efforts of such students as Lothrop Stoddard, Madison Grant, William McDougall, and H. H. Laughlin.

Undoubtedly there are social reasons why the restricted and excluded peoples should be kept out of the country, at least to some extent. As a whole they are culturally more difficult to absorb than the more favored north Europeans. Try as we will, however, unless we are willing to spend untold millions on the development of our embryonic Border Patrol we shall continue unable to apprehend more than a mere tithe of those who attempt entry by evading the inspection which would instantly list them as members of undesired groups.

Individual defects of mind or body, like racial characteristics, are relatively easily observable by inspectors at ports of entry. During the fiscal year which ended June 30, 1930, about 241,000 immigrant aliens and 204,000 non-immigrant aliens were admitted. During the same period some 8,000 aliens were denied admission. The surprising fact is that only a relatively small number of these refusals were based on the more serious physical and psychological defects of the applicants.[8]

Twenty-nine were barred because of mental defect; one hundred and two because of "loathsome or dangerous contagious disease." In view of the fact that there are frequent charges that immigrants are a menace to our native stock, such a report of the Commissioner General of Immigration requires explanation.

The small number of refusals directly charged to disease and other individual defects is partly attributable to the fact

---

[8] All statistics of immigration in this chapter are taken from the *Annual Report of the Commissioner General of Immigration* for the year mentioned.

In spite of the fact that the deportation figures cited later in this section are for the fiscal year 1931, the detailed statistics of incoming immigrants are not used for this year in the discussion of immigration legislation, although they are readily available. This is because the number of alien immigrants admitted in 1931 fell below 100,000 for the first time since the Civil War, and the number of departures exceeded the arrivals of the immigrant class. While this unusual situation may be traced directly to unfavorable economic conditions in the United States, the somewhat arbitrary policy of refusing immigrant visas because of the oversupply of labor already in the United States so interfered with what might be called the natural trend in immigration that there would be little profit in their analysis here.

that many inferior immigrants denied admission are hidden in such listings as "likely to become public charges," under which heading 252 were barred. Many thousands more of would-be immigrants were prevented from setting sail for the United States by the improved legislation and administration which now provides for foreign inspection at the major countries of origin by immigration inspectors, government medical men, and steamship examiners, and directs our consuls to deny their visas to obviously ineligible applicants in all countries. "The effectiveness of the system of preexamining abroad of intending alien applicants, with the assistance of experienced immigrant inspectors serving as technical advisers to American consuls, continues to be reflected in the percentage of rejections at the seaports. In the past year [1930] less than six-tenths of 1 per cent of the applicants presenting themselves at seaports were rejected, or 1,853 out of 348,036, or about 53 in each 10,000."[9] Others, knowing our standards for admission, do not attempt to pass inspection. For these reasons it is difficult accurately to estimate the number of defective and diseased aliens kept from entering our territory.

While such healthy effects of our immigration legislation are to be desired, there is nevertheless one important unsought result, and that is the increased pressure of smugglers on our borders. We have through wise restrictions on diseased and defective aliens added a large group of potential border runners to those already mentioned in the discussion of the debarred peoples. This is not an argument for the abolition of physical qualifications for admission, but merely the statement of an evil which necessarily follows their application and makes our immigration restrictions harder to enforce.

Personal ideals and conduct may also furnish us with standards for the exclusion and deportation of unwanted aliens. A matter of taste, however, becomes involved when we do not want an alien because he believes in anarchism, or polygamy, or has been divorced for adultery or convicted of a crime in-

[9] *Annual Report of the Commissioner General of Immigration for 1930,* pp. 11-12.

volving "moral turpitude." One might well consider the impossibility of obtaining an accurate definition which would enable an immigration inspector to determine which immigrants were "anarchists, or aliens entertaining or affiliated with an organization advocating anarchistic beliefs," and therefore subject to exclusion. "Moral turpitude" is a vague term over which officials may well squabble. Adultery, a belief in polygamy, prostitution and immoral intent are certainly hard to detect, as are several other types of technicalities barring individuals. It may safely be said that any admittance test which amounts to nothing more than a question of personal opinion or the admission of or conviction for an "immoral" act, cannot be enforced except in isolated instances. This is well demonstrated in the annual reports of the Commissioner General of Immigration since such provisions have been in effect.

During the year under discussion, forty criminals and thirteen belonging to the "immoral classes" were barred. To shift for the moment to the fiscal year 1925, solely because the figures are more readily available and not because there is any likelihood that they vary much from those which might be found for 1930, we find two anarchists, eleven vagrants, two professional beggars, and two paupers listed as having been refused admission. In both 1925 and 1930 about 450,000 aliens were admitted, and those listed above as belonging to the undesirable classes mentioned were all who could be barred at the ports of entry! The countless pages of Congressional committee hearings and debates, all the public agitation against such dangerous people, have saved us from the attacks of this handful of the unwanted. Further explanation is required.

Obviously, the law is not being enforced, unless you are willing to assume that Europeans are not subject to the world's vices as are the citizens of our own country. Of course the figures quoted do not state the case quite fairly. Many individuals have been deterred from applying for admission by the knowledge of our restrictive laws, as was the case in regard to mental and physical requirements. Our foreign consuls have stopped others. Possibly a few other causes of exclusion should be added to those already mentioned to make it complete, as, for example, "chronic alcoholism," which in 1925 kept eight aliens from our shores. Reason tells us, however, and so does the Immigration Service, that not all of the scant half million who entered could have obtained admission honestly.

Social and economic conditions in the United States which may be unfavorable for the admission of immigrants are given slight consideration in the law itself. Immigrants are, on the whole, admitted in bunches, so many of such nationality in a certain period of time, according to the law. A closer correlation between conditions in the United States and the number and types of immigrants might well make our laws more enforceable and more just to aliens and citizens alike, but so little experimental work in this field has been done that we can do no more than express a hope.

As a result of the economic depression which began in the fall of 1929, our Immigration Service and the Department of State have cooperated in so twisting an old law that they have been able to restrict the number of immigrants admitted during a period of great unemployment in the United States. The nineteenth-century law refusing admission to "aliens likely to become public charges" was intended by its makers to apply to aliens who, because of some quality of their own, might be unable to support themselves if admitted. In spite of this intention, and no doubt wisely so, our consuls, acting under State Department orders, have been refusing visas to immigrants who could not show that they would be able to keep out of public institutions and care if admitted during the depression. This policy has been applied to non-quota as well as to quota countries. It has, for example, been applied rigorously to Mexican potential immigrants. In effect, the administrative branch of our government has exercised legislative powers in its unintended interpretation of this law. It would seem safer for Congress to provide the remedy.

Let us now assume for the sake of argument only that the legally established tests for admissible immigrants are the best which can at present be devised, and that prospective immigrants are being subjected to them with discrimination. Granting such to be the case, loopholes for illegal entry would still be plentiful in the many exceptions which permit aliens to land in excess of quotas and in some cases after superficial examination.

Alien seamen, for illustration, have been allowed to land for sixty days for the purpose of reshipping for foreign shores. When these seamen decide that their occupational preference lies in the coal fields of Pennsylvania, the mills of Birmingham, or the wheat fields of the Middle West, it becomes a difficult and expensive task to obtain their deportation. It is estimated that 38,000 alien seamen deserted their ships in United States ports during the fiscal year 1924, and about 20,000 during 1925. During 1928 there were 12,000 recorded desertions, declining in 1929 to 11,000, to 9,000 in 1930, and to 3,341 in 1931. when economic conditions in the United States were least attractive. Many of these have of course left the country. How many we do not know, nor is there any way of finding out. This one loophole in our legislation, however, is considered of such importance by Congress that during 1924 and 1925 over five hundred pages of testimony were taken by House and Senate committees dealing with this problem alone, and no practical means for stopping the leak was disclosed.

For a second illustration of the loopholes in immigration legislation we may turn to the Quota Act of 1924, which, be it good or bad in principle, has as its main purpose the limitation of the number and a qualitative selection of industrial and agricultural workers who may become more or less permanent residents of our country. This purpose is in part defeated by important special exemptions from the normal quota provisions.

It has been indicated that about 450,000 aliens were admitted during the fiscal year 1930. Of this number, 241,000 were listed as immigrants, 141,000 of whom were charged to the various quotas and 100,000 admitted as non-quota immigrants. The remaining 204,000 admitted were "non-immigrant aliens." These non-immigrants included temporary visitors for business or pleasure, aliens in continuous transit through the United States, ministers of religious denominations, and students.

Such groups present tremendous problems to our enforcement officers, problems which have not been solved and will not be solved except through an increase in governmental employees and expenditures. University officials will tell you that they must constantly be on their guard in admitting foreign students in order to avoid serving as aids in violating immigration restrictions. Europeans have heard the call to religious work just as they made up their minds to emigrate to America. A pleasure trip has many definitions. It is not impossible for an alien to change his status from one of the above groups to a group in the limited class. The job, then, is to catch and deport him.

The deportation of undesired aliens after they have entered our land is even more difficult than their rejection at the port of arrival. Commissioner-General Hull stated in his report for 1925 that "The experience of the fiscal year just closed has demonstrated the accuracy of the statement made a year ago that the deportation of aliens found to be unlawfully in the United States is rapidly becoming one of the most important functions of the Immigration service." Of the 7,233,595 unnaturalized aliens found in the United States by the census of 1920, possibly 20 per cent were here illegally, according to the same report. In 1921, the number of aliens deported was 4,517; in 1925, 9,495; in 1930, 16,631; in 1931, 18,142. That there are tens of thousands more remaining illegally is admitted by the Immigration Service and by the legislators who drafted the acts now in force, and this fact is accepted by them as a matter of course.

Many of the illegal residents are such because of their illegal entry. They have sneaked across the border, entered as seamen, or passed inspection falsely. Most of them cannot now be located except by some such radical measure as a complete alien registration. Our immigration officials and the Secretary of Labor have from time to time suggested the advisability of such a registration as the only way out of a difficult situation. However, if these aliens have escaped our boundary guards, how much more tedious and expensive will it be to detect them in our cities and on our farms?

Other aliens have rendered themselves obnoxious while legal residents in the United States. Certain criminals, political radicals, paupers, prostitutes, and other immoral aliens are legally but not always actually deportable. Whatever the merits of such reasons for deportation, adequate enforcement measures have not been provided. For example, 2,719 aliens were deported in 1931 as belonging to the criminal and immoral classes: eighteen of them apparently as anarchists, 856 became criminals after entry, 917 were criminals at time of entry, 335 became prostitutes or inmates of houses of prostitution after entry, and so on. Five hundred and seventy-eight became public charges from causes existing prior to entry. Three hundred and seventy-four were mentally or physically defective at time of entry. The remainder of the deportees, about 14,500 in number, were deported for reasons listed as "miscellaneous classes" in the Commissioner General's report. Most of these miscellaneous classes were aliens who had not complied with the technicalities of the law, including those who did not have proper visas, who did not leave the country after the expiration of a temporary permit to enter, who failed to pass the literacy test, etc. Again, either our aliens are surprisingly well behaved or the law is not being enforced.

According to Dr. H. H. Laughlin, a powerful supporter of our present laws, "Of course, the present law contemplated keeping out of the United States all aliens who are likely to become public charges, but there are so many loopholes in the administration of the law that when one makes a first-hand investigation of the custodial institutions of the country he finds many aliens in them in violation of the purpose of our immigration laws, particularly of the act of 1917.

"For example, during our survey of 1922 we found in 445 of the larger custodial state institutions in the United States approximately 44,587 foreign-born white persons who entered the United States in violation of the spirit of the law. The reasons they have not been deported are, first, some have been in the United States longer than five years and consequently they are not deportable under the present law; second, many of these state custodial institutions, of which there are approximately 700 in the United States, do not feel that it is incumbent upon them to take the initiative in deporting deportable persons."[10]

Dr. Laughlin might have added other reasons of practical administration which make it probable that only a few of our present deportables ever will be deported. A simple list of such reasons would be as follows:

(1) Unwillingness of local agencies to cooperate in the enforcement of a national law.

(2) The vague legal definition of several causes for deportation, such as the provision for the expulsion of certain political radicals.

(3) The administrative difficulties of the task of locating, convicting, and expelling offenders.

(4) The expense of the process.

(5) The necessity for obtaining passports, which may be refused or reluctantly given in deportation cases by such countries as Russia, Turkey, Poland, Germany, and England. Arrested individuals may also withhold information essential to the securing of a passport, although government records containing this information are available for those entering in recent years.

(6) The inevitable opposition of public opinion if the law were carried out to the letter.

It is consequently not unfair to say that our deportation legislation has been so designed that it could not be justly enforced in regard to even a fair percentage of our illegal residents. On the contrary, it is subject to grave misuse, as are all such blanket laws, for purposes of persecution and political advancement, as was so commonly charged during the régime of a former Attorney-General with presidential aspirations. However, in view of the general postwar 100-per-cent Ameri-

[10] *Proposed Deportation Legislation.* U. S., House of Representatives, Hearings before the Committee on Immigration and Naturalization, 68:2, December, 1924. Serial 1B, p. 55.

canism agitation, supported and kept alive by numerous active and powerful patriotic propagandist organizations, such as the American Legion, the Daughters of the American Revolution, the Ku Klux Klan, etc., there is little likelihood of any real change in the near future.[11]

It is thus evident that whatever benefits have resulted from our immigration and deportation laws—and there have been important benefits therefrom—there are nevertheless unjustifiable violations in spirit and letter which are all too frequent (although unavoidable by the nature of the situation) which permit thousands of aliens illegally to enter and illegally to remain in the United States. We must turn to a consideration of the means for amelioration of present conditions. Three major suggestions can be made. They are the usual ones offered for the repair of any system of laws which does not function smoothly.

First, we may rely on more, and more stringent, laws, and an enforcing staff increased in numbers and efficiency. This is the plan which now seems to be in favor with our lawmakers, our Immigration Service, and the public. It is usually the first and most obvious proposal. A casual reading of Senate and House committee hearings demonstrates the frantic search for laws without loopholes. The Immigration Service is asking for more men and money. A Border Patrol has recently been established to supplement the regular immigration inspection staff, and is doing good work, but since its very beginning it has been insisting that it cannot do efficient work without additional funds. More immigration inspectors are constantly being requested for our ports and for deportation proceedings. Deportable aliens have admittedly been allowed to remain because money was not available to pay their passage out of the country. There is no end to these requests

[11] For detailed discussion of the deportation laws of the United States, see Constantine M. Panunzio, *The Deportation Cases of 1919-1920*, Federal Council of Churches of Christ in America, Commission on the Church and Social Service, 105 East 22nd Street, New York, 1921, 104 pp.; Jane Perry Clark, *Deportation of Aliens from the United States to Europe*, Columbia University Press, New York, 1931, 524 pp.; National Commission on Law Observance and Enforcement, *The Administration of the Deportation Laws of the United States*, Government Printing Office, Washington, D. C., 1931, 179 pp.

in sight. If there were, we might feel inclined to grant the wishes of the proponents of this plan. Meanwhile, it might be well to think of the effects of a policy which is resulting in separate national police systems to enforce each separate set of national laws.

Second, there is the possibility of adapting our immigration laws to actualities rather than to pseudo-scientific race theories. This could be done by excluding, admitting and deporting aliens in accordance with their individual qualities, scientifically determined, and with proper regard for the industrial and social capacities of our country. Such scientific tests would supersede our present regulations, which are in part—a rather large part—based on the application of undemonstrated racial and social myths. It is interesting to note that no recognized leading anthropologist, biologist, psychologist, or social scientist was called to testify before our Congressional committees in the hearings prior to the adoption of our present major laws. Most of the testimony taken was given by people who, regardless of their scientific or practical qualifications, were unquestionably biased. There is little reason to wonder why our laws are not functioning.

Third, a policy of "hands off" has many advocates who believe in it not only for sentimental reasons, but also because they are convinced that natural laws of population alone can solve such problems. As an immediate program this seems inadvisable, if only for social reasons. There is no likelihood of its adoption, for its adherents are today relatively few. We should dismiss it from consideration and confine our efforts for immediate improvement to the first two suggestions. However, it may be well to remember the possibility that the ultimate solution to our immigration problems may be based on the idea of natural population laws, as the advocates of a "hands off" policy stoutly maintain.

After all, people do not migrate between countries having equal ratios of resources to population in large numbers, and in view of the rapid expansion of the United States since the Civil War, it may not be so many years, historically considered, before the motive which is causing these hundreds of thousands of aliens to press upon our shores will disappear. For the present, we must guard against the relatively temporary troubles which necessarily accompany periods of population adjustment.

Science, not race prejudice, not one-hundred-per-cent Americanism, not economic selfishness, not religious bigotry, not even pseudo-science, must furnish that temporary guard. A few flexible protective measures which are in accord with modern knowledge of race and race relations can now be recommended in general terms. They have, it is believed, the merits of the scientific method and of an elasticity which permits adjustment of changing conditions. They will not stop all immigration law violations, for smuggling, at least, will continue, regardless of the scientific or unscientific nature of our legislation, as long as residents of other countries have any incentive to come to ours. Improvement should nevertheless result from the adoption of the following recommendations:

First, eliminate the impossible mental and moral desirability tests from the present legislation. As a substitute for the present scatter-shot method, it is suggested that broad powers to exclude or deport objectionable aliens be given to responsible officials who will act on individual cases rather than blindly follow blanket laws.

Second, immigrants should be selected on their individual merits rather than on a racial or national basis.

Third, the quantity and quality of immigrants admitted should be limited by the economic and social needs of the United States, determined from year to year by a fact-finding commission.

Fourth, adequate supervision of resident aliens should be maintained through the cooperation of the federal government with existing public and private agencies, such as hospitals, jails, courts, police, schools, philanthropic associations, and the like. In view of the multitude of existing social facilities which could be utilized in alien supervision with but little annoyance to the agencies or to the foreign element, it seems worse than useless to establish a cumbersome national immigrant registration system.

Fifth, a governmental program for the social assimilation of the immigrant is badly needed. It could be developed as a part of our fourth recommendation.

These recommendations find little opposition among students of race and population problems, and could be of great value in a program for immigration law enforcement. Their enactment, however, will be impossible until the scientific facts on which they are based are known to more than a handful of specializing students. In proportion as they are made increasingly scientific, we may expect exclusion, restriction, and deportation immigration legislation to be effective elements in a complete program for the adjustment of racial and nationality minority group relations. They are all a form of segregation, looking for peace through separation, but may be none the less useful on that account.

THE LEGAL SEGREGATION OF COLORED MINORITIES

There has been practically no agitation against the admission of as many Canadian immigrants as have applied, perhaps because their competition has not been realized outside of a few border cities even in times of depression, on account of the ease with which they disappear in the native white population. This friendly attitude has been a factor in our persistence in refusing to exclude Mexican and other tropical American aliens, of whom the Mexican immigrants alone far outnumber the Canadians, the other Latin American immigrants being few in number. Unless we were willing seriously to affront all Latin America, and Mexico in particular, it would not be wise to permit Canada to be the only non-quota country in this hemisphere, or Mexico the only quota country.

Estimates vary as to the number of Mexicans who have been in the United States in recent years. The census for 1930 lists 1,422,533 persons, or 1.2 per cent, of our total population as Mexican, not including 65,968 persons of Mexican birth or parentage who were returned as white. The census definition of a Mexican includes "all persons born in Mexico, or having parents born in Mexico, who are not definitely white, Negro, Indian, Chinese, or Japanese." In previous census counts, Mexicans were included with the white population, so that we have only estimates as to the number of non-white Mexicans in the United States in previous years. The census estimate for 1920 placed this number at 700,541, or 0.7 per cent of the total population. Estimates based on the surplus of entries over departures since 1919 indicate that the total Mexican population of the United States in 1926 was 890,746. Illegal entry, not difficult from Mexico, complicates any estimate of the high point between 1920 and 1930, especially since a good share of Mexican immigrants have been temporary immigrants, crossing and recrossing the border with only short intervals between, with the economic conditions in the United States in the last census year, 1930, at such a low ebb that the attraction of the country for immigrants was probably much less than it had been during the previous four or five years.[12]

Whatever the greatest number may actually have been— and it is not likely that we shall ever know accurately—it was certainly enough to attract the unfavorable attention of citizens of the United States who, unlike many agricultural and some industrial employers who profited by cheap labor, saw only the social maladjustment produced by this form of competition and the clash of cultures resulting from their entry. The prompt and insistent suggestion of the majority of natives who have realized the extent and potentialities of the antagonisms against these new arrivals has been to settle it all by quota or even more stringent restrictive legislation— a suggestion which has not yet been found acceptable by Congress.

The Chinese, like all other immigrant groups, were at first

[12] For discussions of statistics of Mexican immigration, see Manuel Gamio, *Mexican Immigration to the United States,* University of Chicago Press, Chicago, 1930, chap. i, and *The Mexican Immigrant,* University of Chicago Press, Chicago, 1930, pp. xvii + 262; Paul S. Taylor, *Mexican Labor in the United States,* University of California Press, Berkeley, 1929, *University of California Publications in Economics,* vol. vi, no. 3, pp. 237-255.

gladly received and encouraged by governmental legislation. The Burlingame Treaty of 1868 between China and the United States gave reciprocal rights of free migration to the nationals of both countries, although the Chinese were specifically denied the right of naturalization. There had been agitation on the west coast for their exclusion before this time, but it was not until about a decade later that the government began to recognize the Californians' arguments and to seek a way to modify this treaty. In 1880 a new treaty was negotiated by which China conceded the right of the United States to "regulate, limit, or suspend" the immigration of Chinese laborers into this country. In 1882 the first Chinese "exclusion law" was enacted, suspending the immigration of Chinese laborers for a period of ten years, after a previous enactment had been vetoed by the President because, in fixing the term of suspension at twenty years, in his opinion it violated the terms of the treaty of 1880. This law, with many modifications, generally in the direction of greater stringency, was in effect reenacted in 1892 for another ten-year period, and again in 1902, indefinitely. The Immigration Act of 1917 by its "barred zone" provision excluded Chinese immigrants and most other Asiatics except the Japanese, who were at that time restricted by the Gentleman's Agreement.

While the Chinese began coming to the United States in appreciable numbers early in the 1850's, the Japanese were of little importance to us as immigrants until about 1898. The Californians and their neighbors promptly saw in this new source of immigration a danger similar to that which they had just escaped through recently enacted exclusionist legislation, won only after a hard battle against the indifference of the people of states to which Chinese migrated in small numbers or not at all. The fight for Japanese exclusion was immediately begun, and by 1907 the Gentleman's Agreement was secured.

This agreement, with a legal status in considerable dispute, was a promise by President Roosevelt that the United States would refrain from passing exclusionist legislation against the Japanese in exchange for the promise of the Japanese authorities that they would issue no passports to laborers wishing to emigrate to the United States. Precipitated by the action of the San Francisco school board in its attempt to segregate Japanese children in the public schools of that city, and a compromise from the beginning, it was never popular with the Pacific coast states.

Charges of bad faith in the administration of the agreement were leveled against Japan. The issuance of passports to picture brides, to adopted children, to laborers bound for nearby countries who later slipped across our borders, to "farmers" who were supposed to be really farm laborers, was cited as evidence of the tricky evasion of the spirit of the agreement by the Japanese government. Although picture brides were not barred by the agreement, which permitted wives and children of Japanese domiciled in the United States to be given passports, the practice was stopped shortly after the World War, and passports were also refused adopted children. The Japanese, in further effort to prevent exclusionist legislation, adopted the definition of laborer devised by the United States Department of Labor. It also curtailed passports to emigrants destined to adjoining countries. The charge that the Japanese in the United States were evading the spirit of the agreement by a high birth rate, or, as it has been facetiously put, by "immigration from heaven," shows that no matter what Japan did to prove good faith—and she had every reason to act in good faith in order to save the agreement, in view of the resentment which her citizens must have shown against any government which through blundering led to exclusionist legislation—nothing short of absolute refusal to admit any Japanese immigrants could satisfy the Californians.

The final break came in 1924, during the consideration of the general immigration act of that year by Congress. In answer to rumors that the Gentleman's Agreement was to be abrogated and that Japan was not to be given a quota similar to those awarded European countries, Ambassador Hanihara at Washington dispatched a note to Secretary of State Charles E. Hughes protesting against any such possible discrimination. This note, as intended, was sent to Congress and was printed in the *Congressional Record*. It received no attention in the Senate debates until three days later, on April 14, when attention was called to the statement in it that immigration discrimination against the Japanese would be followed by "grave consequences." It seems that in diplomatic correspondence the term "grave consequences" implies a threat of war. This was too much for the Senators to take from an oriental nation, and they promptly put into the act the provision that "aliens ineligible to citizenship" were barred as immigrants. This was done in spite of the fact that as soon as Ambassador Hanihara heard of this interpretation of his note he apologized and explained that such was not his meaning.

It is inconceivable that he intended a threat of war. He had been ambassador to the United States too long to think that such a threat, which Japan was unprepared to carry out, could frighten the Senate into more liberal treatment of Japanese immigrants, or have any other effect than arouse an indignant, unfavorable response.

Had Japan been put on a quota basis similar to that voted European nations, the United States would have gained in good will, not to be lightly disregarded in our relations with a nation situated as is Japan, and in valuable, friendly diplomatic and commercial favors. As it turned out, we lost irretrievably by this gratuitous insult to a friendly nation, all to save the face of our sensitive Senators, who fearlessly showed their defiance of threats and gained votes, in order to save the population of the United States from the danger to racial purity and social disintegration which would have followed the admission of the less than 200 Japanese immigrants who might have been admitted on a quota basis. There is a trace of national adolescence in the action.

Again we have the segregation solution to minority problems. This act, of course, applied to the Chinese and other Orientals, including those of India, already barred under the act of 1917, as well as the Japanese. Shortly after the Californians, afraid of being swamped by the Chinese, had their fears allayed by the Exclusion Act of 1882, the Japanese began arriving in appreciable numbers, and then, when California's safety had been again assured by the law of 1924, the Filipinos arrived on the scene.

According to the census of 1920 there were only 5,603 Filipinos in the United States in that year. As an indication of how difficult it is to estimate the size of any population element, it may be mentioned that "guesses" as to their number in 1930 and the year or two just before, ranged from 25,000 to 80,000. It is not without point that the smallest guess was that of a Filipino organization, while the largest was that of a labor organization. The most careful estimate of all, that of Bruno Lasker, put the number at 56,000.[13] When the actual census tabulations for 1930 appeared, the number turned out to be 45,208.

There have been anti-Filipino riots, and white people have complained against the unfair competition of these new oriental arrivals who work hard sometimes for smaller wages than the standard rate allows. Instead of attempting to work out a program for the adjustment of those already here and aiming at restrictive legislation which would select a reasonable number for admission, the cry from those who do not profit from their labor and fear their competition has been, "Keep them out!" Segregation is again suggested as the solution, but in this case it is not so easy of accomplishment as it was in the case of the Chinese, Japanese, and other Orientals. While not citizens of the United States, Filipinos come from islands in the possession of and governed by the United States. Consequently they are not excluded by the clause in the act of 1924 referring to "aliens ineligible to citizenship," for they are not aliens. There is apparently no legal reason why the natives of any islands under the jurisdiction of the United States who have not been granted citizenship may not be excluded. Legality, however, is not the only question to be considered, for there are practical considerations in the way of the exclusion or severe restriction of Filipino immigration

[13] Bruno Lasker, *Filipino Immigration*, University of Chicago Press, Chicago, 1931, p. 21.

while the Islands are still demanding their independence and other nations have their eyes hungrily fixed on these outlying possessions of ours. The feeling has gone so far that many people, especially workers and their representatives, are willing to sacrifice the Philippines by granting them their independence if that is the only way of preventing even two or three hundred thousand from migrating to the United States.

We think today of the segregation of Negroes as something apart from that accomplished by immigration barriers, as more of a local matter to be accomplished by ordinances, state laws, and the heavy hand of the white man. Yet one of the compromises of our Constitution made possible a Negro immigration barrier, for it permitted legislation against the slave trade after 1807. The slaves, of course, were involuntary immigrants, but immigrants nevertheless, and since Africans have never shown any enthusiasm for voluntary emigration to the United States this provision was as effective a bar to the further introduction of Negroes as though it had prohibited the admission of freeman and slave alike.

Before the slave trade was prohibited by the federal government, individual states in the south, late in the eighteenth century, prohibited the importation of additional slaves. The slave trade was prohibited because of a variety of reasons ranging from pure humanitarianism to hard cash motives, but there can be no doubt but that prominent among them was the fear of the black competitor and a dread of the ultimate cost of his introduction to the nation. It may be recalled that Massachusetts, New York, and California, to say nothing of the colonies before the formation of the United States, also took matters into their own hands and attempted to restrict their population increase by laws prohibiting the admission of unwanted Europeans and, in the case of California, Orientals, some time before the federal government gave relief.

Legal attempts to segregate the Negro, however, have gone further than the refusal to permit more of them to enter the United States. More than in the case of any other group, legal efforts have been made to continue to keep the white man and the Negro apart as much as possible long after his admission to the country. These laws have required separate education, separate transportation, separate recreation, separate public conveniences, such as hotels and restaurants, and separate residential areas.

"Between 1881 and 1907 all the Southern states enacted laws separating the races on railroad cars, street cars and schools, laws excluding Negroes from jury service and the primaries, while the Northern states were enacting Civil Rights Bills. On the wild wave of the poor white's coming to power, few voices dared to be raised in protest. Coming to power meant coming into political office and the redoubling of the fear of losing this power through colored adherents to the opposing party. There were evasions of the amendments, intimidations, circumventing procedure, and movement toward a codification of the new common law, a fixing of those complaints of Negroes which are heard to the very present. Legislation was enacted which aimed at securing for themselves an economic advantage which the old system had denied them."[14]

Intermarriage was prohibited. Political privileges were restricted. Negroes were prevented from entering some occupations reserved for white people on occasion by law, usually devious in nature; but generally custom and tacit understanding were sufficient to secure this kind of segregation without supporting legislation. Wherever possible, we shall discuss the specific types of segregation in the chapters dealing with the activities involved. Segregated education is included in the discussion of the schools, recreational segregation in the chapter on the use of leisure time, and so forth. Some of the more general phases of segregation legislation may be included here, but with the mental note that most segregation, as enforced on any minority, is accomplished without the necessity for being bolstered by legislation, which, after all, can do no more than give formal authority for a course of action already popularly accepted.

With few exceptions, there is nothing in the federal Constitution, including the Civil War Amendments, contrary to those

[14] Charles S. Johnson, op. cit., pp. 13-14.

types of legal segregation just mentioned, provided the matter is a local one properly subject to state regulation. Interstate commerce, of course, is reserved for federal legislation. "Due process of law" must be observed. Theoretically, "equal facilities," as in education, must be provided. For us, these national safeguards of the rights of minorities have little significance, for whenever a reasonably self-sufficient community or political unit wishes to nullify them, it can do so, frequently by law and always by common consent.

Consider for a moment the legal history of residential segregation. Law after law has been discarded as unconstitutional by state and federal courts. For years it was thought that there was no legal way of keeping Negroes from leasing or owning property in white districts. Within the past decade it has been established, however, by decision of the Supreme Court, that it is easily possible, so far as national provision against racial discrimination is concerned, to make use of the right of private contract to accomplish the same purpose. Thus, if it is not contrary to state law, an agreement may be entered into between property owners binding them not to allow their property to be used by Negroes, Jews, Italians, Swedes, or, I suppose, red-headed, blue-eyed people.

Let us assume that even this manner of insuring the racial integrity of a given district were made illegal. Would there be any pronounced difference in the distribution of racial and nationality minorities in the cities of the United States? Obviously not, for residential grouping, whether it be in "nigger districts," Chinatowns, Little Italies, Ghettos, or what not, has gone unconcernedly ahead not only where laws and ordinances have been temporarily illegally enforced, but also where they have been thrown out of court, and where the legislators have not even bothered their heads about the matter.

Of course, legislation could make the boundaries of these settlements more definite and rigid. It could, if permitted, prevent the instances where minorities break out of old settlements, sometimes to live alone surrounded by group strangers, sometimes to start new colonies of their own people. If this were rigidly prevented, majority property owners would be the first to fight against it, or at least to beg for exceptions. Except in absolutely static communities, where business is neither expanding nor contracting, where residential, industrial, trade, and other zones are fixed once and for all, any such severe restriction on the shifting of tenants and owners would cause enormous financial losses to majority property owners, whose property value and income are closely related to the free supply of buyers and renters. This is especially true during the transitional period when a given parcel of land is passing from one classification to another, say from a first-class private-home classification to one adapted to retail stores or perhaps apartment houses.

Legal segregation of despised and hated minorities already within the country has been tried in other parts of the world. The Russian government under the Tsars established segregated districts for Jews, most suggestive of similar orders regarding Negroes issued by southern states and municipalities. The Jew in Russia, however, could be legally forced to live within the pale, while the American Constitution forbids such official recognition of similar practices which are nevertheless unofficially accomplished in the United States.

In essence, the phenomena of residential segregation are economic rather than legal, social, or anything else. We can commend the program of the National Association for the Advancement of Colored People, and other Negro organizations and friends of minorities, who have for many years been giving generous assistance in the expensive process of legally attacking all forms of legislation which aim at the separation of minorities from the majority. They are as valuable, economically as well as otherwise, to the majority as to the minorities their purpose it is to defend. They are not, however, hitting at the foundation of the system, which rests on factors much more basic than laws, the secondary expressions of primary human purposes. Legal segregation of Negroes has been and must be a failure, an attempt to secure interracial peace which has fallen of its own weight, while some blindly continue to prop it up and others wastefully spend their efforts tearing it down, all oblivious of the fact that its own weaknesses cause it to crumble in a society where each person is dependent on the welfare and cooperation of the others.

Like the Negro, the Indian was already in the country before serious efforts could be made to keep him at a distance. Exclusion legislation was of no avail, and deportation was obviously out of the question. The Negro, however, was well scattered among the white people in the areas in which he lived. He had no tribal organization to hold his people together in groups with which governmental bargains could be made. The individual Negro could speak only for himself. Furthermore, he was economically so interwoven with the white man's activities and welfare as to be, in this respect at least, inseparable. The white man from the first was dependent on the Negro's efforts. Indian-white relationships, however, were on a different basis. Agreements could be reached with whole tribes who were economically independent of the white man, and from whom the white man expected to gain little but farm land and other natural resources. Racial friction between the Negro and the white man, and between the Indian and the white man, consequently could not be solved by identical segregation programs, although segregation was resorted to in both cases.

Early in the history of relations between the colonists and the Indians attempts were made to prevent racial disturbances by separating the two groups not only on a social but also on a geographical basis. While the prejudice against the Indian as a "racial inferior" handicapped him in earning his living, kept him from taking part in the political organizations which governed him, and "put him in his place" in other social affairs as well, these measures of discrimination were as a rule found inadequate to satisfy the white man's desire for racial purity and economic advantage. As a result, the reservation system was developed to segregate the Indian geographically, on the theory that interracial conflict could thus be avoided or minimized. The most important experiment of this sort was the attempt to isolate some forty distinct tribes in Indian Territory.

The main body of Indians thus isolated was made up of the so-called Five Civilized Tribes of the southeastern United States, namely, the Chickasaws, Cherokees, Choctaws, Creeks, and Seminoles. These tribes occupied large areas which they had acquired partly by purchase and partly by grants from the government, although title to a considerable portion was contested. The pressure of white population on these areas was increasingly heavy, largely because of the valuable agricultural and timber lands included. Some white discontent with Indian neighbors grew out of the sporadic racial disturbances which seemed impossible to avoid. The discovery of gold on Cherokee land in Georgia increased the white greed for the Indian lands, and the demands of this group became too strong to be resisted by the government. The suggestion of President Monroe in 1825 to move all Indians living east of the Mississippi to a region which is now part of Arkansas and Oklahoma, where the Choctaws had agreed by treaty to go in 1820, met with great favor, except among the Indians themselves. Consequently an enormous area was set aside in this region and the eastern Indians were sent to live there, many by military force against bitter opposition and under brutal conditions. For example, one-fourth of the Cherokees sent out under military escort died on the way. A considerable number had already moved out voluntarily in the hope of bettering their condition. A few were able to escape the westward drive and have left some scattered descendants in the east. Most of them went because they had to. By 1840 all the most important eastern Indian groups were moved into this area.

The Five Civilized Tribes were assured a perpetual right to govern themselves as "nations," and "a government within a government" was thus established. The tribes native to the region were eventually given areas in which they were to live, and others were brought in from places as widely scattered as Oregon, California, and Texas. It was a mixture of all kinds and sizes of Indian tribes, ranging from small groups of disorganized prisoners of war to the relatively advanced and powerful Cherokees. Innumerable degrees and varieties of cultures were represented. Little account was taken of tribal animosities, and in several instances old-time enemies found themselves compulsory neighbors. It was the task of these Indians to organize a government which would secure and maintain peace and prosperity.

A weak confederation of tribes was established, patterned in a fashion after the national and state governments of the east. Laws were developed and in some cases even printed, courts were established, elections were held, and the various functions of government were carried on after a manner. However, no real working government was ever secured—only the empty form of one which never functioned efficiently. Tribal habit and tradition prevailed.

It had been assumed that at least the Five Civilized Tribes were far enough advanced to maintain a republican form of government which would assure some semblance of law and order. This assumption was based on the erroneous belief that these tribes had for the most part abandoned their old habits and standards in favor of the "superior" European civilization of their white neighbors. Many were agriculturists or petty traders or artisans. Numerous well kept farms were owned by them. A fair proportion could speak English. Some had a little schooling. Practically all were living a relatively settled and peaceful life. Most of these Indians, however, had been agriculturists long before the advent of the Europeans, and their farms could therefore hardly be taken as evidence of the adoption of the white man's culture. They had been living fairly quiet lives with only occasional wars, each tribe in its own well defined territory, for generations. In other words, many of the conditions which the white man thought were evidences of cultural advance were only slight changes in long-established tribal customs. They were still tribally minded and their forced attempt to establish a representative and democratic form of government in Indian territory was necessarily a failure from the start. Conditions in their new home required a civil form of government, and no people can change suddenly from tribal to civil life without long years of preparation.

The attempt at isolation was also a failure. White people of all sorts rushed into the Indian reservations in a continuous stream. Many of these were welcomed by the Indians as business men, laborers, traders, missionaries, farmers, and bootleggers. No real attempt at white exclusion was made either by the United States or by the Indians. Crooks discovered here a real haven of refuge, for the United States courts had no jurisdiction over anyone in the Territory, and the Indian courts had none over offenses committed anywhere else and cared little what the white residents did among themselves. Thirty thousand white children in the Territory had no school facilities. Two hundred and fifty thousand white settlers had little or no government protection. Indian courts handed down decisions on the basis of tradition, and soon became notoriously impossible as courts of justice. During the Civil War the land was overrun by the armies of both the South and the North. Some of the Indians had been slave owners even before being moved west, and enlisted with the South, while others were opposed to slavery and fought for the North. After the war they were compelled to free their slaves and admit them to full and equal citizenship. Intermarriages between white, black, and red were common, and all races and degrees of mixture were admitted to tribal membership, with the result that tribal laws and customs broke down and failed to maintain their former influence for order and justice. Health and educational, legal, and industrial conditions became intolerable, and Congress finally decided to put an end to the impossible situation, regardless of their former solemn assurances that the Indians and their heirs could occupy and govern their lands in Indian Territory forever.

A commission was therefore established in 1893 during the administration of President Cleveland, known as the Commission to the Five Civilized Tribes, or the Dawes Commission, to negotiate with these tribes for the dissolution of the tribal governments and the allotment of their land to their individual members. No such agreements were completed until after the Curtis Act of 1898, which provided that if no terms could be agreed upon the Commission was to go ahead anyway

with the allotment of lands and the other work it was supposed to do in wiping out the Indian government. In 1889
United States courts had been established in the Territory.
The allotment which began in 1899 marked the end of the
experiment. Unoccupied territory near the center of the area
had already been opened to white settlers in 1889, and in 1890
the western part was made into the separate Territory of
Oklahoma. In 1907 all that remained of Indian Territory was
included in Oklahoma when that state was admitted into the
Union. Some of the land is still held in trust for Indians to
whom it has been allotted. A small amount of the land of the
forty-odd tribes is still unallotted, but is controlled by the
Indian Office rather than by the Indians. The attempt to
segregate the Indian geographically has been definitely abandoned.

There are still many reservations of various sizes ranging
from a few acres, like those of the California Indians, to the
enormous territory set aside for the Navajos. A few were
created as late atonements for early injustices; most are the
result of our established policy of buying peace by segregating
an "inferior race" on lands which it was thought would never
be wanted for any other purpose. These lands were usually in
out-of-the-way regions and frequently of doubtful value, but
time after time thousands of acres have been chopped off without the voluntary consent of the tribes for whom they had
been set aside. The white population increased faster than
was expected. Transportation improved, and the West was
opened to settlers. Unsuspected mineral and agricultural resources were discovered. White civilization moved on and the
Indian happened to be in the way. While almost all agreements with the Indian have been broken in some respect, there
is no doubt but that the agreements were impossible when
made. Neither the Indians nor the government foresaw or
could have foreseen the remarkable expansion which this country has undergone in the last century, an expansion which will
before long destroy every reservation, wherever located, as
a place where the Indian may continue to live his own life
in a segregated community.

CHAPTER VI

CITIZENSHIP WITH RESERVATIONS

A NEGRO born and reared in any place on earth may become a naturalized American citizen by complying with the same regulations as a European immigrant. Our courts are forbidden to issue naturalization papers to Chinese, Japanese, and other Orientals. Indians born in Canada have been refused the privilege of citizenship, although Mexicans, be they pure bloods of the same racial stock, have been made citizens on application as though they were white. The Ainu of Japan, biologically white, are in effect Orientals before the law. These are but a few of the capricious contrasts which may well bewilder the student of race relations if he allows himself to be misled by anthropological classifications which have no standing in the eyes of the law or by his false expectation that common prejudices always find recognition in the statute books.

Leaving out of account minor technicalities, any person born in the United States proper is automatically born into citizenship, regardless of his racial origin. "White persons" (since 1802) and "aliens of African nativity" and "persons of African descent" (since 1870) may be granted citizenship by our courts if they are properly qualified as individuals. Negroes were thus granted the naturalization privileges of white aliens after the Civil War as a part of the general movement to give them equal rights subsequent to the abolition of slavery; but it has been consistently held that peoples who are neither "white," in the more popular meaning of the term, nor African can achieve citizenship only by birth in this country under existing legislation. Our government can, of course, grant or refuse citizenship to anyone it pleases, and in the absence of permissive naturalization legislation definitely referring to the group to which an individual belongs, he will be refused citizenship regardless of his personal qualities.

There is no need for us to become bogged down in the morass of naturalization constitutional provisions, laws, treaties, and court decisions, which not even an experienced jurist may hope to cross without misstep. As students of group relations rather than of lawmakers' whims, it is for us to chart the guiding contours of the citizenship terrain which may lead us to an understanding of the relations of minorities to a government by an antagonistic majority, instead of wasting our time plotting out the details which take us nowhere except to court.[1]

EXPERIMENTS WITH INDIAN VOTES

The American Indian has received his citizenship in a greater diversity of ways than any other minority. A brief description and comparison of these ways will give us a framework for later discussion of the citizenship status of other minorities. An authoritative statement by the Honorable Edgar B. Meritt, formerly Assistant Indian Commissioner, may be quoted at length.

"The act of April 9, 1866 (14 Stat. L., 27), now Section 1992 of the Revised Statutes, provides that 'All persons born in the United States and not subject to any foreign power, excluding Indians not taxed, are declared to be citizens of the United States.' The question of citizenship is as a general rule an individual one to determine which facts in each particular case must be considered. There are a number of different ways in which Indians have become or may now [1923] become citizens. Some of the most important are as follows:

"1. *Treaty Provision.* In some of the treaties or agreements with certain tribes of Indians provision was made whereby Indians desiring to become citizens might become such by

---

[1] For more detailed information concerning naturalization, see J. W. Jenks, and W. J. Lauck, *op. cit.,* Appendix C-(a), Naturalization Laws and Regulations; C. H. Maxson, *op. cit.; How to Become a Citizen of the United States,* Foreign Language Information Service, 222 Fourth Avenue, New York City, 1927.

complying with certain prescribed formalities somewhat similar to those required by aliens.

"2. *Allotment Under the Act of February 8, 1887.* In the act of February 8, 1887 (24 Stat. L., 388) [generally known as the Dawes Act], Congress provided for the allotment of land to the Indians in severalty and in Section 6 thereof declared that Indians so allotted should become citizens of the United States and of the State in which they reside.

"3. *Issuance of Patent in Fee Simple.* In the act of May 8, 1906 (34 Stat. L., 182) [generally known as the Burke Act], Congress amended the act of February 8, 1887, so as to postpone citizenship of Indians thereafter allotted until after a patent in fee had been issued to said Indians. Provision was also made whereby patent in fee might be issued by the Secretary of the Interior to competent Indians before the expiration of the twenty-five-year trust period [provided by the Dawes Act]. Therefore, Indians whose trust patents are dated subsequent to May 8, 1906, and who have also received their patents in fee simple have become citizens under said act.

"4. *Adopting Habits of Civilized Life.* Section 6 of the act of February 8, 1887, both before and after its amendment of May 8, 1906, provided 'That every Indian born within the territorial limits of the United States who has voluntarily taken up within said limits his residence, separate and apart from any tribe of Indians therein, and has adopted the habits of civilized life is hereby declared to be a citizen of the United States, and is entitled to all the rights, privileges, and immunities of such citizens, whether said Indian has been or not, by birth or otherwise, a member of any tribe of Indians within the territorial limits of the United States, without in any manner impairing or otherwise affecting the rights of any such Indian to tribal or other property.'

"5. *Minor Children.* The Interior Department has held that where Indian parents became citizens upon allotment, their minor children became citizens with them, and that children born subsequent thereto were born to citizenship.

"6. *Citizenship by Birth.* (a) An Indian child born in the United States of citizen Indian parents is born to citizenship.

(b) Legitimate children born of an Indian woman and a white citizen father are born to citizenship.

"7. *Soldiers and Sailors.* Congress in the act of November 6, 1919, provided that Indian soldiers and sailors who served in the recent World War, and who have been honorably discharged may be granted citizenship by courts of competent jurisdiction.

"8. *Marriage.* The act of August 9, 1888 (25 Stat. L. 392), provided that Indian women who married citizens of the United States thereby became citizens of the United States.

"9. *Special Acts of Congress.* Sometimes Congress makes provision for a particular tribe of Indians or a particular group of Indians to become citizens. For instance:

"(a) In the act of March 3, 1901 (31 Stat. L., 1447), provision was made for the extension of citizenship to the Indians in the 'Indian Territory' by amending Section 6 of the act of February 8, 1887 (24 Stat. L., 388). . . .

"(b) In the act of March 3, 1921 (41 Stat. L., 1250), citizenship was extended to all members of the Osage Tribe of Indians in Oklahoma."[2]

It should be added that on June 2, 1924, a year after this summary of the citizenship status of Indians by Commissioner Meritt was published, all Indians born in the United States were made citizens without further formality. This act has finally ended the struggle for Indian citizenship which had its beginnings in the days of the first colonists. It has not, however, removed all Indians from the protected status of government wards, nor has it insured them the use of the ballot. While the national government has the exclusive authority to determine who shall and who shall not be citizens, actual participation in political affairs and the exercise of individual liberty on terms of equality with the native white majority do not necessarily follow formal citizenship.

Citizenship, like all other "rights," not only confers privileges but also imposes duties and obligations. While many humanitarians have expressed their regret at the injustice of the denial of citizenship to Indians not taxed, it is not difficult

[2] In G. E. E. Lindquist, *op. cit.,* pp. 440-441.

to defend this former Congressional restriction. The fact that the entire country once belonged to the Indians may arouse our sympathy for their fallen estate, and should perhaps make us more eager to assist those who are in need, but it certainly does not lead to the conclusion that all Indians should be encouraged to active participation in our government. The legal fiction that tribal Indians, although born in the United States, were not subject to the jurisdiction thereof kept many from citizenship until the inclusive act of 1924 was passed, and can be justified by the observation that these Indians, still holding fast to their preliterate culture, were not prepared to perform the duties of citizenship.

This is a conflict of theory and fact. The accepted theory is that citizenship may be determined by the geographical accident of place of birth. The fact is that neither birthplace nor ancestry assures fitness for political participation. In other words, the right to take an active part in the government of the United States follows from circumstances which do not always guarantee the ability and training necessary to the proper fulfillment of the accompanying political obligations. In democracy some degree of homogeneity is assumed, regardless of differing opinions on specific issues; otherwise government by ballot could not function.

From colonial days it was recognized that the Indian was culturally unfitted to be admitted to the body politic, although he lived within its territorial limits. The first solution to this political problem was in effect the easy fiction that Indian tribes in the United States were nations within a nation, nations having no status in international affairs proper, but characterized by a quasi-independence in domestic affairs, a concession made necessary by the gulf between European and Indian cultures. In accordance with this awkward solution, relations between tribal Indians and the federal government, which had exclusive jurisdiction, were regulated by treaty until this procedure was forbidden by act of Congress in 1871. The "nation within a nation" fiction was then replaced by the less awkward but equally fictitious legal interpretation that they were not technically subject to the jurisdiction of the United States. This pretense, too, was abandoned in 1924.

Yet while Indians as a whole have been culturally unfitted for political equality in a democracy of European tradition, there have been from the beginning individuals and tribes who have come to an understanding of European standards and customs and have adopted them, thus becoming qualified for citizenship. If the rate of acculturation for all Indians had only been the same, the question of admission to citizenship could have been settled in one act applicable to all aborigines. Unfortunately, no people is able to slough off one culture and grow into another at a rate of speed uniform for all individuals. Thus we have today in the United States Indians who have forgotten their Indian ancestors and others who cling to pre-Columbian manners. It is no wonder that citizenship has been conferred on Indians in so many ways.

Perhaps the least justifiable of all the Indian citizenship laws was the act of June 2, 1924, conferring citizenship on all native-born Indians. As a political move and as a sympathetic gesture it can be understood, but there can be no question but that many of the thousands of Indians who were still under special government restriction and supervision in that year were unprepared to assume their newly acquired status. The fact that it was specifically provided that the acquisition of citizenship was not to terminate the guardianship over such Indians as were still wards of the government when the act was passed, shows that Congress itself did not have confidence in the restricted Indians' ability to handle their own affairs, much less help govern others. Until there is reasonable cause for belief that an individual is competent to live as an independent person relatively free from the confusing handicaps of an alien culture and able to fulfill his duties to society and the state unhampered by conflicting foreign standards, the privileges of citizenship should be denied him.

It is beside the question to point out that many native-born white people have the privileges of citizenship unjustified by the ability or willingness to meet their social and political obligations. It is a fundamental error in our government, which need not have been extended to all minorities.

When it has been so extended in communities where newly created minority citizens without fitting responsibilities have been sufficiently numerous to constitute a threat to majority control, the ordinary consequences of citizenship have been promptly nullified by the native white majority. Citizenship, it must be remembered, does not carry with it the privilege of the ballot, which is, within limits, awarded by the several states. In Arizona, for example, restricted Indians whose lives and property are still under the protection of the Indian Bureau, may not vote, for the state constitution disqualifies persons who are legal wards. This issue has been fought through the state courts, which have upheld the disqualification of restricted Indians, and, it seems to us, quite properly so from a social point of view. Indian wards of the government pay no taxes on their property, contribute nothing directly to the local government, may not sell or lease their own lands, if any have been allotted to them, and are otherwise protected from starvation and exploitation. This very protection should disqualify them as active participants in government, for it is either unnecessary or an evidence of incompetency. It certainly limits their liabilities and responsibilities beyond the point where the right to the ballot is justified.

Similarly, when the Dawes Act of 1887 was passed, local political devices withheld the vote from Indians who were citizens by virtue of receiving their allotment of tribal lands. Since title to these lands remained with the government for twenty-five years after their allotment to individual Indians, they could not be taxed for any purpose. This meant that these Indians were enjoying the benefits of their lands to the same extent as were the white people in the same state or community, but without the same responsibilities and risks. White and Indian farms were scattered throughout the same areas, through the government's practice of opening to white settlement at a reasonable price the surplus lands unallotted to tribal members. The lands bought by white settlers were taxable; the Indians' lands were not until title in fee simple was awarded them. Thus the roads were built, the schools supported, the courts and other local governmental functions all paid for by white men's money. Indian citizenship, as might be expected, became meaningless. Bottomless ballot boxes, intimidation, arbitrarily enforced voting qualifications, and all the other tricks by which a dominating majority keeps minority citizens from the polls were put into use in the sections of Indian country most affected. Fortunately, so long as they were wards of the government the disfranchised Indians had little to worry about and cared less. They did not need the vote for self-protection as does the Negro in our southern states, for they had a substitute for the ballot more powerful than the ballot itself.

The Burke Act of 1906 was an attempt to correct the basic fault in the Dawes Act which conferred citizenship without imposing corresponding obligations. By postponing citizenship until title passed from the government to the individual, a more equitable basis for citizenship was provided. The provision that Indians might be declared competent before the expiration of the twenty-five-year period fixed by the Dawes Act was also an improvement. The assumption had been, of course, that in twenty-five years an Indian would have plenty of time to learn how to manage and hold on to his allotment, an utterly false assumption. Time is not the ruling factor in the situation. Some Indians were competent to handle their own affairs on the day they received their allotment; others never became competent. It is as foolish, and perhaps based on the same logic, as the great American myth that the twenty-first birthday marks the arrival of enough wisdom and discretion in an American-born person to warrant the use of the ballot.

Indian citizenship through treaty provision was justifiable to the extent to which it was a recognition of tribal acculturation and to which it avoided being a compromise based on the bargaining strength of a troublesome tribe. Children of Indian citizens usually have been even better qualified than their parents for citizenship status. It is, however, an amusing comment on a man-centered nation that legitimate children of an Indian *woman* and a white *father* were born to citizenship, somewhat in contrast to the policy of slavery days when personal status followed that of the mother, and children of free white fathers and slave colored mothers were slaves. It is also a subtle compliment to feminism that beginning in 1888 Indian women who married citizens thereby acquired citizenship for themselves.

In principle and practice, perhaps the wisest Indian citizenship provision ever enacted was that section of the Dawes Act which granted citizenship to those Indians who "adopted the habits of civilized life." If an Indian born in this country left his tribe, settled down in a community with non-Indian culture, lived as his new neighbors lived, what reason could there be for denying him full citizenship status? Yet until 1887 there was no way in which such an individual could become a full-fledged member of the body politic, for he was neither white nor Negro. Since capacity and desire for the fullest possible community cooperation rather than racial origin should be the fundamental tests for admission to citizenship, it is well that this intolerable situation was corrected by this wise provision of the Dawes Act. It would perhaps have been better had some special machinery been established to determine just when an individual was sufficiently well along on the transition from tribal to civil life, but this would have been expensive. However, with only a handful of Indians making the change each year, the communities in which they settled were themselves well able to pass informal judgment.

Now that we have given all Indians citizenship in one grand gesture we feel that amends have been made for a century and a half of mistreatment. As usual, however, it will continue to be the Indians' white neighbors who will limit the extent of the aboriginal citizens' political participation, and not the people's chosen representatives in Washington.

THE NEGRO IN POLITICS

Some of the first Negroes brought to colonial America apparently enjoyed the same political status as did white redemptioners. Slave status, however, under which the Negro had a mixture of the legal characteristics of a person, of real estate, and of a chattel, became the common status of Negroes long before the Revolutionary War and remained so until the Civil War. Indians, incidentally, were also subject to slavery both under tribal custom and at the hands of white colonists from New England to the South. In that part of the continent settled by the British most Indians were free, and therefore subject to the process of annihilation, while Negroes were brought in and protected under slavery, with only a small percentage achieving a freedom in itself limited by local law and custom.

Generalizations about slave laws are well-nigh futile. We need risk only a few observations. Each colony and state had its own separate slave regulations, sometimes imposed by the mother country, sometimes copied from the codes of nearby governments, sometimes original in their efforts to meet local conditions. Slavery and its attendant customs usually came first, to be followed by legislation recognizing and formalizing already accepted practices, yet not infrequently embodying restrictions and penalties more severe than local sentiment would permit to be enforced.

Slaves, of course, were not considered citizens. The question was raised time and again whether free Negroes should enjoy the full status of free white people; and although the courts eventually decided that they should, the common practice in slave states was to hem them in with legal as well as with informal restraints. There is a constitutional compromise in which a slave counted as three-fifths of a white man, which speaks volumes about the real attitude of the times toward the Negro.

Contradictory laws and practices can be brought from the records of all parts of the United States. Louisiana was less brutal in her legislation concerning Negroes than was the rest of the United States with its British legal tradition. Free Negroes voted in some states, but not in others. They were tried in inferior slave courts in a few districts, but not in others. Regulations concerning legal testimony, jury duty, property rights, family rights, all varied from state to state for free and slave blacks. Education, the right of assembly except for worship and limited recreation, the right to remain within a state if freed, the conditions of manumission, were subjects for legislation in each state, and no two states followed identical practices, nor did any one state have to hold to the same set of Negro laws for any length of time. To attempt here to bring order out of this chaos would be without justification.

It is perfectly well known that the political status of free and slave Negroes up to the Civil War period was sharply restricted. Except for the purposes of detailed, historical monographic research, citations from the multiplicity of laws regarding the rights of Negroes serve only to confuse the reader, for they could not be typical without being unreasonably extensive, nor could they invariably be accepted as indicative of actual practices, for there was a disconcerting practice of disregarding slave laws when they turned out to be unnecessary nuisances, as they frequently did. It takes more than just a few generations to develop a standardized, efficient legal system regulating such a complicated institution as slavery; and since slavery had but a brief, sporadic existence in the United States among, for the most part, people who were without traditional guides for slave owners, other than those of mushroom growth in this country and adjacent islands, the result was an uncodifiable tangle of legal experiments which worked because of their plasticity. The one sure thing was that the Negroes themselves had nothing to say about it.

With the Civil War came emancipation, enfranchisement, and guarantees of equal rights for black and white.[3] If any-

---

[3] The following extracts from the Constitution of the United States and the Amendments to the Constitution are of particular significance in the study of race relations:

Article I, Section 2, paragraph three (in part).— Representatives and direct Taxes shall be apportioned among the several States which may be included within this Union, according to their respective Numbers, which shall be determined by adding to the whole number of free Persons, including those bound to Service for a Term of Years, and excluding Indians not taxed, three fifths of all other Persons.

Amendment XIII, Section 1.—Neither slavery nor involuntary servitude, except as a punishment for crime whereof the party shall have been duly con-

thing, northern politicians did their best to give the Negro a favored status which in effect would have made him almost a ward of the government, although not in the sense that the Indian has been. Although a reaction to slavery was naturally to be expected, it would have been a mistake to give the freedmen any more protection from private or public persecution than is afforded a citizen of any other color. Fortunately, the United States Supreme Court and the post-Civil War decline in emotionalism and increase in political sanity prevented the consummation of such attempts at special Negro legislation protection as the Fourteenth and Fifteenth Amendments and Sumner's Civil Rights Bill originally intended. No specific reference is made to the Negro in the Fourteenth Amendment, and it is amusing to note that, in the years from 1868 to 1914, of some 575 cases involving this amendment coming before the Supreme Court for adjudication, only five per cent dealt with the Negro. "By far the greater proportion of the litigation under this act has been concerned with the federal regulation of industrial combinations. Organized capital rather than the Negro race has invoked the protection of the Fourteenth Amendment against state interference."[4]

The Fifteenth Amendment, with its purpose of insuring Negro suffrage, has met with about the same degree of success as the other legal attempts to protect the Negro through federal intervention. It has been established by court decision that the federal government cannot confer the right to vote, and that it is properly within the jurisdiction of the several states to restrict suffrage on the basis of property, educational,

---

victed, shall exist within the United States, or any place subject to their jurisdiction.

Amendment XIV, Section 1.—All persons born or naturalized in the United States, and subject to the jurisdiction thereof, are citizens of the United States and of the State wherein they reside. No State shall make or enforce any law which shall abridge the privileges or immunities of citizens of the United States; nor shall any State deprive any person of life, liberty, or property, without due process of law; nor deny to any person within its jurisdiction the equal protection of the laws.

Amendment XV, Section 1.—The right of citizens of the United States to vote shall not be denied or abridged by the United States or by any State on account of race, color, or previous condition of servitude.

[4] J. M. Mecklin, Democracy and Race Friction, The Macmillan Company, New York, 1914, p. 231.

and other qualifications, so long as race, color, and previous condition of servitude are not among the restrictions. Beyond this the Fifteenth Amendment may not go, and it has thus become possible for the states in the exercise of their normal powers to disfranchise Negroes almost at will by the use of qualifications which legally have no connection with race, color, or previous servitude, but in fact operate to disfranchise Negroes in far greater proportions than white people.

We are reminded of our previous discussion of the Indian, who was granted citizenship before he was ready for it by the Dawes Act of 1887, and was disfranchised by the white people who might have suffered from ignorant, irresponsible, Indian voting. So long as the federal government held control of the South through its military threats or through the northern-managed Reconstruction, the Negro could vote regardless of the southern white man's wishes. Where and when the grip of the North was relaxed, intimidation and fear kept the Negro away from the polls to which he was legally entitled to go, and it was not long before illegal threats were supplemented or replaced by legal trickery in the inevitable process of keeping the southern government lily white.

Every state in the South today has laws which, while absolutely square with the federal Constitution, nevertheless have as their purpose the disfranchisement of the Negro. Many of them are of such a nature that they might well be copied by the entire country. There are, for example, many reasons why voting should be limited by property and intellectual tests. Why should not a person be made to show ownership of a few hundred dollars' worth of property before registration, or, failing that, be made to read a section from the Constitution and to show that its meaning is reasonably well understood? White primary laws, unconstitutional in their original form, in a district where nomination by one party means election, are another matter.

As a rule, however, the difficulty is not with the laws themselves, generally of high-sounding purpose, but rather with their administration. Thousands of white people have been disfranchised by laws aimed at Negroes. Tens of thousands more would be barred from the polls if these laws were properly enforced. There is the story of the Negro graduate of the Harvard Law School who was not allowed to register in a southern state because his interpretation of a section of the Constitution did not suit an illiterate registrar. Indifference and fear, however, keep many times more Negroes from voting than do state laws and unfair registration officials combined.

Many northern people have the impression that Negroes never vote in the South. This is far from correct. "In most of the border states, such as West Virginia, Kentucky, Maryland, and even Tennessee and Virginia, there is a considerable amount of voting on the part of Negroes. This is probably due to the active two-party rivalry in these states. In Baltimore some 28,239 Negroes are registered. There is much less voting, however, in other sections of the South. Dr. Woofter has estimated that about 3,500 Negroes are registered in Atlanta, 2,000 in Savannah, and 1,000 in Jacksonville. Mr. Kent states that there are only 595 Negroes registered in the entire state of Louisiana."[5]

Quoting from the editorial page of *Opportunity, Journal of Negro Life*, for July, 1931, we find the following interesting facts and comments.

"On the same general subject [Negroes in politics] but from another angle is a striking editorial in the Louisville *Times* of June 13th, captioned 'An Immobile Bloc,' which reads in part as follows:

" 'Eighty per cent of the Negro population of Louisville eligible to vote is registered, as against 62% of the white population. The census figures revealing this disparity demonstrate the effectiveness of the local Republican organization and at the same time the ineffectiveness of the Negro population in realizing its own possibilities as a voting unit.

" 'Of 33,171 Negroes eligible to go to the polls, all except 6,666 are registered, and of the 26,505 registered, all except 673 are registered Republican—which is the way they unfailingly vote.

[5] C. S. Johnson, *op. cit.*, p. 343.

" 'Altogether there are 132,159 registered voters in Louisville. Imagine what influence could be commanded by a bloc of 26,505 of these voters capable of being swung from one of the two major parties to the other or to a third party. Imagine how the politicians would quail before the threat of such a swing, if they supposed the threat could be translated into fact. Blocs far smaller than this—in fact, blocs that have been largely mythical—have yielded enormous influence.'

"The *Times* is a Democratic paper and there will be those who see in this statement a subtle partisan argument calculated to divide the Republican vote. But even if this were the motive which inspired the above editorial, its essential truth cannot be denied. If the Negro voters of Louisville were organized into a black bloc, all things being equal, the Negro voter would be in a position of tremendous power."

The black bloc has become a powerful reality in practically all northern cities, where machine politicians have come to depend on it for the controlling votes which hold them in power. In the old days, it was the ignorant, somewhat bewildered immigrant who furnished the foundation of votes on which were built the machines of New York, Philadelphia, Chicago, and other cities. These are increasingly being assimilated, and with assimilation comes a diffusion to replace their old concentration in minority city districts, and an independence and enlightenment which have already seriously reduced their political tractability. Immigration legislation, following the World War, which was itself the first serious recent check on the supply of immigrants, has prevented the building up of new voting units of European origin. Fortunately, from the political gangs' point of view, the Negro cityward migrant came along just about the right time, with a tractability and political complaisance beautiful to behold, especially since he did not have to be naturalized before he could vote.

In every northern city with an appreciable percentage of Negro voters the machine politician is depending on the colored vote to remain in office in spite of political knavery. The tendency is for Negroes to vote Republican, for they have had sad experiences with the Democrats in their southern home. This makes it easy for the politicians in normally Republican cities, for it reduces the rewards which must be given to leaders and voters whose votes are relatively safe anyway. The result of this tendency is poor bargaining power, so that the Negroes are left with little to show for their support. Where immigrant leaders in the past have been accustomed to acquiring political preferment and financial gain, while their followers divided plenty of small favors and jobs, their Negro successors today are content with pitiful rewards of slight value in comparison with the service rendered, yet they are grateful for even the crumbs. They have never had much, and they are shrewd enough to know that they will not get much until they begin shifting their traditional votes.

It seems likely that this will happen in northern cities, and perhaps even in the South, but not for many years. Negroes have swung to the Democrats in Democratic New York City. They have, on one occasion, supported and, in a sense elected, a reform mayor in Philadelphia. Tammany has given them their reward for whatever switching they have done. The Philadelphia reform mayor made many promises but forgot them after election. This typifies the experience of all voting minorities. It is perhaps the explanation of their worst influence on American government.

Poor people, ignorant people, living in an unfamiliar, semi-hostile environment, need a friend in court. There are so many small favors which even a petty ward heeler can do for them. The immigrant, the city Negro, both are in contact with government in a direct way which the better-established voter seems not to realize. The policeman is real to them, not just a traffic cop or a uniformed friend of nursemaids. Jobs on ash carts, garbage wagons, in the city hall as scrubwomen or janitors, jobs of any kind, however menial, are appreciated by the handicapped minorities. Personal favors, even to a casual friend, mean a lot to such people, and they swing their vote to the man who has the machine and the political sense to grant them open-handedly. Perhaps if there had been no Irish, Italian, German, Jewish, Polish, Negro, and other congested city areas, inhabited by minorities fighting for existence, some other tractable blocs would have been found. In any event, these are the voters who have kept the great American gangs in power, with the Negro doing yeoman service at the present time.

The Emancipation Proclamation was not issued with the Negroes' welfare as the prime consideration. It did not even have much influence on their status at the time, for it was rather an announcement of policy than a final executive decree. Rather than a humanitarian act, it might better be called a political and military move, designed to pacify the abolitionists at home and abroad and to hamper the Confederate military machine by the creation of discontent among slaves and others. This should not be considered a disparagement of Lincoln's proclamation, for its actual purposes were as justifiable as the mawkish sentimentality which has since been attributed to it. Attention is merely called to the proclamation's disregard for the slaves' immediate needs in contrast to the exigencies of a national situation.

Negro enfranchisement was equally unmindful of the freedmen's interests. Nor were the nation's interests given first consideration. The Republican party was simply frightened at what it had done or might be blamed for doing in the prosecution of the War of Secession. The rebel states could not be kept out of the Union forever. Their resentment at the treatment they received at the hands of a Republican government was bound to mean, felt the Republican chiefs, that lean years would soon be in store for the political party responsible. A political trick, disguised with liberal references to natural equality, justice, humanity, freedom, and democracy, gave freed slaves the vote at a time when white rebels were disfranchised, and scalawags and carpetbaggers were the only white people allowed to participate in the government of the southern states.

The merits of the military and civil Reconstruction periods, of the Freedmen's Bureau, of the Negro voters and office holders, of their despised white bosses and henchmen, of the whole period from the Civil War until the Negro and carpetbagger were driven from power, are matters of dispute. There apparently were some efficient and honest carpetbag governors. There were some capable and upright agents of the Freedmen's Bureau. There were some Negro politicians beyond criticism. On the other hand, mismanagement, selfishness, and plain knavery were perhaps even more common. The point at issue, however, is not how poorly or how well the South was governed during the first years of colored freedom and suffrage, but rather how anything else could have been expected from the emancipation and the political participation of thousands upon thousands of inexperienced, untrained, previously dependent colored people of newly acquired citizenship status.

The vote should be a privilege to be earned by evidence of ability and willingness to use it with discretion. A few free Negroes had shown their ability in the use of the ballot before the Civil War, but not a large enough number to act as political leaders for the emancipated masses. Only eleven per cent of the Negroes in the United States in 1860 were free, and only a small proportion of these voted, many of them in northern states where they could not be of assistance in the reorganization of the South. Furthermore, these free Negroes had to a considerable extent received their freedom because of something meritorious in their conduct, or else they had been born and bred in freedom. In either case, they were far better prepared for freedom than were the other 89 per cent. Mass enfranchisement of a minority is difficult to justify, although in the case of the Indians in 1924 there were so few of them that sentiment could perhaps well be allowed to outweigh political caution. There were too many freed slaves in a politically, socially, and economically disrupted, war-torn area to warrant wholesale Negro enfranchisement shortly after the Civil War. Individual merit should have been the basis for the gradual enfranchisement of the freedmen.

Had this been the basis of procedure, it is likely that a much larger proportion of Negroes would be voting today, and voting more intelligently and less on a blind tradition. The desire of Republican leaders to cash in on Negro gratefulness for Civil War services must be blamed for an appreciable amount of Negro non-voting today, as well as for some of his useless, straight-ticket party voting. There is irony in the fact that the "Solid South," not so much a consequence of the war as of post-war irritations, has robbed the Republicans of the fruits of their hypocritical bargain.

THE NATURALIZATION OF ALIENS

Orientals, as has been mentioned, may not become naturalized American citizens. There is no scientific excuse for this racial discrimination, and it is especially difficult to understand since we permit their children to become citizens by virtue of the fact of birth in the United States. In view of the wide differences between oriental and occidental cultures, oriental exclusion, or rather restriction, is desirable to reduce culture conflict and its attendant maladjustments. The handful of Orientals in the United States, however, includes some, particularly among the Japanese, who are in every way fit to participate in the government of their local communities and of the nation.

It is doubtful whether their original omission from our naturalization laws was anything more than an oversight, for there were practically no Orientals in the United States until after the middle of the nineteenth century, and even then they were largely restricted to the west coast. Apparently they were overlooked because our early legislators had never even seen an Oriental, much less suspected them as potential immigrants. Since our courts have held that only peoples specifically mentioned in our naturalization laws may be naturalized, the precedent for refusing them citizenship is of long standing. There are, however, a number of cases in which Orientals have been naturalized, but our courts are now definitely forbidden to grant them citizenship papers.

In other words, a barrier originally created by indifference rather than purpose is now one consciously maintained. The Burlingame Treaty of 1868 specifically refused to grant the right of naturalization to Chinese. Legislation, executive orders, and court decisions have removed any doubt which may have existed about the eligibility of foreign-born Orientals for American citizenship in the earlier days.

Among the reasons for this discrimination may be mentioned the popular myth that white and yellow peoples are racially so different that they must be forever separated. "East is East, and West is West" is quoted at people who suggest a more receptive attitude to our oriental residents, although it would be a less popular quotation if the racial theorists who use it could remember the whole poem instead of one or two lines which give a false impression of Kipling's meaning. However, Orientals have shown that they can adopt western culture and contribute to it, so, since citizenship does not imply intermarriage—witness the Negro in our midst—this argument becomes as meaningless as the Kipling quotation.

We as a nation have not thought much beyond this point regarding Chinese naturalization, but our popular rationalizations regarding the Japanese have been most ingenious. Dual citizenship, for example, has been much overworked. It is true that if we allowed Japanese to become naturalized as we do European immigrants, the Japanese government would continue to claim naturalized persons as Japanese citizens. Voluntary expatriation is recognized by the Japanese government, but it involves the red tape of formal notification to that government in accordance with definite rules and stipulations of which our naturalization laws take no cognizance.

It is, in essence, the age-old conflict of the two basic methods of determining allegiance, *jus sanguinis* and *jus soli*. Shall ancestry furnish the test, or shall it be place of birth? Obviously, if both are used, as they are by every civilized country in the world, there will be conflicts. Further, if voluntary expatriation and naturalization are recognized, there will be still more conflicts unless all nations enter into treaty relationships recognizing each other's systems of citizenship determination. Japan is not alone in disputing our naturalization and other citizenship laws.

We have had misunderstandings with practically every European nation on this same question. A long-drawn-out dispute with Germany over the citizenship of a man we both claimed was settled by the inconclusive method of permitting him to escape from Germany into another country. Italy since the World War has claimed as citizens men whom we also claimed. A list of such disputes would be interminable. Treaties, however, have been used to straighten out most such difficulties. Japan is peculiar in this respect, mainly because she has entered the family of nations so recently and with a civilization which was not of the same common origins as were those of the European and American countries. Such disputes, however, are anachronistic trivialities, technically interesting to the legal mind, but insignificant in portent even in time of war.

Blood is not thicker than water. Allegiance, it has been found, does not follow ancestry. "Once an Englishman, always an Englishman" is patently false. It would be unfortunate for us in the United States if such a principle could be established. A change in skin color does not alter this fact. The Negro is intensely patriotic, as blatant a 100-per-cent American as any provincial tourist. The same is true of most American-born Orientals, so that the fact that Japanese citizenship continues through generation after generation born on foreign soil is a pure technicality. Owing to the dissimilarity of cultures, it is more difficult for a Japanese or Chinese immigrant to change allegiance, but it is possible and it has occurred. Why, then, should we not recognize the fact by formal naturalization?

Equally absurd is that charge that Shintoism, with the Mikado at its head, does not permit "Americanization" because allegiance to the Japanese Emperor, as head of the Shintoist church, is put before allegiance to the United States. In the first place, Orientals coming to the United States include many Christians. Furthermore, oriental faiths adapt themselves to American conditions just as European religions have done. One is reminded at this point of the similar charge that Catholics make poor citizens because of their allegiance to the Pope, a charge that is today smiled on with indulgence by the well informed. Neither squabbles over technical citizenship nor the restraints of foreign faiths can prevent the process of assimilation into the American community and culture if the immigrant, of any race or nationality, and his children become permanent residents in the United States.

The speciousness of the charges of non-assimilability against Orientals becomes apparent when it is remembered that they are also damned if they attempt to assimilate. They are damned if they do, and damned if they don't. Most Chinese make little attempt to assimilate, considering themselves as temporary immigrants, and they are therefore not so seriously inconvenienced by the naturalization barrier against them. The Japanese, on the other hand, intend to stay here, want their children to become real Americans, and there is consequently no excuse, once they have been legally admitted, for not granting them the same citizenship privileges so freely offered even undeserving Europeans.

In a newly settled country it is only natural that citizenship privileges by adoption should be quite liberal. Our pioneer fathers were most generous in their willingness to admit newcomers, of the proper kind, to governmental participation. "The liberality of our naturalization laws dates from the colonial period, when in effect the naturalized citizens had all the privileges of the native-born. During the period of the Confederation (1781-1789) naturalization was left to the individual states. The ratification of the Constitution gave Congress the power to establish a uniform rule of naturalization; and in 1790, shortly after the inauguration of Washington, was enacted the first naturalization act, which required a two years' residence and confined the benefits to free white persons. From 1790 to 1854 fifteen laws dealing with naturalization were adopted, the term 'free white persons' being retained in all; and after 1802 five years' residence was required, this remaining substantially in force until 1906."[6]

Although the nativists have constantly urged more severe naturalization requirements, sometimes going so far as to demand no naturalization at all, they have not been as successful in gaining their ends in this respect as might have been expected. Their demands for immigration restriction have

[6] G. M. Stephenson, op. cit., p. 242.

been reflected in our laws, but we have been less willing to deny citizenship to aliens already in the country who have shown their good faith. It seems that we have in recent years decided to protect our laborers from some immigrant competition, but have failed to see why the aliens already admitted should be refused naturalization, since they will not become more serious competitors on that account. The slight tightening up of our naturalization laws in the last century or so is sociologically unimportant. The process is still so simple and ill-considered that it may be said to be something in the nature of a flimsy barrier which may be readily scaled by aliens whether or not they have shown themselves capable of appreciating the privileges and exercising the duties of citizenship.

In the normal naturalization process today, these are the basic requirements: The immigrant must have lived in the United States for at least five years, including six months' residence in the county where the application for citizenship is made. Having formally indicated the desire to become a citizen, he must not leave the country for more than six months without good reason, and under no circumstances may he stay away for more than a year without facing the necessity of starting all over again. Two witnesses who are citizens must testify to the facts of his residence, his moral character, his belief in the principles of the Constitution, and his general fitness for citizenship. He must show that he is familiar with the principles and form of our government, including that of the state and local community in which he resides. He must have faith in our government. He may not be an anarchist or polygamist. He must be able to speak English, and some courts require a reading knowledge of our language. He must be twenty-one years of age. He must have been legally admitted to the United States. If he can fulfill these requirements, and if he has made no mistakes in filing his "first papers" declaring his intention to become an American citizen and his final petition asking for citizenship, he will probably be admitted.

There are, of course, numerous possible complications. If he was in this country during the World War, he may have something in his record for those years which will be held against him. If, after declaring his intention of becoming a citizen, he changed his mind and obtained exemption from military service because of neutral citizenship, he may never become a citizen of the United States. Even if he had not filed his first papers, but claimed military exemption, he may still find citizenship difficult to obtain in some courts.

Courts do not all follow the same rules in naturalization. Perhaps we had better say that courts do not all interpret the rules in the same way. When the law says that the prospective citizen must understand and believe in the Constitution, a thing which the Supreme Court has had difficulty in doing, there is considerable latitude permitted the courts in determining the fitness of a petitioner. Should a woman who admits that she would refuse to bear arms for the United States in time of war be denied citizenship, knowing that she would not be permitted to do so even if she wanted to? Should a man whose conscience would not permit him to bear arms except in what he believed to be a just war be doomed to remain an alien, although conscientious objectors were given special privileges during the World War? There are so many matters of opinion involved.

Until September 22, 1922, when the Cable Act was passed, a woman lost citizenship when, if a citizen, she married an alien, or gained it when, if an alien, she married a citizen. After this date, the citizenship status of women remained unchanged by marriage, except that the process of obtaining citizenship was made easier for the alien woman who married an American, and that citizenship was more easily lost through marriage to a foreigner who did not live permanently in the United States, or by formal renouncement in a court having authority to naturalize. The American woman who married an alien ineligible to citizenship still lost her American citizenship.

The Cable Act was viewed as defective by some feminists because it did not put men and women on an identical basis in regard to citizenship. It was certainly defective in that it left some women without a country, for foreign governments still clung to the old idea that a woman's citizenship followed her husband's. Recent legislation, however, has corrected some of its faults, and we may say that men and women are treated essentially alike in this respect. This movement, however, is more the result of "women's rights" agitation than of any national minority program.[7]

Soldiers and sailors, veterans of the wars in which we have participated, and minor children constitute the most important groups not already mentioned who have special naturalization privileges. It is assumed that children of citizens will, if properly reared, grow up into good citizens themselves, although if this is true it is difficult to explain why adopted children and stepchildren should not be given the privileges awarded other minors. Military service, in peace or war, is also assumed to insure or to be evidence of those qualities which we demand in citizens. One may be skeptical on this point without being petty.

It is at least as easy to lose American citizenship as it is to gain it. Naturalization papers may be canceled for fraud or error. A naturalized citizen who leaves the United States for more than a reasonably brief visit, particularly if he returns to the country to which he originally owed allegiance, may be presumed to have lost his American citizenship. In fact, any citizen, whether by birth or naturalization, may renounce his American citizenship, which is lost by the simple procedure of acquiring citizenship in any other country. The only exception is that in time of war American citizenship may not be renounced, primarily as a matter of expediency.

Now what does all this amount to, laying legal details aside? We have not attempted to furnish a complete statement of naturalization provisions, but only to select those major requirements which should be sufficient to show the way the wind is blowing.

According to our laws, and leaving special cases out of consideration, the tests of fitness for naturalization are the time

[7] For a discussion of the citizenship of women, see Sophonisba Breckenridge, *Marriage and the Civic Rights of Women*, University of Chicago Press, Chicago, 1931, pp. xi + 152.

spent in residence in the United States after legal entry, the
ability to produce two witnesses to support the petitioner
with sworn testimony, and a perfunctory examination by the
naturalization examiner or the court to determine the applicant's knowledge of the English language and his understanding of and belief in the United States government. The other
technical requirements are so obviously unrelated to the qualities to be desired in citizens that they need not be brought
into the discussion.

Time spent in the United States is no measure of Americanization, if we may use the word. An alien just off the boat
may be far more worthy of being admitted to our body politic
than one who has been here for decades. For administrative
and other practical reasons, however, it is desirable that some
minimum time elapse after arrival before citizenship is
granted, but we must be careful not to assume that length of
American residence is in any degree a test of fitness.

The dependence of the sworn testimony of two witnesses,
secured by the petitioner himself, is a modern survival of an
antiquated method of determining facts. Scandals connected
with this type of witness have been common. There is evidence that in a number of our larger naturalization centers
individuals have made tidy sums by charging petitioners a
fee for falsely swearing to the moral qualities and American
residence of these prospective citizens. Only in the occasional
exceptional case where the suspicions of the court are aroused
by some slip or circumstance is any adequate investigation of
the witnesses made. Our government is most naïve in the
faith it puts in the oaths of strangers.

While no one may hazard a guess as to what questions will
actually be asked in any examination, a few samples, prepared
as guides for immigrants, may be quoted.

"Q. What form of government has the United States?
A. A republican form of government.
Q. What is a republican form of government?
A. It is one in which the head of the government is
elected.

Q. Who made the Constitution?

A. The representatives of the thirteen original states.

Q. When was the Constitution adopted?

A. It was adopted by Convention of September 17, 1787, and was declared in effect in 1789.

Q. When does the President take office?

A. On the 4th of March following his election.

Q. Who were the Pilgrims?

A. They were among the first immigrants to this country, coming from England to seek religious liberty in the new world.

Q. What is the most common kind of local government?

A. City government.

Q. What was the cause of the Civil War?

A. Slavery. Negroes were owned in the southern states as slaves. The northern states believed this was wrong. The southern states, in order to maintain slavery, attempted to secede from the United States. The northern states insisted on maintaining the Union. So war developed.

Q. When was George Washington inaugurated as President?

A. 1789.

Q. Has each state a capital city?

A. Yes."[8]

What is it that can be measured by such questions as these? Nothing more than memory, and some preparation guided by Americanization teachers and friends who are familiar with the sort of thing likely to be asked. Certainly a thousand or ten thousand memorized facts similar to these are no measure of the qualities we should desire in citizens.

Citizenship qualities should be measured, not by such formalized bits of information, but by the way a person lives and meets his responsibilities. Why not have paid government employees attached either to the courts or to the federal naturalization office, perhaps preferably to the latter, whose

[8] *How to Become a Citizen of the United States.* These questions and answers were selected at random from 116 listed in this 47-page bulletin.

duty it would be to go into the home community of immigrants applying for naturalization for the impartial investigation of pertinent facts? What are the applicant's habits of
work? The grocer and other local storekeepers can tell whether
he meets his financial obligations regularly, and so can his
landlord. The parish priest, minister or rabbi may be called
on with profit. So may the school teacher, the attendance
officer and even the policeman on the beat. A brief visit to
the immigrant's home itself would be worth while. There are
so many sources of information, private and official, which
could be utilized but are not, that it is a pity they have been
so long neglected.

Few will dispute their worth. The opposition to their use
generally relies on threats of "frightful cost" and "obnoxious
governmental paternalism." The cost would indeed be staggering in prospect were it not for the fact that restricted immigration is cutting down the numbers of potential applicants
to a reasonable figure. If naturalization is worth while at all,
it is worth doing well, and there is no more "paternalism" in
such proposed investigation than there is in any other governmental work well done. We could afford to accept the testimony of voluntary witnesses in the days when our population
was but a fraction of what it is now, when anonymity was
more difficult of achievement. Those days are gone, and it is
our duty to bring our naturalization procedure as up to date
as we have made our banking laws, only there is not the same
incentive.

Perhaps if we had not built up such a powerful stereotype
of the immigrant as a political radical we should be willing
to admit him more readily as a citizen. Our immigration laws
are evidence of this fear, and so are our naturalization laws,
which prohibit the naturalization of anarchists. The law and
the courts are both most particular that the petitioner be
politically orthodox in behavior and beliefs. He must convince
his examiners of his implicit faith in the American form of
government. This, as has been indicated, is a simple matter of
accomplishment, truthfully or otherwise. It would be better
if we paid less attention to this formal bugaboo and concen-

trated on the immigrant's actual conduct as a member of an American community.

It is probable that there are proportionally more political radicals of all varieties among immigrants than among the native born. Radicalism is a sign of discontent, and so is immigration. Furthermore, radicalism flourishes best among failures, and immigration is usually an evidence of failure in the land of birth. Poverty and exploitation are bound to lead to thoughts of amelioration through political reform, in some individuals.

Minorities, however, are not free from traditional restraints which act as a social balance wheel. No matter what the provocation may be, only a small fraction of any minority can be expected to seek relief through political violence or extremes. They bring their political faiths with them, and European political mores have been fairly conservative during the period of greatest immigration. There is no telling what may happen in the future, but the past is clear.

Even the Negro, with more cause for discontent than most, is poor soil for radical propaganda. Much has been made of some alleged attempts on the part of Soviet Russia to foment discontent among black American workers, admittedly the most exploited group in the United States. No conceivable campaign could do more than furnish a focus for the discontent of a handful of our twelve million Negroes. The vast majority are so thoroughly American in their views that, unhappy as they may be, the words Bolshevism, socialism, communism, and radicalism are epithets. This being true, what need we fear from the bulk of European immigrants, whose background is also conservative and who suffer less exploitation in this country, for a shorter time, until their assimilation is accomplished?

The immigrant, however, invariably comes to this country with a foreign political background against which in comparison is thrown the political system with which he comes in contact in the United States. With his native country far behind him, he is likely to idealize some aspects of the government under which he was reared, and then tactlessly brag about the way things were done under Kaiser, King, Parliament, President, or Dictator in the old country. Sometimes this has the appearance of radicalism; at best it is tinged with un-gratefulness and a lack of manners. The native American finds such comments annoying, and frequently ends the con-versation by suggesting a return to the old country, if it is so perfect over there.

However irritating such comments may be from an alien guest, they may well be called a blessing in disguise. In our more introspective moments, nearly all of us Americans will admit that our government contains imperfections and anachronisms. We who have been born and brought up under the evils of gang rule, graft, political incompetence, inadequate representation, and some of the other weaknesses of democ-racy, American plan, have developed mental callouses and are no longer sensitive to them. The alien, coming from perhaps an even less desirable form of government, nevertheless is more appreciative of both the strength and weaknesses of the American political scheme because of his unfamiliarity with it.

The immigrant has been a tool of corruption because of his ignorance and political tractability, but a tool in the hands of native politicians, in the unsavory meaning of the term, who lost their control over him in proportion to his assimila-tion. He has furnished his quota of radicalism, and more; but radicalism, even if it has taken root, does not flourish among social classes free from exploitation and in a position to grasp opportunities for progress. He has been hypercritical, and in this fault lies his greatest political contribution, for it has been an antidote to the stagnation of monotonous cultural homogeneity.

We have attempted to maintain the thesis that citizenship should be awarded to racial and nationality minorities as their individual members demonstrate their cultural absorption and their sincere desire to function as cooperative members of the communities in which they live. The educational processes by which this end may be fostered are discussed in another section of this study. Formal education, however, can be but a small part of a working program leading to full minority participation in government.

Impatience has sometimes led us to undue speed in granting citizenship to minorities, as has also despicable political chicanery. There is not a single minority, except foreign-born Orientals who have been denied naturalization entirely, which has not had citizenship granted to many of its members long before they were prepared for it. Negro enfranchisement is the best example, and the results of this error in procedure, a desirable objective prostituted by political strategy, are typical. The Indian suffered similarly. There have been times when immigrants were allowed to vote (and the political advantages to a city gang can be readily inferred) before they were able to fulfill the very elementary federal citizenship requirements. One state, Arkansas, has held on to the practice, formerly quite common, of granting suffrage to an alien who does no more than formally declare his intention of becoming a citizen, that is, one who has taken out his first papers, up to the present decade. With this practice now discredited, we still have a long way to go before our citizenship standards are what they should be. This also applies to our practice of granting citizenship to every person born in the United States, with the privilege of suffrage automatically accompanying it at the age of twenty-one, mental competency assumed, restricted only by a scattering of residence, tax-paying, property-ownership and alleged intellectual tests, none of which succeed in sifting the wheat from the chaff.

Millions of eligible aliens, about 40 per cent of the foreign-born of voting age in the United States, have never bothered to apply for citizenship. They are content to live under a government by others. Many who have been naturalized do not exercise the franchise. Other millions, belonging to the majority of old American stock as well as to minorities, care little about the privileges of citizenship to which they have been born. A democracy such as ours cannot function at its greatest efficiency with so great a proportion of disfranchised, voluntary or otherwise, participants in community life.

Elected politicians tend to spend the public's money in protecting the people and in improving their lot in such a way as to hold and gain votes. Paving, street lighting, sewers, police service, the benefits of government in general, all tend to be dispensed where they will do the most good to the dispensers, the elected politicians. Disfranchised Negroes get no more than a bare minimum of these services. Non-voting immigrants suffer the same way. The experience of non-voting Indians has been the same. Even the native-born communities which neglect to exercise the franchise or are not sufficiently numerous to sway an election are neglected whenever possible, although not to anything like the extent of similarly unfortunate minorities. This may be a defect in our governmental system, but it is a fact to be reckoned with.

This should not be interpreted to mean that immigrants should be forced into naturalization, or that non-voting minorities should be driven to the polls by legal or unofficial penalties. For example, the practice of refusing employment, public or private, to aliens leads to little more than sullen compliance with such arbitrary rules, and not infrequently to a resentful defiance which is a handicap to good citizenship.[9] A European-born assistant professor in a leading American university was recently told that his promotion depended in part on whether or not he was willing to become an American citizen. He had intended to become naturalized, but when this pressure was applied he changed his mind in resentment. We should hardly want citizens who became so for such mercenary motives.

Citizenship and political participation is a privilege to be earned, and not an obligatory status to be thrust upon anyone. It carries with it duties as well as rewards. When the duties are fully understood and appreciated by minorities, the privilege should be offered them. When the rewards of citizenship, in a positive and not in a negative sense, become apparent to them, they will seek to qualify themselves for it.

[9] For a discussion of the effects of majority compulsion in such group relationships, see Herbert A. Miller, *Races, Nations and Classes*, J. B. Lippincott Company, Philadelphia, 1924, pp. xvii + 96.

CHAPTER VII

MINORITIES AND LAW OBSERVANCE

CONTRARY to popular belief, crime is a subject which deserves only brief space in a treatise on racial and national minorities in the United States. The problem is not a serious one, all things considered, and what statistical evidence we have about it does not support the common assertion that our minorities are criminal plague spots. Were it not for this widespread fiction, the whole subject could be disposed of through incidental paragraphs in other chapters.

RACE, NATIVITY AND CRIME

If we define crime as a violation of the law, it becomes apparent immediately that we are at a loss for any means of measuring criminality. The number of people in jail bears an unknown relationship to those who have committed identical offenses but have escaped commitment to a penal institution. The number of criminals convicted by our courts depends as much on the efficiency of the courts and of the police as it does on the number of criminals in the community. The number of arrests is an even more faulty index of criminality, for many are arrested on unwarranted suspicion, while more, guilty in fact, elude the officers of the law. The number of crimes committed is also beyond our ken, since such data are not collected except by a few private organizations, such as insurance companies and bankers' associations, and by some police departments which list in their reports the "crimes known to the police."

All comprehensive criminal statistics at present available belong to one or the other of these classes. No matter how carefully they are gathered and sifted, they cannot be made to measure *actual* criminality. It is, of course, useful in many ways to know the detailed statistics of *apparent* criminality, but this usefulness is slight when the purpose is a comparison of the amount and nature of native white criminality with that of immigrants and Negroes.

Let us consider the statistics of known crimes first. Many crimes are discovered and reported for which the perpetrators never come under suspicion. Their race and national origin must therefore remain undisclosed. Furthermore, in those cases where the color or nationality of the criminal is reported, the evidence in support of such classification is likely to be slim and biased. Negro criminals have "high visibility." Racial antagonism not only makes white people in official or private capacity more willing to report Negro criminals, but also more anxious to ascribe a crime to a member of that race. Other races, and aliens, are similarly treated in proportion to their visibility and the community antagonisms to them. Criminals have been known to make use of racial stereotypes in their disguises, and many a crime attributed to Negroes, Italians, Chinese, Indians, and other minorities has been the product of native white ingenuity in disguise. Thus, while the number of crimes known to have been perpetrated is perhaps the best index of actual crime available, its usefulness in group comparisons is doubtful.

The number of arrests is just as useless. While the color of an arrested person is likely to be recorded with reasonable accuracy if such records are kept, many jurisdictions make no attempt at such differentiation. There is even greater indifference to recording European nationalities, and where the attempt is made it is usually unreliable. Jews are commonly recorded as a separate race. Children of immigrants are listed as though they were immigrants themselves. Naturalized immigrants may or may not be counted as Americans. Immigrants purposely mislead police officials as to their nationality, fearing deportation or discrimination, or for no reason at all. Errors of these types are so apparent and frequent that reliable statisticians are wary, and unbiased students would not use such figures at all except in desperation at the general lack of information on the subject.

The innocent as well as the guilty may be arrested. The

more inferior the status of a minority, the more careless police officials tend to become in making arrests among them, so that Negroes, Chinese, south Europeans, Mexicans, and others of similar station may be taken into custody on suspicions so vague that native white people in similar circumstances would not have been disturbed. Thorsten Sellin has cited a case in which, during a two-day period, every Negro who happened to walk past the place where a criminal attack was reported to have occurred was arrested and held for identification by a woman of questionable character who reported the crime. Only one of the thirty-odd Negroes arrested could have been guilty, and in no instance was there any evidence justifying the arrest except presence in a public park within forty-eight hours after a crime was alleged to have been committed; yet the number of Negro arrests in the northern city where this occurred was appreciably swelled.[1] This may be an extreme illustration, but the irresponsible attitude of police officers shown in it is not exceptional. The fact that there are commonly fewer convictions in proportion to arrests for Negroes than for white people is additional evidence of unjustified arrests, if evidence is needed.[2] Until the proportion of innocent and guilty persons arrested is more nearly the same for all population groups, statistics of arrest will be found wanting for our purposes.

What of convictions? Racial bias in arrests cannot help but be reflected in court, for the trial cannot begin until some suspect is brought before the bar of justice. The prosecuting attorney is a representative of the people, chosen in accordance with their will, and not immune to their prejudices.

[1] Thorsten Sellin, "The Negro and the Problem of Law Observance in the Light of Social Research," in Charles Johnson, op. cit., p. 448. Some of the facts in this case known to the writer but not mentioned by Dr. Sellin have been added to his statement.

[2] For detailed statistics of Negro and immigrant crime, see Charles Johnson, op. cit.; Thorsten Sellin, "The Negro Criminal," in Donald Young, editor, "The American Negro," The Annals of the American Academy of Political and Social Science, November, 1928, vol. cxxxx; Carl Kelsey, "Immigration and Crime," in Clyde L. King, editor, "Modern Crime," The Annals of the American Academy of Political and Social Science, May, 1926, vol. cxxv, pp. 165-175; National Commission on Law Observance and Enforcement, Report on Crime and Criminal Justice in Relation to the Foreign Born, Government Printing Office, Washington, D. C., 1931.

The jury, consisting of twelve people who are at least as opinionated as the average in their community, able not infrequently to serve because of their mediocrity, convicts or acquits on the basis not only of law and fact, but also of personal prejudices. Our experience with the jury system and prohibition violations shows how easy it is for verdicts to be rendered contrary to established fact and legal duty. Preconceptions regarding minorities lead to verdicts equally indefensible in the eyes of the law.

If arrests and convictions give us such faulty comparative statistics, their errors can only be compounded when we arrive at tabulations of commitments to prison and prison population. Suspended sentence and parole are escapes from prison more readily available to people of native white stock than to minorities. Probation and pardon are favors more easily obtained for prisoners of white American ancestry than for friendless colored people and foreigners. The alternative of a fine in place of a jail term not only is offered to members of the white majority more frequently than to others, but is also more likely to be paid, and commitment escaped. Longer sentences, too, are more likely to be dealt out to members of alien and racial minorities than to people of native white stock. What reliance, then, can be placed on the statistics of prisoners sent to jail or incarcerated in our penal institutions at a given time?

It may be added here that while our statistics of immigrant crime are faulty beyond repair, the situation is even more hopeless when we wish to study the behavior of their children, born in this country. They are, of course, citizens of the United States by virtue of their place of birth; and as such the task of distinguishing them from the older white stock, if they themselves are white, is beyond the facilities, abilities, and desires of our criminal authorities. In their case, as in the case of all individuals belonging to minorities, we must look to limited, private investigations or to the future for statistical analyses of crime which do more than travesty scientific method.

Still unconvinced as to their comparative worthlessness, the reader may wish to know what conclusions can be drawn from our official criminal statistics concerning the *apparent* criminality of minorities. A surprise is in store for those who blame the immigrant and the Negro for crime waves and a steadily increasing prison population.

In short, the immigrant as a whole, judged by whatever official criminal statistics you will, furnishes a smaller proportion of *apparent* criminals than does the native born. *Real* criminality, it must be remembered, simply cannot be deduced from such statistics. Let us quote from the conclusions of Miss Alida C. Bowler, based on tabulations of 4,854,602 cases.[3] This study of nativity and crime is the most recent and the most trustworthy available. Miss Bowler found, and Miss Abbott, under whose direction the study was made, concurred in the findings:

"1. That in proportion to their respective numbers the foreign born commit considerably fewer crimes than the native born.

"2. That the foreign born approach the record of the native white most closely in the commission of crimes involving personal violence.

"3. That in crimes for gain (including robbery, in which there is also personal violence or the threat of violence) the native white greatly exceed the foreign born.

"4. That in the commission of certain types of offenses there is considerable variation among the different nationalities within the foreign-born group, but that the detailed data as yet available are insufficient, both as to quantity and ac-

---

[3] "This figure contains some duplications, in that many of the convictions and some of the commitment cases have also appeared as police arrests. But each represents a somewhat different phase of the case, and thus becomes a distinct statistical entity."

Police arrests, from 34 cities	3,548,876
Felony arrests, State of New York	24,867
United States prohibition indictments	26,685
Convictions	651,337
Commitments to institutions for petty offenders	524,149
Commitments to Federal and State prisons and reformatories	78,688
Total	4,854,602

National Commission on Law Observance and Enforcement, *op. cit.*, p. 195.

curacy, to warrant the formation of any final conclusion as to the comparative criminality of any particular groups.

"5. That there is insufficient information available to warrant any deductions as to criminal activity among the native born of foreign parentage as compared with those of native parentage."

Not one of these five conclusions is a reversal of the opinions on the matter long held by the leading students of crime and nativity.[4] It is not to be hoped, however, that the myth of high immigrant criminality will now be dispelled in so far as it rests on "official" statistics. The immigrant is too convenient a scapegoat.

Criminologists and immigration "experts" are themselves to blame for some of the popular confusion on the subject. A burden of crime has been laid on the back of the most recent immigrant since before the Revolution. Each group of latest arrivals has had to bear its cross, a heavy burden of public criminal accusation, usually attributed to some impossible inherent defect or peculiarity predisposing to the violation of our laws.[5] Scholarly attempts to get at the root of the matter have published and republished faulty statistics in the sterile belief that figs might be gathered from thistles. Involved techniques and contradictory conclusions have left the layman bewildered and impatient, but certain of one

---

[4] Professor Carl Kelsey, for example, reached the following conclusions about immigration and crime in 1926:

(1) Immigration has added to the complexity of our problem of crime and to the difficulties in the administration of justice.

(2) There is no reason to believe that the immigrants themselves are contributing unduly to the volume of crime.

(3) There is evidence that our penal machinery is none too well adapted to the present situation.

(4) The crux of the problem seems to lie in the activities of the children of immigrants.

(5) The problem seems to be social rather than biological in origin.

Carl Kelsey, "Immigration and Crime," op. cit., p. 174.

[5] To quote Miss Edith Abbott, "Complaints that immigration has increased the burdens of pauperism and crime have been numerous in every period of our history." Historical Aspects of the Immigration Problem, University of Chicago Press, Chicago, 1926, p. 539.

Section IV of this volume, entitled "Pauperism and Crime and other Domestic Immigration Problems," contains well selected documentary material illustrative of this attitude.

thing, that "statistics proved" some correlation between immigration and crime.

Let us demonstrate this process, but without burdening our text by copying the involved tables on which our generalizations are based. The Bureau of the Census has published in the latest of its volumes on prisoners committed to state and federal prisons and reformatories a mass of statistics for the year 1926. Miss Bowler, in her work just cited, after analyzing this census material, lists the "countries having a higher percentage of commitments than of population" as follows:[6]

"For all charges: Austria, Canada, Greece, Italy, China and Mexico.

"For homicide: Austria, Greece, Italy, Yugoslavia, China and Mexico.

"For rape: Austria, France, Greece, Italy, Poland, and Mexico.

"For robbery: Canada, England, Scotland, Wales, Greece, Italy, and Mexico.

"For assault: Austria, Greece, Italy, Yugoslavia, China, Japan and Mexico.

"For burglary: Canada, France, and Mexico.

"For forgery: Canada, England, Scotland, Wales, France, Greece, China, and Mexico.

"For larceny: Austria, Canada, Greece, Russia, and Mexico.

"For liquor violations: Austria, Greece, Hungary, Italy, Yugoslavia, and Mexico.

"For drug violations: Greece, Italy, China, Japan, and Mexico.

"Those countries whose commitment percentage in no instance exceeded their proportion of the foreign-born male population 21 and over were Czechoslovakia, Germany, Ireland, and the Scandinavian countries."

Now what do we know about *actual* criminality and nativity? Before answering, think back to our system of criminal procedure and its possibilities for inequalities in the administration of justice. Then make allowance for the fact that

[6] National Commission on Law Observance and Enforcement, *op. cit.*, pp. 155ff.

crime is a social phenomenon which is never found evenly distributed among the various types of persons in a community, nor is it a stable unit in itself. In modern civilization men are more likely to be criminals than women. Violations of the law are the same neither in quantity nor in kind in urban and rural areas, in manufacturing and agricultural districts, or even in somewhat similar communities in different parts of the United States. There is apparently a correlation between occupation and crime. Very young children under the law may not be convicted of crime, nor is crime so common among young people just over the minimum legal age, nor in the older age groups, as among those in the prime of maturity. Mentality, literacy, economic status, and other conditions too numerous to mention must also be taken into account. Now, since all these correlatives of crime, as measured by arrests, convictions, commitments, and prison population, vary from one minority group to the other—and this statement includes the native-born colored minorities as well as the alien—almost any conclusions you may care to draw about minority criminality, *apparent* or *actual*, can find some justification, depending on what statistical refinements your particular bias leads you to use. The problem is statistically insoluble except by the method of scrapping present data and beginning afresh.

Negro *apparent* criminality, unlike that of the immigrant, is appreciably greater than that of the native white. Taking into account racial discriminations in criminal procedure and penal treatment, allowing for unfavorable population distribution, sex ratios, age groupings, economic status, intellectual development, and the other common correlatives of officially determined crime, Negro *actual* criminality may still be expected to be higher than that of our white population. On what basis may this statement be made, if statistics are omitted from the discussion as of little worth?

In this day of statistical fetishism it is dangerous to fall back on non-statistical observation and simple reasoning in social science, but it is the only recourse left in the dilemma created by the slipshod methods of our criminal authorities.

Instead of using the method of counting *actual* criminals, a method unusable in a community where most crime goes undetected, let us examine the nature of crime itself, analyze its characteristics, and then see what minorities are so fashioned that crime may flourish among them.

Starting with the only workable definition, that crime is a violation of the law, we are immediately beset by the necessity for distinguishing between crimes of varying social significance. To break a speed law is obviously not such a serious anti-social offense as murder or theft. This, however, gets us nowhere, for so are some murders and thefts more dangerous to society than others. The best that can be done, unless we wish to write a book on criminology alone, is to leave out of account those legal offenses which are publicly condoned by our legal authorities themselves, in reflection of public sentiment, and not attempt to classify the rest except as special occasion demands.

Laws are purposely broken because desire for some illegal end outweighs the individual's restraints due to the threat of legal penalty, social disapproval, or personal motivation toward law observance. Opportunity, of course, is also a factor. A starving man may refrain from stealing because he fears imprisonment, public degradation, his own "conscience," or because there is nothing he can lay his hands on. We are consciously leaving out of account hereditary differences in mentality, emotional stability, and other biological factors, for there is no reliable evidence that these factors in conduct vary between races and nationalities. They may rather be considered as constants which cannot be made to explain differential crime rates. The other factors, however, are certainly not constants.

With the exception of a limited number of crimes, especially those involving white people or their property, public officials, usually white, have never shown an interest in Negro offenders as intense as that in white violators of the law. Negroes will have their gin. They cannot be stopped from overstepping legal bounds in sex relations. Petty thieving can be only slightly checked, for it is in their blood and does no serious harm. So runs the defense of this indifference. When the solution of a crime involves no great effort, or when a white person is wronged, the forces of law and order spring into action, but the lesson of indifference and security from police interference has already been learned too thoroughly to be obliterated by these restricted zones of police activity and prejudiced prosecution. Freedom from legal restraint in some criminal activities, even though partly counterbalanced by official diligence in regard to others, may be expected to lead to greater group criminality.

Liquor-law, speed-law, and sanitary-regulation violations carry with them slight social disapproval in the United States today. For some reason or other, the public at large has not yet built up the same social tradition of ostracism from "decent society" for these offenses that it has for many others, especially those which have their roots far back in European civilization and have been definitely censured by the church. Negroes have only recently adopted the white man's culture, and with striking imperfections. Their "social conscience" will require a long period of training while they continue to absorb the culture of their white neighbors and discard their remaining idiosyncrasies.

Regardless of external pressure, individuals refrain from crime for personal reasons related to moral training, habits of conformity, personal acceptance of imposed standards of conduct, security and success in the existing social order, and the like. Need the point be labored by again repeating what is established elsewhere showing colored America's handicaps in these respects?

Individualism is also not conducive to law observance, and the Negro is today as great an individualist as our pioneer fathers were in colonial times. Add to this the still further decrease in social restraint accompanying a cityward migration, with its disturbance of sex and age groupings and its disruption of family and community ties, and enough of the picture has been presented to convince the most skeptical that a high *actual* crime rate is the natural crime rate for the American colored population, not because of race, but because of inferior caste status.

Although the European immigrant also suffers from an unnatural sex ratio and a peculiar age grouping, both tending to increase the crude crime rate, his *actual* criminality as well as the *apparent* is probably below that of the native white stock. This is true in spite of the fact that in addition to unfavorable sex ratios and age groupings, his economic, educational and social status is generally inferior.

The European immigrant comes from lands where legislation similar to our own has been in force for generations, and where law observance has been achieved not only through threats of punishment but also through years of traditional training which has attached a deep-seated, moral meaning to forms of conduct which to us, with an individualistic pioneer background, are still matters of personal choice. He may come from countries where governments are overthrown if they function badly, but observance of the fundamental laws of human relationships, as he understands them, are not to be lightly disregarded. Why should we be so naïve as to expect immigrants to come from countries with low crime rates to the United States, and then change their nature overnight and become the source of crime waves?

This might happen if a large percentage of lawless were included in our European immigration, but we have no reason to believe that this has been the case in recent years. Even in earlier days, when paupers, vagrants, family black sheep, and convicts were "assisted" from England, Ireland, Germany, and other European countries to the United States, these "anti-social classes" were more the unfortunate debtors, unemployed, and petty miscreants than what we today would call criminals.

The only other condition under which we might be led into expecting immigrants to be great criminals would be if their European standards of conduct were in some way the opposite of those recognized by our laws. The truth is that they are essentially the same, with the European standard, if anything, the stricter of the two. This does not mean that there is no cultural conflict when the European immigrant settles in the United States, but that however serious such conflict may be in some respects, it is not the kind that leads to serious infractions of our laws except in the unusual instance. Quite likely, if these immigrants had remained in Europe, their criminal element would have remained much smaller than it turned out to be in this country, but it is still smaller than that of our native white population.

Again on *a priori* grounds, we may expect their children to be more lawless than either their parents or the descendants of old American stock, for they may be caught between two cultures and find difficulty in accepting the restraints of either. So-called gangs and racketeers have commonly been found to be made up more of children of immigrants than of immigrants. This problem is discussed in its relation to sex delinquency in the section on minority family life, and the same principles developed there may be extended to crime in general. Whatever the extent of this problem of the first American-born generation of European ancestry may be, it quickly solves itself as they and their children pass from minority status and disappear into the native white majority without a trace of their original "inferiority" to haunt them.

The Mexican and other colored immigrants, including the Filipino among the Orientals, constitute a different criminal problem, to the extent to which their color gives them permanent minority status, and to the degree to which their cultures vary from our own more than do those of European immigrants. The Mexican, according to the census tabulations of state and federal prison commitments referred to above, is the only group of foreign nativity which has a greater proportion of criminals committed to penal institutions in all classes of crime than its proportion of the total population. Indian physical characteristics serve as distinguishing permanent features of Mexicans, their social status in all respects, judged from the native white point of view, is low, and their culture, a mixture of Indian and south European, with later modifications, is in sharp contrast to our own patterns. These conditions, for which they may be held accountable but not responsible as a people, suggest the desirability of their restriction as immigrants, but are not sufficiently serious to justify exclusion. Chinese, Japanese, and Hindoos, similarly situated, have already been excluded. The regulation of Filipinos, owing to their residence in United States territory, will cause us more embarrassment.

The colored peoples of South America, including Central America and the Caribbean islands, have sent us only a few streams of immigrants, and these have escaped much notice because of their identification with the native-born Negroes in the communities in which they have settled. It will be difficult to draw any conclusions concerning their criminality because of this fact; but it is probable that they have less real criminality than the native-born Negroes because of their generally superior social status in tropical America and the consequent more ready absorption of the standards of their home country. This, by the way, does not apply to all who might come, but only to the majority of those who have thus far migrated to the United States.

This is enough to establish the fact that minority criminality is not a unique problem, but rather one which will adjust itself automatically, sometimes rising and sometimes falling, as each particular minority makes adjustments in such non-criminal aspects of group life as population distribution, work, play, and social status. We do not cure disease by treating symptoms, nor may minority crimes be materially reduced except by striking at the causes.

CULTURE CONFLICT AND THE LAW

Ignorance of the law does not relieve one of accountability for violations, nor does an honest conviction that the law is in error. In this axiomatic statement lies the heart of the problem of minority law observance and law enforcement.

It has been established that minorities are marked by cultural peculiarities. If of alien birth, they are likely to be ignorant of some of our legislation which the rest of us take for granted as common knowledge. In any event, all minorities of racial and national origin find cause for sincere dispute in legislation which to them is unquestionably unjust. Our legis-lators and jurists are cognizant of this fact but, as a rule, hold to the opinion that no legal recognition may be taken of it. This, however, is not always the case.

Public officials of all grades have been known to close their eyes in excuse of offenses because, with uncommon insight, they chanced to appreciate some minority point of view in conflict with statute law. Such leniency, if leniency it is, must be regarded as illegal, and offers but occasional and uncertain relief to bewildered minorities, unable to understand why justice and the law should not be synonymous.

In a few instances, however, the government has seen fit to recognize merit in minority special pleading. In slave days, for example, special legal machinery was created to deal with slave offenders, and in some districts free Negroes were also subject to the jurisdiction of slave courts. This illustration, however, may not be apt, for its existence was coincident with the institution of slavery, a minority status now outlawed. A contemporary illustration of the same principle is still available in our courts of Indian offenses. Their right to existence, however, has been disputed.

In 1925, the year after all Indians born in the United States were granted citizenship, an Indian ward of the government was brought before an Indian court charged with a sex offense against a young girl. He pleaded guilty and was sentenced to some sixty days' labor on a reservation farm. He escaped, but was soon apprehended and placed, manacled, in a crude Indian jail to serve the remainder of his sentence. As he was a repeated offender and had shown signs of vindictiveness, he was closely confined in order that he might not again gain his freedom before the expiration of his sentence. The jail, being old, small, and rarely used, was far from adequate for the purpose it was serving from a health point of view. Numerous influential people interested themselves in the alleged injustices of this case, so that Congress, the Indian Office, the Indian Rights Association, the American Indian Defense Association, and even the President were bombarded with protests against the treatment which he received. Many of these protests emphasized in no uncertain terms the common belief that the Office of Indian Affairs, through the Indian courts and judges, was exercising too great an unchecked power over its wards who were accused of certain criminal offenses.

The need for special machinery to handle Indian offenses was brought to a legal focus by the domestic difficulties of Spotted Tail, a Sioux leader of the latter part of the nineteenth century. After his unceremonious appropriation of the wife of a crippled Indian named Medicine Bear, he offered the offended husband compensation for his loss. While these negotiations were being carried on, a friend of Medicine Bear named Crow Dog made the matter a blood feud and on August 5, 1881, shot Spotted Tail to death. James McLaughlin, a former federal agent to the Sioux and later a United States Indian inspector, comments on the importance of this case as follows:

"The event which put a period to the romantic adventures of Spotted Tail was fraught with important consequences, for it resulted in establishing the status of the Indian before the law. Crow Dog went into hiding until his friends had made compensation to the family of Spotted Tail for his murder. The adjustment was made according to tribal custom, and the affair was settled so far as the Indians were concerned; but Spotted Tail was a man of too much importance for the authorities to permit his assassin to go unpunished. Crow Dog was arrested and brought to trial, was convicted, and the case appealed. The contention was made on behalf of Crow Dog that, he being an Indian and not a citizen of the United States, the court had no jurisdiction; that having been dealt with according to the custom of his tribe for the offense, he was not amenable to prosecution by federal or other courts. The United States Supreme Court, to which the case was carried, took this view of the case and discharged the accused man. The decision resulted in the enactment of legislation which brought all Indians under the laws of the states or territories in which they reside, making them amenable under the laws thereof for felonious crimes not punishable by the federal code."[7]

It was on March 3, 1885, that Congress made Indians who were still under the supervision of the Indian Office punishable under the federal courts for eight specific crimes, namely, murder, manslaughter, rape, assault with intent to kill, assault with a dangerous weapon, arson, burglary, and larceny. As a rule, other acts held criminal under federal and state codes, committed on Indian reservations and restricted allotments by a restricted Indian, were not punishable by either federal or state courts.

Courts of Indian Offenses were consequently established to cover crimes not mentioned in the law of 1885. These included such crimes as assault with intent to commit rape, robbery, mayhem, adultery, forgery, receiving stolen goods, kidnaping, fraud, perjury, unlawful cohabitation, statutory rape, bigamy, incest, polygamy, lewdness, wife and family desertion, soliciting females for immoral purposes, disturbing the peace, etc. A number of special Indian offenses were also assigned to these Indian courts, including the violation of various regulations laid down by the Indian Office governing the conduct of its wards in accordance with authority granted by Congress.

The authority for these courts apparently rests on the "general power of the Secretary of the Interior to make rules and regulations for the management of Indian affairs."[8] Congress has recognized them by appropriating salaries for the judges, who are administratively appointed. The two main advantages of the Indian court system over the alternative proposal to place all Indians under the jurisdiction of the nearest federal or state court are that it is cheaper to be tried under the Indian court, and that the decisions are more likely to be in accord with local tribal custom. Considerable latitude is permitted both in procedure and in decisions, although the

[7] James McLaughlin, *My Friend the Indian*, Houghton Mifflin Company, Boston, 1910, p. 74.

[8] Lewis Merriam, *op. cit.*, p. 760. This volume contains an excellent discussion of the status of Indian offenders as well as an analysis of the general legal status of all Indians.

maximum sentence has been 90 days in jail or at hard labor, or a few dollars' fine.

On one occasion, two boys guilty of a minor offense were both sentenced to plough a ten-acre section for their parents, and the elder boy of the two, who had a greater degree of guilt, was also compelled to fence his section. All things considered, the judges have usually done good work, for, although ignorant from a lawyer's point of view and working without the guidance of definite statute law, as a rule they have been leading citizens of their community selected by the reservation superintendent for their fitness for the job. No doubt there have been judges appointed for reasons other than merit, but these seem to have been a small minority.

It has been the opinion of the Commissioners of Indian Affairs that the Indian courts are the best possible means for handling minor offenses until such time as the Indians might reasonably be expected to give up their tribal customs and standards and come entirely under the white man's law. Most Indians are already under federal and state courts, for they have left their tribal ways of life and are living as ordinary citizens. There are only about thirty Indian courts at the present time, and it would be difficult to find additional Indian communities suited by tradition and isolation for such special legal consideration.

Meanwhile, it has been pointed out that the Indians who are still wards of the government are in a transitional state and should be treated differently from their white neighbors. Education has consequently been emphasized and penal treatment has been minimized wherever possible. The Indian courts have been noticeably more lenient with offenders than the state and federal courts, and rightly so, according to those who feel that laws should have a real meaning to the governed.

Perhaps one more illustration of Indian culture conflict and the law may be used to clarify the problem. A white man named Hugh Boyle was killed by the Cheyennes in 1890 near the Lame Deer agency. The United States authorities demanded the surrender of the two Cheyennes guilty of the murder in order that they might be punished by hanging. The Cheyennes as a body offered horses, blankets, and other wealth in payment for the offense of their fellow tribesmen in such amount that had their offers been accepted the whole group would have been beggared. According to the Cheyennes' beliefs a murder could in this way be offset and the wrong involved righted. After long negotiations they were at last made to understand that the white man's demand for justice could not be satisfied by a transfer of any amount of wealth. A threat of war convinced them of the wisdom of making concessions to the white man's point of view, which they still thought peculiar.

Death by hanging, however, was unthinkable to the Cheyennes, for it was believed that at death the soul passed on to its future existence with the last breath, and hanging would prevent its passage. The souls of the murderers would thus be unable to free themselves and be left imprisoned in their bodies. A compromise was offered under which it was agreed that the murderers would ride up to the agency at an appointed time, shooting at the white defenders, and be killed by the return fire, thus dying as true warriors and in such a way that their spirits might be free.

As agreed, the two men rode at full speed, firing at the troop of cavalry and at the Indian police drawn up at the agency, and were killed after wounding one soldier and killing a horse. One died on the first charge, but the other rode past the troops, turned and rode past again, and was finally shot. During this period practically all the members of the tribe were standing about the surrounding hills watching. There were no disturbances.

The bodies were claimed by the Cheyennes and buried according to their custom. It is interesting to note that on the night before, special ceremonial dances in which the two men took part were held in preparation for the morrow.[9]

Such a compromise between Indian and white culture deserves sympathy. Whenever deemed practical, similar compromises have been made by our government and its officials

[9] James McLaughlin, *op cit.*, pp. 303ff.

in dealing with Indian criminals. Their general success suggests that it would have been a wise policy to have extended the practice, if our purpose has been to secure law and order among the Indians and to provide a maximum of interracial peace. Why, however, should the Indians be such an exception? Would it not have been possible to effect similar compromises in our criminal prosecutions of other minorities of alien culture?

The greatest objection to such an extension of the principle grows out of the fact that the Indians are the only minority who have been even imperfectly segregated in areas distinctly their own. South European immigrants, Mexicans, and Asiatics, all of whom have a cultural background in conflict with our criminal laws, have settled in districts already appropriated and controlled by native white people. Considered purely from an administrative viewpoint, this seems to make such legal discrimination almost impossible. The practical difficulties seem insurmountable, although the need is no less than in the case of the Indians. Sentimentalists may also add that the Indian deserves special recognition because he was here first, while immigrants have voluntarily placed themselves under the jurisdiction of the government of the United States. This latter argument has no scientific value, for the "voluntary" element does not alter the social problem involved.

No longer is it considered scientific by criminologists to make the punishment fit the crime; individualization of treatment is now the goal of scientific penology. Individualization, however, implies consideration of the entire ascertainable heredity and training of the criminal before treatment is recommended. To use a hackneyed analogy, in crimes as in disease, we are insisting more and more firmly that the most effective course of action is dependent not solely on the malady which directed attention to the case, but on a complete knowledge of the patient as a functioning unit. To leave minority backgrounds out of account is as fatal to effective treatment as it would be to disregard mentality.

Much depends on the objective of our criminal legislation.

If the purpose is to punish, to obtain vengeance, to insure retributive justice, then the guilty individual is of no concern save as a subject for torture. While our present laws are thoroughly saturated with this primitive, ineffective spirit, the physical and mental torture of offenders which it implies serves ends which are spiteful and of little social worth in comparison with such penal motives as prevention and cure. Society must be protected from the individual who cannot obey the rules of the game, and the victims of crime should receive recompense for their loss and suffering. A penology of vengeance, incorporating a belief in the need for earthly expiation, pays small dividends. It is bound to be discarded with increasing understanding of crime and criminals.

It cannot be discarded, however, until the law permits greater latitude to our courts and to our penal administrators. This seems to be on the way. Some provisions for individualization have already been accomplished. Unofficially, prosecutors, juries, and judges make allowances in special cases. Maximum and minimum sentences, suspended sentences, probation, parole, pardon and penal alternatives are part of the law. They are even now occasionally used to modify penalties awarded minority members with extenuating histories. Is it, then, such an impossible task to extend the principle to its logical conclusion?

If our desirable penal objectives may be said to be the protection of society and its members from criminal injury, and not just revenge, why not extend the principle of individualization to minorities, as is already being done in a haphazard, occasional manner and has been done more thoroughly for our Indians and Negroes in slave days? The "practical" difficulties, of which so much has been made, are the result of a scientifically unjustifiable criminal system and are not insuperable.

The case may be reversed for argument, and applied to ourselves, the governing majority. By forced treaty, the United States in company with European nations, has obtained the privilege of "extra-territoriality" in China and other eastern nations. This means that American citizens charged with criminal conduct in these countries have not been under the jurisdiction of the local courts and laws, but have had the right of trial under conditions and regulations with which they were familiar. As this is written, the newspapers are making much over the demands of Chinese that an American citizen, a hospital official in China, who shot a native under conditions which apparently led him to suspect burglary, be tried in Chinese courts under Chinese law. Our protests, sanctioned by a one-sided treaty, are founded upon the belief that oriental criminal law is too different from and inferior to our own to be applied to our nationals, even if they have voluntarily taken residence in China.[10]

Without going into the merits of extra-territoriality, which is not easy to defend in principle, our refusal to relinquish this privilege is proof that, when our own citizens are involved, as a minority in a foreign land, we believe that cultural background should be taken into account in criminal cases. The shoe here is on the other foot, but in this day when intellectual leaders no longer think in terms of superior and inferior, but just different, cultures, how can we demand the extreme of extra-territoriality without granting some recognition to the cultural problems of alien minorities in the United States?

This is not a suggestion that other nations be allowed to establish courts to try their citizens domiciled in the United States. We are sufficiently enlightened to make due allowances ourselves, not because any minority has a legal "right" to special treatment, but because such procedure is the sensible one for our own safety and protection.

It may be said that at least one minority, the Negro, because of long residence in the United States, deserves no special consideration in criminal prosecution on account of minority status. This observation is shallow, for it fails to recognize that a slave history and caste distinctions have forced on the Negro a culture in some respects more alien than that of many of our

<hr />

[10] For a brief statement of the problems and status of extra-territoriality in China, see James T. Shotwell, "Extra-Territoriality in China," in J. B. Condliffe, editor, *Problems of the Pacific*, University of Chicago Press, Chicago, 1929, pp. 345-355.

immigrants. This is one reason why Negro criminality is so much higher than that of the immigrant.

Actually, this suggestion that minority peculiarities of culture be taken into account in the disposition of criminal cases does not place aliens and colored peoples in a special class before the law. It is merely a special instance of the general principle of individualization. To the extent that every resident of the United States has had a cultural training different from that of every other resident, the same rule should be applied. The moral delinquent of the slums requires a different penal technique than does the criminal of wealthy parentage. The Iowa farm boy who runs afoul of the law should not be given the same treatment as the city urchin. Such classifications are infinite among both native white stock and minorities of racial and national origin.

Whatever special pleading there may be for minority offenders is exceptional because of a difference of degree, not of kind. The difference is so great, however, that it constitutes the basic problem of minority law observance.

LYNCH LAW

Lynching is another phase of the relationship between minorities and law observance. Although generally defended on the ground that it is caused by minority—especially Negro—criminality, it is more a problem of majority lawlessness.

Detailed descriptions would appear so horrible to the reader, unprepared by mob mindedness for inhuman brutalities, that they rarely find their way into public print. An aged colored man, with hands and feet chopped off, is reported to have been thrown into a river to drown. A feeble-minded boy is chained to a schoolhouse roof and burned with the building. A Negro, fastened with staples to a beam in a burning barn, given a razor to cut himself loose, is shot and pushed back into the flaming building, according to a word-of-mouth account. Another Negro, chained to a post, is burned slowly with leaves and light trash until life seems about to depart, when gasoline is used to prevent an anti-climax of unspectacular, quiet death. Burning, shooting, hanging, mutilation, and clubbing—

alone, in combination, and with ingenious added tortures—
have been perpetrated by mobs of citizens in every period of
American history.[11]

From a social and psychological point of view, however, it
is improper to restrict an analysis of lynching to those instances in which death results from mob action. Tarring and
feathering, riding on a rail, flogging, maiming, driving out of
town, and wanton property destruction should be similarly
classified, for the setting, the motivation, and all the attendant
social phenomena are not so changed by a victim's death as
to warrant separate study.

Defined in this way, there is no record of the number of
lynchings which have taken place in the United States. The
impossibility of keeping count of all forms of lynch law is
probably the excuse for the common misinterpretation of this
form of behavior so as to include only that in which actual
murder occurs. Since there may be a correlation between the
number of lynchings resulting in death and the others of less
physical violence, some of these statistics may be quoted.

"There have been lynched in the United States 4,951 persons in the forty-six years beginning in 1882 [when the
Chicago *Tribune* first began recording lynchings involving
death] and extending through 1927. Of the victims 3,513 were
Negroes and 1,438 whites. Ninety-two were women—sixteen
of them white and seventy-six colored."[12] "From 1890 to 1900
there were 1,665 persons lynched; from 1900 to 1910 there
were 921; from 1910 to 1920 there were 840; and since 1920
through 1927 there were 304. The averages, therefore, for the
four divisions of time, successively, are thus 166.5, 92.1, 84.0
and 38.0."[13] There were 11 lynchings in 1928, ten in 1929,
twenty-one in 1930, and 13 in 1931. Allowing for fluctuations

[11] For descriptions of lynchings, as well as for discussion of their extent,
causes and significance, see Walter White, *Rope and Faggot*, Alfred A. Knopf,
New York, 1929, pp. xiii + 272, iv; James E. Cutler, *Lynch-Law*, Longmans,
Green & Company, New York, 1905, pp. xiv + 287; Raymond T. Bye, *Capital
Punishment*, Com. Philanthropic Labor Yrly. Meeting of Friends, Philadelphia, 1919, 106 pp.; Scott Nearing, *Black America*, Vanguard Press, New York,
1929, 275 pp. (This book contains photographs of lynchings.)

[12] Walter White, *op. cit.*, p. 227.

[13] *Ibid.*, p. 19.

in variation with temporary social stresses, murder by lynch law has decreased to a point where it is relatively unimportant, considered solely as a type of murder. Considered in relation to deaths in automobile or railroad accidents, or to other forms of murder, the number is insignificant.

The number of mob murders, however, is not the important consideration. Back of them are hundreds, perhaps thousands, of unrecorded instances each year in which unauthorized, emotionally aroused, and irresponsible mobs have taken the law into their own hands instead of trusting in the legal authorities. Even if we knew the exact number of overt acts of mob violence and threats of violence, the far-reaching influence of this type of behavior would still be tremendously underestimated. The attitude which tolerates and encourages such conduct is present in thousands of individuals for each one who actually participates in coercive mob action in any given year.

The cause of lynching as it exists today is neither criminal brutality nor the inability of established authorities to cope with an excessive amount of crime. Some people have been lynched for brutal, bestial offenses which, it might be argued, no legal penalty could expiate. There have, no doubt, also been situations needing correction which the law could not afford, hampered as it is by technicalities. The excuses offered by the mobs themselves for their murders indicate no extraordinary need for the replacement of legal agencies by popular "justice."

Cutler's analysis of the reasons for lynchings between 1882 and 1903 resulting in the death of the victims showed them, on the whole, to be quite ordinary crimes, with a scattering of unusually revolting offenses and a much larger proportion of trivial charges. Proof of guilt, not easy to obtain even by deliberate court procedure, is beyond the capacity of a mob, so that it may be said to be a social accident when the victim has actually committed the act for which he is lynched. To quote from Cutler: "With regard to the causes assigned for the lynchings a wide variation is observed. Only 38 per cent of the Negroes, against 53.5 per cent of the Whites and Others, were lynched for Murder. Rape stands next to Murder in order of importance in both cases, but while 34 per cent of the Negroes were lynched for Rape, only 11.5 per cent of the Whites and Others were lynched for that cause. Minor offenses, Arson, Theft, and Assault appear of much more importance as causes for the lynching of Negroes than for the lynching of Whites and Others.

"Those who assume that the majority of the Negroes lynched in the South are lynched for the crime of rape against white women, and that the lynching of Negroes is therefore justifiable, will find very little satisfaction in an examination [of Cutler's statistics]. . . . In the classification of the cases the writer has put every case where both rape and murder were assigned as the cause, under Rape. It is possible that if a careful investigation were made of all the cases credited to Murder, it might be found that the motive in some cases was rape but that the actual crime committed was murder, and that it was for rape as well as for murder that the Negroes in such cases were lynched. . . . The statistics, however, cannot be made to show that more than thirty-four per cent of the Negroes lynched in the South during the last twenty-two years have been lynched for the crime of rape, either attempted, alleged, or actually committed; and it is safe to say that if rape were connected with the offense in any case, that fact would ordinarily be stated in the report."[14]

Investigations by Raymond Bye and Walter White, which include lynchings in the years since Cutler's study, are in accord with this quotation. Bye cites such trivial excuses for murderous lynchings as stealing an overcoat, insolence, disputing a white man's word, slapping a boy, and brushing against a girl on the street.[15] It is clear that the nature of the alleged and actual offenses punished by lynching does not explain the phenomenon of lynching, for they range from the trivial to the heinous. Proof of guilt is unimportant to the mob, and only in exceptional cases, even in the South, do even serious offenses lead to mob action.

[14] James E. Cutler, op. cit., pp. 177-178.
[15] Raymond T. Bye, op. cit., p. 69.

Although a great majority of the victims of lynchings in the United States have been Negroes, this does not mean that if there were no Negroes in the country there would be practically no lynchings. Lynching is not a form of social behavior restricted to Negro-white relations, nor is it essentially a phenomenon of race relationships, in spite of the fact that most people lynched in the United States have belonged to some minority of racial or national origin.

Cutler refers to "the small number (108) of Indians, Mexicans and foreigners that have been lynched during the twenty-two years [covered by his study]. In the years when the larger numbers were lynched they were distributed as follows: in 1883, seven Mexicans, four Indians, and one Chinaman; in 1884, six Mexicans, one Indian, one Japanese, and one Swiss; in 1885, six Chinese and two Indians; in 1891, eleven Italians (at New Orleans), two Indians, and two Chinese; in 1893, five Italians, two Indians, two Mexicans, and one Bohemian; in 1895, five Italians (at Walsenburg, Colorado), two Indians, and two Mexicans. In all, forty-five Indians, twenty-eight Italians, twenty Mexicans, twelve Chinese, one Japanese, one Swiss, and one Bohemian were lynched during the period 1882-1903."[16]

This is likely to create a false impression in the mind of the reader, for the period in question was one when antagonism to these groups was not at high tide. Bye says nothing whatever about the lynching of aliens. White mentions, too briefly in a general study of lynching, the deaths of a few aliens at the hands of mobs, but omits reference to Indians, although more Indians have been lynched, using the mob murder definition, than Negroes.

"A white man would be found murdered and scalped, apparently at least by an Indian. No one could know exactly what tribe might have committed the murder. . . .

"In the face of such a situation the frontiersman very frequently applied a sort of lynch law. A group would merely go out and kill the first Indian they saw. In such cases, without exception, the Indians would eventually take revenge, and

[16] James E. Cutler, *op. cit.*, pp. 171-172.

another Indian war might be the result."[17] Indians were shot down on trumped-up charges or merely as a part of an extermination policy. They were burned alive, drowned, disemboweled; their hands and feet were cut off, and other mutilations were practised. Babies as well as women and children were ingeniously tortured. Every form of death ever applied to Negroes has undoubtedly had its counterpart in the murder of Indians. Incidentally, Indians also lynched white people in equally cruel ways.

Evidence of the lynching of Chinese is readily available in the history of the Pacific states.[18] From the middle of the nineteenth century until 1882, when Cutler's figures begin, was the period when California's antagonism to the Chinese was at its height. Remembering that the census never found more than about 107,000 Chinese in the United States, the number of individuals of this nationality lynched is seen to be proportionately larger than in the case of the Negro. Japanese, also few in number, have had their share of lynchings. To gain a proper perspective, lynchings should always be viewed in their numerical relation to the size of the group to which the victims belonged.

On January 22, 1930, a twenty-two-year-old Filipino youth was shot while in bed by a carload of white men firing into the camp building at Watsonville, California, where a group of Filipino workers were staying. Mob action against Filipinos has occurred on a number of other occasions.[19] In view of the fact that this group numbers less than 50,000 and has but recently migrated to the United States, the lynch attitude toward them is well developed.

Newspaper accounts and the public reaction to anti-Filipino

[17] William Christie MacLeod, *op. cit.*, p. 374. If details are needed, this volume contains sufficient to establish the fact that Indian massacres and "wars" frequently belonged to the category of lynchings. This is particularly true where the "soldiers" were merely citizens on an Indian hunt, and quite commonly they made no pretense at having legal sanction for their murders.

[18] For a description of the west coast attitude toward the Chinese in the early days, see Mary Roberts Coolidge, *Chinese Immigration*, Henry Holt & Company, Inc., New York, 1909, chap. ii.

[19] For "two illustrative cases of acute antagonism to Filipino immigrants," see Bruno Lasker, *Filipino Immigration*, University of Chicago Press, Chicago, 1931, pp. 358-368.

mob demonstrations show how it happens that we are only partly conscious that such behavior, where Negroes are not involved and no one is killed, is also lynching. When "citizens' committees" of agitated white people warn Filipino immigrants to "keep moving," dynamite a club house, or otherwise coerce them, the *incident* retains its identity and is not lost by description as "another lynching," as would be the case if its elements more closely fitted our stereotyped lynch concept. Filipinos are still a novelty. They fit into no comfortable mental category, as do Negroes or criminals of any race. If there is opposition to the mob, a different stereotype of "race riots" is employed. Thus our stereotype of lynching is based on too narrow a definition, one which actually excludes all but a very small percentage of the lynchings which occur.

Accordingly, when a Negro is shot by a small group of white people, it is recognized as a lynching. The similar treatment of a criminal of any race is also so classified. But if the victim is neither a criminal nor a Negro, or is not killed, the public looks on it as a separate and unique incident, as a riot, a murder, a flogging, or as some other type of behavior distinct from lynching. Actually, whenever unauthorized individuals take the law into their own hands and exercise coercive force in vengeance for an alleged offense or in defense against some fancied threat, the essential elements of a lynching are all present.

This means that all lynching is mob action. The phenomena of crowd psychology at a football game, a theater, or in an election crowd lack the characteristics of a lynching, although these may sometimes easily be added by an untoward incident. No one holds that a background of race conflict is essential to a lynching in the strict meaning of the word, and, as has been stated, it is just as meaningless to make the differentiation between mob action and lynching on the basis of the death of the victim. Perhaps the phrase "coercive mob behavior" should be used when death does not result, in view of the popular meaning of the term, but to the present writer this seems needlessly cumbersome.

Lynching, stripped of its confusing non-essentials, is a manifestation of a conflict of group interest. The common assumption, based on the statistics of deaths at the hands of mobs, that "it [lynching] seems to be found only in unstable societies where frontier conditions prevail, or where racial mixtures create a pressing social problem,"[20] is a misleading one which tends to confuse the ordinary settings of American lynchings with their cause. The frontier is connected with lynching because it throws into sharp contrast the antagonistic interests of conflicting groups. The Indian and the white man, the Oriental and the Californian, the forces of law and order, and the bad men of Vigilante days in the west were antagonistic frontier groups where the alignment was clear cut, for a person's status and interests were readily discernible. With the legal authorities sometimes non-existent, generally indifferent to lynching, and practically always impotent in clashes of interest groups, mob action seemed the only effective type of action, so that the tradition of quick, popular justice became prevalent in frontier communities.

In older communities where group interests become entangled so that individuals stand in many relationships to their fellow citizens, some frontier distinctions tend to fade, and so does lynching. A particularly atrocious crime may set an individual apart so that public vengeance may be taken against him, but the criminal classes are indistinct and are treated with popular indifference. The more homogeneous communities, such as small rural districts and the foreign areas of cities, where conflicting interests can be most quickly and generally recognized, still turn most readily to the recourse of mob action.

Race distinctions, supposedly indicative of a conflict of interests, are still as observable as ever, and have for this reason remained an important factor in lynching. Wherever lynching of a racial minority has materially decreased, it has most likely been the result of lessened competition, real or fancied, from that group. The Indians and the Chinese, for example, no longer suffer much from lynching, but then they are no longer serious competitors of the white man. Negro lynch-

[20] Raymond T. Bye, *op. cit.*, p. 12.

ings, too, have fallen off, and this may be ascribed not so much to a recognition of the evils of lynching, *per se,* as to decreasing clashes of interests between black and white in the south. There has, however, been an increasing clash of interests between these groups in the cities, and here Negro lynchings, usually spoken of as race riots, have become more common.[21]

There are a number of types of lynchings not generally so listed which may be used to illustrate this essential factor of interest conflict, common to all. In times of strikes, the workers who have walked out, a compact interest group, are prone to attack members of conflicting groups, such as strikebreakers and mill owners and executives. At hotly contested elections, when the outcome is thought to determine issues of bread and butter, vital to conflicting groups, mob coercion and murder are not unusual. In time of war, copperheads, slackers, hyphenated Americans, and conscientious objectors are in danger of lynching. In all these cases, the conflict of interests is apparent, even if it is only a fancied conflict.[22] Similar basic conflicts should not be lost sight of in frontier or racial lynchings where they are also always present.

This suggests the futility of anti-lynching laws, of interracial commissions, and of educational programs in warring against mob action. Laws taking the prosecution of mob mem-

[21] A comprehensive study of the Chicago race riots, illustrative of this point, may be found in The Chicago Commission on Race Relations, *The Negro in Chicago,* University of Chicago Press, Chicago, 1922, pp. xxiv + 672.

[22] The Philadelphia *Daily News* for July 24, 1931, the evening of the day on which this was written, carried the following news item:

ONE WOUNDED BY BOMBING IN COAL DISORDER

"PITTSBURGH.—A garage in which six nonunion miners were sleeping at the Wildwood mine of the Butler Consolidated Coal Co. was damaged by a bomb explosion, one man being injured.

"Shortly after three men fired on a cottage occupied by three nonunion miners employed by the same company. About six volleys were fired, but none was injured.

"Fearing repetition of Tuesday's attack, when they were fired upon from ambush, 300 miners of the Standard Mining Co. at McKinleyville, W. Va., refused to return to the pit."

This incident has the essential characteristics of a lynching, although it is not probable that it will be catalogued as such by the public.

The same edition carried notice of political riots in Mississippi and prohibition mob disturbances in Georgia and Pennsylvania, all being in essence lynchings.

bers out of the local courts into the federal would be only a well meant gesture, for even federal judges are human, reflect local sentiment, and must depend on the cooperation of local witnesses who are convinced that lynching is justified to preserve group welfare. It is for this reason that local legal authorities are usually without either the power or the will to prevent or prosecute such offenses. To impose a heavy fine on the county in which lynchings take place, a suggestion based on the theory that the substantial property owners of the community would be spurred to prevent them in order to save their pocketbooks, could have but little effect, for the stronger belief would still persist that such coercion was necessary to group protection.

Interracial commissions and other educational programs are valuable to the extent that the clash of group interests is fictitious, and can be shown to be so. Usually such programs reach only the more substantial elements in a community, people who as a rule are neither leaders of nor participants in mob action. Why should they be? They have achieved personal security, and are not directly in conflict with the minorities who are the object of lynchings. Their interest is a secondary one, derived from the masses directly in conflict with Negroes, Chinese, strikers, or other competing groups. This is the fundamental explanation of the fact that mobs, with few exceptions, are composed of the handicapped social classes who cannot be reached by appeals to justice and humanity.

It has been claimed that some lynchings have been justified because they were committed by organized citizens who have calmly met the necessity for taking the law into their own hands, rather than by inflamed, unreasoning mobs which could not be expected to accomplish anything more than ephemeral, destructive, and chance results. Labor officials have been among this group. The Ku Klux Klan and the Vigilantes will serve our purposes as illustrations of this type of defense.

The original, post-Civil War Klan was not a unified organization throughout the South. It was a method of gaining control of southern communities adopted by white people who believed that the Reconstruction government was intolerable. It spread from place to place by imitation, and not without great changes through faulty borrowing and adaptation to local needs. Its better elements abandoned it to the ne'er-do-wells as soon as southern legal machinery came under the control of the more substantial citizenry. Its basic method was intimidation through fear inspired by playing on Negro superstition, threats of physical violence, flogging, driving out of the community, and sometimes actual murder. If one may generalize in spite of wide variations in procedure between units, it can be said to have been primarily a form of mob coercion, modified by the guiding plans of capable leaders who were honestly doing what they thought best for their communities. It soon degenerated, however, and had not the slightest justification for existence after legal power was again available to the rebels. Its need dissipated, it soon died out; and mob action thereafter could no longer be disguised as the constructive leadership of an organization of the best blood of the South.

The similarity of the original Klan to the Vigilantes of the West is a neglected subject. The Klan had its secrecy, its ritual, its oaths, its purpose of establishing a desired social order, and its illegal, coercive procedure. So did the Vigilantes. The Vigilantes made more use of the rope and gun, but they were dealing with dangerous outlaws who could not be intimidated by empty threats or ghostly robes and trickery. In both cases, a device found to be successful by one community was copied by others. Both numbered the better citizens among their members at the start, citizens who had no faith in the existing law and order, who dropped out when the government began functioning to their liking. The only justification for either lies in the extent to which misgovernment and lawlessness necessitated private action, a debatable point.

The modern Klan which was organized following the World War is not the lineal descendent of the original Klan. In fact, it bears little relationship to it except for the unauthorized borrowing of ritual and regalia and its demands that the Negro "stay in his place." It is actually a revival of nativism, previously organized politically in the Native American Party, Know-Nothingism, and the American Protective Association. Its published program is the salvation of the United States from the Jews, who are believed to have been subjected to such continued oppression in Europe that only the subservient, tricky stock without the inherent qualities which are characteristic of the true American have survived, and from the Catholic, whose allegiance to the Pope makes it impossible for him to become a true American. It also claims to be the friend of the Negro, who must be protected from himself and "nigger-lovers" who are misguided in their efforts for his advancement, since his nature is such that he will find greatest happiness if he "stays in his place." The worth of such a program needs no comment, although one may well wonder at the enormous Klan membership achieved on such a basis.

From the beginning, the modern Klan was a commercial organization, planned to reward financially those who obtained members, and to enrich its leaders in a campaign to sell group antagonisms throughout the country, a product which had no cost of production. In practically every part of the country there is hatred and fear of either the Jew, the Catholic, or the Negro. Millions of members were obtained from all sections of the United States. It became a powerful political weapon in the hands of its leaders, capable of grave abuses, as in Indiana, where its influence was sold for cash. The power for evil of any such secret organization, with its emotional appeal to 100-per-cent Americanism and race prejudice as a means for whipping members into line, far outweighs any good it may accomplish through the care of deserving poor and the protection of American institutions.

Its real appeal, however, is in the escape from self-realized mediocrity which it offers the inconsequential element in our population. The rural store clerk, doomed to measure out butter and eggs for the rest of his life, may achieve significance by becoming a knight of the invisible empire, hooded and robed, guarded by secret ritual and password, a defender of the nation! So, too, the college freshman becomes a person of fictitious but gratifying importance when initiated into a fraternity, with its status-conferring mystery of brotherhood. Hundreds of fraternal orders, clubs, and societies include ego-exaltation among the benefits conferred upon their members.

It is a curious comment on humanity that the same psychological motive which draws white men into the Klan is also responsible for an alleged Negro characteristic commonly ridiculed by these same men. Negroes are supposed to have a "primitive" love of dressing up, and if one may judge by the uniforms they wear on parade, there seems to be some basis for this supposition. Most of the white fraternal orders have their colored counterparts, for there are colored Elks, Masons, Knights of Pythias, and the like, with a large supplementary list of uniformed societies separately invented by Negroes. Their uniforms are generally in bad taste, their societies are poorly managed, and membership is frequently restricted only by the necessary dues. Yet members are readily available. Why? Not because of any primitive Negro qualities, but for the same reason the freshman joins a fraternity, the clerk the Klan, and other status-lacking white people join high-sounding societies. The ordinary Negro knows his life is futile, that he does not really matter in the affairs of his community; but if he can have membership in a fraternal order, dress up at meetings once a month and parade once a year, he can at least achieve the illusion of importance. In this respect, the Klansman and Negro are brothers under the skin.

Psychologically, it is a healthy thing that those of us who are mediocre should have some such escape. However, when our escape takes the form of a self-established supergovernment, and gives dangerous power to irresponsible Dragons, Wizards, and Emperors, as in the Klan, it is time to call a halt. There are sufficient innocuous fraternal orders in existence without creating a new Frankenstein monster. The modern Klan, however, is already far on its way to oblivion, probably to rise again in some new form on a later wave of nativism.[23]

The threat of ultimate mob coercion is the uncontrolled weapon in the hands of the leaders of all organizations which

[23] For a detailed readable account of the modern Klan, see John M. Mecklin, *The Ku Klux Klan*, Harcourt, Brace & Company, New York, 1924.

consider themselves the self-appointed saviors of the nation. Not one of them has justified its existence as a public guardian. If this variety of lynch law, where opportunity for constructive guidance is more available than in any other form, has failed so disastrously, what can be expected of sporadic local outbursts? If the government were broken down, if the people had no recourse at the polls and through the courts, then lynch law might for a brief time, while legal order was being reconstituted, enjoy an honored function. Such conditions may have existed in the past, but are not now in evidence.

CHAPTER VIII

LEISURE AND ITS USES

LEISURE time is that time of the day or night which is not devoted to the task of earning a livelihood, or securing a formal education, or to the necessity for restoring the fatigued body to its normal vigor, or engaging in some duty which civil society demands of its members. The amount of such leisure which a given individual has at his disposal will depend on many social and individual factors, such as age, occupation, wealth, etc. For most persons the problem of how to utilize the leisure hours must be solved, and never before has this problem been so important. As civilization has advanced the average man has found more leisure thrust upon him. Working hours have, on the whole, declined, modern inventions have lifted numerous burdens from the shoulders of housekeepers, and laws have been passed to protect the child and the adolescent from too early an entry into fields of productive labor. Of course there are still countless thousands who are forced to spend their lives in drudgery, and whose working day or social situation is such that there is little time or energy left for anything but eating and sleeping.

With increased leisure have come increased facilities for its enjoyment. Our industrial era has not only shortened the working day, but has also produced the radio, the motion picture and the motor car. Educational advance has been followed by demand for more libraries, magazines, books and travel. Recreational demands have been partly met by a mushroom growth of commercialized sports, public amusement parks, and dance halls.

The use to which leisure hours are put is of the greatest importance to society. Play, which takes up a considerable part of leisure time, is an important function of life, a powerful restorative of tired nerves, minds and bodies. If it is properly used, the personality development of the individual may be guided in socially desirable channels. On the whole, leisure-time activities may become educational and democratizing agencies of the highest order. Where they take the form of competitive play mental alertness, physical strength, and a spirit of give and take may be developed.

Improper use of leisure time may, on the other hand, be socially harmful. Anti-social attitudes may be created. Instead of breaking down barriers raised by caste and class, race and religion, it may help to construct walls of intolerance and misunderstanding. If facilities for the proper use of leisure are unavailable or denied to large groups of the population, the social friction arising from such conscious or unconscious discrimination may seriously undermine the social progress of a nation.

RECREATION IN COUNTRY AND CITY

The difference between the country and the city has always been great. The city dweller has in all times felt himself superior to the rustic, while the farmer has looked with envy or suspicion on town folk. Life in the city has, to the average man, held a great fascination. It has undoubtedly provided a greater variety of social contacts, and both physical and mental stimulation have been greater there than in the country districts. For a real understanding of their leisure activities it is therefore necessary to examine the social setting of the racial groups under discussion.

Rural and urban environments may be considered from several points of view. Statistically speaking, our census has classed as rural any population which dwells in isolation or in small village communities or centers having fewer than twenty-five hundred members. Useful as this arbitrary division is for many purposes, it is not sufficient for the understanding of social processes. Rural patterns of thought and behavior may be present in urban communities. Conversely, persons or groups living in rural communities may have a distinctly urban outlook on life. Some of the immigrant colonies in our great metropolitan areas, the migrant Negro dwellers of the northern industrial centers, are typical illustrations of groups which for a long time preserve their rural heritage while living in the city. The typical suburban community may be mentioned as an illustration of the other type. The importance of this distinction will be apparent in the discussion which follows later in this chapter.

The leisure time available to an individual, as well as the ways this time may be spent, are determined to a certain degree by his residence and his occupation. The farmer's leisure days and hours are neither the same in number, nor do they fall in the same time of year as those of the factory hand. Furthermore, they cannot be used in the same way by both. The facilities for recreation are not likely to be the same in nature or extent on farm and in city. Here account must be taken not only of individual advantages and handicaps, but also of community ideals and traditions. Certain trends emerge from an examination of the rural and the urban environments.

Both rural and migratory elements in our population have less access to what might be called institutionalized leisure activities. Organizations designed to meet the needs of growing boys and girls have not penetrated far beyond the confines of our cities. The Y. M. C. A. and the Y. W. C. A. do a little work among Negroes, but so far as rural and migratory Negroes are concerned their efforts may be said to be nonexistent. Boy Scouts and similar girls' organizations also fail to reach the non-urbanized groups. The rural Negroes and Indians, Orientals, European and Mexican immigrants who are located outside the large centers of population derive practically no direct benefits from these nation-wide organizations whose constructive programs could be of great value to them.

Our farming and village populations have found little reason to spend public money for parks, playgrounds, community and recreation centers, libraries and other means for employing leisure moments. There are no doubt some exceptions to this rule, but on the whole the generalization is correct. The recreational needs of the rural dwellers have been met to some extent by the church, which has been of the greatest influence in this respect. This does not mean that the country church has deliberately developed recreational programs. In fact, the city churches have been forced to greater exertions in this line in order to compete with a variety of powerful counter attractions. Without very definite planning, however, the country church in innumerable communities has been a most important focusing point of leisure activities. Going to church itself may be a leisure-time activity, accompanied as it is by the stimulation of music, sermon, prayer and social contacts. Church suppers, sewing circles and picnics grow out of and gratify recreational requirements as well as religious needs. Camp meetings have more than a religious aspect. It should be noted that under present conditions the influence of the rural church on spare-time occupations leads to emphasis on emotional and time-killing pleasure to the neglect of physical and intellectual development.

While the church is important in the rural area, it cannot compete with the home, which was, and still is, a true center of recreational activities. Much was made on the farm of the events in the home, such as births, christenings, funerals, weddings, all of which gave occasion for celebrations and family gatherings. Many of the older recreational traditions and customs of the farm were also characterized by their emphasis on community effort, whereby productive labor and play were combined. Corn husking, grain threshing, barn raising, maple sugaring, butchering, town meetings, fairs and a host of other affairs of a similar nature had a recreational function of great value. Many of these characteristics of rural recreation may still be found in the immigrant groups in our large cities, who, because of their isolation, have maintained patterns of thought and action typical of their rural origin.

Commercialized recreation is less prevalent in the country than in the city. It is natural that theaters or motion picture houses, amusement parks or other commercial ventures, seek the cities where most patrons of these enterprises may be found. In late years improved means of transportation, such as automobiles, street cars, railways, etc., have in a measure offset this handicap, but until the country dweller finds his cash income materially increased he cannot enjoy these forms of recreation to the extent the city dweller does.

The seasonal aspect of rural labor also influences leisure-time activities. Free hours are scarce, bodies are tired, and minds are dull when the fields are being plowed and the crops planted, cultivated and harvested. At other times of the year, particularly in the winter time, leisure is relatively abundant. Seasonal variations of this type are not limited to farmers. Certain industries where sales have peaks at Christmas and at Easter, or in summer, winter, fall, or spring, are large users of the cheap labor of immigrant groups. Recreational resorts, such as Atlantic City, employ more Negroes when the vacation season is at its height than in the winter months. As a rule, however, the country dweller has less opportunity to find extra work than those who live in an area with many diversified industries. Time which might otherwise be turned to profitable labor therefore must be filled in with makeshift pastimes.

The rural attitude toward the use of leisure in economically unproductive pursuits has been distinctly unfavorable. The prevalence of child labor on the farm is not an accident, though many who see the urban child relatively free from the necessity of long hours of labor and encouraged to employ his leisure time in play and education, cannot help but wonder at the apparent stupidity of farming parents. The explanation must be sought in the force of traditions and conventions which have grown up in the rural mind. The soil is a hard taskmaster; work must be done when the time is right and not when it pleases the individual. When one is close to want, and fields respond directly to the amount of labor expended on them, it is easy to understand why even temporary idleness becomes a sin. As a result of changes which have swept over the entire country in recent years, much of the social life of rural districts has disappeared, with the limiting of the use of the few facilities for recreational activity that still remain in our more sparsely settled sections.

There is not much for our rural neighbor to choose from when he wishes to employ his leisure moments. We sometimes envy the country youth his opportunity for the open-air enjoyment of hunting, fishing, and care-free rambles through field and forest, but we forget that he lacks the material equipment of diversified play, and that glorious nature does not always retain its attractiveness in the eyes of those who are constantly seeing it. The claim has been made that for the older country children at least play activities are more varied than those of town children.[1] But on the whole we may say that diversity is not a characteristic of the leisure-time activities of the rural districts.

The family which selects, or is forced into, the farm or the village as its home is therefore driven to a few badly balanced leisure-time pursuits which do little to promote individual or social welfare. Intellectual growth is not encouraged, for manual rule-of-thumb labor is dull, and there is little opportunity for checking its stunting effects through mental diversions. Reading facilities are few. Private philanthropy has shown a lack of interest, or has found the task too great save in isolated instances. Only rarely has community cooperation tried to solve recreational problems, and commercial ventures have hesitated to enter the rural districts for fear of economic failure. There is little left except highly individualized physical activity, catering to the simple senses, and serving no real purpose other than to while away the passing hours.

In this rural environment live about two-thirds of our Negroes, one-eighth of our European immigrants, most of our Japanese and Mexicans, and practically all of our unassimilated Indians. We still urge newcomers to shun the city and grasp the opportunity to become assimilated on our farms and in our villages. We are deluded by the fact that ignorance, backwardness and viciousness are less obvious in rural than in urban areas. Because in other times and under other conditions our forefathers conquered on the farm in spite of natural handicaps, we assume that their descendants can do the same. But today the tables are turned, and our urban areas offer a superior, more varied, and better-balanced diet from which to appease the appetite for leisure enjoyments. The movement

[1] H. C. Lehman, "A Comparison of the Play Activities of Town and Country Children," *Pedagogical Seminary*, September, 1926, vol. xxxiii, pp. 455-476.

of the Negro into industry and the settling of the more recent immigrants in our cities consequently mean that these groups will be better served so far as leisure-time activities are concerned than their rural friends. If recreational agencies may be regarded as assimilative and educational agencies, it is clear that the city furnishes today the real opportunity for cultural assimilation and the breakdown of those barriers which have in the past made difficult the amicable relations between races and nationality groups.

No adequate data exist concerning the leisure activities of any large racial group. The few studies made have been concerned with institutionalized activities and have not covered fair samples of the group studied. A few years ago an investigation was made in Detroit of the earlier chief recreational pursuits of one thousand heads of Negro families recently migrated from various parts of the South. While the results are subject to the general criticisms made of all analyses depending on recalled impressions, the returns are quoted in Table I on the following page.

These results are obviously inaccurate in detail. An analysis of the table should convince even the casual student that the data are only suggestive. Some leisure activities are evidently given too prominent a place, while others have been minimized or excluded. Is it possible that almost half of the Negroes questioned spent their leisure chiefly in hunting and fishing while only fifteen "worked around the house"? Interest in the opposite sex evidently played no important rôle, if these figures are to be accepted. Perhaps there was no clear definition of leisure time which permitted comparable answers. Maybe wishful recollection played a significant part, and perhaps there is here more evidence of the well established fact that the Negro has learned the lesson of giving the questioner only that information which he thinks might be harmless or pleasing.

In spite of these facts, the list given shows a tremendous emphasis on time-killing pastimes, a lack of intellectual and athletic pursuits, a total absence of commercialized forms of recreation, and but little institutionalized leisure.

TABLE I[2]

Fishing	193
Hunting	175
Hunting and fishing	92
Sitting down	88
Church	77
Lodge	63
Reading	48
Doing nothing	47
Visiting	47
Singing and playing musical instruments	23
Talking	19
Knocking about	16
Working around house	15
Gambling	14
Card games	13
Drinking liquor	10
Lying around	24
No answer	36
	1000

In a recent survey of the Negroes of Richmond, Virginia, 698 men and 889 women were asked what they did for amusement. "Going to church" was placed first by 198 men and 331 women; "movies and theaters" by 134 men and 254 women; 91 men and 176 women "played with their children" or "enjoyed their homes and friends." Reading was reported by 101 men and 88 women. And 91 men and 93 women had no amusements or recreations whatever. "Smoking, hunting and fishing were extremely popular with men. Society or lodge meetings, sewing and fancy work, were favorites of the women. Music, singing, and playing of musical instruments were named repeatedly by both men and women. Almost everything in life was mentioned by a sprinkling of both as an amusement: 'walking,' 'drinking,' 'eating,' 'sleeping,' 'praying,' 'resting,' 'working,' 'gardening,' 'traveling,' 'sitting around,' 'using snuff,' 'helping

[2] Forrester B. Washington, "Recreational Facilities for the Negro," in Donald Young, editor, "The American Negro," *The Annals* of the American Academy of Political and Social Science, November, 1928, vol. cxxxx, No. 272, p. 272.

to make others happy,' 'policy playing,' 'automobile riding, etc."[3]

There is no need to dwell at length on the differences exhibited by these two studies. The urban environment of the second group may be partly responsible for the divergence in the responses, but it is likely that variations in the method of investigation may have been the cause. Furthermore, white investigators were used in the second, and not in the first, study. It should be noted that commercial amusements stand high in the second list. In both instances we may be certain that the race attitudes of the white groups were, to a great extent, responsible for both the nature and the extent of some of the leisure activities reported, for these attitudes have forced the Negro into certain types of recreation, and have also been responsible for the development of certain customs and traditions which in turn give sanction to, and encourage, these activities.

TRADITIONAL USES OF LEISURE

The African background of the American Negro has had practically no influence on his leisure-time activities. This makes his leisure problems peculiar when contrasted with our other racial elements. Indian play customs, for instance, have been kept alive both by red man and white. European recreational memories are strong in the minds and habits of millions of immigrants. The fact that native American customs, even though modified by local forces, have continental roots, has made it relatively easy for European immigrants to fit in their leisure activities. The recently transplanted Oriental, with his Asiatic cultures, faces adjustments of a different nature. But the Negro has almost entirely forgotten what he did with his leisure time in Africa.

This may seem surprising to some people. It may even be claimed that the contention is not wholly true. The Negro in the West Indies and other parts of tropical America, for instance, has no doubt remembered some of his African games,

[3] The Negro Welfare Service Committee, Richmond, Va., *The Negro in Richmond, Virginia,* 1929, p. 87.

drum rhythms, music, folk tales, etc. Contrary to public opinion, however, it appears that in the three hundred years since the first Negro set foot on American shores—and many arrived within the last century and a half—the memories of the non-material recreational culture of his native continent have been almost completely wiped out.

There may be faint traces of the African drum still surviving in American Negro rhythmic expression, and broad hints of African origin in the folk songs developed on this continent. The shrewd gazelle of African folk tales may have taken on the appearance of Bre'r Rabbit, and the wicked leopard, that of the American fox. There are striking similarities in some stories and proverbs.

Beliefs in such survivals have been fostered by stage and story presentations of the Negro which do not even claim to have a factual basis, although their influences on an audience are just as powerful. Drums, palm trees, pseudo-tropical music and dances, native dress and decoration, help to put a show or a book across to people who are anxious to believe. In real Negro life these anachronisms are more foreign than the customs of the ancient Israelites. Suffice it to say that the wildest scientific hypothesis current in academic circles today would not grant enough survivals of African leisure-time activities to alter perceptibly the course of race relations. Fictitious beliefs in their existence, however, are no doubt a powerful influence.

Slave traditions and customs are more recent, and have not been so far removed in their influence as have the cultural traits of Africa. Slavery discouraged the education of its victims, and thereby destroyed intellectual recreational activities. Indeed the slave system, as developed in the south, was not conducive to intellectual development of either the white or the colored group. Only a very few of the specially favored classes were able to keep mentally alert. Educational incentives were lacking where a plantation caste system, with its dependence on crude labor, created beauty, wealth and leisure for the elect, but doomed the rest to an existence in which hope of advancement found little place.

The absence of incentive for personal improvement was a

characteristic of the slave régime. The oft-cited exceptions, where Negroes were encouraged to improve their minds and economic status, only show by their rarity the real rigidity of the system. Leisure tended to be employed in killing time, gratifying the senses and establishing personal status. Sex interests were exploited, dogma settled controversy, religious emotionalism dominated church affairs, individual feats of strength and skill were encouraged, and athletic contests minimized. Showing off to win public approval became good form. Gambling was an accepted diversion. Hunting and fishing helped to pass many empty hours. The futility and the lack of balance in leisure occupations and objectives are strikingly shown in the records of these times.

A background such as this cannot be dropped in two or three generations. If some Negroes appear lazy today, part of their desire for leisure at the expense of personal advancement may be explained in terms of plantation life. If hunting and fishing, loafing, gambling, stimulating parties and dances, exaggerated accounts of personal exploits, overemphasis on sex, or other pointless or vicious activities are used to pass the time, some reason therefor can be found in slavery. Little effort has been made since the Civil War to throw off the influences of the days of servitude. In fact, white people, by their very efforts "to keep the Negro in his place," have done their utmost to prevent the emancipation of his leisure.

Aside from the slave traditions which have guided the Negro into specific forms of recreation and have kept him out of others, an additional cultural survival of a more negative aspect can be discerned.[4] To the present day the Negro's per-

[4] An interesting remnant of this tradition may be mentioned. During slave days the Negro servants who were forced to minister to their master's needs on the great religious holidays, such as Easter Day and Whitsuntide, were given the day after for their own celebration. "The Monday following Easter and that following Whitsuntide are still observed in certain parts as holidays for the Negroes, who never think of this custom as a relic of slavery." C. G. Woodson, *op. cit.*, p. 142. "It has become something of a general practice for colored people to take possession of Rock Creek Park the first Monday after every Easter. White people seem to understand that this is the Negro's day and either remain at home or go elsewhere." W. H. Jones, *Recreation and Amusement among Negroes in Washington, D. C.*, Howard University Press, Washington, D. C., 1927, p. 100.

sonal conduct, if it did not affect a white person, has been of no
concern to the dominating white group, except as a target for
idle curiosity. If a Negro wished to make a fool of himself in
his own time, well and good. If he wished to just "set around"
during his free hours, let him "set." If he broke into boisterous
laughter, loud song, eccentric dance, or uncouth rough-and-
tumble, why should anyone bother about it? The result is that
the modern American Negro, except for a thin upper class, has
fewer inhibitions than the white man regarding recreational
activities which serve as physical and emotional outlets. The
Negro who feels like bursting into song, although he lacks voice
or training, is more free to do so than the inhibited white person. The contacts between the sexes are less governed by
ancient rules. The colored child need have less fear than his
white neighbor of being frowned upon for unseemly conduct.
And this freedom, to a degree, continues on through later life.
While this may result in bringing the Negro more passing
pleasure, it serves no purpose except perhaps the one of fostering healthy minds, not tortured by arbitrary social rules. This
may be adequate justification for its existence, but it does not
reduce race friction. It makes contacts between white and
colored more strained, for what may, in truth, be natural can
only seem "primitive" or "savage" to the custom-bound white
man, who is seeking justification for his race attitudes. There
is reason to believe, however, that, fortunately or otherwise,
this remnant of a slave tradition is rapidly passing as the Negro
enters more and more into the white man's cultural standards.
Slave traditions will ultimately be found only in history, sentimental song, and story. Meanwhile the effects of slavery and
of the Reconstruction days which followed still color the leisure-time activities of white men as well as of black.

The European immigrant came to our shores with a host of
recreational customs and traditions which in their nature and
variety depended on his social status and his nationality. In
countries with high literacy, intellectual diversions of certain
types were of course more common, and in the more highly
industrialized countries, class-conscious workingmen had developed labor organizations which in part through their educa-

tional and social functions gave considerable opportunity for leisure enjoyments. As a rule, the family was the center of recreational life. The European's love for music expressed itself in the organization of bands and orchestras, male choruses and choirs, and, in south Europe in particular, the opera offered leisure enjoyments of a high standard. Gymnastic clubs, patriotic and dramatic societies, and religious organizations all played significant rôles. Last but not least, the beer gardens, cafés, taverns and restaurants served as recreational agencies on a large scale, particularly since many of them, at least in the cities, added musical programs frequently of very high standard. The immigrant who came to the United States with these leisure habits well established found great difficulty in continuing them. The more recent immigrant who usually came alone, severing his family and his community ties, found the adjustment most difficult; and in his case the disorganization of his personality was greatly assisted by the unfavorable substitute recreational activities into which he was forced. In most cases he was ignorant of the language, and this fact, coupled with a cultural equipment which made him appear "strange" in the eyes of the native American, effectually debarred him from participation in the social life of his adopted country. Thrown upon his own resources he was forced, while groping for a knowledge of American life, to devise means to recapture in his new environment some of the leisure pleasures which he had known at home. The result was the transplantation to the United States of many of the recreational and other forms of leisure activities common abroad.

In the immigrant sections of our large cities there grew up restaurants, cafés, beer gardens, gymnastic clubs, study circles, discussion groups, labor organizations, foreign-language papers, etc., and in the immigrant homes the recreational life of Europe survived. The skat tournaments and the *Schützenfeste* were not unknown in the small German farm communities of the Middle West. Yet there was a difference. The process of transplantation caused many of the immigrants' leisure activities to change both form and function. Even new types of such activities came to be developed. The absence of a close-

knit community group, or the weakening of the social standards of the old country, caused lodges, clubs and other associations to take on new functions, prominent among which was
that of economic aid in times of stress. The desire to maintain
cultural contacts with the homeland produced patriotic societies such as the Sons of Italy, and gave to the foreign-language press certain characteristics, such as an emphasis on old-
country news and on personal happenings, which, so far as the
latter element is concerned, caused it to resemble the typical
local news sheet of the American community, which lacks a
counterpart abroad. Even the immigrant church, which at
home was reserved for worship, became a community church
which sponsored educational and recreational programs. Import houses supplied the immigrant with foreign books, food,
and appliances.

The effect on race relations of this flowering of alien leisure
activities has been great, perhaps greater than has ordinarily
been assumed. It has been felt by both native American and
immigrant. To the former the attempt to keep alien customs
alive meant inability or unwillingness to enter into the American life. The "strangeness" of the immigrant thus became
emphasized, causing the development or strengthening of unfavorable race attitudes, which in turn made the American less
desirous to assist the immigrant through his most difficult
period, the transition between his arrival and his assimilation,
and by its very nature the most important for the progress of
race relations.

The survival of the transplanted leisure activities of the
immigrant depends to a large degree on the extent to which
they differ from those of the native Americans. The north
European culture is, on the whole, very similar to the American. Britons, Germans, and Scandinavians find the process of
assimilation, therefore, less difficult than do the south Europeans and the Slavs. The high level of popular education in
northern Europe, the relatively great industrialization, the
familiarity with representative government, and the Protestant
religion, gave to immigrants from this area greater facilities for
assimilation than those coming from countries predominantly

agricultural, with low literacy and the Catholic faith. Even the British worker, however, found on his arrival that tea drinking was ridiculed, ale illegal, football of a different variety, and cricket a gentleman's pastime reserved for exclusive country clubs. His habits were essentially those of the native American, however, and his knowledge of the language permitted him to make the transition to American life with relative ease. Finally, he did not bear the social label of an "inferior race."

The more recent immigrants have created more serious problems in race relations, or at least problems which are at the present time more keenly felt. The cultural differences mentioned have given to their leisure institutions greater variety and persistency, and this has helped to create friction or tension between them and the native Americans. Religious national holiday celebrations have been known to create ill will. At best, they have aroused curiosity of a socially undesirable kind. In her book on *The Immigrant and the Community*, Miss Abbott refers, for instance, to the celebration of the Greek Good Friday, which usually comes about two weeks after Good Friday is observed by the western world. "The stores in the Greek colony are draped with purple and black, and there are rows of lighted candles in the windows of the tenements and the shops. At midnight a solemn procession of Greek men and women who make up the colony follow the priest and the sepulcher, which is borne from the church. The American who watches them for the first time, as they march down the street carrying their flickering yellow candles and chanting their Greek hymns, asks himself if he is really in the United States."[5]

The leisure activities of the immigrant tend to become incorporated into American life or to disappear. The religious festivals become in their new setting quite different in nature, and frequently only a few shreds of empty observance are left. The national holidays lose their original significance. The patriotic fervor which can be maintained in the midst of the international or party strife of the home country cannot survive in the matter-of-fact life of the new world, and these days tend

[5] Grace Abbott, *The Immigrant and the Community*, Century Company, New York, 1921, p. 293.

to become occasions for parades, picnics and dull speeches. The folk dances, beautiful as they may be, cannot live in the tenements of New York or on the truck farms of New Jersey. The gymnastic association, which in the old country stood for all-round physical development, hearkens to the call of American sports, and turns its attention to the production of winners in athletic contests.

Many of these leisure habits are also adopted by the native American, a process which is significant, since it not only helps to establish in the immigrant's mind a feeling of respect and appreciation of alien culture traits, but because it helps him in his adjustment. Foreign motion pictures, operas and musical compositions of other types are appreciated by native and immigrant alike. Bavarian beer gardens, French and Italian restaurants cater to an American trade. An important rôle in this process has undoubtedly been played by the growing interest in foreign travel.

The disappearance of alien leisure activities will come only when the second or third generation has become fully emancipated from the European background, a process which in some of our rural communities is less rapid than in our large cities, which are still on the whole real crucibles of Americanization, notwithstanding the argument about the failure of the melting pot. To the children of immigrants many of their parents' leisure activities seem unreal, for they lack the strong emotional fixations which determine their parents' attitudes to traditional forms of behavior. Trained in American ways, they are more likely to be interested in baseball than in cricket and to prefer jazz to opera.

Recreation in the Orient is quite different from that in the United States. It is not possible to characterize the leisure habits of the hundreds of millions of Orientals, but since we have received eastern immigrants mostly from a few localities in China and Japan, and practically none from other parts of Asia, some cautious generalizations may be permitted about their recreational background, if only to illustrate a difference and without regard for detail.

The seclusion of women in the Orient hinders Asiatic acceptance of American customs. Mixed dancing, for illustration, is foreign to both the Chinese and the Japanese mind. Social gatherings of any kind where sexes meet on equal terms are still rare, in spite of the recent feminist movement which has swept through certain sections of the Orient. Women did not appear on the Chinese stage until the second decade of this century, although paid girl entertainers who were well trained in song, music, dance, and conversation have been common for generations. Sex, however, has been a frankly recognized element in oriental life far beyond what has been permitted by Christian prudery of the past century. Concubinage has been accepted as a matter of course. Sex themes in Japanese prints have frequently been of such a nature that in the United States they could not be openly displayed. Mixed nude bathing has been common and unaccompanied by any thought of lewdness, for nakedness for such recognized purposes carried no intrinsic sexual significance. The bases for family life and relations between the sexes are so unlike in Orient and Occident, and at the same time so related to leisure customs, that easterner and westerner easily misinterpret each other.

Physical exercises and competitions are not well represented in either China or Japan. Archery, fencing and other remnants of past days may be found among the upper classes, but the common people have little opportunity for such sports. Wrestling has been highly developed. Outdoor play is restricted to the few, and parks and open spaces for such use cannot be found except in temple grounds and on private estates. Indoor games, on the other hand, are almost universal in their distribution.

Conventionalized art is much appreciated. Symbolic representation takes the place of western realistic style. Not only is this true in painting, but also in the drama. Stage presentations in which scenery has no place, voices are unnatural, men take women's parts, themes are ancient legends, and actors are skilled in avoiding the appearance of normal human beings, are humorous or boring to the western mind. A Eugene O'Neill play no doubt would have the same effect on most Orientals. It might even be disgusting. During recent years the motion picture has penetrated the parts of the Orient from which our immigrants come. While the pictures displayed, usually American, are not true portrayals of occidental life, they nevertheless help to accustom the Oriental to the peculiar ways of the American.

As a result of these differences from American custom, neither the Chinese nor the Japanese in the United States have made any real attempt to enter, or have been admitted, into the general recreational activities of the country. This statement applies only to those born and brought up across the Pacific, for the younger generation, like the American-born children of Europeans, have not maintained close cultural contacts with their parents' native lands.

This difference between Asiatic and American-born Orientals can be illustrated by habits of dress, speech, religious belief, playground interests, courtship customs and the like. Societies and clubs, so common among the older generation, are also found among the younger people, but purposes and intensity of interest are not the same. The recreational aspects of the older organizations which encouraged and provided opportunities for spending leisure time as it was spent in the Orient are not a characteristic of the more youthful groups. No longer are the old games played, the distinctions between the sexes so rigidly upheld, the leisure time passed in typically oriental fashion, except by those who came to us after a childhood training in oriental culture. They have been unable, or have not cared to make recreational adjustments to their new home. Their children would find the recreational restrictions of China or Japan irksome.

An illustration of this condition may be given: "The Chinatowns of the Pacific Coast are as packed with clubs as a New England town, but these clubs belong to men rather than to women. If you were, quite literally, to rip the roofs off the two gay blocks of Vancouver's Chinatown which are its Main street, its Broadway, and its Fifth Avenue, you would find, like rich frosting on a cake, a multitudinous array of clubs— family clubs, county clubs, reading clubs, political clubs, decorated according to the wealth and taste of the members with red oil-cloth and priceless carvings, or with crystal candelabra, delicate Chinese embroideries, and portraits of the ancestors. An examination of top-floor Chinatown would reveal not only that the Chinese have a political life, but that the Chinatown Chinese of the Coast come of pioneer stock, that they are by tradition fundamentalists, and that they have family trees which go back a little farther into the dim mythical spaces of time than do any other family trees except those of the Irish.

"Chinatown's clubs are a shadowy counterpart of Chinatown's three quite separate generations. The older generation of Chinese, who still predominate in Chinatown, live in a very remote world where all the paradoxes are made taut; a world which is at once very stable and very frail, a world which is packed with pleasant sensations and worn smooth with loneliness. Less remote from the Westerner is the generation which is Chinese-born but which has been affected by the Chinese revolution and the Chinese Youth Movement. These young men are aggressive and wildly discontented; they seethe with ideas, and are passionately devoted to the new China which is coming into being. The native-born, who have Chinese Native Sons' Parlors up and down the Coast, know little about either the old China or the new; England, and especially Victorian England, seems closer to them than the aphorisms of Confucius or the dreams of Sun Yat Sen."[6]

It is no longer considered scientific to speak of the American Indian as though all members of the race were essentially similar in physique or culture. Tribes are now the largest units permissible. However, so far as leisure-time activities are concerned, some interpretations common to a large number of the unassimilated Indians still remaining in the United States may be ventured.

Similar games were found by the earliest investigators among all tribes inhabiting what is now the United States. These were games of chance and physical dexterity, and occupied some prominence in community life. Probably all of them originally had some ceremonial significance, although this element often

---

[6] Winifred Raushenbush, *The Survey Graphic,* May 1, 1926, vol. lvi, pp. 154-155.

faded in the course of time, continued existence depending on the amusement value. Games requiring mental skill, as do bridge and chess, were lacking. Athletic contests, such as ball games, races, and archery, were a major diversion. There were also "personal, fraternal, clan or gentile, tribal, and inter-tribal dances"; and "social, erotic, comic, mimic, patriotic, military or warlike, invocative, offertory, and mourning dances, as well as those expressive of gratitude and thanksgiving."[7] Many of these could not by any stretch of the imagination be called leisure-time activities, but others were distinctly so. Secret societies and other well-knit group organizations were effective, as among most preliterate peoples, and sometimes were associated with various diversions. Leisure, however, was a scarce commodity as compared with present-day conditions, except at particular seasons of the year, and was well provided for by custom and tradition.

The coming of the white man upset these orderly provisions. All Indians, in the course of time, were to a degree Europeanized. Means of livelihood, religion, morality, family life, and other phases of Indian culture could not fight off the onslaughts of European civilization without mutilation. Leisure was reduced for few, changed in time of occurrence for others, and increased for most. The government rations system supplied many tribes with food, and work became almost useless. Division of labor on a sex basis originally assigned warfare and hunting for some tribes to the men, and farming and domestic duties to the women. Hunting and fighting drifted into the background as game was ruthlessly destroyed by rifle and plough, and the business of war was stamped out years ago. This left some men with plenty of leisure and their women with too much work, until the old sex traditions were conquered by those of the white man, a process which was rarely completed for the older generation. For the majority, Christianity disrupted their so-called paganism without taking its place more than superficially. Government by family, clan and tribe lost most of its old sanctions. Since their leisure activities

---

[7] *Handbook of American Indians*, Smithsonian Institution, Bureau of American Ethnology, Washington, D. C., 1907, part i, p. 381.

were as a rule bound up with these other customs and traditions, recreational adjustment was necessary.

The adjustments actually made could hardly be described as happy. Alcohol was not unknown before Columbus, but its use was not extensive until provided by the white man at a time when it could furnish a cheap means for forgetfulness, stimulation, and relief from inactivity. The absence of restrictive traditions concerning its use eased the way to overindulgence. Prostitution was almost unknown in many tribes, but "civilization" soon caused its spread. Gambling was a simple outgrowth of new conditions and familiarity with games of chance, and it is not without significance that almost the only games adopted on a large scale from the white man were card games. With no real understanding of the European culture forced upon him, and with the waning of his own, his recreation, like that of the rural Negro, turned to time killing and sense gratification, and, in some cases, to empty personal aggrandizement.

Much Indian leisure was originally spent in group affairs, such as the various feasts and dances. Remnants of this culture trait apparently may still be found in the modern Indian's fondness for gatherings represented in various parts of the country by fairs, camp and other religious meetings, the peyote cult, and dances. In themselves, these may all be harmless. Most of them, however, are accompanied by excessive drinking, sex indulgence, economic waste, and other undesirable features. Certainly they are not helpful in the Indian's assimilation of European civilization efficiently. Fairs, of course, stimulate agricultural and handicraft production through display and competition, but this function has tended to be thrust into the background in favor of the social aspects of such events. The religious side of some meetings and the development of racial consciousness and pride of others is, no doubt, also beneficial, but there are other ways of gaining these ends with fewer concomitant evils. Unless carefully guarded, traditional ceremonial functions may be too easily prostituted by commercialization to be of real worth. Since the ordinary white man looks on affairs like these as evidences of "savagery" and racial inferiority, they can hardly be said to promote rational race relations.

Business men have not failed to see the opportunity for exploiting the handicapped unassimilated Indian. Pool rooms flourish in Indian communities, as they do in Negro and second-generation immigrant areas. The saloon with its modern descendant, the speakeasy, is gathering in the Indian's money. Dance halls of a cheap sort flourish, some restricted to Indian use, others permitting mixed assemblages. Gambling, too, has been commercialized. Few Indians there are who cannot from time to time scrape together enough cash to indulge in these amusements. Motion pictures and the radio are gaining headway. On the whole, his cultural heritage, or lack of it, has suited him well for occupations such as these. His children, owing to their poverty and rural residence, are growing into the white man's ways—except in the use of toys and childish games, which they have always had—at least as slowly as those of any minority group in the United States.

The Mexican is biologically an Indian. Culturally he has retained many Indian traits greatly modified by Spanish influence. Indian games, for example, have been retained without much change in form. What remains of Indian leisure customs naturally does not fit him for the life of a southern farm laborer, railway hand, or casual migratory worker. What is Spanish is no more suited for existence in communities of north European origin. Little successful effort is being made to solve his recreational problems, and little can be made until he becomes a more settled element in our population.

Obviously what has just been said about the differential traditions and customs of minority peoples in the United States would be of no use to a reformer interested in the leisure adjustment of any specific individual or community. It is neither sufficiently comprehensive nor minutely detailed to do more than indicate the types of problems involved and serve as illustrative material for the interpretations which have been offered. Volumes have been written on the cultural history of all of the important minority groups, and most of the unimportant ones as well. From these may be learned superficially thousands of cultural variances in leisure habits of European, African, Asiatic or native American origin. Actually, one must have first-hand knowledge of the people to sense their personal community significance.

RACE ATTITUDES AND LEISURE ACTIVITIES

Ask any roomful of native white Americans to picture an ordinary Negro youth at play. It would be surprising if among the mental images provoked by such a question were not some involving dancing, singing, gambling or just loafing. Substitute German for Negro, and "beer drinking" springs to mind. The word Irish will conjure up something akin to fighting—or at least it would have done so half a generation ago.

These answers are almost certain to be based on the assumption that here are typical activities which may have more than a mere social basis. Yet the evidence to show that certain races have or lack special inherent qualities which qualify them for, or debar them from, certain leisure enjoyments, is most meager. The theory, so common in the James Fenimore Cooper type of literature, that preliterate peoples, living as they do, have inherited special qualities of sight, hearing, patience, endurance, at the expense of others, is false. These traits, found in some American Indians and not in the group as a whole, are the result of training and not of breeding. Negroes are not born with an "instinct of rhythm" or an insistent urge to burst into "blues," jazz, and close harmony. Nor is their emotional make-up essentially more "savage" and "animal like" than that of the white man. Like practically all other leisure habits, German beer and Irish whiskey-drinking can more easily be explained by the cultural historian than by the biologist.

In sports depending on physique some races may be handicapped and others especially qualified. Woman, with a body well built for child bearing, is not expected to compete with man in feats of speed and strength. So, too, the tall Scot and the short south Italian may not be well matched in wrestling, although many south Italians may be expected to defeat the ordinary Scot in such contests. Whatever physical handicaps various races may have when compared with other groups, they cannot in any sense be held to bar them from any known form of leisure activity.

Similarly, whatever mental differences may exist between races—and there is no proof that all races are either mentally equal or unequal—inferior native intelligence does not bar any minority group in the United States from intellectual leisure occupations similar to those of any other people. Lack of education and intellectual traditions, however, may do so. The southern rural Negro can hardly be expected to be as fond of, or as proficient in, contract bridge as the white man of more advanced educational status, but there are many Negroes of different background and training who play contract of a superior quality. In fact, Negro bridge clubs are common in our cities. Regardless of whether this may be properly called an intellectual pursuit, it is an evidence of differences in individual intellectual status which illustrates our point and suggests ways in which race relations may be linked up with individual intellectual status.

Negroes do not use libraries even where they are available as do the mass of native whites, neither do recently arrived, poor, unlettered immigrants from Europe, Asia and Latin America. Apart from the language handicap, public libraries are neither a part of their tradition nor are they mentally equipped to utilize these recreational media. When they do begin to find their way into these buildings, the books selected most frequently are not those which top the native white list. The number and type of books, magazines, and newspapers purchased vary similarly between groups.

Money and education are both necessary for many of our more desirable recreational pursuits. The frequency of our attendance at plays and motion pictures, and the nature of the plays selected, are related to mental training and income, and so are the ownership of a radio set and the programs selected by the listener. The automobile is an expensive toy and beyond the easy reach of the poorer economic classes. It costs little, however, to play sand-lot games, attend simple parties or picnics, or while away the time in the many ingenious forms of loafing.

In spite of the fact, then, that members of all races and nationalities are by nature endowed with the ability to utilize almost any known form of recreation, group differences in residence, tradition, education, and income force special groups into divergent leisure-time activities. One more selective factor, race attitudes, remains to be mentioned.

Most studies of race relations have stressed the restrictions of race prejudice to the neglect of the leisure influences which we have just discussed. The restraining hand of the white man's antagonism has been more frequently discussed than the barriers of location and individual status. The average Negro is more likely to become enraged at being kept out of a theater, a restaurant, or a library by race prejudice than by lack of education, availability, or income. Similarly, some Russian Jews with money and bad manners can see nothing but Gentile discrimination in their exclusion from clubs and hotels. It is always less painful to blame such restrictions on the blind prejudices of others than on one's own characteristics. When, however, these restrictive attitudes are applied to a whole people, including many of higher cultural attainments than ninety-nine per cent of the entire population, race prejudice can be said to be the main reason for the barrier against the superior individuals. Since these individuals include an exceptionally large number of the articulate leaders of their groups, it is no wonder that speeches and literature of protest should be indifferent to all factors save prejudice.

Both the extent and the nature of leisure-time activities are limited by race attitudes of and toward majority and minority peoples in the United States. What the white man thinks about the Negro, be it true or false, may keep the latter out of a theater or restrict him to the upper gallery. What the Negro thinks about the white man may make colored people forego the pleasures of a playground or a library where they might readily be admitted, if not welcomed. Jews may be denied social invitations because of their supposed crudities, and they in turn may hesitate to make advances to Gentiles because of baseless timidity and resentment. There is no way as yet devised for the accurate measurement of such attitudes except by the study of their effects in everyday life, and it is to these manifestations in race relations that we now turn.

As has already been mentioned, studies of leisure habits of minority groups have been largely confined to organized or institutionalized recreation. This means that what the Negro, the immigrant, and the Indian do with most of their leisure can be known only from general observation, a treacherous source of information. Only a small proportion of the ordinary individual's leisure is spent in formal play-groups or in commercialized amusements. Yet it is concerning this small proportion that we have the most reliable data.

Public parks are open to all comers except where southern tradition predominates, and there are some available to both whites and Negroes even in the south. From the fact that a park is technically open to all races and nationalities it cannot be inferred that it is in fact equally available to all. It may be inaccessibly located for those who need its refreshment most, for play space is notably found most abundant adjacent to non-congested areas. Again, the minority group may drift or be driven by popular disapproval into definite sections of a park not always the most desirable in location and advantages. During the Richmond, Virginia, survey, 1,145 families were visited by the investigators. Of these families more than three-fourths made no use of the parks. The most frequent reasons given were that they had "no desire" to use them, or that they "never thought about them," or "did not care for them." Many said they were too far away, and a few claimed that they did not "feel free in the parks," that there were no "colored parks," and that existing parks had "no privileges for Negroes."[8] The July, 1927, census estimate gave the Negro population of Richmond as 55,919, the white as 138,525.

Antagonistic majority groups on occasion cede a section or even an entire park to their despised and hated competitors. This type of semi-voluntary segregation may be said to be the rule when the minority group is easily distinguishable by skin color or imported cultural traits viewed as symptoms of infe-

[8] The Negro Welfare Service Committee, Richmond, Va., op. cit., p. 77.

riority. One can always point to exceptions where black, yellow and white occupy adjoining benches, or picnic grounds where the recent immigrant rubs shoulders with old American stock, but these contacts are likely to be superficial physical accidents and imply toleration rather than sympathetic understanding and friendship. The minority groups profit by such toleration, but its significance as evidence of cooperative race relations must not be exaggerated.

Separate parks have been found necessary only for Negroes, and then only in the southern states. While other groups have been restricted in their use of public open spaces, the problem has never become serious enough to warrant special provision for them. Practically all southern cities, however, have set aside some plot of ground where the Negro may find relief from city streets and buildings. As a rule these parks do not compare in area, equipment, or upkeep, even when allowances are made for the disproportionate size of the white and colored populations in the community served. They may be nothing more than vacant lots or fields adorned with whatever of the original vegetation has been able to survive. Ball grounds, tennis courts, golf links and other special sports areas are commonly laid out in white parks, but rarely in colored. Ground keepers, police supervision and other essential staffing are rarely on a par with that in white parks. There are exceptions, however, such as in Lexington, Kentucky, where colored park standards are about the same as the white. The trend, however slight its manifestations may be, is undoubtedly in the direction of more adequate Negro facilities, as is evidenced by the fact that it is not so many years since the ordinary white man in the south thought the idea that Negroes needed parks of any sort preposterous.

Discrimination in playgrounds is more noticeable, possibly because they are more expensive to equip and maintain than parks, and also because they imply closer contacts between the people using them. Here segregation is practised in every section of the country in spite of denials by officials. One might expect that where young children were involved racial lines would fail to be observed with strictness. Possibly if the children were left alone, this might be approximately true.

Some New Jersey school yards have a wire fence through which white and colored children may look at each other but have no further contacts. Throughout the south white and colored children must not use the same playground at the same time, although it is well known that even before the Civil War they romped together without parental disapproval, as they still do when not using a public playground. Of the seventeen southern cities studied by Forrester Washington in 1927, nine had playgrounds for whites only, two had segregated playgrounds for Negroes, and six had no such facilities for either race. Of forty northern cities included in the same study, one had complete playground segregation, thirty-four had some segregation, and five claimed to have no segregation at all.[9]

In the north the segregation in playgrounds is simple in interpretation. There, Negroes are something of an unknown quantity. Their numbers have increased tremendously, however, in recent years. There are no well understood rules governing contacts between the races which all may follow and, so doing, permit children to play with Negroes with no danger of losing caste in the neighbors' eyes. Further, the tales which have reached the Northerner, unaccustomed to the Negro by long years of constant association, have become the basis of racial beliefs which would be ridiculed by the true Southerner if applied to any Negro of his acquaintance. At a distance, the North has seen only the South's racial antagonisms, and has learned nothing of the less spectacular, commonplace facts about colored individuals which enable white people below the Mason and Dixon line to say one thing about Negroes in general, and act quite differently in individual cases. Race antagonisms are not absent in the north, and with the fears engendered by ignorance of the harmlessness of childhood interracial recreation, playground segregation is at least understandable.

In the south, formal interracial contacts on public playgrounds must have some secret social significance not possessed by the associations of plantation yard, stream, field and street. Perhaps there are not enough swings, teeter boards, and slides to go around. Or it may be that city playgrounds are primarily used by children whose parents have no assured social status

[9] Forrester B. Washington, *op. cit.*, p. 275

and must be careful lest they lose what little prestige they have from being white. These suggestions are, of course, half serious guesses included solely to demonstrate the inadequacy of any explanation except the one that southern public opinion has ruled playground association to be unthinkable. The result is that one of the real sources of racial understanding, early years of play association, is being weakened.

It is perhaps fortunate that playgrounds are so unimportant in the life of the American child, relatively speaking, in so far as race relations are concerned. In another sense it is unfortunate. Where playground segregation exists the minority group loses in per capita equipment, both qualitatively and quantitatively. The Negro, as a race, has proportionately fewer playgrounds with less equipment and, in more cases than not, no trained supervision at all.

In Tulsa, Oklahoma, where the Negro comprises eleven per cent of the population, there are thirteen playgrounds for white children, covering a total area of one thousand acres, with equipment valued at seventy-five thousand dollars and an annual appropriation of one hundred thousand dollars for running expenses, while the Negro children have only two acres of ground, with thirteen benches and four swings.[10] In the Richmond survey it was observed that there were six municipal playgrounds maintained for Negro children, open on the same basis as those for whites. The supervisors were paid twenty-five dollars a month and were not technically trained. One of the playgrounds "appeared to be merely one of the many open fields in the district," and the colored parents objected to it because it was swampy, too near a railroad, poorly equipped, not sufficiently supervised and a hangout for men, women and bad boys.[11] A good sign is that some of the more advanced cities are putting in trained workers, usually but not always colored. The Playground Association of America has a colored division which is doing good work. But after all, minority groups get what is left, if anything, and a larger propor-

[10] E. K. Jones, *The Negro in Community Life*, Proceedings of the National Conference of Social Work, 1929, p. 394.

[11] The Negro Welfare Service Committee of Richmond, Va., *op. cit.*, pp. 80-81.

tion of such children have to find their recreation elsewhere under less auspicious circumstances.

The organized play and recreation provided through organizations such as the Boy Scouts and the Girl Scouts have been closed to the Negro. In late years a few colored troops have been formed, but their very rarity makes them of little except local importance. Woofter found that it was practically impossible to organize colored troops in the south, since white troops took advantage of a charter provision which gave them the power to deny to the Negroes the use of the title and the uniform. In one city the scout master suggested that a large number of Negro boys organized by welfare workers call themselves the Brownie Club.[12]

One further factor should be mentioned because it operates in depriving the Negro child of opportunity for play, even though it is but remotely affected by unfavorable race attitudes. The economic status of the Negro group makes it necessary for these children to spend in productive labor a certain share of what would normally be considered leisure time. In a comparative study of leisure activities in Richmond, questionnaires were answered by 2,700 children in the sixth and subsequent grades, and then compared with results secured from the sixth and seventh grades of a white school in a poor district. While the study was very crude and open to a host of valid objections, the results are suggestive. Almost forty-four per cent of the Negro children stated that they had not had any opportunity to play the day before, while only sixteen per cent of the white children had been in the same position. Only fifteen per cent of the Negroes had spent no time in work, to forty-one per cent of the whites. "In all kinds of unorganized activities, such as visiting, going up town, sitting on the front porch, in all the things, in fact, which are not work, study or play, twenty-five and four-tenths per cent of the white children had spent above five hours the day before, as compared to six and two-tenths of the Negroes."[13]

[12] T. J. Woofter, Jr., *Negro Problems in Cities*, Doubleday, Doran & Co., Inc., New York, 1928, p. 294.

[13] The Negro Welfare Service Committee of Richmond, Va., *op. cit.*, pp. 82-83.

Our urban immigrants have suffered similarly although not to the same degree. South European children have been pushed aside as undesirable play companions in public places. The Oriental on the west coast receives a reserved welcome or none at all. The Mexican child is distinctly unwanted by neighboring native white parents. These people are likely to live in slums, and there are few congested areas in the country which have adequate playgrounds. This is not necessarily purposeful discrimination, but the result is almost the same.

Some cities have built recreation centers with gymnasiums, game rooms, reading rooms, auditoriums, dance space, and other provisions for indoor occupations. With few exceptions, these have been available for white people only. Even where technically open to all who wish to enter, the majority group usually takes possession to the exclusion of all others, who naturally do not wish to go where they are not welcomed. Recreation centers, since they imply even closer contacts than the playground, and are also more costly, are still more racially restricted.

When park, playground, or recreation center boasts a swimming pool, racial segregation is almost sure to enter. For some reason or other, swimming in the same public pool or from the same beach with a member of the colored race is more distasteful to white people than any other common form of athletic activity. A racial clash on a public bathing beach in Chicago in 1919 precipitated the disastrous riots in that city. Atlantic City authorities have been careful to keep Negroes from the beaches popular with the white people unless, of course, they enter in the extenuating capacity of nursemaids. Seaside, lake, and mountain resorts where Jews are restricted do not seem to have the same basis for their action. There seems to be some fear of contamination from bathing in water through which a brown body has passed. To the Nordic, a dark skin perhaps symbolizes dirt. Others fear disease infection, although in ocean, lake, or well kept pool such danger is slight. That this fear is not essentially founded on sex standards which would balk at the exposure to the Negro's gaze of white girls in bathing suits is indicated by the opposition to racially mixed bathing in sex-segregated Y. M. C. A., Y. W. C. A., college, and other enclosed pools. The use of the shower rooms often attached to public swimming places is also quite generally forbidden to Negroes. In one large northern pool, a Negro who wishes to buy a locker ticket is politely asked if he is a member of "the association." Since this "association" is purely mythical, he can show no evidence of membership, and withdraws without insisting on his legal rights.

Yet racially mixed bathing can be found in all sections of the United States. A few pools may be used by all who will, although here again semi-voluntary segregation is the rule. The more informal the bathing arrangements, the less likelihood there is of trouble. The country swimming hole may be freely used by Negroes in one community, but not by those in adjacent neighborhoods. Sometimes a place down stream is tacitly reserved for colored swimmers, while on a hunting or fishing trip brown and white members of the party will unconcernedly refresh themselves in the same pond. Thus even in this activity no universal rule is followed.

The accompanying tables[14] will give an idea of the actual

[14] Forrester B. Washington, *op. cit.*, pp. 274-275.

The seventeen southern cities covered by Washington in his survey included:

Atlanta, Ga.	Lexington, Ky.	Orlando, Fla.
Baltimore, Md.	Macon, Ga.	Richmond, Va.
Birmingham, Ala.	Memphis, Tenn.	Savannah, Ga.
Columbus, Ga.	Nashville, Tenn.	Tampa, Fla.
Houston, Tex.	New Orleans, La.	Washington, D. C.
Jacksonville, Fla.	Norfolk, Va.	

The forty northern cities were:

Atlantic City, N. J.	Kansas City, Mo.	Port Huron, Mich.
Berkeley, Calif.	Lansing, Mich.	Rock Island, Ill.
Buffalo, N. Y.	Mason City, Ia.	Sandusky, Ohio
Burlington, Ia.	Milwaukee, Wis.	Scranton, Pa.
Canton, O.	Minneapolis, Minn.	South Bend, Ind.
Cincinnati, O.	Montclair, N. J.	Springfield, Mass.
Cleveland, O.	Moorestown, N. J.	St. Joseph, Mo.
Colorado Springs, Colo.	New Bedford, Mass.	St. Louis, Mo.
Decatur, Ill.	New York, N. Y.	Toledo, O.
Des Moines, Ia.	Newark, N. J.	Van Wert, O.
Detroit, Mich.	Oakland, Calif.	Watertown, N. Y.
Duluth, Minn.	Philadelphia, Pa.	Wichita, Kan.
Fort Wayne, Ind.	Pittsburgh, Pa.	Zanesville, O.
Indianapolis. Ind.		

extent to which urban recreational facilities have been provided for Negroes, whether by public or private agencies.

Vacations are now recognized as necessary to the efficiency and mental health of American workers. A proper vacation implies a proper place to spend it, and at a reasonable cost. With the coming of cheap transportation by excursion train or car, some change of scene is within the reach of the ordinary city worker who can save a mere trifle. Minority groups, however, may not be accepted at the most accessible resorts.

Jews, for example, are not wanted at many summer places. Eagle's Mere in the Pennsylvania mountains restricts this group. Several leading Atlantic City hotels will not permit

TABLE II

PUBLIC RECREATION IN SEVENTEEN SOUTHERN CITIES

	Facilities for Whites Only	Complete Segregation of Whites and Negroes	No Facilities for Either Race
Playgrounds....................	0	8	3
Parks...........................	4	13	0
Recreation centers...............	3	3	11
Bathing beaches..................	3	11	4
Swimming pools..................	10	6	1

PUBLIC RECREATION IN FORTY NORTHERN CITIES

	Facilities for Whites Only	Complete Segregation of Whites and Negroes	Some Segregation	No Segregation	No Facilities for Either Race
Playgrounds....	0	0	7	33	0
Parks..........	0	0	0	40	0
Recreation centers........	0	2	23	12	3
Bathing beaches	5	11	12	0	12
Swimming pools	3	2	29	3	3

PRIVATE RECREATION (SOCIAL SERVICE) IN SEVENTEEN SOUTHERN CITIES

	Facilities for Whites Only	Complete Segregation of Whites and Negroes	No Facilities for Either Race
Recreation centers, settlements, community centers	7	3	7
Playgrounds	9	2	6
Y. M. C. A.	2	15	0
Boy Scouts	14	3	0
Swimming pools	10	6	1
Summer camps	12	5	0
Camp Fire Girls	15	2	0

PRIVATE RECREATION (SOCIAL SERVICE) IN FORTY NORTHERN CITIES

	Facilities for Whites Only	Complete Segregation of Whites and Negroes	Some Segregation	No Segregation	No Facilities for Either Race
Recreation centers, settlements, community centers	5	24	6	5	..
Playgrounds	0	1	34	5	..
Y. M. C. A.	2	22	6	10	..
Boy Scouts	0	14	14	12	..
Swimming pools	..	4	30	6	..
Summer Camps	..	13	9	18	..
Camp Fire Girls	..	18	22	10	..

them to register. There are seaside, lake and mountain resorts throughout the country which welcome only Gentiles. However, this exclusion has been adequately met by the development of Jewish summer resorts throughout the United States, and the erection of accommodations for members of this faith in all the larger vacation centers, as at Atlantic City.

Probably no other white minority group which has sufficient money and cultural polish to fit into the accepted standards of vacation life is absolutely barred from the ordinary summer resort. Indians, being rural and western, do not need such places, and they would usually be accepted if they wished to make use of them. Mexicans have not yet found it necessary to meet the issue. Orientals are so few that some vacation plans can always be carried out if time and money are available. Negroes are left with makeshift vacation resources.

Before the World War Negroes were developing summer resorts for their exclusive use on a relatively large scale. There is an excellent Negro summer resort in Michigan, and another in Mississippi. Several colored seaside resorts flourish along the Atlantic coast. On the whole, however, these can be patronized only by the few who have the time and money to spend a good portion of the year away from home on vacation. While there are some Negro resorts which can be enjoyed by poor Negroes, the number of this class actually able to patronize them is small. A pseudo-vacation is obtained by many of the working colored people by securing jobs at seashore or other resorts where they can earn their living and still have vacation in off hours and through a change of scene. In Philadelphia, for illustration, it is common for colored cooks and maids to go to Atlantic City and other nearby resorts for summer work, thus breaking the monotony of their routine and obtaining some semblance of a real vacation away from the home city and without starving. This is no doubt better than no vacation at all, but the problem has not been faced. The majority of this group must continue to think of vacation as a short period free from work but otherwise no different from the rest of the year.

Free libraries, supported by taxes or private gifts, are not necessarily free to all. A colored Ph.D., or a self-tutored halting reader, applying for permission to use books in dozens of southern cities, would be told to use the Negro branch library, usually containing from two to ten thousand random volumes. In two or three cities he would be allowed to get the book desired, but would have to take it out of the building to read. At least one city in the far south, El Paso, Texas, would permit him full use of its library service, but there only about one and one-half per cent of the population is colored, compared with sixty per cent Mexican. In the north and west he would have no difficulty at all except an occasional lack of courtesy from racially sensitive employees. In some southern cities he would be told that there were no public books for members of his race. A dozen cities or so, including New York, Chicago and Baltimore, have special Negro branches, or branches used largely by Negroes, but would place no restrictions in the way of any colored person who might want to use the main library or any other branch. There seems to be no rule governing the situation, except the one that in regions most anxious to "keep the Negro in his place," that place is not the public library used by white people.

A few specific illustrations may help to visualize the situation. Cities with no provision for library service to Negroes include Charleston, S. C., with 32,000 Negroes; Dallas, Texas, with 24,000; Mobile, Ala., with 23,000; and Shreveport, La., with 17,000. The 62,000 in Atlanta must use the two Negro branches with a total of 6,700 volumes, a five-thousand-dollar appropriation, 9,000 registered readers and 31,000 volume circulation. The 100,000 Negroes in New Orleans must use one branch with 13,000 volumes, with 2,000 registered readers and 37,000 volume circulation. One library kindly gives all duplicates to Negro preachers and teachers for use by colored citizens. Boston, with a colored population neither large nor concentrated, and practically all other northern cities with or without pressing "Negro problems," pay no more attention to their colored readers than to any other group which may need or want a slightly different selection of material.[15]

No other minority group in the United States receives such library treatment. Foreign-language people may be handicapped because of their inability to use English, but they are definitely urged to use our libraries to their utmost. Rural peoples, like the Indians, may not find libraries in their neighborhood, but that is a geographical accident, publicly regretted.

[15] Louis Shores, "Public Library Service to Negroes," *The Library Journal*, February 15, 1930, vol. lv, pp. 150-154.

While all minority groups suffer some limitations in using libraries during the leisure time at their disposal, only in the case of the Negro is it a racial attitude which keeps out those who have both the ability and the desire to improve or merely pass their leisure in reading publicly owned books.

Of course, if all libraries were thrown absolutely open to all races, a larger proportion of Negroes would fail to use them than of native whites. Their education is inferior. Their traditions do not emphasize reading in libraries. Their leisure interests have been developed along different lines. No great sums of money have been spent in popularizing the use of public libraries among colored people as among the white. Thus one of the most efficient means for diminishing group cultural variations and race friction is relatively closed, particularly in the section of the country where most Negroes live.

While public leisure-time facilities may be neglected through indifference or race antagonisms, some form of commercialized amusement is sure to spring up where there are enough people of any color or nationality to make it worth while financially. The form of amusement may have to be molded to suit local ideas, but one may be certain that any recreational device known to be profitable, unless it involves race mixture contrary to custom, will be offered in proportion to the demand. The demand from minority groups, quite naturally, will be suited to their time, purse, and ideas of desirability. It may be supplied by members of the groups themselves, or by some thrifty member of the majority group who is never lacking when there is an opportunity for turning an honest or even a tainted penny by catering to "inferiors."

Motion pictures probably take first rank among the better-organized commercialized amusements in their influence on minority group opinions. Only the colored races endure discrimination in admission to the movies. There is some tendency to restrict oriental attendance at motion picture houses in areas where anti-oriental feeling is acute, but Indian money is as good as the white man's at the ticket office. Low-class Mexicans and other immigrants are no more desired than crude, unkempt native whites, and no less. The relatively presentable immigrant need have no fears if he has the price of admission. The Negro, however, unless he is willing to sit off by himself, is rarely a desired patron except in houses which make a specialty of catering to him.

In the south the Negro has his choice of taking the poorer seats offered him, finding a colored house, or staying away. Some centers have no houses to which Negroes are admitted; but when competition or hard times reduces profits below the danger line, some way can usually be found whereby the Negro's money can be exchanged for admission to special seats which by some magic have been made proper for his occupancy. Of course, there is always the chance of running a house for Negroes only, and some such places exist in all the larger cities and most of the smaller ones. The majority of these houses are small, poorly ventilated, dirty, and ill kept, and the type of picture is rarely of the best. Yet they are patronized in part by individuals to whom such conditions are revolting, but who accept them occasionally rather than be subjected to annoyance in white theaters or see no shows at all. Only in a few of the more prosperous cities may southern Negroes view the best pictures under happy circumstances either in a properly cared-for section of a white theater or in one of the few first-class colored houses.

There are a few motion picture theaters in the north where segregation and exclusion are openly practised. Still more rare is the kind which pays no attention to the color of its patrons. As is well known, northern states quite commonly have civil-rights acts in legal force, but while these may be looked on as nuisances by managers who wish to draw the color line, they never prevent racial discrimination. An offended person may enter legal suit under some circumstances, but verdicts for the plaintiff, in recent years, are rare. It is so hard to get legal evidence, and if a discriminating ticket agent or usher admits acting beyond the orders of the management, judgment against the theater is impossible unless the employee can be proved a liar.

The non-southern motion picture theater usually finds it unnecessary to take direct action against Negroes. If there are only a few who wish admission from time to time, there is no problem. If there are enough to make it profitable to admit them, as in some New York houses, the answer is easy—let them in, but try to keep them off by themselves so as not to offend white patronage which is also desirable. If colored requests for tickets become too frequent to pass unnoticed and still do not really matter in the day's receipts, there are a thousand and one ways of discouraging the colored applicant so that the word is soon passed around to stay away, for suave side-tracking and public embarrassment outweigh and destroy the amusement value of the screen.

Commonly, as in Philadelphia, courteous ushers solicitously guide the colored patron to a balcony seat. In one nationally known first-run house a buzzer can be heard as the Negro enters. Uniformed ushers materialize on all sides and form a guard of honor lining the path to an unofficial Negro section. Strong men of character or violent emotions may break through the line, but not the ordinary individual who is easily overawed by a show of military force or the danger of becoming the center of public attention. But if quiet determination not to be segregated is shown, or if the manager's presence is insisted on, the line of defenders fades and the dark visitor is permitted to find any seat he can alone. Rarely will a manager risk a show of force. It is much easier to let it be known that embarrassing opposition will be encountered, and Negroes will stay away.

This is only one of numerous means for accomplishing the desired purpose. Ticket sellers are a bulwark of defense. Ticket takers do their share. It is all so easy, so long as one avoids open admission of discrimination on a color basis, that civil-rights acts have become nothing more than dim threats to incautious managers.

The legitimate theater takes much the same attitude as does the motion picture house. Since, however, they sell tickets for specific seats, ticket sellers and the guardians of the doors here bear the burden of preserving the light complexion of the audience. Tickets may be sold in a colored block, preferably in the balcony or higher. In the south, of course, admission is to the upper gallery where Negroes only may sit. Special gallery entrances, frequently by side street or alley, may then be expected, so that there may be no contacts between the races in the lobby or on the stairs. Accommodations in these cases are rarely other than distinctly inferior. In the north, while there is a tendency to place the Negro in as high and out-of-the-way a seat as possible, a strict "nigger heaven" has been found impracticable.

Theater discrimination, however, is relatively less important in race relations than is that found in the movies. Since only Negroes encounter racial barriers to this leisure activity, and since most Negroes either do not have theaters of any sort in their community or belong to an economic class which cannot afford this kind of recreation, the effect on the masses is slight. The financially more fortunate Negroes in the south suffer most in this respect. A dark Negro in Washington, D. C., for example, cannot see a good play or hear good music in the theaters of that city, for there are not enough colored people in the city to support a first-class segregated theater, as is possible with motion pictures or cheap vaudeville and shows which appeal to the uncultured but have no socializing values. It is interesting to note that in Washington segregation is so important that Negroes have been hired by theaters to spot colored people light enough to pass as white who have been taking advantage of their complexions to see plays from which they are supposed to be barred by race. In the north and west, possibly due in part to the hard times through which the legitimate theater has recently been going, the superior group of Negroes, which alone could be expected to profit by attendance at high-class theatrical performances, is increasingly finding reasonable accommodations available. The regrettable feature of the situation is that the cheap, sensational sort of show has been strengthened by theatrical segregation and is now available to Negroes, and well patronized, in all the larger cities.

It may be taken for granted that what is or is not heard or seen on stage and screen must be taken into account in interpreting the life of any group. All minority groups except the Negro may listen to and view the same shows, photoplays, and musical presentations, as any other members of their same community and economic class. Race prejudice is for them no serious barrier in this respect. As has been shown, the Negro is in a different position.

The educated Negro in all northern and some southern urban areas is, in spite of handicaps, able to avail himself of the same facilities of this kind as is his white neighbor. Most white people would be surprised to listen to the superior colored person's conversation about composers, musicians, singers, actors, playwrights, and productions. In interest and quality it is the equal of that found in comparable white groups. Galling restrictions based on race antagonism have produced a mental irritation not conducive to cooperative race relations in many of the cultured Negroes, but they have not kept them from participation in the artistic life of the country.

The Negro masses, however, have automatically been driven into the trashy sort of show. Little choice is left to them. They may go only where their money is the most important item, and that means where cheap thrills, sex, and exaggerated high-society life are the attraction, which draws them into either Negro or mixed houses in large enough numbers to make their patronage pay. In this they are no different from other poorer classes who find sensual eye-and-ear entertainment most attractive because it does not tax the intellect, yet affords a stimulating diversion. The major difference for the Negro is that the path up from the lower levels is narrow, steep, and marked by painful barriers.

Motion pictures in general are a mediocre leisure diversion from a social point of view. Based as they are on large-scale production, distribution, and exhibition, they must be simple and exciting enough to appeal to the greatest possible number of potential customers. They must be liberally sprinkled with the cheap devices of sentiment and emotion, free from any taint which might require intellectual effort by the audience, and characterized by complete conformity to the stereotypes of the masses. Now and then an exceptional play appears, but it must attract a tremendous patronage to warrant wide exhibition, something it rarely does. This is not an indictment of the motives of the motion picture industry, but rather of the modern social and economic order which decrees the prosperity of such leisure-time activities.

All the evidence shows a wide and increasing use of motion pictures for recreation by all minority groups in the United States. While one may regret the general acceptance of this form of amusement at the expense of healthful physical recreation or intellect-building diversions, it does nevertheless act as a means for assimilation. It is not as though the native white population were avoiding motion pictures. If this were the case, and it is far from such, then they could unqualifiedly be said to be adding to the differentiation of minority groups. As it is, except as the Negro is held apart, motion pictures actually are a powerful force in unifying all national elements. That is, they are doing so by being a focal point of interest for all groups.

It need only be mentioned here that so long as motion pictures rely on native white pocketbooks for their existence, they will continue to confirm and spread the racial beliefs of the majority. Negroes and Orientals may be servants and villains, but rarely heroes except in a subservient manner. Mexicans, too, must conform to the nation's idea of what Mexicans really are, which does not seem to be a very complimentary idea. South Europeans in the past have been villains and vamps, both male and female, while heroes and virtuous heroines have been portrayed by northern types. This is less true in recent years, as we have become more familiar with our newer immigrants and, on occasion, even conscious of the individuality of a handful of colored people. The legitimate theater, too, has had to keep in line with popular racial prejudices, although some of them have been violated in scattered shows. We need not expect, however, that either stage or screen will take a position out of keeping with national racial feelings. Their influence in this respect will continue to be that of conserving rather than changing the ideas of the audience.

Dancing among Negroes has been well commercialized. Probably every minority group of any size, wherever located, has some convenient dance hall which, if not exclusively devoted to its use, is at least tacitly understood to be a rendezvous for its members who wish that kind of recreation. Filipino dance halls in the west, Mexican in the south and west, oriental in the regions where they have settled, and those catering to the various European nationalities in the areas where they have congregated, are well known. Where the basis for differentiation is cultural and not skin color, individuals may expect to desert their own peoples' dance halls and patronize any they can afford as soon as outward cultural assimilation is well accomplished. The colored races, however, have not had this opportunity for change.

Of course this change, which is possible for the European immigrant, may not amount to much. Public dance halls run on a commercial basis are notoriously places of moral danger, regardless of which races or nationalities attend. Their connection with drinking, gambling, and prostitution has been so common that all municipalities have been compelled to attempt some supervision and regulation in the public interest. Negro dance halls, however, have perhaps had less supervision than those of any other large population element. Colored morals, for many superior white people, are more a subject of amusement than of concern, so if their dance halls go beyond the limits of white decency, what of it? Who should be concerned except the few superior Negroes, whose voice is ineffective?

As a result, Negro dance halls, owned by white and colored men alike, frequently have been wide open. Alcoholic drinks are sold either in the building or nearby in all the poorer halls, and most of the better ones. Prostitutes use them as a hunting ground. Lascivious dancing is almost unchecked save by the couple's inhibitions. And nobody who matters cares. Conduct which has been reliably reported from New Orleans to New York can hardly be believed by one not familiar with the situation.

The patrons of these affairs may, on occasion, include representatives of all colored classes, but as a rule they are drawn almost exclusively from the poorer and tougher elements who constitute a larger proportion of the colored people than of the native white. But even though the patrons are drawn from the least desirable element, the convenient presence of such places of temptation for the initiated reflects a phase of American life which could not exist to the extent it does without the support of race prejudice.

White people are rigidly excluded from nearly all of the Negro dance halls. Their intrusion on "slumming parties" is bitterly resented, and even if white men or women wished to partake of the fun on terms of absolute equality they would rarely find a welcome. Perhaps this exclusion has aided the continuance of an intolerable condition.

Night clubs, which have in the popular mind become an integral part of the everyday recreational life of all Negroes, are few in number. Outside of New York, where perhaps a dozen or two may be found—the number depending on the prohibition padlocks and business failures—no city has more than two or three, and most have none worthy of the name. And in New York, the most prosperous ones are those which depend on up to ninety per cent of white patronage for their existence. Were it not for the fact that a type of "Negro literature" has given the cabaret false prominence in colored life, it, could be entirely omitted from our discussion, for its significance may truly be said to be imaginative. Since, as described, it so nicely fits the ordinary concept of what Negro recreation should be, the cabaret has been eagerly accepted, with a certain morbid satisfaction, as a characteristic diversion of the race. It may be a long time before the obvious facts to the contrary succeed in convincing white people of their actual rôle.

Commercial amusement parks, with few exceptions, have been unwilling to admit the Negro in any part of the country. Of course he is being admitted to some northern parks, but his welcome has on the whole been thin. The intimacy of roller coaster, shooting gallery, and mirror hall has been deemed too great to permit the same facilities to be enjoyed by both the top and bottom races of the country. This form of segregation is merely another phase of national racial attitudes, although the intensity of antagonism is perhaps here magnified by the quality of white people who predominate. Amusement parks rely on the dimes of the less successful white people for their existence. This is particularly true in the case of adults; and adults, not children, are the backbone of the trade. Many of the smaller parks are infested with a rough element quite out of proportion to the intrinsic harmlessness of the average concession. Patrons such as these would naturally be the loudest in their objections to the presence of Negroes, since their own social status is not of the best.

This exclusion is particularly unfortunate, for the relatively harmless, open-air type of amusement popular in such parks could furnish the poorer colored people a recreational outlet far superior to the central city commercialized devices. Since the World War amusement parks exclusively for colored patrons have sprung up throughout the South and in some sections of the North. They are surprisingly well patronized, considering their less favorable and less extensive equipment when compared with white parks, and are serving a healthy function in spite of the customary accompaniment of toughs, questionable conduct in the dance pavilion and "parties" which must be expected at such places. They are designed to serve the masses, and this is the class which needs such service most among Negroes. It also includes most colored people. If the facilities are sometimes abused, this is no condemnation of the entire scheme. Dance halls, pool rooms and the like are far worse, and have fewer redeeming features.

Another form of commercialized recreation for Negroes should be mentioned, not because of its intrinsic importance but because of the implications in the popular attitude which make it possible. This refers to the so-called "race records" for the phonograph. One of the larger companies producing records has for some time been issuing a special series for Negroes. Some have been harmless reproductions of sermons and church services. Not a few have been so obscene in content, either by direct word or by obvious double meaning in songs recorded that it is difficult to understand why they have been permitted to be sold. The reason, no doubt, is that there is no direct censorship of phonograph records, and that white people as a whole consider Negro morals so low that they cannot be damaged. It may be significant that these records have been announced in a catalogue separate from the general offerings of the company. Recently, it is understood, the worst of these records have been discontinued. A race prejudice which permitted a powerful and responsible corporation to issue them if only for a short time must in the nature of things be indifferent to even worse lapses if confined only to the Negro. This attitude explains much of the Negro's slowness in adopting a recreational code more nearly like that of his white neighbor, who is apparently neighbor in a geographical sense only.

The commercial amusement facilities in the cities studied by Forrester Washington are listed in Table III.

Pool rooms are a major recreational source of evil peculiar in their special manifestations to the United States. While their growth may be most malignant in congested urban areas, they also flourish in towns and villages scarcely larger than a crossroads. Playing pool, it may be necessary to explain, never occupies the time of more than a scattering of the patrons of commercial pool rooms except during off days and hours. There are, of course, any number of well kept, high-class pool and billiard parlors which can be accused of nothing more serious than wasting people's time and money. These are not the ones to which we are referring. They are exceptional, and minority peoples are not often found in them other than as help.

An institution so flourishing as the low-class pool room is usually a response to a definite social need. A place to pass empty hours with congenial companions is a real need for city people as well as villagers. Farm boys, too, may drift to town on occasional nights to get the stimulus and response of poolroom and other gatherings where any reasonably good fellow is certain to be accepted into a superficial but gratifying companionship if he falls properly in line with existing group customs. The home itself may be satisfactory both as to parents and accommodations, but fail to supply the social requirements of the younger members of the family. Sometimes these can be met through church, club, and other groupings with social

TABLE III

COMMERCIAL AMUSEMENT IN SEVENTEEN SOUTHERN CITIES [16]

	Facilities for Whites Only	Complete Segregation of Whites and Negroes	Some Segregation	No Segregation	No Facilities for Either Race
Moving picture theaters......	4	3	10	0	0
Picture and vaudeville houses.......	2	2	10	..	3
Outdoor amusement parks...	2	10	0	0	5
Legitimate theaters........	3	0	11	0	3

COMMERCIAL AMUSEMENT IN FORTY NORTHERN CITIES

	Facilities for Whites Only	Complete Segregation of Whites and Negroes	Some Segregation	No Segregation	No Facilities for Either Race
Moving picture theaters.....	0	0	33	7	0
Picture and vaudeville houses.......	0	0	24	16	0
Outdoor amusement parks...	3	0	19	11	7
Legitimate theaters........	0	0	26	14	0

contacts. Adequate circles of intimate friends may prove sufficient. Gangs of either sex, although we do not call them by such a harsh name if their membership is made up of girls, form automatically to provide a recreational outlet of social stimulus

[16] Forrester B. Washington, *op. cit.*, p. 276.

and satisfaction. In any event, meeting places are required, and here the pool room vies with club room, home, saloon, and country store.

Negro pool rooms are a characteristic of all colored areas. Immigrants are not so addicted to their use as they were to the saloon, which was a natural substitute for familiar old-country gathering places. Other resources more in keeping with tradition may still be utilized, and the necessity for further readjustment be thus avoided. Children of immigrants, and immigrants on whom custom has but a slight hold, have contributed more than their share to the popularity of the pool table and its surroundings. To the Negro the pool room has occupied such an accustomed place that he takes it for granted much as does the Greek his coffee house.

The social character of the common pool room may perhaps best be indicated by observing that in Philadelphia police officials are required to keep constant recorded check on all such places in their individual districts. This order may in a measure be due to overzealous reformers, but the general disrepute in which pool rooms are held can be well substantiated by investigation. Investigators of colored pool rooms have repeatedly found them to be linked up with prostitution, drink, and gambling. At best they are hangouts where futile loafers may be exposed to bootleg liquor, prostitutes, and varieties of games of chance. At their worst they are overrun by vicious criminals who find them convenient for their purposes. The occasional decent establishment does not lend virtue to its disreputable brothers.

There is, however, no way of cleaning up this condition except by providing other facilities which will serve their function attractively and efficiently and without their attendant undesirable features. Since there appears to be no immediate prospect of such facilities, the pool room will continue to assimilate the Negro and the poorer American-born children of European parentage into national fellowship through one of the worst commercialized recreational institutions of the United States.

Commercialized vice is a form of recreation which makes a

strong appeal to minority groups. Prostitution, gambling, and the use of alcohol and other drugs are means for sensual gratification available in some form or other to people of any color or origin. Profits from their illicit commercialization are so attractive that someone seems always ready to supply an effective demand. White men and black cater to the vicious habits of either race. European and native lose their nationality in these trades. The only group distinctions which have held are those between Negro and white, and even these have broken down to a remarkable degree in the vicious types of recreation.

"Numbers" is a gambling invention highly profitable to the organizers, which has such a heavy colored following in New York, Philadelphia and other cities that it is considered a feature of Negro life. The organizers may be white or colored, and so may the gamblers. The scheme is in essence for the gambler to select three numbers to appear in the next day's New York clearing house or other financial reports in a specific place. The bets are small, ranging from one cent on up to several dollars, and if a "hit" is made, the payoff is six hundred to one. Since there are a thousand possible combinations of the numbers from zero to nine, the banker has little chance of losing unless many people select the same number on the same day, and that number happens to "hit." All kinds of hunches are played, for example, some number that Amos 'n' Andy happen to mention over the radio; and the winnings, if any, are large. A very small sum is risked. There is no chance of crookedness unless the man with the money defaults, which is both a rare and dangerous occurrence. Runners are employed to make collections. The organizer can hardly help getting rich. Under such circumstances the appearance of race prejudice may give way before economic pressure. In order to illustrate what such pressure can do, it may be worth mentioning that one metropolitan newspaper tried to avoid even the appearance of cooperating by refusing to publish the financial reports depended on by "number" players. Circulation competition compelled the staid and respectable publisher to swallow his conscience with unseemly haste.

In these cases it is usually the white man who participates

as manager or player in what is considered "nigger gambling."
The Negro does not participate in interracial poker games,
although he may play an excellent hand. Poker has social
connotations which craps have not. Horse racing is, of course,
a white man's sport, but colored money is commonly good
enough to be taken by bookmakers. In spite of apparent exceptions, the rule is that in gambling the white man may step
down occasionally to try to take the Negro's cash playing the
colored man's game, but the Negro may not step up and take
the white man's cash in the games thought to be above his
place. Colored pool and billiards are apparently not the same
as white, or else the social aspect enters again here, for interracial playing is rare. Yet the fact that a leading professional
billiard player married an oriental girl did not bar him as a
popular tournament competitor. The limits beyond which one
may not go must be learned by rule of thumb.

In commercialized prostitution it is also the white who may
step down to associate with colored prostitutes and mistresses
without losing caste. This statement is made deliberately, in
the face of indignant denials by those, particularly in the south,
who insist that such race relations are rare and are socially
penalized. It must be agreed that there are plenty of scrupulous
individuals who are honestly indignant at such conduct, but
there are many more who seem to be indignant in public only,
and still others who are indifferent. At this time we are speaking only of commercialized illicit sexual relations, and there is
no question but that the racial lines may here be crossed without penalty other than that which would be visited on any
similar moral indiscretion in which race were not involved.

On the other hand, any crossing of the racial line by Negroes
visiting white prostitutes would arouse the greatest emotional
indignation in practically *all* classes of white persons. This
does happen from time to time—how frequently there is no
way of knowing—and is considered sufficient cause for lynching, no matter how welcome the colored patron or how degraded the white prostitute. Several lynchings are known to
have been the outgrowth of such relations.

Commercialized sex relations seem to be an unavoidable accompaniment of a caste system which is permitted to grow out of the presence of minority racial and national groups in a community controlled by some self-appointed superior people. Native Indian women living in or near white communities were commercialized from the earliest days of pioneer settlement. Oriental women have been outnumbered by the men, but even so, oriental prostitutes have been available for white trade. Immigrant girls have been an important source of supply for houses of prostitution. This may be little more than another way of saying that such women are always recruited from the exploited, poverty-stricken social classes, for minority groups are likely to be made up largely of such classes. There is some reason to believe, however, that another factor in the situation is a psychological attraction, possibly nothing more than novelty, which seems to be found by many in sex relations with members of a different race or culture. Members of a group of inferior social status may also be put in a state of mind where yielding to illicit sex relations with an individual in the superior group may not only involve little mental conflict but also be a source of personal satisfaction, an elevation of status. This was certainly commonly true under American slavery, and some hangovers from these earlier times may still be observed, although they are rapidly disappearing.

Strangely enough, such intimate contacts do not improve race relations. They may have quite the opposite effect. The superior group comes to the point of view, quite likely, that the inferior has a lower moral standard and is probably more emotional and oversexed, as is the common opinion concerning the American Negro. The patrons who take advantage of the situation never apply the same reasoning to themselves. Meanwhile, the morals of all groups deteriorate and race contacts become more and more strained.

Alcohol, like prostitution, lowers racial barriers to some slight extent. On one southern plantation where Negro workers must drink below a spring in the fields while white workers drink out of the spring itself, a jug of moonshine is passed from individual to individual without regard for color. In New York in colored cabarets and speakeasies where white people are admitted, members of both races rub elbows with little thought of contamination. Such illustrations, however, are exceptional, and were rare before prohibition. Throughout the United States drinking has been a ceremonious procedure, involving a spurious fellowship; and where the ceremonies are observed, the Negro is excluded from participation. Except for thrill-seekers on slumming parties, white people do not "lower" themselves to drink with colored. The white man who may tacitly be permitted a colored mistress must not be observed drinking on terms of equality with a "nigger." It has been observed that southern white bootleggers like to deal with Negro patrons, for they do not dare to report infractions of the law.[17]

Indian and white, however, may be and nearly always have been permitted the common use of the bottle. There have been saloons in pioneer communities where Indians were not welcome, but there were nearly always certain friendly Indians with whom one could share a drink. Orientals have been more restricted in their indulgence of their taste for strong drink. Clubs controlled by white people, of course, in communities where Chinese are common, have barred all yellow people, no matter what their personal accomplishments may have been. This applies both to China and the western coast of the United States. Japanese have encountered similar exclusion. Europeans, on the contrary, have found their money good for a drink in any public saloon where other white people of their class were at home. Even the lowly Mexican has customarily been admitted to the native white man's drinking places. Nevertheless, frequently such groups have by preference patronized particular saloons almost to the exclusion of others where they could have been accepted. This, however, is at least a semi-voluntary segregation. The Negro's segregation has been compulsory.

Rent parties are a form of commercialized recreation patronized exclusively by Negroes of the poorer classes. Families out of work and funds in Harlem and in other Negro communities have in recent years sometimes adopted the device of announc-

[17] C. G. Woodson, *op. cit.*, p. 136.

ing a public party to which all who wish may come. Food and
drink are served, some kind of music is offered, and small fees
are charged. The proceeds are theoretically used to pay the
rent. Landlords with empty apartments or houses have been
known to use the same method to make both ends meet. If a
white person enters, the party usually dissolves. So, too, if
Negroes of the upper classes visit a party on a slumming tour,
the regular patrons quietly drift away, leaving the affair to
the interlopers. In essence, the scheme is private commercialization of home parties so as to provide income for the host
and pseudo-social recreation to poor Negroes with inadequate
normal social leisure facilities. It has flourished among a limited
number of colored people because it has met, however inade-
quately, a need not otherwise provided for in a congested city
area occupied by handicapped individuals without social and
economic resources of a decent standard.

Restaurants, although not essentially recreational in nature,
not uncommonly have a recreational aspect. As a place to meet,
loaf, and talk they are sometimes the competitor or successor
of the old-time saloon. Where dancing and cabaret features are
added, eating becomes a secondary matter. Sometimes they
are a pathetic attempt to keep alive certain food and other
cultural survivals of the home country. They may also be
purely financial ventures surviving because a gullible native
white public thinks it is getting local color in Chinese-Ameri-
can, Italian-American, Russian-American, and other hyphenated but pseudo-foreign restaurants. The real Chinese restaurant is tucked away where none but Chinese may easily find
it. The true Greek and Turkish restaurants, American descendant of the coffee house, serve cold fish, peculiar meats
and vegetables, sticky rich pastries and thick coffee which a
one-hundred-per-cent American would find unpalatable. When
European restaurants in the United States actually serve a
primarily immigrant clientele, they supply a real recreational
need. Usually, if there is any appreciable number of a particular nationality, some such place will spring up and serve the
community needs and be a real factor in the adjustment of
the immigrant to his new home. The pseudo-foreign type,

however, serves the immigrant as nothing more than a means of livelihood, while it creates false ideas of European and oriental culture in the American mind. Restaurants with Negro trade, on the other hand, are always built on the trade of colored customers, for they are rarely patronized by native whites unless they are of the cabaret type. There are many such restaurants for Negroes of the poorer classes, both for food and recreational purposes. It is the superior Negro who has no such facilities. While there are many restaurants in the north and west which will serve Negroes, these are the ones which make a business of selling only food, not recreation. In the south, of course, no white restaurant serves Negroes except behind a partition or in some obscure corner. This means that cultured Negroes who want food in accordance with their means and needs and a place to entertain their friends or to while away the time after the theater, are without facilities, for they are not sufficiently numerous, outside of New York City, to support segregated institutions. A few ventures have been relatively prosperous, and some substitutes, such as private clubs, have had a little success; still this recreational need of the upper classes may be said to be unfilled.

No considerable group of people is able to spend more than a small portion of its leisure time in public and commercialized amusements combined. The actual number of hours so spent, however, may not be so important as the manner of spending them. Public facilities for recreation tend to be wholesome and positive socializing forces under trained guidance and supervision. There is a wide range of choice in commercialized amusements running from symphony concerts and first-class plays to pool rooms and tough dance halls available for selection in the United States, limited only by time, money, and race prejudice. The Negro more than any other group is compelled by antagonistic attitudes to restrict himself to a mere handful of the lot, and to depend exclusively on his own initiative and resources in disposing of the rest of his leisure.

These resources are so limited that there is little left to do but loaf, talk, court, give parties, form clubs, play cards, and read a bit. Of these, straight unadorned loafing, usually in congenial groups, takes the lead. Any place, be it field, parlor, street corner, or barber shop, will do, so long as loafing is permitted without interference. Talking, bragging, story telling, singing, dancing, or just sitting will do to pass the time. Attempts to get out of the rut are futile, although the wealthy, well-born, and better-educated Negroes have created a leisure life that is remarkable in richness and good fellowship. Even in this class, however, the emphasis is perforce on transitory pleasures, in spite of attempts at self-improvement by clubs for the study of Negro life and history and other subjects.

There is no need to pile illustration upon illustration to demonstrate this wasteful use of leisure which cannot be avoided under present conditions. It is far better to call attention to the accepted recreations of those colored people who have to a degree passed beyond the limits of the racial place popularly assigned to them by prejudice.

Many of this type play excellent golf, tennis, and contract bridge. In fact, they play as much and as well as any comparable white group, and they have formed their own country clubs and national sport associations. It is always a source of surprise when one has his first experience at being beaten in these games by colored competition. Chagrin is mixed with a feeling that the world is upside down, for these are white men's games in which Nordic supremacy is taken for granted. After the first few experiences the element of surprise fades and the Negro is looked on as any other individual competitor. Unfortunately, only a few white men have ever had this experience. Bridge clubs where Negroes follow the rules and accepted styles of play intelligently seem preposterous to the uninitiated white man. Tennis is a bit more understandable. Golf clubs, and there are a number of Negro clubs, simply must be of the Octavus Roy Cohen variety, but they are not. The Negro immigrant from the British West Indies has brought with him a liking for and skill in cricket, much to the surprise of New Yorkers, white and black, who have been taught to think of this sport as distinctly a white man's game.

Private dances without gin, ill-fitting clothes, or razors do not fit the white man's stereotype of the Negro. Nor do clubs in which good birth and breeding are the first essentials for membership. Yet these things exist in every large colored community in any part of the country. A club dance attended by Negroes at the top of the list in cities like New York, Philadelphia, Washington, Nashville, or Atlanta compares more than favorably with the average similar white function sponsored by individuals of like education and economic advantages. Gowns of late styles from up-to-the-minute shops are worn, evening clothes fit, the music is good, elderly people attend and are not resented, the dancing is decorous, and conspicuous drinking is distinctly frowned upon. There are naturally always a few individuals out of harmony with the general tone of such an affair, but they only serve to set off the well mannered, wholesome, and whole-hearted spirit of the rest. The boorish drinking and other conduct taken for granted at socially elect white country clubs would cause a Negro to be firmly escorted from the floor at a comparable colored dance. While the buildings in which these affairs are held are shabby when compared to those available for white functions, the conduct is not.

This is the group which reads the best books, sees the best plays, if in the north, hears good music, travels extensively in this country and Europe, attends the annual Thanksgiving Day game between Howard and Lincoln, and is never at a loss for something interesting to do in spare moments. It is not large, but it is growing rapidly. No longer does the college graduate or newly rich real estate operator gain automatic admittance to the upper circles. A limited aristocracy whose family achievements date back before the Civil War is as proud and as jealous of its great names as is Boston of its Cabots and Lodges. Social subclasses are forming on such bases as color, birth, education, money, and mere personal taste. Interlopers with neither depth nor background are instantly spotted, sometimes tolerated, but never accepted. Meanwhile, for these groups, ever increasing in number and size, standards of manners, morals, and taste frequently superior to those of the white upper middle class are long since accepted and followed as a matter of course.

There is reason to believe that these groups will continue to grow in size until they are proportionally as large in our colored population as in the white. In the light of this trend the blatant shortcomings of the masses become less discouraging. European immigrants, except perhaps Jews, cross the line from their minority group to the majority upper classes with no more restriction than the native farm boy of pioneer ancestry who makes good. The Jew has had to create his own social classes, although many individuals mingle freely with Gentiles of all levels. The cultured Indian or Latin American finds congenial circles opened at his wish. The Oriental of great achievement may get glimpses into the social life of the white elect, but little more. So the Negro, if outstanding, may be permitted brief but closely guarded visits to the white social stage with the definite but unmentioned understanding that he has a guest card without full privileges and for a short time only. He must build and is building his own facilities for leisure enjoyment.

In summary, it may be observed that, first of all, minority groups are restricted in opportunity for the use of leisure time. This restriction may be the result of location, tradition, individual handicaps, or prejudice. It varies directly with the degree of isolation, cultural inertia and conflict, personal limitations, and group antagonism. It applies to all or only some of the minority people, and is either temporary or relatively permanent in direct proportion as the distinguishing characteristics of the minority are transitory or permanent, that is, cultural or biological, in nature. North Europeans find their limitations in leisure opportunity slight, temporary, and not equally applicable to all individuals. At the other extreme, Negroes, distinguished by color and other biological features, find the barriers oppressive, relatively fixed, and insurmountable by all classes.

Flowing from this lack of opportunity there is a change in direction of leisure activities. Intellectual and organized physical forms of recreation tend to be sacrificed to wasteful time killers and sense gratification. Public and private funds and organizations for recreational guidance and facilities prefer to work with the majority people. The minority elements must rely largely on their own resources, which, being limited, are adequate only for a few of the less expensive, simpler pursuits which do not imply complete cultural assimilation.

This means in turn an intensification in the utilization of the limited leisure activities available. Cultured Negroes, for illustration, spend what appear to the white person of comparable status a startling amount of time visiting each other and attending all sorts of parties and other social functions, to the detriment of normal home life and other recreational pursuits. Similarly, there is a popular opinion that when foreigners go in for athletics, picnics, clubs, drink, weddings, and other important celebrations, and even loafing, they go in whole-heartedly and without reservations. This opinion is not unsubstantiated by the evidence, for with limited opportunities it is quite natural that the blasé, indifferent recreational attitude of the surfeited native white American would be less prevalent in a group which has less from which to choose.

Differential leisure activities delay assimilation by reinforcing discriminatory group attitudes. Social contacts, so helpful to sympathetic understanding, are prevented. One can hardly hope to appreciate the better qualities of the Negro if he is seen only at work, work which is customarily held in low esteem. If white people could observe Negroes of an equal or a superior class during their leisure hours their prejudices would have to be less generalized. Further, if a minority group is forced into the intensive use of a few leisure occupations, beliefs in special aptitudes and handicaps are fostered. Negro singing has been enjoyed by hundreds of thousands of white people, as has Negro dancing, with the result that the race is credited, or debited, with some inherent, peculiar aptitudes for these accomplishments. He is seen shooting craps but not playing bridge, so the one is considered a racial trait and the other beyond his capacity. The Italian gets wide publicity as a gunman, but not as a patron of the opera, where he sits in the gallery, so he is by nature a criminal and, since vague rumors of his musical appreciation have reached the masses, occasionally interested in the musical arts. All of these beliefs are false, for they grow out of limited opportunity and faulty observation.

It follows that leisure-time activities could be used to break down socially undesirable race attitudes if artificial barriers were discouraged. Negro college athletes, nonexistent in the south, rare but outstanding in the north, are a healthy symptom of what might be done, and with little protest from the campus or public. Interracial competition is likely to emphasize caste distinctions and lead to ill feeling, if not closely guarded. What is needed is not competition of this kind, but rather cooperation on mixed teams, in common theaters and other recreational buildings, and on the playground. There is no sign that such cooperation is increasing. The contrary is probably more nearly correct, especially in such cities as Philadelphia where the colored element is growing and at the same time finding its own facilities increasingly adequate. Other minority groups are being assimilated more and more by this method.

If interracial cooperation is now beyond the realm of possibility in most parts of the country for Negro and white, there is still the chance for improvement in race relations through the utilization of the leisure activities of minority people as an educational medium. School and college have long since realized the educational value of extra-curricular activities, and have definitely guided and encouraged students in their play. The adult grows intellectually only as he learns in his work and spare time, and the greater opportunity lies in the second of these two. Considering the types of work carried on by minority groups, spare time is practically the one time permitting intellectual growth. Physical health, too, needs proper leisure exercise. Build up the minds and bodies of the socially inferior peoples of the United States, and their cultural assimilation, together with more friendly race relations, will be well on the way.

CHAPTER IX

THE VITALITY OF MINORITIES

DEATH and taxes have the reputation of being two certain, ties in the lives of all men. Since the first rule of sound taxa, tion is to secure the greatest amount of feathers with the least amount of squawk, we may take it that minorities, politically inarticulate as they are, contribute their share to the public treasury. Death, however, is supposed to be indifferent to the protests of his victims, so that his hand might be expected to fall with equal weight on men of all colors and of all national origins. It seems, nevertheless, that even death is a respecter of persons, for he takes the poor before the rich, the black, red, yellow, and brown before the white, and the foreign-born before the native.

THE DISCRIMINATING INCIDENCE OF DISEASE AND DEATH

In the death registration area in the United States in 1920 white people furnished 91.4 per cent of the total population, but only 88.1 per cent of the total deaths. The colored people, with only 8.6 per cent of the population to their credit, supplied 11.9 per cent of the deaths. Native whites of native parentage, 52.9 per cent of the population in this area, furnished 45.2 per cent of the deaths; native white of foreign or mixed parentage, 23.8 per cent of the population, furnished 22.2 per cent of the deaths; foreign-born whites, 14.6 per cent of the population, furnished 19.6 per cent of the deaths. In regard to specific European nationality groups, the Irish have the highest death rate, the Scandinavians the lowest. The Germans and the Italians have mortality rates which are about the same. The British, including the English, Welsh, Scotch, and Canadians, seem to have mortality rates which occupy a median position between the rates of the Irish and the Scandinavians. The Russians—mostly Jews—have a remarkably low death rate. In brief, while the foreign-born show a death rate between those of the colored and native-born white groups, there are serious variations between the different nationalities, but no generalizations can be made on the basis of a distinction between old and new immigrants.

Considering infant mortality alone, "There is a wide variation in infant mortality among the immigrant groups, the range [for infants born to mothers of the most important nationalities] being from 66.4 deaths per 1,000 births, among the children of Scandinavian mothers, to 121.8 among the offspring of Polish mothers. That is, the Polish infant mortality is almost twice that of the Scandinavian.

"As between 'old' and 'new' immigrants, the former appear to have an advantage, having an average rate of 78.5 against 98.9 for the latter. Yet the babies of Russian mothers show a superior vitality, having a death rate of only 71.8 per 1,000 births, which is but slightly higher than that of the offspring of Scandinavian mothers, and is lower than that shown by the children of native mothers. On the other hand, the Irish infant mortality is distinctly higher than that of the 'old' immigrant group as a whole."[1]

Death not only mows down immigrants of some nationalities at an earlier age than others, but also varies the type of scythe used. Thus the Irish are cut down by tuberculosis and diseases of the circulatory system, in the areas studied by Professor Carpenter, more often than are immigrants of other nationalities. The Italian suffers great losses from deaths by violence and from disorders associated with pregnancy, childbirth, and lactation. Whooping cough, influenza, and scarlet fever seem to be hard on the British but easy on the Germans. Such comparisons, however, are of doubtful value, for they probably reflect housing, working conditions, population density, necessary adaptations to environment, and other factors which vary not so much with nationality as with haphazard incidents of migration. In all the areas studied by Professor Carpenter, the Germans, for example, have the highest death rate for diph-

---

[1] Niles Carpenter, *op. cit.*, p. 207. All the comparative mortality rates so far mentioned have been taken from this source, pp. 197ff.

theria and croup, 38.7 per 100,000 in Chicago, and also the lowest for the same diseases, 9.1 per 100,000 in Philadelphia.[2] This last illustration alone shows the dangers incident to the comparison of the causes of death among immigrant nationalities; so that until the death registration area in the United States is more inclusive and until much more is known concerning the inherent and environmental causes of the diseases most frequently resulting in death, all that can be said is that specific diseases vary in importance with the nationality of immigrants in the United States. They also vary with much more significant phenomena than national origin.

When color rather than national origin is used to differentiate groups, there is naturally much more popular insistence on the significance of race in mortality and morbidity rates. Among colored peoples exceptionally high death rates and the unusual frequency with which certain diseases strike take on the appearance of racial characteristics, although similar phenomena in the subdivisions of the white race are readily viewed as accidents of residence, occupation, and class status. For illustration, a lesser frequency of venereal disease in the native white stock than in the Negro has been interpreted in terms of morality and hygienic precaution on the part of those of European origin and, at the same time, as a peculiar susceptibility to skin diseases on the part of the African. While this dual interpretation is no longer popular, it affords an example of the emphasis on environment when a white group is involved, and on racial heredity when skin color intrudes. Nevertheless, there are more striking differences between the death and disease rates of colored minorities and the white majority in the United States than there are between those of minorities of European national origin and the white majority.

In 1925 the registration area death rate for whites was 11.2 per 1,000, while that for Negroes was 18.2 per 1,000. "This means that the colored death rate was 62.5 per cent higher than the white. This is, in general, the situation at the present time. If we limit ourselves to the rural part of the registration states, the excess is only 50 per cent; but in the cities of the registration area, the excess is about 90 per cent."[3] In view of the recent cityward migration the high Negro death rate in urban areas, particularly in northern states, has assumed great significance in discussions of the future of the colored population of the United States. The consensus of medical opinion attributes it not to any inability of the Negro to survive in northern climes but rather to his lack of adjustment to city life and rigorous conditions north of the Mason and Dixon line. "At every age period, from infancy to old age, and for each sex, the death rate for colored persons is in excess of that for whites. In every age group, save one, the excess is more pronounced among females than for males. Colored infants of both sexes suffer from death rates approximately two-thirds above that of the whites. In early childhood, the margin is even larger. From five years of age up to adolescence, the margin is 57 per cent excess for males and 72 per cent for females. The most pronounced differences, however, are found between 15 and 25 years, where the death rate for colored boys and young men runs nearly two and a half times that for the whites, and where the mortality among colored girls is more than two and three-quarters times as high as for young white women. . . . The latest reliable figures show a life expectation, at birth, of 44.24 years for colored males and of 46.39 for colored females, as compared with 54.16 years and 58.64 years, respectively, for the whites."[4]

The responsibility for the shorter life expectation of the Negro can be placed on high death rates from a limited number of diseases. Organic diseases of the heart, tuberculosis, pneumonia, external causes (excluding suicide and homicide), congenital malformations and diseases of early infancy, cerebral hemorrhages and softening, and cancer were responsible in 1925 for 58 per cent of Negro deaths.[5] No legitimate purpose would be served here by citing detailed mortality and morbidity

[3] Louis I. Dublin, "The Health of the Negro," in Donald Young, editor, "The American Negro," *The Annals* of the American Academy of Political and Social Science, vol. cxxxx, November, 1928, pp. 77-78.

[4] *Ibid.*, pp. 78-79.

[5] Charles S. Johnson, *op. cit.*, p. 144. Chapters X, XI, XII, and XIII in this volume contain detailed statistics concerning Negro health which are more than adequate for the student of race relations in the United States.

rates for Negroes, for those which are available are of questionable value to our study except as they show an excess or relative rarity for one population group in comparison with another. The registration area does not include the entire country, nor are its figures equally reliable for racial and national minorities in contrast with those for the native white stock. Hospital reports, as well as those of clinics and private physicians, fail to be representative because of the differential use of such medical facilities by population groups. Life insurance statistics naturally depend on the representative status of the insured, so that even the 2,500,000 Negroes insured by the Metropolitan Life Insurance Company whose health records are carefully kept and are conceded to be more typical and more accurate than those of the Census Bureau, afford statistics which illustrate trends but may hardly be claimed to be exact. Such statistical sources as these have established the fact that the leading causes of Negro deaths just mentioned differ considerably from the leading causes of white deaths.[6]

According to the statistics of the Metropolitan Life Insurance Company for 1927, the Negro tuberculosis death rate was 226.2 per 100,000, more than three times that for the whites, which was 73.4 per 100,000. "Organic heart disease followed tuberculosis very closely with a rate of 211.6, or nearly double that for the whites. Third in numerical importance was chronic nephritis, with a rate of 122.1, also double that for the whites. Cerebral hemorrhage, another 'degenerative disease,' also takes double toll of life among the Negroes that it does among whites. Pneumonia was responsible for a death toll of two and a half times that for the whites. These five diseases, together with fatal accidents, which also run higher among colored persons, account for two-thirds of the mortality of Negroes. Other causes in which the death rate of Negroes, in 1927, was approximately double that of whites, are typhoid fever, whooping cough, bronchitis and puerperal conditions. Their influenza death rate was two and a half times higher,

[6] An excellent statistical analysis of comparative white and Negro mortality rates is that by Elbridge Sibley, *Differential Mortality in Tennessee,* Fisk University Press, Nashville, 1930, 152 pp.

while certain other causes like acute nephritis, malaria, pellagra and homicides run from three to eleven times higher. . . .

"There are, on the other hand, a number of items in the mortality and morbidity history of Negroes which are more favorable for them than for whites. The acute communicable diseases of childhood, such as measles and scarlet fever, occur less frequently among Negro children, and when they do are less often fatal. Similarly, erysipelas, certain forms of cancer, diabetes, Addison's disease, leukemia and anemia, locomotor ataxia, acute anterior poliomyelitis, chorea, diseases of the ears, gall stones, diseases of the spleen and urinary calculus, all show lower death rates for this race."[7]

The incidence of syphilis and other venereal infections is difficult to determine for any population group. Individuals afflicted with venereal diseases may be ashamed to ask for medical treatment, they may believe them not sufficiently serious to warrant treatment, they may use home remedies or seek the aid of quack doctors; and, even in mortality statistics, syphilis and gonorrhea remain concealed in other less embarrassing diseases to which they contributed without leaving any record in the published death rates. Nevertheless, it is safe to say that there is a higher venereal disease rate among American Negroes than among white people in this country, and that this higher rate is responsible for a large proportion of the excess of Negro deaths, officially listed as due to tuberculosis, cerebral hemorrhage, pneumonia, and other forms of illness which might not have been fatal without the complication of the "social diseases."

The Filipino is so recent an immigrant that his health records in the United States proper are of doubtful value. Apparently he has an ordinary amount of syphilis and a rather high rate of gonorrheal infection. His resistance to tuberculosis and pneumonia is apparently low. Amœbic dysentery is common in the Philippine Islands and is undoubtedly more frequently encountered among immigrants from there than among natives of continental United States. Leprosy may still be found in the Philippines, but inspection at the port of entry and public

[7] Louis I. Dublin, op. cit., pp. 79-80.

health measures have destroyed any danger of its introduction and spread in this country. About 25 per cent of the Philippine population is infected with hookworm, but this disease is readily controlled. Since there are diseases which are more prevalent in the Philippines than in the United States proper it is necessary that the medical inspection of immigrants from these islands be most careful, but beyond this there seems to be no need for worry. Modern medical knowledge has made it possible for government inspection to insure a healthier immigration from any part of the globe than was dreamed of a generation ago. If immigrants from the Philippines or from any other section of the world were not more free from dangerous and loathsome diseases than our native population, it would be a reflection on our medical inspectors at ports of entry. Their higher mortality and morbidity rates in this country must be due either to racial susceptibility or to their living conditions in this country, and not to any infection existing at the time of admission.[8]

It is no doubt true that most of our worst diseases were brought to the United States from other parts of the world. The first explorers carried with them germs which were to breed diseases unknown to the pre-Columbian Indians. Medical science, however, has despaired of determining the place of origin of practically all diseases and is more interested in combating them than in tracing their genealogy. The immigrant, however, and particularly the colored immigrant, has had to bear the popular blame for the introduction and spread of ill health far beyond his share. It always seems more fitting to fix blame on a stranger than on ourselves. Further, the immigrant has been less healthy than the native, so that there is an apparent logical basis for the charge that he has constituted a grave danger to the health of the entire population. In fact, he has been such a danger, but no more so than any other population class of similar economic and educational status.

As the cerebro-spinal meningitis epidemic on the Pacific

[8] The facts concerning the health of the Filipino immigrant have been taken from Bruno Lasker, *Filipino Immigration*, University of Chicago Press, Chicago, pp. 106ff.

coast in 1929 was attributed to Filipino immigration, so earlier outbreaks of smallpox and bubonic plague were blamed on the Chinese. The meningitis epidemic was promptly shown not to have been of Filipino origin, but anti-Filipino agitation still holds this oriental immigrant responsible. Possibly some or even all of the earlier epidemics in California had an obscure oriental origin, but it is not likely that in the absence of any oriental immigration whatever all epidemics would have been avoided. Rodents on merchant ships may introduce bubonic plague. Smallpox was in the United States long before the oriental immigrant arrived. Undernourished, ignorant, badly housed immigrants may serve as breeding places and centers of infection for epidemic and endemic diseases, but the occasional infected individual who passes medical inspection undetected is not a serious threat to the health of a community today unless its sanitary and health officers are allowed to neglect their duty.

Chinese and Japanese immigrants on the Pacific coast are no longer considered a special health problem, a source of extraordinarily dangerous infection, as they once were. Their mantle in this respect, as in many others, has been passed on to the Filipino and the Mexican. Even at the height of oriental immigration it was hard to make charges of disease-breeding hold against the Japanese, for their rural residence, their rapid Americanization, and their material progress quickly gave the lie to such accusations. Their predecessors, the Chinese, however, included a majority who for at least part of each year lived in congested city districts which could hardly be said to be healthful human habitations. Overcrowding in ramshackle buildings without sewers in San Francisco's Chinatown, perhaps no worse than that to be found more recently in New York's East Side immigrant tenements, shocked even the white owners of the lodging houses leased to Chinese who earned their living renting bunks in tiny rooms to transient men of their race. So long as these unfit properties were profitable, however, little was done about it, especially if graft was paid the health officers. These Orientals were accused of being a filthy people because they lived in the only districts open to them in a prejudiced community. According to Dr. Mary Coolidge, the characteristic diseases of working Chinese were "constipation and inactive liver, tuberculosis—and among the Alaska fishermen, ulcers on the legs. These are the result of opium smoking, excessive tea-drinking, intermittent labor, lack of fresh air and the habit of bandaging cuts without antiseptic dressing. They [the Chinese] are exceptionally free from venereal diseases, partly because of their generally cleanly habits of body; and from bacterial diseases because they rarely drink unboiled water. In the slack season, about Chinese New Year, the fishermen and laborers from the interior come into Chinatown and there they often remain inactive for several months, laying themselves liable to the diseases of their class."[9] This last comment, "laying themselves liable to the diseases of their class," is the key to the health problems of all immigrants, regardless of color, for medical science is insisting with increasing assurance that their high mortality and morbidity rates are class phenomena, influenced more by housing, income, sanitary education, and general minority status than by either blood or their disease records from abroad.

The health record of the Indian affords perhaps the best opportunity for the determination of the relative importance of class or caste status and racial heredity as factors in the incidence of disease and in death rates among American minorities. There are still tribes which retain much of their pre-Columbian culture. We have some knowledge about the specific diseases which have been given them by the white man in recent years—more than about any other American minority, even if we are still in some doubt as to whether the Indian gave syphilis to the white man or whether the white man gave it to the Indian. Further, a larger proportion of Indians lives in relative isolation from other peoples than is true of any other minority. Their health record shows several outstanding peculiarities when compared with that of the rest of the population of the United States.

In a study of Indian health the following facts were obtained

[9] Mary R. Coolidge, op. cit., p. 416.

for 1925 concerning those Indians living in jurisdictions which reported vital statistics for that year:

TABLE I

Estimated Indian population in reporting jurisdictions	180,884
Indian deaths reported	4,629
Indian deaths per 1,000 estimated Indian population	25.6
Deaths per 1,000 in death registration area (U. S. Census)	11.8
Indian deaths from tuberculosis	1,132
Indian deaths from tuberculosis per 1,000 estimated Indian population	6.3
Deaths from tuberculosis per 1,000 in death registration area (U. S. Census)	0.87
Indian deaths under 3 years of age	1,309
Indian deaths under 3 years of age expressed in per cent of all Indian deaths	28.3
Deaths under 3 years of age in death registration area expressed in per cent of all deaths	16.2

It can easily be seen from these figures that Indian health compares most unfavorably with that of the white population of the United States. The fact that the Indian death rate from tuberculosis is over seven times the white tuberculosis death rate, that one-fourth of the Indian deaths are from tuberculosis, that in Arizona the Indian tuberculosis death rate is seventeen times that of the death registration area of the United States, and that about one in every ten Indians has tuberculosis, requires explanation. The extraordinary number of deaths among Indians under three years of age also warrants investigation. Trachoma, an eye disease which ranks next to tuberculosis in frequency of occurrence among the Indians, does not show in the death rate but is nevertheless extremely important, for it invariably weakens the eyesight and may easily result in total blindness. Venereal diseases have been alleged to be unusually common among the Indians, but no accurate statistics can be quoted to prove the point.

So far as other diseases are concerned, no unusual condition of importance has been noted.[10]

RACIAL IMMUNITIES AND SUSCEPTIBILITIES

Three general explanations of this health problem among the Indians have been offered: first, that the Indian is racially susceptible to certain diseases, especially to those which have been newly introduced; second, that the Indian Office has not secured adequate health service for its wards; and third, that the changed conditions under which the Indian is living have created his present peculiar health difficulties, difficulties which will not disappear until his transition from tribal to civil life is completed. It is our task as well as the task of the Indian Office to determine which of these three theories, if any, is the most logical cause of the high Indian death and disease rates. It is of course possible that all three theories may be partly correct, but even if this is true it is desirable that their relative importance and influence be established if a rational program for Indian health work is to be devised.

Little is definitely known concerning the susceptibility and immunity to diseases of the Indian or of any other race. A number of tribes have been almost wiped out by diseases which are not at present serious among the white population. Measles, whooping cough, and plain colds have caused enormous death rates in certain tribes. Smallpox, pneumonia, syphilis, tuberculosis, and trachoma have been especially violent in their attacks on the red man. Typhoid fever and insanity, on the other hand, do not seem as serious among the Indians as among their white neighbors. Facts such as these are not infrequently explained by the theory that some of these diseases at least are new and that the Indian has not been subject to them long enough to build up a racial immunity through the weeding out of those stocks most susceptible to them. We are not sure which diseases are really new to the Indian and which are merely breaking out with increased force because of changed living

[10] The above facts concerning the Indian health situation have been taken from Lewis Merriam, *op. cit.*, chap. viii, pp. 189-344. This study in administration under the auspices of the Institute for Government Research contains the best analysis of the health record of any American minority yet published.

conditions, for complete records over a sufficiently long period of time are naturally not available. If it is ultimately established that the Indian is especially liable to such ills as tuberculosis and respiratory ailments in general, as has been alleged, a health program must either grant the necessity for a long and inhuman process of partial immunization through natural selection or establish an even more elaborate preventive and curative medical attack on these diseases than is necessary for the rest of the population.

The Bureau of Indian Affairs has the duty of providing adequate health service for the Indians still under its supervision. The health figures just quoted for Indians include only tribes for which the Bureau is still responsible. An analysis of the health service provided for them discloses serious faults, a few of which may be noted. Salaries are low and living quarters for both nurses and doctors are in many cases so cramped and undesirable that positions have been filled with difficulty. Large numbers of vacancies in the Indian health service and the high turnover of medical employees are evidence of the niggardly financial policy of Congress. The average age of the doctors indicates the use of the medical positions as a means for supplementing small incomes of relatively unsuccessful elderly men. Some of the work has been done by doctors who bid for the contract to handle sick Indians in a certain area as a side line to their private practice. The tendency is frequently, but not always, for these contract physicians to devote a grudging minimum of time to this aspect of their work, as they get the jobs for a fixed sum regardless of the amount of work done. In not a few instances the territory to be covered has been too large for the staff, both in area and population. Two physicians, for example, at the time of the Merriam study served 2,400 square miles including 7,800 people.

Little preventive work is done by either the doctors or the nurses, who in many cases do no more than pass out drugs as requested from a supply which in the past has been neither well selected nor fresh. Institutional facilities are in some places overcrowded and in others not half utilized. A bare beginning has been made in health education. Few reservations have had anything like a well rounded health program in efficient operation, though the situation has rapidly improved since a capable medical man, borrowed from the Public Health Service, was given charge with definite instructions to install Public Health Service standards, with emphasis on prevention as well as on cure. Even Congress has shown a recent disposition to be more generous with funds for Indian health work. A good share of the Indian health difficulties, however, is not solely the result of inadequate personnel, funds, and program, but is also to be accounted for by the territory to be covered and the prejudices and habits of the Indians themselves.

That the Indians under the supervision of the Indian Office as a group have not yet been able to complete the transition from simple tribal life to the new economic and social conditions which they are meeting under the dominating white civilization is an admitted fact. Problems of sanitation were much simpler in the small, temporary, primitive tepee, hogan, and wickiup than they are in the permanent modern houses which many Indians are just learning to use. Ventilation is assured in the primitive dwelling in spite of every effort to close the chinks. Similar efforts in a well built house of European type result in foul air which breeds disease. House cleaning and sewage disposal were not problems when the tepee was moved several times a year, but a different situation arises when a fixed frame building is used. In short, the Indians have not yet all learned that age-old living habits and customs which were perfectly satisfactory and healthful in their original types of homes will breed disease in the new. There is also, of course, the difficulty in convincing the older generation of the superiority of the white man's medicine over the superstitious remedies of tribal medicine men. Indian women and their families in some districts still resist the offered help of the white doctor in child bearing and child rearing, though in recent years this attitude is becoming less common as the advantages of the new practices and remedies slowly become known and are accepted as helpful. Suspicion of the motives and value of the white doctors has been common, and the blunderings of the inefficient and careless men in the service have not helped in securing the confidence and cooperation of the vanishing American who still thinks in terms of the departed glory of his past generations.

As an illustrative case we may cite the following statement prepared by the Indian Rights Association in 1925 in an attempt to induce the Bureau of Indian Affairs to extend its medical service among a group of Indians who preferred to treat their sick in their own primitive way:

"In Santo Domingo Pueblo the government doctor is not allowed to administer needed relief to the sick even when they desire it, a case in point being that of a woman in agonizing child birth. She was an old school girl. It is a part of the tribal religion to refuse medical aid of white doctors. It is a matter of official record that within the last few years every child under three years old in Santo Domingo died of diphtheria. The government school teacher was not permitted to give even orange juice to the afflicted children. This is one example of what enforcement of the native religion means. Only recently the nurse supplied by a well known welfare organization was refused permission to work in the Pueblo of Tesuque, where many uninformed people have felt that the native primitive life should not be in any manner interrupted. Unless it is interrupted to the extent of securing protection of the health, morals and progress of the Indians themselves, there will soon be no primitive life to protect, as sin and filth exact the same penalty from an Indian they do from a white man."[11] Leaving out of account the matter of sin and morals, is the Indian Office justified in forcing medical service on Indians whose surviving customs and religion forbid it?

Another illustration of incomplete transition from one culture to another may be found in the matter of food. The fairly well balanced diet of fish, game, and agricultural products of the tribal Indians has been upset by wanton destruction of fish and game and the substitution of two or three cereals, a few

[11] From an unpublished statement prepared by the Indian Rights Association of Philadelphia, Pa., on January 23, 1925.

vegetables, and a limited quantity of beef and pork as the new staple foods. Starches have been found to occupy too prominent a place on the Indian bill of fare, and little has been done to educate these people to an appreciation of the value of balanced rations. In fact, the new food habits we have taught them have been decidedly unbalanced. The army rations which used to be distributed so freely were limited in variety to a few standard articles such as pork and flour. Even the boarding schools of the present quarter century have been unable to do much in the way of food education on an average of eleven cents a day allowance per pupil for food plus whatever could be raised with student labor. The most favorably situated schools need at least thirty-five cents a day plus what can be raised on the place.[12] There is not the slightest doubt in the minds of those who have studied the Indian health problem that an adequate balanced diet would diminish if not practically eliminate many of the present complaints. The present deficiency, however, is due not only to poverty but also to an ignorance which we white people have rather fostered than remedied.

The fatalistic attitude that the Indian as a race just has not the inherent resistance necessary to fight off tuberculosis, colds, measles, smallpox, diphtheria, trachoma, and other diseases which take a heavy toll, had better, in the light of the foregoing facts, be relegated to the background. Improved diet, health education, and medical facilities on a par with those of even a backward Pennsylvania village would undoubtedly cut the Indian death and disease rates so that they would compare favorably with those for white people in the United States. The Indian has at least one health advantage in his rural residence. Granting for the sake of argument certain racial susceptibilities which at present may neither be proved nor disproved, it must be remembered that even highly susceptible individuals may, with the aid of modern medical knowledge and a public health program, be protected from the ravages of the very diseases to which they may be susceptible. There

[12] Lewis Merriam, *op. cit.*, pp. 327ff.

is no need for the fatalistic attitude that natural selection must be allowed to lay its inhuman hand on any race or people in the United States.

With a few substitutions of detail this discussion of Indian health could be made to fit the situation of the Negro or any immigrant minority. It could even be made to apply to backward communities of native white stock. The three possible major factors in mortality and morbidity are racial immunities and susceptibilities, ignorance of healthful habits and practices, and inadequate health resources. Of the three, the first is of the least importance, and authoritative recourse to it in explaining differential rates is becoming increasingly rare.

The lack of hygienic knowledge on the part of both the Negro and the immigrant is notorious. Superstitious nostrums and incantations have survived unbelievably among minorities in an age of science.[13] Such dangerous folk beliefs have been brought to this country by immigrants, have been borrowed from the white man by Negroes, and have survived among the Indians from the days when the primitive medicine man was the only doctor available. Health campaigns, including those of a purely educational nature, have bothered little with minorities. Negro masses still fear white hospitals and doctors and have few of their own. Immigrants also distrust remedies with which they are unfamiliar. Among such peoples the theory that ill health is a visitation is as strong today as it was among the older white stock a generation or so ago. The diet of the Negro, with its lack of milk and vegetables and its preponderance of starch and fatty meats is as unbalanced as that of the Indian. The vaunted southern Negro cooking, with its romanticized hot breads, corn concoctions, pork, fried chicken, pot likker and other messes of starch and grease, may tickle the palate, but it irritates the digestive system, and is a diet of

[13] For detailed descriptions of Negro folk medicine, see Newbell N. Puckett, *Folk Beliefs of the Southern Negro,* University of North Carolina Press, Chapel Hill, 1926. Even a casual reading of this excellent study will demonstrate the relationship between colored mortality and ignorance. It will also show that the superstitious medicine of the American Negro is not African in origin, but a development in the United States, borrowed with modifications and additions by one peasant class from another.

necessity rather than of choice.[14] Immigrants hang on to their national dishes, such as Italian spaghetti, Chinese rice and tea, Hungarian goulash, Mexican chili, and the like, but are unable to maintain a balanced ration in this country in many instances as they did in their homeland where they were familiar with and in a better position to secure other foods necessary to round out a healthful diet. It is understood, of course, that many immigrants have come from overcrowded lands where unbalanced diets were their lot, and that their unhealthy food habits have frequently persisted in the United States. One must learn how to balance a diet and like it, how to prevent disease through fresh air, exercise, sanitation, and medical precautions, to trust hospitals, doctors, and nurses, and to eschew home remedies involving bitter tastes, unholy odors, and magical attributes.

Furthermore, these things cannot be learned by a minority which is not allowed the facilities to put them in practice. Poor people of inferior caste and class are less welcome both in hospitals and as private patients than are those of better economic and social status. The common transitional tenant status of minorities of racial and national origin means that they live under unhealthy conditions, in overcrowded houses with inadequate plumbing and a lack of other physical facilities. It is useless to teach the elementary principles of decency and sanitation to people who have no bathtubs, who are jammed

[14] It has too frequently been assumed that healthful food and rural residence are invariably associated. "With respect to pure food the Negro in the country is far from being amply supplied. In the small farm districts of the upper South, where Negroes are independent farmers observing the need for a rotation of crops or working for small planters who do, the food supply is not much of a problem. Such farmers produce a large portion of the food they consume. However, in the sugar and cotton plantation districts, where the one-crop idea has not yet been uprooted, the Negro tenants and laborers must live on such food as is supplied to them by the plantation commissary; and their inadequate income together with the terrorism in vogue makes it impossible for the majority of such persons to improve their daily fare. They buy most unsatisfactory food and pay for it the highest prices. The average man must live on rough corn bread cooked without lard, fried fat bacon or pork, salt fish, sorghum or molasses, hominy or rice occasionally, and coffee or tea along with sufficient sugar sometimes to make a little dessert. . . . If brought in, the best vegetables would never reach these peasants, for such eatables would find a much better market among persons more favorably circumstanced." Carter G. Woodson, op. cit., pp. 4-5.

into cramped, ill-ventilated quarters, and whose toilet facilities are such as to spread disease. Add to these inadequacies in the way of minimum material requirements for health the low wages of exploited labor, labor which is characterized by long hours, dust or damp, heat or cold, heavy and dangerous in nature, the type of work which is least desirable of all, and one need not look further for the causes of the prevalence of tuberculosis, pneumonia, typhoid, the degenerative and filth diseases, or even sheer exhaustion, which kill off minorities who enter our industrial system. The rural agricultural minorities as a rule have better health records than their urban brothers, in spite of less adequate medical service, and this fact indicates the importance of housing and working conditions in their mortality and morbidity rates.

It may seem that too much attention has been paid to Indian health and not enough to the Negro and the immigrant. The Mexican, for example, has barely been mentioned. In view of the fact that the Mexican is racially an Indian more than anything else, it has been deemed unnecessary to detail his physical troubles, for they are no more racial than those of the Indians born in the United States, so that all that could be done would be to pile up additional illustrations of the health effects of ignorance and inadequate resources. The Negro and the European immigrant, however, have no such blood kinship with the Indian, our major illustration of the factors in minority ill health, and a more detailed analysis of the conditions which are killing them off more rapidly than the native white stock might reasonably be expected. These conditions, however, are so obviously environmental, incidents to culture conflict and minority status in general, that no purpose would be served here by quoting superstitions, customs, the evidence of housing surveys, or occupational and other handicaps in detail.

If further support of the position that racial susceptibility is a matter of minor importance in the health of the Negro and of the European immigrant is necessary, it may be obtained from a brief examination of the trends in disease and death rates of these peoples. The incidence of the various diseases among American Negroes is changing, and their death rate is decreasing except where it has been temporarily raised by urban migration. The European immigrant's diseases in this country are not the same in importance here as they were abroad, and his descendants rapidly approximate the health records of the native white stock.

Who would hold today with the prominent New Orleans physician of some four score years ago that "The Negro constitution . . . is not subject to phthisis, although it partakes of what is called scrofulous diathesis; and this condition is due to the fact that the pulmonary apparatus of the Negro is adjusted to the consumption of less oxygen"?[15] Thomas Jefferson also held this view regarding Negro health. "The infections most common to Negroes in the early nineteenth century were listed as abscess, furuncles, fluxions, tumefactions of glands, erysipelas, false peripneumony, worms, œdemia, bilious gastritis, dysentery and visceral obstructions."[16] These quotations indicate a quite different opinion concerning the peculiar diseases of Negroes in the earlier days. It is also a matter of record that Negro slaves were noticeably healthier than freedmen, an observation which suggests that proper precautions under the leadership of interested and capable white men may do much to reduce the high death rate of Negroes who neither know enough nor possess the facilities to protect themselves from unnecessary illness and early death.[17]

"The Negro in America, far from being destined for extinction, is steadily improving his death rate and adding to his life span. The appalling mortality of the Reconstruction Period —35 to 40 per 1,000—has been cut to about 17; and this is no higher than prevailed for a number of European countries before the World War. The Negro is getting a share, if not his full portion, of the benefits of sanitation and public health work in this country. His expectation of life, today, is the same as that which the white man in America had only thirty years ago. . . . Our figures prove that the Negro race is physically

[15] Charles S. Johnson, op. cit., p. 135.
[16] Ibid.
[17] Striking evidence of the inadequacy of Negro hospitals and doctors may be obtained from Negro Hospitals, Julius Rosenwald Fund, Chicago, 1931, 57 pp

well organized, and under improving environmental conditions will continue to add to his life expectancy."[18] If the Negro's death rate has already been reduced to such an extent, and without giving him an education and environment anything like that of the white man, the theory of racial susceptibility in his case has indeed lost most of its force.

Similar comparisons can be made in regard to the vitality of European immigrants. The Irish, for example, make a worse showing in the United States in both infant and total mortality than they do in Ireland. The Russians have low general and infant mortality rates in the United States, but a high infant mortality rate in Russia. The Italians have a low general but an excessive infant mortality rate in the United States, but high rates of both in Italy. Other immigrant groups maintain about the same mortality rates here as in their home country.[19] The children of immigrants, furthermore, as has already been mentioned, have death rates which are considerably lower than those of their parents, and are not afflicted with the same diseases in the same proportions as are their parents. It is not probable that there has been significant selection either in the resistance of the immigrant stock in comparison with the non-migrants who have remained in Europe, or in the survival of American-born children of immigrants with the greatest resistance to disease. Inherent racial susceptibilities and immunities of importance, if they existed, would be too firmly fixed to permit the observed variations in vitality.

It should now be evident that there is no such thing as absolute racial immunity to any human disease, and that there is also probably no such thing as racial susceptibility sufficiently serious to condemn a people to a process of elimination which could only be halted when natural selection had done its work. No doubt there are proportionately more individuals in one race than in another who are especially susceptible to, say, tuberculosis, syphilis, or measles. The white man is perhaps more likely to die of yellow fever than the Negro; but what of it, if the germ of yellow fever is controlled as in the Panama

[18] Louis I. Dublin, op. cit., p. 82.
[19] Niles Carpenter, op. cit., p. 208.

Canal Zone or in the entire United States? The control of two varieties of mosquito has meant the control of yellow fever and malaria. Sewers and shoes are effective weapons against hookworm. Artificial immunization to smallpox, typhoid, and diphtheria has been accomplished. Tuberculosis is no longer a grim reaper who usually kills his victims. Since there are different degrees of susceptibility and relative immunity among individuals, it may be expected on *a priori* grounds alone that such variant individuals will be distributed unevenly as between races. Their importance in vital statistics, however, varies inversely with a people's hygienic knowledge and resources.

In other words, such immunities and susceptibilities as may exist between the peoples of the earth—and there is little agreement as to either their nature or extent—have already been rendered so ineffective whenever the full force of our scientific knowledge of health has been applied that we may be assured that the health record of any American minority could be so controlled as to approximate that of the old American stock. Further, the danger of the introduction of epidemics from abroad has been so reduced that it is correlated only with American indifference, carelessness, and popular ignorance.[20] Minorities, of course, still remain potential sources of infection both for endemic and epidemic diseases, but the majority has only itself to blame if by the neglect of the simplest of health measures it permits such conditions to continue.

It was once thought that peoples were so adapted to specific environments that migrations to radically different climates from those to which they had been fitted by generations of natural selection inevitably meant their ultimate extinction through the ravages of diseases against which they possessed no racial armor. Even moving from rural to urban areas, with the attendant shift from agricultural to industrial pursuits,

[20] During the fiscal year ending June 30, 1930, 191 aliens were debarred from entering the United States and 1,042 aliens were deported on account of physical and mental ill health. The number debarred, of course, takes no account of the thousands who were refused visas abroad or who did not apply for admittance because of the knowledge that they would be refused on account of ill health. *Annual Report of the Commissioner General of Immigration for the Fiscal Year Ending June 30, 1930*, pp. 160, 164.

has been held to be unalterably fatal for the more "primitive" peoples. The Indian, for example, has been supposed to be a case in point, for he has practically vanished before the encroachments of industrial civilization. Our previous discussion, however, has suggested other explanations of his appalling health record than his inherent racial chacteristics. So, too, the Negro is still held to be on the way to extinction in the United States because of his inherent adaptation to a tropical rather than to a temperate climate.[21] His high death rate and decreasing birth rate in the cities to which he has been migrating have been used to support this position by reputable scientists and even by a philanthropist who has spent millions for Negro education and health in the United States. Such theorists, however, apparently overlook the problems of cultural adaptation incident to all migrations in their haste to accept a biological interpretation of these phenomena.[22] Even if the Negro

[21] Professor Hankins' point of view on this question is expressed in the following quotation:

"The transfer of the Negro to the West Indies and the southern states did not involve any great climatic change and hence little physiological derangement. Their death rate in the South is high but probably not for climatic reasons. Their northward movement has, however, resulted in a very great mortality from tuberculosis, and other respiratory diseases. At the same time the Negro excels the white man in resistance to measles, scarlet fever and other skin diseases, and cancer.

"It is by no means certain that the Negro as a pure stock could establish himself in our northern cities. In any case, his death rate has, up to the present, exceeded his birth rate in the northern states. He is therefore, being subjected to vigorous climatic selection. At the same time account must be taken of the fact that the northern Negro has more white blood in his veins than the southern. It is not improbable that his climatic adjustment is facilitated thereby. In that case those strains having the larger proportions of white inheritance would, other things being equal, tend to be preserved at the expense of the purer Negroid strains. A certain amount of race substitution would thus accompany climatic selection." Frank H. Hankins, *An Introduction to the Study of Society*, The Macmillan Company, New York, 1928, p. 185. Quoted by permission of the publishers.

It will be noticed that Professor Hankins minimizes the outstanding necessity for the Negro's cultural adaptation to northern and urban health requirements. It seems to the present writer that until full opportunity is given the Negro for cultural adaptation to the American environments in which he finds himself and until the offsetting influence of modern medical knowledge is taken into account, it is a dangerous procedure to emphasize a possible but unproved significant process of climatic selection in this instance.

[22] The relationship between urban population density and death and an analysis of Negro housing in American cities may be found in T. J. Woofter, Jr., *Negro Problems in Cities*, Doubleday, Doran & Company, Inc., New York, Part II, "Housing."

fails to adapt himself to the American scene any better than he is adapted at the present time, it will take centuries to reduce his proportion in our population to an insignificant percentage. Although it would be a comfortable solution to American racial problems, from the majority point of view, there is not a minority in the country which will be so considerate as to kill itself off by a suicidal death rate. Extinction through racial degeneracy offers no escape from race friction in the United States.

CHAPTER X

SEX AND FAMILY RELATIONS

FAMILIES IN THEIR SETTING

It is customarily taken for granted that the family life of racial and national minorities in the United States is not all that it should be. Negro immorality—sometimes patronizingly referred to as "unmorality"—is a foregone conclusion supported by high illegitimacy, divorce, and desertion rates as well as by common story and gossip. New immigrants mistreat, overwork, and tyrannize their wives and children, if all one hears and reads is to be believed. Mexicans are supposed to spend most of their spare time courting ladies to whom they are not married, to the neglect of a squalling brood and a slovenly wife at home. Indian men have the reputation of shifting the heavy work on to their wives' shoulders and of taking little interest in normal domestic affairs. Chinese and Filipinos in this country are rarely married and are thought to spend too much time with American girls of doubtful character. These beliefs and others of a similar nature are a part of the American tradition. For many of them there is some basis in fact. Rarely is their popular interpretation in terms of cause even approximately accurate.

In the first place, it is difficult to judge minority family life in terms of idealized majority standards. The majority ideal of permanent monogamy, with no extra-marital sex relationships and with the perfect cooperation between family members which is the outgrowth of a smoothly functioning family unit, is not so frequently encountered among our native-born white population as might be desired. Perhaps if minorities were to be compared with the practices rather than with the ideals of their superior neighbors they might not seem so remiss in their family responsibilities. There is also the fact to be considered that deviations from a social standard may be increased in visibility because of association with other minority peculiarities, such as skin color, dress, or language. The illegitimate child of colored parentage fixes itself in the majority consciousness as evidence of *Negro immorality*, while a white child of unmarried parents is merely evidence of personal sin and not of racial vice. There are also less sympathy and understanding and a greater willingness to display the shortcomings of a group other than our own.

Then, too, the family is today recognized to be a social institution which takes on various forms and functions in accordance with the needs and possibilities of the community in which it exists. The patriarchal family is ill adapted to the needs of an industrialized community, and few students regret its passing in the American city. It has always been necessary to adjust the forms and functions of the family to changes in other aspects of social organization. Since racial and national minorities in the United States exhibit peculiarities of economic and social organization not so commonly found in the majority, their family life must be viewed in the light of these peculiar characteristics.

It has been shown that minority working people do not enter all occupations in the same proportion as do native-born white wage earners. There is a piling up of workers in the unskilled and semi-skilled jobs, balanced by a scarcity of opportunity in the skilled and professional occupations, which must be reflected in minority domestic relations. Low income influences housing, recreation, education, and nutrition, all of which are associated with family life. More women are compelled to enter gainful occupations as well as to do an excessive amount of work in the home. Children must contribute to the support of the family at an earlier age. Some of the occupations heavily loaded with minority women and young people are in themselves morally hazardous, such as domestic service and menial labor in certain types of restaurants, pool rooms and other commercialized recreational establishments. Work requiring migratory labor, such as railroad and other construction work, seasonal industries, and the occupations which require individuals to be separated from their families are proportionally more dependent on immigrants and colored people than are the more settled forms of employment.

A consequence of the low economic level of minorities frequently overlooked is the resultant limitation of the number of social classes which are found in them. There is an almost unlimited number of class distinctions to be found among native-born white people, and each class has a set of family standards which differ in degree if not in kind from those of other classes in the same population element. These majority classes are basically distinguished by varying levels of income, education, achievement, prestige-giving ancestry, and what not. Thus it is possible to have an infinite variety of ideals of family life within the group, a possibility which is severely restricted among minorities. This is not to be interpreted to mean that there are no class distinctions among minorities, but rather that there is a greater concentration of individuals in the less favored classes who naturally have the greatest difficulty in approximating family standards set by the majority on an assumption of a relatively high economic status.

The United States prides itself on its high standard of living, theoretically accessible to all, but in fact beyond the reach of a much greater share of Negroes and immigrants than of others. Nevertheless, our books are written and our sermons preached with moral instructions in them which cannot be obeyed by any poverty-stricken class, be it black or white, native or foreign. Native whites of good old American stock may fail just as miserably as any foreigner, Negro, or blanket Indian; but not so many of them do, nor is their failure seized upon as evidence of racial degeneracy. When whole minority communities seem to disregard our family virtues, the explanation lies not in themselves but in our entire population, which permits and not infrequently demands that minorities be homogeneous in regard to class status. Needless to say, that class status must be of the lowest.

Economic and class status are of course not alone in the determination of family standards and practices in minorities. The social history of a group, apart from its economic aspects, is in itself a powerful factor. It has taken generations for the circumspect Bostonian, the Pennsylvania villager, and the Charleston blue blood to build up a tradition which tends to hold each succeeding generation fast in a network of social restraints which had their origin on the other side of the Atlantic, centuries ago.

No minority has such an unbroken mesh of rules and sanctions to restrain wayward, antisocial conduct. The invisible imprint of a thousand slave traditions remains to mar the family life of the American Negro, but African domestic rights and duties have left no mark. The ancestral threads have been broken, and the Negro must now painfully yet rapidly bend himself to the family standards and ideals of the white man, who has had centuries to accomplish the same end. So, too, the Indian, who had reached a tolerable pre-Columbian solution of his domestic problems, satisfactory to himself if not to missionaries, was taught to look with shame on the customs of his parents, while still unable to appreciate or utilize the peculiar form of monogamy professed by Christians to be the only moral expression of sex.

Only those immigrants who chanced to come from England, Germany, and Scandinavia have been able to weave their ancestral domestic pattern into that of their new home, making only the gradual and minor alterations required of everyone regardless of place of birth. The American family is not static, but has constantly made adjustments to a changing environment. These adjustments the old immigrant has also adopted, more or less reluctantly, but at least in company with the envied majority. In themselves, they have seemed extensive, but in comparison with those forced on the new immigrant from south Europe, from Mexico, China, Japan, and the Philippines, they pale into insignificance. The wonder is that this new immigrant has been able to maintain even a semblance of family normality, defining normality in terms of majority ideals.

The social prejudices of the majority have influenced minority family life largely through the characteristic indifference of the majority to the morals of individuals beyond the pale.

While one is supposed to shake one's head at the moral threat of the Negro to American civilization, the peccadillos of a colored maid or janitor are more a subject for humor than censure. By some strange quirk of pseudo-logic, it is only when all Negroes, all Orientals, all Italians, are under discussion in relationship to their influence on the morals of the United States as a whole, that their delinquencies arouse the 100-per-cent American. Under other circumstances, we laugh about them: "What else do you expect from such people?"

Of course, an individual's delinquency, especially if it be that of a minority male who has evidenced undue interest in a woman of the superior group, may be seized upon as typifying the delinquency of his race, whereupon his punishment is for the sins of his people instead of for his own. The Negro who "insults" a white woman is not burned because of his individual conduct, but as a representative of his people. The Filipino club, wrecked by a mob in Watsonville, California, was attacked not to save the virtue of the white girls hired as paid dance partners—there was already some question of their character—but as a symbol of a group attitude which needed only a slight excuse to serve as a focus of attention in order to produce violent action. This type of interest in minority morals has no noticeable constructive influence on the domestic life of anyone. The minority may be frightened, scared into an attitude of hypocritical submission, but that is all. The important thing for us to consider here is not the occasional, vicariously administered group chastisement, but the constant, penetrating indifference to the family morality of minorities.

The attitude of minorities toward familial legislation is likely to be one which leads to obedience only if there is fear of detection. It is difficult to be sincerely respectful in regard to a law which one believes foolish or pernicious. The Chinese family, for illustration, could not exist under the law of this country, yet it has served the Chinese well for many centuries in a form more stable than that of our own family. Can the Chinese immigrant be expected to obey our domestic legislation except through fear, a poor reason for obedience, until he has been thoroughly assimilated into our culture? In so far as every minority has different views as to what constitutes a normal family, and what are its normal functions, to that extent our laws confuse by attempting to substitute artificial rules. At least they seem artificial to minorities before assimilation has progressed far enough to make them understandable.

There is an old story of an Indian chief who agreed to abide by the white man's law and have only one wife instead of the several who would have been permitted under tribal law. Later, when his wife grew old, he asked the white man's permission to get rid of her and take a younger woman into his family in her place. He was honestly puzzled by the curt refusal he received, for, as he put it, "his wife was old, and he wanted but one [wife]—the one he didn't have."[1] He obeyed the decision, but his obedience was superficial and without understanding, a type of obedience common in all minorities.

The Italian father may be just as puzzled when he is forbidden to take his child out of school in order to send him to work and to collect the wages for the family treasury. Similarly, a central European girl may wonder why she is accused of immorality because she has given sexual privileges to her promised husband, a perfectly proper course of action in her home country. Cultural conflicts such as these are unavoidable where minorities live subject to the laws of others. The laws can hardly be relaxed or altered so as to make exceptions in such cases. Their administration can, of course, be tempered with understanding and allowance for variant standards, but at best the conflict remains, and must remain until cultural assimilation has been completed. Minority disrespect for the law meanwhile will also remain.

The law, on the other hand, has not infrequently shown its disrespect for minorities and their morals—perhaps not actually the law, in most cases, but its administrators. The only way in which the law itself reduces minority family stability is in its restrictions on racial intermarriage, a subject discussed

---

[1] James McLaughlin, *My Friend the Indian*, Houghton Mifflin Company, Boston, 1910, p. 64.

in the chapter on race mixture. It may be suggested here, however, that when the law refuses its sanction to the union of individuals, one of whom is entirely of European ancestry, while the other is a mixture of European and Indian, Chinese, Japanese, or Filipino, or perhaps has only a drop of Negro blood, a certain amount of sexual freedom is thereby encouraged. The minorities will hold themselves morally less dear when they are "Jim Crowed" by law, while the European will have legal precedent for his egotistical superiority, and a rationalized excuse for paying not always unwelcome attention to the women of minorities in his vicinity, women who may be the mistresses but not the legal wives of white men. A majority of the states in the Union give encouragement to this condition through "racial integrity" legislation, although it is well known that few interracial marriages occur when they are legally permitted, while miscegenation goes merrily on in all districts where colored minorities live, regardless of laws designed to insure the perpetual purity of the old American stock.

In the administration of domestic legislation, minority offenders are likely to be punished with penalties proportionate in severity to community racial prejudice, provided the offenders manage to annoy the judge and jury into thinking of them as representatives of the criminal element of their people. This may happen to anyone, but rarely does, for in spite of the belief in the essential immorality of minorities, few serious charges of immorality against them ever go to trial. As a rule, the administrators of the law are not interested in the morality and family life of minorities in their jurisdiction. To their way of thinking, there really is not much use in wasting time and money trying to make Negroes forswear seduction, Indians support their broods, or "Hunkies" quit beating their wives. Only when the offenses have something to do with the more favored classes will the sheriff, prosecutor and judge bestir themselves.

This is illustrated by the careless supervision of Negro and immigrant dance halls and other forms of commercial recreation likely to be accompanied by sex exploitation. Throughout the country they are bothered but little, so long as native white people stay away and public indignation is not aroused. The common official attitude toward the domestic difficulties of Mexican immigrants is, "Why bother, so long as they keep it in their own district?" Bigamy is seldom prosecuted in the case of Indians, Mexicans, Negroes, and south Europeans, and then only in a reluctant spirit and with the firm conviction that a verdict of guilty cannot possibly do any good. The seduction or rape of a colored girl by either a white or a colored man is viewed with skepticism and no indignation by the ordinary white official, and this attitude has its counterpart, though less flagrant, when similar offenses against the daughters of recent immigrants from southern and eastern Europe are reported. Thus both the law and its administration are factors in the differentiation of minority family standards and practices.

The mere geographical distribution of a minority may increase or diminish peculiarities of family organization. Acculturation is much slower in rural regions. For illustration, the courtship practice of "bundling" survived in rural Pennsylvania for generations after it was completely forgotten by people of the same European origin living in nearby cities. The Swedes of rural Minnesota are today culturally more Swedish than their cousins who settled in urban centers. The rural Indian of the Southwest has no rival in the maintenance of pre-Columbian culture among the Indians of the East, although a few eastern Indian farmers and mountaineers remember bits of folk lore, while city dwellers of the same blood already think of themselves as Negro or white. The Negro migrant to the city has in the past fifteen years made greater strides in the absorption of European culture than did his father and grandfather combined. In passing judgment, then, we should expect the rural dwellers to show less facility in adopting majority family standards than will be found among those who have been predominantly urban.

Thus far minority family peculiarities have been explained in terms of culture and environment, with the greatest emphasis on the economic and traditional factors. Is there, then, no biological cause of group family differentiation which merits equal prominence in the discussion? The answer is no, with the exception of one item, itself culturally determined, and this in spite of the fact that popular belief gives great weight to theories based on inborn race differences. The one exception to this negative statement has to do with a biological fact which is largely the outgrowth of cultural differentiation, namely, the numerical ratio between the sexes. The sex ratio varies noticeably between minority groups, and in none of the larger groups, except the Indian, is it approximately the same as that of the native-born white people of native parentage. Some comparison of these sex ratios, expressed in terms of the number of males per 100 females, will be profitable.

The sex ratio for native white people of native parentage in 1930 was 102.3, that is, there were 102.3 males for every 100 females in this group.[2] That for the Chinese was 394.7, a decrease from the high figure of 1890, when it was 2,678.9. Taking first this excessively high ratio, let us see what it means in the development of family life. Obviously, it means first of all that a pitifully small percentage of Chinese in this country can live as members of a family unless they marry women of some other national origin. This, however, rarely happens, and we consequently have the socially unhealthy condition of a minimum of family life among the 74,954 Chinese in the United States in this year. The word "unhealthy" is used because it is assumed that the normal human existence involves marriage and family relationships. Furthermore, since the sex impulse does not atrophy when family life becomes impossible, sex irregularity is a result. A few oriental women have been imported for immoral purposes. White prostitutes have not been lacking. In recent years there has been an increasing dependence by the Chinese on mulatto mistresses. Racial antagonisms on the part of white people, Chinese, and Negroes have prevented any great amount of

[2] All sex ratios are taken from the 15th Census, *Population Bulletin, Second Series, United States Summary, Composition and Characteristics of the Population*, pp. 8, 13, 64.

racial intermarriage and have required all interracial sex relationships to be kept as secret as possible, but they have nevertheless taken place, and on a lower moral plane than if race
prejudice had not been a factor. Those Chinese who have been
so fortunate as to obtain brides, however, have apparently
appreciated their virtues, for divorce and desertion have been
extraordinarily uncommon. This, perhaps, means no more than
the fact that that which is scarce and difficult to obtain is
highly valued and not quickly relinquished. Whatever the
motive, marriageable Chinese girls in the United States may
be happy that they need not worry about obtaining a husband
or fear being soon cast off.

The Filipino sex ratio for 1930 was 1,437.7, a rate so high as
to cause another unhealthy condition similar to and probably
more pronounced than that among the Chinese. The Japanese,
fortunately, came to the United States with the intention of
remaining and becoming an integral part of the communities
in which they settled. Thus they have brought their wives
with them, or have sent for them, whenever possible, and have
settled down to family life more than any other oriental nationality. Even so, their sex ratio in 1930 was 143.3, far too
high for the uniform establishment of normal domestic institutions.

Immigration has been a population movement in which
males have predominated. Thus, colored and white immigrants
have included more men than women, whether they came from
Europe or Asia, from the northern or southern section of their
home continent. The foreign-born white population of the
United States in 1930 showed a sex ratio of 115.1, not so high
as that of all colored immigrants combined, but still sufficiently abnormal to lead to the usual problems accompanying
an excess of males. In the case of the white immigrant, the
tendency of a high sex ratio to emphasize sex and personality
disorganization is checked by the possibility of marriage with
native-born girls of either native, foreign, or mixed parentage.
For reasons mentioned in the chapter on race mixture, it is
socially advisable that their choice settle on the native-born

girls who have most in common with them because of foreign parentage of the same nationality.

In the recent years of restricted immigration and legislation favoring the admission of feminine members of the families of foreign-born residents, the sex ratios of all alien groups have crept closer and closer to the 100 mark. There is good reason why, if our Congress has the domestic welfare of the country at heart, there should be increasingly strict legislation for the purpose of making the family rather than the individual the unit of future immigration. Meanwhile, we cannot afford to miss any opportunity to reunite families parted by migration or fail to encourage the assumption of familial responsibilities by those aliens among us who are without the steadying influence of home ties.

The American Negro is the largest population class which has a significant excess of females over males, as indicated by a sex ratio of 97.0 in 1930. The rural Negro, however, has a sex ratio of 101.7, very nearly that for the total population of the United States, which was 102.5. The rural sex ratio, however, was 108.3, and it is better to use this figure as a basis for comparison. The urban Negro for the same year had a sex ratio of 91.3.

The sex ratio of the rural Negro is, then, so nearly normal, if we may assume the normal to be a trifle over 100, that his domestic relationships can hardly be influenced by the slight variation which exists. The urban Negro, however, especially in the larger cities such as New York (91.9), Detroit (107.6), Birmingham (88.7), Los Angeles (89.3), San Francisco (135.8), Washington, D. C. (89.1), Chicago (97.5), New Orleans (98.1), Cleveland (100.0), and Philadelphia (97.6), shows extreme variations in both directions, with a few cities having just about the proper balance.

This means that in those cities where there is a noticeable excess of males due to an influx of industrial laborers, such as in San Francisco, sex and familial maladjustment similar to those found among the Chinese may be expected. Where the women are more numerous than the men, a different tendency is found. Under such conditions women, being in excess, are "cheap," men have less incentive to marry, and there is an unfortunate competition for husbands rather than for wives. Experience teaches us that in modern society marriage depends more on the supply of men than women. However much it may irk us to admit the fact, we are still living in a man-centered world, so that when men are scarce and women plentiful, marriage bonds seem less inviting to masculine judgment and women must make themselves especially attractive by granting concessions in the way of sex privileges and perhaps financial considerations if many are not to be left without even a brief moment of masculine companionship.

Although disturbances in the sex ratios of racial and nationality minorities in the United States, largely caused by differential migration rates between the sexes, may be said to constitute a biological factor in family maladjustment, no truly inherent racial influence can be established. Yet it is a duty to lay the ghost of racial sex differences which still wanders through the literature on the subject. The explanation of the origin of such beliefs is not a difficult task. Family life does differ between races and nationalities. There is a greater amount of sex freedom in some groups than in others. Therefore, say the crossroads scientists, nature must have endowed some peoples with stronger sex impulses, with less power of restraint, with more insistent urges to a variety of sex experiences. While there are some physical differences in the sexual characteristics of the peoples of the world, no scientific evidence has been produced to demonstrate that their functioning differs in sufficient degree to account for variations in the observance of the accepted standards of American family relationships.

When we attempt to excuse the Negro's easy virtue by off-hand references to his recent transplanting from primitive Africa, where he was free to live the unfettered life supposedly normal for "savages," we are placing reliance on a rationalized argument which has no evidence to support it. Savages, so called, are not free to conduct themselves without restraint.

Indeed, many tribes penalize sex offenders, such as adulterers, seducers, and illicit mothers, much more severely and certainly than do we in this enlightened land. Peoples living in tropical and subtropical regions, such as the Mediterranean nationalities, have not been bred into an inherently oversexed, unstable, emotional lot. Nor have the northern peoples been bred into hereditary ascetics.

Differences in behavior need no such rationalized apologies when there is an abundance of evidence that cultural and environmental facts, differing from group to group as they do, suffice to clarify the problem of causation involved. Peoples of varying occupations and economic levels, cultural histories and traditions, and sex ratios, cannot live with identical family patterns. It would be regrettable if they tried to do so, for their domestic institutions could not function in harmony with the others, or satisfy their needs.

HUSBANDS, WIVES AND CHILDREN

Negro men prefer light-colored women as sweethearts, wives, and mistresses. Light complexions, hair that is neither kinky nor of the deepest black, features that are not too Negroid, are assets to the colored girl in her relations with colored men, for they make her more desirable and give her opportunities denied her darker sisters. The evidence for this statement is abundant. Herskovits, to cite the best scientific study of the subject, has found a remarkably high proportion of wives with less pigmentation, objectively measured, than their husbands. In a Harlem group he found the husbands lighter in color in 29.0 per cent of his cases, the wives lighter in 56.5 per cent, and both about the same color in 14.5 per cent. "The average proportion of black in the color-top was 72 per cent for the husbands and 67.7 per cent for the wives, a decisive difference showing how much lighter, on the average, the wives are than their husbands. And lest it be argued that there is here involved a sex-linked characteristic, I may say that the average [proportion of black] for all the men of the entire Harlem series is 69.5 per cent, while that for all the women is 69.8 per cent—results which have no statistical significance as far as difference is concerned."[3]

Casual observation should be sufficient to convince the most confirmed skeptic of the truth of our original statement. Skin bleaches, as advertised in all Negro newspapers, are used as a standard cosmetic by colored girls. Ribald jingles and jokes about the black girl's handicaps in courtship are a part of Negro life. The sensitiveness of the dark-complexioned woman in the presence of those with near-white skins is a common sign of lack of personal adjustment to an accident of birth.

One of the best lines of indirect evidence is that the more successful a colored man is, the more likely his wife is to approximate the type who can pass for white. This confers such an advantage on the light girl that even if she can "pass" without fear of detection, she is less likely to do so than a man, since by remaining a Negro she stays in a group in which she is especially privileged, while if she crossed into the white group she would be just another woman among thousands, her complexion and features no longer a peculiar asset. The woman, of course, pays only secondary attention to the appearance of her husband, since in our civilization her main objective is to secure a good provider who can and will take the best possible care of her.

Here we have a factor in the selection of the marriage partner not found in the majority group. It may be said that young men of old American stock also pay attention to complexion and hair color in their courtship; but in this case it is more a matter of personal preference than of group standards, for while a man may prefer a blonde to a brunette, a light skin to an olive, the reverse may also be true without exciting surprise in his friends, but not if he is a Negro. The scion of an old New England family of the highest social status may take a blue-eyed, red-headed, pink-cheeked girl to a dance, or he may take just the opposite type, and in neither case will eyebrows be raised nor tongues start wagging if she is in other respects socially presentable. The favored colored boy who selects a

[3] M. J. Herskovits, *The American Negro,* Alfred A. Knopf, New York, 1928. pp. 64-65.

Negroid type as his companion may be praised for his courage in defying convention or criticized for thrusting her upon his friends, but he cannot escape comment.

There is a tendency for Negro women of similar color and prominence of European features to flock together, imperfect in practice, but a tendency just the same. A sorority at a leading Negro college until a few years ago was said never to have admitted anyone who could not pass for white, and when the unwritten rule was broken it was supposed to have been the result of pressure by college authorities anxious, perhaps, to build up race instead of class consciousness. Such cliques, however, are not just of two varieties, those who can and those who cannot pass for white. They run the whole range of biological possibilities, modified, of course, by personal qualities which may gain admittance for a woman not eligible on the sole basis of physical appearance. This suggests that the differentiation is not solely for convenience in relations with the outside world, but is rather a partial acceptance of European standards.

The reasons for this preference are in dispute. Perhaps no one reason will suffice. Certainly, the lighter one's wife is, the more privileges she will have in her contacts with the white world as well as in the colored. While many Negroes violently deny this preference to be an aping of the white man's standards of beauty and desirability, the most obvious explanation is that the Negro has been so thoroughly acculturated that he has even adopted an approximation of the white man's ideal physical type as his own. The colored woman, for her part, has adopted the ideal of a husband as being primarily concerned with income and attention rather than with appearances.

Negro children play with white dolls, and a series of campaigns to popularize brown-skinned, black-eyed dolls have been successful only in a small way. So, too, their favorite motion picture actresses and actors are white, although race consciousness and the availability of tickets have popularized a few outstanding colored actors of both the screen and the legitimate stage. Advertisements in the colored newspapers designed to attract Negro patronage significantly avoid Negroid features in their pictures of girls, included supposedly because of the appeal of their type to potential Negro buyers.

Other minorities show similar preferences in the selection of feminine companions in proportion as they have forgotten their alien culture and have absorbed that of their new home. Intermarriage is common between all white groups, and for a variety of reasons, not the least of which is the physical appearance of the woman, who in most cases belongs to the native-born class, while the husband is more likely to belong to a minority. Irish children show no great preference for Irish dolls, nor is there any pronounced selection in the toys of Jewish, Italian, Scandinavian, and other minority children to conform to ancestral type. Greta Garbo, a Scandinavian type closely approximating the American, has as much appeal for the reasonably well assimilated Russian, Greek, and Indian as for the Swede or old American, although she would probably have been considered too thin, pale, and sexually unattractive had these same people encountered her before their ancient standards of beauty were contaminated by contact with the north European in a dominant rôle. It may be assumed that even a Hottentot, who now looks upon advanced steatopygia with great favor in a bride, might be converted by acculturation to an admiration for the formless flapper type.

Advertising posters designed to gain new customers for brands of cigarettes, refrigerators, or automobiles through pictured "sex appeal" do not vary the type of girl portrayed in accordance with the national or racial origin of potential buyers.

All this is evidence that the process of assimilation does not stop short of ideals in the selection of the marriage partner, but may even go so far as to idealize physical types rarely found in the minority group itself. Just as Negro parents are happy when their girls do not have Negroid skin, hair, and features, which they call "bad," significantly enough, so do Jewish parents rejoice when their daughters can pass for Gentiles. They know that it means a better chance to make a desirable marriage, since minority men will be a bit more-anxious to win the girl of their own group who looks as though she might belong to the majority, not because they want anyone to think she does belong to the majority, but because they have accepted the majority's tastes in feminine appearance. This phenomenon is more readily observable among Negroes than white minorities, because skin color can be measured more easily than Jewish or Mediterranean features, and also because other matrimonial influences such as social status and income play a less important rôle.

There are, of course, several minority groups and many minority individuals of whom all this is not true. It depends on the degree of assimilation. Chinese, Filipinos, and, to a lesser extent, Japanese, have, because of recency of arrival and relatively strict social isolation, retained their alien concepts of desirability in women, although the scarcity of women of Chinese and Filipino origin in the United States has forced them into the extra-marital companionship of others. The younger generation of Japanese, born and brought up in this country, seem to be accepting American standards, for assimilation is inevitable where even the most superficial out-group contacts occur.

Majority styles themselves change in matters of dress, manners, and appearance, and with considerable rapidity. It may be said with confidence, however, that with the modern breakdown of group isolation through improvement in travel and communication, minority standards in the selection of husbands and wives will increasingly approximate those of the majority in similar social classes and communities. Where, as in the case of the colored peoples, this tends to put a premium on those who because of race mixture are European in type, and at the same time seriously to handicap those marriageable girls who preserve the racial features of their parentage, the result of this acculturation is most unfortunate for the development of the minority. The black girl will hold herself, and will be held, more cheaply, with a consequent straining of family ties. The same will be true of the Oriental, the Indian, and those European peoples still thought of as inferiors who have inborn physical characteristics making it impossible for them to meet the newly acquired physical ideals of their potential husbands.

In another way, the result of this selective process will be a more rapid and efficient adjustment of minorities to American life. Even though physical features cannot be greatly altered to meet the new demands of marriageable youths, language, dress, manners, and habits can be changed more or less quickly, depending on incentive. Men, having more contacts with the outside world than women, assimilate more rapidly. As they change, a powerful incentive is given these women to do their best to measure up to the new demands, so that differential assimilation between the sexes is diminished and the entire group is more quickly adjusted to the requirements of a majority-ruled community.

Regardless of how upsetting it may be for a man to find that his greatest admiration is for a type of woman most rare in the group from which he must select his bride, the effect shows itself not so much in the number of bachelors, old maids, and deferred marriages as in family tensions. The acculturated Jew who is unable to get a wife who resembles a Gentile, the Negro disappointed in not finding a wife without "bad" features, or the American-born Japanese boy who knows only a few eligible girls, all alien in appearance, behaves just as does the boy of old American white stock who cannot obtain a bride qualified for the Follies. He marries someone less acceptable in this one respect, and is compensated, no doubt, by other redeeming qualities, makes the best of it uncomplainingly, and usually is not severely disturbed by the unattained ideal.

The marriage rate itself may be calculated for any race or immigrant people in the United States if a few variables are known. What is the sex ratio? What proportion of the group is under fifteen or over fifty years of age? Is it an urban or rural group? In what proportions are the occupations followed unskilled, semi-skilled, skilled, or white-collar jobs? How far has cultural assimilation gone? Making due allowance for these variables, we may expect the percentage of individuals who get married in any group to be just about the same as that for any other group. There is no reason for thinking of high or low marriage rates, such as the low one for the Chinese or the high one for the European-born residents in the United States, as though they were expressions of the biological nature of a species, of some quaint, outlandish culture pattern, when they are merely natural symptoms of American conditions under which the people are living.

Much has been made of the swarms of children supposed to be the inevitable accompaniment of all immigration which includes a fair share of women. It is something of a popular belief that immigrant wives and their feminine descendants tend to breed at a rate approximating the biological limit, especially Orientals, Mexicans, and south Europeans.

The truth of the matter is that foreign-born women do have more children than native white women, and that even though there is a slightly higher death rate among children of foreign mothers, their average number of surviving children is still higher than that for native-born mothers. According to Carpenter, who used birth registration area figures for 1920, "Although the native mothers show only 3.0 children ever born, as compared with 4.0 for the foreign-born mothers, they had 2.7 children still surviving, as against 3.4 for the foreign born."[4] These figures, based as they are on the number of children per mother, make no allowance for the contribution of the excess of foreign-born men, some of whom marry into the native white group, although the native-born women they marry are to a great extent themselves of foreign parentage. The numerical inferiority of foreign-born women, it must be remembered, is being constantly reduced by our recent immigration policies.

The differential between the native and immigrant birth rates is not a matter of inherent fertility, as has been carelessly assumed by pseudo-scientists in their attempts to alarm the nation with prophecies of a threatened replacement of pioneer stock by descendants of recent arrivals. Waiving for the time being the question whether such a replacement would be more than a sentimental loss, there is still considerable doubt as to the existence of any serious tendency in this direction.

[4] Niles Carpenter, *op. cit.*, p. 184.

It has been estimated by William S. Rossiter, in his Census Monograph, *Increase of Population in the United States: 1910-1920,* that "approximately 47,330,000 out of the 58,421,-957 native whites of native parents represent 'the contribution of the original stock to the population of the United States.' This does not mean that all of these 47,330,000 persons were directly derived from the pre-Revolutionary population, but that there was in 1920 a group descending in varying degrees of purity from the original native stock, whose combined heredity represented the 'numerical equivalent' of 47,330,000 pure-bred representatives of that stock. On the basis of this calculation about 11,092,000 of the native whites of native parentage are the 'numerical equivalent' of the descendants of persons immigrating to this country subsequently to the colonial period, who, with the 36,399,000 whites who are foreign born or the children of foreign parents, or of mixed native and foreign parentage, make up a total of about 47,491,000 who are in some sense foreign."[5] While some estimates place the number of foreign representatives at a higher proportion of the total white population than do Rossiter and Carpenter, the old American stock is holding its own surprisingly well in view of the millions of immigrants who have poured into the country during the past century.

This is more readily understood when attention is called to a few additional significant facts. The native white stock is more heavily rural than the foreign, and the rural birth rate is much higher than the urban. In fact, the native white stock is not reproducing itself in the city, but the same population element is supplying a large surplus of births over deaths in farm areas. The foreign stock, on the other hand, is predominantly urban, where the tendency to small families is most pronounced, so that we should expect even this group with its large family traditions to yield to the pressure and show evidence of family limitation as soon as assimilation is well under way. This is actually what happens.

The resistance of European traditions to the pressure of the new American environment, however, is too strong in the

[5] *Ibid.,* pp. 4-5.

foreign-born generation to permit it to reduce its average family size to that of the native-born whites. The first generation born in the United States has less respect for European ways of doing things and shows a marked tendency to family limitation. Unfortunately, we have no data on the family size of the following generation in the census reports, although inferences can be drawn from private studies, with reasonable confidence in their accuracy, that in size their families are the typical American families of their home communities. Since the small family is mechanically best adapted to industrial urban life, foreign peoples make the necessary adjustment in domestic standards just as quickly as the hold of their alien traditions permits. This tendency, coupled with the fact that aliens in the United States are shorter lived than natives, plus the rural distribution of our colonial stock, accounts for the survival and relatively rapid increase of pioneer family lines in spite of immigrant competition.

In regard to the alleged greater fertility of the new immigrant, it should be mentioned that birth rates in all European countries have declined during the past fifty years, that the north European once had a birth rate in this country higher than that of the recent immigrant, and that until well into the nineteenth century our colonial stock increased as rapidly as any population in the world for which we have accurate figures. Regardless of possible differences in the upper limits of potential fertility which there may be between the peoples of the world, it is evident that the number of actual births can be quickly reduced when circumstances warrant a reduction.

The size of the average Chinese, Filipino, and Japanese families also shows a definite trend toward conformity to native white standards. Such a small proportion of the Chinese in the United States are married that we may dismiss them from further discussion here. Unless the Filipinos materially increase the number of women migrating to this country, they, too, will continue to find the possibilities of family life severely restricted. The Japanese, however, introduced a sufficient number of women before their exclusion in 1924 to make possible an ordinary surplus of births over deaths in the future. Nevertheless, the charge levied against the Japanese that they would swamp the Pacific coast by an extraordinary high oriental birth rate has not been supported by experience, for their family size has decreased as has that of the European immigrant. The Mexican shows no peculiarities in this respect to mark him off from the European, in spite of his different racial ancestry. Family size among the Indians born in the United States is naturally a function of their environment and economic status.

The Negro has long had the reputation of being most prolific. This reputation has some support in fact, for the average number of children per Negro mother in the birth registration area in 1920 was 3.6, with 3.1 living, compared with the somewhat lower figures for native white mothers previously mentioned.[6] The Negro in this country has always been a rural resident, so that it should be no surprise to find that he has more children than the white man, who is more evenly distributed in both city and country. It has been noticed that the Negroes who have migrated to the cities in the past fifteen years have tended to fall into step with their white neighbors in the matter of family limitation by having fewer children than their relatives who stayed in the rural south. It is statistically unfortunate that most Negroes live in those states where birth registration is least complete and that Negro birth registration is worst of all, so that such government figures as exist must be used with reservations in comparisons of communities or of different years. From direct observation, however, it is known that the Negro can and is willing to reduce his birth rate when he learns the necessity and methods for doing so.

An insight into the attitudes of minorities toward the problems of family limitation can be given by a study of the patients applying for advice and treatment at the birth-control clinics established in some American cities, including Philadelphia, New York, and Baltimore. The evidence thus far is that applicants are drawn from religious denominations and racial groups in proportions which correspond closely to the proportions which they represent in the total population of

[6] Niles Carpenter, *op. cit.*, p. 184.

the communities having access to the clinics. Even those immigrants having a religious tradition opposed to the use of contraceptives send their numerical share of applicants. The Negro, too, who breaks away from his rural residence also breaks away from his rural cultural heritage and seeks information which will permit him to limit his family size in accordance with his newer status.

The frequency of illegitimate births varies between minority groups to a startling extent, giving rise to theories of their relative morality which show little understanding of the problem. The number of babies born out of wedlock is not necessarily a measure of comparative morality, for, leaving out of consideration for the moment the question of the propriety of varying moral standards in American minorities, there still remains the fact that only a small proportion of extra-marital cohabitation results in live births. Contraceptives, abortives, miscarriages, and natural infertility prevent our securing any reliable measure of sex delinquency from birth-registration statistics of illegitimacy. While there is no reason to believe that any racial and nationality elements in the United States population are significantly less fertile than any others, it is well known that the knowledge and use of contraceptives and abortives are not evenly distributed, and there is reason to believe that uninduced miscarriages are less common in some stocks than in others because of the varying incidence of disease and other environmental contributing factors. Paying no attention to its moral implications, there is still much to be learned about minority family life from illegitimacy rates.

Measuring illegitimacy by the number of such births reported per 1,000 total births, and using the statistics of the birth-registration area for 1920, we find that the rate for white mothers of foreign birth (5.2) is decidedly lower than that for white mothers born in the United States (16.7). The old immigrants also show higher rates than the new. For example, the following rates may be cited: For mothers born in Canada, 15.0; Scandinavia, 8.3; Germany, including German Poland, 6.6; England, Scotland and Wales, 10.6; Italy, 2.5; Ireland, 10.1; Russia, including Russian Poland, 2.5;

Hungary, 5.0; Poland, 4.0. The Negro rate on the same basis was 125.6, while the other colored peoples combined showed a rate of 44.7. The differences between urban and rural rates are not particularly significant, although as a rule they are higher in urban than in rural areas.[7]

If we think in terms of the social organization of these minorities, one explanation, if not justification, stands out above all others, namely, that the degree of independence of the individual from, or his subjugation to, the family as a social and economic unit makes the care of children born to unmarried mothers relatively simple or difficult, as the case may be. The new immigrant's concept of the family under which he operates in this country as long as possible, is of a rigid, semi-patriarchal type which is both a production and a consumption unit. The father is the ruling head and main support. The wife or mother, children and whatever other attached adults, such as brothers, sisters, uncles, aunts, or cousins, there may be, cooperate in the household duties and in earning supplementary income. In such a scheme there is little room for an extra baby or two, and a powerful tradition has grown up in Europe, where this concept developed, to prevent these accidental burdens, without the father bearing his share of the cost.

The higher standard of living possible in the United States makes such children, deprived as they are of their natural father's care and protection, less of a burden on the mother's family if she stays with them, permits the growth of satisfactory institutions and child-placing agencies for their care if necessary, while the spirit of individualism which has extended even to women permits the mother to earn sufficient money to pay for the keep of her illegitimate baby and herself if the occasion demands.

A surplus of men, furthermore, as is found in immigrant groups, increases the proportion of marriageable girls who are able to find husbands, so that from a purely statistical approach we should expect those groups with the highest sex ratio to have the lowest illegitimacy rates, although the type

[7] Niles Carpenter, *op. cit.*, p. 245.

of rate here used tells us nothing about the origin of the fathers involved. Nevertheless, we cannot attribute a scarcity of illegitimate births, as distinguished from illicit sex relations, to a high sex ratio except to a minor extent, for this is not invariably the case, nor would it be in keeping with the fact that when the sex ratio approximates 100 there may be either many or few children of unmarried mothers.

The Negro rate of 125.6 per 1,000 births, for example, would be difficult to understand were it not for the fact that the male has never assumed dominance in the United States, that the family is a relatively loose-knit, personal relationship, and that the unmarried mother may without mental conflict or social disapproval do what she would probably do if she were married, that is, work as a productive economic unit, independently of family connections. American Negroes have proportionately the largest number of women gainfully employed of any important minority in the United States. The children born out of wedlock are less a handicap and burden to the women and their families of this group than to any other.

Of course, it will be said that the real reason for the great number of illegitimate Negro births lies in the lack of social disapproval of such events in the colored race. It is true that the stigma attached to Negro bastardy is relatively slight except for the select and numerically small upper classes, either in the minds of colored or white people, and that with a lesser penalty attached, together with but slight knowledge of contraceptives, careless immorality must be expected. In this connection one is reminded of the southern white girl, daughter of a university professor, who, until she was some ten or twelve years of age, thought there were two kinds of babies, white and illegitimate. An atmosphere such as this itself breeds further laxity. Also, we sometimes lose sight of the fact that an important reason for insistence on formal marriage is the necessity for the legal determination of property rights, and since the property rights of most Negroes are hardly worth bothering with, we have here an additional reason why so many colored couples simply live together in what is delicately but inaccurately called common-law marriage.

It is not at all likely that Negroes, with their high illegitimacy rate, have any less knowledge of contraceptives and abortives than have the recent immigrants with their low rate. To claim that the lack of social disapproval of such conduct is the cause of the high illegitimacy rate among Negroes is to put the cart before the horse, for the lack of disapproval in large measure follows the event made possible by the social and economic status of Negro women and the prevalent type of family organization. Had there been any necessity for doing so, Negro men and women would rapidly have built up a pressure of social tradition and personal inhibitions similar to that which acts as the immediate but not the ultimate source of restraint which keeps down the number of illegitimate births among immigrants and native whites.

FAMILIES OF THE PAST

When the social forces and personal drives which shape up the family form and routine in a group continue after a change in any or all of the institutions other than the family, they become ends in themselves instead of remaining means to an end. This type of cultural lag may be harmless, but is much more likely to assume a serious aspect if readaptation is not soon effected. Possibly no harm is done, for example, by the European immigrant's tendency to hold fast to a concept of the family which includes distant relatives as actively or potentially assisting members of an enlarged, functioning family, although the apparent impossibility of adapting such a unit to a useful purpose in an industrial society has made most of us forget that it was once a part of the culture of our own ancestors. Harmless familial anachronisms are hard to find, but even the casual student of the American family is familiar with dozens of illustrations of a disturbing nature.

American Indian family life furnishes us with a damaging picture of the social and personal injury which may result from an attempt to force too great adaptations in too little time. In using this minority as illustrative of this general principle we must avoid the assumptions that all pre-Columbian tribes had identical domestic institutions or that they have all faced similar transitional adjustments. Nevertheless, we may risk a few generalities which will be relatively accurate for most tribes, and the different degrees of success which they have achieved in absorbing a modified European culture may aid in clarifying the problems involved.

We have already referred to the Indian's inability to appreciate the European's belief that polygamy is immoral. This view is now accepted by most Indians, not only because of constant missionary activity and legal threats, but also because polygamy does not seem to be a family form suitable to their present manner of living.

Another difficult adjustment had to do with the revision of the concept of family descent and the correlated methods governing property inheritance, children's support and education, and woman's status in domestic affairs. Indian tribes in what is now the United States had both a bilateral and a unilateral theory of family organization. That is, in addition to recognizing the biological relationship of both the maternal and the paternal ancestry of a given individual, an additional scheme based on descent through female ancestry only, known as matrilineal descent, was used in some tribes, including the Iroquois, while a scheme based on descent through the male line only, known as patrilineal descent, was found in others.

Customarily, under matrilineal descent valuable personal property was inherited through the female line only instead of through both the maternal and the paternal relatives as in our European culture. In some such tribes a father had more responsibility for the care and training of his sisters' sons than for his own. Under this system, known as the avunculate, the child and its maternal uncles may have a closer relationship of duties and privileges than under our own, and the child is insured excellent care and education. The mothers, naturally, tend to assume a more important place in their children's lives and in other domestic affairs than under a purely bilateral arrangement. As soon as the Indian yielded to European influences, the matrilineal system disintegrated, and this disintegration invariably occurred before the fathers understood and accepted their new obligations and status. The mother lost prestige and influence in assuming the status of European mothers, and no little difficulty was experienced in defining their new status as well as that of each family member.

The Pueblos of the Southwest are at present in the process of discarding matrilineal descent and its corollaries, and there seems to be no way of avoiding a troublesome break in their family life, during which many individuals will be left without adequate standards and protection. It is one of the duties of the federal Indian Bureau to see to it that the transition is as easy as possible. Only a few Indians are left in the United States who still adhere to the matrilineal system. Most of them have forgotten its significance, which, by the way, was never that of a matriarchate, although vestiges survive in places, as among the Senecas of New York, who include many who still believe in the system of matrilineal descent to the extent of insisting that inheritance be determined on that basis, much to the annoyance of the more modern tribal members.

More than half the Indians of the western hemisphere were patrilineal, but although this manner of tracing descent is more easily understood by the European than is that of the opposite system—for there are so many things in European culture which smack of patrilineal origin—they too had to give up the old ways and, after a transitional period, take up the new when the white man took control.

The march of European culture through the New World had a devastating effect on the Indian family, especially on that of the eastern agricultural area, because of the conflict of ideas as to the proper division of labor between the sexes. The Indians of this area in particular considered agriculture to be woman's work, although this did not hold true for all tribes. Some of the southwestern tribes, for example, assigned the cultivation of maize and other foods to the men, but throughout the hemisphere this arrangement occurred only when hunting became an unimportant occupation. Thus in those areas where the cultivation of food plants was woman's work, the men were not left idle, for there was plenty left for them to do in the way of providing meat and of insuring safety from external foes. The many other tasks necessary for tribal existence were also parceled out so that both sexes had plenty to do and neither wasted much more time than the other. The white man, however, promptly laid low as much of the forest as he could, put the plow to as much soil as he could, and depleted all varieties of game, so that the Indian was compelled to depend increasingly on cultivated crops, which naturally increased woman's burden and turned the man into what we glibly named a "lazy savage." After the Indian was decisively defeated in battle, fighting also became one of the lost arts. Having thus removed two of the Indian's chief male occupations, the despoiler, innocent of anthropology and psychology, expected him to plunge right into farming, and roundly condemned him, when he failed to do so, for living on his overworked wife's efforts. For him to do otherwise would have been as disgraceful to his masculine pride as it would be today for the ordinary white man to take over the family cooking, dishwashing, and infant care. What is more, no self-respecting Indian woman would have wanted to live with a man who lowered himself by agricultural work even to ease her own lot.

Now that for nearly all the Indians in the United States the old division of labor has faded from tribal memory with the passing of generations under European domination, idleness is no longer thrust upon the husband, the wife is less overburdened, and farms may prosper under the cooperative labor of both men and women. Thus one cause of "laziness" has disappeared, but at a high cost of transitional family disorganization. The Indian has given us examples of the heavy strain on family organization—and there were destructive strains on his other social institutions as well—which were the immediate consequence of his being relegated to the position of a minority group upon the ascendency of the transplanted European. He was, however, not the only sufferer, and probably not the worst.

Not a trace of African family forms and processes was given opportunity to survive when the Negro was brought to the

United States. Tribal life was destroyed partly by the sale and purchase of individuals from scattered parts of the dark continent in all the slave districts in this hemisphere. What traditions survived this distribution quickly lost significance in the New World and were gone in a generation or two, except in some relatively unimportant isolated areas, including perhaps some of the Sea Islands. The Negro's problem of family adjustment today is one of completing his acculturation, already well under way but turned into a false channel by the exigencies of slavery.

Slavery in the south was based on the individual, and in spite of the relatively stable family organization permitted on most plantations and required on those which were best managed, the slave was not deluded into believing that his owner's prime interest centered on anything but the slave himself. The family was merely a means for keeping individual slaves housed, fed, and contented, for producing more individuals, and perhaps for satisfying moral and religious scruples which ran counter to the owner's economic interests. The black man has learned his lesson well. An individualist the white man made him, and an individualist he has remained, modified only a trifle since the Civil War.

In this respect his family standards and ideals—or, from an old-fashioned point of view, his lack of them—fit him for the industrial life he is beginning to enjoy. Perhaps he is for the same reason handicapped for small-acreage farming, where individualism may not be carried too far. It seems regrettable that this attitude, no drawback in plantation slaves but a bit ahead of the times in our most modernized industrial cities, should be a characteristic of a minority which for the greater part is struggling along on an agricultural system designed for the close-knit family groups such as those of the Pennsylvania German or Scandinavian western farmer.

Our European immigration has always included, and still includes, a majority which has been raised to respect and obey the dictates of a family set-up which was the product of small, family-operated farms. There have been, of course, hundreds of thousands of immigrants who were subject to the influences of industrialization before setting sail for the United States, but a large proportion of these had not yet thoroughly absorbed the new-fangled notions of the new order. The European farmer or farm laborer who went to the farm in the United States was able to adjust his family customs slowly and without severe growing pains. His life here could continue much the same as it had been ordered in the old country, for was he not a farmer in both places, and is it not possible to take one's time in the process of acculturation in the isolation of rural areas where contacts with the outside world are less involved than in the city? But since in the last few decades farm lands in the public domain have been exhausted and the only paying occupations open seem to be in mill and factory, the farm families of Europe have been transplanted to the cities of America; and while the older generation has fought to hold fast to stern traditional ways, the younger has seen that they are alien, has discarded them as old-fashioned, and is left in a state of revolt against the outmoded customs without a constructive substitute.

Although the north European has fewer family adjustments to make than any other of our racial or nationality minorities, be the change ever so slight for him, he must still pass through a transitional period until he has achieved a working arrangement which will permit him, his wife, and his children to strike a balance between freedom from home restraint with its attendant inhibitions and personal conflicts, and limitations imposed by the domestic folkways of the land of birth. It may well be said that the necessity for casting off the old and putting on the new in sex and family relationships is not restricted to immigrants, Negroes, or Indians. Of course not. Every native family which moves from one place to another in the United States, which changes from one social or economic status to another, which merely continues to exist as the world around it takes new forms, must undergo similar transitional periods with their strains and stresses. Like most such things, the difference is one of degree, for the degree of difference between the domestic adjustment problems of racial and nationality minorities and those of the majority, well established.

at home and in control, is the difference between immorality and morality, sin and virtue, crime and law observance.

Marriage as an unbreakable contract is an invention of the Christian, an outgrowth of the sacramental theory of marriage, now abandoned or modified by all major religious denominations except the Roman Catholic Church. The attitude of minorities toward the legal recognition of family dissolution will serve as an another illustration of the conflict of cultures.

The United States, following the lead of its Protestant settlers, has refused legally to recognize marriage as an unbreakable, lifelong contract, although the reasons for which it may be terminated in the various states range from adultery only to personal inclination of either party. One state alone, South Carolina, refuses any divorces. The American people have become even more liberal in their attitude toward legalized family dissolution than the law itself, and now wink knowingly at false divorce testimony, close their eyes at family desertion except for the entrance of the economic motive when wife and children can find no new support, and do little to prevent the substitution of illicit relations for the mockeries of artificially maintained home life.

The Indians, a few still pagan, and many of the Christians among them only superficially converted, have few scruples against severing relations with wife or husband when mismating becomes evident. The census returns for the past three or four decades, during which the Indian returns have been most nearly accurate, show a higher average proportion of divorced men and women than can be found in any other minority.

This must of course be used with hesitancy as absolute evidence of the group attitude toward divorce, for, like all such statistics, they are meaningless unless interpreted in the light of the number of remarriages, the prevalent occupations and income, geographical distribution, and so forth. It is because of the necessity for such modification that few family statistics are here used; their implications could only be guessed, and it is at least as safe to start one's line of reasoning with known facts from the culture of a people as to depend on figures which attempt the numerical expression of the facts of domestic relationships which have yet to be reduced to measurable, quantitative terms. It would of course be possible to rework census data with the aid of intricate and ingenious formulæ, but no formula ever devised can make good statistics out of bad ones. It is more honest not to disguise guesses with manufactured tables and charts.

To use a non-statistical approach, a knowledge of the fact that Indians 'constitute the minority least influenced by Christianity, with the exception of a small number of Orientals, leads us to conclude that both divorce and family desertion should be relatively free from social penalties and the restraints of an opposing personal ethics. What few reliable facts we have seem to bear out this hypothesis. The Indian who is still an Indian culturally sees no immorality in correcting a mistake, and acts accordingly.

What the future trend in this respect will be is hard to say, but if missionary efforts continue among the surviving tribes as in the past and at present, the Indians may find themselves in an even more awkward position. Missionaries are notorious for the conservative quality of their moral teachings which, if effective among the Indians, will tend to bring them around to a point of view on family dissolution which will be out of date in native white communities before the few remaining "uncivilized" red men have had time to learn what the white men really think.

The Negro, unlike the Indian, has completely forgotten that he, too, once looked on marriage as an earthly contract, with only incidental religious implications. Since considerably less than a quarter of a million Negroes in the United States are claimed by the Roman Catholic Church, the sacramental concept of marriage has not been directly substituted for their earthly African views except for this number. Protestantism, however, is filled with the ghosts of the Catholic doctrine, so that when the American Negro adopted the white man's religion he also acquired the belief that divorce was a disgrace. Between one-half and one-third of our Negro population, however, holds no church membership, and it is well known that many of the rest have only a veneer of what the church authorities would call true Christianity. Nor has their cultural absorption from the white man gone far enough to produce a horror of the divorced man or woman, or even of the family deserter, equal to that which is still part of our European and early American tradition except in an unmeasurable minority. Since missionaries and moral reformers leave the Negro to work out his own salvation pretty much by himself, it is not likely that he will ever accept the modified Catholic attitude, now on the wane among the American-born white people.

The north European comes to us with ideas on divorce which differ little from those of the American majority. The new immigration, however, including as it does the Catholic and the Jew, both far less individualistic than the north European, runs afoul of the prevalent American practice in ways just opposite to the conflicts of the colored minorities. The Jew and other recent arrivals of non-Catholic ancestry make their adaptations in a generation or so, for among them divorce is something to be avoided if possible, but on occasion it is regarded as an accepted remedy, distasteful but unavoidable, like bitter medicine and major surgical operations. The Roman Catholic, however, has a propagandist and authoritative institution in his church which wages constant warfare on the spread of a tolerant attitude toward divorce among her people, thus increasing and prolonging the bitterness of group prejudices beyond what otherwise would be their normal intensity and length of life.

Yet one may not speak too hastily in criticism of the now unfashionable, strongly cemented family with its all-inclusive functioning. True, it is out of style in our cities, and even in the emancipated rural districts, but when the individual finds himself in trouble it is well to have a family which accepts a multitude of obligations to its members, even to the distant cousins. It has been observed that the Negro who lands before the bar of justice is a lonely figure, compared with the young Jew, so frequently supported, comforted, and perhaps embarrassed by a flock of relatives who have come to see him through. The individualist may have the greater freedom, but he also stands alone in trouble. The widow or wife who has lost her husband by desertion or divorce may expect help from her family, and as a matter of right instead of as charity, if her people have not become too individualistic. Financial aid in time of unemployment, sickness, or business failure, or perhaps much-needed backing in a new commercial venture, may come from relatives when all other sources are dried up. There are so many things which may happen, disastrous to the victim if the bond of blood is weak, yet not without remedy in the family circle that holds together.

No doubt, in the eyes of the individualist, the state should provide old-age and mothers' pensions, unemployment insurance, employment service, social agencies for the care of dependent children, and all the other welfare devices to help the citizen in trouble, but it has not done so. Anachronistic kinship sacrifices still have a function remaining, and those minorities who have weakened and do not now accept such family obligations as a matter of course suffer most in time of need.

FAMILIES IN TRANSITION

No picture of the family life of minorities could be revealing without an attempt to give it form by a few bold strokes of unifying generalization. We have already generalized about their differences and about a scattering of points in common. There remains the task of reducing the detail to an integrated whole.

A twin pattern, product of the process of acculturation which is the common problem of all race conflict, may be seen in the domestic standards of all American racial and nationality minorities. *Within the minority individual there is an absence of those personal restraints which could produce conformity to the acceptable varieties of sexual and familial behavior, and, as these restraints are inculcated, no two members of a given community or family are likely to absorb them with equal rapidity or thoroughness.* At some point in the process of acculturation there must be at least one generation, perhaps several, depending on the degree of social isolation.

which is left without a socialized compass in which it can have faith to guide its behavior.

Considering first the absence of expected restraints, the so-called immorality of the Negro furnishes a case in point. Why should Negroes be so lax in their sexual behavior and so careless in their observation of family responsibilities?

The sex impulse is a natural impulse, which, however, is severely restricted in its expression in most cultures by social rules, no doubt necessary for the protection of offspring and adults, which for many individuals inhibit a normal functioning. Sexual frigidity to some degree is now known to be ordinary in girls of European and American training. A system of sex education which from early youth instills a concept of sex as unclean and bestial could have no other effect except to hinder free expression in sex relations after marriage as well as before, for when, for the purpose of keeping our young people chaste, this function has been convincingly taught as a nasty yielding to base passions, this aspect persists long after sanctification by marriage grants permission for indulgence. Such a lesson thoroughly learned cannot be brushed aside by a brief courtship and a legal ceremony. Since the double standard of sex morality still exists and boys' wild oats are condoned if frowned upon, frigidity should be and is less frequently found to a serious degree in the husband than in the wife.

There is reason to believe that the ordinary colored girl in this country is not subjected to the same constant nagging and threats regarding the importance of chastity as is her white neighbor. While this is not true of all colored families, there is sufficient difference between the white and colored people in the United States to lead to a great deal less sexual frigidity among Negro than among white women. White people have behind them, except for the few who have lost it, a continuity of generations of tradition reaching back to early Europe and before, modified in minor ways from time to time, but with an enduring emphasis on the value of virginity and the inevitable, irredeemable sinfulness of sex delinquency. Such an attitude cannot be made part of a culture pattern in two or three generations, and that is all the Negro has to fall back on. He started over again under slavery, and slave morality was not of much concern to slave owners. The value of a slave did not depend on chastity. While a majority of Negro slaves probably lived in reasonably strict monogamy, this was as much through personal inclination as through a conviction of moral necessity. There is evidence that on some plantations it was a badge of prestige and honor for a colored girl to be selected as a white man's mistress, and sometimes slave mothers strove to secure this favor for their daughters. Regardless of the exact frequency of occurrence of attitudes similar to these—and there is no historical proof of their exact extent— the fact that they existed in even a fair minority of cases would be sufficient to delay the adoption of the white man's professed Christian standards even if the slaves had not known the white man's indifference to their violation.

Since emancipation there has been little more encouragement of chastity among Negroes. Colored maids are not refused positions or discharged for open illicit relationships except in unusual instances, although a white girl would be driven out and denounced for less flagrant lapses. With only minor penalties enforced, and frequently none at all, what incentive or possibility is there for parents and preachers to drive home to colored children the moral lessons which we take for granted in white communities?

It is a question whether this absence of social restrictions and individual inhibitions is a blessing or a curse. In so far as it is responsible for the Negro being out of step with the dominating white man's professions it is a handicap to the Negro and a source of moral danger to the white man himself. To the extent that it permits a more normal, in the sense of natural, sex life to the Negro, it may be a blessing in disguise, a blessing which the Negro is doing his best to reject, for he is trying hard to acquire the inhibitions now lacking, or at least to conceal their absence, to show that he is the white man's moral equal. He cannot help but feel the lack to be a disgrace and shame, but it is still not an easy one to overcome.

A quotation from Mecklin is apt. "A question of fundamental import for the Negro home is the position and influence of the Negro woman. She is as wife and mother undoubtedly the central figure, and there is something elemental, even heroic, in her nature. One feels that in her are preserved the best traditions of the race. She is not infrequently the real head of the household. This may be partly the result of the common slave owners' policy of issuing food and other equipment to the women and otherwise exalting their position as the stable element in the slave family, and as a measure of moral values she must be reckoned with first of all in the Negro home. A Negro writer has given us the following interpretation of the deepest instincts (*sic*) of her nature. 'The Negro woman with her strong desire for motherhood, may teach modern civilization that virginity, save as a means of healthy motherhood, is an evil and not a divine attribute. That while the sexual appetite is the most easily abused of all the human appetites and most deadly when perverted, that nevertheless it is a legitimate, beneficent appetite when normal, and that no civilization can long survive which stigmatises it as essentially nasty and only to be discussed in shamefaced whispers. The Negro attitude in these matters is in many respects healthier and more reasonable. Their sexual passions are strong and frank, but they are, despite example and temptation, only to a limited degree perverted or merely commercial. The Negro mother-love and family instinct is strong, and it regards the family as a means, not an end, and although the end in the present Negro mind is usually personal happiness rather than social order, yet even here radical reformers of divorce courts have something to learn.' "[8]

It is suggested that a lesser amount of sexual frigidity in the colored girl (and there is perhaps a similar lesser amount in colored men) contributes to the desire which some white men have for colored mistresses. The theory is that the more natural responses of the uninhibited women of the darker race gain favor in contrast with the restraint of the white. The truth of this theory has not been adequately demonstrated, but it may well be a factor adding to the racial cross-

[8] John M. Mecklin, *op. cit.*, pp. 213-214.

ing which has made approximately three-quarters of our Negro mulattoes.

A lack of artificial restraints characterizes the entire family life of the American Negro of all classes, although the upper levels closely approximate majority standards. Rarely is identity achieved. The attitude toward sex offenses, for illustration, contains less subjective moralizing and more of a practical recognition of objective facts. Without intending in any way to belittle the colored minister, for he is the most powerful leader of the masses who need him, it may be said that Negro parishioners give greater latitude to their preachers than do white congregations of corresponding social levels. For example, there is one well-known if illiterate evangelistic preacher whose promiscuous relations with several members of his congregation are familiar to hundreds of Negroes in New York, Philadelphia, and Washington. His church has been filled to overflowing for years, mostly with members who do not approve but take no action. Of course, he draws only from a credulous, emotionally susceptible, ignorant stratum, but the significant fact for us is that Negroes of all classes who know of his conduct smile tolerantly, recount his latest reputed adventure with a humorous twist, shrug their shoulders at such foolishness, but do not trouble themselves with ineffectual attempts at reform. Even the outraged know the uselessness of action in this particular case. There are others like it.

When another preacher recently discovered his wife in a compromising situation in the same week that she made a similar discovery concerning him, and their friends were left in no doubt about the facts, the final adjustment of the tangle was the acceptance of a new charge in another city, away from the scene and source of their trouble, where they could pick up the threads of their old relationship, which is what they both really wanted to do in spite of their lapses. It should be noticed that they were able to solve their domestic problem the way they wanted to, that is, in accordance with their true feelings and with no busybodies to bother them. Their friends did not give them the cold shoulder, a new church was willing to accept them although knowing the circumstances of the move, and, strangest of all to the European way of thinking, the husband did not feel personally disgraced by his wife's conduct, nor was it necessary for him to reestablish his status by repudiating her for physical unfaithfulness.

The relations of parents and children also seem on a healthier basis in this respect. The father and mother whose daughter errs, bitterly regretful of her sin as they may be, are not likely to feel they have to cast her out of their home for the honor and safety of the family. The East Lynne gesture in parent as in husband would be repudiated if suggested. The family, to their quaint way of thinking, exists to serve its members, and not its members to build and worship an institution as an end in itself. If a son or a daughter is in trouble, has incurred the Lord's wrath through sin and needs a refuge, why, that's what the family is for! This simple acceptance of the family as a human creation, its right to existence to be judged by its human usefulness, is in relieving contrast to the fetish we Europeans have made out of our domestic institutions, which, to our way of thinking, apparently must be preserved no matter what the cost in human suffering.

While sexual jealousy is as sharp in its pain among Negroes as among white people, it is perhaps more readily assuaged. There is no doubt but that a deserting wife or husband can be taken back with less mental conflict than would be the case if the Negro were thoroughly Europeanized. Personal pride, the fear of pitying or sympathetic gossip, and the belief that a woman who has sinned is forever lost, make it difficult to effect a reconciliation between estranged white couples, but not between average Negroes. It is even easier for the guilty wife to bring herself to return to her betrayed husband, for the "conviction of sin," the basic factor in much personality disintegration among white girls who have been seduced, is likely to be absent or of weak strength.

Naturally enough, Negroes who realize the gulf between white and colored family standards—and the number is not small—are now attempting to bring their people into line. In other words, at a time when white people are just beginning to realize the penalty they are paying for a system of sex education based on ignorance and the fear of disease, unwanted babies, eternal punishment, and all the nastiness with which we have invested sex, Negro leadership and white advice, instead of warning against these mistakes, hold out the prospect of a time when the colored people will accept the same false views. It is the reverse of the program of mental hygiene which now has the support of our progressive educators.

The immigrant from Europe or Asia also lacks the domestic restraints and attitudes which we expect of him, but he has a different set which do not make his assimilation any easier. The old restraints and customs must first be weakened and destroyed or sublimated, and the new slipped into their place with as little delay as possible. The Indian, too, has been caught in this process, but then so has the Negro, only we made short shrift of his African "savagery" and left him dangling with a confused mixture of Christian and slave codes, leaving us all bewildered in turn when he did not automatically insist on "higher" standards than he was permitted.

We have been equally bewildered by the inability of every other minority with a different cultural history from our own to turn itself into "Americans" over night. Excepting the Negro, every minority still contains thousands of individuals who in their original environment were mentally molded to a set course of sex and family behavior so that it has become a real part of them, fixed with a permanence which seems to be but is not hereditary. Unlike the Negro, their behavior is culturally restrained to an extent beyond that of at least the less provincial of our native youth. As a rule, they hold fast to their early teachings with a tenacity no less than that of the native stock. It is not often that they find their way into our courts.

When they do, it is either because they, like other people, include a small percentage of mavericks, or because they persist in the belief that the morality of their native civilization is just as high now as ever. Some, like the Indian and certain Orientals, believe in limited polygyny, although none have practised it extensively. Others, like the south European, are more lenient toward concubinage and prostitution. Usually, however, this foreign generation gets into trouble because it tries to hold to a family system which is too ironclad for modern taste; but since our laws hark back to similar customs in our own history, and reformers are generally more zealous in maintaining the old than in fostering innovations, we have the paradoxical phenomenon of liberal praise for the very causes of social maladjustment. Perhaps it is just as well, for there is nothing much to be done about it anyway. Only a small percentage of human beings seem able to change with the times, once maturity has been reached.

The second generation, that is, the first born and reared in the United States, is differently situated. It encounters the difficult task of growing up in two worlds. Here, for example, is a girl, the daughter of parents perhaps Spanish or Chinese, who believe she should be cloistered from an early age until marriage. She soon learns that this is simply not being done, that it is "un-American." There is then a danger, far from certainty, however, that she will repudiate her parents' efforts, rebel against them and run wild. She must have time to learn that in the absence of enforced seclusion and chaperonage, American civilization has provided other safeguards operating through the training of the girls themselves instead of through external compulsions. This illustration is, of course, not the only one which could be found. There are other conflicts of the same order regarding every aspect of sex conduct.

What of the American-born girl of immigrant parents whose mother was, in American eyes, the family drudge, living to do the will of her husband? What will be her attitude toward wifely duties when she grows up and realizes, as she must, how "foreign" her mother's actions were? Will not the son, too, tend to resent parental domination, and show his independence and Americanism by overdenial of restraint? With this conflict of cultures present in the home of every child born in this country of alien or Indian parents, the wonder is that it is no greater source of dissatisfaction and disturbance than it is. The percentage of misfits—familial agnostics, they might be called—is high, but somehow or other most of them muddle through, and their children in their turn, if there is no color bar to hold them suspended in transition, usually lose their status as members of minorities.

The twin effect of this acculturation process previously referred to is the disturbing influence of the unevenness with which it is accomplished by individual community and family members. It is the unusual family which can synchronize the absorption of its members into the community life of the strange home. The family, however, is a plastic and adjustable institution, so that, provided there is the slightest relative uniformity of transition, it can be held together and kept functioning with signs of only minor tensions, unhealthy but not absolutely destructive.

So long as the Indians stayed together in tribal activities, differential acculturation was kept at a minimum. A few individuals naturally made the first contacts with the white man, and some permitted the advice of their tribal brothers to go unheeded as they experimented with the frontiersmen's innovations. But until actual tribal disintegration set in, the tribe as a whole accepted or rejected the horse, the gun, the Bible, or the plow.

It was a source of parental complaint that Indian children were forced to go to governmental schools, particularly to the non-reservation schools such as that at Carlisle, for the heretical significance of the white man's educational program was immediately sensed. The children came home strangers, and in the parents' eyes were lost through cultural heresy, from which they had to be lured or driven back to the blanket. Only where tribal life survives today is there a semblance of early culture left. In no case, however, is there sufficient tribal unity now to resist the ravages of differential acculturation.

For years, governmental authorities have urged that Indian custom marriage and divorce be replaced by federal and state legislation demanding observance of the white man's standards. In one report they pointed out, theoretically in favor of their point of view, that in certain districts where Indians were early subjected to state law, the young men soon discovered that although the old form of marriage was no longer binding, some of the girls, in less contact with the outside world, did not know about the change. The result was a number of courtships followed by custom marriage and then, at the whim of the legally unrecognized groom, desertion, with the more civilized seducers secure in the knowledge they could not be held legally responsible. There have also been numerous cases where legal husbands have divorced their wives, knowing that a legal divorce could not be obtained, but safe because their wives were still thinking in terms of a vanishing culture. The annihilation of the tribe as a functioning organization has made this inevitable whether the white man's or the Indian's marriage and divorce law is legally recognized.

Such knavery has a dramatic quality which arrests attention, but the number of these scoundrels, products of transition though they be, is small. The hopeless part of the picture is that of honest, sincere, and kindly husbands, wives, and children who, in spite of good intentions, cannot help but antagonize each other. The young man who has been to Haskell Institute may readily learn to be ashamed of the primitive dress, habits, and ideas of his parents, and the girl he marries must be quick to grow with him if he continues contacts with European civilization. Too often the scene centers in a mother who cannot understand her son's brusque treatment, a father who is out of touch with wife and son and resentful of them, and a son whose affection, truly strong for both parents, is unwillingly concealed from them by an opaque cultural wall unwittingly erected.

Change only the name, the time, the place, and you have a description of an immigrant commonplace. Think of Tony, his Mary, and their boy Joe instead of Spotted Dog, Wounded Deer, and Running Elk. Tony has been in the United States two years, has saved enough to pay his wife's passage. When he meets her at the train he is puzzled. She is not the girl he married. The trouble is, she is the girl he married but he is not the man she married. He married her in Italy, where she was the village belle. In America, against the background of American girls' clothes and manners, and in the light of his new acceptance of Americanisms, her beautiful peasant festival dress seems tawdry, her jewelry foreign, her hair out of style and even her manner of greeting out of place. Puzzled, faithful, but not so proud, he takes her to her new home. Joe is born, grows up, runs with a "wise" gang, and is ashamed and disobedient. The family may or may not hold together. Tony may have a mistress or two, seeking something he cannot find. Mary is not likely to take a lover. She lives out her span in solitude. Joe strikes out for himself. Yet usually the family survives, but at a cost beyond words.

Now select three Chinese, Japanese, Filipino, Mexican, Greek, or Danish names, and reconstruct the scene. It is the same, except in intensity. Only if there is an isolated ethnic group, corresponding vaguely to the early Indian tribes, like the Norwegians and Swedes in rural Minnesota, the Germans in Wisconsin and Pennsylvania, the French in Louisiana, in which practically all contacts take place within the group, can differential assimilation be minimized, because the new culture under such circumstances must seep in gradually, spread a bit more evenly, than when the individual goes outside his group from time to time and is more exposed to new ideas than those who stay at home.

Thus the horse culture and use of firearms spread through and were accepted by Indian tribes as a whole. So the use of the self-binding reaper, the threshing machine, and other agricultural improvements became a part of the culture complex of isolated rural nationality groups. In such a process as this the entire community participates and becomes familiar with the innovation in rapid order. This is quite different from what happens when the husband and son leave the home every day and learn to use new machinery, become accustomed to advanced ideas, but cannot readily communicate their new attitudes to those who have no similar outside contacts.

The march toward uniform domestic institutions is impeded by many obstacles, but it is sure. Minorities are sometimes met part way by the majority; sometimes they must follow an ever advancing front. But they follow.

CHAPTER XI

THE BLENDING OF RACES

THE worship of racial purity, by-product of nationalism and the obligation of all true nativists, is a stigma of provincialism characterizing individuals and communities that live in the past. The "Daughters" and "Sons" of this and that, whose ancestral exploits overshadow their own futility, are a variety which tends to glorify unmixed descent from someone or other. Modern representatives of the breed of the Pilgrim Fathers, the Huguenots, the Cavaliers, the Quakers, and the Creoles may have no personal adventures and hard-won victories to recount, but the pioneer blood in their veins can be called on for reassurance of the possession of high qualities, twice blessed if uncontaminated by the admixture of less historic strains. The "native sons" of the West are showing symptoms which presage an attack of living in the past on the reputations of exalted frontiersmen who, in their day, could make no claim to superiority based on ancestry. Minorities themselves have their aristocracies of blood, so that there are Irish, German, Jewish, Italian, Polish, and even Negro families secure in their belief in an inherent greatness which needs no present-generation achievement in proof, although they are but a brief span removed from the first ancestor to demonstrate worth in his own right. Nations of mongrel origin follow the example of individuals, and, when they are no longer too busy forging ahead to look backward, point to their past contributions to civilization, arrogant in the possession of the blood of former world leaders.

Purity of blood, however, is a relative matter both for individuals and for nations. Strictly speaking, "pure races" may be found only in isolated, backward regions of the globe inhabited by unprepossessing, primitive peoples. The typical American, if there is such a creature, would needs be a hybrid of many European and some colored stocks. A moment's consideration makes evident the mathematical impossibility of family purity, for ancestors increase in geometrical ratio as one goes back generation after generation, so that even after making due allowance for inbreeding, the total sources of any American's inheritance only five or six generations removed are staggering. Let anyone who is proud of noble ancestry, who traces descent to the *Mayflower*, to the Huguenots, to an Irish king, an English lord, an Italian count, calculate the number of forbears he has had since his first known ancestor, and the relative unimportance of a few drops of vaunted blood will be apparent. Can the reader state with certainty the name and exact racial stock of all of his great-great-grandparents, or of his great-grandparents? Where the individual's race fades in unrecorded history, can the nation—and all nations have suffered infusions of strange blood through immeasurable migrations—speak with certainty?

All modern nations must admit that they are mongrels, ignorant of the proportional contributions of countless racial stocks. Why, then, this modern emphasis on racial and national integrity? It rests, of course, on the belief in the inherent superiority of some stocks over others, a belief which science refuses to support and popular opinion cannot agree upon. With the major exception of the American Negro, every people on earth believes it is at least the equal if not the superior in quality of every other people. Who can say which people, if any, is correct in its assumption of superiority? For the present we can only say that peoples vary in outward characteristics and may also vary in inner qualities, the latter being a pure assumption. Why worry, then, about race mixture?

The worry is due to both ignorance and disregard of history and the biological sciences. It has, however, some justification in its contribution to both group and individual welfare, for antagonism to biological amalgamation may aid in group survival through reinforcing group unity, and to individual success through avoidance of conflict with taboos, regardless of how irrational they may be in the light of biological science. In other words, while the biological defense of the doctrine advocating the maintenance of racial superiority through racial purity may not be attempted with success—and it is equally impossible to defend any doctrine of race improvement through race mixture—the social consequences of the amalgamation of varying stocks may be shown to be unfortunate in its consequences in specific instances.

BIOLOGICAL THEORIES OF RACE MIXTURE

The uncertain support of biological theories of the consequences of race mixture is made evident by the current existence of conflicting beliefs concerning its effects.[1] There is one school of thought which holds that race mixture, as such, produces offspring inferior to both parent groups; another, that the offspring are midway between the parent races; another, that they are, at least in some respects, superior to both parent races; and another, that the racial factor is of no significance whatever, and that only the quality of the individual parents need be considered. Only the last school has any reputable academic following today.

The leading scientific exponents of the first school, the one holding that mongrels, because they are mongrels, tend to inferiority, have been Jon A. Mjøen and C. B. Davenport. Dr. F. H. Hankins has summarized Professor Mjøen's position as

---

[1] For comprehensive discussions of the relation between race, race mixture, and group potentialities for the development of a complex and "great" civilization, see Eugene Pittard, *Race and History*, translated by V. C. C. Collum, Alfred A. Knopf, New York, 1926. Pittard includes a useful bibliography. See also Friedrich Hertz, *Race and Civilization*, translated by A. S. Levetus and W. Entz, The Macmillan Company, New York, 1928, pp. xii + 328. An extensive bibliography, valuable for its continental references, may be found at the end of each chapter. See further, F. H. Hankins, *The Racial Basis of Civilization*, Alfred A. Knopf, New York, 1926, pp. x + 384; Theophile Simar, *Étude critique sur la formation de la doctrine des races au XVIIIe siècle et son expansion au XIXe siècle*, Maurice Lamertin, Brussels, 1922, 403 pp. A publisher's announcement of a translation of this volume which, however, never appeared, has misled several American authors to the citation of an English edition which is highly desirable but not available. An extensive bibliography, rich in French and German references, is included. See also Jean Finot, *Race Prejudice,* translated by Florence Wade-Evans, Archibald Constable and Co., Ltd., London, 1906, pp. xvi + 320. A fourth French edition of *Le préjugé des races,* somewhat revised, was published in Paris by Felix Alcan in 1921, pp. xi + 543. The original edition was published in 1905, also in Paris.

follows: "Professor Jon A. Mjøen argues that the increased development in the F₁ generation in both animals and humans [an increased development which is not disputed] must be looked upon as abnormal and consequently as a source of weakness. Mjøen also argues that immunity against disease is reduced by crossing; that 'crossing between widely different races can lower the physical and mental level'; that 'prostitutes and the "unwilling to work" are found more frequently among types showing strong race mixture than among the relatively pure types'; that there is an increase in tuberculosis and other diseases as also a reduction in mental balance and vigor; and finally, that there is an increase in criminality as evidenced by increased tendency to lie, steal and drink to excess."[2] Dr. Davenport's position is typified by his findings in Jamaica, where he and Steggerda found the Negro-white mixtures inferior in many respects to either parent race.[3] There is no question concerning the factual findings of these men and of others who report similarly. Their interpretations of their facts in terms of race crossing, as such, are properly subject to criticism.

It is an accepted principle of biology that, barring inexplicable mutations, descendants in all living species are endowed with only inherent characteristics which were represented in the inherent qualities of their parents. When individuals of different "races" of hogs, sheep, chickens, cows, or horses are crossed—and our illustrations might have been taken from the plant kingdom as well—no new and peculiar qualities are thus produced. Fertility may be changed, probably increased, as may also size and vigor, particularly in the first hybrid generation. Increased variability in biological characteristics is also supposed to be an attribute of mixed peoples, although Dr. Herskovits has shown that this is not true of the American Negro, in spite of the Negro's known mixture with white and Indian blood, to say nothing of his

---

[2] F. H. Hankins, *op. cit.*, p. 337. Dr. Hankins cites as authority for his statements concerning Mjøen's position, "Harmonic and Disharmonic Race Crossings," *Eugenics in Race and State*, pp. 41-61, and "Harmonic and Unharmonic Crossing," *Eugenic Review*, 1922, vol. xiv, pp. 35-40.

[3] See chap. xii.

pre-slavery race crossings.[4] As students of race relations in the United States, we can afford to disregard the effects of race crossing on fertility, size, vigor, and variability until a relationship is established between them and group potentiality for absorbing and contributing to western culture. No biologist or physical anthropologist can claim that the effect of race crossing on these traits has significantly influenced the course of American history.

The claim, however, that mongrels are an "inharmonious" product of the ill-assorted amalgamation of divergent race traits is a challenge to the potentialities of any mixed people. It rests, however, too heavily on the measurement of group characteristics which are social as well as biological. Disease resistance, tuberculosis, mental stability, poverty and pauperism, inferior social status, have been found to be more prevalent in some mixed groups than in either parent race, but such phenomena as these are too largely dominated by the social environment to furnish much of a clue to the effects of race mixture. Only if the mixed group lived under identical environmental conditions, including the social as well as the physical, could they be ascribed to the process of race mixture. No study of race mixture which has been used to establish the claim that the amalgamation of widely differing races produces "inharmonious" offspring has ever found that parent and offspring groups were living under anything like identical social and economic circumstances. To maintain that this is because mixture itself makes it impossible is circular reasoning.

We shall have to be content with the conclusion of the biologists that neither group inbreeding nor group outbreeding is in itself harmful or beneficial. It depends on what stock one starts with. Unfortunately for many mixed peoples, their ancestors responsible for race crossing have not been of the better or even of the average quality of the parent races. Negro-white crossing in the United States, for example, has

[4] M. J. Herskovits, *op. cit.* This is by all odds the most careful study of race crossings in the United States. The results of several years of painstaking fieldwork are summarized and interpreted in social as well as in biological terms, yet the style is clear, the thought stimulating, and the book brief.

commonly been of the inferior white stock with perhaps a somewhat better selection of the colored stock. This generalized statement is not seriously disturbed by the common knowledge that numerous white people of superior achievement have been known to have had mulatto children. Race crossing takes place between the classes of the two groups which have the most contacts which may lead to familiarity, and these have been between the poorer whites and Negroes in the United States. Whatever selection of superior individuals has occurred has been of the better physical, and perhaps mental, types of Negroes, who because of their more attractive qualities were chosen by white people as their partners. It is well known, for example, that in the case of Negro-white marriages, it has been almost invariably the white man or woman who was the inferior mate. The tendency is that whenever a majority member "stoops" to sex relations with an individual of minority status, some selection is made on the basis of apparent superiority on the part of the "inferior" partner, but not in the case of the majority member, for all members of the "superior" group, no matter how debased, have a superior status by virtue of birth. In recent years, however, scientists have become more and more skeptical of the theory that class distinctions and acknowledged leadership are necessarily correlated with inherent ability, so that the tendency to negative selection among the majority, and positive selection among the minority, individuals responsible for race crossing may be based on cultural achievement and status unrelated to inherent qualities.

Whether or not there is any biological selection in race crossing, the general rule is that the parent on one side or the other, and frequently on both sides, is of inferior social status, and this fact alone would account for much of the apparent inferiority of human hybrids which Mjøen and Davenport ascribe to the biological effects of race mixture. Further, the status of the hybrid is likely to be less definite than that of either parent group. He is frequently illegitimate. If there are cultural differences, he is caught between two conflicting cultures. Having the blood but not the social status of the "superior" race, he may easily find himself unadjusted to the facts of his existence. The minority itself may spurn such bastards. Is it any wonder that human hybrids have been found who gave the appearance of "inharmonious" amalgams?

The final argument against the school of thought which asserts the inherent inferiority of mixed peoples because of their mixture is that the groups on which they base their defense are exceptional. Mixed races, after all, are the races which lead the world today in what we call civilization. If it be argued that these mixed peoples are mixtures of closely related parent groups, it may be pointed out that mulattoes in the United States, in South Africa, in Latin America, have been superior to the pure blacks in the achievement of material and intellectual success. Eurasians in Hawaii, in the Philippines, in the United States, and in those parts of Asia where they have not been made outcasts by a racially arrogant, pure-blood, dominant oriental majority, have shown themselves in no way biologically handicapped in the struggle for earthly rewards. If reference could be made only to the American mulatto, who is admittedly more successful than the full-blooded American Negro, the claim that race mixture is intrinsically harmful would be refuted, for where a group such as the human hybrid is a relative success in one place and relative failure in another, it is illogical to explain the failure, but not the success, in biological terms.

In the United States the social and economic position of mixed races of widely varying parent stocks is actually midway between the positions of the parent stocks. Popular prejudice relegated such hybrids to the caste of their socially inferior parent. Thus the mulatto is a Negro, the Eurasian an Oriental, the Indian-Negro a Negro, the Jew-Gentile a Jew, and so forth. The attempt to fix a special status for hybrids by the use of the names sambo, quadroon, octoroon, mulatto and mestizo, once all bases of class distinctions in the United States, has failed to the extent that few people today can accurately identify the type and degree of race mixture to which each refers. As caste distinctions decrease in rigidity it is more a matter of indifference with which parent group the mixed individual is identified, so that the Irish-American, German-American, and Italian-American are admitted to either majority or minority status. Where such indifference is displayed there can be no theory of harmful results of race crossing, although the Nordicists are fighting hard to instill a feeling of group consciousness and superiority into the tall, blond, blue-eyed, dolichocephalic north European. Thus far their efforts have been relatively fruitless, for the Nordic is continuing to intermarry quite freely and without social ostracism with all white stocks except the Jewish. When the Jewish and the colored groups are involved, but with the exception of the Indian, caste is lost by intermarriage, and the offspring are denied majority membership. They accept this minority membership perforce and sullenly, and disprove its logical basis by achieving a general level of success superior to that of their "inferior" parentage, although not equal to that of the majority.

If one believes in the inequality of races but has not been won to the view that race mixture is inherently harmful, it seems logical that mixed peoples should be midway in quality between their parent stocks. Since offspring inherit qualities from both father and mother, it is to be expected that mulattoes would be inferior to the white race but superior to the black. In confirmation of this theory are cited the achievements of whites, mulattoes, and pure Negroes, which rank in the order named. It is a mere assumption, however, to attribute this ranking to biological qualities, an assumption which is found to be unjustified when cultural factors are considered.

Mulattoes have always stood in a position which could well be envied by the unmixed Negro. They have been favored by the white man, sometimes because of blood relationship, and more frequently because of the inference that their white blood makes them superior to other Negroes. They have been in some instances educated by their white parents, who could not bring themselves to cast off entirely the obligations of kinship. They have been set up in business or in farming. They have been given favored positions as house servants and artisans under slavery and after. Most of all, since they look more like a white man than does the full-blood, it is assumed that they must be more like a white man, and therefore superior as employees. Even today the colored girl with European features and with a light skin can demand and obtain higher wages as a waitress, cook, or servant than the black girl. Colored men of pronounced white features also have the advantage over black men in obtaining the better-paid, more responsible positions available to Negroes in white industries. The common preference for the "mammy" type of servant or the "darkey" type of gardener, butler, odd-job man, and flunkey is not in opposition to this statement, for the very preference for these types helps keep them in the dead-end employments just mentioned, certainly not employments which lead to advancement. Dark Negroes themselves look up to and envy their lighter brothers, although they may hate them for their accidental advantage of complexion. The mixed Negro is also at a psychological advantage because he, too, believes in the superiority of the white man, feels that his white blood makes him superior, and knows that he is the recipient of extra favors from all sides because of his bi-racial parentage. If this is not sufficient to destroy the validity of the theory of an intermediate biological group, which depends so much on evidence of this nature, attention may be called to the fact that there has been no adequate proof of racial inferiority or superiority, so that there may consequently be no proof that mixed peoples are limited by birth to a position halfway between their parent races in quality.

There are but few adherents of the theory that the mixture of two widely varying races, say the white and the yellow, black or red, produces offspring superior to both parent stocks. There are, however, many who accept the belief that a mixture of racial stocks within one of the major color divisions leads to race improvement. Israel Zangwill's drama *The Melting Pot* did much to popularize this notion in the United States, where it has held the greatest sway. In essence, it holds that the United States has been a huge caldron in which the peoples of Europe have been poured, melted down, the dross drawn off, and the remainder, a superior blend of the best qualities of all European nationalities, has been saved to populate the country with a superrace. No doubt it is possible to fuse scrap metal, skim off the impurities, and produce an alloy of superior quality, but that has nothing to do with human biology. Analogies are dangerous, for to be used as proof they must logically be identities, which by definition they never are. Further, they are likely to carry conviction to the undiscriminating masses by their ease of superficial comprehension and by their dramatic qualities. We should not, however, be prejudiced against this theory merely because it was popularized by an analogy, but should look to see what true evidence there is in support of it.[5]

In brief, the evidence is that the mixed population of the United States has made remarkable material progress in the century and a half of its existence. As has been previously explained, this progress may better be attributed to an abundance of resources in comparison with the total population and to scientific and technical improvements in the arts which chanced to come to fruition during the few years of the existence of this country. A fusion of nationalities also chanced to occur at the same time, so that the one event might readily be mistaken for the result of the other. The further mistaken belief that inbreeding leads to hereditary degeneracy, and the corollary that outbreeding is an automatic remedy for biological weakness, has a share of the responsibility for the erstwhile popularity of the melting-pot theory. It may be accepted that inbreeding may produce a "double dose" of hereditary defects, but, with the exceptions of changes in fertility, size, vigor, and perhaps variability, which have just been pointed out as socially unimportant characteristics in the brief span of modern civilization, no possible improvement from race mixture has been scientifically demonstrated. When one crosses a breed of cattle known for its quantity production of milk, but not for richness of quality, with another breed known to produce a

---

[5] A thoroughgoing criticism of the melting-pot theory which, however, inclines too much toward the racial doctrine of north European supremacy for the present writer's taste, is H. P. Fairchild, *The Melting Pot Mistake*, Little, Brown, & Company, Boston, 1926, pp. vi + 266.

high butter-fat content in its milk, but little quantity, the result may be a hybrid characterized by the productivity of great quantities of milk with a high butter-fat content, one capable of producing but little milk and little butter-fat, or one ranking somewhere in between these two extremes. So when two human stocks are crossed it is a biological gamble as to whether the good, bad, or indifferent qualities of either or both parent groups will be preserved in the offspring. Of one thing we may rest assured, and that is that there will be no absolutely new features introduced by the crossing itself.

Since there is no biological evidence that mixed races are either hereditarily inferior to both parent stocks, intermediate between them or superior to them, the only remaining possibility is that it is the inherent quality of the individuals responsible for the crossing which matters. This may be disappointing to those who rested secure in the belief either that they possessed native greatness because of racial purity or that their supposed superior natural endowments were the result of a melting-pot process, but it may also give comfort to those who feared a poverty of capacity because of mixed ancestry. It assures no one of success or failure because of racial purity or racial crossing. It amounts to little more than the common-sense observation that biological inheritance is limited to direct ancestors and may not be extended to include contributions from an entire race. Individual variations in ability between members of the same race are far greater than any possible variations between the averages of two races. This being true, familial and not racial heredity must assume responsibility for the quality of human hybrids.

Were it not for the possibility that race crossing may be biologically selective, as previously suggested, the entire matter could be dismissed so far as biological evidence is concerned. The selection of human mates, however, is a complex affair, and the possibility that when races cross, inferior tends to mate with inferior, superior with superior, or inferior with superior, needs examination. The dominating race, of course, usually claims that only its inferior members would mate with racial inferiors. and that even its unregenerates select the su-

perior individuals of inferior racial status for such relationships. Such a tendency has been observed in numerous specific
illustrations of racial crossing. Unfortunately for the biological
aspects of this observation, civilized men select their wives
and mistresses more because of their social and their purely
physical attributes than for their mental qualities. Only by
some specious argument that sexually desirable social and
physical qualities are correlated with potential ability, a correlation which remains to be proved, could modern selection in
racial crossing be shown to be biologically significant. Here
again, no valid generalization can be made except that the
theories of Weismann and Mendel have accepted no amendments from Gobineau, Chamberlain, Mjøen, Davenport,
Grant, Stoddard, McDougall, et al.[6]

HE SOCIAL CONSEQUENCES OF RACE MIXTURE

Anthropologists insist that there is no great people which
is not a racial mixture so varied and complex that the relative
proportions of the contributing blood streams are hopelessly
lost. At best, the biological meaning of the term as applied to
mankind is only a group of mixed individuals who have been
so isolated in recent generations as to require a degree of
inbreeding sufficient to fix a limited number of distinguishing
hereditary characteristics so that their variations around a
norm will be somewhat restricted. At worst, it is used to refer
to a group politically unified or possessing a common language
or culture, a reference which has no biological significance
whatever unless by accident. How, then, has it come about
that serious thinkers have dared to interpret the history of
civilization as a function of hereditary racial qualities?

[6] The leading authorities holding the view that civilization is dependent on
race, including many more than those whose names are here mentioned, are
adequately discussed in the works of Hankins, Hertz and Simar previously
cited. A few of the more recent publications of this type may be listed: Madison
Grant, *The Passing of the Great Race*, Charles Scribner's Sons, New York,
1916, pp. xxi + 245; Lothrop Stoddard, *The Rising Tide of Color*, Charles
Scribner's Sons, New York, 1921, pp. xxxii + 320; J. W. Gregory, *The Menace
of Color*, J. B. Lippincott Company, Philadelphia, 1926, 264 pp.; and Hans F.
K. Günther, *The Racial Elements in European History*, translated by G. C.
Wheeler. E. P. Dutton & Co., Inc., New York, 1926, pp. vi + 279.

Aside from the will to believe in one's own innate superiority, and the psychological predilection of human failures and the insecure to the formation of "defense mechanisms," both of which are fundamental to the wide acceptance of racial doctrines, history and contemporary culture lend credence to a racial interpretation of history. Have not the world's greatest recorded cultures been the product of white peoples? Certainly our history texts and courses by their neglect of oriental and African history and their emphasis on the ancient civilizations of the white man alone do little to contradict this belief. This emphasis is perhaps justified by the fact that our own direct cultural ancestors are of the greatest importance to us and that but few records of the civilizations of colored peoples are available. Justified or not, such an attitude, carried as it is throughout our literature, tends to create a racial arrogance in the white reader and student. Further, is not modern civilization the product not only of the white man, but especially of the north European white man? Have not the greatest contributions to "progress"—progress is such a difficult word to define—been made by the Nordic, the Aryan, the Teuton, the Celt, the Gaul, the Greek, the Etruscan, the Iberian, or, more recently, the American? It matters little to group patriots that the nations called Nordic are racially mixed or that the Nordics were "savages" when Greece and Rome were in their glory. They have but recently and grudgingly come to admit that "Aryan" refers to a language and that there is no such race. What difference does it make to the race-proud Frenchman that the Celts and Gauls have an unknown racial origin? More than five hundred students of the author continued to rank the "American" as the superior "race" *after* completing a course on race relations! The "will to believe" the personally most favorable interpretation of history is strong!

History has been interpreted in terms of the "great man," of climate and geographical resources, of cultural diffusion, of the differential birth rate, and of heaven knows how many other "principal factors," but none of these affords such a sense of personal satisfaction and security to a superficially educated democracy as the one in terms of race. It is comforting to think that the leading civilizations of the past arose because of the superior quality of their people, usually white, and declined because of infusions of inferior blood, for if this is true, then the civilization of our own race may be eternally maintained by the simple expedient of group inbreeding.

The golden age of Greece must have been the product of the innate superiority of the Athenians, for what other people has produced fourteen "geniuses" in such a brief span of years? It is pertinent to point out that probably not more than two of these fourteen geniuses were Athenians except by adoption, just as the geniuses of Germany have not all been unmixed Teutons, those of France not all Celts and Gauls, those of England not of unmixed British stock, and those of the United States not all "native sons." If an explanation of Greek supremacy is required, need we look to racial hypotheses when it is evident that a factor more susceptible to proof is at hand, namely, the location of Greece at the crossroads of the world in her time? Located as they were, the Athenians attracted to their midst not only world commerce but also the great thinkers and the material and intellectual inventions of the world. A similar phenomenon can be observed in the history of Paris, London, and New York. Could any of these cities have achieved their greatness if the impossible had occurred, and exactly the same people had made their homes in Central Africa, Asia, or Australia? The crossroads of the world have moved their position with every major change in demand for resources, improvement in communication, and advance in the economic arts. Egypt, Persia, Babylon, India, China, Rome, Venice, Spain, and France, to cite but a few of the many possible illustrations, were at the world crossroads in their day, rose to glory because of the pyramiding of cultural advantages, and faded not because of racial impurities but because the world moved on.[7]

[7] An opposing point of view to that of the present author is expressed by Professor East when he writes as follows:

"The general attitude of society towards creative work may have had much to do with giving a Golden Age to Greece, a Renaissance to Italy, an Elizabethan period to England, a Napoleonic Era to France; but the essential

England may be cited as a modern example of the same process. Her resources and location made it possible, almost inevitable, that she should be the mistress of the seas, the leader of the Industrial Revolution, the world banker, the center of learning, art, and literature for a little while. An island without the natural resources demanded by modern industry, such as copper, oil, or a climate suitable for cotton, she seems doomed to comparative unimportance as contrasted with her pre-World War rôle. Has there been a racial change? Yes, her world preeminence has introduced some new blood, but the recent mixture has been proportionately slight compared with those of more than two centuries ago. Her mantle seems to be falling on the United States, and we shall no doubt accept it as a tribute to our racial superiority, blissfully indifferent to the knowledge that it is not only second hand, but more worn than that, for has it not been the property of at least a dozen peoples within the past three millennia?

If this be an economic interpretation of history, make the worst of it. It is intended, however, to be no more than a purgative emphasis on locality, natural resources, and cultural concentration as factors in the development of civilizations far more potent than race. Why blame the fall of Egypt on an admixture of Negro blood, as has been done? Who were these Roman citizens, that they built so well, only to fall victims to a declining birth rate among the pure patricians, the increase of slaves, and wandering hordes from the north? Did world conquest destroy the Persians by its accompanying race mix-

requisites for each was the inherent greatness of a few individuals, a biological greatness which passes, leaving us to mourn. Were this not true, why is it that Italy and Greece are but shadows of their former selves? Can any one seriously maintain that either country, now immensely expanded in population, does not give the same opportunities for creative work that it gave some centuries ago? Galton concluded that the ablest race in history was built up in Attica between 530 B.C. and 430 B.C., when from 45,000 free-born males surviving the age of 50 there came 14 of the most illustrious men of history. Today we look at Greece, and with incredible naïveté ask why Greece has fallen from her proud estate. The answer is simple. The Greece of today is biologically different from the Greece of Pericles. The peculiar combinations of germ-plasm which gave her a commanding position have segregated out and disappeared." E. M. East, *Heredity and Human Affairs*, Charles Scribner's Sons, New York, 1927, pp. 165-166.

ture? Every leading civilization, from the time of the supremacy of China to the present, rose to its greatest heights while the process of race mixture was taking place, and has remained nationally feeble ever since its fall, in spite of the fact that race mixture practically ceased in every case at the time of its decline. Perhaps it may be said that once the mixture took place, all hope of revival was lost. Strange, is it not, since every one of which we have record was a racial *mélange* centuries before its flame burned brightest. Perhaps we may be permitted to change the metaphor and describe, no doubt as some racial theorists would, the final outburst of grandeur as the swan song of a dying people. It is discouraging for the racial purists that the song has not customarily been most beautiful while the people were at the height of their "untainted vigor."

It has been said that when two peoples come to occupy the same territory their biological intermixture is inevitable. This does not mean that they will invariably intermingle their bloods freely, nor that there are not instances in which social barriers of caste are so impassable as to be more difficult to overcome than a geographical barrier of ocean, mountain, or desert was before the development of communication. For practical purposes, however, social isolation, supported only by ancestral distinctions of breed without the aid of physical ramparts, is never absolute. Even royalty has been known to mate with commoner. Sexual adventures into forbidden fields are too attractive for many reasons to expect that an entire race will observe a taboo of endogamy.

Race contacts which result from exploration, immigration, and from military expeditions have customarily included an excess of males among the mobile group. The sex impulse is a constant factor in the lives of men, and history tells us that where women of their own stock are not available not all males whose home family relations have been broken or interrupted will refrain from accepting the favors of such women as they may find. Soldiers and sailors on foreign soil have been responsible for much race mixture, usually but not always of an illicit nature. The hardy adventurers who first settled the eastern region of the United States, and their successors, the pioneers of the West, began a mixture of white and Indian blood which is not likely to cease until the Indian has disappeared from this country. Later pioneers, known by the less heroic name of immigrant, also found it inconvenient to be always accompanied by their womenfolk, but few remained celibate on that account. A group with a sex ratio well over a hundred in a strange land where tradition is a faulty, inadequate guide, never fails to include some who doubt the need for racial purity or are callous concerning their responsibility for mongrel offspring.

Traditional attitudes toward race mixture and morality are a more effective means of social control in a community which solidly accepts them than when they are the mental baggage of migrants of scorned minority status. The pressure of public opinion does not lie so heavily on those who have moved away from relatives and friends, and by so doing acquired a concealing mantle of relative anonymity to cloak their adventures. Taught to observe some particular sexual code, the migrant frequently finds himself surrounded by respectable people who have no respect for the peculiarities of his beliefs. Doubts arise, and without the restraining force of public disapproval, the most is made of them. A Jew may marry a *goy*, a Chinaman a white girl, an Italian a Protestant American, or a Magyar someone of less vaunted ancestry in this country, while at home such a *mésalliance* would have been unthinkable. A marriage or illicit relationship which at home would have meant disgrace and ostracism involves a much lesser penalty here, or none at all.

Yet it is not only the migrant who is responsible for the initiative in race mixture. The presence of minority women of inferior social status is a temptation to illicit relationships, for such women are held cheap by the men of the higher social classes, who feel less compunction about their seduction than they would regarding women of their own class. The white man's attitude toward Negro womanhood reminds one of the ancient code of chivalry which recognized no obligation of decency or humanity toward members of the weaker sex unless of superior caste. Women of an inferior out-group seem to be considered legitimate prey to superior males who readily rationalize despicable conduct. Why bother about a few more fatherless halfbreeds born to squaws, niggers, greasers, wops, and such? Women of inferior status who under a more normal social environment would effectively resist illicit advances are made more amenable to such suggestions by the handicaps of the majority attitude toward them. This does not mean that a very large proportion of native white people or of any minority participate in race mixture. The proportion of such individuals, while unknown, is probably small, but it is a major source of miscegenation.

Many white people find Negroes of either sex so repulsive that they honestly wonder how it is possible that there are so many mulattoes in the United States. The Oriental, the Mexican, the Jewish, and some other of the recent immigrant types affect numerous individuals of old American stock in a somewhat similar way. Minorities, it has been suggested, gradually come to accept American standards of attractiveness. The native, of course, has developed these standards to begin with, and when minority appearance with regard to physical features, dress, and manners is too "outlandish" there is likely to be a sexual repulsion of great effectiveness in limiting race mixture. Two conditions, however, in addition to the high sex ratio and weakening of tradition already mentioned, make it possible for this initial repulsion to be overcome. First, familiarity with minority characteristics changes one's perspective, so that what were previously disgusting habits of behavior and dress and repulsive physical qualities may soon become matters of indifference or even positive attractions. Second, minorities quickly begin to approximate the majority in appearance through acculturation and interbreeding.

The Negro, perhaps because he is least like the native white stock in appearance, affords the most clear-cut illustration of this process. The thick lips, kinky hair, dark skin, bodily odor, group customs, and manners of the relatively pure-blooded Negro in the United States are not normally sexually attractive to the white man. Yet there are millions of mulattoes living in the United States, and it is an obviously farcical rationalization to account for their presence in terms of "pathological miscegenation." Some Negroes had white blood before they were brought to this country. A large proportion of the increase in mulattoes in the United States has come about through the intermarriage of mulattoes and without the direct infusion of any more white blood than there was in the parent generation. The racial repulsion of the Negro must have been overcome in thousands of white men who had the excuse of neither a high sex ratio nor of restraints broken through migration. Naturally, many of the race crossings were between white men and mulattoes with a minimum of Negroid features and characteristics. The black girl, however, has not been without her white lovers.

Slavery, with its compulsory interdependence of black and white, gave both the opportunity for miscegenation and the familiarity which removed the repelling force of Negro habits and features. Since the Negro's introduction to the United States there has never been a time when there were no opportunities, even necessities, for interracial familiarities, without "social obligations," which reduced the psychological prominence of race differences. Meanwhile, Negroes have been gradually approaching the white man's standards of attractiveness as they have learned what kind of clothes to wear, how to bleach their skin artificially, how to straighten their hair, how to speak good English, how to conduct themselves as the white man prefers, and, not the least of all, by the infusion and diffusion of white blood in their veins with a consequent increase in their interracial attractiveness.

With the major difference that the original racial distinctions were not so startling, this process has been taking place in regard to the factors facilitating group crossing between every other minority and the native white stock. In every case, whatever initial repulsion may have existed has gradually been reduced in effectiveness by familiarity, assimilation, and amalgamation. Unquestionably there would be some race mixture in the United States without the encouragement of any of these three factors, but the amount would be reduced by their absence, and the social penalties and individual psychological maladjustments incident to miscegenation at the same time might be expected to be materially increased. We should still be a mongrel nation, biologically speaking, but with a smaller proportion of mongrels produced by recent direct crossing.

The desire for variety in sexual experience has probably been overemphasized as a cause of racial crossing. There is more reason to believe that relatively few individuals actually desire a variety of sexual experiences, but rather that man is readily conditioned to seek somewhat uniform sex stimuli and responses. Sex fetishes related to articles of dress, odors, physical qualities, personal mannerisms, etc., are easy to acquire, and commonly become a practical necessity in cohabitation. This, of course, tends to decrease direct race mixture unless offset by other factors.

There is no need to fall back on some hypothetical, innate desire for variety of experience to explain interracial marriages and illicit relations. In addition to the factors already mentioned, there is a positive attraction between individuals of different races or nationalities in the attendant slighter influence of inhibitions and restraints, with a consequent greater freedom for a natural and unhampered expression of the sexual impulse. It has already been suggested that the American Negro's relative lack of sexual fetters may explain a considerable amount of miscegenation. Even a different set of fetters, which may be mistaken for an absence of restraint and frequently means the absence of the particular fetters which have been inhibiting an individual in his relations with women of his own group, can serve as a release. Thus, to a man chafing under the sexual restraints of a New England community, the equally severe restraints of the Spanish may spell freedom. Further, inferior social status in a sexual partner may break chains which permit no normal sexual expression with a person of equal social status subject to the same moral code.

The last few paragraphs have perhaps reinforced the popular impression that in race crossing the man is usually of superior social status compared to that of the woman involved. While this is true, its interpretation is a matter of dispute. The prevailing double standard of morality, condoning violations of the code by a man which would be utterly condemned in a woman, naturally has greater force in restraining women than men from illicit sex indulgence. This, for example, is one reason why marriages between colored and white people in the United States more often involve white women and colored men than the reverse. A man of superior status is less likely than a woman of his class to feel the need of marriage to lend whatever sanctity is possible to a mixed relationship, while the women of inferior status, knowing their inferiority and respecting the man's superiority, can hardly demand marriage. The explanation, then, of this sexual disproportion in race mixture is cultural rather than biological. Women have no more of an innate disgust or aversion for relations with members of a different race than have men. The popular belief to the contrary is largely the product of a masculine hope and egoism which has interpreted a phenomenon of feminine education and economic dependence as an inherited preference.

It might seem that these factors of abnormal sex ratios, anonymity and cultural change in migrants, increasing interracial familiarity through contacts which are unavoidable, and the positive attractions of miscegenation through their peculiar freedom from irksome restraints and inhibitions, would lead to the rapid and unavoidable intermixture of all groups living in a given community. In a sense this is correct, but it must not be forgotten that there are also forces which tend to preserve racial purity. They are never one hundred per cent effective, but they exert a restraining influence which must not be underestimated.

Perhaps the least of these restraining forces is the law. A majority of the states in this country have enacted "racial integrity" legislation. According to Professor Reuter, there are twenty-nine states which have laws prohibiting the intermarriage of whites and Negroes, including all of the southern and most of the western states.[8] In Arizona, Indians, Mongolians,

[8] E. B. Reuter, *Race Mixture*, McGraw-Hill Book Company, Inc., New York, 1931, p. 82.

and Negroes, and their descendants, are not permitted to marry white persons. In Georgia a white person may not marry an individual with even a trace of African, West Indian, Asiatic Indian, or Mongolian blood. In Louisiana neither Indians nor white persons may marry anyone with a trace of African ancestry. In Nevada, a state not otherwise noted for its defense of the marriage bond, members of the black, brown, yellow, and red races may not marry a white person. Oregon includes persons of one-fourth or more Negro, Chinese or Kanaka, or more than one-half Indian blood in the forbidden class. In South Dakota a member of the Caucasian race may not marry an African, Korean, Malayan, or Mongolian. In Pennsylvania there are no legal restrictions on interracial marriages at all. In other states even illicit sexual relations between members of different races are subject to special punishment, as in Florida, where adultery between a Negro and a white person may be penalized by twelve months' imprisonment or a fine of one thousand dollars. The legal definition of the "inferior" race may include any degree of mixture from one-half down to the slightest trace. A forbidden interracial marriage may be void from the beginning without specific legal prosecution, or it may be necessary to institute suit to establish the facts. The penalty may run as high as several years' imprisonment and a heavy fine.[9]

Such legislation is little more than a political gesture, satisfying to prejudiced white constituents who feel that "there ought to be a law" against race mixture, but who do not realize that actual marriage has contributed but a trifle to the amount of colored blood which has been diluted by white in the United States. There are few marriages between white and colored people in the northeastern states where the law is silent on the question. Possibly, in the eyes of rabid racial enthusiasts, if only one mixed marriage is prevented by legal enactment, the law is justified. It would be difficult, however, to justify such an extreme position, at least until illicit interracial relationships in the southern and western states had

[9] *Ibid.*, chap. iv, pp. 75-103. All specific references to state interracial legislation in this paragraph are taken from this source.

been reduced to a number of interracial marriages as small as that in the northeast. Even where there are no laws against miscegenation, public sentiment is an effective barrier against it. In every state in the Union there is public opposition adequate to keep marriages between white and colored people at a biologically unimportant minimum regardless of the law, but there is no state which has developed a public sentiment against illicit race mixture sufficient to prevent extensive miscegenation. Those who fear race mixture should remember that biology never inquires into the legal status of mates.

Public sentiment against race mixture is not restricted to members of the white majority. To the degree that colored minorities have achieved group consciousness they, too, penalize severely their members who form legal or illicit alliances with individuals of other groups, including the yellow as well as the white. The common assumption of white people that every Negro would like, whether he admits it or not, to obtain a mate from the superior majority is erroneous. During slavery a white lover even outside of the bonds of matrimony conveyed a certain prestige. Today there is a tendency to conceal such relations by the colored partner who wishes to avoid ostracism by Negroes themselves, except among some of the very inferior classes. Among the more substantial Negroes, regardless of the behavior of a handful of emancipated Harlemites and their like in other cities, it is fatal to the social and business standing of a Negro to be suspected of familiarity with a white person of the opposite sex. Negroes are not ignorant of the fact that few if any white people attempt to mix with them socially unless they wish to write a book or find a colored lover; and they have in consequence erected a barrier between the races which is practically impassable, except for superficial contacts, to the best-intentioned white person in the world. This barrier is now so strong that Professor Herskovits believes it sufficient, as a supplement to the white attitude, to prevent further serious dilution of Negro blood with white by direct intermixture.

According to Herskovits, "The pressure within the Negro community, as well as that of the larger community of which it forms a part, against sexual relations between Negroes and Whites, is of great importance in this connection [his claim that American Negro inbreeding differs only in degree from that of a geographically isolated group]. I do not mean, of course, that there is a complete cessation of such mixture; for it seems unlikely that this will ever come about, no matter how strong the social disapprobation may become. But I believe that the amount of crossing at present is negligible in comparison with what it was in the time of slavery and shortly thereafter, and I further believe that these results [of the study of Negro's physical type] point to such a conclusion.

"It might be argued that my work was done among university students, in families which were firmly established both in the city and in the country, and that in such groups one would expect more rigid standards and fewer interracial meetings. But if we consult Dr. Ruth Reed's study of the unmarried mother in Harlem, we find that in five hundred cases of illegitimate birth among Negro women, only eight of the fathers were white men. I have talked to a large number of Southerners who might be expected to know the amount of racial crossing in the South, and they agree that the amount of illicit relationship, with resulting primary crosses, is amazingly small, although it is certainly larger than Dr. Reed found to be the case in New York."[10]

Such race consciousness, strong enough to be considered by Professor Herskovits as an approximate substitute for geographical isolation in fixing the American Negro as a physical type, is less developed in the Negro than in the Oriental. Unlike the Negroes, the Chinese and Japanese have not forgotten their original cultures. They have not the tradition of slavery and inferiority which might make them look on interracial alliances as elevating rather than as degrading. Practically all Orientals are so unsophisticated—in our eyes—as to consider themselves and their history superior to the white man and his recent industrial culture. Here, then, is another minority barrier to race mixture. It is a barrier which may be encountered among all minorities to a greater or lesser degree,

[10] M. J. Herskovits, *op. cit.*, pp. 30-31.

depending on the extent of their American acculturation, the pressure against them as minorities, and their similarity in appearance to the native white majority. It is a thousandfold more effective in keeping down race mixture than any conceivable legislation.

There is a real basis and justification for popular pressure against the mixture of peoples who may readily be distinguished from each other either because of racial features or because of cultural differences. Neither the direct participants in such marriages or illicit unions, nor their children, are in a position favorable to personal happiness or material success. There are cultural standards prevailing in the United States and in most other countries which will not permit felicitous interracial unions. The fact that they are cultural obstacles must not be used to minimize their significance, for cultural facts are as substantial barriers in human relations as granite mountains. Further, so long as group solidarity has any survival value for the individual, it is dangerous to allow it to be weakened by the tolerance of intergroup relations destructive of unity.

Sex relations, legal or otherwise, involve a readjustment of personality and behavior in terms of the sex partner. The readjustments go so far as to involve relatives, friends, and acquaintances. The marriage of a native white American with an Italian, an Irishman, or a Mexican, for illustration, promptly brings up the question of religion, for the native is likely to be a Protestant and the alien a Catholic. If both partners take their religion seriously, but marry nevertheless, there is an immediate conflict which may be mitigated by true affection, but not eliminated. As has been remarked, marriage involves enough adjustments without incurring the extra risks of theological differences. This, of course, is only one of the added risks of intergroup marriages, for there are hundreds of other possibilities of friction in cultural differences, such as those concerning the relative status of husband, wife, and children, the standard of living, patriotism, and even favorite foods. Since every minority of racial and national origin has cultural standards which differ from those of other minorities and the majority of native white stock, the chances of domestic felicity in intergroup unions are materially reduced.

If, however, the sexual partners themselves are so happy as to overcome their personal differences of culture, relatives and associates must be reckoned with. Even a father, mother, brother, or sister, to say nothing of mere acquaintances, has less incentive to "put up" with "peculiarities" in an addition to the family circle through marriage. The tolerant force of personal affection is needed to overcome group suspicions and the annoyance of "outlandish" habits and, perhaps, appearance. An example of a Catholic-Protestant marriage comes to mind, where the couple themselves never gave the slightest outward indication of any marital rift, but the Protestant relatives, of fine old American stock, never accepted the Catholic bride. They even went so far as to ascribe immorality to her, claiming the connivance of her family and priest, "so that there would be Catholic children to inherit Protestant property"—all without any evidence whatever. This, of course, is not an inevitable consequence of Catholic-Protestant marriages, but it illustrates a marital danger which would have been avoided had this Italian Catholic girl married a fellow Catholic, and had the American Protestant boy married a Protestant. There is no need to prove the point up to the hilt by adding illustrations of the same dangers lurking in Jewish-Gentile, Oriental-white, or Negro-white marriages. Even Indian-white marriages, now commonly accepted as proper, are not free from the dangers of cultural conflict unless the Indian has become completely Europeanized or the white partner completely acculturated to Indian customs and beliefs. The family may be a social unit, but it is one which can function smoothly only if it has the cooperation of the community in which it resides.

The terms "half-breed" and "mongrel" have not acquired their sinister connotations out of thin air. Children of mixed marriages are much more likely to be social liabilities than those whose parents accept a common culture. Of course, the usual interpretation of this fact ascribes it to a mixture of bloods when it is the mixture of cultures which is to blame. Children do not just grow up into stalwart citizens; they require guidance. Where the influences of father and mother are at cross-purposes there are bound to be greater chances for the children to reject the guidance of both. The crime rate for children born in this country of foreign or mixed percentage, higher than that of either parent group, is evidence of this fact.

Supplementary to this form of cultural maladjustment is the likelihood of personality disturbances. Where class and caste distinctions between the parent groups are slight, as between the Irish and German Catholics, the aristocratic Portuguese Jew and the American Gentile, the Swede and the Englishman, the accompanying problems of personality adjustment are perhaps no more serious than when an heiress marries a chauffeur, or a college professor an illiterate waif. When, however, marriages or illict sex relations occur between individuals of sharply differentiated cultures the resulting children will find themselves in an unfortunate situation. As Professor Reuter has put it, "The mixed-blood individual is in a fundamental sense a member of different and exclusive groups. Each group has its rules and definitions in accordance with which the wishes must find their satisfaction; each impresses a set of beliefs and behavior standards; each develops a body of sentimental loyalties. As an aspirant for membership in the culturally advanced group, the mixed-blood approves and upholds its ideals and standards. But as a member of a special caste or as an unaccommodated member of the excluded racial group, he embodies the ideal and standards of the minority. Thus, within the individual, incident to the real or potential membership in opposing groups, there is mental disorder, a conflict between opposing group loyalties. In last analysis the conflict is but the counterpart of the external situation. The covert conflict is irresolvable so long as the mixed blood is denied admittance to the idealized group and remains unaccommodated to the other.

"Individual escape takes varied forms, which do not require enumeration here. This tendency to overcompensation for inferiority status is familiar to every observer of racial and social phenomena, as is also the tendency toward formalism, bohemianism, egocentrism, and introversion.

"The mixed blood is thus an unadjusted person. His immediate group has no respected place in the society. In ideals and aspirations he is identified with the culturally dominant group; in social rôle and cultural participation he is identified with the excluded group. He is, in consequence, a man of divided loyalties. It is only when the resulting conflict is resolved by the mixed blood's accommodation to the socially defined place—membership in, and leadership of, the backward group—only when he identifies himself with it, participates in life on that basis, and finds the satisfaction of his wishes in that group organization that he escapes the conflict resulting from his divided heritage. It is only through an identification of himself with the social group to which the social definitions consign him that he can find a tolerable life and develop a wholesome personality."[11]

Historically speaking, group pride and prejudice has been a much more useful means for social control than it is today in any industrialized nation. When each community, nation, or race lived as an independent population unit, and the gain of one, such as the acquisition of additional territory, was the loss of another, group integrity was a social asset. Now, however, there is a division of labor not only between individuals in the same ethnic unit but also between nations and peoples. Today native white American, immigrant, Indian, Oriental, and Negro prosper or join the unemployed as the nation is economically sound or disorganized. Economic depression in the United States is reflected in Bolivian tin mines, Argentine wheat and cattle ranches, Brazilian rubber and coffee plantations, Japanese silk markets, African diamond workings, and so on. The United States in turn is not independent of prosperity abroad.

The old tooth-and-claw struggle for survival in competition with neighboring peoples is giving way to the necessity for intergroup cooperation, a demand of industrial specialization.

[11] E. B. Reuter, op. cit., pp. 215-216.

The old hatreds between French and German, Italian and Austrian, white man and black, Occidental and Oriental, once meant great gain for the top dog, but now spell starvation for both victor and vanquished. The refusal of the United States to recognize Soviet Russia has gained us little, and has had to be modified by hypocritical commercial relations through a kind of back-door arrangement. Tariff barriers similarly seem to cost more than they gain, for retaliation is easy by nations which produce commodities we need and are purchasers of our products as well as competing producers for our markets. The significance of all this in the problems of race mixture lies in the fact that the attendant group contacts break down social as well as political barriers and destroy the necessity for group integrity. Indeed, they make it impossible.

As the need and possibility of political isolation—call it nationalism or provincialism if you will—are in the process of destruction, so class and caste distinctions have already come to be recognized as hindrances to progress. Democracy is an empty word unless it means the free recognition of ability, native and acquired, whether it be found in rich or poor, alien or native, black man or white. Minorities in the United States consume as much of our national wealth as they are permitted by group prejudices and productive capacity. When their productivity is artificially held far below their potentialities, the final result is not that there is more left for a dog-in-the-manger majority, but that a selfish majority is defeating its own purpose by limiting the total national productivity to the detriment of the welfare of American residents as a whole. The days are gone when one class in the western world may long prosper at the expense of the masses.

Temporary and individual gain, however, may still result from holding tight the lines of race and nationality. For example, labor as a whole suffers from the exclusion of Negroes and other minorities from the benefits of union organization, but individual workers may for a time ride along in an impermanent security from minority competition. It is this ever-present possibility of immediate gain which helps keep alive a belief in the value of racial solidarity even where economic forces may be shown to make it a detriment rather than an advantage in mass competition. Industrialism and the consequent detailed division of labor are recent inventions of mankind, and it will be long before the lessons of intergroup cooperation which they are teaching us will be learned so thoroughly that race mixture will be freely permissible.

What of the outcome of this struggle between the forces tending toward race mixture and those conducive to a maintenance of racial purity? Unless there be another economic revolution, no less radical than the Industrial Revolution, it seems that the increasing interdependence of all mankind will eventually—far in the distant future—convince the civilized world of the essential unity of the human race. The idea is growing in prevalence, and race mixture is keeping pace with it. For the present, however, and until cultural conflicts have been materially reduced, the individual who mixes his blood with that of another group of racial or national origin must run the danger of bringing a curse of personal unhappiness and social ostracism upon himself and upon his children. He may find compensating satisfactions in so doing, and he may be doing humanity a service in speeding the day when caste and class lines will have dwindled to nothingness, but to those who believe that the cost of such martyrdom far exceeds the gain, the sacrifice will hardly recommend itself.

CHAPTER XII

RACE AND ABILITY

A LEADING anthropologist, Dr. Clark Wissler, has said that one of the outstanding cultural traits of the United States is a blind belief in education as the key to individual progress and the solution of all social ills. Centuries hence, long after the boasted civilization of America has gone the way of Egypt, Babylon, Greece, and Rome, some archæologist coming upon a university library miraculously preserved will be dumfounded and amused by the naïve faith of an entire nation confident that the one perfect social food and medicine combined was served by its schools.

If we were to survey the accomplishments of formal education in regard to race relations during the past century or more, this faith in education would be severely shaken. The first thing we should discover, and one which has been generally overlooked, is the relative unimportance of the classroom in the creation of social attitudes. The growing child learns more, and more readily, from his parents and playmates than from his teacher and his schoolbooks about the supposed qualities of Indians, Negroes, Jews, and other minority peoples. How easy would it be, for illustration, to root out by schoolroom methods alone the eastern youngster's idealized mental image of the storied redskin? The southern concept of the Negro is driven solidly into children's minds by word and deed almost from the day of birth, and no course in anthropology or other social science is likely to do more than produce a superficial lip service to academic fact in students with a lifelong, penetrating background of racial prejudice. The teachers themselves are of the same stuff as their community and cannot be expected to break the chain of public opinion. Change through the school must necessarily be slow.

GENERALIZATIONS ON THE MENTALITY OF PEOPLES

As a rule, what is taught in the classroom about race and race relations is no more than a humanized reflection of popular beliefs. A few individuals may take a different approach, and a few special courses on immigration, the Negro, and other subjects in which race and racial achievement may be mentioned, can be found, but they are limited in number. Judging by the time and emphasis given them, they cannot be said to be an important part of present curricula. Perhaps nothing else should be expected, for an important function of the school is to fit the child to live in harmony with his neighbors, not to fight against their traditional attitudes. The teacher too far out of line with the accepted standards of the community and its school board may expect to be asked to "tone down" or look for a new job.

Our schools of all degrees should serve several purposes in the training of our youth, regardless of race, nationality or group prejudices. These purposes may roughly be described as how to make a living, how to live as a community member, and how to get the maximum enjoyment out of life. Granting these purposes, it might be assumed that they would be equally applicable to all individuals regardless of color or national origin, but while this may be true in theory, it certainly is not so in practice in the United States.

Minority groups are usually at the bottom of the economic and social scale. They are handicapped by a lack of familiarity with the customs and standards of the dominant group, by a lack of established relatives and friends, and by the unwillingness of prejudice to grant equality of opportunity. Recent immigrants and the colored races may be welcomed as laborers in unpleasant, rough jobs when there is plenty of work to go around, but there is effective resentment against them when they are too successful, or unemployment becomes pronounced. The result is that their income and living standards are lower than the average, and their first problem is that of making a living. Consequently public opinion stresses the necessity for minority group education which will be of economic value, and pays little attention to formal training which will help them to get the maximum enjoyment out of life.

Minority peoples are usually socially as well as economically maladjusted. Crime rates may seem too high, as among immigrants and Negroes. Housing and health are likely to be inferior. Family and moral standards leave much to be desired. In short, all kinds of social behavior out of line with the standards of the majority tend to become apparent to the country as a whole. The mass answer to conditions such as these is an educational program which will, in theory, eliminate these social ills.

For the white immigrant who is patently handicapped by foreign language and tradition, attention has been centered on school work which will increase his familiarity with the English language and with American ideals. It is dimly realized that in a few generations he will be absorbed into the total white population, and immediate efforts are made to speed up and facilitate his cultural assimilation.

The Negro, however, is looked on as more of a biological problem, debarred by color from ultimate absorption and limited by inherited mental inferiority in the acquisition of formal education. The Oriental is also thought to be barred from absorption by his color, but even race prejudice has been unable to convince the masses of his inherent inferiority in view of past centuries of Chinese achievement and the rapid rise of modern Japan. The Indian is popularly conceded to be worthy of whatever education he will accept, although in the early days of this country he was put on a par with the Negro. The Mexican educational problem has not yet intruded itself on the popular consciousness. All of these generalizations are false or unproved to the extent to which they are supposed to rest on inborn mental traits.

If there is any necessity for special educational treatment for any immigrant or racial group in the United States it must be based on cultural divergencies and not on racial traits. Undoubtedly the newly arrived Italian immigrant may profit by special courses in history, civics, hygiene, and English. So may immigrants from any part of the world, and many of our native population as well. While the colored child may also be expected to gain by special schoolroom and curricular attention, the benefit from exceptional programs is less pronounced and may be outweighed by the injurious results of separate treatment of Negro and white students. All this amounts to nothing more than saying that throughout the country there are differences in background among white and colored, native and foreign born, which must be taken into account in the school system. So long as social classes exist teachers will have to allow for group differences which they create and represent. Racial groupings in this respect are not peculiar.

Allowances must also be made for individual differences in pupils. It is in many ways foolish to attempt to teach children of all degrees of intelligence in the same class and then expect results equal to those which might have been attained by a system of selection based on mentality. If, as many people believe, there is a correlation between inherent potential ability, race, and nationality, it logically follows that to mix children from all parts of the world indiscriminately in the same school classes is unwise.

The belief that humanity has by nature been divided and subdivided into races and subraces, each of which varies in mental qualities and handicaps from the others, is so widespread and at the same time so forcefully challenged, that some reasonably accurate conclusions concerning its validity must be reached before education and race relations may be discussed.

Beliefs in the mental inequality of races have not been based on the result of scientific investigation. Very few scientists have been willing to make any such generalizations, and those who have done so have bolstered rather than created popular beliefs in sympathy with their findings. Logically, one would expect that actual inherent mental differences would lead to racial discrimination. As a matter of fact, it is race prejudice which has caused the acceptance of the doctrine of inherent mental differences.

Practically every large group of people in the world believes itself equal if not superior to all others, perhaps with the exception of those who, like the American Negro, have been taught to accept their unproved inferiority by a dominant class. "The chosen people" were complacently certain that they were the anointed of God. The British sincerely believe their rule in India, Egypt, and South Africa to be a part of the "white man's burden." Germans feel the heavy responsibility of pushing forward their *Kultur*. The Japanese, so self-assured that they have been called the "Germans of the Orient," have no doubt about their powers. Teutonism, Anglo-Saxonism, Slavism, Iberianism, Nordicism, and Aryanism—and perhaps we should now add Mussolini's Italianism and the "manifest destiny" of the white American—are racial doctrines similar to hundreds of others less well known through lack of a Gobineau, a Chamberlain or a Stoddard to give them circulation in the disguise of science. There are so many such theories "proving" racial supremacy, all in conflict with each other, that one becomes skeptical of their slightest validity. To claim essential racial equality on that account, however, would also be a prejudiced conclusion. Facts themselves, not specious theories, must be examined.

The measurement of racial potentialities is in its infancy. It is only within the last few decades that any real progress has been made in the comparison of individual inborn qualities. The comparison of groups has had to wait on the technique for the measurement of individuals, a technique not yet removed from the realm of speculation and tentative experiment. Several widely varying approaches to the study of racial capacities have been utilized with indifferent success. Not one is claimed by its own adherents to yield final results.

Historically speaking, racial capacities were first approached through broad cultural comparisons. Probably all tribes and nations have made some contrast of their own achievements with those of strangers with whom they came in contact. The extent to which these contrasts were followed in early times by inferences of biological nature is in doubt. There is little reason to believe that the Greeks looked down on the barbarians as racial inferiors, although they may have despised their cultural traits. The Jew gained confidence through his faith that he was Jehovah's favorite, but the Old Testament does not tell us that he thought the Egyptian and Hittite lacking in intelligence, nor was he himself held in light esteem by his enemies and conquerors. The Moors and the Spaniards were not bothered by theories of mentality and race; they were too busy settling issues of territorial control. The first American discoverers and colonists patronized the Indians for their heathenish and savage ways of life, but the natives who adopted European culture were accepted like any other human being and as a matter of course. In past centuries when the natives of Africa, America and Australia were first encountered by white adventurers they were frequently killed or enslaved with ruthlessness, not because of their mental inferiority but with the justification that they were unbelievers, strangers, and enemies. It is only in recent times that the claim of biological inferiority has been used to justify prejudiced discrimination and ill treatment.

Of course, there may have been some vague thought of inborn racial differences when one people compared its achievements with those of another, although the evidence in support of this statement is weak. Strict tribal endogamy, for example, may sometimes have been supported by unformulated racial theories, but the strongest sanction for such customs which tended to preserve racial purity grew out of the value which lay in cultural uniformity, not racial integrity. Jew and Gentile, Protestant, Catholic, and heathen, Mohammedan and unbeliever, were forbidden intermarriage for religious reasons which disappeared with conversion. A Christian knight on crusade might take to wife any infidel of proper social status encountered on the way provided she accepted the Cross; otherwise she could only be his mistress. Within the last century and a half popular opinion has clothed class and nationality cultural differences in a biological terminology. Racial heredity has become more important in the people's minds than environment and personal inclination.

Theoretically, there is no unconquerable obstacle in the way of determining racial capacities by means of comparisons of cultural achievements. Actually, it has thus far proved to be impossible to accomplish. British and Italian cultures differ in many respects all the way from religion to leisure-time activities, but to what extent, if any, these variations may properly be attributed to race is another matter. Racially, the north Italian and the neighboring German are closely related; culturally, their differences are greater than those between north and south Italian, of quite different European stocks. American Indians have been counted as one race in spite of noticeable tribal variations, but the cultural achievements of the Incas, Mayas and Aztecs were so far more complex than those of the Yurok, Utes, and Omahas as to seem beyond comparison. The culture of the Mayas in pre-Columbian times, judging by modern European standards, was much in advance of that of the Nordics of north Europe at the height of Greek and Roman glory. Now their relative positions are quite altered. The American Negro and the African have few cultural similarities not of common European origin. The ways of the "heathen Chinee" may be peculiar, but his descendants in western centers slip easily into the pattern of their new home with or without intermarriage. Such facts are confusing if we are trying to learn about racial potentialities.

Group contacts which make possible the borrowing and interchange of ideas and inventions count for more than is usually admitted. Upon contact with western civilization, Japan blossomed into a first-class power in the family of nations. The great civilizations in history have without exception, as previously stated, been located at the crossroads of the world. China, Persia, Egypt, Babylon, Greece, Rome, Venice, Spain, England, the United States, all were or are veritable clearing houses of trade, commerce, and thought at the peak of their grandeur. We need not enter the argument as to which was cause and which was effect. Such debate is futile here. The similarity is too pointed to be left out of account in racial judgments.

The trouble grows out of the practical difficulties in the way of equalizing the environmental handicaps and advantages so influential in determining the trend and speed of cultural development. We can never know what might have happened had Africans inhabited Europe and Europeans lived in Africa. If the Rocky Mountains had chanced to be located near the eastern coast of North America and the low Appalachian hills on the western coast, the whole course of growth of the United States might have been altered beyond belief.

Who knows what the American Indian might have achieved had he been able to borrow oriental grains, cattle and fowl from all over the world, Greek thought, Roman law, Jewish nationalistic religion, and a constant stream of additional inventions, as did the Englishman? Two runners of identical physique may be expected to run a dead heat if they travel identical paths after identical training, but only then. No two peoples, even when living in adjoining territory or in the same city ward, have fulfilled the rigid requirements which would make practical the comparison of cultural achievements, free from differential advantages and handicaps, in such a way as to permit biological generalizations concerning potential ability.

Nevertheless, it is possible to say that all races have sufficient mentality to survive in any geographical or cultural environment in which any other race has survived, and, when permitted, to compete on terms of apparent equality. The white man has not done so well in certain tropical areas, and the Negro has not always thrived in temperate climates. These racial eliminations, however, have been because of physical and cultural rather than mental inadequacy. Brains were not what was lacking.

If broad historical comparisons do not afford final conclusions, perhaps cultural studies of peoples living side by side, geographically if not socially, may give more positive results. Countless social studies as well as general observation tell us that minority groups in the United States do not get along as well as the majority. American-born children of immigrants and Negroes furnish a higher proportion of our jail population than their numbers warrant. Negroes and some foreign groups have too high an illegitimacy rate. Poverty is more common, as is unemployment, among alien and colored people than among the native born of white parentage. Why? Is Negro and Italian illiteracy due to mental weakness or to other limitations of a non-hereditary nature? A good deal depends on whom you ask. A Georgia cracker or a scion of Virginia "white trash" will explain away Negro maladjustments with the contemptuous statement that "niggers" just are that way. Old New England stock may be certain that French Canadians, Portuguese and Italians have so much poverty and crime because of their Latin ancestry. The minority groups themselves may even come to believe these explanations, but their leaders are sure to reply that it is all due to external forces over which their people have no control.

The truth remains unknown. Both sides have some facts on which to go, but neither can speak with finality on the basis of evidence derived from cultural comparisons. One can no more sum up the conduct of a group and the influences which have guided it, and then say that this shortcoming was due 90 per cent to environment and that failure 90 per cent to heredity, than one can make similar generalizations concerning the life history of an individual. All that can be said is that this thing was done and that was not. Why and why not in terms of race or environment are out of the question.

Since the answer to the question of racial potentialities is not to be found by present methods of investigation in analysis of cultural material, so plentifully available but difficult of interpretation by students of race, the obvious thing to do is to turn to the laboratory approach. This has been done extensively during the last few decades both by physical anthropologists and other biological scientists who have carefully dissected, measured, and studied the bodies and functioning of individuals of all races, and by the psychologists who have invented a multitude of ingenious measuring devices generally known as mental tests.

The physical anthropologists have measured the human body. The shape and size of the head, height sitting and standing, the length of arms, legs, fingers, and toes, the hair structure, the color of skin, hair, and eyes, weight and other racial characteristics have been painstakingly gathered for thousands upon thousands of human beings and skeletal remains. On the basis of these findings mankind has been classified in from one to forty or more races and subraces by scientists of unquestioned integrity and standing. It is interesting to observe at this point that while biologists have refused to divide animals into races on bases such as the cephalic index, physical anthropologists have considered this measurement as adequate for the division of mankind into races.

While physical anthropologists today, no matter what their lists of races may be, do not claim that the features which they have measured have any necessary correlation with mental capacity, it is not long since it was possible for racial theorists to obtain respectable followings who accepted specious doctrines based on such supposed correlations between the physical anthropologists' findings and cultural potentiality. The weight of the brain, which varies from race to race, superficially impressed laymen, rather than students, as a means for estimating group ability. The Negro brain is lighter than the white brain, just as woman's brain is lighter than man's, but no important conclusions can be drawn from this fact. If the human brain is neither exceptionally large nor exceptionally small, that is, if it varies in size within reasonably wide limits—and the average brain weight of all races falls within these limits—no relationship between these minor variations and mental capacity can be observed. The shape of the head, usually expressed as the cephalic index, the relation between the length and breadth of the skull, has been the basis of whole schools of racial theorists who have attempted to show the innate superiority of people possessing this or that shape; but now, while people are still classified as long heads, round heads, or something in between, anthropologists recognize no cultural significance in such variations. We are not even certain that head form is a racially permanent characteristic, for the descendants of several European immigrant groups in the United States who have been carefully measured show a tendency to vary from their ancestors toward a medium-shaped head. Brain structure might be more significant than shape or size, but no one seems to be sufficiently skilled to identify unlabeled brains as white, yellow, red, brown, or black by laboratory examination of their structure. There is reason to believe that there are differences in the nervous systems which are racial in nature, but the evidence is as yet so tenuous that, even if interpretations of their significance were not absolutely lacking, as is the case, they have no known bearing on racial capacity.

When it comes to such superficial features as pigmentation of skin, eyes, and hair, type of hair and its bodily distribution, bodily structure, facial features, and the like, we are more at a loss than ever to know their meaning. Some of these outward characteristics may be the result of generations of selective adaptation to geographical environment, but, if so, they are of decreasing importance under modern artificial living conditions, and any race today can apparently survive in temperate and subtropical regions. With the popularization of the Darwinian theory of evolution the idea took hold, always in untrained minds, that the various races might be steps on the evolutionary trail, leading from the lower animals on up through the darker races to the white. This on its face is absurd, for any race may be "animal-like," depending on the characteristic selected for comparison. Dark skin and full lips are not animal traits, but hairiness is, and this would put the white group at the bottom of the scale of races. Protruding jaw and sloping forehead might be called animal features, and would put the darker peoples on the lower steps. Our admiration for the high forehead, the "highbrow," is partly the result of our belief that the further we get away from the appearance of the lower animals the more superior we become, but it has no justification in fact, for there is no evidence that a sloping forehead is a sign of even slight inferiority. Perhaps the fact that Greek sculptors, from whom we get some of our standards of beauty, exaggerated the foreheads of their statues, has something to do with our opinion. Finally, there are greater variations in all these characteristics among individuals of the same race than there are between the norms of any two races.

It may be possible in the future to look at a man's skin, head, hair or other racial feature and then generalize vaguely about his aptitudes or handicaps, but it is highly doubtful. None of the outward racial characteristics have any known direct connection with the inward mechanism of reasoning or emotion. We may look at the hair color and other features of a cow, if we are properly trained, and tell something about her qualities as a milk, cream and beef producer—valuable knowledge in the case of cattle. There is no immediate likelihood that we shall be able to know anything of the cultural capacities of a human being simply because we know his race.

THE NEGATIVE EVIDENCE OF PSYCHOLOGY

Pure biological science in its various branches has been unable to furnish much information about the relationship between biological characteristics and cultural potentialities, for the simple reason that its field has been so defined as to require concentration on structure and functioning under laboratory conditions. Numerous biologists, anatomists and physical anthropologists have gone beyond these limits in interpreting their data in social terms. With few exceptions their results have been shallow, and the exceptions have been successful, not because of the scientists' strictly biological training but through their broader social knowledge. A biological scientist may find, as did Hiro Ide of the Wistar Institute of Anatomy and Biology, that in a given number of cases the median and sciatic nerves of Negro and white cadavers differ noticeably in structure.[1] The interpretation of this difference in terms of mental capacity or social behavior is another matter.

The psychologists perhaps more than any other group of students have attempted to combine social and biological investigations. While they have had some success in this effort, their results are far from final in any racial comparisons. The work which has attracted most attention in this field has gone

[1] Hiro Ide, "On Several Characters Shown by the Cross-sections of the Median and Sciatic Nerves of Human Males According to Race," *Journal of Comparative Neurology*, vol. li, no. 2, December 15, 1930, pp. 457-487; and "On Several Characters Shown by the Cross-sections of the Median and Sciatic Nerves of Human Females and a Comparison of these with the Corresponding Observations on the Male Nerves from Whites and Negroes," *ibid.*, vol. li, no. 2, December 15, 1930, pp. 489-521.

under the general name of mental tests. As indicators of racial capacity for education they have many weaknesses, which, however, do not necessarily condemn them utterly as so many protagonists of racial equality have maintained.[2]

There is no doubt but that racial and national minority groups in the United States are inferior to the older native white stock if both intelligence and intellect are considered together. It is wiser not to do this, for intelligence, being inborn mental ability, should be thought of apart from intellect, which may be defined as intelligence plus training and experience. It is a different thing to say that Negro children are at present intellectually incapable of competing on terms of equality with native white children in our schools, than insisting that their inherent intelligence, which cannot vary much from generation to generation, prevents them from acquiring and using the same educational training afforded white children. The one is a temporary problem, perhaps due to economic and traditional handicaps, while the other requires lasting educational treatment for the group inferior in intelligence. Granting without the possibility of argument that immigrant, Indian, oriental and colored children, taken as a whole and admitting special cases, are intellectually handicapped, the question of intelligence remains to be solved.

Shortly after the World War students and laymen were struck with the possibilities of utilizing the Army mental tests which were given to 1,700,000 men in the military service of the United States. They were commonly referred to as measurements of intelligence and were administered to a large number of individuals of all social and economic classes. To many they seemed to provide an opportunity for settling the vexing questions concerning the relation between inborn ability and success in life.

It was found upon analysis of the results that there was a distinct correlation between occupation and score which was

[2] For bibliographies of publications on racial psychology, see Frank G. Bruner, "Racial Differences," *Psychological Bulletin*, vol. xi, no. 10, October 15, 1914, pp. 384-386; R. S. Woodworth, "Comparative Psychology of Races," *ibid.*, vol. xiii, no. 10, October 15, 1916, pp. 388-397; Thomas R. Garth, "A Review of Racial Psychology," *ibid.*, vol. xxii, no. 6, June 15, 1925, pp. 343-364.

too close to be due to chance coincidence. The average scores of laborers were well down the scale, while those of engineers, doctors, and other professional people were up near the top. The superficial conclusion was that people who succeeded did so because they were born with brains, while those who failed were never given a chance by heredity. Of course there were plenty of exceptions, but these were passed over by careless thinkers as "unusual cases."

It was also found that the Negro and other minority groups made poor showings when compared with old native white stock. The median score of colored men, for illustration, was significantly lower than that of white men. This fact, however, lost some of its significance, or rather it acquired a new significance, when it was observed that Negroes in northern states such as Ohio, Pennsylvania, Illinois, and New York did better than white men from Kentucky, Mississippi, Arkansas, and Georgia. It was useless to suggest that northern Negroes included many migrants from the south who might be expected to be superior to the race as a whole, for there was not the slightest evidence that the more intelligent colored men were the ones who moved into northern industrial communities. If the conclusion was accepted that the Army mental tests demonstrated the superiority of the white race, and especially the old white stock, then it must also be accepted that the average northern Negro man is superior in intelligence to the average white man in a number of southern states. When this issue was realized there was amusing haste to point out the economic and educational handicaps of the South which would account for the differences.

The point of the matter is that the Army tests were never designed to measure native intelligence. Their purpose was to select quickly and efficiently the various types of men who could be expected to fit most readily into specific jobs ranging all the way from labor battalions to officers' training schools. This the Army tests accomplished with surprising although not perfect efficiency. When we remember that education, both formal and informal, as well as inherited brains, were factors in producing effective military laborers and officers, there is less chance of misinterpreting Army test results.

Dr. Carl C. Brigham's analysis of the Army tests given to approximately 90,000 white and 20,000 colored recruits and published in his *A Study of American Intelligence* contains the most comprehensive investigation of Negro-white differences as yet made.[3] The average mental age of white drafted men was found to be 13.1, while that of the colored drafted men was only 10.4. Over 85 per cent of the Negroes, furthermore, were found by these tests to be inferior to the average of the white drafted men.

Brigham's results have been widely quoted. They still are, for that matter, although in 1930 Dr. Brigham had the courage to deny his earlier findings when, after a review of existing types of tests for the study of comparative abilities he announced that "comparative studies of various national and racial groups may not be made with existing tests," and that "one of the most pretentious of these comparative racial studies—the writer's own—" is "without foundation."[4]

It would be useless here to cite the results of the hundreds of comparisons of Negro-white mental ability which have been made by dozens of trained psychologists both before and after the Army tests were perfected. One study, however, should be mentioned because of the endorsement it has received in biological circles, namely, Davenport and Steggerda's *Investigation of Race Crossing in Jamaica.*[5] Anthropometric and psychological measurements and comparisons were made of black, brown, and white groups, each group containing one hundred persons divided equally on the basis of sex. On the basis of the psychological tests—tests of musical capacity, form discrimination and substitution tests, copying geometric figures, drawing a man, criticism of absurd sentences, repetition of seven numbers, cutting a figure out of folded paper, ball-and-field test, manikin test, the Knox moron test and

[3] Princeton University Press, Princeton, 1923, p. 210.

[4] C. C. Brigham, "Intelligence Tests of Immigrant Groups," *Psychological Review*, March 1930, vol. xxxvii, pp. 158-165.

[5] Carnegie Institution, Washington, D. C., Publication No. 395, 1929, pp. x + 516.

the Knox cube imitation test, and eight Army alpha subtests —the authors found that the whites ranked on the average first, with the blacks second, and the browns last. The position of the mulattoes is interesting, for in the United States most similar comparisons have favored this group instead of full-blooded Negroes, the explanation given being that the white blood in the mulatto gave him a decided advantage.

In spite of the impressive nature of the report of this investigation, with its tables, diagrams, and statistical refinements, it is open to all the criticisms made of other studies of a similar nature. The small samples of the groups would probably be adequate were we sure of their representative nature. Unfortunately the authors appear to have chosen their subjects in a most haphazard manner, the only criterion of similarity being a "low economic level." The psychosocial environment of the persons tested was ignored. Certain "social data" were secured but they were of no sociological significance. (The questionnaire used for this purpose contained items such as these: Do you have malaria very often? Do you have any birthmarks? Do you walk fast? etc., etc.) Finally, the study, so far as the psychological tests are concerned, must be considered in the light of Brigham's criticism already mentioned. In other words, it is only one more addition to our inconclusive literature on race differences.

Recognizing that general intelligence is not the only inherited mental quality on which success in modern life is dependent, attempts to measure special abilities and temperamental or emotional traits have also been made. These have raised questions concerning racial ability to solve abstract or concrete problems, to verbalize, to remember, to distinguish tones, to maintain rhythms, to resist fatigue, to exercise inhibitory power, and the like. Certain racial differences have been claimed, but the experiments have been neither sufficiently extensive nor adequate in technique to warrant quoting in a study of race relations. Only a summary of the findings of mental, special-ability, and temperament tests is here required, and that of Dr. Viteles will serve our purposes. He has stated concerning Negro-white tests that:

(1) "On practically all tests of mental ability, groups of Negroes are consistently inferior to groups of whites.

(2) "Although in every instance there is considerable overlapping between the two races, there is a consistently higher proportion of inferior scores and smaller proportion of superior test scores among Negroes than whites.

(3) "There is evidence to the effect that the amount of difference between the groups increases with age.

(4) "A selection of Negroes and whites from similar social levels reduces the difference between the two races.

(5) "Weighting of educational differences serves likewise to reduce the inferiority on test scores on the part of the Negro.

(6) "According to certain of these studies, the findings of which are not undisputed, increases in the proportion of white blood in the mixed Negro serve to reduce the amount of Negro inferiority.

(7) "Although the evidence is limited, there are suggestions of qualitative differences in mental ability between the two races following from investigations employing tests of specific mental abilities.

(8) "Experimental evidence on differences in temperament between the two races is extremely meagre."[6]

Many psychological studies have been made of the problem by improved methods since Dr. Viteles reached these conclusions in 1928; but even the most careful of these, that by Joseph Peterson and Lyle H. Lanier, entitled *Studies in Comparative Abilities of Whites and Negroes*, has done nothing to cause him to change his earlier generalizations on the value of these studies.[7] On the basis of four different tests of general ability, two of mechanical ability, one of musical talent, and one will-temperament test, this volume painstakingly compares Negro and white children and college students in New York, Chicago and Nashville, and expresses the opinion that

[6] Morris Viteles, "The Mental Status of the Negro," in Donald Young, editor, "The American Negro," *The Annals* of the American Academy of Political and Social Science, November, 1928, no. 229, vol. cxxxx, pp. 166-177.

[7] Mental Measurement Monographs, Serial No. 5, The Williams & Wilkins Company, Baltimore. 1929, pp. iii + 156.

white children, considered as a group, are superior by birth to colored. Every possible attempt is made to rule out confusing factors of differential incentive, health, home conditions, and the like, and the authors are convinced that they have been relatively successful in doing so. They do not claim perfection, for the concluding sentences of the monograph state that "What the net effects of these differences in samplings (favoring the whites) really are on the test scores, we cannot say without further investigation. It is best not to speculate on them here."[8] Until racial mental tests are more refined in their control over sampling so that there may be no question that extraneous social influences on scores are eliminated, it is best not to use them as conclusive evidence of racial capacity.

The results of mental tests of immigrants are similar to those of American Negroes, although they have regularly scored higher than the colored people, with the English-speaking and north Europeans—Irish perhaps excepted—at the top and the south Europeans at the bottom. The World War Army mental tests have been mentioned in connection with Negro-white differences. Since they have also been used as arguments against European immigrants they may be brought in again at this point. Dr. Brigham in his work already cited found the comparative scores, on a scale running from 0 to 25, as given in Table I on the following page.

These figures have been widely quoted as evidence that immigrants from southern and western Europe have not the ability to become efficiently assimilated into the American culture stream. They are included in Dr. Brigham's recent sweeping condemnation of his earlier work, and are quoted here because, if one may judge by past experience, they will probably be cited in support of racial doctrines for some time to come in spite of their author's low estimate of their value. The arguments showing them to be valid as testimony demonstrating racial differences in innate capacity are essentially the same as those which have been previously mentioned in regard to the Army mental tests and Negro-white capacity.

Since no comprehensive survey of immigrant intelligence

[8] *Ibid.*, p. 152.

TABLE I[9]

AVERAGE SCORES IN ARMY MENTAL TESTS (COMBINED ALPHA, BETA AND INDIVIDUAL TESTS)

United States officers....	18.84	Belgium..............	12.79
England..............	14.87	Ireland..............	12.32
Scotland.............	14.34	Austria..............	12.27
Holland.............	14.32	Turkey..............	12.02
Germany.............	13.88	Greece..............	11.90
U. S. white draft.......	13.77	Russia..............	11.34
Denmark.............	13.69	Italy...............	11.01
Sweden..............	13.30	Poland..............	10.74
Norway.............	12.98	U. S., colored.........	10.41

has as yet supplanted Dr. Kirkpatrick's study, his opinion may be cited as typical of the conservative attitude toward mental-test comparisons of white races and nationalities. He is convinced that innate capacities vary as between European stocks and in favor of those people of north European culture. Like the other workers in the field, he is not of the opinion that the tests have been so devised and applied that inborn traits alone determine group differentials in the scores, but he believes it reasonable to assume that the relatively consistent superiority of the older predominant immigrant stocks is indicative of desirable inherent qualities. This belief is being more seriously questioned as additional tests with improved technique are reported and scrutinized.

What has been said about the Negroes and the immigrants applies equally to Indians and Orientals. These groups have in recent years been tested, but in general we may say that the environmental variable has not been so well eliminated that the results may be considered as evidence of mental status. The language handicap has invalidated verbal tests, and factors such as poverty, irregularity in school attendance, differential habits or traditions of study, nutritional and occupational factors, have rendered the test results inconclusive.

"After all, such tests are cultural in nature and require the

[9] C. C. Brigham, quoted in C. Kirkpatrick, *Intelligence and Immigration*, Mental Measurement Monographs, Serial No. 2, The Williams & Wilkins Company, Baltimore, 1926, p. 125.

subjects to express themselves through cultural media. There is no special magic in triangles, squares, circles, numbers, animal pictures, and similar simple devices, which will automatically eliminate the influence of formal and informal education, varying incentive, malnutrition and the like. No one really claims there is, except the pseudo-scientists and laymen who use the work of others as it was never intended to be used.

"Another point to be considered is that artificial tasks administered under experimental conditions are not necessarily indicators of general or specific abilities essential for competition in modern civilization. Boys who are dropped from college may make the best of business men. French Canadians, Chinese, South Europeans, and others, who score low on another man's test are not thereby proved unfit to till the soil, build great cities, or create a lasting art.

"The inference should not be drawn, however, that such experimental work is thought to be without real value. The only suggestion here made is that the results should be used in their proper field of application. Army mental tests were useful during the World War for practical army purposes, but not in the post-war period for biological interpretations. Schools and colleges may use mental tests for admissions and other administrative purposes, but racial theorists should be most cautious in utilizing such materials as the basis for prophesying racial futures. Industrial plants may profitably encourage psychological measurements as an aid in personnel selection, but the further interpretations of the results obtained in attempts to make them apply to race relations as such requires qualification. *It is their misuse rather than their use which causes trouble.*"[10]

There are those who admit the futility of attempting to determine racial capacity through broad cultural comparisons and laboratory experiment. They nevertheless insist that Negro and sometimes other minority group children as well

[10] Donald Young, "Statistical Studies of Race Relations," in Stuart A. Rice, *Statistics in Social Studies,* University of Pennsylvania Press, Philadelphia, 1930, pp. 74-77.

show a lack of capacity by their failure to achieve results in the classroom equal to those of native white children. It is brought out in support of this position that Negro school children seem to be inferior in tests of addition, spelling, reading, and handwriting even when they have the same teachers and live in the same neighborhoods as their white competitors. They also show a tendency to do poorer work as they advance in the public school grades, and for the most part they drop out as soon as the law allows.

Differences between schoolroom achievement of colored and white children do exist, but they are not uniform throughout the country. White city children as a rule do better in their classes than city Negroes, and rural whites show better results than rural Negroes. There are exceptional instances, not so uncommon as might be expected, where colored children show superiority in some subject to white children of similar economic and social status, but it is safe to generalize that Negro-white comparisons in school achievement are unfavorable to the colored children in their results.

The clue to the answer to this problem may be found in the fact that urban Negro children consistently do better than rural white children, and that northern Negro children make a better showing than do the white children of some southern states where the school systems are inferior and white families live in ignorance and poverty. So long as the colored element is held apart from the rest of the population in a rigid caste system which does not permit a single colored individual ever to forget his African ancestry, retarded colored school children can be taken for granted. Whether the retardation will continue or decrease to the vanishing point as Negroes are afforded wider opportunities for cultural development is a disputed question to which our present knowledge yields no satisfactory answer.

Few Negro children reach high school; fewer still are admitted to our colleges. A discouragingly great number drop out of primary school before they reach the higher grades. It has long been noticed that colored pupils do well in the very first years of their formal education but slow down rapidly as they get along in years, soon falling so far behind the comparable white age group as to cause despair at the thought of working with them. This is commonly explained by laymen and school teachers, who should know better, as being due to the arrest of mental growth in the Negro at an early age and at a point much lower on the intelligence scale than that at which the white child's brain growth is checked. The economic factor which compels Negro children to enter gainful occupations at an early age is forgotten, although it is well known that these children belong to a group which has been forced to lean heavily on child labor. An additional fact which rarely comes to the white man's mind is that Negroes are not born with full knowledge of their racial status, and when it dawns on them, while they are still in grade school, that they must spend their lives as "niggers," barred by prejudiced restrictions on their employment from making full use of even a common-school education, and otherwise subjected to the restrictions of a despised and hated race, school incentives quickly fade.

Children of other racial and national groups also show tendencies to lag a bit in school work, the amount of retardation and inferiority varying directly with their economic and social handicaps. If they belong to groups, as nearly all do, which may improve their status through assimilation and even amalgamation, the achievement differential may be slight. In some instances the reward may be so great that handicaps apparently become added incentives and lead to superior scholastic work. The Jew, for example, who is likely to have a strong traditional respect for education, has found that the one way to overcome the prejudice against him is to succeed in professional occupations such as medicine and teaching, and advantage of this opening has been eagerly taken. For all white minority groups there is a lessening of oppression with educational advancement. The opposite is not infrequently the case with Negroes, especially in the south.

In this discussion of racial capacities there has been but one reference to mental testing and race mixture. In Dr. Viteles' summary of the results of Negro-white mental tests the disputed finding that "increases in the proportion of white blood in the mixed Negro serve to reduce the amount of Negro inferiority" was recorded. There is no question but that most outstanding American Negroes have some white blood, the few exceptions to the contrary notwithstanding. This observation on the surface appears to support the mental tests which award superiority to the mulatto, although it should be remembered that a number of psychological examinations of mixed bloods have found no correlation between ability and degree of white infusion. Indeed, it is not at all startling to discover that the majority of Negroes of real achievement are not full bloods when it is recalled that seven or eight Negroes out of ten in the United States probably have some white blood. This fact alone makes it almost a mathematical certainty that any appreciable colored group, leaders or failures, would contain a majority of mixed bloods. It is almost as true that most Negro criminals are mixed with white blood as it is that colored doctors, lawyers, educators, and individuals of cultural refinement and wealth may generally find a light-complexioned bar sinister in their genealogies.

Other factors than mathematical probability are, however, involved in the greater frequency of success of light-colored Negroes. It may be said dogmatically that in the United States the light-complexioned Negro is favored by both whites and Negroes over his darker cousins. The white man apparently feels that the more nearly a Negro looks like white people the more nearly like them he must be, and therefore it follows that he is a superior Negro. In certain personal service and menial occupations dark Negro types seem to be preferred, witness the "mammy" of southern white sentimentality. Although this observation will be bitterly disputed by many who claim personal fondness for the supposed superior dark Negro and spurn the "white" or "yellow nigger," most white people, especially in the north, do not act in accordance with their line of argument. There is also considerable keen jealousy of the lighter types on the part of dark Negroes, while the lighter types hesitate to associate with the dark. The lighter Negro, however, usually has the advantage when it comes to opportunities for real advancement, economic, intellectual, or social, in spite of a wide variety of attempts to pull him back. Light-complexioned girls are in demand as wives and, other things being equal, may expect to secure the more desirable men as husbands. This in turn tends to increase the proportion of white blood in colored family lines of note.

The American Indian is also a mixed blood to such an extent that it is rare to meet a member of that race, other than in the southwest, who one can be sure is free from white or Negro ancestry. There are no reliable statistics on the amount of racial mixture of any large groups in the United States, but it is safe to say that not a third of those listed by the census as Indians are biologically pure Indians. In those sections of the South where they are known to have Negro blood they are treated as nearly like Negroes as possible. In other parts of the country a small amount of Indian blood entitles them to full classification as Indians. No rule can be found, for their community status depends more on white public opinion, regardless of biological facts, and on the degree of their cultural assimilation than on ancestry. The term "half breed" as applied to Indian mixtures in the past has been a term of reproach, implying indisputable inferiority. Such automatic disapproval has now faded, and no wild theories about the effects of Indian mixture on inborn abilities are at present current.

Negro blood alone seems to count unalterably in public opinion as having deteriorating cultural effects when mixed with that of other races. Oriental-white mixture is not favored, but in the United States it is not taken for granted that Chinese or Japanese mixture with white produces mentally inferior offspring. Racial crossing between the various subdivisions of white stock are given little if any biological significance except by racial purists, who are far in the minority. Negro blood, however, when mixed with that of any other race, white or colored, must be more potent, for it is rarely if ever supposed to be without significant biological effect. Paradoxically enough, sometimes Negro-white mixtures result in "bad niggers" thought to be far inferior to the more desired

"Uncle Tom" type, and, when the mixed individual shows evidence of ability, it is the white blood which is responsible. As a matter of fact, there is no known correlation whatever between race mixture and inherited capacity.

Perhaps the one conclusion which indisputably follows from every kind of racial comparison is that races overlap so much in capacity that they come very near to coinciding. Any individual from any race may be matched exactly in inborn ability by some individual in another race. No race in the world has been without its geniuses who would be geniuses under any conditions. Also, no race in the world has been without its idiots. It is possible that there may be more superior individuals in the white than in the colored races. There may even be more people of great capacity among the north Europeans than among the Mediterranean nationalities, although this is improbable. There is similarly a slight chance that the colored races contain a greater proportion of mediocre and inferior individuals than the white. In other words, while the upper and lower limits of capacity are beyond serious question the same for all great races, the distribution of capacities has not been proved to be identical. But—neither has it been shown to be unequal.

It is not unreasonable to assume that since biological processes have differentiated mankind into types with observable physical differences, there may also have been an accompanying differentiation of mental traits and capacities. The commonly cited special mental qualities attributed to the colored races and European peoples can all be explained in cultural terms, however, and, since this is true, it is an unscientific procedure to explain them laboriously by resorting to far-fetched hereditary theories. Temperamental characteristics, such as those of the Italian, likewise need no biological analysis in view of the copious evidence of climate and tradition as to their origin.

For instance, we are told now and then that homicides are common among Italians, and that the reason is their peculiar "hot-headedness" which prompts them to use the stiletto—or, better, the gun—on slightest provocation. As a matter of fact, any study of the names of murderers in our large urban, particularly eastern, centers will yield an astonishingly high number of Italian names, and the same is true of the list of victims. A curious thing has been observed, however. These persons were almost always born in Italy. Their children and grandchildren, born here, choose more American ways of committing crime, and tend to become thieves instead of murderers. What has been ascribed to a temperamental peculiarity is thus shown to be only a culture trait.

It may be expected that at some future time racial differences in capacity will be scientifically established, just as there may be differences between man and woman. It is not long since women were thought to be incapable of serious intellectual effort. They have only recently been given the vote, and are still considered ineligible by virtue of their sex for certain political functions. They are not wanted in executive positions in commerce and industry, although they have penetrated into occupations which a few decades ago were thought beyond their mental powers. Their legal rights have been and are even now, although to a lesser extent, restricted. Their capacities are supposed to be, through long biological selection, peculiar to their reproductive functions, and their emotions are claimed to disqualify the majority from sustained, impartial rational activities. There are progressive schools which refuse them admittance, largely because of a traditional attitude which considered them incapable of making use of an education planned for men. Just as there are physical differences between man and woman, so there may be accompanying mental and emotional differences, but these need not be looked on as superior and inferior qualities. The similarities are so much greater than the divergencies, viewed in proper perspective, that most of our sex discrimination in industrial society is without any biological foundation whatever. The watermelon is not intrinsically inferior to the cantaloupe; preference of one to another is a matter of taste. So, too, any differences in racial capacities which may be established in the future need not be differences of superiority or inferiority. A Shakespeare is not inferior to an Einstein; their capacities have led to different products, neither of which can be belittled. Every race has its contribution to make, and no one may judge between them.

In the last analysis, every race in the United States has made profitable use of our entire educational system. Negroes have learned to read and write in any language taught. They have graduated from high school and college with honors. Many have been elected to honorary scholastic societies such as Phi Beta Kappa. A goodly number have received Ph.D.'s from leading universities, earning them on the same standards as white students. Professional schools have had colored people graduate near the top of their classes so frequently that it is no longer news. The fact that other races and nationalities have been even more successful than the Negro in our schools is too well known to need elaboration. If the proportions of individuals of these minority groups who have successfully competed in our schools, colleges, and professional schools is smaller than that of the native white stock, and if they have on occasion been somewhat retarded in their progress, that is no reason for limiting their educational opportunities, unless it can be shown beyond all reasonable doubt that they are by racial nature barred from equal competition. Since no such inferiority has been proved, and regardless of the fact that absolute identity of capacity has also not been established, there is at present no warrant for differential educational treatment.

CHAPTER XIII

THE EDUCATION OF AMERICAN MINORITIES

IN THE previous chapter it has been shown that the mental capacities of minority nationality or racial groups in the United States have not been proved inferior to those of native white Americans. We may therefore assume that all these groups are capable of profiting by equal educational opportunities and that such opportunities should be offered them. Perhaps we should go even farther and demand that special efforts be made to create for them educational programs which will have a greater assimilative power than those of today. The education we have offered in the past to our immigrants and the various colored groups has generally failed so far as race relations are concerned. This failure has largely been due to the fact that we have remained blind to the strength and the essence of cultural conflicts which arise and are perpetuated wherever individuals or groups with different concepts of life and different habits, traditions and manners are forced into contact. The groups in conflict do not necessarily have to originate in different countries. They may come from different social classes within a country and even from different age groups within the same family. The clash does not come only between native and foreign ideas and traditions, but also between country and city, capital and labor, the old and the new generation. A few illustrations of these conflicts will be offered.

The European, particularly the south European, family may be said to be a close-knit unit with the functions of husband, wife and children clearly defined, as was pointed out in the chapter on minority family relationships. Daughters are carefully chaperoned, and little freedom before marriage is permitted them. In the United States a more individualistic family pattern is accepted, permitting to the various members of the family a greater freedom of action. The immigrant soon discovers that the standards of the new country are at variance with those which governed him at home. Gone are the restraints which were part of his old community and family life. The new standards he does not understand. Before he has come to grasp the American's way of life he passes through a period of transition frequently characterized by conduct which is in accord with neither European nor American traditions.

While a people transplanted from an alien culture may have the greatest difficulties to overcome in the process of adaptation to new conditions, any cultural change may bring similar difficulties. Not the least of these are the difficulties faced today by the migrant Negro or any Negro whose social horizon is widening. Whatever we may think of the color barriers of the South, the fact remains that the ordinary southern Negro before the World War was well orientated in his social life, his conduct being definitely regulated by strongly intrenched customs and traditions. Since the war the Negro is no longer certain of the justification for these traditions. His entrance into industry and his northern hegira have weakened the old barriers. The result has been the disorganization of his social life, the breakdown of standardized conduct patterns, and the groping for a new basis of behavior. That basis has not yet been found, and the transition from the old to the new has produced a wide range of cultural conflicts.[1] Many of the crudities, excesses, and stupidities of the American Negro are but evidence of his transitional position. A lack of thrift is to be expected of a people only lately freed from slavery and peonage. Notable success in science and the learned professions—and both the Negro and the Indian have been backward in these fields—cannot be expected in the absence of the spurring traditions which are part of the cultural heritage of many immigrant groups. Many of the ludicrous mistakes in matters of taste and manners which the Negro makes and which the

[1] The Negro has already completed one cycle of such cultural change. During slavery his life was completely defined for him by his white master. The Civil War and the Reconstruction Period brought a transition, and it took many years before the South had again established a social system in which the free Negro had a well defined place.

white may regard as "typical of Negro character," are perfectly natural considering the Negro's cultural background.

On the whole, however, the cultural assimilation of the Negro is not so difficult as that of other racial and nationality groups, for basically the Negro's culture is Anglo-American, and he has not been faced so much with the need for discarding old standards as with that of enlarging and perfecting them. In the case of Orientals, Indians and European immigrants, on the other hand, the process involves in greater or less degree a substitution instead of an extension of culture patterns.

In this assimilative process formal education plays an important rôle, and it will be the purpose of this chapter and that which follows to examine the problem of the nature, the extent, and the function of such education in assisting minority groups of this country in acquiring the native white American's way of life.

VOCATIONAL EDUCATION

In the development of educational programs for the minority groups mentioned, two trends have manifested themselves, because of the fact that it has been quite generally assumed by the dominant groups: first, that people of inferior status require special types of education; and, second, that it is highly desirable to supply this education in segregated schools.

The special type of education usually suggested is one that will provide a training in the semi-skilled and skilled trades, such as agriculture, the building trades, mechanical work, personal service, and the like. Unskilled labor is being increasingly recognized as expensive to the entire community, and in spite of the growing mechanization of certain types of industry which permits a few hours of instruction to take the place of long apprenticeship, workers without any special vocational training in school or by experience are a drug on the market. Native white workers naturally tend to be unfriendly to the added competition which results from the entrance of alien and colored hands into their occupations, even though the more influential classes who determine school policies are relatively unaffected by such antagonisms. On the other hand, the latter are inclined to place little faith in the possibility that "inferior" peoples may profit greatly by classical and professional education except in isolated instances. Self-styled superior individuals are prone to look down on skilled manual workers as well as on crude laborers, so it is not surprising that we find these trades, just a trifle up the ladder of social evaluation, offered in good faith and ignorance as economic bait to persons subjected to racial discrimination.

There have been kindly, well-intentioned racial theorists who have sincerely believed that a peasant people needs few if any intellectual leaders, but must rather rely on increasingly successful manual laborers who will eventually produce group leaders and people capable of being led in the paths of progress. Their contention has been that group progress must be built on a solid dirt foundation such as only farmers and artisans may set. Opposed to this point of view have been radical spokesmen of the oppressed peoples and classes, confident that far-visioned, intellectual leadership, not directly the product of the soil, can best chart the course of racial progress. Such debate is purely academic and no one well acquainted with the facts of race history would take one side to the exclusion of the other, yet it has been worn to fine shreds by white people attempting to justify the vocational emphasis in Negro education.

In this debate leaders of minority groups themselves have taken conspicuous part. Most white people still believe that Booker T. Washington placed his faith for the future of the American Negro in trained colored manual workers, and that W. E. B. Du Bois is relying on the development of intellectual Negro leadership which can successfully wrest from the white man's grasp equal social opportunities. Neither man, however, has exclusively held to the one or the other point of view, for both have realized from the beginning that both vocational and academic education were part of a whole pattern from which Negro progress might be expected. Du Bois, it is true, has antagonized white opinion by his bitter insistence on complete Negro participation in every aspect of national life and education. Washington accomplished the difficult task of conciliating white people of North and South by his public emphasis on manual labor and vocational training carried on in full recognition of the color line, while at the same time he did not alienate more than a handful of the people of his own race. Both men have tried to achieve identical goals by tactical methods in harmony with their respective personalities and capacities.

No judgment as to the final influence of these divergent methods of attacking the problem can be rendered. Although the bold attacks and the intellectual power of Du Bois may challenge greater admiration, the fact remains that Washington obtained the instant cooperation of influential white men in both north and south. For a colored leader to receive even a grudging tribute and limited support for a progressive educational project throughout the country is no mean achievement. Washington approached genius in the way he played his cards in the game of race relations. The monument which best keeps his memory alive is Tuskegee Normal and Industrial Institute, in Alabama, a school patterned after the model of Hampton Normal and Agricultural Institute at Hampton, Virginia, founded in 1868 by General Samuel Chapman Armstrong for the education of Negro and Indian youth in vocational subjects, as is indicated by the adjectives "Normal" and "Agricultural" in the name. These adjectives have lately been dropped and the official name now is Hampton Institute, but the professed spirit of this school and the scores of others throughout the south is still embodied in the practice of teaching subject peoples to work efficiently with their hands and then teach others of their kind to do so also. When the white man is asked to mention Negro leaders in whom he has confidence the names of Washington, an early disciple of General Armstrong and a Hampton product, and Major R. R. Moton, an aide of Washington and his successor at Tuskegee, may be expected to head the list. Du Bois is well known, but he has not the white man's confidence, for his name is not associated with the patient training of Negro labor.

Northern and southern favor alike has been granted to Negro individuals and institutions which have stressed colored education in agriculture and the tasks of industry. Negro teachers, willing to pass on the lowly torch of racial pride in agricultural and industrial jobs well done, have consistently achieved the patronizing encouragement of the white man who knows the national value of skilled workers.

Only in the last decade or so have Negro institutions with the academic traditions of Atlanta and Fisk been able to compete at all successfully with the Hampton and Tuskegee type of school for the lavish gifts of white foundations and philanthropists, who gladly give to those who do not demand too high a place for their people. The appeal of the latter, however, still has the better chance of success.

A case in point is the joint Hampton and Tuskegee campaign for a $10,000,000 addition to their endowment a few years after the World War. Five gifts ranging from $250,000 to $3,600,000, totaling $5,350,000, were secured from white capitalists. The goal of $10,000,000 was easily passed. An analysis of the campaign literature shows a shrewd knowledge of what the white man of wealth and position wants the Negro to be and to do. One typewritten pamphlet of about thirty pages, which is claimed to have been an important item in securing the largest individual gift, illustrates this point. In essence, it was a carefully prepared statement of the vocational work being done by the two institutions, containing numerous illustrations of the good influence of Hampton and Tuskegee farmers and workers on the communities in which they settled. Farm products were shown to have increased under their influence. Buildings were improved. An industrial strike was avoided. Race relations were peaceful, and everybody apparently prospered when the Hampton-Tuskegee spirit of hard and skilled, if lowly, work penetrated a community. No mention was made of the increasingly important academic work being done by both institutions. Such information is best kept in the background when white cooperation and cash are desired. The pamphlet was a gem of racial strategy, and typified the front which has long been displayed to the white race as occasion demanded.

There is, however, a growing spirit of discontent with the Hampton-Tuskegee plan of education among a large group of Negroes. Many factors have contributed to this restlessness. Not the least of them has been the monotonous, conciliating reiteration of the theme that these schools and their imitators contain the key to the solution of race relations in the United States through the opportunities offered colored youth without provoking the antagonism of the dominant race. The impression is given the white people that Hampton-Tuskegee Negroes know their place—not too high a place—and this impression has been given credence by the recognition of racial barriers on the campus, as at Hampton. Even southern white people can find little to object to in the forced catering by officials, students, and alumni to the accepted Negro-white caste system. Colored people more and more are resenting this compromise position.

It is of course recognized by all that this type of educational institution has been of remarkable benefit to colored and white people alike. Every race needs vocational education for a goodly portion of its boys and girls, and the Negro is less prepared to accept and utilize a classical education than any other group in the United States. The criticism is not of the nature and quality of the teaching, for academic as well as vocational education is provided, but rather of the attitude which, consciously or otherwise, is fostered by these institutions among colored students and the white race as a whole concerning the Negro's place in the American economic order.

Two Negro colleges of academic tradition, Atlanta and Fisk Universities, have already been mentioned. Howard University, in Washington, D. C., also provides a good training in classical subjects as well as in medicine and other professions. There are many such schools, too numerous to mention by name, with academic standards ranging all the way from those of mediocre high schools for whites to those of fairly good colleges. A comparatively small number of colored boys and girls are adequately equipped to benefit by a first-class college education, and it may be said that, instead of adding to the number of these institutions, it would be better if many of them were eliminated and the rest encouraged to improve their standards. It is a regrettable fact that not a single Negro college in the United States could stand comparison with any one of several dozen leading white colleges in the country in regard to equipment, teaching personnel, or student body.

The vocational ideal has also penetrated the public school systems of the country, but its application to Negroes has taken a curious turn. In spite of the generous white support of private agricultural and industrial institutions for Negroes, and the popular belief that such education is best for our colored youth, the public schools have been reluctant to afford opportunities for colored vocational training. This inconsistency is easily understood, for well-qualified vocational teachers are none too plentiful and vocational school equipment is expensive. It costs more to give a child of school age a good vocational education than a superior classical education. Consequently colored children have been literally compelled to take academic courses in the public schools of the South, and to a lesser extent in the North, through the poor quality of the vocational work offered them or the total absence of such facilities. This policy has been defended by the statement that in many trades taught in public vocational schools no work opportunities exist for Negroes because of the race prejudice which bars them from skilled trades now thought of as almost exclusively white. There is some truth to this argument, but it is probably of slight importance in the determination of educational policy when compared with the economic factor.

The fact that colored parents frequently resent any suggestion that their children take vocational rather than classical high school courses has helped to close this type of education to many boys and girls who could profit by it. In Philadelphia, for illustration, advisers have been upbraided by fathers and mothers of Negro students who have been guided into manual training instead of college preparatory courses when there was no possible chance of later college study. Such guidance, sincerely and intelligently offered, has been mistaken as evidence of race prejudice by colored parents who were convinced that it was only another attempt to keep Negroes from their intellectual rights.

There is every reason to believe that the emphasis placed on vocational training instead of academic education for Negroes is due to the general belief that mental inferiority of this race makes its members incapable of being anything but "hewers of wood and drawers of water."

The Indian, too, has been thought to need vocational education more than any other type, but in recent years less because of any supposed inability to pursue successfully a purely academic career than because his economic status obviously requires training suitable to his pursuits in later life. In the early days of President Grant's peace policy toward Indian tribes provision was made to send farmers, blacksmiths, and other artisans to live in Indian country to serve, by example and actual teaching, as instruments for improvement of the Indians' economic efforts. The Indians themselves were in many cases eager to secure such instruction and some treaties stipulated that vocational instruction should be provided by the government. Unfortunately the pay was poor and many unqualified individuals were sent. Some good was done, but the carelessness and the pinch-penny policy followed by the Administration produced negligible results.

Indian schools at the present time still teach vocational subjects, but in an antiquated style which would not be tolerated in white public institutions. There is little or no connection between the subjects taught and their possible usefulness to the students. Harness making has been included in at least one school where automobile mechanics is neglected, although there is no chance for the Indians to earn a living at the trade. Excellent printing is also an outstanding example of a useless trade well taught, for there is a minimum of opportunity for Indians to be admitted to printers' unions, or to secure jobs on newspapers or in publishing houses. Too often the vocational work is nothing more than a means for getting work done so that schools may survive on the small allowances granted by the government. Agriculture, for illustration, shows an almost perfect correlation with institutional food needs, and only rarely is there any connection between the type of farm work in which instruction is given and the agricultural possibilities of the land which the student is known to have available at home. Household arts receive attention in girls' classes, but again the cooking and sewing for the institution seem to be of more importance than the home needs of the students.

There has been no influential propaganda in recent years to convince the country that Indians by virtue of their racial peculiarities need training in the skilled trades. Where they are qualified, they are permitted and even encouraged to go to white colleges for academic or professional education. The University of Oklahoma, in the heart of Indian country, has some two hundred students with known Indian ancestry, some being of pure Indian blood. Few Indians, however, have made notable success of their academic or professional training, and it would apparently be desirable to increase the facilities for farming education if only because of their geographic location in agricultural centers. What is needed, in short, is a coordination between the vocational education offered them and the economic opportunities which they are likely to encounter. The quality of instruction, of course, should be improved, for at present it is on a low level.

Indian vocational education is furthermore hampered among tribes, such as the Pueblo groups of the Southwest, where the economic traditions of aboriginal culture persist. In such communities there is always a progressive group which wishes to take advantage of improved farm machinery, seeds, stock, and agricultural methods. The opposition of the conservative element is then a real problem, for there is strong white support for the "vanishing red man" who clings to the traditions of his ancestors regardless of the consequences of his battle against the overwhelming force of the white man's civilization. This is to be differentiated from the opposition of conservative Negroes to innovations of the younger ones, which are innovations within one cultural pattern and not shifts from one distinct general culture to another.

Even the oriental and the Mexican immigrants escape the restrictive influence of the kind of doctrine which tries to drive Negroes into special types of schools. Chinese and Japanese students are common in all the more important universities, thanks to the educational policy of their governments and, in the case of those students born in the United States, to the anxiety of oriental immigrant parents to improve the status of their children. Latin Americans have long made use of our facilities for classical education, and the recent influx of despised Mexican laborers has not canceled a popular high regard for wealthy and cultured individuals from the countries to the south of the United States.

The Negro thus bears the brunt of an educational attack which is based on the belief that group improvement must be founded on a rise in the productiveness of the masses through training in manual labor, with intellectual leadership in a minor rôle. With the possible exception of the Indian, his is the only minority group in the United States which receives little popular acclaim for mental progress. Progress in the manual trades is patronizingly rewarded, but white doors close instead of open when a colored man shows signs of thinking. There are of course a few white people who recognize intellectual merit when they see it in a skin of any color, but popular opinion considers evidences of brains in a Negro a sign that he is not staying in his place. The intellectual Indian, north or south European, Mexican, or Oriental finds doors opened to him which his brethren may not pass, and with the exception of the Oriental, the reception within is on terms of practical equality. Even the Oriental need fear insult only from the lower white classes and those with a provincial outlook. The Negro, however, expects toleration as his reward for hand labor or doing nothing at all, and resentment, persecution, or closed doors when he allows the white man to see evidence of mental capacity. The exceptions to this statement do not invalidate the rule.

AMERICANIZATION

There is no sharp feeling that European immigrants should be restricted to vocational education, for it is recognized that they must in two or three generations disappear as distinguishable groups. True, it is felt that most of them must be physical workers rather than, members of the intellectual classes, but this does not as a rule imply a belief in a distinction of kind. Their education, it is realized, must be allowed to rest on individual qualities, and while it is suspected that a relatively high number of their children will be restricted by racial inheritance to manual labor, too many successful doctors, lawyers, writers, artists, and scientists have come from every part of Europe to permit the acceptance of any racial theory of vocational education. On the other hand, the adult immigrant's ignorance of American customs and ideals has, in recent years in particular, and never more strongly than in the years of or immediately after the World War, caused private or public agencies to stress the need of education of a special type for this group. "Americanization work" is the generic name given to these programs.

Americanization does not lend itself to facile definition. Certainly the goal of our efforts to educate the immigrant should not be to make him look, dress, talk, and behave like some mythical one-hundred-per-cent American who is supposed to typify all that is desirable in our civilization. There can, of course, be no uniform pattern to which all immigrants should be molded. Vermont would hardly be satisfied with a revamped immigrant suited to the habits and ways of southern California, nor would New Orleans be content with a Butte, Montana, product. To attempt to isolate some minimum pattern to which all Americans could subscribe despite community, class and individual variations is futile, for good and unimpeachable American citizens may have nothing more in common than accidental birth and residence within the territorial limits of the United States. Uniformity is not only inconceivable, but it is also undesirable as both a cause and a symptom of stagnation. But without an accepted pattern, how can we hope to Americanize our immigrants?

The answer is obscured not by the intricacy of the problem but by the verbal dust thrown into our eyes by well-intentioned patriots who thought in terms of conformity and loyalty without reference to their actual sources. It was thought that there was some body of knowledge and a national spirit which could be given to aliens in small doses of American history, government, hygiene, mental arithmetic, and the English language. Evidence of Americanization was the completion of the most elementary courses in such subjects and a desire to take out naturalization papers, with an acceptance of the duties of peace and war thereby imposed.

Actually, Americanization has little to do with any of these things. An alien may take a college education specializing in American history and government, live a healthy life and take out naturalization papers, and still not fit into American life. On the other hand, he may be uninformed about George Washington and the Continental Congress, ignorant of the details of representative government, live in a contagion-breeding tenement, remain a technical subject of a king, and still be a blessing to the community. Possibly such an individual could not properly be called "Americanized," but if so, it is the concept which is out of line, not the useful but handicapped tenement dweller.

The only real meaning which the term Americanization may possess, other than the hypocritical and superficial wartime definition in terms of nationalism, is the simple one of adult education. There is no need for Americanization to differ in content or purpose from the education of native-born citizens. Of course, there is usually the problem of reeducation, implying a modification of an alien culture into adjustment with that of the United States, but such reeducation is also desirable for a large number of individuals of old American stock. It is doubtful whether the reeducation of lagging native citizens is any easier than the Americanization of aliens, for the alien at least realizes he is in a new environment, while the American is more likely to be cocksure of himself and his ideas. The technical problems of pedagogical method peculiar to the education of the immigrant are not sufficient to require the coining of the nationalistic but essentially meaningless shibboleth, Americanization. "Immigrant education" is less misleading and does not tend to warp instruction in the direction of patriotic drum thumping. Give the immigrant, his children, and the native American an education which will prepare them for useful participation in community life, with the same objectives for all and minor variations in technique, and the school need not bother further about cultural assimilation and national loyalty.

The immigrant should of course be assimilated with the help of the school, which implies the development of cultural compatibility without the destruction of individuality; but obvious compulsion should never be used to gain this end, for the result of such procedure is likely to be outward conformity and an inner feeling of rebellion. Compulsion is a common accompaniment of Americanization work. Factories, we have pointed out, are urged not to employ aliens unless they have obtained their first papers indicating a desire to be naturalized. Schools frequently refuse to hire citizens of foreign lands as teachers. These things are done in time of peace; during war the pressure upon neutral aliens to give an outward sign of Americanization becomes terrific. Many yield, for there is little else to do when the means of livelihood are at stake; but it is doubtful whether such forced converts are as desirable as those who quietly adopt the customs and ideals of their community and perhaps neglect to have their new status publicly recorded. Most immigrants become truly Americanized automatically if given a chance without oppression and exploitation. Guidance and protection, not force, are needed.

It has been held that there are many kinds of men scattered over the world, but only one true civilization. Even the amateur student of history now knows that actually mankind is a relatively homogeneous unit, if groups are compared with groups, while civilizations, radically at variance with each other, may be numbered without limit. It is when individuals who represent diverse civilizations as a whole, or perhaps possess merely some minor conflicting cultural traits, come into contact that friction is likely to result. Here the school may play an important rôle in synthesizing conflicting cultural elements, but it cannot do so by riding roughshod over the standards and traditions of a minority group. It must take them into account if only to destroy them. They must always be the point of departure in any constructive program, and frequently it is wisest to preserve at least a few minority traits which may be accepted with profit into the dominant culture while making the assimilation of their possessors less humiliating and painful.

No culture is so perfect that it will not bear improvement by borrowing from almost any other culture. It is a sign of provincialism that schools in the United States have generally sought to assimilate minority peoples by cultural absorption without thought for the preservation of the best and most adaptable traits of the stranger. This attitude is now, fortunately, becoming obsolete in the best educational circles, and some decrease in cultural conflict may confidently be expected from this willingness to see virtue in a stranger's peculiarities.

The culture of the minority group is never completely lost even where no formal effort is made to preserve some of its features. Every nationality and racial group in the United States, even though its origin can no longer be sharply distinguished, has left some evidence of its existence in the form of cultural borrowings by the majority group. The Indian has left his imprint on our language through the many words and place names borrowed from him. Our table is richer by the corn, potatoes, succotash and other foods he has contributed, and to our agricultural customs we have added his system of corn culture which was originally taken over intact by the white man. The whole line of southern development shows the influence of the Negro's participation. Borrowing from the Oriental started long before the discovery of America. European immigrant contributions are so well known and numerous that illustrations are unnecessary. In helping to select alien cultural contributions for adoption, and in calling attention to the origin of those already accepted as an integral part of the civilization of the United States, the school can perform a significant function.

Cultural assimilation is least painful for the immigrants whose native cultures most nearly resemble those of this country, and most distressing, perhaps, for the ones who, like the Oriental, have little in their early training in common with our ways of life. It is, however, a necessary adjustment, and the schools as well as the less formal educational agencies must help to make it a reality. How to do this without disrupting individual standards, thus leaving thousands of new arrivals, for a time at least, with weakened guides and sanctions for behavior, is an unsolved problem.

Inevitable as this problem of transitional lack of standards may seem, there is some hope that its socially undesirable effects may be lessened by a formal educational program which will take account of the worth-while qualities of alien cultures. Indeed, some progress has already been made in this direction, although its relative importance has been exaggerated. The Indian Bureau is now attempting to get local agents and teachers to make use of whatever cultural survivals, such as Navajo blankets and Pueblo pottery, may help its wards until they have been thoroughly Europeanized. The recording and popularizing of folk lore, songs, and other cultural traits of various minority peoples in the United States may have some effect in delaying the disintegration of the restraining influences of their special cultures, but the total effect of such artificial efforts is relatively slight and hardly worth the cost except for historical and æsthetic purposes. The school approach, it seems, must not operate through attempts to delay the disappearance of alien cultures or to bring them back after they have faded, for neither is possible to a sufficient extent to be socially significant in the solution of this particular problem, but rather to concentrate on the inculcation of new standards and ideals as rapidly as possible without disparagement of the old.

A school properly equipped and manned may be one of the most effective means for bringing conflicting groups together in harmony. The efficient way to do this, however, is not to separate children and parents either physically or intellectually any more than absolutely necessary for the accomplishment of the ultimate purpose, which is cultural adjustment to the environment which will prevail in later life. Unless all members of the family unit—and the family is a much more compact, efficiently functioning unit among many minority groups than among people of native white stock—are assimilated into their new surroundings at harmonious rates of development, there either will be family friction, probably sufficient to destroy its essential unity, the children consequently being deprived of the advantages of family life, or else the strength of family and communal bonds will cause a reversion to their former habits and beliefs after their release from the influences of school.

Children born in this country of immigrant parents, especially if their parents have not come from northwestern Europe, are assimilated much more rapidly than the older generation by forces operating both in and out of school. The school alone concerns us here, and in so far as it permits parents to adhere to alien standards and beliefs while it teaches conflicting ideas to the children, it is neglecting its duty. If school children are taught one thing at home and another in school, the obvious result is a degree of disregard for both. Immigrant parents, we must repeat, are notorious for their conflicts with their children, producing a lack of control dangerous in formative years. The child is pinched between the old world and the new, and breaks away from the restraints of both with a skeptical rebellion born of conflicting cultures.

So long as we have a division of labor on a sex basis, and children fail to follow their fathers' educational and occupational footsteps, there is no reason to expect any real reduction in culture conflicts caused by differential education of family members. A suggestion that the family or community be transformed into the unit with which the schools will deal in place of the individual child, is a matter for academic interest only at the present time. There are too many costs in the way of its acceptance. If it has any merit at all, it lies in calling attention

to the penalties which we pay for belonging to an individualistic society, and possibly, realizing these penalties, we may do
what little we can to prevent too sharp a break between alien
and American cultures, the older generations and the young.

Some optimistic schoolmen and Americanization workers
will promptly claim that the family and community are already accepted as the unit on which sound educational programs are being built. Sporadic attempts at adult education
are being made among both the native and foreign-born population, but their effect in easing individuals through their
transitional period may be largely discounted. Most minority
group adults are not reached by any formal educational program at all, and those who do stumble into Americanization
classes and similar attempts at education find them too brief
and shallow, as a rule, to keep them abreast of the younger
people of the community. Parent-teacher associations are also
a step in the right direction, but a short one. Perhaps the most
helpful feature of the situation is the fact that children unconsciously educate their parents during their hours at home, and
it is a comment on our adult educational program that the
younger generation has been able to do more to keep their
elders up to date than all the efforts of our skilled adult
teachers.

But in spite of our children's efforts it seems that there is
bound to continue a combination of formal and informal education which will produce rapid results in the younger people,
slower assimilation in the fathers, and a minimum change in
the mothers. The younger generation is less bound by old-
country traditions, which they have received second-hand in
a country where they are not accepted. The older men who
have been reared abroad change with reluctance, but since
they are the breadwinners in constant contact with the world
of industry and trade, they cannot help but absorb some of
the customs and ideals of their new home country. Wives and
mothers, however, especially if they were reared in lands where
woman's place was in the home, have the fewest and most
superficial contacts with American civilization, and conse-

quently hold fast to old-world standards more rigidly than their husbands or children.

Too often the immigrant is guided toward economic exploitation, insanitary and inadequate housing, political corruption, and all the rest of the mistreatment which customarily goes along with being a "wop," "dago," "hunky," "kike," or other derisively branded foreign product. These are the very things from which he must be protected if his cultural assimilation is to be painless, rapid, and complete. It is patently futile to elaborate on the evils of economic radicalism and the universal benevolence of capitalistic industrialism in an Americanization classroom, when the mature students are spending their days in underpaid, exhaustive labor in sweat shops and mills without souls. Why waste money in propaganda to spread a knowledge of physical and mental hygiene among immigrants and their children when they may live nowhere save in disease-breeding, overcrowded areas where families and boarders of both sexes and all ages are crowded into quarters so small and ill equipped that sufficient privacy and conveniences for the development of ordinary standards of modesty, decency and morality are beyond possibility? What value is there in teaching the superiority of democratic and representative government, the integrity of Washington, Jefferson, and Lincoln, and the equality of all before the bar of American justice, when votes are openly bought by cash or favors, political graft is taken for granted, and justice lends a ready ear to the ward heeler? The immigrant believes what he sees and experiences, not what he is taught by Americanization workers in a few short hours of instruction.

In spite of this conflict between teaching and reality, it is not suggested that adult immigrant instruction should be discontinued. It is, however, futile to attempt to convince immigrants of the ideal qualities of American institutions when they know perfectly well from first-hand sources that the ideals are practically unattainable by minority groups, or perhaps even mythical. What is needed is both a readjustment of living conditions to conform more nearly to announced American standards, and a revision of teaching in the direction of reality and away from meaningless and impractical fictions. The improvement of immigrant living and working conditions is not the function of the school, and may not be further discussed in this chapter; yet from such reformation will be expected the greatest results in the way of fundamental immigrant education and assimilation, for the informal training of everyday events and circumstances is the basic source of standards and conduct.

The functions of the schools in the assimilation of minority groups are to furnish mental tools for the job of living in the United States, and to crystallize workable ideals and standards acceptable to the community. Neither of these functions is being performed in more than a perfunctory manner, and then only for a minority of the aliens within our borders.

It is usually stated that a knowledge of English is the first prerequisite to proper assimilation. To an extent this is true; but it must not be forgotten that the Pennsylvania Germans, and other rural groups as well, have been "Americanized" for generations in spite of a limited knowledge of the English language. Language is only a tool, and while it is essential that the communication tool of the community be learned quickly and thoroughly there may be advantages in not discarding the old too soon. Identical thoughts can be expressed in English, German, Italian, or Chinese, and it is much easier to grasp ideas expressed in the speech of childhood than in one learned in later life. This means that while all immigrants should probably be taught a minimum of English necessary to their functioning as community members, much assimilative work, especially that involving the inculcation of social standards, may be best carried on in the childhood tongue. Foreign-language newspapers, much reviled as unpatriotic propaganda sheets, are an efficient assimilative agency, for in spite of a tendency to emphasize foreign news and glorify the country of their readers' birth, they have found it necessary to include American items and editorials which reflect the point of view of the new home, and perhaps do more to "Americanize" immigrant subscribers than could any unfamiliar publication in a difficult secondary language. Any program of assimilation which considers its first duty to be the wiping out of all alien tongues without delay, and fails to make use of the best tool for conveying ideas to the immigrant, that is, his primary language, is paying more attention to surface polishing than to true assimilation. It is not the means of expression, but the attitudes and actions which count, for they require no greater substitute of English in the foreign-born generations than is dictated by the English-speaking contacts of the individual.

The measure of assimilation, accomplished by community and school influences, can be nothing more than the individual's service to the society of which he is a part. He may contribute to his community's welfare by doing manual or intellectual labor of the best possible quality. The relations of an individual to his government are a criterion of adjustment, as are his relations to his family and the community at large. He may be a radical or conservative in political and economic views, so long as he has taken advantage of the opportunities offered him and acts honestly in accordance with his lights. The tests of an assimilated immigrant are identical with those which a native citizen of *Mayflower* ancestry must pass if he wishes to be counted as a credit to his country. It is to meet such tests, and nothing more, that school and society must unite in guiding and directing the alien in our land. Minority and majority groups alike require educational institutions which will serve this end, regardless of race, color, nationality, or creed.

CHAPTER XIV

EDUCATIONAL SEGREGATION

So FAR as the Negro and the other colored groups are involved, the school is not at present an important agency in reducing racial frictions. It is a social institution which reflects the opinions of the group governing it. Teachers and officials are effective mouthpieces of community opinion, and so long as the community at large believes in the inferiority of certain minority groups and in the need for race barriers, just so long and no longer will the school support and inculcate these beliefs. However, we may consciously strive for an elimination of injustice produced by these beliefs. Even a country such as this, governed by certain race and national prejudices, may demand that race, color, or nationality should not provide bars to equal opportunities in education.

SEPARATE SCHOOLS FOR MINORITIES

No racial or nationality group in the United States has had its children educated in entirely separate schools from those patronized by the youth of old American stock. But there has been a degree of educational segregation in our school system which has kept large numbers of immigrant and colored children apart from those of native parentage. The factors which have produced this segregation have not been the same in all cases, nor have the effects been identical. There is, however, a sufficient similarity running through the school segregation of Negro, Indian, oriental and European immigrant children to warrant comparison.

The sharpest cleavage has been between the education of colored and white children, particularly in the south, but also in northern areas where Negroes have concentrated. To the southern white parent it is unthinkable that his children and those of any Negro should attend the same classes. In the north the feeling is less keen, but wherever it is possible to do so, the tendency is to encourage separate schools for Negroes, especially in the elementary grades, and to a lesser extent in high schools. With the exception of Lincoln University in Pennsylvania and Wilberforce University in Ohio, however, it has not been thought necessary to erect separate college facilities. Private schools in all sections of the country bar Negroes, although an occasional colored student may slip in unnoticed where public disapproval has no strength. In those regions where segregation has long been practised there are no signs of a change of policy; where such policy has been weakly supported or absent, the tendency is apparently toward increasing separation.

The issue is clear and increasingly important, for as the white people of the North are apparently swinging over to the southern attitude, the Negroes of the entire country are coming to the point where their objections, shielded from the white man where strategically desirable, must be given weight. Few Negroes favor segregation: none may do so openly among their own people without arousing bitter feeling, except it be in a hopeless spirit of compromise in order to obtain the best schooling possible for their children from antagonistic white communities. To some extent the argument reminds one of the dispute regarding separate education for boys and girls. This similarity will become apparent as the discussion develops. Reasoning by analogy, however, will not settle the issue. If segregation is advantageous to the community, it should be accomplished; if disadvantageous, it should not. If it is a matter of no real importance, popular opinion may decide without danger.

There are communities, including most of the South and some sections in the North, where white public opinion is so strong and bitter that it becomes automatically advantageous to the entire population, colored and white, to enforce the color line in schools. There is no argument strong enough to overcome the race feeling in states and districts where the emotional race traditions of the South are firmly established. Factual arguments have no weight when they are put in the balance with such prejudice, and attempts to unify the school systems under these conditions would fail, and in their failure would produce open racial ruptures more devastating than any possible evils to be corrected.

This observation may create the impression of hopelessness concerning any possibility of reducing southern educational segregation at the present time. If so, it is in accordance with the facts, for even the most violent colored opponents of educational segregation have refused to battle in such areas and have concentrated their efforts on the improvement of colored schools so that they may not lag too far behind the white.[1] There are few localities in northern states where the issue may not be fought out on some basis more intelligent than that of race feeling, and the exceptions may nearly all be found in the border areas of southern New Jersey, Pennsylvania, Ohio, Indiana, and Illinois. Where segregation exists or is being contemplated in districts other than these, the case is far from hopeless, and the final course of action may be influenced by intellectual and political arguments.

It has already been stated that the Negro does not require a different type of education from white children except as his limited background may demand slightly different treatment. Morally, the Negro should be taught the same standards as anyone else. The country would be better off politically if the colored element were molded into an improved citizenship more qualified to take an intelligent part in government. Industrially and professionally, educational objectives should be the same for all peoples of similar environment. What cultural handicaps the Negro has are not necessarily permanent in nature, and may best be removed through a unified educational program which will take account of individual variations without making them worse through public overemphasis.

Separate schools, then, cannot be defended because of differential racial qualities, for none have been established. There

[1] An intimate account of the founding, early struggles, moderate success and legal termination of the outstanding experiment in Negro-white coeducation at Berea College in Kentucky, may be found in Edwin R. Embree, *Brown America*, Viking Press, Inc., New York, 1931. pp. vi + 311.

is no more force to the argument that Negro children (for illustration, recent migrants from southern farms) need a segregated school to bring them up to the level of community standards than there is to one that all poor children, foreign or native born, who come from handicapped classes should be isolated in the same or similar special buildings. This would be an impossible procedure.

If, however, segregation should prove advantageous to the white man there is no profit in opposing it, for it will be increasingly adopted regardless of its effect on the colored groups. This is a question of practical politics, and since the white man controls the school boards it may be expected that he will first protect his own interests with little thought of altruistic motives. As a matter of fact, the white man apparently loses more than he gains by this device.

It has been held that the presence of colored children from inferior homes retards the educational progress of white school children. There is an element of truth in this opinion, for if a teacher is compelled to regulate her efforts to the abilities and speed of the backward students, obviously the superior individuals may idle along with a minimum of application to school tasks and thus waste opportunity for advancement more in accordance with capacity. It is also true that Negro children as a group are more retarded educationally and do poorer average work than white children, apparently a reflection of their home and class status. The fact that some Negroes do superior work does not alter this fact. If colored children are permitted to be a drag on other students, some remedial measures should be taken.

The remedy, however, is not necessarily segregation. White children also differ in capacity for school work, and even in strictly white institutions some students may loaf along while others must work at top speed to achieve satisfactory results. Since low capacity with its attendant retarding influence on superior children can be found in all groups and is not a racial phenomenon, the solution may be to grade students, regardless of color, in accordance with their capacity, native or acquired, to keep in step with the other similar members of their class.

Simply to put all Negroes in one school and all whites in another would mean that the superior white and colored pupils in both schools would be denied opportunity to receive the quality of instruction they deserved.

The moral and health standards of the Negroes are known to be more lax than those of the ordinary white community. Their use of language is likely to be careless and ungrammatical, and full of mispronunciation and vulgar idiom. In other words, the average Negro would hardly serve as an acceptable model of personal conduct and expression to people with progressive standards. It is beside the point that many Negroes are superior in every way to a great number of white people. The general run of Negro behavior is less in accordance with the social conventions than that of the white man. Thus it is claimed that colored pupils are a source of contamination to the white. This charge, too, has some truth in it, but there is danger of contamination from children of all races. On this basis numerous white children should be segregated from others with superior home training, but no practical way has been devised for accomplishing this purpose.

It might seem that since colored people as a class come from poorer social environments it would be best to put them all off by themselves, in spite of the superior qualities of the few, in order to obtain the greatest good for the greatest number. This, however, would not accomplish the desired result, for the school is not the only source of contact between races. It is not even the most important means whereby undesirable social traits are passed from one race to another. Complete segregation of Negroes and white people has never been approached for either children or adults, for there are countless points of contact through domestic servants, children's maids, other employee-employer relationships, and casual meetings at work or play. The extent of such borrowings may be illustrated by the recent white craze for Negro music and dances. The presence of white blood in a majority of American Negroes is not without significance. In view of the fact that "contamination" cannot be avoided through school segregation or any other form of segregation as yet invented, the answer to this argument seems to be a program for cleaning up the distasteful conditions at their source by expending every effort to raise the standards of the Negro and not by continuing to allow him to break conventions of morals and taste undisturbed, on the theory that he is injuring only himself.

Racial intermarriage is a threat which drives white Americans wild. If two races go to school together, it is violently stated, miscegenation, legal or illicit, must increase. There are plenty of contacts outside of the school between the sexes of different races to allow more than sufficient opportunity for a maximum of race crossing. There are powerful social forces at work in every state of the Union which will continue to restrict marital eligibility in accordance with group conventions, and this means that interracial marriages will remain in a forbidden category whether or not the children are segregated in school. Not every classmate is a potential husband or wife for the American girl or boy even in white schools. There is no noticeably greater amount of sexual relationship of any sort between colored and white people in those northern communities where all children attend the same school than where they are divided by race; and it may even be that there is less than in the south where, in spite of educational segregation, *ante bellum* traditions and the presence of an underprivileged caste encourage miscegenation, contrary to legal and other policies.

Certainly separate schools for Negro and white pupils are an unreal situation in the north, if not in all parts of the country. The Negro has to live in constant contact with white people. Just as certainly white people cannot avoid frequent contacts with Negroes if any live in their community. It is perhaps best to start these contacts as early as possible.

The idea of racial segregation in schools is not new, nor has it been restricted to Negro-white relationships. All colored races have been excluded from some school or other in the United States, and so have certain immigrant peoples. It has been tried on the Indian, and without success. In frontier communities the Indian child was deemed a source of contamination to white children, and separate schools were established. The most reliable argument, however, has been that the Indian required a special education, although this has been shown to be unfounded except as Indian opportunities for economic advancement have been culturally limited. In certain parts of the South where Indian and Negro mixture has been common, antagonism to Indian-white coeducation is still strong, sufficiently so to force the Indian into Negro schools, or where, as is quite the rule, the Indian resents being classed with Negroes, into special schools. Today, however, where prejudice against the Negro does not complicate the situation, Indians are admitted to public schools and colleges, and even the best of private secondary schools, without discrimination. Educational authorities are agreed that it would be ideal if all Indians were able to attend educational institutions with a good proportion of white students.

This will be impossible of achievement for many years to come. The Navajos, for example, with their large southwestern reservation, will require separate schools for years to come if for no other reason than their geographic isolation from white people. This is also true where there are other Indian groups with few or no white neighbors. Cultural differences, still strong in some tribes but rapidly disappearing, are not sufficient by themselves to justify separate schools except in the eyes of sentimental individuals who mourn but cannot stop the passing of Indian civilizations in the United States. The fact that Indians are now admitted to the most exclusive college fraternities even in Indian country, as at the University of Oklahoma, indicates an attitude toward that race which will speed the passing of segregated Indian educational institutions.

Popular opinion in California, in the period centered about 1860, made little distinction between Negroes, Indians, and Mongolians. They were all inferior colored races, and as such it was thought desirable to provide some separate schools for the lot. Either this opinion was not sufficiently strong to lead to their actual establishment, or else there were too few children of colored origin requiring school facilities to warrant the expenditure of tax money for the purpose, for in spite of a number of state statutes, largely permissive rather than mandatory, looking toward the removal of children of colored races from white schools, no separate school was established for Orientals until 1885, when a Chinese school was opened on the edge of the Chinese district in San Francisco. In fact, in these early days there were only a few hundreds of Chinese and Negro children in the state, and not all of them applied for admission to public schools, while the Indian children constituted a school problem largely by their non-attendance. It is thus easy to see why a popular belief that the colored races should be educated in separate schools resulted in neglect in the development of such schools.

In 1905, the San Francisco Board of Supervisors ruled that the Japanese children should attend the oriental school, although it was inconveniently located for them. This action was defended by referring to the danger of contamination of white boys and girls from contact with children of a supposedly less moral race, some of whom were noticeably older than their white classmates. The retarding influence of a foreign-language group of inferior caste was also cited. That these were not the real explanations of the segregation order is evidenced by the fact that there were few Japanese children in the public schools, and only a small number of these were more than a year or two over age when compared with white fellow students. These, incidentally, might properly have been removed from classes of younger children without the necessity of segregating all students of their race. There is ample testimony, adequately verified, that Japanese children were not sources of moral contamination and that they did not slow up the school work of the white children. Obviously, the origin of the Japanese school segregation order was the increasing anti-Japanese feeling which accompanied the growth of immigration from that country. The order, put into effect in 1906 by the School Board, aroused so much antagonism among Japanese both here and abroad, and the issue seemed so trivial to non-Californians, that after President Roosevelt's intervention it was withdrawn. The Gentleman's Agreement limiting immigration from Japan was an outgrowth of this ruling.

Such segregation for aliens or citizens is undoubtedly legal under the Constitution so long as equal facilities are afforded the minority group. Of this there can be no question. It is another matter, however, when the necessity, wisdom, or good taste of such a procedure is considered. That race feeling is the cause of oriental school segregation is attested by the present situation.

In all parts of the United States where Chinese and Japanese are numerically unimportant the question of separate education receives scant attention. This is not necessarily because it would be too expensive to segregate oriental children from white, for they could be required to attend Negro schools where they exist, so far as the federal government is concerned. Under the law of the land, there is no insuperable barrier to putting into practice a ruling that the children of any or all colored races shall attend segregated schools. Yet even in the Pacific coast states, where anti-oriental antagonism is keenest, little segregation of the pupils of Chinese or Japanese ancestry exists. In San Francisco a majority of oriental children go to a segregated school, but some oriental children are found in other schools. In other parts of California may be found schools or classes containing only Orientals, but this is practised for the lower grades only, and there are so many cases where no separation can be observed that no generally observed rule may be said to exist. In Oregon and Washington there are some schools where Orientals predominate, but absolute segregation by law or custom has not been deemed desirable or necessary by any effective group of citizens.

The situation thus resembles that in which northern Negroes find themselves so frequently. Schools predominantly colored spring up in colored communities, but there is no hard and fast rule which demands separate facilities. In the same city there may be strictly colored schools, schools predominantly colored, schools with a minority of colored pupils, and schools with only a thin sprinkling of colored students. In high schools and colleges, while the attitude may be unfriendly, absolute segregation has proved impractical. The South alone has been able to maintain sharp lines of cleavage between the races in all types of educational institutions; the Negro alone has been the object of sufficient sustained antagonism to be the basis of a dual school system from kindergarten to professional school.

Where the segregation of the children of immigrants has been accomplished, it has been the result of concentration of a foreign element in some area, of the voluntary withdrawal from the public schools of some alien group, or of the creation of private institutions, unsupported by taxpayers, which have refused or restricted the admission of minority group children. Since there are both urban and rural areas populated almost entirely by immigrants of one nationality or another, it naturally follows that the schools of the neighborhood will reflect the race or nationality of the community. Here there is segregation without planned discrimination to handicap the children. If segregation of pupils with common cultural traditions and limitations should ever prove advantageous to majority or minority peoples, an example might be here anticipated. Italian children predominating in one school, Jewish children in another, Polish children in another, native white in still another, should make it possible for sympathetic teachers to take account of peculiar customs and standards in order to assimilate the unadjusted students into the main cultural stream of the country without any retarding influences, without any childish race friction or feeling of inferiority. Yet educators who have had experience with the education of immigrant children as a whole do not favor the extension of such segregation, and actually fight to reduce it to a minimum. If it is not successful here, under such favorable conditions, why should it be expected to produce desirable results with colored pupils, black, brown, yellow, or red, when accompanied by the additional handicaps due to color?

Voluntary segregation in special schools by minority groups has been properly looked on with suspicion by a large proportion of the American people. Japanese supplementary schools have been cited as evidence of the unwillingness of these people to permit their children to become assimilated. This is criticism unjustified by the facts, for these schools have been little more than an attempt to provide opportunity for American-born Japanese to learn the language and some small amount of the history and tradition of their parents. It has not been their purpose to make Japanese out of United States citizens, but rather to keep alive some vestiges of an ancient traditional culture in the minds of a young generation of good American patriots, for such American-born Japanese have proved to be. Where the purpose is to maintain allegiance to a foreign government, as has been the case with some supplementary schools and their teachers, there is reason for disapproval; but attempts to develop a patriotic ferver for a land which the children have never seen have not been popular with parents or pupils, and their results have been negative. It takes more than a few hours of formal instruction a week to offset the influences of real life.

Immigrants of every nationality have tried by some schoolroom method to give their children a respect for the achievements of their ancestors, and we should respect them for their efforts to pass along some understanding of the land of origin to their children, who may well be better American citizens for it. A line may be drawn, however, when such instruction becomes subversive to American citizenship and has the purpose of building an active patriotism for some foreign country. It is well for the Irishman to be familiar with Ireland's history, and proud of it; but when familiarity and pride become emotional loyalty strong enough to hamper the United States in the prosecution of war even slightly, as during the World War period, cultural assimilation is retarded. Fortunately, it has been impossible to create a foreign loyalty in any large proportion of American-born children of whatever European or oriental ancestry, and such attempts have been more of a petty annoyance in bad taste rather than a serious political problem.

Just as minority groups have supplemented or supplanted the public schools with privately supported institutions of their own, so have various classes of native white stock considered the public schools inadequate for the education of their children. This has led to the founding of private schools of many varieties. The existence of these cannot be explained solely on the basis of superior instruction, for the great majority of private institutions neither surpass nor equal in educational efficiency the better public schools in all sections of the country. There may be any number of reasons why parents send their children to private day or boarding schools, of primary, secondary, or college rank, but among them must be included class and caste consciousness. Even if pupils are not sent to institutions for this reason, they nevertheless are likely to be reinforced in any belief in the innate superiority of the native white stock.

This follows inevitably from the fact that private schools generally, from kindergarten to college, are segregated schools so far as the more despised minority peoples are concerned. Negroes rarely, if ever, are admitted to primary and secondary private schools. Few of them enter the more elect, smaller privately controlled colleges. In districts where there is anti-Jewish feeling, the Jews too come under the ban. Of course, every minority group is limited in its attendance at private educational institutions if only because of insufficient income, but the adequate income of a few Negroes and many Jews does not make them welcome at the private school of ordinary rank.

The private schools of a sect composed entirely of old American stock may be cited for illustration. The Society of Friends, usually known as the Quakers, maintains a number of private schools giving instruction in subjects ranging from the elementary grades to college. Negroes are generally refused admittance to the schools and colleges in or near Philadelphia under Quaker control. They are decidedly not wanted, even in such liberal Quaker colleges as Swarthmore and Haverford, although an occasional exception has been made. Jews are in a similar position, although the exceptions in their case have been more numerous. There is a recent case where the son of a Jewish alumnus of one of the best Quaker preparatory schools was refused enrollment because of his parentage about the same time that his father was invited to contribute to the school endowment. The defense that Quaker schools are for Quakers does not remove the fact of segregation. It does not even answer the charge of racial and class discrimination, for non-Quakers are admitted relatively freely if they do not belong to the Negro race or the Jewish faith.

It may seem unfair to single out the Quakers as an illustration, but perhaps they open themselves to special criticism through their praiseworthy liberal teachings regarding race relations, and their well known interracial committees which have worked hard to reduce race friction. When Judge Parker of North Carolina was proposed for the United States Supreme Court by President Hoover, himself a birthright Friend, Quakers played an important part in securing his rejection by the Senate, partly because of his earlier utterances showing prejudice against the Negro. In view of such avowed beliefs their segregated schools are open to comment.

Private schools and colleges under other control tend toward similar segregation. Inconsistently enough, students from foreign countries, regardless of race, appear to be quite generally welcomed in private institutions, while American-born youths of immigrant parentage are excluded. Oriental students rarely encounter discrimination when they apply for admission. Latin Americans are also welcome, although it is well known that Brazilians, Cubans, and Porto Ricans commonly have some African ancestry. Foreign students of any color or creed may find welcome in first-class private schools and colleges, usually without extensive search, and their presence is not infrequently mentioned with pride by officials, as though they added tone to the institution. The same stock born in America encounters a different reception.

Thus voluntary school segregation, whether by the accident of place of residence or purposeful withdrawal from public schools by minority or majority groups, is a common phenomenon in the United States and is a powerful factor in maintaining and strengthening racial and cultural barriers. There may be sufficient benefit derived from such separation to counterbalance the consequent group misunderstandings and friction, but the fact remains that a lack of interracial cooperation is one of the products of the system.

THE COSTS OF SEGREGATION

The theory that racial and cultural groups require education of a special type and in special classes has led seventeen southern states and the District of Columbia to develop dual school systems, one for whites and one for Negroes. These states have all accepted in principle the doctrine that educational opportunities should be the same for all persons regardless of color, but in actual practice this doctrine has been honored in its breach. The result has been that segregation has invariably meant inferior education for the minority group, and not only in these states but everywhere in the United States where the practice prevails.

The inferiority in educational opportunities expresses itself in numerous ways. The instruction rendered is poorer because the teachers are not properly trained or paid, nor do the schools possess proper material equipment. The shorter school terms, furthermore, reduce the assimilative power of the student. The inadequacy of the elementary school instruction makes it difficult to pursue high school studies with success, and the insufficiency of preparatory training reduces materially the chance of college entrance or graduation. The lack of proper education in the elementary stages thus makes itself felt throughout the entire system, including the university and the professional school.

No school can successfully carry out an educational program unless the financial basis is adequate. In the case of the Negro, at least, the dominant white group has consistently refused to use the taxpayer's money for the education of the Negro child or youth on a basis of equality with white children. Charles S. Johnson gives a table which shows the proportions of state educational funds devoted to Negro education compared with the proportion of the Negroes in the age groups of six to thirteen inclusive in seventeen states.[2]

[2] Charles S. Johnson, *op. cit.*, p. 262.

TABLE I

State	Per Cent of State Funds Spent for Negro Education	Per Cent of Negroes in the Total Age Groups 6–13
South Carolina......	10.66	54.9
Mississippi..........	10.51	53.0
Georgia.............	13.33	43.5
Louisiana...........	9.98	39.3
Alabama............	8.40	38.9
Florida.............	7.91	36.9
North Carolina......	12.13	31.5
Virginia............	11.09	31.3
Arkansas...........	15.99	25.9
Tennessee..........	11.93	22.9
Maryland...........	9.67	17.8
Texas..............	12.00	16.2
Delaware...........	13.78	14.4
Kentucky...........	8.02	8.2
Oklahoma..........	4.73	7.2
West Virginia.......	4.65	4.7
Missouri............	3.15	4.1

It will be noticed that in some of these states the proportional amount spent for Negro education is approximately the same as that spent for white education. These states have a small number of Negroes, and it has been definitely proved that in the south at least there is a definite correlation between the size of the Negro population in a community and the money spent for the education of that group. The higher the proportion of Negroes, the smaller the per capita expenditure for Negro children. In the survey of Negro Education in 1916, the comparisons in Table II were presented to illustrate this fact.

It was found in the same survey that the average per capita expenditure in the southern states was $2.89 for colored and $10.32 for white pupils.

A good share of this discrimination is no doubt due to the economic handicaps of the South. Where communities are far from prosperous. funds for education are limited, and if there

TABLE II[3]

County Groups, Percentage of Negroes in the Population	White Teachers' Salaries	Negro Teachers' Salaries	Per Capita White	Per Capita Negro
Counties under 10 per cent...	$ 7,755,817	$ 325,579	$ 7.96	$7.23
Counties 10 to 25 per cent....	9,633,674	1,196,788	9.55	5.55
Counties 25 to 50 per cent....	12,572,666	2,265,945	11.11	3.19
Counties 50 to 75 per cent....	4,574,366	1,167,796	12.53	1.77
Counties 75 per cent and over	888,759	359,800	22.22	1.78

are not enough to go around white children are taken care of first. It would be a rare white school board which would lower the efficiency of the schools for white children in order to raise the Negro standards. The ever-present belief that Negroes are spoiled by education anyway makes it possible to defend a discriminatory policy which would otherwise be patently unfair.

It is a truism to say that in the last analysis it is the teacher of a school who determines the value of the education imparted. If teachers are grossly underpaid, only poorly prepared or otherwise unsuccessful individuals will enter the profession. While the existence of a color bar to some degree vitiates this generalization, it is on the whole correct. White teachers in the south average higher salaries than do the colored. In the 1916 survey mentioned, information secured from various states brought out the facts in the following table:[4]

TABLE III

	Average Annual Salary, White	Average Annual Salary, Negro
Alabama....................	$355.53	$158.78
Florida....................	305.02	168.70
Georgia...................	318.63	119.35
Kentucky.................	322.70	310.05
Louisiana.................	529.04	159.89
North Carolina...........	196.83	118.59
South Carolina...........	333.28	110.54
Virginia..................	322.69	172.63

[3] Department of the Interior, Bureau of Education, *Negro Education*, Bulletin No. 38, 1916, vol. i, p. 7.

[4] *Ibid.*, vol. i, p. 34.

While conditions have greatly improved since then, great inequalities in pay still persist, as may be seen from the following quotation:

"The schedule of salaries in Lexington provides a minimum of $1000 for white elementary teachers, and a maximum of $900 for colored elementary teachers. The minimum for white high-school teachers is $1400 while the maximum for colored high-school teachers is $1200. White teachers receive $35 additional pay for summer-school work, and Negro teachers $20. The annual increment for white teachers is $50, for Negro teachers $25.

"In Memphis, the minimum salary for white elementary teachers is $1000, and the maximum $1600. The minimum for the colored elementary teachers holding certificates is $720, and the maximum is $1020. In the high schools, the white teachers receive a minimum of $1400 and a maximum of $1920; the colored teachers a minimum of $1020 and a maximum of $1680.

"In New Orleans, the minimum salary for white elementary teachers is $1200. The maximum is $1750 for teachers without degrees, with an additional $150 for holders of the bachelor's degree, and an additional $150 for holders of the master's degree, or a maximum of $2050. The minimum salary for the colored elementary teachers is $1000. The maximum is $1550 for teachers without degrees. Negro teachers holding degrees formerly received additional pay as indicated above for the whites, but this has been discontinued.

"In the high schools, white teachers receive a minimum of $1400 and a maximum of $3300 (holders of the bachelor's degree). Colored high school teachers with the bachelor's degree receive from $1100 to $2300."[5]

It is evident that the salaries of these teachers leave much to be desired. In 1916, seventy per cent of the teachers in the "black belt" states had *less than six grades of elementary education.* Serious efforts have been made in the last few decades to improve this situation, and, largely through the aid of

[5] T. J. Woofter, Jr., *Negro Problems in Cities*, Doubleday, Doran & Company, Inc., New York, 1928, pp. 205-206.

philanthropy, many teacher-training schools have been founded. It will take a long time, however, before there are enough Negro teachers to meet the need even in part. There are approximately five million Negroes under nineteen years of age, and the latest estimate indicates that there are only forty-seven thousand Negro teachers in elementary and high schools.[6]

Since the World War and the beginning of Negro migration northward, the South has realized that Negro labor forms the very foundation of its economic system. To prevent the withdrawal of that labor to northern industry many southern states have tried to provide inducements for the Negro to remain, and improved educational facilities have formed a part of the incentive. To some extent these constructive efforts are reflected in Table IV compiled from data given in a recent federal report.

It will be noticed that the enrollment has risen in the high schools and that the average number of days in attendance has increased, as has the length of the school year. No improvement appears to have been recorded in the enrollment in public elementary schools.[7]

[6] Department of the Interior, Bureau of Education, *Survey of Negro Colleges and Universities*, Bulletin No. 7, 1928, p. 2.

[7] The following quotation not only affords a summary of certain significant facts concerning Negro education but also possesses value as an evidence of the attitude of colored leaders toward the segregation policy of the South.

"The report of Dr. Ambrose Caliver, specialist in the education of Negroes, United States Office of Education, has been published for the years 1928-1930. During the ten years' period, from 1918-1928, thirty million dollars was spent for Negro schoolhouses in eight states, and two hundred and seventy million for whites. The Negroes form 30% of the population.

"In one-third of the counties of the South, Negroes are without high school facilities. There are 578 counties in the former slave states, of which 282 have no high schools. The average length of the school year in the country was 171.5 days and for the Negroes, 131 days. Throughout the country there are thirty pupils for each teacher, while among Negroes there are forty-five. The average annual salary for Negroes is far below that of the whites. In Mississippi, whites receive $545; Negroes $386. In South Carolina whites $769; Negroes $302. In Virginia, whites $822; Negroes $472. In North Carolina, whites $838; Negroes $487. The proportion of state funds devoted to Negro education shows even greater discrepancies. On the other hand, there has been a great increase in the income and property of Negro land grant colleges, and the private colleges have also increased in buildings and endowment." *The Crisis*, January, 1932, p. 463.

TABLE IV

STATISTICS OF EDUCATION OF THE NEGRO RACE 1918-1926 [8]

Public Schools for Negroes in 18 Southern States	1918	1926
Children (Negro) 5 to 17 years of age inclusive......................	2,860,134	3,226,935
Pupils enrolled in public school......	1,963,572	2,218,312
Pupils enrolled in public high schools reporting.....................	12,583	55,083
Average number of days attended by each pupil in the year...........	70	93
Average length of school year, in days	106	132
Per cent of Negro school population enrolled.......................	68.6	68.7
Per cent of total pupils in high school	.64	2.48
Schools for Negroes in Continental United States		
Pupils in public high schools reporting		
Boys...........................	7,143	38,129
Girls..........................	14,827	60,576
Pupils in private high schools reporting...........................	9,032	10,261

It is only recently that the South has recognized the need for public higher education for the Negro, and some public high schools have been erected since the war for this purpose. The general standards of these schools do not appear on the whole to be very high, for only a few years ago a student of this question wrote:

"As the schools for colored pupils become higher in grade the standards become relatively lower. In such items as salaries of teachers, preparation of teachers, courses of study, and

---

The report from which these figures were taken was published by the Department of the Interior, Office of Education, *Biennial Survey of Education in the United States, 1928-1930,* chap. xvii, "Education of Certain Racial Groups in the United States and Its Territories." In addition to a discussion of Negro education, this chapter contains brief analyses of educational work among the Hawaiians, Porto Ricans, Filipinos, native Alaskans and Indians. Bulletin No. 20, 1931.

[8] Department of the Interior, Bureau of Education, *Statistics of Education of the Negro Race 1925-1926,* Bulletin No. 19, 1928, p. 5.

laboratory and literary facilities, the contrasts between the Negro and the white high schools are greater than the contrasts between the Negro and the white elementary schools. . . . Richmond did not begin to develop a good Negro high school until 1916-1917, and did not have a modern high school building for colored pupils until 1922-1923. This building contains 962 seats, had an enrollment in its second year of 1032, and in 1925-1926 of 1196. . . . There was no public high school for colored pupils in Atlanta until 1923-1924. It was built to accommodate 1000 pupils, but 1565 enrolled on the opening day. The enrollment for 1926 was 2215. This school became a four-year high school in 1926-1927."[9]

The following data from recent surveys give a good idea of the extent to which the education of the Negro is retarded in comparison with that of the white. In Arkansas in 1927-1928, 368,255 white and 110,853 colored children were enrolled in the public schools. These figures represent 79.4 and 70.7 per cent respectively of the white and colored children of school age in the state. The average daily attendance in percentages of the enrollment was 73.6 for the whites and 70.5 for the Negroes. There were employed 10,697 white and 2,383 colored teachers. The average salary of the white teachers was $667 and of the Negroes $436. The average length of the school term was one hundred and fifty days for the whites and one hundred and thirty-two days for the Negroes. While only about one-fourth of the white children were enrolled for six months or less, over forty per cent of the Negroes attended for such periods. Per school child enrolled, the value of white school property was $78.02, that of colored school property, $27. During the year referred to, new buildings and improvements were made at the cost of $2,774,267 for white and $211,-982 for colored children. This in spite of the fact that during this year over $39,000 was given to the state by philanthropic agencies specifically interested in Negro education.[10]

[9] T. J. Woofter, Jr., *Negro Problems in Cities*, p. 208.
[10] *Negro Schools in Arkansas, 1927-1928*, State of Arkansas, Department of Education.

From the recent Richmond, Virginia, survey the following extract is presented:

"Interesting light is thrown on some of the education problems of Negroes in Richmond by a study of the 1927 report of the Richmond Public Schools. The total value of land and buildings used for white pupils was $6,215,502, for Negro pupils $712,932. The report shows also that the per capita cost of instruction in the white high schools was $70.72, Negro schools $34.06; the per capita cost of instruction in white elementary schools $50.79, and Negro $23.72. The average annual salary of white elementary teachers was $1,484, Negro $923; white high school teachers $1,985, Negro $1,224. The principals of all Negro schools were—and are—white. All school nurses also were—and are—white. These are paid considerably more than the Negro teachers. The 949 kindergarten children are white. (One Negro kindergarten was established in 1927-1928.) The average enrollment to each class room was 47 for Negro teachers, 33 for white teachers. Twenty-two white schools and two Negro schools have motion picture equipment. None of the Negro schools are equipped with a gymnasium due, partially at least, to the fact that Negroes in Richmond have taken over white neighborhoods and have fallen heir to many of the old school buildings constructed before the day of the school gymnasiums. All of the mentally retarded children enrolled in special classes are white; all the children enrolled in sight-saving classes are white; all of the speech-reading classes are for white children."[11]

The lack of equal educational opportunity for the Negro becomes greater the higher he rises in the hierarchy of schools, for not only does he lack the wealth needed to acquire a higher education, but he is also handicapped by insufficient preparatory training. Yet the development of Negro leadership is dependent to a large extent on higher education.

"There are 3,500 Negro physicians and surgeons in the United States, or approximately one colored physician to every 3,343 Negroes. The white race has one physician to

[11] The Negro Welfare Service Committee, Richmond, Va., *op. cit.*, pp. 89-90.

every 553 persons. A serious lack of Negro dentists prevails. There is only one to every 10,540 Negro inhabitants. In technical lines an even more pronounced shortage of trained men is revealed. There are in the United States only 50 Negro architects, 184 engineers, 145 designers, draftsmen, and inventors, and 207 chemists. Professional and technical education can be obtained in institutions of higher learning only.

"Although the number of Negro clergymen serving as pastors of churches or preachers of the Gospel is approximately 19,600, the training of a large number is extremely limited. Many have not received the benefit of a secondary education and others have never been graduated from college, much less obtained the advantage of proper training in schools of theology. The average number of graduates from Negro theological seminaries is less than ten a year, when the actual demand for qualified Negro ministers is over 100 annually. The responsibility of providing leadership to direct the ethical, the religious, and the spiritual life of the large Negro population is one that rests upon higher education."[12]

It is gratifying to know that the decade 1916-1926 saw a great development in this field of education. The survey just quoted showed that in 1916 there were only thirty-one institutions for Negroes offering college work, while in 1926 there were seventy-seven. The enrollment rose in this decade from 2,132 to 13,860, or 550 per cent.[13] This does not mean of course that all of these institutions have reached the standards of the better colleges for whites. Salaries of teachers are still lower than those of colleges for whites, and the laboratory equipment and the libraries are poorer.

Of the seventy-nine institutions recently studied by the United States Bureau of Education, only fifteen had libraries of over ten thousand volumes, and in many cases these libraries were overburdened with useless books, "the donations for the most part of retired clergymen and others."[14]

On the whole, therefore, segregated professional training for

[12] Department of the Interior, Bureau of Education, *Survey of Negro Colleges and Universities,* Bulletin No. 7, 1928, pp. 3-4.
[13] *Ibid.,* p. 56.
[14] *Ibid.,* p. 47.

the Negro has not reached white standards. Patterned, after white seminaries, Negro theological institutions emphasize systematic theology, homiletics and church history, but generally in a superficial manner. The quality of instruction is inferior, and little effort has been made to revise curricula to bring them into harmony with recent trends in education for the ministry. Admission requirements are low, as might be expected while there is competition for students, and at least as much attention appears to be paid to evidence of a direct and demonstrable call to church service as to intellectual qualifications.

No Negro medical school can compete with a score of leading white institutions. Lack of money, teachers, equipment, and students is sufficient to account for this failure, and it is remarkable that two or three colored schools of medicine, notably that of Howard University, are doing as good work as they are. Desirable interneships are rare, and there are probably less than a hundred to supply the colored needs of the entire country. Negro doctors, of course, are not permitted to serve their interneship in the ordinary hospital, private or state supported, nor may colored girls train for nursing in the vast majority of hospitals. The total number of colored hospitals is so small, and their facilities so limited, that there is no chance of their taking care of the medical training needs of American Negroes during the present generation. In dentistry the situation is worse.

The restrictions of segregated training for the teaching profession can be inferred from what has previously been said about separate schools for Negroes. University training for the practice of law is attainable in the south only in segregated schools, and is of inferior quality. Outside of the ministry, medicine, dentistry, teaching, and the legal profession, there are few opportunities for colored professional attainments; and however limited the facilities for the study of the branches of engineering and other professions not mentioned specifically may be, it is without purpose to extend the discussion by reference to educational shortcomings until there is greater need for men so trained. Preachers, doctors, teachers, and

lawyers are needed in large numbers if the colored element is
to be properly served, yet a segregated educational system has
failed to furnish the American Negro with anything like a
minimum number of first- or even second-rate professional
schools.

One way out of the dilemma of segregated professional
schools has been for an increasing number of Negro students
to drift into northern institutions. Qualified theological students are finding their way into northern seminaries in greater
numbers, where the color line is not drawn so sharply as in
the pulpit, although they are unwelcome, if not flatly barred,
at most. The leading northern medical schools will admit a
few Negroes each year, but not too many. One of the best
medical schools in the country has a policy of admitting not
more than two Negroes a year, which is half of the number of
women permitted to register. Northern law schools are a bit
more liberal, and law degrees from such schools as Pennsylvania and Harvard are reasonably easy to get by qualified
Negro students. Northern teachers' colleges discriminate least
of all against colored students. The difficulty is, having a
degree, to get a teacher's appointment, but that can hardly be
blamed on schools of education.

Only a small number of colored students from southern
segregated schools are intellectually qualified to pursue a college education, and fewer still can hope to do passing work in
northern professional schools. Starting with inferior segregated
primary schools, the retarding influences of a poor beginning
continue on up the educational scale until they keep the colored product of the system from a higher education. Colored
schools of college or professional grade encounter constant
pressure to hold down their admission requirements, or else
the products of a segregated system cannot qualify for entrance. White colleges and professional schools, which do not
want Negroes anyway, find place for few who have not gone
through northern unsegregated public schools. The starting
point for any corrective measures must be at the bottom of
the scale. Adequate primary schools must precede good high

schools, and good high schools are required to furnish students for good colleges.

So far as higher and professional education is concerned, it would be a wise policy to wipe out the majority of schools now in existence which have only colored students, preserving only the leading institutions and concentrating on their improvement for southern Negro advanced education. In the north there are sufficient facilities for Negro college and professional education, in spite of unfriendly attitudes on the part of white students, faculty and administrators, to take care of all Negroes who are prepared for advanced education. Additional openings will be found as more qualified applicants appear. When colored students become so numerous at any northern institution that they attract serious attention, race feeling may become strong enough to cause open friction and ill will, but that day does not seem imminent.[15]

Indian students also have been given inferior educational facilities when segregated. Such treatment seems to be inherent in the system. Boarding schools have been operated within the past decade on a per capita cost of $200 per year, and eleven to eighteen cents per day has been the cost of the food of Indian boarding students.[16] In 1926 only 83 per cent of the Indian children between the ages of five and seventeen were in school, in contrast to the 90 per cent of all children in this age group in the country who were in school.[17] A higher proportion of these Indian children was educationally retarded than was the proportion of all children of the same age. Indian illiteracy compared with rural illiteracy for the same states in 1920 was 67.8 per cent to 20.4 per cent in Arizona, 61.6 to 2.5 per cent in Utah, and 23 per cent to 1.4 in Oregon. For the entire country the illiteracy rate in 1920 was 6 per cent, while for Indians in the sixteen states with the greatest number of Indians it was 36 per cent, and in three of these

[15] For references to recent literature on Negro education, see Department of the Interior, Office of Education, *Bibliography on Education of the Negro*, comprising publications from January, 1928, to December, 1930. Bulletin No. 17, 1931.

[16] Lewis Merriam, *op. cit.*, p. 348.

[17] *Ibid.*, p. 356.

states it exceeded 60 per cent.[18] Teaching standards and salaries were low and equipment was inferior. The hopeful aspect of the situation is that public and official opinion is shifting, and it appears that there is a decreasing need for segregated Indian schools, although the present generation will not witness their total elimination. Meanwhile, with race prejudice against the Indian almost gone, public interest in Indian affairs may be stirred up to the point where it will insist that school children of this race shall have facilities of at least a minimum standard of decency which would not shame a third-rate backwoods and poverty-stricken country.

Other racial and nationality groups have educational opportunities in accordance with their economic and intellectual status. South and north European alike may attend public schools in their vicinity, nor do colleges and professional schools bar them to such an extent that intellectual advancement becomes difficult. German, Pole, Italian, Greek or any other nationality, including the Latin Americans, may be found in any institution for which their cultural attainments and income are adequate qualifications. Some schools and colleges not supported by taxes may be less friendly than others toward students of non-native stock, but there are plenty of institutions of all kinds to take care of youths without colored ancestry. The fact that a fine New England college limits Jewish enrollment by dividing the country into districts for admission purposes, so that the section of the United States where most Jews live is the least favored district, or that other colleges use "intelligence tests" and "personal interviews" to restrict Jewish enrollment, is beside the point. There are enough other institutions to meet Jewish educational needs. The colored group alone, and particularly the Negro, is forced by race antagonism into a position of educational starvation. Perhaps malnutrition would be a better word, for the Negro gets just enough schooling to keep him from intellectual death but not enough to permit healthy mental growth.

Where minority groups are permitted to attend schools and colleges predominantly native white, their relations with both

[18] *Ibid.*, p. 357.

student body and staff are inevitably on a separate plane. This creates an unhealthy mental attitude in the minority students, but does not seem to bother the majority until the minority through heavy enrollment becomes something more than a curiosity.

Colored and white students may seem to get along well together, yet there is probably no school or college in the United States where the Negro boy or girl can slip easily into the life of the campus and encounter none of those subtle limitations on interracial associations which exist in the United States even where ordinary barriers appear to have been removed. At any large eastern university which accepts Negro students quite freely, such as Harvard, Columbia, or Pennsylvania—and these are three universities which Negroes attend because of the prestige of their diploma, combined with a minimum of discrimination—the casual observer would see no sign of prejudice in the average classroom, on the athletic fields, or on the campus. Yet the peace is only an armed truce regarded with hostility by the Negroes and general indifference by the whites, except where some specific incident may focus public opinion.

Social activities are studiously avoided by Negro college students who need no orders, for they know where not to go. Negroes have found it difficult to obtain rooms in Harvard and Pennsylvania dormitories, although they may get in. Campus restaurants in Cambridge and Philadelphia may or may not serve colored students. Student activities are carried on without colored representation. The few honors and recognitions which are awarded to colored students are worn to shreds and become pitiful in their poverty as they are repeatedly paraded to demonstrate Negro accomplishment in competition with first-class white students. No Negro is deluded into the belief that he is or can be a normal part of campus life in a white college, and practically none of them really want to be, except in protest. Colored and white students in all schools and colleges, excepting perhaps the lower grades with pupils who do not yet recognize the fact of race, maintain an isolation which is impenetrable by occasional interracially minded individuals of either group. While this isolation is as much the fault of the colored students as of the white, the direct effect is on the Negro, who tends to grow sour at the injustice, real or fancied, of his school position. Racial coeducation does reduce to some extent the abysmal ignorance of white and black about each other, but the social isolation enforced with bitterness by Negroes and careless assurance by white students does not permit basic changes in attitude, and frequently the coeducational school becomes in the eyes of the white a real danger to race solidarity. Only a couple of years ago some Filipino students at a large middle-western university formed a social club which had for its purpose the bringing of whites and Filipinos together in a spirit of good fellowship and understanding. On the basis that this might mean increasea social contacts between the members of the club and the white girl students of the university, an official of the institution felt called upon to write a letter to the club suggesting that its members "confine their social life to mingling with members of their own group or with the young men of the university."[19]

The Jew, too, with adequate educational facilities, is nevertheless in a mentally unhealthy position when he attends Gentile institutions. Fraternities do not admit Jewish students, so they, like the Negroes, have been compelled to form their own. While academic honors may go to the Jewish boy and girl, campus recognition is awarded them sparingly. They are accused of being grinds who learn without understanding. Gentile cheating is not uncommonly excused as a defense against "Jewish dishonesty." While this social isolation is not as extensive as that of the Negro, it is sufficiently so to cause ill will between the two groups and to encourage prejudice.

There seems to be no way of eliminating these group planes in educational life. A socially inferior group, conscious of its position, tends to keep to itself by its own volition as well as by compulsion from above. This same phenomenon of class distinction is found in educational institutions when there are no racial, national or religious bases for discrimination. Physi-

[19] Editorial on "Race Prejudice in Nebraska," The World Tomorrow, January, 1930, No. 1, vol. xiii, p. 7.

cal differences or alien cultural peculiarities are solid foundations for discrimination which cannot be wiped out in a few years. The handicap of being unwanted but formally accepted cannot at present be avoided by the outstanding minority groups of the United States who enter the general educational system.

In opposition to a common belief, school segregation tends to increase rather than prevent race conflicts. Keeping colored and white children in different buildings and playgrounds prevents fights between them while under school supervision, but it magnifies race distinction and bitter feeling in the long run. The white pupils appreciate their superior position, and the colored are filled with resentment and tend to accept their inferiority with disastrous results. Very young children of all colors mix peacefully in class and play, and it is not until race consciousness is introduced by their elders, which usually takes place over a period of several years before high school age, that group aloofness, bickering and open fights occur. After having been separated in the grades, it is in the later school years, when racial consciousness is full blown, that students of the two races are commonly thrown together in northern high schools and colleges, where they let each other alone and have few clashes of any sort. Race friction in later life, it seems, is increased by school emphasis on distinctions in color, and this exceeds in social importance the scattering petty quarrels of immature children which sometimes occur in mixed schools. It is to the white man's advantage to reduce race friction between adults if it can be done to even a minor extent at the slight expense of only a few childish squabbles.

Negro teachers are rarely put in charge of white students even where classes are predominantly colored. Public opinion is thought to be too strong against such a practice in all sections of the country. It is therefore argued that a segregated school system for Negroes provides teaching and administrative positions for colored people otherwise ineligible because of race prejudice. This point is offered in support of segregated schools by sincere white school officials who see no other way of employing well-trained colored teachers clamoring for jobs.

In the south this is actually the case, but northern Negroes view this explanation with skepticism, for they know instances where Negroes have taught white children with favorable results.

In the New York City public schools a colored teacher may have only white pupils, mixed classes, or only colored students, and the white boys and girls do not come from only the poorer immigrant families. In Philadelphia, colored teachers are not knowingly permitted to have any white pupils. In order to accomplish this, certain primary schools in colored districts are reserved for Negro children, and colored teachers on the list eligible for appointment never secure positions except in these colored schools. As a matter of fact, white students have accidentally been enrolled under colored teachers, with their parents' approval and with happy results. Several cases are known where teachers with Negro blood in undetectable quantities have been appointed to white schools in Philadelphia, but when this was discovered their appointments failed of renewal. There are other cases in point, but these are sufficient to show that under conditions which prevail in all the larger northern cities colored teachers need not be barred except in segregated schools. There is no inherent reason why a white child should feel any more degraded by learning the multiplication table from a competent Negro teacher than discipline from the colored hand of a Mammy. White children obey colored teachers as they do white, if one may judge by illustrations from New York. To argue for segregated schools because they provide positions for Negro teachers is not only false so far as the North is concerned, but it is also pedagogically unsound in that it views the schools as an economic opportunity for adults instead of an educational gateway for children.

While northern segregated schools may offer a temporary advantage for qualified colored teachers, the children's losses by such segregation are out of proportion to possible gains. The Negro student fights less with white children in the school yard, but interracial tension is increased at other times and places. Colored teachers may be more sympathetic with colored children than are white teachers, but this is a criticism of white instructors and school officials who permit discrimination, and the problem can be solved by other means than separation. Undoubtedly colored teachers understand their Negro charges better than do white teachers, but perhaps the best way of increasing interracial understanding is to increase normal contacts instead of destroying them at every minor threat of friction.

We should do well to heed Moton's shrewd observation: "The white man's knowledge of Negro life is diminishing, and the rate is accelerated by the present-day policy of segregation. This operates practically to make an ever widening gulf between the two races, which leaves each race more and more ignorant of the other. Without contact there cannot be knowledge: segregation reduces the contacts, and so knowledge and understanding decrease. With the decreasing knowledge come increasing distrust and suspicion, and these in turn engender prejudice and even hatred. So a vicious circle is established whose ultimate effect, unless counteracted, must be a separation of the races into more or less opposing camps, with results as disastrous to the spirit of American institutions as to the genuine progress of both races."[20]

The belief that Negro pupils gain incentive from the knowledge that members of their race are competent to instruct them in the public schools is ludicrous, when applied to segregated schools. It has merit only when the child sees people of his color winning appointments and success in open competition with the dominant race. The pre-adolescent school child's admiration for the teacher is rapidly reduced as a source of inspiration by the inevitable later knowledge of the real reasons for segregation.

Negroes may perhaps be trusted to know better than their white neighbors whether a segregated school is best for colored children. Of course it may be argued that colored parents would naturally wish their children to be educated in association with the superior caste, and that Negro teachers could

[20] R. R. Moton, *What the Negro Thinks,* Doubleday, Doran & Company, Inc., Garden City, N. Y., 1928, p. 5.

hardly be expected to prefer racial isolation with its implications of inferiority. Nevertheless, it is significant that Negroes as a whole fight segregation whenever there is any possibility for success, and even where they are outwardly resigned to the all-powerful pressure of race prejudice, they are still among themselves bitterly, if hopelessly, resentful of the system of segregation. No Negro leader can openly favor school segregation except for strategic reasons, and maintain his leadership. The Negro has made up his mind that segregation handicaps his children and the entire race.

Colored and white students do not mingle in activities other than those of the classroom or superficial schoolyard play. Few illustrations of lasting, intimate friendships on terms of equality have grown out of school or college contacts between the races where no separation has existed. Interracial participation in games is common, but it usually stops at that point. A colored boy may be accepted as a member of a school track, football, baseball, or basketball team, and travel with his teammates in good fellowship, but the pressure of prejudice from both white and colored groups is nearly always too strong to permit the ripening and continuation of such friendly contacts beyond the superficial manifestations of school associations. Colored boys and girls rarely are invited to the parties at the homes of white associates, infrequently accept if they are asked, and practically never return such overtures.

The same is true in college associations. Negro college students maintain their own fraternities, hold their own dances, and otherwise provide an adequate social life for themselves. Membership on athletic teams does not alter the situation. Strangely enough, Negro college students resent their exclusion from the social activities of their white classmates and occasionally try to break such restrictions. For illustration, three or four couples recently attended a class dance at a large eastern university, but their purpose, as they expressed it among themselves, was not to have a good time but rather to show that they could go if they wanted to. Curiosity about white students' dances was an additional motive. One colored girl in the party was invited to dance by a white classmate, but flatly refused, although the invitation was well meant and without a tinge of condescension. There was no intention, on the part of the colored students, of real participation in the affair other than attendance and a few dances with the members of their own party.

This attitude may be further illustrated by an experience of the writer at a Negro fraternity dance. The reaction to his participation by half a dozen students from the university at which he was a member of the teaching staff was significantly similar to what might be expected if a colored man attempted to take part in a white affair. They wondered if he was gathering material for a book, suspected his motives in dancing with a charming colored girl, and, gathering in little indignant knots, wondered what they could do to prevent the violation of their group integrity. A colored man would have been violently ejected from a white affair of similar nature; the colored boys were more subtle if not less indignant in their methods of attaining the same end. Only a few of the two or three hundred Negro guests welcomed the white visitor, who was thoroughly enjoying himself on a proper invitation. It may be taken for granted that the white man's personality had little to do with the antagonism to his presence, which was the product of group consciousness and would have been the same at any similar occasion in any part of the United States.

Voluntary educational segregation may become a serious threat only when it takes the place of the public school system instead of supplementing it, and then inculcates ideals and standards at variance with those of the community. To the extent to which the Roman Catholic parochial school system supplants the public school and teaches cultural elements foreign and antagonistic to those of the United States as a whole, it delays the assimilation of Irish, Italian, and other immigrants of that faith, and increases group conflict. There can be no quarrel with purely religious instruction or sentimental efforts to hold fast to alien culture elements which do not clash with fundamental American ideals, but it is doubtful whether the parochial schools restrict themselves to these fields. This is no place to raise the question of parochial school efficiency;

subject matter and point of view alone are of concern in a study of race relations. An illustration may suffice to demonstrate possible sources of friction in group relationships between parochial school immigrant children and others.

Parochial school teachings concerning the family are at variance with both law and popular opinion in many parts of the United States. Without going into the merits of the case, it can be shown that the attitude toward divorce taught Catholic children may clash with that popularly accepted and with the spirit of our divorce legislation. Every state in the Union except South Carolina now permits divorce. Whether this is wise legislation is aside from the question. The fact is that no stigma is attached to divorce by an increasingly large number of Americans, and the fostering of an emotional attitude antagonistic to this point of view does not aid the assimilation of recent immigrants and their children. Other family attitudes taught, including those regarding the duties of husband, wife and child to each other and to society might be elaborated, but would only serve to labor the point.

In numerous ways the parochial school tends to preserve old-world attitudes not altogether in harmony with American culture patterns. In theory at least, teaching is controlled from the Vatican and by Church officials, the overwhelming majority of whom were reared in Latin cultures. This is of course in a measure offset by a teaching personnel of American background, but it is difficult to see how a conflict of cultures and strained race relations can be avoided under such conditions. One cannot criticize the objectives of the parochial school system, for there are no objective tests as yet devised which will serve as measures of cultural values. The fact of conflict resulting from Catholic and non-Catholic educational systems in the same community cannot be disputed.

Another illustration of the means whereby our educational agencies may create or perpetuate culture conflicts can be drawn from our experience with the Indian. The early theorists about Indian education evolved a scheme whereby children of the aborigines were removed from their parents at an early age and taught the white man's ways far from the retarding influences of tribal home life. This was to be done through the non-reservation boarding school, located at some distance from the homes of its students, and teaching the simple elementary subjects of the ordinary white school as well as certain vocational subjects, such as farming, carpentry, tailoring, home economics, and the like.

The school formerly located at Carlisle, Pennsylvania, and now abandoned, is the most widely known illustration of this type. Here Indian children were brought after its founding and given an inferior grade-school education in conjunction with badly planned vocational training. They were in the heart of a prosperous white community, far away from "contaminating" tribal influences. Like the majority of Indian schools even today, neither the teaching, the curriculum, nor living conditions were of sufficiently high standard to have found acceptance in the better white school systems.

An appreciable number of Indian parents—how many we have no way of finding out—disliked intensely the effects of the Carlisle school on their children, some to such an extent that mere infants had to be taken to school by threats and armed force. This dislike was only natural, for it soon became common Indian knowledge that children taken to Carlisle at an early age returned after a few years strangers in appearance and in spirit. This frequently happens, of course, when a native white son or daughter returns from boarding school or college with habits and ideas out of line with those of the parents. But the Indian child was likely to return to his home not with a few bits of radical information and two or three habits disrespectful to his parents' ideals, but with a purposefully taught lack of veneration for the civilization which his parents held most dear. It is not peculiar that such a child was viewed as lost by parents who had little left on which to center the attention of their advanced years.

The Indian boarding-school child had three choices. He could stay out of Indian country and try his luck in the white man's centers. For this he was poorly equipped, since a smattering of elementary subjects and a superficial knowledge of some trade are not enough to offset the handicaps of an original differentiated culture and racial feeling. No Indian school has been of college grade; most have been glorified grammar schools, vocational and academic. Even the so-called "outing system" whereby students were placed with neighboring white families for a few months in order that they might learn at first hand how white people lived did little permanent good, although it is a scheme which still has possibilities if properly used. As actually operated, it amounted to farming out children for the profit of white families who found their labor helpful. The Indian child of the non-reservation boarding school simply could not be equipped as well as the white child who had no comparable handicaps.

The second choice was to return to Indian country, thus avoiding competition with individuals better trained in the white man's ways, and fight to put into use his Europeanized training. This met with the solid opposition of the tribal elders as well as that of his parents in many instances, and resulted more often than not in failure. The pressure of age-old tribal customs and the constant wearing opposition of the powerful, older and conservative group usually forced the surrender of conflicting western ways of life.

But one choice remains, that which leads to an easy yielding to the force of tribal opinion. Drifting back into tribal life is the least difficult of the three choices, and too many have taken it. This "going back to the blanket" has been denied by Indian Bureau and school officials to be sufficiently frequent to be of any significance. The evidence, however, is quite clear that although only a few actually go all the way back to tribal life, practically no students from unassimilated or partly assimilated tribes have been able to resist the popular pressure of their people to slough off much of the veneer of the white man's culture.

The present policy of the Bureau of Indian Affairs is to eliminate all young children from non-reservation boarding schools, reserving this type of school for older and more advanced pupils. Yet in 1926 about two-fifths of the 70,000 Indian children reported by the Bureau as enrolled in some school were in this type. Reservation boarding schools are subject to about the same objections in the way of education of children away from their parents as are those away from Indian country, although they usually permit closer contact between parents and child, so that educational changes will not seem as sharp as if the separation were more effective. The ideal is, of course, a local school, public for both white and Indian if possible, where families may remain intact, and parents, if they do not grow with their children, may at least not be startled by the sudden vision of months of change in their offspring.

This ideal of common public school education for Indian and white children is attainable for a large proportion of our Indian population even under present conditions. It is also a practical objective in a constructive educational program for the other racial and national minority groups in the United States, Negroes in the southern and certain areas of the border states excepted.

This exception is conceded, however reluctantly, even by the greater number of the bitterest opponents of Negro school segregation. In spite of the fact that the weight of evidence indicates that school classification of pupils should be on the basis of individual ability and attainments rather than by ethnic divisions, public opinion in the excepted areas is so emotionally powerful that the potential benefits of a mixed school to the Negro and to the community at large are destroyed by the inevitable explosion which would follow the most timid attempt to introduce a unified school system where the "Southerner's complex" exists.

CHAPTER XV

THE CHURCH AND RACE RELATIONS

JAHVEH, God of the ancient Hebrews, was a bloodthirsty, jealous and deceitful God who favored His chosen people to the destruction and damnation of all Gentiles. The mellowing passage of centuries has endowed Him with a fatherly attitude toward all mankind, for today He is no longer a tribal God, but universal in His protective interests and powers, so that even those outside the fold of His organized churches are numbered among His children. The theologies of Christianity, dominant faith in the United States, and of Judaism, the only other important cult in the country, both accept the concept of a paternalistic God who views all humanity as a brotherhood equal in his sight and alike worthy of salvation. But, while there is no hierarchy of color or nationality in their creeds, the tenets of the "brotherhood of man" and the "Fatherhood of God" find readier intellectual acceptance than social application.

The unchallenged intellectual acknowledgment of the doctrine of man's equality before the Lord has led to the expectation by minority peoples that through religion and the church might be found the way to interracial peace. Christianity especially, with its doctrines of the Golden Rule and human fellowship, has been the hope of the oppressed who have failed to realize the distinction between an ideal religion and its earthly expression through a man-made church. It has been said that perfection is rarely attained in this world, and, judged by its practices contrasted with its avowed ideals in race relations, the Christian church, in all its major sects, has failed to reach its professed standards.

No criticism is here intended of religion, which is a matter of faith and cannot be subjected to cold analysis. It is the institutionalization of religion by men through the church, with its theologies and practices, which is open to comment, especially since theologies and practices fail to agree. The instruction to go and teach all nations has been followed; but only the converted heathen with the proper skin color have been "brought into the fold"—if that expression has any meaning beyond church membership. "Faith without works" is truly sterile in race relations.

RELIGIOUS DIFFERENTIATION

The interracial work of the church has to some degree been handicapped by a lack of church unity in dogma and practice, encouraged by the belief in a personal interpretation of the Scriptures, and a personal worship of God which grew out of the Renaissance period. In this belief we may seek the foundation for the two hundred or more varieties of Christianity, each with its separate church, existing today in the United States. Here are forms of worship to fit the religious needs of practically all the different social groups in the country, for it is clear that these needs are not identical in all men. Differences in natural endowment and cultural background and training inevitably lead to religious differentiation. Beautiful Easter music may serve subjectively as either an emotional outlet or an artistic form of recreation, and the fact that it is commonly assumed to be a worshipful expression pleasing to the Supreme Being does not alter the circumstance that identical words, musical arrangement, instruments, and choir, may not be equally appreciated by a wealthy New York congregation, a rescue mission, and a rural church in the black belt. The conversion of a farm Negro may require an emotional revival meeting which would only amuse or disgust the Boston Unitarian. These differences rest on variations in the cultural background of these groups, and not on innate race differences, but they nevertheless form effective bars to unification in theologies and forms of worship.

Minority groups are, as a rule, poor in worldly goods. The immigrant came to our shores largely to improve his economic position, and the transition years were usually lean. The Indian has not recovered from the destruction of his preliterate economic system and the disastrous effects of a rationing system which robbed him of his independence, his ambition and his initiative. The Negro is still struggling to rid himself of the fetters which have chained him to the bottom rung of the economic ladder. All denominations cannot appeal effectively to these groups. The reason is not merely economic. The poor classes are also the ignorant classes. Their worship takes more emotional forms, and the church which relies strongly on an emotional appeal or emphasizes superstitious beliefs will attract them, as compared with one which appeals to intellect and to cultivated, æsthetic tastes.

The intense participation of rural Negroes in frequent revivals, with their emotionalism of dramatic exhortation, group singing and shouting, public repentance and spiritual rebirth accompanied by exciting twists, jerks and shakes apparently beyond physical control, needs no racial explanation, for almost identical religious manifestations may be found among the Indians and backward white people. Superstitious healers and charms or incantations for securing a desired object or event are also evidences of group intellectual status rather than of racial quality, for hardly any of the magical formulæ and devices in use by American Negroes fail to have their counterpart among southern "white trash," certain immigrants, and other handicapped classes. There is reason to believe that the Negro has borrowed practically all of his supernatural beliefs, altered to a degree by modifications and adaptations in the process, from his white neighbors. Thus the poverty, ignorance, and general social status of different groups lead to forms of worship in keeping with their total situation.

Such minority groups may also be held to a particular church by tradition and inertia. The American Negro is a Protestant, usually a Methodist or a Baptist. Except in Maryland and the Catholic districts on the Gulf of Mexico, he is rarely found in the Catholic Church, which claims some 200,-000 colored members in the United States. As this distribution indicates, his church traditions began with those of his white neighbors, and their force still holds him in the customary sects, regardless of modifications which he may have introduced into their rituals. The Indian, too, in his church observances reflects the influences of the white man in that so far as he has accepted Christianity, it has been the Christianity of his neighbors and, more particularly, of the missionaries sent to him. He is a Catholic or a Protestant in proportion to the effectiveness of early missionaries, as he in some instances, where assimilative forces have been weak, remains true to his pre-Columbian faiths as well as he remembers them. The south European remains a Catholic, the Jew does not become a Christian, and the north European is predominantly Protestant. The fact that all these faiths have been modified by a generation or more of exposure to American influences, yet have retained their fundamental tenets and their traditional adherents, demonstrates the strength of cultural inertia in church affiliations. Even the Oriental who has come to our shores untouched by the influence of Christian missionaries, as have many Japanese, clings to his traditional forms of worship, although there is more white opposition to the Buddhist temple than to the African Methodist Episcopal Church, which is at least Christian.

Culturally, the Italian immigrant needs an Italian Catholic church in which to worship. Obviously, a Quaker meeting or any other Protestant service might seem blasphemous to an adherent of the Church of Rome. It is less obvious that even within the Church of Rome there are racial and national groups which find difficulty in common worship. Italian and Polish Catholics, for illustration, are best served in separate parishes not only because of language differences, but also because of other cultural divergencies which would limit the sphere of influence of a common church. French Canadians, also Catholic in faith, similarly are more at home worshiping with their own group than in a parish of mixed national origin. Scandinavian and German Lutherans build churches of their own, maintaining national lines of cleavage, not out of willful desire to be different, but because their personalities have been so developed that they need to worship in the particular ways taught them in childhood. One cannot throw off traditional worship as a cloak whose style is of no importance, and enter into the spirit of any chance church serving the same God, but in a strange manner.

In addition to individual differences in wealth, education and cultural background, which strike peculiar averages for varying racial and national groups in the United States, church separation is also encouraged by the compulsions of class and caste. In slave days Negroes were commonly forced to worship in special seats apart from the white members of the congregation in a common building or else were given separate churches, with or without pastors of their own. The abolition of slavery, however, has not abolished social distinctions, and we still have the spectacle of theological seminaries which will not admit Negroes, and churches which will not share communion with fellow believers of darker hue. Even where no bar is publicly raised against Negroes, and such bars are common, a white congregation is likely to resent the attendance of Negroes, especially if there is an appreciable colored community nearby. When a Brooklyn, N. Y., pastor of southern extraction recently announced that Negroes were not wanted in his congregation regardless of their credentials, the storm of protest was probably exceeded by the open and tacit approval of his policy, at least in sections of the country where Negro districts may be found. Other minority groups encounter similar discrimination in churches, although the openness and the intensity of objection to them decreases as their distinguishing features, such as color, language, or dress, are less noticeable.

Church affiliation, then, may be due to a number of factors. Few Negroes, for illustration, belong to the Society of Friends. This may be explained by a number of circumstances. Quakers as a group are a well-to-do sect, intellectually advanced and proud of their birthright. They employ no pastors and conduct their meetings with a minimum of ritual and emotionalism. They have no set creed, and so long as one lives a righteous life and searches for the truth in religion, he may go so far as to doubt the inspiration of the Bible, the Divinity of Christ, or the existence of God, and still remain in good standing in at least one Quaker sect, for there are several divisions in the Society of Friends. Thus we have here a highly intellectualized faith, paradoxically speaking, for which most American Negroes are ill fitted by tradition or personal attainments. There are a few colored Quakers, but there is no evidence that the number will soon materially increase even with an increase in intellectual Negroes, for Quakers do not feel kindly toward proselyting although they do support missionary work—in which, however, social work rather than conversion is the motive. Since the Society of Friends has developed into a group with great respect for ancestry and emphasis on congenial social relationships—witness the use of "thee" and "thy" and of Christian names when addressing fellow members of the Society—it is understandable that interlopers, especially if of an inferior status, should be privately discouraged although theoretically welcome. Thus Negroes may expect to find neither religious contentment nor the open hand of fellowship in a Christian sect justly noted for its broad ideals and charity for the oppressed of all nations.

The same factors—individual characteristics, group traits, and antagonistic attitudes—although they are not mutually exclusive categories, which hold Negroes and Quakers apart, serve as barriers which limit if they do not prevent the religious assimilation in unified churches of other racial and national groups. There is, however, considerable variation in the relative pressure exerted by each of these factors from group to group. Group traits, such as language and culture history, are perhaps of the greatest importance in keeping apart the Irish Catholics and the French Canadians in the northeast, the Norwegian immigrant and native Lutheran in the central west, the southwestern Indian and white Christian sects of the southwest. Individual characteristics keep the poor immigrant out of the established and prestige-bearing congregations throughout the country. Again, color may take first rank in barring some Negroes and Orientals from white communions into which they might otherwise fit. In probably no case is any one of these factors operative by itself; a conjunction of two or three in varying proportions is the rule.

These facts may be regarded by some persons as an indictment of the church for its failure to support and to act in accordance with the tenets of the founders. An unbiased examination of the data of social history should convince anyone, however, that the church does not shape social policies so much as it reflects them. No great religion has been able to create a church which maintained its fundamental principles of human relations without change. Truly international and interracial as are the great religions, their churches are in the main conservators and supporters of the current beliefs and practices which govern the social intercourse of their members.

The World War yielded numerous examples of this fact. Intense nationalism was preached from the pulpit and approved by the pews. The "brotherhood of man" was for a time forgotten in the interest of winning the war. Politically, economically, racially, the church, then, gives rich evidence that it rests not on the Rock of Ages but on the shifting sands of human prejudices, beliefs, and emotions.

The race and nationality antagonisms of the United States have been increased instead of decreased by church separation, dictated by the individual needs of the minority and majority groups or by the social pressure of the latter. Such separation has taken two forms: either the minority group has formed a sect of its own, or the dominant group has set aside separate churches within its denomination for their use.

The Roman Catholic Church includes parishes especially for Negroes, Italians, Poles, French Canadians, Germans, Irish, and others. Nationality lines are observed by Protestant sects such as the Lutheran, Reformed, Presbyterian, Episcopalian, and others. Northern churches without real southern tradition prefer people of color to worship in separate buildings in spite of theological identity. Southern Christian denominations demand separate buildings, if not absolute separation in central organization as well. It is interesting to note that before the Civil War, when the Negro's inferior status was legally assured, it was sufficient distinction to have physical segregation only without the modern prevalent denominational separation of Negroes. Indians, too, have their own churches, although there is little objection to their belonging to white institutions, except in the case of Indians tainted with Negro ancestry. Even Chinese and Japanese Christians find religious fellowship with their white neighbors not unmixed with racial prejudices.

Such differentiations may be found within the religious institutions of minority peoples as well as in the churches of the majority. Judaism, however, is perhaps a clearer illustration of this point, for Jewish synagogues do not cater equally to Jews of all national origins. German Jews, Russian Jews, Portuguese Jews, and English Jews have their quarrels among themselves. In part these quarrels are related to the generalized differences between the Orthodox and Reformed congregations; but beyond this factor, and at least equal to it in significance, is the cultural antagonism between the descendants of former generations of Jewish immigrants and the recent arrivals who are referred to in private by their co-religionists of superior American status as "kikes." This attitude toward recent immigrants of the same faith on the part of well-assimilated Jews is both a result of resentment at being carried down in public opinion by the newcomers' peculiar traits, and also of their new but thoroughly absorbed standards which make them look down on foreign cultural characteristics like any American of older stock. To us its significance lies in the fact that a church not favored by the majority of the population may in turn be cool to the advances of more handicapped co-religionists. An interesting sidelight is shed by the fact that a group of American Jews who urged the Department of State to intercede in behalf of some mistreated Russian Jews were obviously embarrassed by the Russians' use of the term "brethren" which implied a closer bond than the preferred "co-religionists." Illustrations such as this demonstrate that it is not a snobbish American characteristic which fosters church separation, but rather that it is a social phenomenon which will tend to occur wherever social distinctions are observed.

The extent of church segregation cannot be definitely measured, but some indices may be offered. American church statistics are notoriously unreliable; but it is probably safe to say that there are approximately 50,000 Negro churches with some 5,000,000 communicants and about $100,000,000 worth of property in the United States today. Just what these figures mean is another thing. A "church" is an unsatisfactory statistical unit, for it may be anything from St. Philip's Episcopal Church in Harlem, with its church building proper, five-story parish house, rectory and three-hundred-acre farm, three-quarters of a million dollars in assets and seventy-thousand-dollar annual budget, to a small "store-front" church in a rented room, formerly used to sell some petty merchandise, with debts instead of assets, and a mere handful of parishioners. The published number of communicants may be restricted to members regular in their attendance and support, or it may be padded by retaining individuals who have moved or who have been otherwise lost to the congregation but without formal notice, for a large membership means prestige and sometimes helps in obtaining financial support.

Separate Negro churches were in existence before the close of the eighteenth century, but until after the Civil War the bulk of colored Christians in the United States were affiliated with white churches. The first separate Negro denomination, the African Methodist Episcopal Church, was organized in 1816 in Philadelphia, followed by the organization of the African Methodist Episcopal Zion Church in 1821 in New York. "The bulk of Negro Methodists, however, were in the South, and were either members of white congregations or of separate Negro congregations not affiliated with any denominational body. Immediately after the Civil War, the majority of them became affiliated with the A.M.E. or the A.M.E.Z. denomination. Within one year after the close of the Civil War the number of colored members of the Methodist Episcopal Church, South, had been reduced from 207,000 to 78,000. The church authorized the organization of the remaining colored members into another separate denomination. The new organization, the 'Colored Methodist Episcopal Church,' was effected in 1870."[1]

The Baptists went through a similar development. "The first Negro Baptist church in America was organized at Silver Bluff, S. C., in 1773. In 1776 one was organized at Petersburg, Virginia; in 1780, one at Richmond, Virginia; in 1785, one at Williamsburg, Virginia; and in 1788, the church at Savannah, Georgia, was founded by Andrew Bryan. There were also many Negro Baptist churches in the North before the Civil War. Among the earliest were the Abyssinia Baptist Church, established in New York in 1800, and the first African Baptist Church, which was established in Philadelphia in 1809. But as in the case of the Methodists, a large majority of the Negro Baptists were in the South and for the most part were members of white churches. Thus, for example, 'in 1845 the Baptist Church of Beaufort, South Carolina, reported 3,323 members, two-thirds of them colored; the First Baptist Church of Charleston, 1,643, and 1,382 of them colored; the Georgetown Church 831, and 798 of them colored; in one association 4,300 members, and 3,800 of them colored. In other states like conditions prevailed to a large extent.' "[2]

In addition to the denominations already mentioned, there are many others which maintain separate organizations for Negro worship. Most large Christian denominations in the United States include some churches for Negroes, so that, including these with the separate colored denominations, we have Negro churches designated as Methodist Episcopal and Independent Methodist Episcopal, as well as the three other varieties previously cited, Missionary, Free Will, and Primitive Baptist; Episcopalian; Presbyterian; Congregational; Roman Catholic, and others. These "others" include innumerable little churches, if they may be dignified by the name, which as individual units are too small and ephemeral to have any importance in race relations, but as a group are indicative of a social condition which in a measure is a response to the

[1] W. A. Daniel, *The Education of Negro Ministers*, Doubleday, Doran & Company, Inc., New York, 1925, pp. 21-22.
[2] *Ibid.*, p. 22.

limitations of prejudices, although they have their white counterparts. "Doubtless some of the founders of these . . . churches are sincere, though ignorant; but it is certain that many of them are parasitical fakers, even downright scoundrels, who count themselves successful when they have under the guise of religion got enough hard-working women together to ensure them an easy living. This little-church movement has also given rise to many cults and much cultism. Ira De A. Reid, of the National Urban League, recently made a survey of the churches of Harlem and found that there had been a rapid growth in the number of religious sects that studied and practised esoteric mysteries. In his report he says: 'There are they who dabble in spiritualism, exhibiting their many charms and wares in the form of Grand Imperial incense, prayer incense, aluminum trumpets, luminous bands and other accessories.' Among these cults some of the names found by Mr. Reid were: The Commandment Keepers, Holy Church of the Living God, the Pillar and Ground of Truth, the Temple of the Gospel of the Kingdom, the Metaphysical Church of the Divine Investigation, Prophet Bess, St. Matthew's Church of the Divine Silence and Truth, Tabernacle of the Congregation of the Disciples of the Kingdom, the Church of the Temple of Love."[3] The list could be indefinitely extended, but would yield nothing more than a directory of all possible forms of religious observance which might be found in any group of several millions of people scattered about a large country in an infinity of social levels.

The only distinction between such a religious directory for Negroes and one for a white, yellow, or red group of similar size would be in the relative strength of each classification, corresponding to the differences in the relative distribution in the various economic, intellectual, cultural and other population classes. Such differences in relative strength may be actually observed when the American Negro church affiliations are compared with those of the Indian, Oriental, white immigrant, and native white citizen. They may most readily be

[3] James Weldon Johnson, *Black Manhattan*, Alfred A. Knopf, New York, 1930, p. 164.

estimated if a mental church scale is imagined ranging in easy gradations from those institutions at the theoretical top which respect science and foster practical programs for social improvement, to those at the bottom which place emphasis on ritual, emotionalism, and dependence on faith in supernatural intervention. It is probable that if one were able to plot a curve of distribution of Negro affiliations on such a base scale a more pronounced skew toward the bottom would be observable than in a similar chart of white people in the United States. Just what such a chart of the other minority racial and nationality groups in the United States would show is a debatable question.

The recent (1926) census of religious bodies indicates that there are twenty-four denominations in the United States entirely Negro. Of these the Negro Baptists rank first with 2,914,000 members, making it the fifth largest denomination in the country. The concentration of the congregations of this body in certain states has made its churches take first place in Virginia, South Carolina, Georgia, Florida, Alabama, Mississippi, Arkansas, and Louisiana. The African Methodist Episcopal Church ranks second, with 487,000 adult members; the African Methodist Episcopal Zion Church third, with 397,-000; and the Colored Methodist Episcopal fourth, with 181,000 members. Eighty-five per cent of Negro church members are found in these four denominations. Thirty denominations in the United States have both white and Negro congregations. The Methodist Episcopal Church, for instance, has 3,743 Negro congregations with 303,000 members. The Presbyterian Church in the United States and the Disciples of Christ follow, with Negro churches totaling 35,400 and 34,700 members respectively. The Protestant Episcopal Church, the Churches of Christ, the Congregational Church, and the Roman Catholic Church also have a number of colored congregations. Most of the rest have only a few such churches. Six have only one colored church each, and five others fewer than nine each.[4]

---

[4] C. Luther Fry, *The U. S. Looks at its Churches*, Institute of Social and Religious Research, New York, 1930, pp. 21, 24, 39.

At least one of the minority peoples, the American Indian, would probably show a church distribution somewhat out of keeping with what would normally be expected of a poverty-stricken, uneducated rural group. His pre-Columbian faiths in relatively pure form have been deserted except for a few isolated individuals, mostly of the older generation. There are said to be some 60,000 Roman Catholic Indians, nearly all in the areas where that church was dominant in pioneer days. Protestant missions of twenty-six different denominations and societies working in the Indian field reported some 32,000 Indians enrolled under their organizations, although six made no report of membership in the study here quoted. Of this number, the Protestant Episcopal denomination reported 9,526; the Presbyterian, U.S.A., 6,594; the Baptist, Southern Convention, 4,176; the Methodist Episcopal, South, 2,388; and the Methodist Episcopal, North, 1,986.[5] What has happened to those Indians who have assimilated so well as to need no missionary guidance and support cannot be said. There are many such in the United States, and they may properly be omitted from this study since they create no problems of race relations and have no separate churches. Among the partially assimilated Indians there are few Christian churches financially supported by themselves, and it is largely due to the necessity for outside help that the development of Indian churches has taken what might be called an unnatural turn.

Free from dependence on white funds to the same degree as were the Negro churches, it is probable that the Indian distribution curve would have skewed further down toward the emotional and ritualistic end of our hypothetical base line. Pre-Columbian Indian religious observances were filled with festivals, rituals, symbolism, and belief in mysterious powers. While their original faiths and practices could not meet the needs of their modern Europeanized customs, their standards and ways of life are still more in keeping with the type of church commonly found in the rural south. It is remarkable that in spite of white religious domination they have found

[5] G. E. E. Lindquist, op: cit., pp. 428ff.

as suitable church facilities as is indicated in the previous paragraph.

The Indian search for a form of religious worship adapted to his needs is exemplified by three fusions of Christianity with his own beliefs and practices, aided by the efforts of native leaders of no mean power. The Ghost Dance religion which spread so rapidly over the plains in the 'nineties contained Indian as well as Christian elements and was temporarily successful in gaining adherents because it was adapted to native tradition and gave promise of a much desired Indian millennium when white oppression would fail and cease. Similarly, the peyote cult, a mixture of Christian observances and beliefs with many of native origin, particularly that of the use of the peyote, spread rapidly because it was in line with old customs and modern needs. The mescal button, or peyote, is the cut-off, dried top of a cactus which produces visionary and ecstatic states of mind when chewed. Before its spread into the United States it had some religious significance among the Huichol Indians in Mexico.

"Before 1890 the use of the plant spread from the Mescalero Apache and the Tonkawaw to the Comanche, Kiowa, and Quapaw, and after this date to the Pawnee, the Caddo, the Delaware, the Southern Arapahoe and the Southern Cheyenne. 'By 1910 the use of peyote had spread through the plains and northwest to the Northern Arapahoe and Northern Cheyenne, Shawnee, Sac, Fox, Kickapoo, Seneca, Quapaw, Kansa, Omaha, Sioux, and Pottowattomie.' Later it spread to the Crow, the Utes, the Menominee, the Muskhogean and the Shoshone. The rapid spread of this practice to some thirty additional tribes in the thirty-four years since 1890 is due to the natural acceptability of a vision-producing drug to a people in whose culture the vision experience plays such a large part, to the reservation life and to the building up of friendly intertribal relations by the preceding Ghost Dance craze."[6]

Another separate Indian cult is found in the Indian Shaker Church which has some hold on the Indians of the Northwest.

[6] Clifford Kirkpatrick, *Religion in Human Affairs*, p. 170. Dr. Kirkpatrick's quotation is from a manuscript by Dr. W. C. MacLeod.

It apparently contains some elements of Roman Catholic and Protestant practices as well as a large proportion of native culture traits. The founder's (John Slocum, a Mud Bay Indian) "original efforts were aimed at the moral elevation of his race. No good Shaker might use tobacco or liquor, and all must duly pay their debts. Since Slocum's day, however, various barbaric rites have become mingled with the original teachings. The Bible is not used at their services. These rites are exemplified particularly in the ceremonies attendant on efforts to heal the sick and to make Shaker converts. The Shakers do not believe in medical aid for the sick, but attempt to heal them with shakings and incantations."[7]

These three fused faiths, the Ghost Dance, the peyote cult, and the Shaker religion, are illustrations of Indian attempts to find a form of religious expression adapted to their individual and group needs. They resemble in their purpose, if not in outward manifestations, numerous Negro sects created by desire for opportunity for worship in ways adapted to the worshiper. They differ more distinctly from the American Christian sects than do those of the Negro, because at the time of their founding and diffusion Indian cultures still had a strong hold on the Indians who adopted them, while the Negro at the time of the creation of his peculiar sects was already fundamentally Europeanized. They were all doomed at the start to a rapid disappearance because they were too greatly at variance with the dominant culture which was already rapidly engulfing the American Indian.

The Chinese in the United States, like the Indians, do not commonly build and support churches of their own. Their ancestral faith is linked so tightly with family organization that the immigration of individuals into this country, a physical desertion of relatives, has prevented the extensive institutionalization of their worship. This fact, coupled with a low economic level as among most immigrants, and their small numbers, has quite understandably militated against the erection of temples, regardless of faithfulness to ancient gods. Some Chinese had already acquired a veneer of Christianity

[7] G. E. E. Lindquist, op. cit., pp. 386-387.

before their arrival in the United States. Others came under the influence of Christian missions in this country. There is, of course, no way of knowing how many have become Christians in reality as well as in outward form; but since it is estimated that only twenty per cent of the American Chinese are reached by mission boards, and since they do not as a rule either join white churches or support Christian churches of their own, it may be judged that the majority do not come under the influence of American churches. In religious organization, they remain a sharply separated group in the United States.[8] In addition to the Japanese Christians there is a goodly number of Buddhists and Shintoists. "The Buddhist churches in the United States are studying and duplicating the methods of the Christian churches, largely in order to hold the native-born Japanese children who not only know English better than they do Japanese but who tend to feel more at home in a Christian than in a Buddhist church."[9] The fact that a larger proportion of Japanese immigrants than Chinese have wives and families, together with their scattering in small farm and town communities, may account in large measure for their supporting churches of all three faiths, while the Chinese support practically none. The rapid assimilation of the Japanese, however, has done little to reduce the separation of their Christian churches from those of white neighbors.

There is powerful antagonism to the mere presence of a Japanese church in some white communities on the Pacific coast. "In 1923 and 1924 there were three such agitations started in the neighborhood of Los Angeles over the establishment of new Japanese churches. In Hollywood, the Japanese attempted to buy a piece of property to use for a Japanese Presbyterian Church; in Long Beach, three Presbyterian churches tried to buy property for a Japanese mission; and in Pasadena, the Japanese wished to establish a Buddhist temple in the same block with two Christian churches. In all three cases, ministers and church members of certain other faiths sided with the anti-Japanese groups in preventing the erection

[8] Eliot Grinnell Mears, *op. cit.*, p. 379.
[9] *Ibid.*, p. 379.

of the new churches; and in two cases their efforts were successful."[10] Where even geographical separation is demanded by Christians, it is fruitless to discuss real unity between native white and Japanese worship.

There is reason to question the adequacy of the segregated forms of worship available to Orientals in the United States. Where the Chinese has remained true to his oriental traditions, he has probably catered to his needs growing out of an oriental background at the expense of the requirements of an essentially individualistic life in the United States. Where he has been influenced by Christian missions, the sect accepted has depended to a greater extent on the effective interest of Christian philanthropists than on its suitability to his immediate needs. Since the Japanese build and support an appreciable number of their own churches, including many varieties, and depend less on missionary assistance, it has been possible for them not only to choose in accordance with their desires but also to modify church practices to fit their new environment and character. Their rapid adjustment to their new home has directed their choice and modifications into channels increasingly closer to those of white worshipers in their communities.

The white immigrant has continued to worship in separate churches after his arrival in the United States more because of his own desires than on account of any real pressure to keep him out of native American sects. The American church attitude toward him has been generally one of indifference. Nominally, he is nearly always a Christian before his arrival, unless he is a Jew, in which case Christian sects have been loath to attempt his conversion, either because of certainty of failure or, more likely, because of anti-Jewish prejudices. Churches which send missionaries to foreign countries to work among Christians of other sects may neglect the foreign Christians within our borders. One amusing example of this attitude has been cited regarding a New York City church "which sold its fine building because there were too many foreigners in the neighborhood, and sent the proceeds to the Board of Foreign

[10] *Ibid.*, p. 381.

Missions."[11] This illustration is, of course, not typical of a general attitude, for there are churches which devote much time and money to work among aliens in the United States. Practical indifference, however, has been so much the rule that the immigrant has had little difficulty in maintaining his separate churches in spite of widespread criticism of foreign sects.

In 1909, two years after the peak of immigration from Europe was reached, and during the decade before the World War when Europe steadily sent great numbers of her people to our shores, a study was made showing the diversity and separation of immigrant churches, which is worth quoting. The immigrant churches in Johnstown, Pennsylvania, were listed as follows:

TABLE I

IMMIGRANT CHURCHES IN JOHNSTOWN, PA., 1909 [12]

Race	Denomination	Number of Members	Year of Establishment
Croatian........	Greek Catholic	150	1907
Croatian........	Roman Catholic	700	1903
Croatian ⎫ Servian ⎬	Greek Orthodox	600	1902
German.........	Roman Catholic	1,500	1855
Irish............	Roman Catholic	1,100	1868
Italian..........	Roman Catholic[a]	300	1905
Magyar.........	Colonist	75	1903
Magyar.........	Hungarian Reformed	300	1903
Magyar.........	Roman Catholic	600	1901
Polish...........	Roman Catholic	1,200	1900
Slovak..........	Greek Catholic	1,200	1895
Slovak..........	Greek Catholic	100	1908
Slovak..........	Lutheran	500	1903
Slovak..........	Roman Catholic	500	1902
Welsh..........	Baptist[b] ⎫		
Welsh..........	Congregational[b] ⎬	700	1854
Welsh..........	Lutheran[b] ⎭		

[a] In Italian section.   [b] In American section.

NOTE. All except those indicated otherwise are in the Foreign section.

[11] H. P. Fairchild, *Immigration*, 1920 edition, pp. 297-298.

[12] Jeremiah W. Jenks and W. Jett Lauck, *op. cit.*, p. 121.

This distribution is of course not identical with any that might be found in some other city or in some other year. Unfortunately, there are no accurate data which supply the facts of church affiliation by country of origin for inhabitants of the United States as a whole. Consequently for information concerning the extent of immigrant church separation it is necessary to rely on a general knowledge of the religious composition of the various European nations and on the numerous church surveys which have been made for specific peoples and areas in the United States.

Even a casual analysis of the 13,366,407 foreign-born white people found in the United States by the census of 1930 demonstrates something of the extent of the tendency to immigrant church separation. Of this number, 1,122,576 were born in Sweden, Norway, and Denmark, countries almost exclusively Lutheran in faith. The Irish Free State, heavily Roman Catholic, was represented by 744,810 individuals. England's 808,672, Scotland's 354,323, and Wales' 60,205 line up well with old established American sects, but nevertheless are kept apart to some extent by national backgrounds. Russia sent 1,153,624 individuals, of whom slightly more than half were of "Yiddish and Hebrew" mother tongue. Poland was represented by 1,268,583 individuals, Italy by 1,790,424, Austria by 370,914, Germany by 1,608,814, and Hungary by 274,450. French Canada sent 370,850, while the remainder of the Dominion contributed 907,569 people. There were in this country in 1930 about 1,500,000 persons born in Mexico or born in this country of Mexican parentage. The countries here cited are the most important sources of immigration, and it is significant that each one of them is associated in the popular mind with at least one great sect. Minor immigrant countries, such as Greece, Albania, Spain, Portugal, Armenia, Palestine, Turkey, and others have similar associations.

The 1926 church census makes it possible to segregate at least some national groups. Without taking into account such sects as Mennonites, Dunkards, etc., which, while restricted more or less to certain nationality groups, have a long history in this country, let us consider some of the more recent immigrant groups. Of eastern Orthodox Churches no fewer than seven separate organizations are listed: the Albanian Orthodox Church with 1,300 adult members; the Bulgarian Orthodox Church, with 596; the Greek (Hellenic), with 94,334; the Roumanian, with 14,874; the Russian, with 67,925; the Serbian, with 10,297; and the Syrian, with 6,452. Jewish congregations were credited with 2,930,332 members. A large portion of the Roman Catholic membership of 13,306,800 was of course drawn from recent immigrant groups, but in addition the Polish National Catholic Church listed 42,331 members, and the Lithuanian National Catholic Church, 993. The Church of Armenia in the United States had 19,712, the Assyrian Jacobite Apostolic Church 1,116, and the Free Magyar Reformed Church 2,289. Three Finnish Lutheran denominations were given: the Suomi Synod with 21,348, the Evangelical Lutheran with 5,228, and the Apostolic with 16,384. While a considerable number of Scandinavians are found in the general Lutheran denominations, the Swedish Augustana Synod reported 233,288 members; two Norwegian bodies, 348,600 members; two Danish bodies, 35,000 members; and the Icelandic Lutheran Church, 1,726. In addition, three Scandinavian Evangelistic Churches reported 48,299.[13] Here is abundant evidence of church separation based on cultural differentiation and tradition.

Studies of four rural immigrant communities published in 1929 under the auspices of the Institute of Social and Religious Research add detail to our picture of immigrant church separation. In the three Virginia counties of Prince George, Dinwiddie and Chesterfield, centered about Petersburg, there were perhaps 3,500 individuals described by the natives as "Bohemians," mostly Czecho-Slovaks, many of whom were born in this country. Religiously they may be divided into four groups: Protestants, Catholics, Free Thinkers, and some indifferent persons distinguished as "nothing." About 1,000 were found to be Catholics, and 1,000 Protestants of the Lutheran, Baptist, Presbyterian and Congregational sects. There

[13] C. Luther Fry, op. cit., pp. 132-138.

is little religious fellowship between these "Bohemians" and their native Virginian neighbors, white or colored.

In Sunderland, Franklin County, Massachusetts, an agricultural community, immigrants first arrived about 1887 and increased during later years of success and failure until they numbered 207 farmers, including 111 Poles, 67 Lithuanians, 25 Slovaks and 4 Latvians. Agriculture became the main occupation of those who remained on either their own acreage or shares. The Poles have become a group more compact socially than if they had gone to a large city, and this with their foreign traits has held them apart from the native New Englanders. The other nationalities have come to. identify themselves with the "Poles." The Poles built their own Roman Catholic Church, but the Lithuanians, with some exceptions, joined the Irish church. The Greek Catholics for a time attended the Roman church, but in 1919 broke with the Poles and established their own church after heated encounters, in a measure the result of postwar events in Poland.

The Danes in the rural community of Askov in Minnesota, all calling themselves American, have held on to the Danish language and the Lutheran church beliefs and practices brought along from Denmark, although modifications to fit the American scene are being brought about by the younger generations.

An experiment in immigrant colonization, begun during the first decade of the present century on reclaimed land near Wilmington, North Carolina, was originally with five tracts, one for Italians, one for a few families from Holland, one for Greeks, one for Germans and the fifth for some English bachelors who were soon succeeded by a group of Hungarian families. The original plan worked poorly, and the Greeks drifted away, to be followed by the Poles. The Italians scattered when prohibition affected their grape culture. Into one tract, now known as Castle Hayne, drifted Hollanders, Poles, Italians, Danes, Hungarians, Russians, and others, including some of native stock. With the success of Castle Hayne and the varying fortunes of the other colonization districts eventually came considerable mixing of nationalities in economic and social affairs. Religious separation, however, held on longer and more firmly than other traditional culture traits, the Poles, for example, maintaining a Catholic church so small that it has warranted only the services of a Wilmington priest who celebrates mass and delivers a sermon once a month.[14]

A majority of immigrants, of course, live in urban areas and the above rural illustrations naturally cannot be taken as representative of anything more than a tendency to immigrant church segregation so far as the non-rural foreign-born residents of the United States are concerned. However, rather than pile illustration upon illustration to demonstrate such separation, it is perhaps sufficient to point out that the larger such immigrant communities of any one place of origin grow —and they do grow larger in urban than in rural areas—the greater is the possibility of maintaining separate religious institutions. The most important offsetting feature tending to decrease urban separation is the fact that assimilation seems to be more rapid in cities with their frequent and involved intergroup contacts than on farms where a high degree of self-sufficiency may easily be obtained. There is no reason to believe that urban immigrant church separation from native institutions is noticeably less in extent than that found in rural districts, if equally unassimilated groups are compared.

THE PENALTIES AND GAINS OF SECTARIANISM

The influence of this extensive church separation of majority and minority racial and national groups in the United States has been a notable factor in preventing healthy interracial contacts. It may neither be said to be an unmixed evil nor claimed as a perfect instrument for group adjustment to American life. While its effects are so widespread—penetrating as they do every aspect of life—as to refuse cataloging, three outstanding results of church separation may be suggested.

Of primary importance is the fact that the immediate religious needs of the Negro, the white, and the Japanese

---

[14] The data on these four rural immigrant communities in Virginia, Massachusetts, Minnesota, and North Carolina have been taken from Edmund de S. Brunner, op. cit., pp. 139ff.

immigrants have been and are better served in separate churches than would be possible in united religious institutions. This statement purposely omits mention of the Indian and the Chinese immigrant, who, as previously mentioned, have been able neither to retain their ancient forms of worship nor control the new. It also omits mention of the possible long-run effects of religious segregation, which quite obviously are not the same as those which follow the immediate satisfaction of the demands of an existing situation.

Negroes and immigrants have to an unbelievable extent been permitted, and perhaps forced, to live their own religious lives without interference, guidance, or interest on the part of the majority sects. It does not seem possible that Christianity, with its tremendous missionary activities, should have practically forgotten the potential converts in its midst, especially in view of the lively interest shown in their non-religious affairs. This callous neglect of their morals and souls has permitted them to work out their own salvation in whatever ways they pleased, and, at a very rough guess, half of them have taken advantage of this freedom to avoid salvation through any church, while the remainder have built and molded institutions to their taste.

Thus the Negro and the immigrant churches have become the only formal institutions definitely controlled by themselves. Their economic life is subject to the will of the dominant majority. Their political activities are no more extensive than the native white man wants them to be. Their education is provided in schools whose finances and policies are matters of grave concern to the dominant classes. Even parochial schools are not free from the watchful eye of the one-hundred-per-cent Americans. Few white men, however, show more than an idle curiosity about the Negro's "superstitions" and "primitive" religious observances, just as not many old Americans bother their heads about the foreigner's faith, unless it be as a point of attack against his political or economic advances, as in the case of the Catholic and Jew. An anti-Catholic political campaign or an anti-Semitic business or school war can hardly be considered an interest in a minority church. The purely religious aspects of a minority church apparently become of interest only when its members threaten success along some other line. Then even the church passes out of the unrestricted control of an annoying minority.

However, in spite of sporadic interference with immigrant religions, illustrated by the Know-Nothing party, the American Protective Association, the modern Ku Klux Klan and the recent anti-Catholic opposition to a Catholic candidate for the presidency of the United States, the immigrant may be said to have been historically free to worship according to his pleasure. The Negro, of course, has not been subject to attacks similar to those directed against the immigrant, for his churches are at least nominally if not always actually identical with those of his white oppressors. Even the anti-Buddhist and the anti-Shintoist agitation on the Pacific coast has had as its purpose more the exclusion of oriental competition than religious salvation. Thus religious freedom has been greater in the United States through church separation than an intolerant attitude toward minority beliefs, noticeable throughout the country, might lead one to expect.

That church separation has had numerous effects on the groups most involved is self-evident. The freedom of religious worship granted by this country has frequently aided in the development of schism, sometimes based on doctrinal differences, but just as frequently perhaps on clashing opinions regarding administrative policies. One result has been a tendency to "over-churching" evident from some of the statistical data already presented. While the average city church in 1926 reported an adult membership of 433, the Negro urban church reported only 199.[15] Such conditions, coupled with the low economic or social status of most minority groups, have made impossible the construction of adequate buildings and the employment of well-trained ministers. In 1926, the average Negro rural congregation worshiped in a church valued at $2,000.00 and received annually from each member $6.20. The urban Negro congregation worshiped in a building worth over $16,-000.00, and each member expended annually $13.06. The

[15] C. Luther Fry, op. cit., p. 2.

average city church, on the other hand, in the same year, reported a building worth $53,500.00, and an average annual expenditure per member of $21.50, the corresponding figures for the rural church being $6,200.00 and $13.27 respectively.[16] The expenditures of the Negro Baptists averaged $9.65 for urban, and $4.61 for rural members.

The same condition was found among recent immigrant groups. In no instance did the average annual expenditure per member of the eastern Orthodox churches rise above $12.34, and in two denominations, the Serbian and Roumanian, it was below $7.00. The Jewish congregations showed an annual expenditure of only $6.51 per member, the lowest of any large denomination. The Roman Catholic Church expended $15.37. These amounts appear in their true light when it is considered that of the twenty-four principal denominations listed by Fry, only three expended less than $10.00 per urban member, the majority expending over $25.00; only six expended less than $10.00 per rural member, the majority expending over $15.00.

Satisfaction in worship cannot of course be measured in terms of beautiful churches, high-salaried ministers, and ample financial resources. In the case of the minority groups of this country the limited resources have, nevertheless, provided expression for religious and other social needs. The diversity of sects has permitted individualization in religious expression. In this process the churches themselves have undergone significant changes both as to doctrinal basis, administrative organization, and function.

God, Jesus, Moses, Adam, and other Biblical characters have changed their personalities as easily as their dress to suit the rural Negro, who could not grasp the significance with which they had been invested through centuries of European and American development. The will of God may be interpreted in a thousand ways, depending on the interpreter. The Supreme Being cannot possibly be envisioned as identical in purpose by colored Georgia peasant, English mill worker,

[16] *Ibid.,* p. 2.

Italian laborer, Indian farmer, oriental truck farmer and native white clerk.

In organization the church has also been modified. The European immigrant, member of a great national church, frequently found the authority of the bishop or priest sent to him by the mother church galling, particularly since he had become aware of the democratic régime in American political and religious life. The result was frequently the breakdown of church authority, which no doubt often caused his unchurching, but just as often led him to organize a new church along more democratic lines. In this manner, for instance, did the Polish National Independent Catholic Church and the Polish Catholic Church of America arise. The first organization was created "as a protest against the domination of the Polish Roman Catholic Church of this country by Irish Roman Catholic groups and a demand for parish control of church property."[17] The second arose as a protest against both the Roman and the National Church, and claims a more democratic organization than either.[18]

The effect of American life shows itself even in changes in the form of worship. The austerity of some of the European churches, with their absence of pews, has been known to have been modified with the purchase of discarded Protestant churches which afforded comfortable seats.

The most important of all the modifications which the church has undergone in the hands of minority groups is the change in function. The church of the Negro and of the immigrant is more than a place of worship. It is the organization which has been forced by the restrictive effects of prejudice, apathy or neglect, to fill many of the social needs of its members which in other groups are filled by recreational and other agencies. And the Negro church is also a safety valve where thwarted desires and emotions may be freely vented.

"The multiplicity of churches in Harlem, and in every other Negro community, is commonly accounted for by the innate

---

[17] Paul Fox, *The Poles in America,* Doubleday, Doran & Company, Inc., New York, 1922, p. 113.

[18] *Ibid.,* p. 114.

and deep religious emotion of the race. Conceding the strength and depth of this emotion, there is also the vital fact that colored churches provide their members with a great deal of enjoyment, aside from the joys of religion. Indeed, a Negro church is for its members much more besides a place of worship. It is a social center, it is a club, it is an arena for the exercise of one's capabilities and powers, a world in which one may achieve self-realization and preferment. Of course, a church means something of the same sort to all groups; but with the Negro all these attributes are magnified because of the fact that they are so curtailed for him in the world at large. Most of the large Harlem churches open early on Sunday morning and remain open until ten or eleven o'clock at night; and there is not an hour during that time when any one of them is empty. A good many people stay in church all day; there they take their dinner, cooked and served hot by a special committee. Aside from any spiritual benefits derived, going to church means being dressed in one's best clothes, forgetting for the time about work, having the chance to acquit oneself with credit before one's fellows, and having the opportunity of meeting, talking, and laughing with friends and of casting an appraising and approving eye upon the opposite sex. Going to church is an outlet for the Negro's religious emotions; but not the least reason why he is willing to support so many churches is that they furnish so many agreeable activities and so much real enjoyment. He is willing to support them because he has not yet, and will not have until there is far greater economic and intellectual development and social organization, any other agencies that can fill their place.

"The importance of the place of the church in Negro life is not comparable with its importance among other American groups. In a community like Harlem, which has not yet attained cohesion and adjustment, the church is a stabilizing force. The integrating value of the churches in Harlem, where there are so many disintegrating forces at work, can easily be underestimated."[19]

When a community becomes large enough and sufficiently

[19] James Weldon Johnson, *op. cit.,* pp. 165-166.

diversified to permit the formation of castes and classes, varying sects must provide outlets for religious expression. Sufficient diversity may, of course, be provided within a unified church organization as in the case of the Roman Catholic Church, where more than usual provision is made for varying group needs through a diversity of religious orders, the intermediary saints and administrative consideration of special community and individual needs. In Protestantism, however, it is apparently necessary that separate sects be provided to supply even the diversity found within the Catholic organization. Consequently, the Catholic immigrant of many' nationalities has, unlike many of his Protestant brothers, been able to remain a member of his ancestral church.

In the light of these facts it is reasonable to claim that the minority churches are performing an extremely valuable service to their members, and that the value of this service is due to its adaptation to peculiar minority group needs. From this point of view the Negro and the immigrant churches are far superior to the churches of the dominant groups, for these churches, governed by the political, economic, and race attitudes of the majority, could never give to the minority groups the religious comfort and the social services which these groups look for in the church. Undoubtedly the picture has its other side. Church separation is likely to retard cultural assimilation, but so long as the dominant groups do not earnestly desire or work for such assimilation, the minority church cannot be blamed for doing work which is highly useful and necessary.

The churches in the United States have been far too conservative to fight for the abolition of group barriers. Individual leaders and congregations have done so, but their accomplishments seem pitiful when contrasted with the restrictive influence of conservative church members and clergy. White and colored churches have been induced to exchange pastors on occasion. Interracial Sunday, part of an interdenominational program for a better understanding between all peoples, has created less of a ripple than "Clean Up Week." The surveys and publications of the Institute of Social and Religious Research have included a number of excellent analyses of immigrant and race questions. Church commissions and committees of an interracial nature have been formed without end. Practical social work as well as preaching has been included in programs participated in by all denominations with varying degrees of enthusiasm. What enthusiasm has been observable, however, has been on the part of leaders who were already convinced of the desirability of an interracial sphere for church work, and it has spread only slowly, if at all, to the conservative church element. Indeed, the interracial material gathered and the experiences recorded have come to the knowledge of only few ministers of the Gospel and a still smaller proportion of their parishioners. A start has been made, but we must not mislead ourselves by imagining that it is a novel feature of church progressivism, for similar starts have been made ever since racial theories first effected church separation. There is no reason to believe that this latest movement will bring success where countless other beginnings failed before the attack was well begun. So long as the churches reflect other aspects of social life, we must expect conservatism to support the hierarchy of social orders.

In many instances it is this very conservatism which is anxious for cultural uniformity, while at the same time denying minorities the privilege of contacts which would promote assimilation. Of course some conservatives wish to obtain uniformity through the exclusion or expulsion of non-conformists, rather than by their assimilation. The Ku Klux Klan, for illustration, is apparently convinced that Jews cannot be assimilated because through generations of persecution in Europe true American biological qualities are supposed to have been eliminated from their character, a foolish assumption on the face of it, since there is no such thing as a true American biological quality, nor may the characteristics of a people be permanently altered in the few generations of persecution which the Jews have undergone. Roman Catholics, according to the Klan, also cannot be assimilated, for their allegiance is first to a foreign church and then to the United States. Negroes, of course, cannot be assimilated, nor can they be deported, but if they are "kept in their place" they and everyone else will automatically benefit. These anti-assimilation arguments of the Klan may be matched by other extremists who believe that racial integrity rather than cultural training is the key to American progress.

However, in spite of extremist opposition to the cultural assimilation of Jews, Catholics, Negroes, and Orientals, every minority trait foreign to the majority which comes in contact with it is likely to be viewed as undesirable by conservative Americans. Quite obviously, one-hundred-per-centism is neither possible nor desirable in a country as large as the United States, for there is much to be gained by cultural variations which are in the nature of adaptations to local conditions, and minority contributions to this adaptation cannot be overlooked with impunity. Using the church as an illustration, it may be observed that the presence and competition of a number of sects may have the healthy effect of preventing religious dry rot. Nevertheless, a greater degree of uniformity than is at present attainable is to be desired, and one factor which is preventing its accomplishment is church separation.

There are of course minority groups and individuals who have only a tenuous church affiliation or none at all. Bohemian Free Thinkers are one illustration of an immigrant group who have revolted against the organized church even before their arrival in this country. The Jews, especially of the younger generation, depend little on their synagogues for the satisfaction of social needs. Only 46 per cent of Negro men as compared with 49 per cent of white men were in some church in 1926, so that church separation may hardly be said to be a direct hindrance to the assimilation of the non-church 54 per cent. Seventy-three per cent of Negro women as compared with 62 per cent of white women were in some church in the same year, and this high percentage is an indication of the extent to which a non-segregated church might aid assimilation.[20] There is no way of knowing what dependence immigrants place on their churches other than as a place of pure worship, but churches with exclusive foreign membership—

[20] C. Luther Fry, *op. cit.*, p. 8.

and this includes the children of foreign parentage—are so common and their multitudinous social activities are so well known that the assimilative service which might be rendered can hardly be overestimated. Of course, if there were no church separation, there would probably be less separation in other phases of social life, and the church would not have to supply the variety of activities which are now found in immigrant and colored churches. But this is mere speculation, and as the facts now stand an opportunity for minority cultural assimilation is being neglected.

Christianity has long been accused of being a religion of submission. It is a religion of peace and suffering, although it may be made to support bitter warfare on occasion. As a rule, however, its teachings that the righteous and the oppressed will receive their reward in the hereafter—and the definition of righteousness is not strength in battle—tend to produce patience and humility in the inferior classes here on earth, for better times are promised those who have faith. While the statement cannot be statistically proved, it is safe to say that Christianity has often prevented open minority revolts. While it may not always bring absolute contentment in the breast of the true believer, it does offer excuses for inaction even under severe provocation.

There are Negro leaders who regret the hold of the Christian church on the American colored population. There is evidence that their task of leadership is made difficult by the colored churches, if their task is to bring better times to their people on earth. The variety of colored sects, each jealous of the others, and the scattered membership in white denominations and congregations, retard unity in political and economic action. The emotional outlet provided by services and revivals and the certainty of salvation through the rebirth of conversion make a colored following hard to hold to a non-religious organization or program. The fact that the colored ministry includes so many who are unprepared for their tasks except by "call" and their natural endowments closes them as an avenue of approach to social reform which they might so easily form if they were possessed of enlightened vision, for their followers are legion. No matter which way the intellectual Negro leader turns, he is blocked by the church, for the church is not in sympathy with intellectual programs and has the strength of being of, not for, the people.

The church may be measured by its ministers, for they not only lead their people on the paths which they believe righteous, but they are also chosen and hold their pulpits as their preachings and deeds reflect those of their flocks. Less than one out of four of the ministers in the three leading colored denominations claim to be college or seminary graduates, as compared with five out of eight for the eighteen white denominations studied.[21] This is not due solely to the limited opportunities for the education of Negro ministers. The fact is that a well-educated minister could not hold a pastorate in most colored churches unless he were a veritable genius, for the colored masses view with suspicion and distrust the black man who has too thoroughly absorbed the white man's culture and science. It is significant that Negro radicals openly fighting for their rights have included only a small proportion of ministers. When the ordinary white man takes stock of Negro leaders who may be dangerous, no minister is likely to be included in the list. The mental picture of a colored minister which comes to the mind of the white man is usually that of a conciliatory, ignorant, hat-in-hand "darkey" somewhat resembling Uncle Tom. While no white man can be certain of such a generalization, it is the author's impression that the Negro stereotype is very much the same. Any church which flourishes under such leadership, even if it does damn white oppression up and down the scale in private, not daring to do so when the white man is around, must have a controlling membership firm in the conviction that the rewards of humility will come in the hereafter.

This acceptance of the existing social order by the Negro church is shown in the spirituals. Their beauty remains unchallenged. "They are the music," says Du Bois, "of an unhappy people, of the children of disappointment; they tell of the death and suffering and unvoiced longing toward a truer

[21] *Ibid.*, p. 62f.

world, of wonderings and hidden ways. In them the slave spoke to the world. Far from his native lands and customs . . . experiencing the pang of the separation of loved ones on the auction block, knowing the hard task master, feeling the lash, the Negro seized Christianity, the religion of compensations in life to come for ills suffered in the present existence, the religion which implied the hope that in the next world there would be a reversal of conditions of rich and poor, of proud and meek, of master and slave. The result was a body of songs voicing all the cardinal virtues of Christianity; patience, forbearance, love, faith and hope."[22]

Swing Low, Sweet Chariot gives its promise that it is "comin' for to carry me home." *Die in de Fiel'* announces that "I'm on my journey Home." *Didn't my Lord deliver Daniel?*, *Nobody Knows de Trouble I See, I Got a Home in Dat Rock, De Angels in Heab'n Gwineter Write my Name, Po' Mourner's Got a Home at Las'*, and a multitude of others which might be selected almost at random, as these were, from *The Book of American Negro Spirituals* and *The Second Book of Negro Spirituals*, edited by James Weldon Johnson, with musical arrangements by J. Rosamond Johnson, and additional numbers in the first volume by Lawrence Brown, show such an attitude by their very titles. Of course, some, like the powerful *Go Down Moses* and *Joshua Fit de Battle ob Jericho*, indicate a more rebellious attitude, but they are not in the majority. It is naturally impossible for an outsider to grasp the significance which the words of any spiritual may have for a Negro congregation, but it does seem that they contain an extraordinary amount of hopeless substitution of heavenly blessings for unachievable earthly comforts. It is pathetic but understandable that America's only real contribution to world music should thus express the passive surrender of its creators.

Christianized Indians have also been the submissive Indians. The early Catholic missions of the Southwest tamed the native tribes by conversion as well as by physical force. Protestant missionaries have been similarly helpful to the

---

[22] W. E. B. Du Bois, *Souls of Black Folk*, A. C. McClurg, Chicago, 1924, pp. 253 *et seq.*

armed forces of the United States. In wars fought by Indians against the white man, the native faiths were towers of strength, while Christianity in its original form was a handicap in battle. In the southwest today, there is little trouble between the government and the "Progressives" who have accepted Christianity; it is the conservative *caciques* or "heathen" priestly officials and their followers who fight the hardest. Indian "prophets" and "messiahs" who have preached the salvation of their people through warfare have been common. It is not without point that the fighters were the ones who achieved the most favorable treaties, while the peaceful tribes, frequently under Christian influence, received scant consideration. After all, it is hardly worth while bribing a man who is already on your side.

It is unfair to create the impression that Christian and friendly Indians have been synonymous in our history, or that it was Christianity which was *the* cause of submission other than force of arms. There have been innumerable instances of kindly disposed tribes who were relatively untouched by the white man's missionaries, and on more than a few occasions converted Indians were as remiss in observing the teachings of Christ as the white man has been when he needed the land of an Indian. Furthermore, conversion to Christianity was frequently but one symptom of Europeanization, which itself would naturally reduce Indian-white warfare regardless of religious beliefs. However, after all due allowance for such instances, it still seems that Christian missionaries saved the souls of thousands of warriors at the cost of the Indians' active independence of spirit, a cost which may or may not be justified by results.

Immigrants who have arrived in this country already thoroughly Christianized present a different problem. Their varieties of Christianity were long since linked up with all possible brands of nationalism, and they remained so during the immigrants' transitional period in the United States. The Norwegian Lutheran, the Dutch Reformed, the Roman Catholic, the Greek Catholic, and dozens of other sects are associated with national culture groups in such a way that they may actually strengthen their membership in resisting majority oppression. The Irish may be cited as an illustration of a group which has made use of Christianity as a force welding them together in their struggle for success in the United States. In such cases it is the nationalistic traditions which have attached themselves to specific sects and not the Christian doctrines as such which give power to the minority immigrants. The Christianity of the Negro, Indian, and Oriental has not yet developed such strengthening associations, for it was given too recently to these peoples by a socially superior group. Judaism has been able to survive and, being wrapped up in centuries of non-religious traditions, has upheld the hands of its followers in their battles against oppression. Thus it has not been the religious teachings of immigrants which have given them their strength, but rather the nationalistic traditions which have associated themselves with their churches through years of growth before migration.

It is still probable that among the mass of immigrants of Christian tradition the teachings of the New Testament have exerted a quieting influence similar to but perhaps weaker than in the case of the American Negro. Even Judaism, originally a nationalistic religion, has become a sleep-producing drug for a minority people secure in the knowledge that they are the chosen of God who will triumph in the next world if not in this. To the extent to which this is true of immigrant religions—and there is no known way of measuring it—a tendency toward submission to their lot has been a product of immigrant churches.

It may be said that such a tendency would be produced by Christianity in minority peoples, regardless of whether they worshiped in separate churches or whether they were accepted into the membership of the majority churches. To a degree this is true, for even the masses of the native white citizens of the United States have received quieting comfort in their lot from their churches. The poverty of the poor becomes less a burden when their thoughts are turned to the life after death, be they white or black, native or foreign, Christian, Jew, Mohammedan or Buddhist. Negro, immigrant, and other

minority individuals who have chanced to join a majority
church have been lulled by sermons, hymns, and prayer just
as certainly as if they were isolated in churches of their own,
and perhaps even more certainly, for as a minority element
in churches controlled by others there is no possibility of
using religious fervor as an aid to revolt.

CHAPTER XVI

ART AND RACE RELATIONS

THERE is an abyss between paintings and chromos, poetry and doggerel, literature and trash, music and noise, dancing and contortions, acting and "performing," which may not readily be defined but is none the less real. In the study of racial attitudes, however, it is rarely necessary to distinguish between the artist and the near-artist, for the potboilers and putterings of quacks and failures make as deep and lasting impressions on the public as the exquisite perfections of the genius.

The public, in fact, is much more impressed by the shabby products of sham artists than by offerings which have won the approval of connoisseurs. The rhymes of Edgar Guest are more real to the masses than the works of Shakespeare. Jazz rhythms and threadbare melodies of novelty orchestras, phonographs, radios, and incompetent musicians appeal to the untrained ear with a compelling power beyond the possibilities of the compositions of a Beethoven or a Wagner presented by a Stokowski. The stickily sweet croonings of a romantic-looking orchestra leader or revue star will suffice as a pedestal on which to place a popular idol while operas starve on alms given for society's sake. The circulation of trashy weeklies climbs into the millions while older magazines in the "quality group" die or drag along on pitiful subscription lists. The Harold Bell Wrights outsell the Edith Whartons. Tap dancers are applauded by the thousands who express their doubts as to the sanity of the followers of the more æsthetic styles. The cartoons of a Bud Fisher are a source of pleasure to millions who never heard of Pennell or Whistler. Motion pictures filled with cheap sentiment featuring stars who cannot act, musical comedies, revues, sex and mystery plays, draw big houses at top prices while the gems of drama grow dusty in libraries.

We need not labor the point by additional citations of such contrasts, for it is quite evident that in the arts it is frequently the mediocre product, or worse, which most readily achieves the widest if most ephemeral circulation.

It therefore follows that racial and national attitudes and artistic achievements are influenced not only by the best in all the arts but also by the worst. Since the poorer products are the more widely circulated, if not the more enduring, the effects of the inferior varieties may be assumed to be the more far-reaching. It is possible to claim that the popular manifestations of the arts are not actually inferior to the classical, but this is beside the point. The task is to discover what have been the contributions to the arts by the minority peoples of the United States, and what, in turn, have been the effects of artistic expressions, crude and sublime alike, on group relationships.

THE ARTISTIC ACHIEVEMENTS OF AMERICAN MINORITIES

The extent to which individuals of racial and national minority groups have contributed to the artistic life of the United States may be over- or underestimated with equal ease, but to measure it accurately is impossible. Without effort, there pass in mental review the spirituals, folk tales and rhythms of the American Negro, the characteristic patterns in textiles, pottery and silver of the Indian, the colorful designs in paint, porcelain and weave of the Oriental, and a chance selection from European-born authors, musicians, actors, and perhaps a sample or two from the graphic and plastic arts. Further thought destroys the clarity and simplicity of the array, as individual artists are jumbled up with traditional group contributions, and the problem of origins becomes a confused blur.

What Negro artists have there been who have notably enriched American life? Their names, alas, are almost entirely unknown, for the Negro's artistic gifts have been largely anonymous, as must be the creations of a peasant folk in contrast with those of an individual genius. Who created the spirituals and who sings them best today? Bre'r Rabbit and

Uncle Remus have folk parentage, and no man can take credit for more than the arrangement and popularization of their exploits. Jazz music and Negro dances have a multitude of interpreters, but their origin is of the people. It is one thing to talk of the artistic contributions of the Negro race and quite another to list outstanding individual contributors.

While the culture of the United States would suffer seriously if the artistic gifts of the Negro were destroyed, yet had a majority of the better-known colored artists never been born, literature, music, and the other arts would hardly have deviated from their present course. The development of race relations and of colored achievement would have been seriously altered by the absence of any of the more important names from the list of Negro artists in any field, but the strictly artistic loss to the country would have been slight.

American Negroes have produced a few gems in poetry, an occasional short story of high quality, a handful of interesting novels, and some plays of reasonably good workmanship. It is difficult and perhaps foolhardy for a layman to pass judgment on the representative publications of millions, but the expressed opinions of recognized authorities are so nearly unanimous as to the poverty of the literary production of colored America that they cannot be disregarded. Making due allowance for the racial prejudices of white experts, it must still be held that colored American authors have been overrated from the days of slavery to the present. There is one prominent colored author who frankly admits that if in some supernatural way he were given the chance to pass for white he would refuse it, for as a white man he would not find it so simple to get publishers to accept his works, nor would so many people, white and colored, be paying his royalties. Interest in subject matter and in the author's race may readily be mistaken for recognition of ability, especially if there is the will to believe.

This is in no sense an indictment of the ability of the colored group, nor should this criticism be understood as an attempt to belittle the literary accomplishments of the American Negro. That Negro blood does not limit the literary heights to which one may climb is amply established by the successes of Dumas and Pushkin, whose works are admired by discriminating multitudes who have no knowledge of their colored ancestry. Tradition, training, and social status, however, do not fan whatever sparks of genius undoubtedly exist in our colored population. Even the ease of publication which budding colored authors encounter tends to lower their standards, for it is difficult to resist rushing into print when no one will openly censure careless workmanship and others have achieved notoriety on similar flimsy foundations. It is a wonder that under such conditions so many reasonably good poems, books, and plays have been produced by a group which has a wealth of excuses for and incentives to mediocrity.

Extravagant praise of ordinary accomplishments is understandable among a people who have had their supposed inferiority hammered into them until they have come to believe it themselves. Unfortunately, it is likely to have a damaging rebound. The poetry of Paul Laurence Dunbar, James Weldon Johnson, Countee Cullen, Claude McKay, Jean Toomer, and Langston Hughes is not without merit, but the prejudiced overpraise which it has received through race consciousness has caused a reaction of criticism to set in, not only among white critics but also in a number of the more conservative intellectual colored circles. The fiction of Jessie Fauset, Charles W. Chesnutt, Walter White, Nella Larsen, W. E. B. Du Bois, and many others, including all the poets already mentioned, may rank with, if not above, the fiction of white authors of average ability. Their reputations should not suffer because no Dumas has appeared among them. Yet because it is racial treason to a powerful Negro element who see prejudice in criticisms not reeking with praise, it has been almost impossible to award them their proper and enviable rank in American literature. Literary perspective has been blurred by the emotional attitudes of both white and colored partisans. When in later years we or our descendants shall at last be permitted to see clearly, it is probable that the best of them will be found worthy of their times and at least on a par with contemporary popular poetry and fiction.

The same prejudices color appraisal of other varieties of artistic creations by Negroes. One painter, H. O. Tanner, stands head and shoulders above the rest of his people. He, however, has found it convenient to leave the United States for French residence, although he is still considered an American artist. One might imagine that oils, water colors, and etchings could readily be freed from the taint of a colored hand, but this is far from the truth. Two or three promising sculptors have made brave beginnings, but none have reached the heights, whether due to lack of inspiration, ability, or opportunity can not be said. Art schools and associations of artists may or may not admit Negroes. White models may refuse to pose for Negroes, or white fellow students may feel contaminated by the presence of colored associates. An artist's signature on his work adds or detracts from its value in the minds of purchasers, and there is only the one American Negro whose name is important enough to stimulate buyers. Of course, as in the case of poetry and fiction, there is a special clientele consisting of a few wealthy Negroes and some sympathetic white people who will buy as much because of the artist's color as because of the quality of his work, but their number is too small to provide an adequate outlet for products of Negro brushes. There is more indiscriminate admiration than purchasing power, and even Negro artists must eat. Where the artist of recognized first rank is constrained to leave the country after a struggle, the student may not expect an easy path to success.

To most Americans the Negro of the stage has been a white man with a blacked face. This is not because there have been no actual Negroes on the stage but because they have been so few as to be numbered in tens while white actors ran into the thousands. It has been difficult for stage producers to visualize a colored actor in anything except a comic rôle, and even then white actors with darkened skins and exaggerated lips have been preferred to the real thing. Al Jolson, a Jewish actor famous for his blackface caricatures, is better known today than any colored comedian. The minstrels, now almost forgotten, were first copied just before the middle of the nineteenth century by white entertainers from the informal slave comedy of pre-Civil War days, and not until a quarter of a century later did Negroes succeed in recapturing a part in the popular and profitable amusement originally a product of their own ingenuity. Some white troupes included Negroes in their personnel, and when after the Civil War all-Negro companies were formed such troupes adopted, even to the extent of blacking their faces, and improved, the stage business developed by white companies. As a comedian the Negro first trod the boards, and as a comedian he was applauded by white audiences. The colored actors whose names became household words included Bert Williams, George Walker, Will Marion Cook, Ada Overton, Bob Cole, Florence Mills, and others whose reputations depended on anything but serious drama.

A sufficient number of Negroes have made good in the more serious plays, however, to demonstrate the adaptability of members of their race to non-humorous rôles. Ira Aldridge was an American-born Negro whose fame as a Shakespearean actor was gained in Europe but spread back to the land of his birth. Charles Gilpin's superb work in O'Neill's *Emperor Jones* will not soon be forgotten by those fortunate enough to have seen him. Paul Robeson has achieved outstanding success in serious drama, but has apparently found Europe more to his liking than the United States. Richard B. Harrison found fame as "the Lord" in *The Green Pastures* after years of disappointment. No list of actors here given should be considered inclusive, for there are many others equally deserving even if their names are not so well known to white people. It is certain that the number of colored actors of merit would have been much larger were it not for the restrictions placed on their stage appearance by race prejudice.

Race prejudice more than anything else has been responsible for keeping the Negro actor in comedy. He may act on occasion, but his part must be humorous. He may dance, but it must be "Negro dancing." He may sing, but it must not be "classical" music except in occasional concerts usually topped off with spirituals. In other words, to be popular with white patrons he must fit himself into the none too flattering white man's stereotype of what a Negro should be like. In relatively recent years colored girls with no acting ability have been permitted to be glorified for the edification of white audiences, like the white chorus girls in the various "revues" and musical comedies. Several Negro plays with Negro casts, notably *Porgy*, have been well received, as they deserved. *The Green Pastures*, a play distinctly in line with the white man's concept of the Negro, has been well played by Negroes and must be listed as one of the great productions of New York in recent years. Every Negro actor who has enjoyed white patronage on the American stage, and every play of Negro life which has made money, from Bert Williams to Charles Gilpin, and from *Uncle Tom's Cabin* to *The Green Pastures*, has had to be careful to avoid arousing white emotions by staying within the bounds of the white man's idea of proper Negro conduct.

The white man pictures the Negro as a natural-born musician, instrumental or vocal, just as he seems to imagine that all colored people are natural dancers. Negro dancing proficiency, however, is supposed to be of an eccentric or emotional type, and so, too, his music must be the uncouth, if pleasantly stimulating, outpouring of a savage and untutored soul. It is readily conceded that only a Negro can sing, play, or dance to plantation or levee music, ragtime, jazz, and the blues. In the spirituals, too, the Negro is granted superiority. Actually, in granting this superiority the white man is mentally pushing the Negro further down the human scale, for while such folk music may be viewed by the select few as a contribution to culture worthy of the highest respect, the masses tend to look on it as something growing out of and appealing to man's grosser nature, a heritage of savagery which should be suppressed by civilized society or indulged in only with apologies.

Let us grant immediately, for there is no possibility of argument, that the Negro's contribution to American culture through his folk music is a supreme gift.[1] It is a gift, however,

---

[1] For well selected and excellently arranged Negro spirituals, see James Weldon Johnson, editor, *The Book of American Negro Spirituals*, musical arrangements by J. Rosamond Johnson, with additional numbers by Lawrence Brown, Viking Press, Inc., New York, 1925, 187 pp.; James Weldon Johnson.

of the American Negro and not of Africa, for there is little or nothing in it to connect it with that continent except the fact that it is usually sung by individuals of African ancestry. European influences, on the other hand, are quite evident both in the musical forms of expression and in the sentiments conveyed by the verses. Furthermore, it is not a gift which can by any stretch of the imagination be called the product of some special biological quality of the American Negro, but one which has grown rather out of his social status as an American peasant.[2] This is as true of the spirituals as it is of the Negro's

---

editor, *The Second Book of Negro Spirituals,* musical arrangements by J. Rosamond Johnson, Viking Press, Inc., New York, 1926, 189 pp.

The introductions to these two volumes by James Weldon Johnson will repay careful reading, although the editor's interpretation of Negro spirituals is not widely accepted today.

For the words of all varieties of Negro songs, including religious, social, work and other types, including a few specimen tunes, an extensive bibliography and adequate discussion by the author, see Newman I. White, *American Negro Folk-Songs,* Harvard University Press, Cambridge, 1928, pp. x + 501. See also Howard W. Odum, *The Negro and His Songs,* University of North Carolina Press, Chapel Hill, 1925, pp. vii + 306; Mary Allen Griscom, *The Negro Sings a New Heaven,* University of North Carolina Press, Chapel Hill, 1930, 101 pp.

[2] To refer again to the conclusions of Professor T. R. Garth:

"It may be stated as a fact that races do not differ in sensory traits either qualitatively or quantitatively. Regardless of the opinion the popular mind has held in this regard, psychological studies of primitive peoples and civilized peoples has demonstrated that there is no difference in this respect. All races of men hear equally well, see equally well, and are equally sensitive to pain. . . .

"In regard to esthetics of different races it is held that regardless of the crudity of primitive art or the virtuosity of the art of cultured peoples there is but one esthetic impulse. This esthetic impulse finds its satisfactions in such forms as rhythm, symmetry, unity, climax, contrast, in art of all races. A thing of beauty finds currency in any race, for beauty is universal. Differences in art may all be accounted for by differences in materials, in tradition, and in technical skill and not in the esthetic impulse.

"The simple matter of color preference of races seemed to afford an opportunity for finding differences, but much to our surprise, if we eliminate the factor of 'education,' as with the case of the young, they are found to agree fairly well. The influence of culture and tribal preferences would seem to have a profound effect. And the chief value of this investigation in color preferences is to show the great modifying power of nurture. It may soar over native tendencies so universally as to make what is acquired appear to be native. . . .

"The tests of musical talent among races so far are few, but representatives of several races have been studied with the musical talent tests. These test results do not indicate differences of an innate character in musical talent, though some superficial evidence appears in tests for pitch and tonal memory." T. R. Garth, *Race Psychology,* McGraw-Hill Book Company, New York, 1931, pp. 208-210.

work songs, popular rhythmic music, and the accompanying dances. The lowly local origin of these tuneful and rhythmic group achievements should not be used to brush aside the Negro's rôle in American cultural life, but should excite the admiration of the American white population which in a greater length of time has produced nothing of the sort. The Negro may be said to have created a substitute for his lost African heritage, while his white neighbors continued to be dependent on the folk traditions of their European forbears, and were relatively unproductive because their needs were well supplied without creative effort. The Negro was compelled to borrow, adapt, and create a folk music as a part of a whole new pattern suitable to his American scene. The product now belongs to the world.

Although these folk creations of the dark "American peasant" are by their nature beyond criticism, the individuals who interpret them to the outer world are not. Just as the American Negro has failed to give to the country a literary genius of the first rank, so has he failed to produce a single outstanding individual in the musical field who could not offhand be matched by dozens of white artists who make no claim of belonging to the ages. If Harry T. Burleigh had been born white, he would probably be as well known as a composer and singer as he now is, but no one would hold him up as an example of musical genius of the first rank. Roland Hayes as a white man would probably draw favorable comments from the critics, but it is likely that his following and monetary rewards would be smaller, and to only a few of the musically elect would his name be familiar. In these cases and others like them, membership in a minority racial group has worked to the advantage of the individual who in spite of prejudice has been able to climb the first few rungs of the ladder of success and demonstrate some measure of talent. Once even slight talent has been shown, although the climb still remains difficult and the rewards are usually small, critics of either race are expected to give unstinted praise and gloss over inadequacies and defects, or else be charged with prejudice. The result has been that the student of Negro achievement is in-

timidated into exaggerations and misled by sympathetic enthusiasts to the point where the laurel of success has been
awarded to a few individuals of reasonable merit, and to many
who are worse than mediocre.[3]

Professor Reuter has been as outspoken, yet temperate, as
any dispassionate student of American race relations on the
literary and artistic contributions of individual Negroes. It is
his opinion that, "measured by objective standards, the contributions of the Negroes in the realm of literature and the
fine arts, as in science and scholarship, have been small and
unimportant. There are no single pieces of work of first or
even second rank, and few individuals of more than local and
racial reputation have appeared."[4] This statement may be
brutal in its frankness, and it may place too low a valuation
on a limited number of scattered literary and artistic products
of American Negroes, but it is certainly nearer the truth than
the uncritical lists of composers, singers, musicians, actors,
painters, and the like, which may be found in a veritable flood
of overoptimistic books and articles, of which James Weldon
Johnson's *Black Manhattan* is perhaps an illustration.

We agree with Professor Reuter that the slight accomplishment of the American Negro in literature, art, and music "is
subject to social explanation and the barren record probably
implies nothing in regard to future accomplishment."[5] This
explanation of the cause of artistic poverty, however, does
not increase the objective merit of quite ordinary accomplishments, although it may help us to understand the too zealous
defense of odds and ends of trash which apparently gain importance from the ancestry of their source. It is not so strange
as it may seem that Negroes and their sympathetic friends,
resenting as they do any implication that colored Americans
should not be expected to measure up to white standards of
achievement, nevertheless are frequently at no great pains to
apply the strictest standards to the artistry of Negroes before

[3] For an illustration of excessive praise by a white author of mediocre
Negro artistic accomplishments, see Edwin R. Embree, *op. cit.*, pp. 233-253.
[4] E. B. Reuter, *The American Race Problem*, Thomas Y. Crowell Company,
New York, 1927, p. 292.
[5] *Ibid.*, p. 292.

advertising it to the world as a real achievement of the colored race.

The more certain one is that Negroes have artistic capacity equal to that of white people the more one is driven to cite instances to prove the point. When first-class evidence is none too plentiful, wishful thinking may make it easy to invest an ordinary product with the attributes of a masterpiece. Thus simple melodies, catchy rhythms, bits of verse, ordinary plays and books, a good but not exceptional voice or stage personality, musical technique of the parlor variety, and splashes of line and color become transformed into evidences of Negro genius, although the equivalent products of white men make no impression on anyone, for they are too common. In this way an ungrammatical pornographic autobiography has become a "human document" and the author a colored "intellectual." Vaudeville teams have been transformed into actors and singers of supposed first rank. Crude dancers slightly above the burlesque level have been similarly exalted. Violinists, pianists, and singers have been able to fill concert halls which would have remained empty at the appearance of equally amateurish white musicians. For a colored critic to call attention to this situation is treason; when a white man does so it is sufficient evidence of race prejudice to cause him to be looked on as an enemy of the Negro.

Happily there are an increasing number of Negroes in America whose personal standards are high enough to keep them from falling into such errors of judgment. Dr. Du Bois, for example, cannot be accused of mistaking mediocrity for genius simply because of the blinding effect of color, but his clear vision has failed to increase his popularity among a large group of leaders who may be referred to as "professional Negroes." The more clear-sighted of the Negroes and students of American race relations recognize the dangers of exaggeration of individual achievement, and are but a little confused by the deceptive plea that only by undue exaltation of ordinary Negro artistic achievement may the younger generation be inspired to attempt the heights.

Any attempt to prophesy concerning the future artistic contributions of the Negro to American culture must rest on flimsy foundations. We have no reason to believe that he is especially qualified by nature in any artistic field, nor have any inborn handicaps been discovered. He has retained little or nothing of the African cultures he brought with him into slavery. What he has developed since then has been in response to his American environment and has reflected the influence of the essentially European culture of his white neighbors. He need yield to none in the peasant forms of artistic expression which have sprung up among his people, regardless of how meager individual contributions have been. In fact, the sorry individual showing, which is sorry only by contrast with the idealized picture of itself which has been foisted upon the public of both races, is indicative of nothing more than the limitations of prejudice and poverty. If Europe has been able to produce a Pushkin and a Dumas, both of whom had no different and no less Negro blood than countless American Negroes but were less handicapped by racial barriers than they would have been in the United States, it is only reasonable to assume that the millions of colored people in this country include a normal proportion of individuals with the potential ability to reach similar pinnacles. Until free opportunity is granted there can be no way of establishing or disproving this statement.

The rare fragments of African art that have become an integral part of the culture of the United States have been introduced almost without exception by white sponsors or by modern Negroes whose interest in the land of their forbears came through study rather than through their social heritage. The American Indian, on the other hand, has retained for himself and has given to the country at large a variety of artistic motives and patterns which have been passed along from generation to generation and from race to race without a sharp break in cultural continuity. Furthermore, the artistic contributions of the Indian, unlike those of the Negro, have been contributions from their original cultures achieved while they were still an independent, isolated people, free from the influences of the white man.[6]

Like those of the Negro, however, they have been the products of groups and not of outstanding individual geniuses. The Navajo weaves blankets of unique design and excellent quality, but the technique and form are of the people, even though the wool with which they work is a material borrowed from the white man. Craftsmen of the same tribe create attractive jewelry, but no Cellini working in silver and turquoise has appeared above the horizon. The same generalization can be made in regard to Indian pottery, music, dances, and other media for artistic expression, although naturally there are individuals who excel their fellows in any of the arts.

These outstanding artists, however, may be criticized and given their proper rank without incurring the wrath of any appreciable number of white people or Indians. Of course there is the tendency, as in the case of the Negro, to exaggerate the merit of an Indian painter or other artist, but it does not amount to racial treason or sheer prejudice if one refuses to give unqualified approval to an ordinary product. Possibly the fact that the Indian no longer suffers from the stigma of an "inferior" race but is rather in a position where an individual who demonstrates real skill or talent finds few social or other barriers raised against his free contact with white people in most parts of the country, is in a measure responsible for the lack of pressure to exalt mediocre accomplishments.

The undue mass homage which is paid to the artistic expressions of all colored peoples has no single explanation, and it certainly cannot be said to be the result of an intelligent appreciation of creations which only a short time ago were regarded as heathenish products of near-savages. What was once considered a grinning ebony idol has become a work of art. Grotesque masks of African and American Indian tribes must no longer be considered "curiosities" by those who make any claim to culture. Bead work, carved and painted decora-

---

[6] For a brief bibliography of Indian songs, dances, handicrafts, stories, and folk lore, see G. E. E. Lindquist, *op. cit.* See also The Exposition of Indian Tribal Arts, *Introduction to American Indian Art,* 578 Madison Ave., New York, 1931, 55 pp.

tions, jangling ornaments, characteristic conventionalized designs and other decorations whose origin lies in the cultures of colored peoples are now admired by the multitudes who know nothing of their intrinsic merits. The sudden popularity of the Negro spirituals is another case in point. This uncritical admiration has gone so far that the minority races themselves have caught the fad and are filled with pride and wonder at the artistic capacities of their people.

This does not mean that there is no high degree of merit in such artistic products of our minority groups; undoubtedly there is, although a layman must speak softly on such a technical question. As a matter of fact, the educated, cosmopolitan white man has for generations acknowledged the quality of preliterate and peasant design, music, and folk lore. For illustration, a select few have long recognized the true worth of American Indian and Negro folk tales, while nearly everyone else thought them nothing more than superstitious stories of ignorant, inferior people, if they thought of them at all. Today these same "superstitious stories" are written up, not infrequently by hack writers, and sold in large quantities to an admiring public. Why this sudden popularity of the artistic achievements of the colored peoples?

Some light may be thrown on the present popular interest in the folk contributions of the American Negro and the Indian by a consideration of the widespread interest in oriental arts. When China, Japan, and other oriental countries were first opened to commerce with the modern western world, travelers brought back all kinds of artistic odds and ends, some of which were real objects of art to the few, while all attracted the interest of the masses, possibly because in their strangeness they stirred the imagination to fanciful thoughts about an unknown people who were mysterious and interesting because of their differences. Today, while similar oriental objects remain in the category of "curiosities" to the ordinary American, an increasing number of individuals profess an appreciation of Japanese prints, Chinese jades and porcelains, and a host of other oriental products, partly because it is the thing to do, and partly because of the appeal of the exotic.

The fact that this is an uncritical admiration is easily demonstrated by even a casual observation of current fads. Cheap coolie coats have sold well at high prices. Carved ivory cigarette holders and other trinkets which the veriest amateur should know to be bastard products made only for the tourist and gift-shop trade have acquired popularity beyond their worth. Red lacquer and gold paint in pseudo-oriental design add to the salability of poor furniture. The list is endless, and without value except as it establishes the true nature of the American worship of the strange in any and all of the arts. In this respect at least the oriental influence on American race relations is fundamentally similar to that of the Negro and the Indian. There is also a similarity in the fact that the white man's admiration goes out to contributions of the oriental peoples of China, Japan, India, and the neighboring lands rather than to the work of outstanding individuals, although again the individual artist gains reflected glory because of his identification with the achievements of his people.

Immigrant art and artists from Europe are both likely to lose their alien identity in the United States, for both blend readily with their American background. There is little of high quality in American art and letters which is at the same time the product of a white man and also distinctly American. The culture of the country is so characteristically European that it is impossible to estimate our indebtedness to any group of recent arrivals, who, all things considered, have been reared in cultural heritages which have infinitely fewer divergencies from our own than they have points in common. The result has been that individual immigrant artists have been less able to capitalize their minority position and have had to depend more on the worth of their products than have American Negroes, Indians, and Orientals.

Exception to this rule should be made, however, in the case of European immigrant minorities whose cultures vary to any considerable degree from the prevailing standards in the United States. For illustration, there has been a vogue for Russian music, literature, and the peasant arts for which their alien qualities are largely responsible. So, too, Italian opera, architecture, pottery, painting, and furniture have been accepted by many Americans solely because of their Italian origin. Almost any European artistic creation from poetry to motion pictures produced in a style with which we are not familiar in this country automatically gains prestige by virtue of its origin, and individual artists who work in the unfamiliar styles are for a while carried along on a wave of popularity for which they are themselves only slightly responsible. It matters little that such fads for the unusual from Europe may be the direct result of propaganda for sales or cultural recognition; the same might be said of the recent fad for the products of American Negro painters and writers, for it too is in considerable measure the result of a deliberate advertising campaign. The essential fact for our consideration is the existence of such fads, however created, and their resultant repercussion on American race relations.

In spite of these European fads and the American reverence for things foreign, we are not in the mental habit of thinking in terms of English, German, French, Swedish, Jewish, or other European arts in the sense that we speak of the artistry of American colored minorities. True, we do commonly refer to Russian literature, French novels, German music, Italian opera, Spanish dancing, English architecture, Dutch painting, and countless additional national arts as though they were something apart from the accomplishments of other nationalities in the same fields. These distinctions, however, are by no means the same as the ones implied when we speak of Negro music, folk lore, dancing, and the like, or even "American Indian art" and "oriental art." The various European sub-varieties of the arts are unconsciously conceded to be on a par with each other, although any one may be preferred. For example, German and Italian music may be admitted to be different, and one may prefer the Italian to the German, and even go so far as to ascribe the differences to racial qualities, but both are granted full status as products of satisfactorily civilized peoples. The artistic products of the American Negro, on the other hand, are applauded not as creations on the same plane as those of the various European nationalities, but rather as something primitive, something which is suspected of being the natural product of a childlike race still not far removed from a state of nature.

In an estimate of the relative artistic contributions of the minority groups in the United States there could hardly be any question but that the white immigrants from all parts of Europe, and their children, have furnished an overwhelmingly greater number of the real leaders in every field than all the colored peoples combined. We need not manufacture a metaphysical explanation of this fact in terms of inherent racial qualities, for social explanations are so numerous and obvious that only a special pleader could be expected to find them inadequate. The too frequent tendency of American intellectuals to accept uncritically the work of Europeans as though it simply must be good because of its source accounts for some of the successes of immigrants. The similarity of the immigrant's background to the cultural standards he finds in the United States, with just enough differences to make him interesting, is also a factor. Above all, the immigrant who sloughs off his distinguishing cultural features, such as foreign language, dress, and other outward stigmas of his minority class, is able to pass as a member of the powerful majority, and the slight traces of European origin which may cling to him are then regarded as social assets rather than liabilities. Regardless of the immigrant's inferior condition as he enters the country, compared with the condition of the native whites, both his economic and social handicaps are far less restricting and rigid than those of any colored group. It is no wonder that our European-born population and their first American generation have supplied such a vast number of artists that to attempt to list them—a relatively easy task with American Negro artists—would be futile. On the basis of the size of the groups, there should, of course, be three times as many artists in the immigrant population as in the Negro, for there are three times as many immigrants and children of immigrants as there are American Negroes. The ratio, however, is actually much greater than this.

Thus immigrants and their children have furnished proportionally both more and greater individual artists of all kinds than all the American colored people. Their achievements, furthermore, are such that they are accepted as members of native white communities about on a par with individuals of old American stock with similar accomplishments to their credit. While the contributions of the colored groups have had an originality in their variance from European patterns which has given them prominence and, in the cases of the Negro and the Indian, may be said to amount to a practical monopoly on true American art, their rôle in American civilization is minor. Their influence on race relations has been through an emphasis on differences instead of similarities, although the effects of this emphasis on race prejudice have probably been somewhat reduced by a concurrent recognition of quality.

The explanation of the qualitative and quantitative differences between the artistic products of American minority groups in terms of cultural history, present economic and social status, and the limitations of race attitudes is sometimes challenged by members of minority groups themselves, on the ground that the various races are born with special artistic aptitudes and limitations which automatically determine the extent and direction of their æsthetic development. This reminds one very much of the now discredited belief that Indians are born with keener eyesight and sharper hearing than white men, a theory once applied to all preliterates, but now so obviously recognized to be a misinterpretation of the effects of specialized training as to be hardly worth discussion. It is also reminiscent of similar theories about the origin of the artistic interests of the various European nationalities, which, too, have been thrown overboard now that careful psychological tests have failed to uncover any significant inherent differences in artistic capacities between races and nationalities.

Fewer such biological misinterpretations would be made if it were realized that what in artistic expression may seem to be primitive or savage in a racial sense may be due to nothing more than a freedom from the inhibitions of Europeanized civilization. The unconventional Negro Charleston or Black

Bottom, which to the white man's way of thinking seems so natural to the colored boy or girl and so undignified in the white, may actually be more natural when performed by a Negro, not because of any special racial abilities but for the reason that the ordinary American Negro may be "undignified" without criticism from his own people or the white man. What is "not being done" by the ordinary white person may be entirely good form for the American Negro for the elementary reason that identical social standards have not been developed by colored and white groups alike, and consequently colored individuals are free from certain inhibiting forces which forbid or demand various types of conduct in their white neighbors.

More specifically, jazz music and dancing, together with other types of rhythmic innovations, can be initiated by colored composers, musicians, and dancers more readily than by white people who are to a greater degree bound by traditions which have to be broken before the colored innovations can even be copied. This same freedom undoubtedly played a part in the creation of the spirituals as well as in the development of secular music. Of course, there is pressure on the Negro artist to follow white leaders and patterns, but it might be said to be a pressure from the outside while he as a person still remains relatively free from unconscious mental training which would tend to keep him in step with the accepted white standards. It is not denied that the American Negro's culture is essentially the white man's culture, but it is unquestionably true that the white man's culture has not been borrowed in its entirety. The white man not only "knows the rules" more accurately than the Negro, but he also has made them more a part of himself, with the result that it is a greater wrench for him to break away from the customary, whether it be in art or in any other phase of social existence.

To the extent to which any minority group in the United States is subject to cultural standards of its own or is free from those of the majority it is also in a more favorable position to create and accept new artistic modes. There are a considerable number of native-born white people who have somehow or other emancipated themselves from conventional social restrictions, but they stand in the rôle of individual pioneers, while in the case of minorities it is rather the group itself which blazes new trails. A Negro author, by virtue of the fact that he is a Negro, may write an autobiography, poem, novel, or essay in which he departs radically in style and content from accepted white standards, and win high praise thereby, while a white man of equal ability would more likely be kept mute by the inhibiting force of traditions and customs of little import to the average colored man. So, too, an unassimilated Indian might feel free to indulge in a Ghost Dance, to make decorated pottery, or to weave a blanket, while his inhibited white friend would consider the same activities as beneath the dignity of a civilized man. In the case of the Indian, however, as in the case of immigrant groups who have not lost their alien culture, the apparent freedom for artistic expression in what the majority thinks of as unconventional ways is likely to be rather subjection to alien standards, although in the process of transition from one culture to another there is the danger that the old social restrictions will be cast off before the new have been accepted, thus leaving the individual relatively free from social restraint. Differing social inhibitions, then, as well as the absence of inhibitions in certain minority groups, must be given their place in an interpretation of the uneven artistic development of American racial and national minorities.

ART AS MINORITY PROPAGANDA

The uneven development of the arts among minorities of racial and national origin is vigorously defended as a normal and proper cleavage in cultural growth, and may be expected to be of great value both to the nation and to the minorities themselves. When some individuals rise to claim that art is art, and that there can be no special varieties which in a sense would be the property of a particular minority, an equally vigorous defense is heard for the theory that ultimate, universal values in this field at least must on occasion be disregarded as a practical ideal in favor of racially and nationally limited forms and standards. Without taking sides in such a perennial debate, it is possible to analyze the practical artistic objectives evident in the products of the various minorities in the United States.

Let us first consider the American Negro. Is it possible or likely that his artistic line of development in the long run will be along a path separate from that of the rest of the population? Would any purpose in a program for the reduction of race friction be served by such a separation?

We have already pointed out that there is no biological reason why the Negro may be expected to differ from the white man in his artistic expressions, and that such theories may be regarded as the product of misinterpretation of social data. This, however, does not dispose of the arguments defending separate cultural development for social reasons. May it not be a practical necessity for the American Negro to bring forth unique forms of the arts which he may call his own in order that he may have pride in the achievements of his people and take courage therefrom in attempting more strenuous tasks? Will not such "Negro arts" attract the favorable attention of the white majority and make them more kindly disposed and appreciative of colored people's good qualities? The answer seems to be no.

It is true that some Negroes have received encouragement, resulting in increased self-confidence, from a knowledge that white people have appreciated the spirituals, jazz, and other unique creations. Most white people, however, think of these things as curiosities, interesting curiosities worth knowing about, but none the less evidences of racial differences which, while they may arouse enthusiastic admiration, do not stir envy. The Negro as a whole, of course, knows perfectly well the real bases of the white man's interest in his achievements, bases which may range all the way from pure intellectual curiosity to morbid thrill-seeking, but rarely include a wholesome desire for participation in any other than a slumming sense. How, then, can the ordinary Negro obtain pride and self-confidence from a source which he knows to be contaminated by insincerity?

This insincerity is not only that of the white faddist. Negro artists themselves produce what the public will buy, and their public is mostly white with a sprinkling of colored intellectuals. Since this public wants "Negro art," that is what is offered. The Negro who paints a picture of a New England landscape is at a terrific handicap in competition with an equal or inferior who sprinkles his canvas liberally with palm trees, monkeys, and tropical background, draws out of perspective and otherwise introduces what passes for "Negro motives." In the same way, Roland Hayes must sing spirituals, colored actors must either be comedians or appear only in plays of Negro life, poems must be about the dark man's yearnings, preferably in dialect, and novels must present "Negro problems." This in spite of the fact that the Negro is an American whose culture is year by year more closely approximating that of the country as a whole and must continue to do so if only because of an economic and social structure so interwoven that group isolation has become impossible.

A few Negro leaders preach the necessity for reviving African art, legends, and general cultural history as a foundation on which the traditions of the American Negro must be built. It is correctly pointed out that what traditions the Negro has are those of a slave caste, an insecure base for the erection of a superstructure of progress. It does not follow, however, that slave traditions can be replaced only by an artificial resurrection of African culture in America. As a matter of fact, it is probably impossible to stimulate such a resurrection, for the gap of generations between the American Negro and his African ancestral cultures is so great and his interest in bridging it so superficial that the task is beyond the strength of all his leaders together.

The ordinary Negro knows little and cares less about African ways of life, and rightly so, for he is African in his distant ancestry only, and not in all of that by any means. He is an American, even though his Americanism in some respects varies from that of the white man. He can never be made anything else. There is, furthermore, no successful precedent known to history for the attempt to make him anything else, for all peoples who have moved from one habitat to another distant one have altered their culture to meet the new situation and have failed to heed calls to return to the ways of their fathers. The Jews are an outstanding example of such failure. The Negro's skin color is not sufficient justification for the hope that he will prove an exception to the general rule of cultural change in any direction except backwards.

The result must ultimately be that with decreasing cultural isolation the American Negro will carry the process of cultural grafting on to the white American stem up to the end, when he will have traditions in common with the rest of the population. Of course as long as he remains a Negro he will perforce remember that he has an ancestry which is not identical with that of the rest of the country. In that respect, however, he will be no different from the white Americans who are proud of their German, Irish, English, Italian, and other ancestry yet at the same time identify themselves with the white population of the United States as a whole. Cultural grafting is not new, and peoples of various racial origins today have as their traditional and ideal heroes men who had no blood in common with them. What white man in the United States fails to include in his list of cultural leaders in whom he takes pride and from whom he gains confidence such men as Shakespeare, Michelangelo, Socrates, Plato, Aristotle, Pericles, Alexander the Great, Hannibal, Julius Cæsar, Napoleon, and others who may or may not be the remotest blood kin to him? The American Negro, however, thus far takes pride only in leaders of Negro ancestry, and finds few of them. There is no reason why, when his cultural assimilation is more nearly complete, he should not take every bit as much pride in David or Socrates as the educated Scandinavian does today, for neither is descended from racial stocks of these cultural heroes. In this, perhaps, lies the clue to the future of "Negro arts" which, if they follow universal precedent, are bound to disappear with the absorption of the Negro into the white man's culture.

Whatever gains there may be in the attempts to develop and keep alive unique arts among the American Negroes, they are of necessity transitional and do little to smooth the rough spots in race relations. They have, of course, served to call attention to the Negro as an element in our population, and it is perhaps desirable for the Negro not to be forgotten. As an advertising medium which has helped to make the country "Negro conscious" their rôle has been important. A few individuals have been spurred on to greater effort by their encouragement. Others have made more money out of "Negro arts" than they would have if lacking this special advantage. Negroes as a whole, however, are probably about where they would have been if the racial point of view had never been emphasized in this field, not even excepting the possible but limited effects of its publicity value.

Propagandist uses of the arts in minority group campaigns for recognition and favor are neither new nor restricted to the American Negro. Sometimes these campaigns have been consciously planned in the best merchandising manner, as in the case of the Soviet peasant arts which are used as bait for securing individual friendship to the Russian government. On other occasions a craze for art objects of a particular national or racial stamp may sweep the country with no artificial stimulation except such as is naturally to be expected of the manufacturers and distributors of the objects in question, as has been the case in any number of fads for things Chinese, Japanese, Italian, or Spanish. The stimulation for these waves of popularity may come from a desire for individual profit, for improved international relations, for improved group relations within the country, for no planned reason at all, or for a combination of any of these reasons.

Mexican arts have thus been shoved to the front in the United States for a variety of reasons. Groups of sympathetic and internationally minded citizens have tried to stir up popular interest because of purely altruistic motives. Artists and their agents have helped for financial reasons. The Mexican government has cooperated for political reasons. Hardheaded individuals have added their bit because it seemed to be a way of accomplishing practical purposes. A few in the process may actually have understood and appreciated the Mexican cultural products which they were pushing along, but only a few. The effects of this campaign can hardly be measured, but there is reason to believe that in spite of the fact that it never reached the mass of United States citizens, it did serve the function of friendship-and-respect-for-our-neighbor advertising, among a select group who help mold public opinion and public policy. Incidentally, it gave some Mexican artists an unusual source of revenue and afforded encouragement to further achievement. An unanticipated possible effect was to influence many who had previously thought of the Mexican as a Spaniard and his artistic products as Spanish in style, and therefore on a level with, if different from, the products of England, Germany, France, or Italy, to change their point of view and come to regard Mexican art as something peculiar in the sense that Negro art is peculiar, and consequently the product of a peculiar people.

The unanticipated effect of such campaigns, previously emphasized in our discussion of American Negro art, is likely if not sure to follow any propagandist program based on national or racial arts. The arts so advertised may not be identical with or even closely similar to the forms which are popularly accepted as standard, for if they are their group source becomes obscured and the artist alone stands out apart from his background. Only when there is some unique quality, readily recognized by the tyro, does art serve as propagandist material. This accounts for the constant use of peasant products, possibly modified by individualistic bizarre interpretations, as group propaganda. There must be a group trade-mark or it will tend to be accepted merely as art and not as a particular brand of art, just as a manufacturer of pork and beans must have a trade-mark to show that it is Smith's we should buy and not merely pork and beans. Unfortunately, in so labeling artistic products they are automatically labeled as inferior since they are advertised as different from the accepted standard (our own), and certainly cannot be superior to it. In view of this tendency the wisdom of such propaganda is doubtful if the purpose is to elevate the social status of the minorities to the level of the majority.

Even when the arts are not purposely used as propaganda

they are nevertheless almost certain to influence public opinion concerning the qualities and worth of minority groups, for nearly all convey ideas in addition to affording gratification of more abstract æsthetic desires. Words cannot be used in song, poem, novel, story or play without reflecting the author's or interpreter's attitudes toward the subject matter. The graphic and plastic arts offer no escape from this inexorable rule. Music and the dance may be relatively free from this general principle, but even in these arts the public as well as the artist have been educated to consider certain forms of expression more "primitive" or less "civilized" than others, thereby influencing group attitudes. It is doubtful whether any artist will be called successful if the ideas which he expresses do not coincide with those of a group from which he may draw followers. The larger the group of followers— whether before or after his death makes little difference to us— the greater will be his influence on public opinion, if only to reinforce and solidify valuations previously accepted. The temptation, of course, is to keep in line in so far as ideas are concerned, if not in regard to mechanical technique, for in orthodoxy lie the greatest immediate rewards. The unorthodox stand out because of their rarity, and while their influence may in the long run be tremendous, their following is likely to be recruited from similar-thinking, if small, groups.

Thus current stereotyped beliefs concerning the appearance, social standards, and conduct of minority groups are likely to be supported by artists of all varieties where they have already taken root and spread to other people in proportion as artistic products themselves are spread. It matters little what the facts are; no racial or national stereotype can even approximate reality. The artist differs from the rest of his group primarily in his artistic ability and training. His social standards and evaluations are absorbed from his environment. However superior or original his artistic technique may be, his creations must give evidence of his social background unless they are absolutely neutral.

Many artistic creations are of course neutral in regard to racial questions; a much greater number show racial bias only vaguely. Thus a New England landscape may be said to be racially neutral, although the minute a person or a cultural product such as a farmhouse, church, or bit of farm machinery is introduced it tends, however slightly, to reinforce the doctrine of the superiority of Americanized European civilization, the product of white peoples. The very absence of the slightest reference to any minority group may be a violation of neutrality, for it tends to give an impression that the normal is a majority characteristic while only the peculiar in minorities is worth portraying. For illustration, if motion pictures used only white old-American actors in plays which made no reference to any minority people in the United States, the effect on social attitudes could hardly be said to be strictly neutral. Quite commonly, however, the practice is the very opposite of pseudo-neutrality through neglect, in that whenever in real life customary racial attitudes would be shown they are also shown in the artist's conception of a similar situation.

Let us take painting as means for clarifying this generalized statement, remembering that as previously stated the word "art" is here used to include all brands of workmanship from the highest down to trash. As a type of painting at first thought far removed from any reference to race or nationality, we may consider Landseer's animal pictures, so popular only a short generation ago as parlor decorations. His animal subjects were animals popularly associated, if not actually so, with European culture, such as favorite European breeds of dogs or wild creatures of the English chase. Does this not emphasize the alleged superiority of the culture of the majority, and therefore of the majority itself? Is this not typical of the pseudo-neutral artists? Maxfield Parrish and Rockwell Kent might have been used in place of Landseer as illustrations of this point.

Portraits by outstanding European and American artists are almost without exception those of white people of the prevailing culture, painted because of their social status or superior physical qualities. Colored or other minority people are rarely painted except as "character studies," and the fact that there are also numerous character studies of white persons does little to offset this fact, for the public of course recognizes that there are all sorts of white people in the majority group but it has only the peculiar minority individuals called to its attention. The minority "character" may be either strong or weak, evil or benign, but the uniqueness is rarely absent. Not only must the minority models possess some unique quality in person or adornment, and usually in both, but their cultural setting or physical environment must also be different from the normal if there is not an obvious master-servant relationship, or there would be no excuse for the painting.

It is a long descent from even reasonably good animal or portrait painters down to comic-strip "artists" as the connoisseur views it, but the influence of the cartoon of either humorous or serious intent on social attitudes is if anything greater than that of its more aristocratic cousin. Cartoons have as their primary purpose the conveying of attitudes and ideas; quite obviously the technique and the æsthetic appeal of great art are absent and unlamented. What rudiments of technique are still visible in the cartoon are adequate to "get across" some simple point to the lowest common denominator in the American population. To be understood by the greatest possible number of readers they must depend on stereotyped figures, such as Uncle Sam, John Bull, and Mr. Common People. Racial and national stereotypes are practically always among those present. Uncle Sam and John Bull themselves are national stereotypes. Hairbreadth Harry, Relentless Rudolph, the Katzenjammer Kids, Moon Mullins, Lord Plushbottom and the rest of the better-known comic characters, with few if any exceptions, fall in line with the popular mental picture of the groups to which they belong. The false impressions created by constant dependence on such stereotypes are not reduced but rather increased in importance by the humorous intent of the comic strip.

These cartoons are read by adults and children with no intent of learning anything. Rather they are time-killers. The fact that the impressions created are unconscious impressions does not destroy their reality. Children look at the Sunday "funnies" even before they can read, with the result that pernicious ideas concerning other races and nationalities are sown in their minds at an early impressionable age. Adults have similar ideas confirmed by the same pictures. In them Orientals are faithful servants, mysterious plotters, or the future invaders of the western world. Negroes are rare in comic strips, possibly because of the fact that they buy a good many copies of the newspapers to whom comic strips are syndicated. The few Negroes who do creep in occasionally are usually jungle savages or American servants. South Europeans are the villains and vamps, while north European types are the heroes and sweet but innocent heroines. Jews, like Abe Kabibble, are always intended to be funny because of language, figure, or "Jewish traits" of behavior. Indians are nearly always noble red men. The cartoonist who attempted anything else than to follow popular stereotypes in such matters simply could not sell his drawings.

The cartoons with serious intent must also follow popular patterns. The German must be either a pot-bellied beer drinker or an overbearing Prussian. The Russian must be of the pre-War aristocratic type, a down-trodden peasant or a bewhiskered, booted and bloused Bolshevik. The Frenchman must have pointed whiskers and a silk hat, the well-bred Englishman needs a monocle but no chin, the Italian must be short and dark, whether he comes from north or south Italy, and so on. Naturally these racial and national stereotypes may be crossed with those of other classes, as, for example, when the drawing is of an English lord, an English socialist, an English farmer, an English bartender, or a cockney. Such double stereotypes are just as effective in creating and bolstering race prejudices as are the single ones. So long as pen and pencil are used to produce cartoons such patterns must be followed. There is no other device whereby the cartoonist is enabled to drive home his point so quickly and surely to his audience of millions.

It may seem that too much attention has been paid this distant cousin of the fine arts, the cartoon. The justification lies in their undoubted significance in race relations, their common neglect as a factor in the situation, and the present writer's belief that the cartoon affords an illustration of the trend in all phases of art. What the cartoon does so crudely in fostering race prejudices is no different in principle from what is done on stage and screen, in book and periodical, in the graphic and plastic arts as well as in music and dancing. In essence, it is the uncritical acceptance of popular myths, less frequently of accurate observations concerning minority groups, and the informal education of young and old into a similar uncritical acceptance of the same generalizations. In truth it is a vicious circle, with only a few individual artists ineffectually striving to break out of it.

Since dependence on stereotypes decreases to some extent with education, it would be expected that those arts which make the widest appeal in the hope of financial returns and therefore have to cater to the less educated masses, would be the ones which are more slavish in their adherence to unwarranted racial and national myths. Such seems to be the case. Cartoons, as previously discussed, are distinctly a financial venture whose success is measured by the number of readers. Motion pictures would naturally fall into this same category, as would also popular fiction and the illustrations accompanying it. Popular music does not escape this classification, although classical music does to a greater degree than is true of the classical in the other artistic fields, probably because of the previously mentioned unimportance of interpretation in terms of reality. Artists and their business associates gain income in proportion to the number of people who buy their products, and since people will buy what they most nearly understand, the necessity for dependence on popular stereotypes by popular artists is an inevitable consequence.

If this statement is accurate, motion pictures should be more slavish in their adherence to race myths than grand opera. This is actually the case. Operas in turn should reflect popular stereotypes more clearly than the little theaters which claim to be more interested in art itself than in commercial success. This again seems to work out in accordance with our general principle, for the little theaters, such as the Hedgerow Theatre in Rose Valley, Pennsylvania, sometimes disrespectfully but significantly referred to as "arty" theaters, have been pioneers in the use of Negro actors and plays. Musical comedies, mystery and other "lowbrow" productions, and "problem plays" such as those of Shaw, rank in the order named in the legitimate theater in regard to popular approval and adherence to popular racial doctrines.

The same correlation between popularity and adherence to accepted racial and national stereotypes is distinctly visible in the music of the streets. Where the accompanying words of "catchy" music convey any ideas at all they too must be orthodox. Not only the words of such music tend to become stereotyped, but the tunes themselves also are forced to conform to some pattern which the majority has been trained to accept as typical. We may call to witness the "mammy" songs, the "darkey" songs of Stephen Foster, the pseudo-American Indian songs, such as "The Waters of Minnetonka," the pseudo-oriental compositions of Rimsky-Korsakoff—for example, the "Song of India"—or the supposedly typical Spanish theme in "La Paloma." In so far as such music is regarded as "primitive" or "peasant" in contrast with the "civilized" varieties, or as it is popularly connected with undisguised sex interest as distinguished from that which has no such elemental connotations, it influences race attitudes by its emphasis on differences generally conceded to be stigmas of inferiority. However much it may be regretted, this emphasis can hardly be avoided if the composer and musician intends to live by his art alone.

In similar vein, the highbrow fiction writer who has neither desire for nor hope of publication in a weekly periodical with a bloated circulation of several million copies may be and not infrequently is iconoclastic in his treatment of racial myths. Writers of novels and stories for the masses, however, as typified by those who publish in the *Saturday Evening Post* and *Liberty*, if they mention race or nationality at all, must be careful to keep in step with their readers' generalizations. Octavus Roy Cohen's stories of Epic Peters, Lawyer Chew, Lady Luck, "The Sons and Daughters of I Will Arise," and other burlesqued darkey characters usually in ludicrous situations, as published in the *Post*, are almost a national tradition. Stories of modern Russia in the same magazine apparently must show the Bolshevists as sinister or misguided fanatics, even though the apparent purpose of the fiction is to amuse or interest rather than to instruct. Perhaps the words "even though" in the previous sentence should be changed to "because," for in all likelihood the actual reason for the monotonous conformity of both fiction and feature articles in this periodical and the others of approximately the same type is not the racial or patriotic zeal of the editors to preserve America for the old Americans, but rather a shrewdly guided desire for sales and profit.

One can scarcely censure the periodicals for this practice, since such slavish conformity is only natural in our social order, and practically all popular writers, including those identified with minority groups who have achieved some measure of fame, follow the same practice even when they have no intention of submitting their manuscripts to a magazine. Ludwig Lewisohn, for illustration, passes along the popular belief that blood is thicker than water in his *Island Within*, which tells of a Jew who deserts Judaism to the extent of marrying a Gentile, but eventually returns to his people for true happiness. Jessie Fauset, a Negro, supports the same theory when in her *Plum Bun* she tells the story of a light colored girl who experiments with passing for white, but finds no real contentment until at last she is back in the bosom of her family surrounded by people of some African ancestry. Stories of the Negro, Jew, Oriental, Indian, or any other sharply defined minority group, whether written by a member of the minority or by a person of colonial white stock, have small chance of large sale if they disturb the mental digestion of the masses by disagreeing with accepted mental patterns.

Uncle Tom's Cabin, one of the most widely read books ever written by an American, was successful as a book and play not because it fought a battle against slavery, but rather because in portraying slavery unfavorably it fitted in with anti-slavery sentiment already rampant in most parts of the western world, and at the same time maintained the popular conception of the Negro as a darkey, more to be pitied than scorned, feared, or hated. Harriet Beecher Stowe's Uncle Tom still remains the stereotype of the kind of Negro fondly regarded by the Southerner as well as by the Northerner because he "knew his place." Thomas Dixon's *The Clansman* and *The Leopard's Spots* also obtained popularity because of their conformity to an accepted mental picture of Negroes, Southerners, and race relations. The motion picture, *The Birth of a Nation*, adapted from *The Clansman*, achieved wide popularity for similar reasons as well as because of the high quality of its acting and directing. Joel Chandler Harris's Uncle Remus stories fit in the same way, although the stereotypes involved in these stories are not the same as those emphasized by Dixon.

It is not surprising that Negroes nearly always write about Negroes and in terms of stereotypes which do not differ widely from those generally held by white people. The Negro is, after all, culturally an American, and while his literature stresses the injustice of the racial situation in the United States more than the writings of white people, the characters and events in his fiction must in essence be the same as those of successful white authors if he is also to be successful. Van Vechten's *Nigger Heaven* gives us a stereotyped view of Harlem life surprisingly similar to that found in Claude McKay's *Home to Harlem* and a number of other recent novels written by Negroes. Paul Laurence Dunbar's dialect poetry shows a spirit of protest growing out of his color, but it also shows a view of the American Negro which grew out of the larger American cultural scene. No Negro author of any considerable reputation has been able to break the bonds of American stereotypes, for he is first of all an American. If he were by some chance to break these bonds it is likely that he would be deserted by Negro and white readers alike.

While the American Negro and the Jew have produced an appreciable number of authors who have written about their own minority group, the other minorities in the United States have to a greater extent been written about by outsiders, being relatively mute themselves. Our literature concerning the

Oriental is nearly all written by Occidentals. Stories about the Indian, from the time of James Fenimore Cooper to the present, have been largely the product of white authors. Immigrant minorities other than the Jewish have produced a great number of writers who from time to time have made use of the phenomena of group relationships in their stories. Monotonously these stories follow and reinforce accepted stereotypes, and are characterized, when written by a minority member, primarily by the natural protests of the underdog.

The popular arts thus habitually reflect popular race attitudes in a rough proportion to their popular acceptance. They tend to be a conservative influence in the social order, constantly repeating and hammering home racial facts and fancies which have found favor with the majority population. This is especially true when the artists are members of the majority group.

It is also true, if with some reservations, when the artists are members of a minority, for while minority artists have a choice between attempting to develop a minority art with distinct differentiating characteristics or entering competition with majority artists in their own field, in either case they must pay tribute to their lay following, which does not wish to be argued or jarred out of racial preconceptions. To the degree to which the minority culture approximates that of the majority, these preconceptions will also approximate each other in the groups considered, and every minority in the United States in these days of efficient communication is being driven to the adoption of the majority culture.

Art is consequently a vital factor in the cultural assimilation of American minorities. Its conservative influence makes for uniformity of racial attitudes, the attitudes which are already most widely accepted. On the other hand, there is the possibility that it may to a much greater extent than at present become a progressive factor in the building of American racial ideals and standards in so far as change may be progressive.

Group attitudes are highly emotionalized, and mere logic supported by cold facts rarely carries much weight in an argument with an emotionally biased individual. There is an emotional appeal in all of the arts, however, which may well be used, under competent guidance, to break down outworn mental sets no longer considered necessary or socially desirable. To select an illustration from a different field, we may refer to a method used by the United States as well as all other participants in the World War. Fiction, usually disguised as fact, although the disguise was not essential to the purpose, was used to arouse emotions against the enemy. Posters showing heroic doughboys going over the top for the glory and honor of their country spurred men on to enlistment. Pictures of beautiful women draped in white robes and the national colors militantly urged the purchase of Liberty Bonds. Music of all sorts was used to arouse the emotions to the proper pitch for fighting a war. Motion pictures and the stage were drawn on to serve the same purpose. Germans were hated as an abhorred race by Americans of recent German descent, partly because of the way the arts were used for propaganda purposes. No art was allowed to shirk its duty, and it is doubtful whether the war could have been fought as well as it was, either in the trenches or at home, without these emotional driving forces.

There is nothing new in such use of the arts, excepting perhaps some advanced techniques, for since time immemorial the drum and trumpet have been instruments of war, as have also carved and painted standards and icons, and folk tales showing the wickedness of the enemy. There is no inherent reason why these same devices which so often have been used to stir the emotions in war may not be guided to advantage in furthering interracial peace. The problem is more difficult for there is less experience on which to draw, and there is less incentive to action in time of peace, but the possibilities are obvious.

Not only do the arts afford a means for emotional appeal otherwise lacking, but they also, viewed as an educational medium, have an ease of understanding which is unsurpassed by facts and figures in books and lectures. The cartoon is an offensive weapon feared by every politician far more than logic and statistics combined. Many a political grafter has been

driven to cover by reforms swept along by the force of cartoons, campaign songs, and pointed comment made understandable through the arts to voters who would have been
incapable of grasping more formal arguments. Individuals
who have no training for the interpretation of mental-test
results, who are bored with arguments for interracial cooperation based on economic interdependence, and have no time to
figure out the dangerous effects of handicapped, illiterate,
poverty-stricken minorities on the majority, could and would
appreciate the same points if the arts were properly used for
such propaganda purposes. Their simplicity and their emotional appeal are well-nigh irresistible if brought to bear on
any group.

Therein lies the rub. They have not, except sporadically,
been brought to bear on the racial attitudes of the American
people other than to support those already in existence. In
spite of German-American, Swedish-American, Italian-American, and other hyphenated societies which exist literally by
the hundreds, if local organizations are taken into account,
minority groups in the United States have not been sufficiently
well organized to put across any planned program of propaganda in the arts. This is largely due to the diversity of
interests in America which begins to dissipate any existing
spirit of national unity as soon as the immigrant lands, and
while something of a sentimental interest remains in the original home country, most immigrants are more directly concerned with America and Americans than with fellow immigrants who happened to be born in the same foreign land.
Such diversity of interests makes any organization of immigrant minorities practically impossible if it involves extensive
propaganda for the betterment of group relations, in spite of
occasional spurts in times of stress.

It might seem that the colored groups, more definitely set
apart by their racial features, should be able to organize with
relative efficiency for propaganda purposes. It is only necessary
to point out that existing welfare and propagandist Negro
organizations, such as the National Association for the Advancement of Colored People and the National Urban League,

and their associated periodicals, *The Crisis* and *Opportunity*, receive pitifully slight support from the people for whom they are fighting. Negro newspapers with their efforts for race improvement also fail to receive the expected support from the people they try to serve. The Indians are in a similar position. Even the Orientals have signally failed to unite for the improvement of their group status in the United States, and most of the propaganda in their favor has been the result of foreign rather than American resident Chinese inspiration, as in the case of the Kuomingtong, whose American members worked hard to help the Nationalists in China, and incidentally helped themselves during a recent revolution. In the same way, the Japanese, Italian, and other foreign governments have from time to time been the inspiration for American propaganda to gain international favor which almost accidentally furthered the cause of American minorities of corresponding national origin. Until a minority group attains something more important in common than national origin or racial similarity—and it is doubtful if any ever will—the conscious use of the arts in decreasing racial prejudices must remain an improbability. The only other source of such activity is the so-called humanitarians, and their past performances do not justify optimism regarding their future influence in this field.

The assimilative rôle of art thus becomes paradoxical. In general it tends to confirm the racial attitudes of the majority toward minorities, and at the same time drives these prejudices into the minds of the minorities themselves. This is evidenced by the common observation that "inferior" minorities look down on other minorities. The Jew has about the same racial attitudes toward the Negro, the Oriental, and other minorities as are held by the majority. The Negro feels the same way about the Jew, the Oriental, and others. It has even come to the point where minorities lose confidence in their own people, although the minority individual may omit himself from his borrowed classification of his people as inferior. The fairly well-assimilated Jew is very likely to have his doubts about his people, and possibly even about himself. The Negro as a

rule certainly thinks of his fellow Negroes as not equal to the
white man. There are of course valid exceptions to this generalization, but the very protests which such a statement
usually provokes in minorities indicate its essential truth by
their violence. It has not been said that the stereotyped arts
are solely responsible for this acceptance of American group
prejudices, for there are obviously numerous other contributing factors, elsewhere discussed, but it is affirmed that artistic
reflections of public beliefs are not the least of these.

CHAPTER XVII

THE PROSPECT

MAN is an impatient animal, eager for solutions of social ills and disdainful of academicians' surveys, hypotheses, analyses, and theories. Action, not cautious and laborious research, is demanded of those who would lead the populace. Thus a Chamberlain, a Gobineau, or a Stoddard attracts myriads of followers by a pseudo-scientific program based on a doctrine of God-given white supremacy—each with his favorite subdivision of the white race—while the very names of Franz Boas, Eugene Pittard, Herbert A. Miller, E. B. Reuter, Friedrich Hertz, and other scholarly students of the peoples of the world are unknown outside of a small intellectual circle. "Give us the solution, and let sterile scholars while away their time with obscure facts which lead but to quibbling books!" is the cry of the masses.

THE FUTILITY OF PANACEAS

Solutions to the problems of race relations have been offered freely, but not by scholars. Deportation of minorities back to Africa, the Orient, Mexico, and Europe, the exclusion of minority immigrants, extinction through "racial degeneracy," geographic, residential, economic, and social segregation, biological amalgamation, cultural assimilation, and a true "brotherhood of man" are among the more common panaceas urged upon communities suffering from complaints as serious as race riots or as trivial as social snobbishness. It is too late for exclusion, deportation is impossible, extinction by a surplus of deaths over births is a phantom, complete segregation of any type has never been accomplished, amalgamation is a will-o'-the-wisp which would lead us through centuries of travail, assimilation is a tedious process dependent on identity of environments and equality of opportunity, and the abolition of class and caste distinctions is a purpose, not a program. The ineffectiveness of all such panaceas is evident from the way group antagonism in the United States has continued to remain endemic, an ever-present social ill which breaks out from time to time with exceptional virulence and without regard for the cure-alls of reformers.

Yet there must be some working program or policy capable of development and of popular acceptance which would be superior to the present confusion of conflicting ideals and practices. On the one hand, racial equality and tolerance are not to be hoped for in the immediate future, but, on the other, it is inconceivable that the present chaos and wanton waste of human potentialities because of unadjusted group relations should be permitted to continue without some concerted effort toward orderly cooperation. Any plan for social adjustment must be a compromise if it is to gain sufficient adherents from opposing sides to put it into operation. Objectionable as it may seem to the idealists who still have faith in an impractical eighteenth-century philosophy of democracy, class and caste distinctions are so imbedded in our social consciousness that they must be recognized in any program for the adjustment of minority-majority relationships.

Since Negro-white relationships offer the greatest obstacles to adjustment, any program which holds out hope for their improvement may be assumed to be applicable, with modifications, to the adjustment of the relationships of any other population elements of racial or national origin in the United States. The open recognition of social castes and classes, the restatement of their justification and limitations, and an extension of opportunities for all individuals regardless of race and national origin seem unavoidable.

The present popular theory—a theory which, surprisingly enough, is not popularly practised—is that a nigger is a nigger, a Jew a Jew, a Chinaman a Chinaman, and so on. The well known phrase, coined by a Negro who has since regretted it, that "all coons look alike to me," expresses the common sentiment that distinctions between individuals of the colored race are unimportant in comparison with their similarities. Since the Negro race is accepted as an inferior race, this means that all Negroes are inferior to all white people. As the prejudiced Southerner so frequently puts it, "No nigger is as good as any white man." There have been, and still are, opinionated racial doctrinaires who have applied similar generalizations to other American minorities: witness the once popular phrase that "the only good Indian is a dead Indian," or other stereotyped characterizations of new immigrants, Mexicans, and Orientals.

This type of characterization demands a rigid caste system under which the social status of an individual is determined by the status of his parents. If the belief that "no nigger is as good as any white man" were put into practice, all Negroes would be forced into an inferior caste. It is typical of castes that one can never achieve higher status than that into which he is born, although high status may be lost. Thus there is an idiomatic phrase "to lose caste," but none "to gain caste." Caste is determined by a permanent mark of inferior or superior breeding, whether it be skin color, a hereditary title of nobility, or an inalienable control of landed estates. Social classes, on the other hand, are less rigid, and an individual may gain or lose class status, for it is based on such transitory qualities as personal wealth, education, military rank, political preferment, and individual achievement.

The alleged caste status of the American Negro has been expressed by Professor Park as follows:[1]

ALLEGED CASTE DISTINCTION BETWEEN AMERICAN NEGROES AND
WHITE POPULATION

All white people
—————————
All Negroes

Similar horizontal dividing lines might be used to express supposed caste distinctions between Mexican "greasers," Jews, Chinese, Japanese, Filipinos, Indians, or some south Europeans, and the old American native white stock, with the latter, of course, always on top. An actual caste system may be

[1] Robert E. Park, "The Bases of Race Prejudice," in Donald Young, editor, "The American Negro," *The Annals* of the American Academy of Political and Social Science, November, 1928, vol. cxxxx, p. 20.

said to exist when an ineradicable stigma of inferiority, such as color, marks a distinct cleavage between two groups; and individuals of the lower status are never accepted in full social equality by the upper group. If, on the other hand, the line can be crossed by exceptional individuals of inferior status, who are then accorded all or many of the privileges of majority status, the distinctions may be better described as those of class. Actually, only the Negro of all American minorities finds the line impassable, and he alone may therefore, strictly speaking, be said to have been assigned to an inferior caste. It is a matter of delicate judgment to decide whether or not the Oriental in the United States may properly be described as having caste status, but since there are individuals of Japanese, Chinese, and even Filipino ancestry who have been granted almost, if not quite, full equality in white American circles, their status had better be distinguished from that of the Negro. For all practical purposes, of course, most Orientals residing in this country might as well belong to an inferior caste based on inherited physical characteristics, but their restrictions are not nearly so narrowly confining as those imposed on even the more successful Negroes. Exceptional individuals of all other minorities may with varying degrees of ease, depending on such things as their place of residence, their personality, or their personal accomplishments, rise far above the status of their group.

It is theoretically possible to have castes without classes, classes without castes, or classes within castes. The latter possibility represents the actual conditions in the United States today. This means that the dividing line between castes and classes should be vertical, and not horizontal, that is, that a proper diagram of group relationships should allow for class distinctions within all groups and not follow the misleading allegation, so defensively asserted by theorists who express a wish rather than an observation, that all members of one group are superior in status to all members of some other group. What Professor Park has said, in discussing Negro-white relationships, might also be said of all minority-majority relationships: "The races no longer look up and down: they look across."[2] We must therefore substitute the following diagram with a vertical dividing line for the previous one with a horizontal division:

HYPOTHETICAL CASTE DISTINCTION BETWEEN AMERICAN NEGROES AND WHITE POPULATION

All white people	All Negroes

The confusion has been one between popular theory and actual practice, complicated by a constantly changing occupational and intellectual distribution within all minorities. While we have continued to accept a higher-lower interpretation of group relationships, more nearly correct a century ago, but never entirely so, minority individuals of all colors and national origins have entered more and more diversified occupations ranging in type from day labor to the skilled professions, and by a process of acculturation they have achieved a complicated social pattern which inevitably produced a social stratification within each minority. Once social stratification became clear cut within minorities, as it had long been in the majority, there were necessarily individuals of minority status who nevertheless belonged to classes socially superior to some majority strata. This situation may be diagrammed as on the following page.

There is no way of knowing just how many social classes there are in any population group, but it may be assumed that there are more in the native white majority than in any minority, and that minorities have a greater concentration in the lower levels. A glance at the next diagram, remembering that the number of classes and their relative size are purely imaginary, immediately establishes the obvious but neglected fact that there are Negroes whose class status, within their

[2] *Ibid.*

HYPOTHETICAL CLASS AND CASTE RELATIONSHIPS OF AMERICAN
NEGROES AND WHITE POPULATION

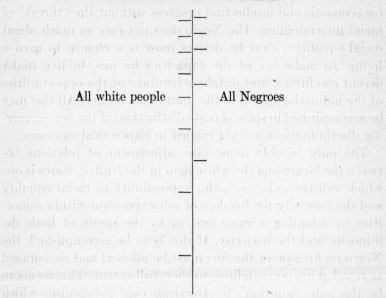

caste, is superior to the class status of any number of white people. This is no more than saying that Negroes like W. E. B. Du Bois, Booker T. Washington, H. O. Tanner, and R. R. Moton have been recognized as of far superior qualities and attainments than white clerks, ditch diggers, and artisans. In *ante bellum* days there was a much heavier concentration of Negroes in the inferior classes, a concentration so great as to afford an aspect of truth to the allegation that all white people were superior to all Negroes in worth and status. Today no minority of colored or European origin is so undifferentiated as to warrant such a generalization.

Why do we not, then, frankly recognize that Negroes like every other people vary in regard to native ability and attainments, and must consequently be treated as individuals in their social relations? Why do we not give up preaching and ranting about a false stereotype of racial uniformity which does not conform to reality in practice? The cult of "white supremacy," of course, may not be destroyed by an appeal to the logic of facts; but if the dividing line between white and black were openly admitted to be such as to foster stratification within each race, there would be increased opportunity for economic and intellectual progress without the "threat" of racial intermingling. The Negro does not care so much about social equality; what he desires most is a chance to earn a living, to make use of the capacities he has, to live under decent conditions, and to take advantage of the opportunities of the industrial age up to the limit of his ability. All this may be accomplished in spite of caste distinctions if the accompanying discriminations are not carried to impractical extremes.

The only feasible immediate adjustment of relations between the Negro and the white man in the United States is one which will recognize both the impossibility of racial equality and the necessity for freedom of self-expression within minorities by adapting a caste system to the needs of both the minority and the majority. If this is to be accomplished, the Negro on his side of the line must be allowed and encouraged to develop his potentialities to their full extent. This seems to be the only "solution" to American race antagonism which promises immediate rewards both to the Negro, who is more anxious to escape discrimination than segregation, and to the white man, who, whether he admits it or not, suffers from the presence and competition of a culturally retarded race.

The vertical division with sub-stratifications on both sides of the line is already in existence, not only between the white man and the black in this country, but also between Jew and Gentile, Oriental and Occidental, foreign born and native. It expresses crudely the relationship between the majority and all minorities, and even between minorities themselves, such as the Chinese and Japanese, the south European and the Jew. It is an unavoidable compromise between an absolute caste system which recognizes no distinctions between individuals of the inferior caste—a system which is dependent on the absence of variations in the economic and social rôles of persons assigned to this status—and absolute equality, which presupposes the elimination of the causes of group prejudices. The former extreme and anything closely approximating it has been eliminated by existing variations in the achievements of the members of any and all minorities; the latter, by the fact that the basic causes of racial prejudices will not permit a mere ideal to counteract their influence. A compromise, however distasteful to the advocates of either extreme, has been the unplanned and unavoidable consequence.

THE CONFLICT OF PREJUDICE AND TOLERANCE

The present compromise between the caste system and racial equality will continue so long as a conflict of individual and group interests, real or fictitious, is believed by both the minorities and the majority to be involved in their relations. Every minority is viewed as a threat to American labor, government, family, church, morals, and racial quality. Minorities, in turn, are constantly looking for insults, economic discrimination, political favoritism, and evidences of social segregation. The unemployed blame their condition on cheap labor, willing to work for a pittance because of "un-American" living standards and habits. Crime in the south is defensively dismissed as a natural product of the presence of Negroes; in industrial centers it is the foreigner who is held responsible for disregard of the law. Vice, divorce, desertion, and even children's disrespect of their parents' wishes have been attributed to the disintegrating influence of alien cultures on the true American family. All this, of course, is largely nonsense, with just enough truth mixed in to convince those who want to be convinced.

Minorities are perhaps even more anxious to be convinced that their failures are the product of oppression, and many of them undoubtedly may be so explained. The tendency, however, is to overwork this type of explanation. The Jew who for legitimate reasons is dropped from college, or refused admittance, is tempted to save his face by references to anti-Semitism. In one university a Jewish faculty member was appointed to the disciplinary committee—he himself is authority for this explanation—in order to forestall charges of unfair discrimination. Let it be emphasized that this type of defensive reaction is not a "Jewish characteristic," as is so frequently charged by Christians; it is a universal minority device for explaining away failures, and is made effective by the fact that it is not infrequently the correct explanation. Furthermore, minorities often have no way of knowing whether they are the subject of discrimination. Recently a Negro college graduate threatened to report a Pullman ticket agent for insolence when a railroad ticket, a Pullman ticket and an envelope were shoved out to him under the wicket without being folded together. The agent sullenly took them back and put the tickets inside the envelope as demanded. Within the next year the present writer, who happens to be white, found that in thirty purchases of Pullman reservations the tickets were placed in the envelope only four times. How, indeed, is a person of obvious minority status to know when slovenly service, discourtesy, discrimination in employment, and other personal affronts— all far from rare in the lives of white men—may be attributed to his group status, his purely personal qualities, or the boorishness of an ill-bred individual? The person who is assigned minority status and yet can keep from carrying a chip on his shoulder is exceptional.

Group antagonisms seem to be inevitable when two peoples in contact with each other may be distinguished by differentiating characteristics, either inborn or cultural, and are actual or potential competitors. Only by eliminating the outward evidences of distinction, such as color, dress, or language, or by removing the competitive factor, may racial antagonisms be destroyed. The Indian, once considered a beast to be hunted down and driven to the waste lands without mercy, has now achieved an enviable status as a "noble red man." Up to the end of the frontier days he was assigned a status about on a par with the Negro, as is witnessed by the fact that Hampton was designed to accommodate both Indians and Negroes, who were to be educated to "work with the hands." Prejudice against the aboriginal American died down as he was eliminated as a competitor of the white man. His distinguishing features remain; the few thousands of his race who have survived into the present century in the United States offer no threat to the rest of the population except in the areas of their concentration, where alone any noticeable antagonism to them can be found.

The Germans and the Irish are two other minorities which were not so long ago regarded with disdain and even hatred by the native-born white majority, yet are today considered as the founders of a most desirable population element. Immigrants from their countries are welcomed as of superior quality. The almost 7,000,000 immigrants from Germany, and their children, are still competitors of our older white stocks, as are also the 3,000,000 immigrants and children of immigrants from what is now the Irish Free State. The disappearance of serious prejudice against these peoples can be largely attributed to the fact that they are no longer highly visible population groups, for the German accent, the Irish brogue, peculiarities of dress and manners, have been largely lost through acculturation. Gone are the shanty Irish, the Paddies and the Bridgets, with their clay pipes and their shamrocks, now to be found only in sentimental historical tales and Saint Patrick's Day celebrations. Gone, too, are marks of German origin, so that even the stereotyped German caricatures of Weber and Fields have lost their humor, to be replaced by those of Al Jolson and Fanny Brice, now also on the wane. There can be no pronounced prejudices against peoples whose outward appearance does not mark them as of special origin.

Popular feeling against the Chinese and the Japanese has been modified in spite of the fact that their inherent racial features still make them easily distinguishable, for restrictive immigration laws have held their numbers to an unimportant minimum. With the threat of any great influx from their countries removed by government action, and their proportion of the Pacific coast population a trifling one, few need fear their competition. Race riots against them are now a matter of history; the popular attitude has become one of practical indifference toward those who are residents of our country. In the absence of legislation which will prevent the arrival of great numbers of Filipinos, should they decide to migrate to the Pacific coast, even the small number who have already arrived may provoke considerable animosity. It is safe to predict that they too will be regarded with indifference even by Californians when the bars are raised against immigrants from the Philippine Islands. The Mexican is distinguishable as an alien minority not only by cultural characteristics but also by his racial features, and the actual competition of those already in this country, together with the potential threat of further immigration, has resulted in the continuance of a strong anti-Mexican prejudice.

Hostility to all of the minorities just mentioned may be controlled and even eliminated, because in each case it has been or is possible for their competition to be checked by restrictions on their numbers, or because, in the case of white minorities, they can be readily assimilated and absorbed by the white majority. Antagonism against the Negro seems destined to preserve its force for generations to come.

The distinguishing features of the Negro will be preserved unless and until he is completely absorbed by the white race through miscegenation, a prospect which is so many centuries removed that it can be disregarded. His numbers cannot be expected to be reduced even in proportion to the total population of the country for many, many generations. Thus he seems doomed to remain an object of prejudice for countless years. A more even distribution throughout the country might conceivably reduce discrimination against him in those sections where he is at present concentrated, but twelve million people of dark skin cannot be so scattered throughout the United States that their effective competition would be diminished to a point low enough to eliminate prejudice. Further, if industry and agriculture were so organized, and if the country were so prosperous that every able-bodied person could find employment, we might expect hatred of the black man to diminish, but this is an inconceivably utopian prospect. It may be observed that the decrease in immigration since the World War, with its resulting removal of hundreds of thousands of Negroes from the areas of heaviest concentration, has improved the relations of the races in some southern communities. There seems, however, to be no hope of change in the near future in the relations between the Negro and the white man unless it be in the direction, previously mentioned, of a compromise caste system permitting a dual but interlocking economic and social organization.

It should not be understood from this discussion that visibility and competition are the only factors in race prejudice. Tradition is a third factor which must be taken into account. The fact that the Negro was once a slave, that all minorities were originally cheap and despised laborers, has a powerful influence on our present attitudes. Human memory, however, is short, and man readily forgets or rationalizes incidents of past generations. Australians today are little ashamed of their ancestors who were sent to their land when it was a penal colony. Indentured servants, or redemptioners, were the original American ancestors of many proud family lines. A goodly proportion of American settlers and early immigrants were criminals and paupers who have left no mark of inferiority on their descendants. The tradition of the Indian as a thieving, untrustworthy, cruel savage has faded in direct relationship to his decline as a competitive element in our population. No minorities need dread that the dead hand of tradition will reach out from the past with sufficient strength to do more than retard their progress slightly, if they are neither feared nor branded.

In our first chapter it was declared that neither the logic nor the emotional appeal of the spoken or written word can make much impression on the stereotyped racial attitudes and beliefs of the masses, so long as the interests of one population group are in apparent opposition to those of another. If this statement is true, the possible influence of reform organizations as well as of individual reformers in the field of race relations is definitely limited to the correction of particular instances of injustice—especially those which are so outrageous as to exceed the limits of popular prejudiced approval—and to campaigns of public enlightenment concerning the basic community of interests among all peoples in the United States.

This is our reason for omitting discussion of the hundreds of organizations and movements for the improvement of race relations and the securing of justice for minorities in our country. What have such organizations as the National Urban League, the National Association for the Advancement of Colored People, the Association for the Study of Negro Life and History, the Commission on Interracial Cooperation accomplished to justify their existence? The answer is: Much in the way of fighting particular instances of atrocious injustice, a little in the way of the dissemination of interracial facts, and nothing so far as any general change in racial attitudes is concerned. Shortly after the World War lynchings of Negroes declined rapidly, and a good share of the credit for this decline was claimed by the Commission on Interracial Cooperation. Seven Negroes were reported to have been lynched in 1929, counting only those who were killed by mobs and not those who were otherwise mistreated, and twenty in 1930.[3] If the Commission was responsible for declines in lynchings, is its negligence also responsible for this increase? Actually, of course, lynchings fluctuate in practical independence of the efforts of such organizations, which have no means of attacking the fundamental causes of lynching. All praise should go to the efforts of the interracial pioneers who are sacrificing much for their ideals and who have fought valiantly for the adjustment of interracial relations. Nothing, however, is to be gained by carrying our confidence in them to the extent of believing that they may do more than battle the symptoms of race prejudice, as a fever may be reduced by the application of ice, affording some relief to the patient but not curing the disease.

The decline in prejudice against the Indian can hardly be attributed to the effort of the Indian Rights Association or the American Indian Defense Association, yet these organizations have aided many an Indian in obtaining justice, secured the enactment of favorable legislation, fought incompetent and dishonest officials, and otherwise given much assistance to a handicapped minority. Prejudice against the Indian, however, would have declined to its present low level had they

[3] Monroe N. Work, *Negro Year Book,* Negro Year Book Publishing Co., Tuskegee Institute, 1931, p. 293.

never existed. The same may be said of the numerous immigrant societies, such as the Japanese Association in America, the Chinese tongs, the immigrant churches, the Society for Italian Immigrants, the Hebrew Sheltering and Immigrant Aid Society, and thousands of others, if local societies are included. "Practically every immigrant race and nationality has formed some kind of organization to assist newcomers of its own kind to self-support in this country. In addition, groups of immigrants of various nationalities have developed other agencies for meeting special problems in connection with finding work, with trade-union control of jobs, and with employers' policies, as well as with efforts to keep down the cost of living."[4] The educational and immigrant protective work done by such societies has been most important in the adjustment of their respective minorities to American life and in the enlightenment of public opinion concerning their qualities and contributions to the growth of the United States.[5]

From the point of view of American minorities and of the country as a whole, there can be no question but that the elimination of group prejudices and antagonisms would be of great benefit. From the point of view of the ordinary individual, however, it is doubtful whether his life would be made any easier, whether he would be better equipped to live among his fellow men, if he were converted into a completely tolerant person in his relations with other population groups. The Negro who would accept white friends as individuals without regard for their color, and on a basis of absolute equality, must reconcile himself to severe penalties of economic and social ostracism by many of his fellows on whom he may be dependent for a living, or at least for a majority of his social contacts. The white business man or laborer who refuses to discriminate in any way against the black or the yellow must remember that he is not living in complete isolation, independent of the pressure of social approval and disap-

[4] William M. Leiserson, op. cit., p. 278.
[5] For a description of Jewish societies, see Harry S. Linfield, The Communal Organization of the Jews in the United States, 1927, The American Jewish Committee. New York, 1930, p. 191.

proval. The ideal of racial tolerance may be a goal, and a socially desirable goal at that, but the first pioneers who achieve it must pay the penalties of all martyrs.

This raises a query concerning the proper purpose of a college course, a program of interracial propaganda, and even of a book on American race relations. Is the happiness of the individual, his personal adjustment to the world in which he lives, to be sacrificed to the ultimate welfare of the nation? Undoubtedly the nation founded on industrialism with its interdependence of all contributing human units will prosper the most if group barriers are broken and freedom of personal development is permitted. Should the tolerant individual—and there are many such if minor prejudices be disregarded—assume the rôle of missionary and urge his fellow men to purge their minds and actions of all prejudice against those of other racial and national origins? Should he do his utmost to make martyrs of his friends, students and readers who may be having difficulty enough to get along in an intolerant world?

The inevitable conflict is one between ideals—ideals of justice, humanity, and immediate sacrifice for the gains of posterity—and the practical exigencies of personal interests which may not be dismissed by an accusation of selfishness. Let us assume that you, the reader, are convinced of the illogical basis of present group prejudices, of the terrific human costs paid for the privilege of despising and hating our neighbors, and of the futility of any attempt to maintain racial integrity. Are you, then, willing to cast aside racial prejudices and dine with a Negro, admit an Oriental to your family circle, or work for a Jew? If you chance to belong to some minority which sneers at and resents the discriminations of those who consider themselves your superiors because of an accident of birth, can you accept all other minorities or even persons of old American white stock on even terms? If you believe that you possess complete tolerance, is it not perhaps that you are in the unusual position of being secure in your economic and social status, or that you are deluding yourself into the belief that you accept all men on their individual merits because certain difficult situations have never arisen in your life? If the answers to these questions are embarrassing to an honest desire to reconcile knowledge and behavior, remember that man is not a free agent and that logic does not rule the world.

SELECTED BIBLIOGRAPHY

Suggested Minimum Library

Coolidge, Mary Roberts, *Chinese Immigration*, Henry Holt and Co., Inc., New York, 1909, pp. x + 531

Fairchild, H. P., *Immigration*, The Macmillan Company, New York, 1925, revised edition, pp. xi + 520

Feldman, Herman, *Racial Factors in American Industry*, Harper & Brothers, New York, 1931, pp. xiv + 318

Gamio, Manuel, *Mexican Immigration to the United States*, The University of Chicago Press, Chicago, 1930, pp. xviii + 262

Gamio, Manuel, *The Mexican Immigrant*, The University of Chicago Press, Chicago, 1930, pp. xvii + 262

Garis, Roy L., *Immigration Restriction*, The Macmillan Company, New York, 1927, pp. xv + 376

Garth, Thomas R., *Race Psychology*, McGraw-Hill Book Company, Inc., New York, 1931, pp. xiv + 260

Hankins, Frank H., *The Racial Basis of Civilization*, Alfred A. Knopf, New York, 1926, pp. x + 384

Hertz, Friedrich, *Race and Civilization*, translated by A. S. Levetus and W. Entz, The Macmillan Company, New York, 1928, pp. xii + 328

Jenks, Jeremiah W., and Lauck, W. Jett, *The Immigration Problem*, R. D. Smith (ed.), Funk & Wagnalls Company, New York, 1926, sixth edition, pp. xxvii + 717

Johnson, Charles S., *The Negro in American Civilization*, Henry Holt and Co., Inc., New York, 1930, pp. xiv + 538

Lasker, Bruno, *Filipino Immigration*, The University of Chicago Press, Chicago, 1931, pp. xxii + 445

Lindquist, G. E. E., *The Red Man in the United States*, Doubleday, Doran & Company, Inc., New York, 1923, pp. xxviii + 461

Locke, Alain, *The New Negro*, Albert and Charles Boni, Inc., New York, 1925, pp. xviii + 446

McKenzie, R. D., *Oriental Exclusion*, The University of Chicago Press, Chicago, 1928, 200 pp.

Mears, Eliot Grinnell, *Resident Orientals on the American Pacific Coast*, The University of Chicago Press, Chicago, 1928, pp. xvi + 545

Merriam, Lewis, and Associates, *The Problem of Indian Adminis-*

tration, The Johns Hopkins Press, Baltimore, 1928, pp. xxii + 872

Miller, Herbert A., *Races, Nations and Classes*, J. B. Lippincott Company, Philadelphia, 1924, pp. xvii + 196

Millis, H. A., *The Japanese Problem in the United States*, The Macmillan Company, New York, 1915, pp. xxi + 334

Panunzio, Constantine, *Immigration Crossroads*, The Macmillan Company, New York, 1927, pp. viii + 307

Pittard, Eugene, *Race and History*, translated by V. C. C. Collum, Alfred A. Knopf, New York, 1926, pp. xxiii + 505

Reuter, E. B., *The American Race Problem*, Thomas Y. Crowell Company, New York, 1927, pp. xii + 448

Stephenson, George M., *A History of American Immigration*, Ginn and Company, Boston, 1926, pp. xi + 316

Thompson, Warren S., *Population Problems*, McGraw-Hill Book Company, Inc., New York, 1930, pp. xi + 462

Weatherford, W. D., *The Negro from Africa to America*, Doubleday, Doran & Company, Inc., New York, 1924, 487 pp.

Willcox, Walter F. (ed.), *International Migrations*, vol. i, "Statistics," compiled on behalf of the International Labor Office, Geneva, with introduction and notes by Imre Ferenczi, 1112 pp.; vol. ii, "Interpretations," by a group of scholars in different countries, National Bureau of Economic Research, New York, 1931, 715 pp.

Young, Donald (ed.), "The American Negro," *The Annals* of the American Academy of Political and Social Science, vol. cxxxx, November, 1928, pp. viii + 359

SUPPLEMENTARY REFERENCES

THE NEGRO

Atlanta University Publications, Numbers 1 to 20, The Atlanta University Press, Atlanta, 1896-1916

Baker, Ray Stannard, *Following the Color Line*, Doubleday, Doran & Company, Inc., New York, 1908, pp. xii + 314

Bancroft, Frederic, *Slave-Trading in the Old South*, J. H. Furst Co., Baltimore, 1931, 415 pp.

Brawley, Benjamin, *A Short History of the American Negro*, The Macmillan Company, New York, 1913, xiv + 247

Brawley, Benjamin, *A Social History of the American Negro*, The Macmillan Company, New York, 1921, pp. xv + 420

Brawley, Benjamin, *The Negro in Art and Literature*, Duffield & Company, New York, 1930, pp. xii + 231

The Chicago Commission on Race Relations, *The Negro in Chicago*,

The University of Chicago Press, Chicago, 1922, pp. xxiv + 672

Cooley, Rossa B., *School Acres*, Yale University Press, New Haven, 1930, pp. xxii + 166

Cutler, James E., *Lynch-Law*, Longmans, Green & Company, New York, 1905, pp. xiv + 287

Daniel, W. A., *The Education of Negro Ministers*, Doubleday, Doran & Company, Inc., New York, 1925, 187 pp.

Daniels, John, *In Freedom's Birthplace*, Houghton Mifflin Company, Boston, 1914, pp. xiii + 296

Davenport, C. B., and Steggerda, Morris, *Investigation of Race Crossing in Jamaica*, Carnegie Institution, Washington, D. C., 1929, pp. x + 516

Detweiler, Frederick G., *The Negro Press in the United States*, The University of Chicago Press, Chicago, 1922, pp. x + 274

Dowd, Jerome, *The Negro in American Life*, The Century Company, New York, 1926, pp. xix + 611

Du Bois, W. E. Burghardt, *Darkwater*, Harcourt, Brace and Company, New York, 1921, pp. viii + 276

Du Bois, W. E. Burghardt, *The Gift of Black Folk*, The Stratford Co., Boston, 1924, pp. iv + 349

Du Bois, W. E. Burghardt, *The Souls of Black Folk*, A. C. McClurg and Co., Chicago, 1903, pp. viii + 264

Du Bois, W. E. Burghardt, *The Suppression of the African Slave Trade*, Longmans, Green & Company, New York, 1896, pp. xi + 335

Dutcher, Dean, *The Negro in Modern Industrial Society*, privately printed, Lancaster, Pa., 1930, pp. xiv + 137

Edwards, Paul K., *The Southern Urban Negro as a Consumer*, Prentice-Hall, Inc., New York, 1932, pp. xxiv + 323.

Embree, Edwin R., *Brown America*, Viking Press, Inc., New York, 1931, pp. vi + 311

Fleming, Walter L., *Documentary History of Reconstruction*, The Arthur H. Clark Co., Cleveland, vol. i, pp. xviii + 493; vol. ii, pp. xiv + 480

Frazier, E. Franklin, *The Negro Family in Chicago*, The University of Chicago Press, Chicago, 1932, pp. xxv + 294

Gillard, John T., S. S. J., *The Catholic Church and the American Negro*, St. Joseph's Society Press, Baltimore, 1929, pp. xv + 324

Gilligan, Rev. Francis J., *The Morality of the Color Line*, Catholic University of America, Washington, D. C., 1928, pp. x + 222

Greene, Lorenzo J., and Woodson, Carter G., *The Negro Wage Earner*, The Association for the Study of Negro Life and History, Washington, D. C., 1930, pp. xiii + 388

Grissom, Mary Allen, *The Negro Sings a New Heaven*, The University of North Carolina Press, Chapel Hill, N. C., 1930, 101 pp.

Hammond, L. H., *In Black and White*, Fleming H. Revell & Company, New York, 1914, 244 pp.

Hart, Albert Bushnell, *The Southern South*, D. Appleton & Company, New York, 1910, 444 pp.

Haynes, George E., *The Trend of the Races*, Council of Women for Home Missions, New York, 1922, pp. xvi + 205

Herskovits, Melville J., *The American Negro*, Alfred A. Knopf, New York, 1928, pp. xiv + 92

Johnson, Charles S. (ed.), *Ebony and Topaz*, National Urban League, New York, 1927, 164 pp.

Johnson, James Weldon, *Black Manhattan*, Alfred A. Knopf, New York, 1930, pp. xxxiv + 287

Johnson, James Weldon, Johnson, J. Rosamond, and Brown, Lawrence, *The Book of American Negro Spirituals*, Viking Press, Inc., New York, 1925, 187 pp.

Johnson, James Weldon, and J. Rosamond, *The Second Book of Negro Spirituals*, Viking Press, Inc., New York, 1926, 189 pp.

Johnston, Sir Harry H., *The Negro in the New World*, The Macmillan Company, New York, 1910, pp. xxix + 499

Jones, Thomas Jesse (director), *Negro Education*, Bureau of Education, Department of the Interior, Bulletin No. 38, Government Printing Office, Washington, D. C., 1916, vol. i, pp. xiv + 423; vol. ii, pp. v + 724

Jones, William Henry, *Recreation and Amusement among Negroes in Washington, D. C.*, Howard University Press, Washington, D. C., 1927, pp. xv + 216

Jones, William Henry, *The Housing of Negroes in Washington, D. C.*, Howard University Press, Washington, D. C., 1929, 191 pp.

Kelsey, Carl, *The Negro Farmer*, Jennings and Pye, Chicago, 1903, 103 pp.

Kemble, Fannie, *Journal of Residence on a Georgia Plantation*, Harper & Brothers, New York, 1863, 337 pp.

Kennedy, Louise Venable, *The Negro Peasant Turns Cityward*, Columbia University Press, New York, 1930, 270 pp.

Kerlin, Robert T., *The Voice of the Negro*, E. P. Dutton & Co., Inc., New York, 1920, pp. xii + 188

Lewinson, Paul, *Race, Class, and Party*, Oxford University Press, New York, 1932, pp. x + 302

Lewis, Edward E., *The Mobility of the Negro*, Columbia University Press, New York, 1931, 144 pp.

Loggins, Vernon, *The Negro Author*, Columbia University Press, New York, 1931, pp. ix + 480

Mecklin, J. M., *Democracy and Race Friction*, The Macmillan Company, New York, 1914, pp. x + 273

Mecklin, J. M., *The Ku Klux Klan*, Harcourt, Brace and Company, New York, 1924, 244 pp.

Miller, Kelly, *Race Adjustment*, The Neale Publishing Co., New York, 1908, 306 pp.

Moton, R. R., *Finding a Way Out*, Doubleday, Doran and Company, Inc., New York, 1921, pp. ix + 295

Moton, R. R., *What the Negro Thinks*, Doubleday, Doran and Company, Inc., New York, 1928, pp. vii + 267

Murphy, E. G., *Problems of the Present South*, The Macmillan Company, New York, 1904, pp. xi + 335

Nearing, Scott, *Black America*, Vanguard Press, Inc., New York, 1929, 275 pp.

Negro Colleges and Universities, Survey of, Bureau of Education, Department of the Interior, Bulletin No. 7, Government Printing Office, Washington, D. C., 1928, pp. vi + 964

Nowlin, William F., *The Negro in American National Politics*, The Stratford Company, Boston, 1931, 148 pp.

Odum, Howard W., and Johnson, Guy B., *The Negro and His Songs*, The University of North Carolina Press, Chapel Hill, N. C., 1925, pp. vii + 306

Olmsted, F. L., *A Journey in the Back Country*, Mason Brothers, New York, 1860, pp. xvi + 492

Olmsted, F. L., *A Journey in the Seaboard Slave States*, Dix and Edwards, New York, 1856, pp. xv + 723

Olmsted, F. L., *The Cotton Kingdom*, Mason Brothers, New York, 1862, vol. i, pp. viii + 376; vol. ii, pp. iv + 404

Ovington, Mary White, *Half a Man*, Longmans, Green & Company, New York, 1911, pp. xi + 236

Peabody, Francis Greenwood, *Education for Life*, Doubleday, Doran & Company, Inc., New York, 1922, pp. xxiv + 393

Peterson, Joseph, and Lanier, Lyle H., *Studies in Comparative Abilities of Whites and Negroes*, Mental Measurement Monographs, No. 5, The Williams & Wilkins Company, Baltimore, 1929, pp. iii + 156

Phillips, Ulrich Bonnell, *American Negro Slavery*, D. Appleton & Company, New York, 1918, pp. xi + 529

Phillips, Ulrich Bonnell, *Life and Labor in the Old South*, Little, Brown and Company, Boston, 1929, pp. xix + 375

Puckett, Newbell N., *Folk Beliefs of the Southern Negro*, The University of North Carolina Press, Chapel Hill, N. C., 1926, pp. xiv + 644

Reed, Ruth, *Negro Illegitimacy in New York City*, Columbia University Press, New York, 1926, 136 pp.

Reid, Ira DeA. (director), *Negro Membership in American Labor Unions*, The National Urban League, New York, 1930, 175 pp.

Reuter, E. B., *Race Mixture*, McGraw-Hill Book Company, Inc., New York, 1931, pp. vii + 224

Reuter, E. B., *The Mulatto in the United States*, Richard G. Badger, Boston, 1918, 417 pp.

Scott, Emmett J., *Negro Migration During the War*, Carnegie Endowment for International Peace, Preliminary Studies of the War, No. 16, Oxford University Press, New York, 1920, pp. v + 189

Seligman, Herbert J., *The Negro Faces America*, Harper & Brothers, New York, 1920, 318 pp.

Sibley, Elbridge, *Differential Mortality in Tennessee*, The Fisk University Press, Nashville, Tenn., 1930, 152 pp.

Sinclair, William A., *The Aftermath of Slavery*, Small Maynard and Co., Boston, 1905, pp. xiii + 358

Spero, Sterling D., and Harris, Abram L., *The Black Worker*, Columbia University Press, New York, 1931, pp. x + 509

Stephenson, G. T., *Race Distinctions in American Law*, D. Appleton & Company, New York, 1910, pp. xiv + 338

Stone, Alfred Holt, *Studies in the American Race Problem*, Doubleday, Doran and Company, Inc., New York, 1908, pp. xxii + 555

Washington, Booker T., *The Future of the American Negro*, Small Maynard and Co., Boston, 1901, pp. x + 244

Washington, Booker T., *The Story of the Negro*, Doubleday, Doran and Company, Inc., New York, 1909, vol. i, pp. vii + 322; vol. ii, 437 pp.

Washington, Booker T., *Up from Slavery*, A. L. Burt Company, New York, 1900, pp. viii + 330

Washington, Booker T., *Working with the Hands*, Doubleday, Doran and Company, Inc., New York, 1904, pp. x + 246

Wesley, Charles H., *Negro Labor in the United States*, Vanguard Press, Inc., New York, 1927, pp. xiii + 343

White, Newman I., *American Negro Folk-Songs*, Harvard University Press, Cambridge, 1928, pp. x + 501

White, Walter, *Rope and Faggot*, Alfred A. Knopf, New York, 1929, pp. xiii + 272 + iv

Woodson, Carter G., *A Century of Negro Migration*, The Association for the Study of Negro Life and History, Washington, D. C., 1918, pp. vii + 221

Woodson, Carter G., *The Education of the Negro Prior to 1861*, G. P. Putnam's Sons, New York, 1915, pp. v + 454

Woodson, Carter G., *The History of the Negro Church*, The Associated Publishers, Washington, D. C., 1921, pp. x + 330

Woodson, Carter G., *The Negro in Our History*, The Associated Publishers, Washington, D. C., 4th edition, 1927, pp. xxx + 616

Woodson, Carter G., *The Rural Negro*, The Association for the Study of Negro Life and History, Washington, D. C., 1930, pp. xvi + 265

Woofter, T. J., Jr., *Black Yeomanry*, Henry Holt and Company, Inc., New York, 1930, pp. x + 291

Woofter, T. J., Jr., *Negro Problems in Cities,* Doubleday, Doran and Company, Inc., New York, 1928, 284 pp.

Woofter, T. J., Jr., *The Basis of Racial Adjustment*, Ginn and Company, Boston, 1925, pp. viii + 258

Work, Monroe N., *A Bibliography of the Negro in Africa and America*, The H. W. Wilson Co., New York, 1928, pp. xxi + 698

Work, Monroe N. (ed.), *Negro Year Book*, Negro Year Book Publishing Co., Tuskegee Institute, Alabama, 8th edition, 1931, pp. xiv + 544

THE IMMIGRANT

Abbott, Edith, *Historical Aspects of the Immigration Problem*, The University of Chicago Press, Chicago, 1926, pp. xx + 881

Abbott, Edith, *Immigration: Select Documents and Case Records*, The University of Chicago Press, Chicago, 1924, pp. xxii + 809

Abbott, Grace, *The Immigrant and the Community*, The Century Company, New York, 1921, pp. vii + 303

The American Jewish Year Book, The Jewish Publishing Society of America, Philadelphia, Annual, 1899-1932.

Antin, Mary, *The Promised Land*, Houghton Mifflin Company, Boston, 1912, pp. xv + 373

Antin, Mary, *They Who Knock at Our Gates*, Houghton Mifflin Company, Boston, 1914, pp. x + 142

Balch, Emily Greene, *Our Slavic Fellow Citizens*, Charities Publication Committee, New York, 1910, pp. xx + 536

Baskerville, Beatrice C., *The Polish Jew*, The Macmillan Company, New York, 1906, 336 pp.

Bernheimer, Charles S. (ed.), *The Russian Jew in the United States*, The John C. Winston Co., Philadelphia, 1905, 426 pp.

Blegen, Theodore C., *Norwegian Migration to America*, The Norwegian-American Historical Association, Northfield, Minn., 1931, pp. xi + 413

Bogardus, Emory S., *Essentials of Americanization*, University of Southern California Press, Los Angeles, 1923, 442 pp.

Bogardus, Emory S., *Immigration and Race Attitudes*, D. C. Heath and Company, New York, 1928, pp. xi + 268

Boody, Bertha M., *A Psychological Study of Immigrant Children at Ellis Island*, Mental Measurement Monographs, No. 3, The Williams and Wilkins Co., Baltimore, February, 1926, 163 pp.

Breckenridge, S. P., *Marriage and the Civic Rights of Women*, The University of Chicago Press, Chicago, 1931, pp. xi + 158

Breckenridge, S. P., *New Homes for Old*, Harper & Brothers, New York, 1921, pp. xi + 355

Broun, Heywood C., and Britt, George, *Christians Only*, Vanguard Press, Inc., New York, 1931, 333 pp.

Brunner, Edmund deS., *Immigrant Farmers and Their Children*, Doubleday, Doran and Company, Inc., New York, 1929, pp. xvii + 277

Burgess, Thomas, *Greeks in America*, Sherman, French and Co., Boston, 1913, pp. xiv + 256

Čapek, Thomas, *The Čechs (Bohemians) in America*, Houghton Mifflin Company, Boston, 1920, pp. xviii + 293

Carpenter, Niles, *Immigrants and Their Children*, Census Monographs, No. VII, Government Printing Office, Washington, D. C., 1927, pp. xvi + 431

Carrothers, W. A., *Emigration from the British Isles*, P. S. King and Son, London, 1929, pp. xii + 328

Claghorn, Kate Holladay, *The Immigrant's Day in Court*, Harper & Brothers, New York, 1923, pp. xvi + 546

Clark, Francis E., *Our Italian Fellow Citizens*, Small Maynard and Co., Boston, 1919, pp. ix + 217

Clark, Jane Perry, *Deportation of Aliens from the United States to Europe*, Columbia University Press, New York, 1931, 524 pp.

Crocker, W. R., *The Japanese Population Problem*, The Macmillan Company, New York, 1931, 240 pp.

Daniels, John, *America via the Neighborhood*, Harper & Brothers, New York, 1920, pp. xiii + 462

Davis, Jerome, *The Russian and Ruthenian in America*, Doubleday, Doran and Company, Inc., New York, 1922, pp. xiv + 155

Davis, Jerome, *The Russian Immigrant*, The Macmillan Company, New York, 1922, pp. xv + 219

Davis, Michael M., *Immigrant Health and the Community*, Harper & Brothers, New York, 1921, pp. xxvii + 481

Davis, Philip, assisted by Schwartz, Bertha, *Immigration and Americanization*, Ginn and Company, Boston, 1920, pp. xii + 770

Drachsler, Julius, *Democracy and Assimilation*, The Macmillan Company, New York, 1920, pp. xii + 275

Fairchild, H. P., *Greek Immigration to the United States*, Yale University Press, New Haven, 1911, pp. xvii + 270

Fairchild, H. P. (ed.), *Immigrant Backgrounds*, John Wiley & Sons, Inc., New York, 1927, pp. x + 269

Fairchild, H. P., *The Melting Pot Mistake*, Little, Brown and Co., Boston, 1926, pp. vi + 266

Faust, Albert B., *The German Element in the United States*, Houghton Mifflin Company, Boston, 1909, vol. i, pp. xxvi + 591; vol. ii, pp. xvi + 605

Fishberg, Maurice, *The Jews*, The Walter Scott Publishing Co., London, 1911, pp. xix + 578

Foerster, Robert F., *The Italian Emigration of Our Times*, Harvard University Press, Cambridge, 1919, pp. xv + 556

Foreign Language Information Service, *How to Become a Citizen of the United States*, New York, 1927, 47 pp.

Fox, Paul, *The Poles in America*, Doubleday, Doran and Company, Inc., New York, 1922, pp. xii + 143

Gavit, John Palmer, *Americans by Choice*, Harper & Brothers, New York, 1922, pp. xxiv + 449

Gulick, Sidney L., *The American Japanese Problem*, Charles Scribner's Sons, New York, 1914, pp. x + 349

Hall, Prescott F., *Immigration*, Henry Holt and Company, Inc., New York, 1908, pp. xiii + 393

Holt, Hamilton (ed.), *Undistinguished Americans*, James Pott and Co., New York, 1906, pp. vii + 299

Hourwich, Isaac A., *Immigration and Labor*, G. P. Putnam's Sons, New York, 1912, pp. xvii + 544

Immigration Commission, Abstracts of Reports of the, 61st Congress, 3rd Session, Senate Document No. 747, Government Printing Office, Washington, D. C., December 5, 1910, vol. i, pp. viii + 902; vol. ii, pp. viii + 900

Janson, Florence Edith, *The Background of Swedish Immigration, 1840-1930*, The University of Chicago Press, Chicago, 1931, pp. xi + 517

Jerome, Harry, *Migration and Business Cycles*, National Bureau of Economic Research, New York, 1926, 256 pp.

Johnson, S. C., *A History of Emigration from the United Kingdom to North America*, E. P. Dutton & Co., Inc., New York, 1914, pp. xvi + 387

Joseph, Samuel, *Jewish Immigration to the United States*, privately printed, New York, 1910, 211 pp.

Kawakami, K. K., *Japan in World Politics*, The Macmillan Company, New York, 1917, pp. xvii + 300

Kellor, Frances, *Immigration and the Future*, Doubleday, Doran & Company, Inc., New York, 1920, pp. xv + 276

Kelsey, Carl (ed.), "Present-Day Immigration, with Special Reference to the Japanese," *The Annals* of the American Academy of Political and Social Science, vol. xciii, January, 1921, pp. v + 232

Kirkpatrick, Clifford, *Intelligence and Immigration*, Mental Measurement Monographs, No. 2, The Williams & Wilkins Company, Baltimore, 1926, pp. xiii + 127

Lasker, Bruno (ed.), *Jewish Experiences in America*, The Inquiry, New York, 1930, pp. xiv + 309

Laughlin, H. H., *Analysis of America's Modern Melting Pot*, United States, House of Representatives, 67th Congress, 3rd Session, Hearings before the Committee on Immigration and Naturalization, Serial 7C, Government Printing Office, Washington, D. C., November 21, 1922, pp. ii + 725-831

Laughlin, H. H., *Europe as an Emigrant-Exporting Continent and the United States as an Immigrant-Receiving Nation*, United States, House of Representatives, 68th Congress, 1st Session, Hearings before the Committee on Immigration and Naturalization, Serial 5-A, Government Printing Office, Washington, D. C., March 8, 1924, pp. v + 1231-1437

Leiserson, William M., *Adjusting Immigrant and Industry*, Harper & Brothers, New York, 1924, pp. xv + 356

Lewis, Edward R., *America, Nation or Confusion*, Harper & Brothers, New York, 1928, pp. xvi + 408

MacLean, Annie Marion, *Modern Immigration*, J. B. Lippincott Company, Philadelphia, 1925, pp. xii + 393

Mayo-Smith, Richmond, *Emigration and Immigration*, Charles Scribner's Sons, New York, 1908, pp. xiv + 316

Miller, Kenneth D., *The Czecho-Slovaks in America*, Doubleday, Doran & Company, Inc., New York, 1922, pp. viii + 192

National Commission on Law Observance and Enforcement, *The Administration of the Deportation Laws of the United States*, Government Printing Office, Washington, D. C., 1931, 179 pp.

National Commission on Law Observance and Enforcement, *Report on Crime and Criminal Justice in Relation to the Foreign Born*, Government Printing Office, Washington, D. C., 1931, 416 pp.

Panunzio, Constantine M., *The Deportation Cases of 1919-1920*, Federal Council of Churches of Christ in America, 1921, 104 pp.

Panunzio, Constantine M., *The Soul of an Immigrant*, The Macmillan Company, New York, 1922, pp. xiv + 329

Park, Robert E., *The Immigrant Press and Its Control*, Harper & Brothers, New York, 1922, pp. xix + 487

Park, Robert E., and Miller, Herbert A., *Old World Traits Transplanted*, Harper & Brothers, New York, 1921, pp. viii + 307

Roberts, Peter, *The Problem of Americanization*, The Macmillan Company, New York, 1920, pp. ix + 246

Rose, Philip M., *The Italians in America*, Doubleday, Doran & Company, Inc., New York, 1922, pp. vii + 155

Ross, Edward Alsworth, *Standing Room Only*, The Century Company, New York, 1927, pp. xiv + 368

Ross, Edward Alsworth, *The Old World in the New*, The Century Company, New York, 1914, 327 pp.

Schibsby, Marian, *Handbook for Immigrants to the United States*, Foreign Language Information Service, New York, 1927, 180 pp.

Seward, George F., *Chinese Immigration*, Charles Scribner's Sons, New York, 1881, pp. xv + 420

Sharlip, William, and Owens, Albert A., *Adult Immigrant Education*, The Macmillan Company, New York, 1925, pp. xviii + 317

Souders, D. A., *The Magyars in America*, Doubleday, Doran & Company, Inc., New York, 1922, pp. ix + 149

Speek, Peter A., *A Stake in the Land*, Harper & Brothers, New York, 1921, pp. xxix + 266

Steiner, Edward A., *The Immigrant Tide*, Fleming H. Revell & Company, New York, 1909, 370 pp.

Steiner, Edward A., *On the Trail of the Immigrant*, Fleming H. Revell & Company, New York, 1906, 375 pp.

Steiner, Jesse F., *The Japanese Invasion*, A. C. McClurg and Co., Chicago, 1917, pp. xvii + 224

Stella, Antonio, *Some Aspects of Italian Immigration to the United States*, G. P. Putnam's Sons, New York, 1924, pp. xxii + 124

Stephenson, George M., *The Religious Aspects of Swedish Immigration*, The University of Minnesota Press, Minneapolis, 1932, pp. viii + 542

Taft, Henry W., *Japan and America*, The Macmillan Company, New York, 1932, pp. viii + 359

Taylor, Paul S., *Mexican Labor in the United States*, University of California Publications in Economics; vol. vi, No. 1, "Imperial Valley," December, 1928, pp. 1-94; No. 2, " Valley of the South Platte, Colorado," June, 1929, pp. 95-235; No. 3, "Migration Statistics," August, 1929, pp. 237-255; No. 4, "Racial School Statistics, California, 1927," November, 1929, pp. 257-292; No. 5, "Dimmit County, Winter Garden District, South Texas," July, 1930, pp. 293-464. Vol. vii, No. 1, "Bethlehem, Pennsylvania," June, 1931, pp. ix + 1-24, University of California Press, Berkeley, California

Thomas, W. I., and Znaniecki, Florian, *The Polish Peasant in*

Europe and America, Alfred A. Knopf, New York, 2nd edition, 1927, vol. i, pp. xv + 1116; vol. ii, pp. vi + 1117-2250

Thompson, Frank V., *Schooling the Immigrant*, Harper & Brothers, New York, 1920, 408 pp.

Van Vleck, William C., *The Administrative Control of Aliens*, The Commonwealth Fund, New York, 1932, pp. ix + 260

Warne, Frank Julian, *The Immigrant Invasion*, Dodd, Mead & Company, Inc., New York, 1913, 336 pp.

Warne, Frank Julian, *The Tide of Immigration*, D. Appleton & Company, New York, 1916, 387 pp.

Whelpley, James Davenport, *The Problem of the Immigrant*, E. P. Dutton & Co., Inc., New York, 1905, pp. vi + 295

Xenides, J. P., *The Greeks in America*, Doubleday, Doran & Company, Inc., New York, 1922, pp. xii + 160

THE INDIAN

Bureau of American Ethnology, Smithsonian Institution, *Handbook of American Indians*, Government Printing Office, Washington, D. C., 1907, part i, pp. ix + 972; part ii, pp. iv + 1221. (While this is the only publication of the Bureau of American Ethnology listed in this bibliography, attention should be called to the fact that many of its bulletins contain valuable information for the student of race relations.)

Coolidge, Dane and Mary Roberts, *The Navajo Indians*, Houghton Mifflin Company, Boston, 1930, pp. x + 316

Coolidge, Mary Roberts, *The Rain-Makers*, Houghton Mifflin Company, Boston, 1929, pp. xiii + 326

The Exposition of Indian Tribal Arts, Inc., *Introduction to American Indian Art*, 578 Madison Ave., New York, 1931, 55 pp.

Gessner, Robert, *Massacre*, Jonathan Cape and Harrison Smith, New York, 1931, pp. x + 418

Grinnell, George Bird, *The Indians of Today*, Herbert S. Stone and Co., Chicago, 1900, 185 pp.

Jackson, Helen, *A Century of Dishonor*, Roberts Brothers, Boston, new edition, 1893, 514 pp.

Leupp, Francis E., *The Indian and his Problem*, Charles Scribner's Sons, New York, 1910, pp. xiv + 369

McLaughlin, James, *My Friend the Indian*, Houghton Mifflin Company, Boston, 1910, pp. viii + 416

MacLeod, W. Christie, *The American Indian Frontier*, Alfred A. Knopf, New York, 1928, pp. xxiii + 598

Radin, Paul, *Crashing Thunder*, D. Appleton & Company, 1926, pp. xxv + 202

Radin, Paul, *The Story of the American Indian,* Boni and Liver-
ight, New York, 1927, pp. xiv + 371
Schmeckebier, Laurence F., *The Office of Indian Affairs,* The Johns
Hopkins Press, Baltimore, 1927, pp. xiv + 591

POPULATION

Carr-Saunders, A. M., *Population,* Oxford University Press, Lon-
don, 1925, 112 pp.
Carr-Saunders, A. M., *The Population Problem,* The Clarendon
Press, Oxford, 1922, 516 pp.
Cox, Harold, *The Problem of Population,* G. P. Putnam's Sons,
New York, 1923, pp. ix + 244
Dublin, Louis I. (ed.), *Population Problems,* Houghton Mifflin
Company, Boston, 1926, pp. xi + 318
East, E. M., *Mankind at the Crossroads,* Charles Scribner's Sons,
New York, 1923, pp. viii + 360
Pearl, Raymond, *The Biology of Population Growth,* Alfred A.
Knopf, New York, 1925, pp. xiv + 260
Thompson, Warren S., *Danger Spots in World Population,* Alfred
A. Knopf, New York, 1929, pp. xi + 343 + x
Wright, Harold, *Population,* Nisket and Co., London, 1923, pp. xiv
+ 178

GENERAL

Blackwood, Beatrice, *A Study in Mental Testing in Relation to
Anthropology,* Mental Measurement Monographs, No. 4, The
Williams & Wilkins Company, Baltimore, 1927, 120 pp.
Bryce, James, *The Relations of the Advanced and the Backward
Races of Mankind,* The Clarendon Press, Oxford, 1902, 46 pp.
Carpenter, Niles, and Associates, *Nationality, Color and Economic
Opportunity in the City of Buffalo,* The University of Buffalo
Studies, vol. v, No. 4, Monographs in Sociology, No. 2, Buffalo,
N. Y., June, 1927, pp. 95-194
Cleveland, Frederick A., *American Citizenship,* The Ronald Press
Company, New York, 1927, pp. vi + 475
Commons, John R., *Races and Immigrants in America,* The Mac-
millan Company, New York, pp. xiii + 242
Dixon, Roland B., *The Racial History of Man,* Charles Scribner's
Sons, New York, 1923, pp. xvi + 583
Duncan, Hannibal G., *Race and Population Problems,* Longmans,
Green & Company, New York, 1929, pp. xv + 424
Finot, Jean, *Race Prejudice,* translated by Florence Wade-Evans,
Archibald Constable and Co., London, 1906, pp. viii + 320

Haddon, A. C., *The Races of Man*, The Macmillan Company, New York, 1925, pp. viii + 201

Hrdlička, Aleš, *The Old Americans*, The Williams and Wilkins Company, Baltimore, 1925, pp. xiii + 438

Huntington, Ellsworth, *The Character of Races*, Charles Scribner's Sons, New York, 1924, pp. xvi + 393

Katz, Daniel, and Allport, Floyd, *Students' Attitudes*, The Craftsman Press, Syracuse, N. Y., 1931, pp. xxviii + 408

Lasker, Bruno, *Race Attitudes in Children*, Henry Holt and Company, Inc., New York, 1929, pp. xvi + 394

Maxson, Charles H., *Citizenship*, Oxford University Press, New York, 1930, pp. vii + 483

Muntz, Earl Edward, *Race Contact*, The Century Company, New York, 1927, pp. xiv + 407

National Conference on the Christian Way of Life, *And Who Is My Neighbor?* Association Press, New York, 1924, pp. ix + 231

Ripley, W. Z., *Races of Europe*, D. Appleton & Company, New York, 1889, pp. xxxii + 624

Speer, R. E., *Race and Race Relations*, Fleming H. Revell & Company, New York, 1924, 434 pp.

Thurstone, L. L., and Chave, E. J., *The Measurement of Attitude*, The University of Chicago Press, Chicago, 1929, pp. xii + 96

INDEX

Abbott, Edith, 231, 600; quoted, 232n
Abbott, Grace, 600; quoted, 276
Ability, racial. *See* Mental ability.
Abrams, Ray, xii
Acculturation, 351
    See also Americanization, Assimilation.
Adam, 527
Adaptation, 340ff., 426
    See also Natural selection.
Advertising, 358f.
African background, 270f., 372f., 546ff., 551f., 561
Agricultural labor, 58ff., 64, 72ff., 77f., 79f.
Agriculture, Chap. III, 263
    diversified *vs.* specialized, 68ff.
    family life in, 373f.
    minority participation in, 60ff.
    southern regional variations in, 66f., 75f.
    See also Agricultural labor, Farm population, Land, Land tenure, Occupations.
Ainu, 195
Alcohol, use of, 158, 172, 269, 282ff., 304, 309, 312f., 317
Aldridge, Ira, 545
Alexander the Great, 562
Alien land laws, 80ff.
Alien registration, 179
Alien seamen, 173
Aliens, registration of, 179f.
    student definitions of, 12
    See also Citizenship, Deportation, Immigration, Immigration legislation, Migration, Naturalization.
Aliens ineligible to citizenship, 167f., 184f.
    See also Citizenship, Naturalization, Oriental exclusion.
Allport, Floyd, 3n, 5n
Allport, G. W., 11n
Amalgamation. *See* Hybrids, Intermarriage, Race mixture.

American Bar Association, 145
American Indian Defense Association, 240, 590
American Jewish Year Book, The, 600
American Legion, 177
American Medical Association, 144f.
American Protective Association, 155f., 259, 527
Americanization, 457ff.
    barriers to, 464f.
    compulsory, 459
    measures of, 465f.
    problems in, 459ff.
    See also Acculturation, Assimilation, Citizenship.
Amos 'n' Andy, 310
Amusement parks, 305f., 308
    See also Leisure activities.
Anarchists, 175, 217, 222
Anatomists, 430
Anglo-Saxonism, 423
Annapolis, 145
Anthropologists, 427ff.
Antin, Mary, 600
Aristotle, 562
Armstrong, Samuel Chapman, 450
Army mental tests, 431ff., 436ff.
Art, Chap. XVI, 278, 461
    African, 546ff., 551f., 561
    as propaganda, 559ff., 567f., 574f.
    race traits and, 124, 547n
    See also Dancing, Literature, Motion pictures, Music, Spirituals.
Aryanism, 401, 423
Assimilation, 179, 200, 216, 268, 276, 319, 356, 385, 406f., 421, 464, 532, 573, 578
    and education, 446ff., 477, 479f.
    cultural grafting, 562
    differential, 461ff., 501
    ideals, 464f.
    standard of living, 464f.
    See also Acculturation, Americanization, Citizenship, Naturalization.
Athenians, 402f.

Moses, 527
Motion pictures, 269, 277, 283, 285, 299f., 303, 308, 358, 378f., 540, 569, 574
See also Art.
Moton, R. R., 450, 583, 598; quoted, 497
Mulattoes, 187, 193, 317, 394, 396f.
See also Hybrids, Intermarriage, Race mixture.
Muntz, Earl Edward, 607
Murphy, E. G., 598
Murphy, Gardner and Lois B., 3n, 8n, 11n; quoted, 9
Music, 269, 273f., 283ff., 319f., 505, 541f., 545f., 570, 574
See also Art, Musical abilities, Spirituals.
Musical abilities, 434, 547n
Mussolini, B., 423

Napoleon, 562
National Association for the Advancement of Colored People, 189, 575
National Bar Association, 145
National Commission on Law Observance and Enforcement, 177n, 229n, 231n, 233n, 603
National Conference on the Christian Way of Life, 607
National Medical Association, 145
National origins. *See* Quota Act of 1924.
National Urban League, 514, 575
Nationalism, 276, 417, 510, 574ff.
Native American Party, 154, 259
Nativism, 82, 154ff., 258f., 527
Natural selection, 429, 443
and health, 340ff., 578
and migration, 53ff.
climatic, 426
in race mixture, 393f., 399f.
sexual, 358ff.
Naturalization, 195f., 213ff., 458
development of, 215f.
legal provisions, 217ff.
suggested changes, 219ff.
See also Americanization, Citizenship, Politics, Suffrage.
Nearing, Scott, 249n, 597
Negro Colleges and Universities, Survey of, 598

Negro migration, 44f., 49, 126f., 484
causes of, 46ff.
compared with Jewish migration, 49f.
misconceptions, 45ff.
See also Migration.
Negro Welfare Service Committee, 270, 287, 290; quoted, 291, 487
Nerves, 429f.
Newspapers, foreign language, 275, 465f.
Negro, 576
Niebuhr, H. Richard, 19n
Night clubs, 305
Non-immigrant aliens, 173f.
Non-reservation schools, 386, 500ff.
Nordicism, 396, 401, 423
Nowlin, William F., 598
"Numbers." *See* Policy playing.

Occupations, 125ff., 345, 432f., 501
hypothetical chart of, 107
statistics of, 101ff., 102ff., 108
See also Agriculture, Industry, Labor.
Odum, Howard W., 547n, 598
Olmsted, F. L., 598
O'Neill, E., 545
"One-crop system," 68ff.
Opportunity, 576; quoted, 208f.
Optimum population, 116f.
Oriental exclusion, 156, 157, 167f., 182ff., 184f.
See also Barred Zone, Burlingame Treaty, Gentlemen's Agreement.
Outbreeding. *See* Race mixture.
Outing system, 502
Overton, Ada, 545
Ovington, Mary White, 598

Padrones, 118
Painting, 544
Panaceas, 578ff.
Panics. *See* Business cycles.
Panunzio, Constantine, 177n, 595, 603
Parent-teacher associations, 463
Park, Robert E., 580, 603; quoted, 581f.
Parker, J. J., 479
Parks, 264, 287f., 292, 294
See also Amusement parks, Leisure activities.
Parochial schools, 499f.
Parrish, Maxfield, 566